CELLULOID POWER

Social Film Criticism from
The Birth of a Nation to
Judgment at Nuremberg

by
DAVID PLATT

The Scarecrow Press, Inc.
Metuchen, N.J., & London
1992

Every effort has been made to locate the copyright owners of material quoted/reprinted herein. Omissions brought to our attention will be corrected in future printings.

British Library Cataloguing-in-Publication data available

Library of Congress Cataloging-in-Publication Data

Celluloid power : social film criticism from The birth of a nation to
    Judgment at Nuremberg / selected, edited, and arranged with com-
    mentary by David Platt.
        p.   cm.
    Includes index.
    ISBN 0-8108-2442-6 (acid-free paper)
    1. Politics in motion pictures. 2. Motion pictures—Political as-
pects. 3. Motion pictures—History. 4. Motion pictures—Reviews. I. Platt, David, 1903–
PN1995.9.P6C44   1992
302.23′43—dc20   91-35568

This book is dedicated to the nine blacklisted members of the Hollywood Ten who stood tall in the "Time of the Toad," when so many others developed brittle spines. We speak of Alvah Bessie (1904–1985), Herbert Biberman (1900–1971), Lester Cole (1904–1985), Ring Lardner, Jr., John Howard Lawson (1895–1977), Albert Maltz (1909–1985), Samuel Ornitz (1890–1957), Adrian Scott (1912–1972), and Dalton Trumbo (1905–1976). They will be long remembered as the first American screen artists in the century-long history of the cinema to be condemned to prison for the crime of opinion. The tenth member, Edward Dmytryk, was freed from jail, removed from the blacklist, and allowed to resume his directorial career when he recanted his views and agreed to name names as a friendly witness before the House Unamerican Activities Committee.

I wish to thank Morris U. Schappes, editor of the magazine *Jewish Currents*, for his support and encouragement in the compilation of this book.

CONTENTS

PART III: SOCIAL AWAKENING—THE 1930s

PART IV: WAR, POST-WAR, AND McCARTHYISM

PREFACE

WILLIAM MORRIS: "Yea, the voiceless wrath of the wretched, and their learned discontent. We must give it voice and wisdom till the waiting-tide be spent." (*The Day Is Coming.*)

MAXIM GORKY: "I have come into the world to cry out against abuses. . . . Everybody lives for something better to come." (*The Lower Depths.*)

WALT WHITMAN: "We have frequently printed the word Democracy. I cannot too often repeat that it is a word the real gist of which still sleeps, quite unawakened, notwithstanding the resonance and the many angry tempests out of which the syllables have come, from pen and tongue. It is a great word whose history, I suppose, remains unwritten, because that history has yet to be enacted." (*Democratic Vistas.*)

DAVID CAUTE: "Sartre has said that there can be no great work of literature which does not contribute to the liberation of man and surely this must hold true of film as well." (*The Compound Cinema,* by Lewis Jacobs.)

CLIFFORD ODETS: "We must not expect very much of a motion picture that is conceived on the cold marble floor of a bank."

LOUIS DELLUC: "Chaplin's face has the same importance that the traditional bust of Beethoven has for a musician or musicologist." (French Film Critic, 1922.)

ALEXANDER DOVJENKO: "Let us not treat the theme of ordinary man as an ordinary theme. A film that is not steeped in human feeling is like a planet without atmosphere." (Soviet Director.)

CESARE ZAVATTINI: "The cinema has used far too few images to open the eyes of our neighbors, to help them understand (and prevent) terrible events." (Italian Screenwriter.)

ROBERT FLAHERTY: "Film is the great pencil of the modern world, and it is unfortunate that men do not use it to full advantage. In communicating his ideas man started with pictures, and in the 20th century he has discovered that pictures—motion pictures—provide a more graphic and cosmopolitan method of communication than the printed word. Film has given mankind its first universal language." (U.S. Documentary Filmmaker.)

ERIC VON STROHEIM: "The biggest handicap of the American cinema is its moral narrow-mindedness. . . . The public at large is not as spiritually poor as the producers imagine. It wants to be shown life as real as it actually is for people. . . . I intend to tailor my films in the rough fabric of human conflicts. Because to make films with the regularity of a sausage machine forces you to make them neither better nor worse than a string of sausages." (In the end Von Stroheim's masterpiece, *Greed* [1924], was taken out of his hands and cut up by a Hollywood butcher. Others directed by him suffered a similar fate. See Jay Leyda's article in *Celluloid Power*.)

JOHN HOWARD LAWSON: "The blacklist constitutes a roll of honor of Americans whose patriotism was not for sale." (Hollywood Screenwriter and one of the famed Blacklisted Ten.)

JACK LONDON: "After God had finished the rattlesnake, the toad and the vampire, he had some awful stuff left with which he made a scab. . . . There is nothing lower."

T HESE ARE SOME OF THE IDEAS the editor of this anthology of social film criticism was searching for when he began putting together his book in the mid-1970s. We believe that *Celluloid Power: Social Film Criticism From "The Birth of a Nation" to "Judgment at Nuremberg"* is unique among collections of this kind. A principal point is that it concentrates in one compact volume material on the century's major controversial films—primarily those dealing with such issues as war, imperialism social revolution, fascism, racism, anti-Semitism and the holocaust, McCarthy witchhunting, the cold war, etc. We refer here to films connected with the fateful years 1905, 1914, 1917, 1929, the 1930s Great Depression, the rise of Hitler and his worldwide gang of thugs, brown-shirted or otherwise, the Spanish Civil War, World War II, Hiroshima.

A glance at the table of contents will show a number of other unique features of the anthology: the high caliber of the contributors, for instance, indicated by a simple listing of some of their names below: Sergei Eisenstein, Jean Renoir, Joris Ivens, Bela Balasz, Lewis Milestone, Harry Alan Potamkin, John Howard Lawson, Jay Leyda, Lewis Jacobs, Leo Hurwitz, Leo Seltzer, Dalton Trumbo, Kevin Brownlow, Roger Manvell, Robert Stebbins, Lorraine Hansberry, Dorothy B. Jones, Timothy J. Lyons, Gale Sondergaard, Arthur Knight, Linda Kowall, Cedric Belfrage, Gary Crowdus, Morris U. Schappes, Russell Campbell, Anthony Slide, Carl Marzani, Albert Maltz, Herbert J. Biberman, Bernard L. Peterson, Jr., Samuel Brody, Ring Lardner, Jr., Lester Cole, Adrian Scott, Alvah Bessie. These 35 are among the 55 or more screenwriters, directors, producers, historians, critics and documentary filmmakers of distinction who are represented with articles and reviews on such diverse films as *The Birth of a Nation, Intolerance, Battle Cry of Peace, War Brides, Shoulder Arms, Passion of Joan D'Arc, Greed, Potemkin, Storm Over Asia, Three Songs About Lenin, The Crowd, All Quiet on the Western Front, ¡Que Viva México!, I Am a Fugitive from a Chain Gang, The Informer, They Won't Forget, Grand Illusion, The Great Dictator, Professor Mamlock, Native Land, The Grapes of Wrath, Gone With the Wind, The Good Earth, The Wave, Fury, Spanish Earth, Citizen Kane, Mission to Moscow, Why We Fight, Monsieur Verdoux, Viva Zapata!, Salt of the Earth, Oliver Twist, Raisin in the Sun, Judgment at Nuremberg, Crossfire, Shoah,* and scores of other films that probe, illuminate and arouse, as well as bang the drums for shabby causes.

An important aspect of *Celluloid Power* is that a very large percentage of the contributors could be characterized as nonconformist. Former political prisoners, deportees, exiles, and victims of witchhunting and blacklisting are in this category, as well as others who occasionally experienced the cold stab of the censor when they sought to dig a little deeper into the social and political corruption around them. We refer to those whose films or film scripts were tampered with and even mutilated by the front office, when they were not censored by state police boards or banned altogether from theatres by self-appointed legions of purity and decency. In many cases it was not so much the content of their films, as their private beliefs, constitutionally protected, that laid them low. High on the list are the Hollywood artists who encountered the ultimate obscenity: censorship by prison.

The United States, of course, is not the only country that threw into jail or forced into exile some of its leading screen artists, including arresting, fingerprinting and demeaning a titan like Chaplin. Suffice it to mention the indignities suffered by film director Ingmar Bergman in his native Sweden and by Jean Renoir in France, the land of his birth. Add to these the persecution by the Hitler regime of some of the world-renowned artists of the 1920s German film renaissance (the makers of *Dr. Caligari, Metropolis, Last Laugh, Kameradschaft, Kuhle Wampe*). As for the brutal censorship exercised by the Stalin dictatorship over such awesome masters of Soviet film art as Eisenstein, Dovjenko, Pudovkin and Vertov during the period of the Moscow Trials and the postwar terror, the record is there for all to see in film historian Jay Leyda's *Kino, A History of Russian and Soviet Film*. The appearance in the 1980s of a number of extraordinary Soviet films, in which the leading characters bear an unmistakable resemblance to Stalin and other despoilers of the socialist dream, reflects the efforts of Mikhail Gorbachev and his associates to open up, reinvigorate and democratize the long, long overdue restructuring of Soviet society.

Perhaps the special strength of *Celluloid Power* lies in the commitment to the idea that films should be more than "a smudge of make-believe," should espouse the causes of the underprivileged, oppose war as a solution of social and political problems, and strengthen efforts to end stereotyped portrayals of Blacks, Jews, Hispanics, Asians, Native Indians and all national minorities, keeping in mind the historic truth of the holocaust that unbridled racism and anti-Semitism go hand in hand with unimaginable horror. Below are brief descriptions of some of the book's ground-breaking contributions in these areas.

Prof. Bernard L. Peterson, Jr. writes about "Oscar Micheaux: America's Legendary Black Filmmaker." Among the numerous surprises of his essay is that Micheaux made three films on the famous Leo Frank case (that of a New York Jew lynched in the South in 1915) a decade or more before the release in 1937 of the noted Warner Bros. film, *They Won't Forget,* directed by Mervyn LeRoy. See Lewis Jacobs' review in the 1930s section of the anthology.

Dorothy B. Jones discusses "The Portrayal of China and India on the American Screen: 1896–1955." In her study Jones notes that the earliest screen images of China were brief newsreels of Chinese cities and Chinatown, USA, shot by cameramen employed by Thomas Edison. These gave way during World War I to humiliating feature-length films by American companies in which Chinese characters were connected for the most part with tong wars, opium dens, gambling joints and "inscrutable" orientals "with tapering fingers and long pointed fingernails poised menacingly." Griffith's 1919 silent classic, *Broken Blossoms,* starring Lillian Gish as an abused woman who is befriended by a humanistic Chinese merchant, was a rare exception in its time. A decade later (1929), said Jones, American audiences also saw a "powerful and spine-chilling" Soviet film, *China Express,* directed by Ilya Trauberg, that pictured China prophetically as an "express train hurtling through the night toward Communist revolution." Among Soviet audiences some wondered how the train was able to get along without the fire-man after he left the engine to lead the revolt. (Leyda).

Russell Campbell's article on "The Red Scare Cycle" tells of a little known but quantitatively large body of long lost silent films with titles like *The Red Viper* and *Bolshevism on Trial,* which painted in lurid colors what was conceived as a threat to America posed by the 1917 Russian Revolution. Such films acquired their special character, said Campbell, "through being part of a co-ordinated government-business campaign to stamp out socialism." In some of the films, the massive postwar strikes in steel, coal and other major industries (several million American workers were involved in them) were attributed to outside agitators in the service of Lenin and the Bolsheviks. (Compare with ABC-TV's 14½-hour travesty, *Amerika* [Feb. 1987], set in Nebraska 10 years after the Soviets have to all appearances conquered the United States without firing a shot. The series depicted the U.S. as "groaning under the yoke of a supposed military occupation" by the Soviets and their allies in the United Nations whom they control.)

Sergei Eisenstein's scenario for his unfinished 1932 epic, *¡Que Viva México!*, is reprinted in its entirety from the legendary journal *Experimental Cinema*. Film history knows no greater esthetic crime than the mutilation by Hollywood "hacks" of Eisenstein's vision of Mexico. See Ivor Montagu's final comment on the case elsewhere in *Celluloid Power.*

Philip Sterling's "A Channel for Democratic Thought" recalls a veritable treasure-trove of early social films (almost all long lost or not readily available silent films) influenced by the socialist and populist ideals of Eugene Debs and Robert LaFollette. Included is the 20-episode serial, *Graft* (Universal, 1916), the plot of which was based on a group of vested interests pooling their power and prestige to raise prices, bribe public officials, prevent labor from organizing and igniting public protest. The titles tell the story: *The Tenement House Evil; The Traction Grab; The Harbor Transportation Trust; The Milk Battle; The Powder Trust and the War; The Patent Medicine Danger; The Insurance Swindlers; Pirates of Finance.*

Linda Kowall continues her worthy effort to rescue from oblivion the forgotten film pioneer Siegmund Lubin, a German Jewish immigrant who came to America in 1876 and six years later settled in Philadelphia as a skilled and highly successful optician (President Grant was one of his clients) before his interest in the new film medium was aroused by the experiments and inventions of Edison and others. Lubin's first film, *Horse Eating Hay,* created a sensation in 1897 when it was first shown to a public that thought it was the real thing and hurried to get out of its way when the horse seemed to move toward them. He went on to produce and exhibit some 5,000 films over the next 20 years and to put

Philadelphia on the map as the world's leading film center before World War I. Far more than any of his contemporaries, Lubin was involved creatively in all aspects of film. Not only did he produce, direct, distribute and exhibit films (he was the first to own a chain of theatres), but he also invented, developed and manufactured better projection machines and movie cameras. He was, above all, a pioneer in the use of films for educational, scientific, medical and humanitarian purposes and made a number of films against social injustice, political corruption and war. Disastrous fires which destroyed the bulk of his master negatives were a major contributor to Lubin's disappearance from the pages of film history, Kowall writes.

Herbert Luft, a concentration camp survivor, examines a long list of American and European films on the holocaust, including *Der Ewige Jude* (The Eternal Jew), one of the lesser known "cinematic curtain-raisers" for the holocaust made by the Nazis in 1940 and often referred to as one of the most evil films ever made. The film portrays Jews as a threat to humanity. To get this idea across, half-starved, ill-clothed and unwashed men, women and children whose human rights the Nazis have trampled on are photographed in order to contrast Jewish "lack of dignity," "lack of hygiene" with the admirable and healthy Germans. Luft writes that the film was "put together so cunningly that the enraged public went out from the theatre onto the street ready to massacre the 'unclean foreign elements.' " Was *Der Ewige Jude* "the most evil film ever made" or should that "laurel" go to Leni Riefenstahl's *Triumph of the Will,* her mammoth documentary salute to the glory of Hitler and the Nazis. The truth is that both films, to say nothing of scores of others along the same lines, have blood on their hands.

Herbert Biberman and Paul Jarrico write about the black-listing of *Salt of the Earth* by Hollywood mobsters. Their independently made film, based on Michael Wilson's powerful screenplay, about a strike of Mexican-American zinc workers—in which the key to victory is a struggle against male domination by the strikers wives—earned its greatest recognition abroad. Today it is heralded everywhere as a work of art that celebrates the greatness of minorities.

Celluloid Power features several articles on Chaplin,

among them French director Jean Renoir's eloquent appreciation of his 1947 masterpiece, *Monsieur Verdoux,* and articles by Timothy J. Lyons, Bela Belasz, Herman G. Weinberg and David Matis. All are relevant to the centennial of the birth, April 16, 1889 of the towering comic genius and film satirist whose name has at one time or another been linked with Shakespeare, Swift, Molière, Dickens, Rabelais, Voltaire and Sholem Aleichem.

The centennial of the birth of Danish film director, Carl Dreyer (Feb. 3, 1889–March 20, 1968), maker of *Passion of Joan of Arc, Day of Wrath, Ordet, Gertrude* and other films, was celebrated abroad, thanks to the efforts of Danish dramatist and film critic Elsa Gress-Wright, a longtime friend and neighbor of the director. Her *Ballad of Carl Dreyer,* in which the drama of his childhood and adulthood is spliced with scenes from some of his famous films, was recently produced on Danish television. There is also an English version of the *Ballad,* a draft text of which has been deposited with the Museum of Modern Art Film Study Center in New York.

The 90th birthday of documentary filmmaker Joris Ivens (b. Nov. 18, 1898) was observed on both sides of the Atlantic. The city of Florence paid a special homage to the artist. In New York, the Museum of Modern Art showed a large number of his most famous films throughout the month of November. He was also honored with a retrospective of 13 films at the annual Anthropos Documentary Film Festival held in Los Angeles early in December.

We honor the memory of Sam Brody, Jay Leyda, Albert Maltz, Lester Cole and Alvah Bessie, all of whom contributed to the making of this book.

PART I

THE EARLIEST YEARS

1 WORLD WITHOUT SOUND: THE 1896 LUMIÈRE FILM PROGRAM

Maxim Gorky

A review of the Lumière program at the Nizhni-Novgorod Fair, as printed in the *Nizhegorodski listok* (newspaper), July 4, 1896, and signed "I.M. Pacatus." Translated by Leda Swan.

L AST NIGHT I WAS in the Kingdom of Shadows. If you only knew how strange it is to be there. It is a world without sound, without colour. Everything there—the earth, the trees, the people, the water and the air—is dipped in monotonous grey. Grey rays of the sun across the grey sky, grey eyes in grey faces, and the leaves of the trees are ashen grey. It is not life but its shadow, it is not motion but its soundless spectre.

Here I shall try to explain myself, lest I be suspected of madness or indulgence in symbolism. I was at Aumont's and saw Lumière's cinematograph—moving photography. The extraordinary impression it creates is so unique and complex that I doubt my ability to describe it with all its nuances. However, I shall try to convey its fundamentals.

When the lights go out in the room in which Lumière's invention is shown, there suddenly appears on the screen a

From Jay Leyda, *KINO: A History of the Russian and Soviet Film* (London: Allen & Unwin, Ltd., 1960; 3rd ed., Princeton University Press, 1983). Reprinted by permission of the author and of Princeton University Press.

large grey picture, "A Street in Paris"—shadows of a bad engraving. As you gaze at it, you see carriages, buildings and people in various poses, all frozen into immobility. All this is in grey, and the sky above is also grey—you anticipate nothing new in this all too familiar scene, for you have seen pictures of Paris streets more than once.

But suddenly a strange flicker passes through the screen and the picture stirs to life. Carriages coming from somewhere in the perspective of the picture are moving straight at you, into the darkness in which you sit; somewhere from afar people appear and loom larger as they come closer to you; in the foreground children are playing with a dog, bicyclists tear along, and pedestrians cross the street picking their way among the carriages. All this moves, teems with life and, upon approaching the edge of the screen, vanishes somewhere beyond it.

And all this in strange silence where no rumble of the wheels is heard, no sound of footsteps or of speech. Nothing. Not a single note of the intricate symphony that always accompanies the movements of people. Noiselessly, the ashen-grey foliage of the trees sways in the wind, and the grey silhouettes of the people, as though condemned to eternal silence and cruelly punished by being deprived of all the colours of life, glide noiselessly along the grey ground.

Their smiles are lifeless, even though their movements are full of living energy and are so swift as to be almost imperceptible. Their laughter is soundless, although you see the muscles contracting in their grey faces. Before you a life is surging, a life deprived of words and shorn of the living spectrum of colours —the grey, the soundless, the bleak and dismal life.

It is terrifying to see, but it is the movement of shadows, only of shadows. Curses and ghosts, the evil spirits that have cast entire cities into eternal sleep, come to mind and you feel as though Merlin's vicious trick is being enacted before you. As though he had bewitched the entire street, he compressed its many-storied buildings from roof-tops to foundations to yard-like size. He dwarfed the people in corresponding proportion, robbing them of the power of speech and scraping together all the pigment of earth and sky into a monotonous grey colour.

Under this guise he shoved his grotesque creation into a niche in the dark room of a restaurant. Suddenly something clicks, everything vanishes and a train appears on the screen. It speeds straight at you—watch out! It seems as though it will plunge into the darkness in which you sit, turning you into a ripped sack full of lacerated flesh and splintered bones, and crushing into dust and into broken fragments this hall and this building, so full of women, wine, music and vice. But this, too, is but a train of shadows. Noiselessly, the locomotive disappears beyond the edge of the screen. The train comes to a stop, and grey figures silently emerge from the cars, soundlessly greet their friends, laugh, walk, run, bustle, and . . . are gone.

And here is another picture. Three men seated at the table, playing cards. Their faces are tense, their hands move swiftly. The cupidity of the players is betrayed by the trembling fingers and by the twitching of their facial muscles. They play. . . . Suddenly, they break into laughter, and the waiter who has stopped at their table with beer, laughs too. They laugh until their sides split but not a sound is heard. It seems as if these people have died and their shadows have been condemned to play cards in silence unto eternity.

Another picture. A gardener watering flowers. The light grey stream of water, issuing from a hose, breaks into a fine spray. It falls upon the flowerbeds and upon the grass blades weighted down by the water. A boy enters, steps on the hose, and stops the stream. The gardener stares into the nozzle of the hose, whereupon the boy steps back and a stream of water hits the gardener in the face. You imagine the spray will reach you, and you want to shield yourself. But on the screen the gardener has already begun to chase the rascal all over the garden and having caught him, gives him a beating. But the beating is soundless, nor can you hear the gurgle of the water as it gushes from the hose left lying on the ground.

This mute, grey life finally begins to disturb and depress you. It seems as though it carries a warning, fraught with a vague but sinister meaning that makes your heart grow faint. You are forgetting where you are. Strange imaginings invade your mind and your consciouness begins to wane and grow dim. . . .

But suddenly, alongside of you, a gay chatter and a provoking laughter of a woman is heard . . . and you remember that you are at Aumont's, Charles Aumont's. . . . But why of all places should this remarkable invention of Lumière find its way and be demonstrated here, this invention which affirms once again the energy and the curiosity of the human mind, forever striving to solve and grasp all, and . . . while on the way to the solution of the mystery of life, incidentally builds Aumont's fortune? I do not yet see the scientific importance of Lumière's invention but, no doubt, it is there, and it could probably be applied to the general ends of science, that is, of bettering man's life and the developing of his mind. This is not to be found at Aumont's where vice alone is being encouraged and popularized. Why then at Aumont's, among the "victims of social needs" and among the loafers who here buy their kisses? Why here, of all places, are they showing this latest achievement of science? And soon probably Lumière's invention will be perfected, but in the spirit of Aumont-Toulon and Company.

Besides those pictures I have already mentioned, is featured "The Family Breakfast," an idyll of three. A young couple with its chubby first-born is seated at the breakfast table. The two are so much in love, and are so charming, gay and happy, and the baby is so amusing. The picture creates a fine, felicitous impression. Has this family scene a place at Aumont's?

And here is still another. Women workers, in a thick, gay and laughing crowd, rush out of the factory gates into the street. This too is out of place at Aumont's. Why remind here of the possibility of a clean, toiling life? This reminder is useless. Under the best of circumstances this picture will only painfully sting the woman who sells her kisses.

I am convinced that these pictures will soon be replaced by others of a genre more suited to the general tone of the "Concert Parisien." For example, they will show a picture titled: "As She Undresses," or "Madam at Her Bath," or "A Woman in Stockings." They could also depict a sordid squabble between a husband and wife and serve it to the public under the heading of "The Blessings of Family Life."

Yes, no doubt, this is how it will be done. The bucolic and the idyll could not possibly find their place in Russia's

markets thirsting for the piquant and the extravagant. I also could suggest a few themes for development by means of a cinematograph and for the amusement of the market place. For instance: to impale a fashionable parasite upon a picket fence, as is the way of the Turks, photograph him, then show it.
It is not exactly piquant but quite edifying.

See Leyda's Kino *(pp. 410–413) for statements on the silent film by such other Russian literary figures as Leo Tolstoy (1908) and Vladimir Mayakovsky (1913). Authors on Film, edited by Harry M. Geduld (Indiana University Press, 1972), is a good source for film comments by American and European writers of distinction such as Frank Norris, Jack London, John Dos Passos, Theodore Dreiser, Bertolt Brecht, Virginia Woolf, Thomas Mann, Jean Cocteau, and others. (DP)*

2 THE PORTRAYAL OF CHINA AND INDIA ON THE AMERICAN SCREEN, 1896–1955

Dorothy B. Jones

CHINESE THEMES

THE VERY EARLIEST motion pictures in this country were of a newsreel or documentary variety—a motion picture record of events and places of interest which appeared between 1896 and 1907.

Among the early motion pictures which have been identified from the records of the United States Copyright Office, are a number dealing with China. In 1896 the American Mutoscope Company issued two brief subjects on the visit of a Chinese celebrity to New York City—these being entitled *Li Hung Chang At Grant's Tomb,* and *Li Hung Chang Driving Through 4th and Broadway.*

Two years later, in 1898, Thomas A. Edison sent a cameraman on a round-the-world trip to get film footage for the company's productions, and in China he visited Hong Kong and Shanghai. Thus it was that the first documentary footage taken in China appeared on the American screen during 1898 in such subjects as *Hong Kong Regiment, Government House at Hong Kong, Shanghai Police,*

Excerpted from a monograph, *The Evolution of Chinese and Indian Themes, Locales, and Characters as Portrayed on the American Screen (1896–1955),* published October 1955 by The Center for International Studies, Massachusetts Institute of Technology, Cambridge, Mass. Reprinted by permission of the copyright holder, Dorothy B. Jones.

Shanghai Street Scene, etc. Seven such subjects in all were released by the Thomas A. Edison company during that year.

Four years later, in 1902, the American Mutoscope and Biograph Company also released several films on China—*Ch-ien-Men Gate, Peking, and Street Scene, Tientsin.* In this early period, too, films were being shown about the Chinese in America. From such film titles as *Chinese Procession* (1898), *Scene in Chinatown* (1903), *Chinese Laundry at Work* (1904), etc., it can be seen that the life and customs of the Chinese have been treated on the American screen from the earliest days of the motion picture.

By 1910 fictional entertainment had become the primary product of the motion picture industry, and films about China and the Chinese continued to serve as subject matter for some of these productions. It is interesting that many of the types of films about China which are still to be found today had their roots back in the first decade of the century. For example, the serial thriller with an oriental villain dates back to this period of film history. Such a serial was *Patria* (Horton, Inc., International Film Service, 1917) with Irene Castle and Milton Sills, with an Oriental in the role of the villain.[1] Also in 1916 a film entitled *China* (Dorsey Motion Pictures) was released by the United Photoplays Company. This was an eight-reel film of the travelogue variety based entirely on documentary footage. The information short subject on China had its prototype in a film entitled *China at Work and at Play* which was released by Universal Manufacturing Company in 1917.

But by far the most important film of this period on China was D. W. Griffith's motion picture *Broken Blossoms* (Griffith, 1919). This film (the alternate title of which on the screen is "The Yellow Man and the Girl") was based on Thomas Burke's *Limehouse Nights,* and particularly on his story, "The Chink and the Child," and was filmed under the personal direction of D. W. Griffith. Lucy, the girl "White Blossom," was played by Lillian Gish and "the Yellow Man" by Richard Barthelmess. Lewis Jacobs describes this film as "a poignant, romantic tragedy of the love and care of a Chinaman for a mistreated girl" and comments that:

Despite its lapses into sentimentality, the whole has a reality and plausibility that represented Griffith at his best, from the opening scenes in the streets of the Orient with the carousing American sailors and the religious solemnity of the Chinamen, to the fog-drenched docks of Limehouse and the lurid interior of the smoking den. Impressive as the atmosphere is, it is equaled by the characterizations. Richard Barthelmess as the Chinaman appears as sensitive and fragile as the story wants us to believe. Slender and pale, with his tilted head, his withdrawn, curved body, and his dreamy countenance emphasized in large closeups time and again, he is a vivid character in contrast to the large, restless, energetic Brute (Donald Crisp).[2]

As a motion picture about China, *Broken Blossoms* was important for a variety of reasons. First, as a film which received enthusiastic acclaim from the critics,[3] *Broken Blossoms* focused attention on things Chinese and started a whole cycle of films with a Chinatown setting. Second, its contrast between the gentleness and poetic sensitivity of the Chinese and the coarseness and brutality of the English villain was, in itself, something completely new to the American screen. Similarly, the beauty and refinement of "The Yellow Man's" shop and living quarters are sharply contrasted with the dirt and squalor in which the Brute and his daughter are seen to live. Thus the philosophy and the way of life of the Far East were given an extremely favorable portrayal in this film. Commenting on this aspect of the film, Seymour W. Stern, well-known as an authority of Griffith, wrote:

Taking *The Chink* of the original story by Burke, he (Griffith) invests him with attributes of almost classic nobility, and so makes him a living symbol of non-existent Christian character. The delicately idealized, poetic *Yellow Man,* the "Christian with yellow skin," with his rare and silent perception of the moral bankruptcy and social evil everywhere about him, becomes, in effect, a touchstone of the tragic failure of the Western world. He also serves as a mouthpiece for the caustic reference, in a subtitle, to those across the sea . . . the barbarous Anglo-Saxons, sons of turmoil and strife. . . . Thus, while primarily a poetic tragedy, *Broken Blossoms* was also, in the broad sense of the term, a theme-picture.[4]

Broken Blossoms was followed the next year by Crooked Streets (Paramount-Artcraft, Famous Lasky Players), the story of an American girl who goes to China in search of rare vases as secretary to an antiquarian and who gets taken into an opium den in Shanghai by a treacherous rickshaw driver. Mr. Wu (Stoll Film Corp., 1920) based on the play by H. M. Vernon and Harold Owen, was also laid in China. In addition to these and other films laid in China, there followed in the 1920's a long series of motion pictures which utilized the Limehouse district of London or the Chinatowns of large American cities as a background for intrigue, mystery and suspense—such films as Outside the Law (Universal Film Mfg. Co., 1921), Shadows (Preferred Pictures, Inc., 1922), The Chinese Parrot (Universal Pictures Corp., 1927), Chinatown Charlie (First National Pictures, 1928), Chinatown Nights (Paramount Famous Lasky Corp., 1929), Chinese Blues (Universal Pictures Corp., 1930), Chinatown After Dark (Action Pictures, 1931), etc.

These films and many others like them used Chinatown as an intriguing background for a movie mystery or a story of crime. This type of film was to be found on the American screen as late as the middle thirties when Paramount presented Limehouse Blues starring George Raft, Anna Mae Wong, and Montague Love, which deals with a similar background set in the Limehouse district of London. Although Chinatown as a background for a mystery or crime film has recurred since the middle thirties (for example, in Chinatown at Midnight—Columbia Film Corp., 1949), it has long since disappeared as a regular film vehicle. In addition to Hollywood films produced with a Chinatown background there were a whole series of such films which came from England during the 1920's localled generally in the Limehouse district of London.

Before leaving the films which utilized the Chinatown background it is worth noting that the earlier films of this series placed the emphasis primarily upon the element of mystery associated with Chinatown—sinister shadows, sliding panels, Oriental faces peering through windows, trembling curtains behind which hid unknown figures, etc. Toward the end of the twenties and into the thirties, however, although these films continued to utilize these devices, the stories themselves began to be more concerned with gang warfare in Chinatown. Influenced by stories published about the Tong Wars, films of this series now become mostly occupied with a portrayal of underworld life in Chinatown—gambling, smuggling, gang warfare, and the life of a variety of sordid characters who were portrayed as peopling the underworld of Chinatown. Thus films of this series merged with and became a part of the gangster era of motion pictures.

Another Chinese theme which dates far back in America film history is the story of the love between an American and a Chinese. One of the earliest known feature films about China is *Broken Fetters* (Bluebird Photoplays, Inc., 1916) which was produced and directed by Rex Ingram. The alternate title of this production was *Yellow and White,* and it told the story of a Chinese girl named Mignon who had been sold to a wealthy Chinese who kept her in his gambling house. Here a young American artist met and fell in love with her. He gambled all his money away trying to win enough to buy the girl's freedom, and later when the two owners of the gambling house quarreled, he was able to rescue and free Mignon. The girl turns out to be in reality the daughter of the former American Consul in Shanghai, who was adopted by a wealthy Mandarin when her father died. Mignon and her artist marry and travel to China on their honeymoon.

The solution offered by this 1916 movie in the portrayal of a great love between an American and Chinese is one which was to be repeated many times on the screen during the next fifteen years. However, probably the two most popular motion pictures which thus resolved a romance between East and West were *East is West* (Universal Film Corporation, 1930) and *Son of the Gods* (First National Pictures, Inc., 1930).

East is West (which had been made once before in 1922 by Joseph M. Schenck) was a saga of little Ming Tong (Lupe Velez) and her American hero Billy Benson (Lew Ayers), with Edward G. Robinson appearing in this, his first "talkie," in the role of Charlie Yong, an egocentric half-caste. Although Billy Benson is determined to marry the little Chinese girl with whom he has fallen in love, he is opposed by his family and friends. In the end it turns out that Ming Tong is really the daughter of a famous missionary who was stolen by Yong when she was a baby. Since Ming Tong is not really Chinese, she is (in the words of a reviewer of the film) "eligible to enter fashionable West Coast society as the bride of Billy Benson."

In *Son of the Gods* this situation is reversed with Sam Lee (Richard Barthelmess) as the wealthy young Chinese who falls in love with an American girl. The marriage appears to be out of the question and both of the lovers are deeply unhappy. Then it is learned that Sam is only the adopted son of Lee Ying, and at last the two sweethearts are free to find happiness together.

East is West is based on a play of 1920 and *Son of the Gods* on a novel which appeared in *Cosmopolitan* Magazine in 1928 and was published as a novel by Harpers & Bros. in 1929. Thus it is probable that this theme is one which was current generally during the 1920's on the stage and in fiction, as well as on the screen.

The problem of miscegenation, however—as it applies to marriage between an American or British person and a Chinese—was not always happily resolved on the screen. In *Broken Blossoms* (Griffith, 1919), which has been described above, the love of "the Yellow Man" for the girl, "White Blossom," was portrayed as a tragedy.

This was similarly the case in *The Red Lantern* (Metro Pictures Corp., 1919) which was released the same year. This film based on the novel by Edith Wherry, deals with the tragic love of a Chinese half-caste girl and the son of an American Protestant missionary in China, a story which is told against the background of the Boxer Rebellion. In the end the girl Mahlee (played by Nazimova), realizing the tragic impossibility of her situation, drinks poison. There are a whole series of films in which one of the lovers meets a tragic death before the match can be consumated. In *Mr. Wu* (based on the play by Harry Maurice Vernon and Harold Owen, which was made into a movie in 1920 by Stoll Film Corp., and again in 1927 by Metro-Goldwyn-Mayer), a Chinese girl who is "betrayed" by an Englishman also dies, and her father seeks revenge against the English family involved.

This theme—the tragedy of a great love between persons of the "white" and "yellow" races—continued into the thirties. Among the films which dramatized this theme were *The Bitter Tea of General Yen* (Columbia Pictures Corp., 1932) which tells of the romance between a Chinese warlord and an American missionary in Shanghai. In this film the Chinese General, who is the hero of the story, commits suicide at the end by drinking poison. The tragedy of an East-West romance is portrayed in a different light in *Shanghai* (Paramount Productions, Inc., 1935) which relates the story of the love between a half-caste (Charles Boyer), son of an exiled Russian nobleman and a Manchu princess, and an American girl (Loretta Young). It is interesting here that the tragic events which decide this young couple's fate do not actually occur, but are pictured as events of the previous generation: when Charles Boyer and Loretta Young decide to marry despite the fact that he is "half white, half yellow," his good friend, the Chinese ambassador, dissuades Boyer from making "the same mistake his parents did," telling the young man that, as the result of the unhappiness caused by such a marriage, his princess-mother committed suicide. Thus it is that the young couple decide not to defy racial prejudices, but to go their separate ways. That the inevitable tragedy of this situation had begun to be questioned by the middle thirties is evident not only in the less extreme resolution of the problem shown in *Shanghai,* but is also suggested in a review of this film by Richard Watts, Jr. in the *New York Herald Tribune,* who wrote:

> Until the scene wherein the social leaders of the international settlement walk out on Mr. Boyer when they find that he has Mongol blood, the picture is interesting and persuasive. Upon the occasion of the big climax, however, the picture becomes slightly incredible. It is not that I doubt that the Shanghai social set could be crude enough to put the half-caste in his place in such melodramatic fashion. It is merely that when hearing of the dire fate in store for any possible alliance between East and West, I could not help thinking of a number of successful romances of this type currently to be encountered in the Far East and thereupon feel that the tragedy of the blighted romance was not as cruelly inevitable as the authors had anticipated.[5]

Another variation of the theme of miscegenation is to be found in films in which the interest of a Chinese man or woman in a white person of the opposite sex is portrayed as a threat or menace. This element is utilized to a certain extent in *Broken Blossoms* (Griffith, 1919), for it is not until the film is well along that we fully understand and appreciate that the Yellow Man's gentle adoration of the girl is a dream which he well understands can never be realized. In *Crooked Streets* (Paramount-Artcraft, 1920) a pretty American girl is threatened by a treacherous rickshaw driver and rescued by an Irish adventurer named O'Dare, and in *Tell It to the Marines* (Metro-Goldwyn-Mayer, 1926) a group of American nurses stranded in Hanchow are threatened by a group of Chinese bandits who are finally beaten off by American Marines. This theme—which was clearly an outgrowth of "The Yellow Peril" literature—was usually dramatized as the fascination of the "Yellow Man" for the "White Woman." But in some instances the situation was reversed—as in *The Mask of Fu Manchu* (Metro-Goldwyn-Mayer, 1932) in which the evil Dr. Fu Manchu (Boris Karloff) uses a strange drug which allows him to guide the will of the handsome hero so that Fu Manchu's daughter, who is attracted to him, can have him for her own.

The number of films dealing with China or prominently featuring Chinese locales or characters began to increase noticeably around the middle of 1925. It was in this period that the Fu Manchu and Charlie Chan films had their beginning. The first film featuring the Chinese detective known as Chan was *The House Without a Key* (Pathé Exchange, Inc., 1926), a ten-part serial in which the veteran Japanese actor, George Kuwa, played the role of Chan which, in this film, was one of secondary importance. Two other films of this series were released in the late 1920's, twenty Charlie Chan films were released in the 1930's, and twenty-four in the 1940's, the last in 1949.

The Fu Manchu films were made between 1929 and 1932. Aside from the characterization of the Chinese villain Fu Manchu and the Chinese detective Charlie Chan which will be discussed later in this report, these films were important inasmuch as they reinforced the association between things

Chinese and mystery. The kind of mystery presented in the Fu Manchu films was one in which the Chinese villain and his accomplices created the atmosphere of evilness and mystery, complete with mysterious shadows, sliding panels, strange drugs with unheard-of-powers, etc. The Charlie Chan films, on the other hand, associated the Chinese not with the creation of the mystery but with the solving of it. It is interesting that although there was a complete shift in emphasis with the introduction of the Charlie Chan films, actually the association between things mysterious and the Chinese continued to be perpetuated throughout both of these series.

We have already mentioned that the gangster films which became popular on the American screen during the late twenties and early thirties, found their counterpart in a greater emphasis upon underworld life in films made against the background of Chinatown. It should also be noted that in this same period a new theme about China emerged which likewise was influenced by the gangster film—namely, the films about the Chinese warlords. These motion pictures (*The Bitter Tea of General Yen,* Columbia, 1932; *The General Died at Dawn,* Paramount, 1936; *West of Shanghai,* Warner Brothers, 1937, etc.) undertook to dramatize the rivalries between military chieftans in China which had been reported in the American press and which were part of the struggle involved in the unification of Nationalist China. However, the warlords—military personalities outside the official Chinese government who were seeking control and domination over certain areas of the country—came to be pictured on the American screen as the Chinese equivalent of the American gangster.

At the same time, during the 1930's a more realistic portrayal of China began to be evident on the American screen. In the early 1930's China claimed the attention of the United States and the entire world with the Manchurian question. It will be recalled that during 1931 and 1932 Manchuria made many headlines, focusing world attention on the Far East in general and on China in particular. With China in the news, factual short subjects and documentaries on China began to appear in greater number on the American screen. In 1932 the Star Film Company released a

60-minute documentary entitled *China Speaks.* This film, based entirely on newsreel footage and concluding with a long message from General Sun, was (according to reviewers) obviously hastily bought together to capitalize on current public interest in China. It was followed, however, throughout the 1930's by a number of travelogues about China. Most of the major motion picture companies distributed at least one such short subject, as, for example, *Drums of the Orient* and *Shanghai* (both released by RKO-Pathé in 1932); *Hong Kong Highlights* (20th Century-Fox, 1936); *Hong Kong, The Hub of the Orient* (Metro-Goldwyn-Mayer, 1937); *China Today* (Vitaphone Corp., 1938); etc. There is a record of at least sixteen short subjects or documentaries about China made during the 1930's—four times as many as those known to have been made during the 1920's.

Not only was an increased amount of documentary footage on China shown on the American screen during the 1930's, but a new and more factual approach became evident for the first time during this period in a feature motion picture about China. It was evident to some extent in *Oil for the Lamps of China* (Warners, 1935) which told the story of an idealistic employee of an American oil company in China who designs an oil lamp which consumes so little oil that the Chinese peasants can afford to use it instead of their primitive torches. But the first important and serious attempt to portray China realistically in a Hollywood feature film was in *The Good Earth* (Metro-Goldwyn-Mayer, 1937).[6]

The Good Earth embodied a completely new approach to the subject of China. In dramatizing the life story of a Chinese peasant family, Irving Thalberg, the producer, and Sydney Franklin, the director, strove to tell the story of the Chinese people, not as strange, mysterious, fictional characters of another world, but as human beings whose life story was very much like the life story of people anywhere else in the world. This film, although far in advance of its time as screenfare, reflected the growing tendency of the American screen to portray the real rather than the fantasy China. The influence of this motion picture not only throughout the country but throughout the world cannot be doubted, and likewise its influence in Hollywood was considerable for it was an extremely successful picture which captured the attention and imagination of Hollywood. It is not inaccurate to say that *The Good Earth* provided the foundation for the more serious efforts of Hollywood to re-create the Chinese scene in a series of war films which were made dramatizing the role of China during World War II.

It was in the early 1940's that the new realistic presentation of China became definitely and clearly established on the American screen. In June of 1941 the March of Time issued its film, *China Fights Back,* which clarified the background of China's battle against the invading Japanese. During the next two years several full-length documentaries on China's role in the war were shown on American screens, including *The Battle of China* (United Artists, 1942) and *Ravaged Earth* (1943). And factual short subjects based on newsreel footage continued to appear—e.g., *Inside Fighting China* (United Artists, 1942); *China* (The March of Time, Forum Edition, 1945); *China Carries On* (20th Century-Fox, 1945); etc.

At the same time Hollywood feature films dramatizing China's role in the war were among the first war films to appear after American entry into World War II late in 1941. The first of these films were concerned with the problem of getting American supplies into China through Burma. *Burma Convoy* (Universal, 1941) told the story of a young American heading a truck convoy traveling on the Burma Road, who helps to uncover and defeat a group of Chinese Fifth Columnists (aligned with Japan) who are interfering with the convoying of supplies to China. *A Yank on the Burma Road* (Metro-Goldwyn-Mayer, 1942) dramatized the story of an American soldier-of-fortune who crosses the Burma-Chinese border before Pearl Harbor and leads a band of guerrillas in battling the Japanese. *China Girl* (20th Century-Fox, 1942) also deals with the early days along the Burma Road. And *The Flying Tigers* (Republic, 1942) and *God is my Co-Pilot* (Warner Brothers, 1943) are stories about the heroism of General Chennault's famed Flying Tigers. While some of these films were melodramatic and based on time-worn movie formulas, others (for example, *God is my Co-Pilot*) made a serious attempt to portray realistically the role of the Chinese in the war and American efforts to get badly needed war supplies into China by way of Burma.

But the most consistent and oft-repeated theme about China during World War II was that of the valiant resistance of the Chinese to the Japanese invaders. This theme was documented in The March of Time and other short subjects on China noted above. It was reiterated in the full-length documentaries—particularly in *Ravaged Earth*. It almost invariably appeared as a secondary theme in the feature films which dramatized American efforts to get war supplies into China (for example, *China Girl* devotes considerable footage to a dramatization of Chinese endurance and resistance). And, finally, a new series of films about China made toward the end of the war concerned themselves primarily with depicting Chinese resistance to the Japanese.

The most important of these films were *China* (Paramount, 1943), which pictures the struggles of the Chinese against Japanese aggression through the adventures of a calloused American oil man prior to Pearl Harbor, whose neutral attitude changes quickly when he comes face to face with Japanese atrocities; *Dragon Seed* (Metro-Goldwyn-Mayer, 1944), based on Pearl Buck's novel, showing how a peaceful Chinese family mobilizes to combat the Japanese invasion; and *China Sky* (RKO-Radio, 1945), which depicts the tenacity of Chinese guerrillas who harrassed the Japanese advance.[7]

Since the end of World War II films laid in China have, for the most part, been action melodramas, espionage or murder mysteries, and love stories which are played in a Chinese setting—Shanghai, Singapore,[8] or, more recently, Macao or Hong Kong. One theme which has reoccurred in quite a number of films since the war is smuggling and black market activities in the Far East—for example, *Singapore* (Universal, 1947) dealt with the smuggling of pearls out of Singapore; *Intrigue* (Star Films, United Artists, 1948) was a story about black marketeers flying food and other scarce materials into Shanghai; *To the End of the Earth* (Columbia, 1948) told a story of the U.S. Bureau of Narcotics in pursuit of smugglers which takes them from San Francisco to Shanghai and elsewhere; *Smuggler's Island* (Universal, 1951) was concerned with the smuggling of gold from the island of Macao to Hong Kong; *Peking Express* (Paramount, 1951) told of the plot of a Chinese Communist leader to double-cross his own government by channeling medical supplies into black market hands, etc. Smuggling continues as a theme even in recent movies about China (as in *Soldier of Fortune*, 20th Century-Fox, 1955). Only a few films on this theme have been important motion pictures, but this series of film is notable because it represents a postwar recurrence of an old theme of illicit traffic of one sort or another which has appeared off and on through the years in pictures dealing with China or the Chinese.

Since the Communists gained control on the China mainland there have been no films which have attempted to give a picture of what is going on in China. Since the Korean War, however, the theme of Communist China as an American enemy had received some attention on the screen, mostly in films dealing with the Korean War—for example, *Retreat Hell!* (Warner Brothers, 1952) which tells the story of the retreat from the area of the Chosin Reservoir after North Korea was invaded by Chinese troops. In such films the Chinese are either characterized objectively, without effect (as in *Retreat Hell!*) or are identified primarily as "Communists" or "Reds," and there appears to be a genuine reluctance to characterize the Chinese as our enemy.

In the recent film, *Hell and High Water* (20th Century-Fox, 1954), which centers about a Chinese Communist plot to drop an atomic bomb on Korea or Manchuria and blame it on the United States, there are two important Chinese characters in the film—Ho Sin, a Chinese Red, and Chin Lee, a Chinese-American who in the end gives his life in order to get the crucial information from the Chinese Communist prisoner. In this film the Chinese Communist villains are primarily referred to as "Reds," but they are counterbalanced by the heroic Chinese-American.

It is interesting that since so many of our associations with China are through missionaries there have been so few films which have undertaken to tell the story of the missionary in China. There have, over a period of thirty-five years, been quite a number of motion pictures about China which had a missionary as an important character in the story—from *The Red Lantern* (Metro-Goldywn-Mayer, 1919) to *The Bitter Tea of General Yen* (Columbia, 1932), *The Story of Dr. Wassell*

(Paramount, 1944) and, more recently, *Hong Kong* (Pine-Thomas-Paramount, 1952).

Of the few films which set out to dramatize on the screen the experiences of missionaries in China, the most outstanding and most widely seen is *The Keys of the Kingdom* (20th Century-Fox, 1944), which was one of the top box-office films of 1944–1945, and which is still shown widely throughout the country in hospitals, schools, etc., in 16-mm. This motion picture, based on the best-selling novel by A. J. Cronin, tells the story of the life of a Scottish priest serving as a missionary in an outlying province of China. This motion picture was hailed as one of the most accurate pictures of China that has ever been shown on the American screen, though the film was made entirely in Hollywood.

In any discussion of Chinese themes shown on the American screen, it should be noted that films from China have been imported into this country ever since films began to be made in that country. These motion pictures, which are traditional Chinese drama recorded on film, have rarely been shown outside of Chinese-American circles. In recent years these films have begun to reflect some occidental influence. For example, in some recent films Chinese characters are shown in certain scenes wearing Western clothes. However, Chinese films have seldom if ever had any kind of general release in this country.

NOTES

1. Interestingly enough, the man who took this role was none other than Warner Oland, who was later to be cast first as Fu Manchu, and then as Charlie Chan. This is the first film in which Warner Oland played the role of a Chinese villain. He had not originally been cast in this part, but at the end of the first day's shooting the director decided that the actor playing the villain did not look enough like an Oriental, and Warner Oland was selected to take his place.
2. Lewis Jacobs, *Rise of the American Film*, pp. 88–89.
3. Released in 1919, *Broken Blossoms* got a record price of $3.00 a seat for its premiere. Critics heaped praises upon the film. Even the conservative *New York Times* hailed it unreservedly as a "masterpiece."
4. From Seymour W. Stern's *Program Notes on Broken Blossoms,*

published in May 1949, by the Great Films Society of Beverly Hills, California.
5. *New York Herald Tribune,* July 20, 1935.
6. *The Good Earth* won two Academy Awards. Luise Rainer won the award as the Best Actress of the year for her role as O-Lan, and Karl Freund won the award for Cinematography for his work on this film.
7. *China Sky* was based on the Pearl Buck novel, but in the motion picture the story of guerrilla warfare is overshadowed by the romantic angle.
8. Singapore—though in fact a city located on an island off the extreme southern end of the Malay Peninsula—has been portrayed generally as Chinese on the American screen. Singapore has traditionally supported a large Chinese population, so that this screen portrayal of the city has some basis in fact.

THE PORTRAYAL OF INDIA ON THE AMERICAN SCREEN

There have been far fewer motion pictures on the American screen portraying Indian themes, locales, and characters than those portraying China. The ratio in favor of films primarily concerned with China and the Chinese is approximately five to one against those portraying India and the Indian people.

As in the case of films about China, the earliest American motion pictures on India were of the newsreel variety, and the first known film of this type was a Thomas A. Edison film of 1902 entitled *Hindoo Fakir.* In 1912 the Thomas A. Edison Company released a series of brief films of the newsreel or travelogue variety which had been taken in India—*Scenes In Delhi, India; Simla, India; Views In Calcutta, India; Picturesque Darjeeling, India,* etc. Three years later in 1915, Dr. Dorsey, head of the United Photo Plays Company, visited India to record the third in his series of six-reel documentaries on the Far East. By this time, however, the fiction film had begun to claim the primary interest and attention of the motion picture industry. One of the first known feature films to characterize the Hindu on the American screen was *The Bombay Buddha* (Universal Film Mfg. Co., 1915) which concerned the theft of a golden Buddah. Although most of the characters in this film story were Occidentals, the Hindu provided the element of mystery in the solution of the crime.

In the interim between World Wars I and II (roughly

1918–1941 inclusive), very few documentaries or short subjects about India were shown on the American screen. It was not until after American entry into World War II that factual films about India began to appear on the screen in this country. Among the first and most important of these were two March of Time releases, *India at War* and *India in Crisis,* both of which came out in 1942, soon followed by a number of travelogues and other types of documentary motion pictures on India.

Although there have been relatively few films shown on the American screen which have concerned themselves with India and the Indians, it is significant that in recent years there has been a great increase of screen interest in India. We have a record of 30 American-produced motion pictures on India (features, short subjects, and documentaries) which have been released since 1940—and this number is almost half of the total number of 66 American films known to have been shown during the entire period 1902–1954. Thus since World War II there has been a striking increase in the amount of screen attention devoted to India, and, as we shall see, the subject matter during recent years also has undergone important changes.

Analyzing the Production Code Administration figures for Asiatic countries portrayed on the American screen between June 1947 and December 1954, it is interesting to note that there are 30 feature films portraying India and that, with the exception of Korea (which was portrayed in 34 different motion pictures during this same period), films on India were second only to China, of which there were 42. (It is worth noting also that during this same period Japan was portrayed in only 22 different films.) In other words, in recent years, and particularly since India has achieved independence, there has been a noteworthy increase in the amount of screen time which is being devoted to India.

INDIAN THEMES

An interesting and significant fact about the subject matter of films on the American screen dealing with India is that it remained consistent over so long a period of time. Indeed, the most important themes about India can be traced back to the very earliest days of the motion picture. The first motion picture about India of which there is any record is, as already noted, a film entitled *Hindoo Fakir* (Thomas A. Edison, 1902), which can be regarded as the ancestor of the many motion pictures which have attempted to portray the religious atmosphere of India. Likewise, an early film entitled *Charge by 1st Bengal Lancers* (American Mutoscope & Biograph Co., 1903) was the first film to focus attention on the famous Bengal Lancers who have been the heroes of the most spectacular adventure stories of the screen laid in India. Similarly, George A. Dorsey's 6-reel travelogue on India released in 1916 highlighted the big hunt in Indian jungles—another theme which has consistently appeared and reappeared over the years. Finally, *Soul of Buddha* (Fox, 1918) was the forerunner of a whole series of motion pictures dramatizing the tragedy which befalls lovers who attempt to ignore the longstanding prejudices which divide East and West.

India, the mysterious, is a theme which has run consistently through motion pictures about that country. The word "mysterious" or "mystic" has always been associated closely with India in motion pictures (e.g., *Oriental Mystic,* Vitagraph Co. of America, 1909), but interestingly enough this has been an entirely different type of mystery from that associated with China. The mystery of India as portrayed on the screen is tied up with the mysticism of religious cults and of Buddhism itself, which has never been fully comprehended by Americans generally nor by most Americans making motion pictures.

One of the first films about India to develop this theme of "mystic India" was *Soul of Buddha* (Fox, 1918) already referred to above. This motion picture told the following story of a famous East Indian dancer (Theda Bara):

> The widowed mother of Bavahari, an East Indian dancer of considerable fame, fearing for her daughter's morals, brings her to the temple where Bava consecrates herself as a religious dancer. While dancing at a religious festival at the temple, Bava falls in front of Sir John Dare, a major in the English army, who aids her. Intervening, the priests, headed

by Ysora, the high priest, rush toward Sir John and would have killed him but for Bava. As punishment for interfering Bava is commanded to pray before Buddha all night, but she escapes, meets Sir John and they are married. Sir John is cashiered from the army for his escapade, and a year later a child is born. Ysora, who has vowed vengeance, kills the baby and Bava leaves her husband. Sometime later in Paris where she is making her premier appearance on the opera stage, Bava is slain by Ysora who is disguised as Buddha, thereby carrying out his full oath of vengeance.

This early feature film on India was advertised as "strange, mystic and grippingly tense." Other publicity blurbs on the picture also referred to its atmosphere of mystery, e.g., "From the temples of the Most High comes Mystery and Death" and "Love penetrates the veil of mystery and lures dancer to death."[1] It is interesting that in this story the Indian priests are the villains and the religion is definitely identified with Buddhism (often Indian religions are pictured as some strange cult which is not clearly identified with any known religious faith).

This theme, the religious mysticism of India, recurs in many motion pictures: *The Green Goddess* (Distinctive Productions, Inc., 1923, and later made by Warner Bros. in 1929), *Stronger Than Death* (Metro, 1920), *The Black Watch* (Fox, 1929), *Son of India* (Metro, 1931), and innumerable other motion picture stories laid in India. In *The Wheel of Life* (Paramount, 1929) much of the action of the picture takes place in a temple of Buddhist lamas in the Himalayas, and the film takes its title from the symbolic drawings which appear on the wall of the monastery which, in one scene, are explained to the hero and heroine (and the audience) by one of the high priests. A more modern version of the same theme is to be found in *The Razor's Edge* (20th Century-Fox, 1946). In this film there is an impressive sequence when the hero, seeking the answer to life, visits an aged priest high in the Himalayan mountains; here he acquires new serenity through the mystic and ancient sources of knowledge and understanding made known to him. That the words "mystic" and "mysterious" have continued to be associated with India in motion pictures is suggested by the titles of such short subjects as *Mystic India* (20th Century-Fox, 1944), *Mysterious Ceylon* (Warner Bros., 1949), etc.

As in the case of China, one of the earliest themes with respect to India was the dramatization of a love affair between an Indian and an Occidental which ended in tragedy. In some films with this theme the tragedy occurred after marriage, as in *The Soul of Buddha* (Fox, 1918), outlined above, wherein the child, and, at the end, the Indian heroine herself, are killed, the latter as a result of her unholy marriage to an Englishman.

In other films with this theme one of the lovers dies before the marriage can be consummated—for example, in *The Black Watch* (Fox, 1929), *Son of India* (Metro-Goldwyn-Mayer, 1931), *The Rains Came* (20th Century-Fox, 1939), *Man-Eater of Kumaon* (Universal-International, 1948).

The forbidden marriage between East and West also is one element in the plot of *The Green Goddess* (made in 1923 and again in 1930) wherein the suave and lustful Rajah of Rukh wants the heroine Lucilla so that she can bear him a child, "a superman born of the combination of the East and the West."

It is interesting that in several recent films the dramatized love relationship between a European and an Indian has ended without tragedy. Thus in *The Diamond Queen* (Warner Bros., 1953) an Indian native girl falls in love with and, in the end, runs away with an adventurous Frenchman. Similarly, in *King of the Khyber Pass* (20th Century-Fox, 1954) the half-caste son of a British officer and a Moslem girl wins the Colonel's daughter. And in *Bengal Brigade* (Universal-International, 1954) a native girl falls in love with a British officer, and this also does not end in tragedy. The relationship is pictured as a friendship between the Englishman and the Indian girl in which the latter desired more than that, but in the end is content to accept friendship, realizing that the Englishman loves another. Such casual and matter-of-fact portrayals of the relationship between an Indian and a European are new to the American screen.

Jungle life and India as the land of the Big Hunt is another theme which for the past forty years has appeared on the American screen. That George Dorsey's six-reel documentary *India* (United Photo Plays Co., 1916) contained considerable footage on this subject is suggested in a letter from Mr. Dorsey describing this phase of his "expedition" to the Far East:

> I had the honor of being the guest of His Highness the Nizam of Hyderabad, on a cheetah hunt planned in honor of His Highness the Aga Khan. . . . His Highness was also kind enough to let us photograph his menagerie. This is his hobby—the collecting of strange animals and birds. He has a number of white elephants. . . . I expect to finish with India in about forty days more. While here we will join a tiger hunt and an elephant hunt.[2]

Though this theme has recurred since 1915 (also in British films shown on American screens, such as *Elephant Boy,* Korda-UA, 1937; *Drums,* London Films-UA, 1938; *The Jungle Book,* Korda-UA, 1952), it has become increasingly popular in the past seven or eight years in "jungle thrillers" laid in India. For example, *Man-Eater of Kumaon* (Universal-International, 1948) is a jungle melodrama about the stalking of a man-eating tiger that is ravaging a native Indian village at the foot of the Himalayas.

In 1949 Sabu and Turhan Bey appeared in *Song of India* (Columbia, 1949) which revolves around the adventures of an Indian prince and princess who enter a forbidden preserve to hunt wild game. *The Jungle* (Sundaram-Berke Productions, 1952) was the story of a Hindu princess determined to find out why her villages were being destroyed by wild elephant stampedes; in the end it is discovered that a herd of prehistoric monsters have been driving the elephants mad with fear. Another jungle melodrama, *Eyes of the Jungle* (Lippert, 1953), tells the story of a doctor doing medical research in India, who emerges a hero for finding out the cause of a strange wasting sickness among the natives. *The Diamond Queen* (Warner Brothers, 1953) is also a tale of high adventures in the jungles of India. Many of these films of recent years include considerable background footage which was shot in the jungles of India. *The Bengal Brigade* (Universal-International, 1954) and some other recent films on India which are not primarily concerned with this theme also contain sequences which picture the jungles of India.

But the Indian theme which has appeared most frequently on the American screen—one that has been dramatized in most of the big Hollywood productions dealing with India—is the story of primitive tribesmen (usually pictured as living just beyond the Indian frontier) who rise up against the British in India with the idea of overcoming and destroying the British Indian army and taking over all of India. This plot against India is defeated by the British Indian army led by gallant British officers. This theme has recurred with remarkable consistency for over a quarter of a century. Some of the more important films which have dramatized this theme are as follows:

1. *The Black Watch* (Fox, 1929), starring Victor McLaglen and Myrna Loy. Based on a story by Talbot Mundy. Directed by John Ford. This picture concerns a "holy war" which is being planned by hillmen living on the Afghanistan frontier, under the leadership of a beautiful woman, Yasmini, whom the hillmen regard as a goddess. Her plan is to overcome the British, while Britain is preoccupied on the continent during World War I, and with her armed tribesmen to sweep over and conquer all India. The hero, aided by loyal Indian subjects, uncovers the plot and prevents the uprising.

2. *The Wheel of Life* (Paramount, 1929), starring Richard Dix and Esther Ralston. Based on a stage play by James Bernard Fagan. Directed by Victor Schertzinger. This story (which is a variation on the theme under discussion) is laid near the Tibetan border in Punjab. Here a group of white people are marooned in a Buddhist monastery, menaced by a tribe of hostile native tribesmen. They are rescued by re-enforcements from the British military post—and Indian troops under British command battle and fight off the wild tribesmen.

3. *The Lives of a Bengal Lancer* (Paramount, 1935), starring Gary Cooper, Franchot Tone. From the book by Francis Yeats-Brown. Directed by Henry Hathaway. This story takes place on the northwest frontier of India near the Khyber Pass, where the dangerous Mohammed Khan

is effecting a coalition of tribesmen to move against the British. The British officers, realizing that they have "300 million people to protect," act swiftly and, with the support of the entire regiment, manage to defeat Mohammed Khan and his tribesmen in their own stronghold.

4. *The Charge of the Light Brigade* (Warner Bros., 1936), starring Errol Flynn, Olivia De Havilland. Original story by Michael Jacoby. Directed by Michael Curtiz. Tennyson's famous "Charge of the Light Brigade" is explained by a story about Suristan on the Indian border. Here Surat Khan, in league with Russia on the eve of the Crimean War, leads the border tribes against a British outpost killing men, women, and children. The 27th Bengal Lancers dedicate themselves to avenging this massacre, and the opportunity comes at Balaklava, when it is learned that Surat Khan is with the Russians. Fired by the memory of the massacre, the Light Brigade makes its famous charge, and Surat Khan goes down under the charge of British horsemen.

5. *Wee Willie Winkie* (20th Century-Fox, 1937), starring Shirley Temple and Victor McLaglen; based on the Rudyard Kipling story. Directed by John Ford. Laid in the Khyber Pass, 1897, the story of how a little girl makes peace between a British regiment in India and a rebellious mountain chieftain, the leader of savage tribesmen who are determined to annihilate the British.

6. *Gunga Din* (R-K-O, 1939), starring Cary Grant, Victor McLaglen, and Douglas Fairbanks, Jr. Based on a story by Ben Hecht and Charles MacArthur, inspired by the Rudyard Kipling poem. Directed by George Stevens. A primitive religious tribe known as the Thugs are shown to be plotting the destruction of British forces in India, and ultimately the domination of all of India. India is saved from this fate by the heroism of Gunga Din, a regimental bhisti serving with the Bengal Lancers, the bravery of the three British officers, and the fighting strength of the British army which destroys the Thug forces.

Pictures with the above-described theme reached highest popularity during the decade 1929–1939. Of the above-listed pictures, the last four—*The Lives of a Bengal Lancer* (1935);

The Charge of the Light Brigade (1936); *Wee Willie Winkie* (1937); and *Gunga Din* (1939)—were rated as Box Office Champions during the years when they were released (i.e., were among the fifteen or sixteen top-grossing films of the year).

It will be recalled that from 1926 on there were many riots in India, and during the 1930's Gandhi and the activities of the Nationalists in India made world headlines. Yet the uprisings against the British as pictured on the American screen during this period were restricted entirely to the portrayal of savage hillmen living on the borders of India— the Afghans, etc. By attributing the fighting in India mainly to border tribes of primitive hillmen, American motion pictures ignored completely the fight for independence on the part of the Indian people as a whole, a touchy subject from the standpoint of international film markets. There was in the 1930's in Hollywood, as elsewhere throughout the country, very little known and understood with respect to what was actually going on in India, and in portraying the Indian conflict in these terms, the hillmen could be portrayed in the role of the enemy and the British Bengal Lancers in the role of the heroes.

Thus during the decade 1929–1939 the British role in India was glorified on the American screen. This was done through a series of rousing adventure films about the British troops stationed there (notably the Bengal Lancers) which told of brave men finding adventure in a foreign land where primitive people, wild animals, poisonous snakes, and treacherous country called upon them to be brave and fearless soldiers of fortune. In defeating the wild tribesmen, the British have been invariably presented as serving the cause of right and law and order, and acting for the good of India by saving the country from being overrun by savage tribes. The "good" elements of the Indian population are shown to work with them willingly; the "bad" elements against them.

The theme of the mountain tribesmen with their plot to overthrow the British and take over all of India disappeared entirely from the screen during the war years. Indeed, during the years of American participation in World War II, not one feature motion picture primarily concerned with India was produced in Hollywood. There were, however, a half dozen factual short subjects about India shown during the war in American theatres, including three highly informative March of Time documentaries.

In the 1950's the savage tribesmen theme has reappeared in a number of motion pictures (e.g., in *Thunder in the East,* Paramount, 1953), but for the most part it has been used only incidentally and in a variant form. In 1954 this theme once again came fully to life in *King of the Khyber Rifles* but with interesting variations. In this film 20th Century-Fox rewrote and remade the Talbot Mundy yarn which twenty-five years earlier had been used as a basis for *The Black Watch,* and gave it panoramic treatment with cinemascope, for which, incidentally, the subject matter was admirably suited. Although *King of the Khyber Rifles* dramatizes the fighting between British garrisons in India and the wild hill people, its hero (Tyrone Power) is, as already noted, portrayed as a half-caste son of a British officer and a Moslem girl; in addition, the famous Sepoy Mutiny against the British is for the first time brought into the story.

Just as *The Good Earth* (Metro-Goldwyn-Mayer, 1937) had been a forerunner of a more factual and more positive approach to the portrayal of China on the screen, so did *The Rains Came* (20th Century-Fox, 1939) occupy a similar position in relation to portrayals of India in American feature films. In this motion picture the British army in India—which had provided the major subject matter of feature films on India for so many years—was completely omitted from the story. In producing *The Rains Came,* 20th Century-Fox spared no expense in its efforts to portray modern India with a maximum degree of accuracy. For the first time this film projected on American screens a picture of Indians ruling in India. Futhermore, *The Rains Came* pictures the government of one of the Indian states (referred to in the film as "Ranchipur") as having a progressive and modern government which, in a time of great catastrophe, proves itself well able to meet the situation courageously and successfully. Although British characters are among the most important in the story, the hero himself is a young Indian doctor (Tyrone Power), who is portrayed as devoting himself unstintingly to the improvement and betterment of the lot of his people.

Although the Indian maharajah and maharini are pictured as living in wealth and splendor (as was generally the case in India at the time the picture was made), they are characterized as wise and benevolent leaders. The Indian people themselves are shown rising to the occasion during a time of floods, earthquake, and plague, volunteering their services in helping their government to meet the emergency. In the end the Indian doctor sacrifices his own personal happiness (his love for a British woman) in order to assume his responsibilities as the new maharajah of the State of Ranchipur.

Here was a new approach to the portrayal of India, a film in which Indian people themselves were shown as having control in the management of their affairs and in shaping their own destinies.

Thus about fifteen years ago the portrayal of India and of British-Indian relations changed on the American screen, and this change has been accelerated since India achieved independence. During World War II, for the first time in almost twenty-five years, Americans learned, through a series of factual short subjects, something about India, her people, her tremendous economic problems, her role in the war, her relationship to Great Britain, etc. Early in 1949 a March of Time documentary (*Asia's New Voice,* Time, Inc., 1949) showed how the people of India had struggled since 1947 to secure their full independence from Great Britain and presented the many problems facing the new Indian government in its attempt to weld the diverse elements of India into a united modern state.

In 1951 the French director, Jean Renoir, gave American audiences a pictorially exciting and provocative view of India in *The River* (Oriental-International, United Artists). This motion picture aroused a great deal of interest and comment throughout the United States, where it was hailed by many critics not only for its artistry, but also as the first feature film which had successfully captured the "feel" of that country.

NOTES

1. *Moving Picture World,* May 18, 1918.
2. *Motion Pictures News,* June 19, 1915.

3   SIEGMUND LUBIN: THE FORGOTTEN FILMMAKER

Linda Kowall

IN PHILIPSBURG, the summer of 1914 ended with a crash that could be heard for miles and seen around the world. On the slopes of Centre County's Collision Field, a stadium formed by nature, five thousand festive, flag-waving spectators gathered to watch the wrecking of two great Pittsburgh & Susquehanna Railroad locomotives. Bands entertained the Labor Day celebrants with musical selections while fifteen cameramen positioned themselves behind protective armor-plated shields along the trains' horseshoe-curved route and waited for just the right light. Finally, the sun blazed through the clouds. The director gave the word. As both trains appeared around their curves, the crowd rose to its feet. "Like two huge horses in battle," wrote an *Altoona Mirror* reporter, the crashing locomotives reared high into the air before crumpling in on each other in an agony of twisted iron, dust, smoke and steam. All agreed it was a spectacular show.

At a cost of more than twenty-five thousand dollars, this scene for *A Partner To Providence*—episode eight in the popular serial *The Beloved Adventurer*—was also in its time one of the most expensive single scenes ever photographed for a motion picture. It was but one of nearly five thousand films produced between 1897 and 1916 by the Philadelphia-based Lubin Film Company, a company whose chief,

---

From *Pennsylvania Heritage* Magazine, Winter 1986. Reprinted by permission of the author.

Siegmund Lubin in 1910. Photo courtesy of Linda Kowall. Photo by Will
Brown.

Siegmund Lubin, was one of the early motion picture industry's most important and colorful pioneers.

Today, Siegmund Lubin is remembered, when at all, as the enigmatic film mogul who saved the careers of Cecil B. DeMille, Samuel Goldwyn and Jesse Lasky, later the founders of Paramount Pictures. To his contemporaries, however, he was "Pop" Lubin, "the Rockefeller of the Movies," "the man who combined dramatic power with the wizardry of finance and made it possible to commercialize the movies." Marie Dressler, Molly Picon, matinee idols Florence Lawrence and Arthur Johnson, the celebrated Jacob Adler, the notorious Evelyn Nesbit Thaw and the then unknown Oliver "Babe" Hardy were a few of the many personalities featured in the films bearing Lubin's famous Liberty Bell trademark.

Lubin's story was the stuff of which dime novelists would weave their versions of the American Dream. In 1876, the nation was celebrating its Centennial and revelling in innocent anticipation of the continuing peace and prosperity the machine age promised when Lubin, a twenty-five year old German-Jewish immigrant from Berlin, disembarked in New York. "When I came here I was like all young fellows, out to get my fortune. I heard there was gold in the West, and so I took a little jewelry to sell to the Indians and went to California," he would later recall, laughing at his own naivety. "Instead, the Indians got what little I had and I came quick back to New York." Lubin spent his next years traveling to numerous fairs and expositions peddling a variety of optical wares and a metal polish he concocted and impishly labeled "Putzpommade." It was an odd occupation for a man possessing a Heidelberg degree and an extensive knowledge of chemistry, physics and optics, but his crash course in American life would serve him well.

In 1882, at the urging of his travel-weary wife Annie, Lubin finally settled in Philadelphia and opened his first optical shop at 237 North Eighth Street. There, the proud peddler-optician (who once fit Ulysses S. Grant with a pair of spectacles) established himself as one of America's first full-service opticians by combining the traditionally separate services of refracting, manufacturing and dispensing custom-made eyewear. Soon, he was able to move to 21 South Eighth Street, an address that was about to become famous as the headquarters of "Lubin, World's Largest Manufacturer of Life Motion Picture Machines and Films."

In late nineteenth century Philadelphia, it was almost inevitable for Lubin's knowledge of optics to develop into a fascination with photography. The city was a major center for technical, aesthetic and commercial advancements in photography. The Langenheim brothers' introduction of the stereopticon slide to the United States opened the way for Philadelphia to become a leading manufacturing center for stereopticon as well as magic lantern slides.

Internationally renowned William Rau, the only photographer to whom Admiral Peary would entrust the precious negatives of his Arctic explorations, was only a few blocks from Lubin's shop. And so by 1894, "S. Lubin, Manufacturing Optician," also began advertising himself as "S. Lubin, Photographer." His specialty was stereopticon slides and, perhaps owing to his proximity to the theater district, he produced the hand-colored song slides being used by spotlight singers in vaudeville houses to promote the popular ballads of the day. From here, moving pictures were just a step away.

For Lubin, the catalyst was Eadweard Muybridge. During his tenure as a visiting professor at the University of Pennsylvania, from 1885 to 1893, Muybridge continued to conduct and hold demonstrations of his remarkable animal locomotion studies. "He showed a horse walking by stereopticon pictures, shown rapidly one after the other. I started to experiment then," Lubin recalled. "It was in the '90s."

In December 1895, the Franklin Institute hosted C. Francis Jenkins' screening of the first motion picture on flexible film shown before a scientific organization. Lubin immediately purchased a machine from Jenkins and soon, the basement of his optical shop took on the aspect of an alchemist's laboratory as he began to experiment in earnest. By 1896, he had built his first projector, the "Cineograph" and produced his first film, *Horse Eating Hay*. It was primitive fare, but his private audience gasped and marvelled. His next opus was a pillow fight between his two daughters and their friends. Remembering back more than eighty-five years to Saturdays at Lubin's optical shop, one of those friends, Marguerite Sessler Goldsmith, said, "We would be taken to the second floor where he had those old-fashioned Chinese screens, the bamboo that wiggled, and of course being kids, we loved that. And then we would sit down and he had the screen and the machine and we would see ourselves flickering all over the place with the pillow feathers. They were the 'flickers,' he called them, and they flicked all right!"

From the optical shop, Lubin's "Life Motion Picture" enterprise quickly invaded his home in a proper Victorian neighborhood at 1608 North Fifteenth Street. There, in the backyard, he built a stage. Scandalized by the sight of vaudeville dancers undulating before his camera in filmy costumes and prizefighters in revealing tights, the neighbors closed their shutters in horror—and then peeked from behind. The Lubin residence soon became a waystation and dressing room for the motley assortment of performers, both animal and human, that populated his early pictures.

Annie Lubin grew tired of the greasepaint in her bathroom. Distressed by the near asphyxiation of her family when some trained monkeys tethered to the stove turned on the gas jets in their escape, she rebelled. Lubin moved his studio to the rooftop of 912 Arch Street, a location convenient to Philadelphia's famous Trocadero Theater, a burlesque house affectionately known as the "Troc," where he recruited much of the talent for his early Life Motion Pictures. Among his Troc recruits was "Mlle. Fifi," a Philadelphia policeman's daughter who later created quite a sensation as the subject of the legendary raid on Minsky's.

The backyard and Arch Street productions did quite well. An avid prizefight fan himself, Lubin scored his first big success in 1897 with a filmed reenactment of the epic bout between "Gentleman Jim" Corbett and "Ruby Robert" Fitzsimmons. Two local freight-handlers donned false mustaches and followed Pop's spirited rendering of the blow-by-blow newspaper account that served as their script. Pop's cleverly worded advertisements put little emphasis on the fact that his *Corbett-Fitzsimmons Fight* was a re-creation, misleading most fans to believe they were watching the real thing. This became the first of many classic prizefights Lubin would recreate—sometimes with the actual combatants themselves—before the camera on his Arch Street roof. A stickler for realistic detail, he was known to pass out one-dollar bills for his "spectators" to bet at "ringside." With as many as 200 screaming spectators jamming Lubin's and adjacent rooftops, the fire department, fearing the worst, usually added to the considerable excitement by staging a raid.

For more genteel audiences, Lubin filmed *The Passion Play*. At a time when the average length of a motion picture was only fifty to one hundred feet (or spanning one to two minutes), the production of a five thousand foot Passion Play film was a monumental undertaking and, sometimes, an ordeal. The scenery, painted vistas of Galilee strung across Lubin's backyard, flapped in the breeze. The actors were even less impressive. The disciples included several gamblers whose absence was assured whenever a hot crap game could be found. Cast for his striking physical resemblance to popular images of his heavenly counterpart, Lubin's "Christ" was quite a tippler. When the dissipated thespian failed to report for his big scene after another binge, Pop advised the assembled cast: "Please you shall go home. We cannot crucify Christ today. He is too drunk."

Besides raids and unreliable actors, early film production was fraught with other difficulties. Photographic emulsions were unpredictable and apt to flake. Processing was an art, hardly a science. The look of things changed dramatically. Red photographed black. White fluoresced. Blue eyes did not photograph at all. Cameras were bulky and heavy and had to be hefted onto freight wagons for transportation to outdoor locations. Exhibitors had their problems, too. It was a lucky projectionist, indeed, who could laboriously crank one hundred feet of film through his machine without seeing the evenings' program scratch, peel, break or explode in flames. New film titles were scarce and flickering, out-of-focus images only added to the audience's disenchantment. Making matters worse, these visual assaults were generally shown in rented halls by itinerant showmen or projected on spittle and fly-specked bedsheets in dingy and cramped little storefronts.

Lubin's dedication to such a dubious endeavor was cause for wonder, but as Pop recalled, "I told my theatrical friends they had no idea of the future of motion pictures. Long before the days of the nickel houses, I saw them coming." One of the first to see motion pictures not only for what they were but for what they could become, Lubin, with his unique combination of technical and marketing skills, played a leading role in the creation of one of the nation's largest industries and most popular art forms from what had promised to be merely another short-lived novelty.

In 1897, amid advertisements for "Buffalo Foot Cycles" and "circus animals for hire," readers of the *New York Clipper* began to see weekly notices for Lubin's Cineograph, "the most perfect of all projecting machines." Although he was not the only one to manufacture and market projectors, Lubin's enticements to "Make a Small Fortune" and his comparatively inexpensive equipment quickly made motion picture exhibition appealing and affordable to thousands of small entrepreneurs. By 1899, he was offering a special "Showman's Package" that included a Cineograph, films, stereopticon slides, records and a Victor Talking Machine— everything needed to present a film program with musical accompaniment—for ninety-nine dollars. Superior lenses produced a sharper image, smoother gear trains cut down on film breakage and, by 1902, Lubin was proudly announcing "No More Flicker!" His "Marvel of the Century" was still far from perfect, but its ruggedness, light weight and portability made it a favorite with barnstorming showmen. "I think this machine was about the first one used throughout this section of the country for putting on professional exhibitions," recalled veteran showman George W. Dawson, whose reliable Cineograph was used to project the films when the Nickelodeon, popularly regarded as the world's first movie theater, opened in Pittsburgh on June 19, 1905.

In addition to sturdy projection equipment, exhibitors needed films in greater variety and quantity, a need Lubin rapidly satisfied by increasing production. To his popular repertory of pugilism and piety, he added patriotism. The Battleship *Maine* was sunk in a water tank while the major engagements of the Spanish-American War were reenacted in Philadelphia's Fairmount Park. Real or re-created, Lubin films of important political and cultural events—the Paris Exposition, the Olympics in Greece, the Boxer Rebellion, the Pan-American Exposition, President McKinley's assassination—provided immigrant audiences with a news source requiring little or no knowledge of the English language and, for rural audiences, brought the outside world to their little towns. Using trick photography, Pop entertained children with films of *A Trip To The Moon* and other fabulous tales. For "gentlemen only," there were "smokers."

By the turn of the century, Lubin was able to supply well over five thousand different films, including little comic episodes, disaster scenes and, of course, every variation of the ever-popular "chase." Most he produced himself, but many were films by other producers which he simply processed through his optical printer and duplicated. It was a common practice, but Lubin's superior skill quickly earned him the reputation as the early film trade's most notorious pirate.

Thomas Edison had never cared for the movies he is unjustly credited with inventing, but Siegmund Lubin's sudden rise to prominence in the moving picture field did not escape the dour Wizard of Menlo Park, who claimed the exclusive right to manufacture and sell motion picture films and equipment in the United States. Edison warned, threatened and then, on January 10, 1898, filed suit against Lubin for patent infringement. It marked the beginning of a ten-year legal and commercial battle during which Lubin continued to prosper in puckish defiance of Edison Company court injunctions, detectives and hired thugs.

Seeking to broaden the largely rural and lower class urban audience for moving pictures, Lubin built what was probably the world's first theater expressly for movies in 1899 on the midway of the National Export Exposition in West Philadelphia. The prizefight announcer Pop had hired as a barker exhorted wary, middle-class fairgoers to peek inside and the Cineograph Theater soon became the expo's most popular attraction. Lubin's first upscale moving picture theater, the Victoria at 926-28 Market Street in Philadelphia, followed in 1902. Designed by architect Franz Koenig in a style best described as early cinema gothic, the Victoria marked a significant improvement in moviegoing comfort; it became the first of a chain of more than one hundred theaters, including the world's first triple cinema in Baltimore, that Lubin opened in Philadelphia, Reading, Allentown, Wilkes-Barre and cities along the east coast.

Unfazed by the ongoing Edison Company harrassment, Lubin also continued to produce hundreds of popular farces, melodramas, westerns and thrillers which occasionally paled beside the behind-the-scenes adventures of his "outlaw" film crews. The cunning producer frequently evaded his pursuers by dispatching a decoy crew to lure the detectives on wild goose chases through Fairmount Park while his genuine cast and crew embarked on a full day's filming in one of several clandestine locations.

Eastern Delaware County, along Darby Creek, was a favorite location. "Here comes Lubie!" schoolchildren clamored as his film crew made its way up Baltimore Pike towards sanctuary in Lansdowne, Yeadon, Upper Darby, Cardington and Addingham (now part of Drexel Hill) where the Lubin Company continued to film until 1910. Fascinated local residents provided a pool of willing extras and Shoemaker's livery stable supplied horses needed in filming outlaw thrillers. Using expertly chosen camera angles, Lubin's cameramen transformed the Addingham hills into the High Sierras and nearby quarries into perilously steep cliffs, thus providing the origin, many oldtimers claim, of the popular term "cliffhanger." Cowboy and pioneer pictures usually featured scenes taken at a log cabin occupied by Lansdowne's mysterious "Dandelion Liz" or at the seventeenth century Swede's Cabin in Addingham, lending these early films a rugged authenticity impossible to duplicate on any Hollywood backlot.

By 1908, "nickel madness" was sweeping the country and, according to *Moving Picture World,* Lubin and New York's Biograph films were the decided favorites of patrons flocking to the new Bijou Dreams theaters opening everywhere. Realizing the futility of continuing to fight them, the Edison Company arranged a truce with its leading competitors, Lubin, Biograph, Vitagraph, Selig, Essanay, Kalem, Kleine, Pathé and Melies. On December 18, 1908, Edison and these producers formed the Motion Picture Patents Company, a film trust that would virtually monopolize the industry for the next five years. With the stroke of a pen, Lubin—once the "outlaw"—achieved recognition as a motion picture patriarch. Siegmund Lubin and the film industry now entered a period of phenomenal growth.

With his Patents Company profits, Pop built a new studio at Twentieth Street and Indiana Avenue in Philadelphia. At its opening in 1911, the complex occupied an entire city block and boasted laboratories and a studio which were among the largest, most technically sophisticated in the world. "Lubinville," as it came to be commonly called, presented a study in contrasts. In the largely immigrant neighborhood known as Stifftown because of the number of corpses once left there as gruesome calling cards by the dreaded Black Hand, cowboys galloped down the street for a day's filming in Fairmount Park and movie-struck mothers and children watched for glimpses of their glamorous photoplay favorites. Crowds of would-be performers—some seeking adventure, others desperate for a way out of poverty—gathered in the street and inside the courtyard, slowing Lubin's glamorous Lozier touring car as it entered the studio gate.

Inside, the advanced processing technology of Lubin's labs added lustre to the company motto, "Clear As A Bell," and to his films' longstanding reputation as the sharpest, clearest images on the screen. The first floor of the large glass and brick studio was capable of accommodating up to five sets and separate crews filming at once. A cavernous loft area above was used for the biggest, most ambitious productions. Liberated from total dependence on the sun, Lubin directors could film indoor scenes under the studio's powerful banks of Cooper-Hewitt tubes and Aristo arc lamps that snapped night into day.

Lubinville's technical efficiency co-existed with creative anarchy. Carpenters hammered and sawed new sets into position. Lights sputtered. Cameras clattered. Directors shouted instructions to the four of five companies of actors taking pratfalls, shooting up a saloon, fighting or making love. Only the pictures were silent. Scenario editor Lillian Rubenstein remembered, "It was not unusual to receive letters from fans with lip reading ability, complaining that Florence Lawrence had jabbered about her hairdresser during a tense love scene, while in another, Arthur Johnson had lamented the state in which his dress-suit had come from the presser's!"

Siegmund Lubin, a man as complex as the intricate workings of his studio, presided over his operation like an eccentric papa. A six foot, three inch giant of a man, he was known for his business acumen and particularly keen sense of humor. A penchant for recounting amusing personal anecdotes in his inimitable German accent prompted reporters to describe him as "a regular Lew Fields." He drank only the finest champagne and always kept his office fully stocked. Pop's reputation as a ladies' man was well-known and his weekends were usually spent in Manhattan where he surrounded himself with beautiful women. "Each of these girls would, generally, be promised a part in his forthcoming opus," recalled Rubenstein. "Invariably, his return to his office after a New York sabbath found the long benches that flanked the anteroom filled with lovely examples of feminine beauty . . . all drawn by the common bond of glittering promises extended by the movie magnate. All day Monday they came, and Tuesday as well, but by Wednesday, the first group would slowly evaporate . . . However, as sure as clockwork, on the following Monday after Lubin's weekend sojourn, the benches would be crowded once more."

Lubin's genuine concern for his rapidly increasing family of employees was as legendary as his weakness for beautiful women. In an era of generally appalling working conditions, Lubinville provided a congenial working environment, good pay by contemporary standards, and full medical benefits in the event of illness or injury. A studio dining room serving free lunches prepared by the Lubin chef was another fringe benefit cited by the newly founded *United Labor Journal* in singling out Lubin for special commendation in 1915. "I have myself risen from the depths of poverty," Pop once said in attempting to explain. "I can feel just as they feel and I know the bond of loyalty between us will last while I live. I want them to feel we are one family."

Although Lubin built his fortune—estimated at eleven million dollars!—on commercial releases, he was perhaps the first film pioneer to recognize the educational potential of motion pictures. As early as 1906, he believed that, "the day is not far distant when the moving picture film will be delivered at the home as is the morning newspaper of today and that the written description of the events of the day before will be augmented by the realistic portrayal of the happening."

Shortly after opening at Twentieth and Indiana Streets, he placed the studio and his own considerable technical skills at the disposal of some of the nation's most prominent physicians. By 1911, Lubin was making filmed studies of patients afflicted with nervous disorders to assist Dr. Francis X. Dercum in continuing work he had begun with Muybridge at the University of Pennsylvania. With Lubin's help, physicians Theodore H. Weisenberg and Charles D. Mills conducted similar studies and lectured widely on their findings. By filming through a microscope to take some of the world's first films of the movement of microbes in milk and changes in nerve cells, Lubin also helped pioneer the field of cinephotomicrography. In addition to taking early time-lapse films of plant growth, Lubin also developed the working prototype of a motion picture X-ray camera, a forerunner of fluoroscopy.

Lubin films were being enjoyed in theaters around the world and, to satisfy the growing demand here and abroad, Pop and his talented stable of producer-directors opened additional studios throughout the country. In Jacksonville, Florida, Oliver Hardy made his motion picture debut with the Lubin comedy company. The Jacksonville studio also produced the first series of films to feature a cast of black actors instead of the customary white actors in blackface. Sadly, the titles of these films alone, *Rastus Among The Zulus* and *Coontown Suffragettes,* speak for themselves. Society pictures and naval adventures starring "Opulent Ormi" Hawley and Earl Metcalfe were filmed in Newport, Rhode Island, while Mexican westerns were a popular staple of Lubin West in Los Angeles. Romaine Fielding, who helped engineer the dramatic train wreck sequence at Phillipsburg, took charge of Lubin's Southwest studio and wrote, produced, directed and starred in some of the first realistic westerns to be filmed on location throughout Arizona, New Mexico, Texas and Colorado. Using the industry's first portable lighting system, which he designed, Fielding also shot the first feature film, *The Great Divide,* ever taken in the Grand Canyon.

In addition to commercial successes, roving cameramen

captured actual documentary footage of contemporary events ranging from the Dayton, Ohio, flood to the opening battles of World War I. During the first three days of July in 1913, Lubin crews traveled to the battlefield at Gettysburg to film the Civil War veterans gathering to commemorate that tragic conflict. The finished one-thousand-foot, approximately twelve-minute, film *Fiftieth Anniversary Of The Battle of Gettysburg,* was intended as a comprehensive record of "the greatest of all reunions." Beginning with the arrival of the fifty-five thousand veterans, the film, proceeded to show the vast encampment before focusing in on the individuals—Yankees and Rebels shaking hands, high-ranking officers and old nurses who had seen service on the field. Lubin flyers described it as a film "which will be preserved for all time for its historical value."

Not satisfied with his accomplishments, Lubin still dreamed of better. To supplement Lubinville, he purchased the estate of brewer John Betz in 1912 and embarked on a plan to create "The Utopian Moving Picture Plant of the World," a self-sufficient industrial village. Part of his land would be farmed to feed the nearly seven hundred employees eventually expected to live and work on the estate in comfort and harmony. His grand notion was never realized, but Lubin did succeed in spending an estimated two million dollars to purchase and transform his five hundred acre estate across the Schuylkill River from Valley Forge into the most elaborate, extensive and expensive motion picture setting in the world. With nearly two miles of property fronting the Schuylkill, a boathouse on the water, fields and quarries, farms, forests and a deerpark, the vast studio-estate that took a day's ride to cover lived up to its description as "a director's paradise." Overlooking it all was Lubin's grand Betzwood mansion, an English Gothic manor house as palatial as the great showplaces of P.A.B. Widener, Edward Stotesbury and other Pennsylvania magnates of the gilded age.

Thanks to Lubin Company engineer Edward L. Simons, Betzwood's scenic resources were soon matched by its state-of-the-art technology. The laboratory was seventy-five percent automated and, to remove all particles that might blemish the final prints, outside air was passed through an "air washer." Betzwood was the world's first fully air-conditioned film lab and Simons also designed and oversaw the installation of the first continuous film printing machine and the first large-scale automatic time and temperature film development process, with a capacity to process more than eight million feet of film each week!

The story of Lubin's expertise and Betzwood's technology saving the careers of Samuel Goldwyn, Jesse Lasky and Cecil B. DeMille has entered the annals of motion picture mythology. When the fledgling producers tried to project their first film, *The Squaw Man* performed a virtual war dance on the screen. Fearing ruin, the desperate trio brought their film to Pop, whose reputation as a technical wizard and as the maverick of the despised Patents Company offered hope to these beleaguered fugitives from the Film Trust. Lubin easily diagnosed the problem as improperly spaced sprocket holes and the film, repaired and processed at Betzwood, went on to make motion picture history as the first Hollywood feature production and the film whose success laid the foundation for Paramount Pictures.

Filming at Betzwood got off to an exciting start in the spring of 1913 with Lubin's epic production, *The Battle of Shiloh,* one of the first big budget pictures to feature the proverbial cast of thousands. Making up this huge cast were the State Constabulary doubling as cavalrymen and five thousand Slavic coal miners borrowed from the mines for two dollars each per day to play Southern infantrymen.

One battle scene had an unexpected outcome. Smoke-pots simulating cannon fire were placed in a long buckthorn hedge. The miners, very few of whom spoke English, were positioned behind the hedge and supposed to retreat when the advancing Blues reached it. "But it didn't happen that way," Harry Webb, a former Lubin horse trainer and stunt-man, recalled. "Those Slavs thought it was for real and came through that pall of smoke bayoneting the Blues and the scene was a wrong-sided route with many Blues being wounded before director's shouts stopped the carnage. 'We no whipped,' a Slav spokesman said. 'We lick them bastards any place you say!' " With that scene reshot according to history, *The Battle of Shiloh* proved a success and became the first of many Civil War pictures filmed at Betzwood.

After *Shiloh,* Lubin directors returned to English-speaking extras and, to the delight of local Norristown residents, "Every time Pop Lubin was ready to film a Civil War thriller, he would send in a call to Carney's Pool Room in Norristown for men to don a Union or Confederate uniform and report at Betzwood to film the scenes," a former Norristown resident recalled. Soon dubbed "Carney's Brigade," this reliable company of mercenaries gladly acted for sandwiches and a dollar or two a day. Brigade members were part of the encampment on the Betzwood grounds when Lubin cameramen and technicians achieved a breakthrough in capturing some of the industry's first successful night-time scenes for *Stonewall Jackson's Way.*

Ever since Stetson began manufacturing the hats and Owen Wister's *The Virginian* defined the legend, Pennsylvanians have carried on a love affair with the West and adopted Pennsylvanian Siegmund Lubin was no exception.

To Pop's surprise, Betzwood came complete with its own resident cowboy in the person of Buck Taylor—hero of Buffalo Bill's first Wild West Show and immortalized in the dime novels of Prentiss Ingraham—who had a ninety-nine year lease on the estate at one dollar a year. Harry Webb, a former Buffalo Bill Show rider himself, was given the job of breaking the one hundred and twenty-five green broncs being shipped in by railcar from Arizona and soon, the white water rapids at Buttermilk Falls gave way to Betzwood as the production center for Lubin's "eastern westerns." Actor Edgar Jones was hired as the star, not for his riding or acting ability but, oldtimers swear, for his resemblance to the cowboy in the Frederick Remington picture hanging in Pop's office. Jones was supported by the Lubin rough riders, a wild bunch who looked the part but could not distinguish a cow from a calf. Most were local boys with the exception of Webb and Smokey Warner who had left the Cody troupe in 1911 for better pay with Lubin.

As a stand-in for the real West, Betzwood could be very convincing. For *A Waif of the Desert,* its open "prairies" were covered with tons of lime and dotted with fake cactus to create the illusion of sprawling Arizona desert. Webb, who was leading a Conestoga yoked with six oxen and a Jersey cow tied behind the wagon, had vivid memories of one of the film's unintentionally exciting scenes. "I, 'ragged and weary,' was plodding alongside my oxen when a footman, just ahead, flushed a 'planted' rabbit from a 'planted' bush. His blunderbuss stampeded my oxen and as I ran panting, 'Whoa, Buck! Whoa, Paint!,' the Jersey was being dragged on her side and my 'family' was screaming at me to 'Stop those silly, bellowing, cows!' As the runaway disappeared over the horizon a whiskered jayhawker yelled, 'California here we come!' "

An Arizona desert one day and the Russian steppes the next, Betzwood was capable of being made to look like virtually *any* place in the world. Taking full advantage of this asset, Siegmund Lubin produced dozens of ambitious and costly features starring famous personalities in popular Broadway plays or tailor-made original scripts between 1913 and 1916. Zany Marie Dressler inspired the mirth of her Betzwood crew and moviegoers alike in her feature-length comedy, *Tillie's Tomato Surprise.* In *Michael Strogoff,* Betzwood became a Russian nobleman's estate. Longtime area residents still remember the Schuylkill River being set ablaze for the film's climactic scene in which the world-renowed Jacob Adler, as Strogoff, made his thrilling escape from a Moscow in flames. With the possible exception of Prince Henry of Prussia and Mary Pickford, Betzwood's most famous guest was Evelyn Nesbit Thaw, once the focus of the ragtime era's juiciest scandal. In her role as a woman who has known both great luxury and persecution in Lubin's *Threads of Destiny,* Nesbit was able to draw on her concern with social causes as well as her better-known identification with the good life for her performance.

Some of Lubin's most popular and prestigious films were his spectacular and expensive disaster epics. For *Through Fire to Fortune* or *The Sunken Village,* about a small town threatened by an underground mine fire, an entire village was constructed on scaffolding over a quarry at Betzwood. At the director's word, the scaffolding was dynamited away to create the image of a village being engulfed by earth and flame. A year after Europe's guns of August had fired, Lubin film crews in Newport burned and dynamited another specially built town and enlisted the cooperation of the navy's Atlantic Squadron to depict an imaginary invasion of America in *A Nation's Peril.* "Lubin Burns Money" shouted the headline on a story detailing the burning of the abandoned Tacony Iron Works (the foundry where the William Penn statue atop Philadelphia's City Hall had been cast) for a scene in *The Gods of Fate,* a film delineating industrialism's tragic human toll. A growing preoccupation with social problems and disaster films may have reflected the distant rumblings of a way of life about to change dramatically for Lubin and the world he so loved. The trainwreck footage for *A Partner to Providence* became a recurring image in films ominously titled *The Valley of Lost Hope, In the Hour of Disaster,* and *The Gods of Fate.*

Paralleling Lubin's cinematic disasters were a rapid series of personal disasters. On June 13, 1914, the film vault at Lubinville exploded, destroying the negatives of every one of the thousands of Lubin pictures produced. The outbreak of World War I proved an equally serious blow to Lubin who still had family in Germany and was heavily dependent on foreign markets for his films. Poor health and the enormous financial burden of legal fees and judgments incurred as a result of the court-ordered dissolution of the Film Trust delivered the final blows. On September 1, 1916, the cameras stopped, the studios were shuttered and the Lubin Film Company disappeared from motion picture history. Of the nearly five thousand films Lubin produced, less than two hundred are known to survive. Printed on highly volatile nitrocellulose stock, those not lost in the Lubinville explosion fell prey to the ravages of nitrate decomposition or were heedlessly scrapped as worthless relics of a sophisticated industry's child-like beginnings.

Lubin returned to the optical shop where it all began. He died at his home in Ventnor, New Jersey, on September 11, 1923.

To Pop, the final chapter of his story was hardly a sad one. Secure in his belief that films were a universal language and, looking forward to the future of the influential industry he had helped create, he assured an interviewer in 1917, "The camera is dispensing more happiness than guns, and will be an institution when the Krupp is silenced and the ships of the nations are free to dance over the waters again." Lubin spent his final years entertaining a special audience—his grandchildren—and tinkering with radios. Pointing to a box of wire coils and vacuum tubes, he told his wife, "Annie, I'm going to make that box talk." "You'll never stop," was her reply.

David Belasco (1853–1931), the pioneer theatre impresario and director, never made a single movie but his name nonetheless deserves to be linked with Siegmund Lubin, as an early contributor to the phenomenal growth of the new film medium. What he contributed at the turn of the century were innovative staging and lighting techniques that would soon become a major preoccupation of the commercial film industry. For example, in his popular 1905 melodrama, The Girl of the Golden West *(later done as an opera by Puccini), the entire second-act was devoted to a poker game in the girl's cabin, while a violent snowstorm rages outside. Belasco's biographer, William Winter, has left us a graphic description of this scene:*

> *Nothing of the kind which I have ever seen in the theatre has fully equalled in verisimilitude the blizzard on Cloudy Mountain as depicted by Belasco in the Second Act of this fine melodrama—such a bitter and cruel storm of wind-driven snow and ice as he had often suffered under in the strolling days of his nomadic youth. When the scene, the interior of the Girl's log-cabin, was disclosed the spectators perceived, dimly, through windows at the back, a far vista of rugged, snow-clad mountains which gradually faded from vision as the fall of snow increased and the casements became obscured by sleet. Then, throughout the progress of the action, intensifying the sense of desolation, dread, and terror, the audience heard the wild moaning and shrill whistle of the gale, and at moments, as the tempest rose to a climax of fury, could see the fine-powdered snow driven in tiny sprays and eddies through every crevice of the walls and the very fabric of the cabin quiver and rock beneath the impact of terrific blasts of wind—long-shrieking down the mountain sides before they struck,—while in every fitful pause was audible the sharp click-click-click of freezing snow driving on wall and window. . . . e operation of the necessary mechanical contrivances required a force of thirty-two trained artisans, —a sort of mechanical orchestra. . . .*

Other famed Belasco scenic effects included a rainstorm in the second act of his production of Tiger Rose *(1917), done so realistically that during the intermission members of the audience going to the lobby were amazed to find no sign of rain. Belasco's ideas, it should be noted, were influenced by the Théâtre Libre, founded by Zola and Antoine in Paris in 1887 as an attempt to inject new blood into a decayed and dying theatre. What Belasco did, however, aside from his sensational scenic effects, were but a pale imitation of Théâtre Libre's social reformism. See Mordecai Gorelik's classic 1940 volume,* New Theatres for Old, *for an account of this vital theatre movement that swept away the "accumulated trash" of a century or more of outworn drama of "Spanish palaces, dashing heroes and sinister villains in black capes," replacing it with "an extroverted approach to reality," and eventually influencing the new art of film. (DP)*

4   A CHANNEL FOR DEMOCRATIC THOUGHT

Philip Sterling

> It is the people's drama; it is democracy's
> expression of the drama . . . it is democracy's
> newspaper.—Dr. Frederic C. Howe.

SOCIOLOGISTS ARE FOND OF repeating that the motion picture is a powerful molder of public opinion but the full import of this truth, and what it does to the films we see, cannot be realized until we achieve a better understanding of the social dynamics in which all propaganda originates.

Formal study has sought to classify propaganda into such vague opposites as "good" and "bad," "conscious" and "unconscious," "altruistic" and "self-seeking." The soundest sociologists, however, have come to recognize propaganda as "a means of social control." Carrying this definition further, one must conclude that propaganda is an ideological expression of the struggle between opposing interests for the leadership of society.

The chief propaganda function of the film is to perpetuate the existing order. It does this by endless and ingenious repetition, by pleasant and spectacular insistence on dramatic patterns cut to the measure of the status quo. But propaganda is not an arbitrary device. It is a recurring link in the endless chain of social cause and effect. In a democratic

From *Films: A Quarterly* (Vol. 1, No. 2, Spring, 1940). Reprinted by permission of the author.

system every manifestation of propaganda is evoked by, and in turn calls forth, some other, opposite type. No propaganda exists without its counter-propaganda. If the chief function of the film today is a fond, uncritical defense of the status quo, we can assume that, from the invention of the Kinetoscope to the last Academy dinner, there has also existed a tradition of protest, of the urge for social change. Not only can this assumption be made; it can be documented, and designated as the democratic tradition on the screen.

The objection may be raised that any examples offered to substantiate a democratic tradition are exceptions to the general rule of film production. Admittedly, films of social criticism do not bulk large by comparison with the total output over the entire period of the motion picture's development. Nevertheless, they have been sufficiently numerous and persistent in their appearance to constitute a recognizable and important aspect of film history.

In the face of growing consciousness among filmmakers, both in and out of Hollywood, that their medium is a powerful social lever, it is necessary to recognize the democratic tradition on the screen as a healthy, vigorous deviation from the stagnant, reactionary norm. Such recognition may serve to hearten creative film workers to whom social truth is precious. It may encourage those who, despite term contracts, are sorely tempted to draw a little truth into the framework of the Hollywood structure. It may give fresh inspiration to those who are struggling, despite puny financial resources and distribution monopolies, to make and show films everywhere and anywhere in the U.S.A. It should reassure anyone who wants to put the people's point of view on film that s/he isn't starting from scratch.

If some of the pictures touched upon in this brief survey are unfamiliar, it is because a discussion of screen propaganda cannot be confined to the most widely known films alone. Mass distribution methods assure even the most mediocre vehicle a vast audience, if it is the product of a major company.

In 1903, when the film emerged as a narrative-dramatic medium, it was disdained by the upper classes as "a cheap amusement for cheap people." But to the underprivileged denizens of swollen urban centers and factory towns, these crude shows promised not only entertainment but information, education and the general sense of well-being induced by humble appreciative contact with the better things of life.

Catering to an exclusively lower-class audience, it was inevitable that the movies should become the protagonists of broad interests common to the mass of its patrons. The law of supply and demand soon made it obvious that among the most successful films were those which portrayed the workingman in combat against grasping employers, greedy trusts, heartless landlords, corrupt politicians, and a host of other social and economic evils besetting the lower brackets.

Early in their history, under the stimulus of popular movements ranging from the Granges to the I.W.W., story films turned unorthodox eyes on politics, politicos and bureaucracy, making them the targets of broad humor. *The Candidate* (1908, Pathé) portrayed the distasteful electioneering duties, the premature victory celebration and the eventual frustration of an office-seeker and his ambitious wife. *In the Government Service* (1908, Pathé) shows a tax collector cooking his breakfast, eating it and composing himself for a nap in full view of exasperated citizens waiting before his wicket to pay their taxes. *The Politician's Love Story* (1909, Biograph) deals with the embarrassment and ultimate sweet surrender of a political boss who finds that he cannot do bodily damage to an unfriendly cartoonist because the cartoonist is a woman. Gene Fowler records that it was directed by D.W. Griffith and that it marked Mack Sennett's debut as a screen writer, as well as providing one of his earliest starring vehicles. *The Politician* (1909, Gaumont) records the discomfiture of a successful office-seeker who is pressed for fulfillment of his campaign promises. (Gaumont and Pathé were French companies but until World War I there was unrestricted commercial interchange of attractions between Europe and the United States.)

It was Will Rogers, however, who achieved the probable high point in movie humor at the expense of politicians. Rogers, a village idler, in *Going to Congress* (1920, Pathé) is picked by the party machine as a docile candidate, and wins the election by promising rain to his rural electorate.

As films gained somewhat in length and dramatic capacity, a more serious type began to concern itself with politics.

The essential pattern, with many variations, consisted of an honest officeholder struggling to protect the people's interests against corrupt business influences. This type has persisted down the years, finding its most recent expression in *Mr. Smith Goes to Washington* (1939, Columbia) but its significance in the second decade of the century is indicated by Louis Reeves Harrison's comments in *The Moving Picture World,* on *The Reform Candidate* (1911, Edison):

"Once in a while," he observes, "there is a veritable revolt against the contemptible methods used in 'practical' politics and such a one is spiritedly shown in the Edison production in a way that throws the spotlight on methods employed by electric traction companies to obtain valuable franchises by felonious perversion of legislative action." Flowery, but enlightening. Would any reviewer for a modern trade paper dare to comment on a new film with such freedom and such concern for its meaning?

From politics it was a short step to more direct criticism of the social and economic structure. Until 1917, there flourished a school of cinematic muckraking closely akin to the muckraking journalism of an approximately concurrent period. Between 1890, when the Sherman Anti-Trust Act was passed and 1914, when President Wilson sought to bolster its ineffectual provisions with the Clayton Anti-Trust Act, monopoly combines were a powerful source of public irritation. This irritation was reflected in films such as D.W. Griffith's *A Corner in Wheat* (1909, Biograph) which contrasted the honest toil by which grain is cultivated with the rapacious operations of wheat pit gamblers. The inevitable punishment of malefactors, on which the Production Code insists so rigorously today, was satisfied in the Griffith film by a dénouement in which the king of the wheat gamblers is buried under an avalanche of grain pouring into an elevator. It is worthy of note, in passing, that such punishment is not visited on Jim Taylor, the mastermind of the political machine, nor on Governor Hopper, his puppet, in such contemporary references to the problems of democracy as *Mr. Smith Goes to Washington.*

The Griffith film, like all the democratically inclined opera of the period was an ideologically active reflection, not merely of current events, but of the attitude evoked by these events in the mass of common people who constituted the motion picture audience.

It must be noted here that the democratic film reflects its times in a fashion capable of stimulating thought and deed. Films devoted to defense of the *status quo* are usually passive reflections of life, for their ultimate function is to dissuade its audiences from the need for change. Consequently they must induce a mood of spiritual and intellectual lassitude. This is what Hollywood's official and conservative spokesman may have meant when he declared, pontifically, "the purpose of entertainment is to entertain."

Even as late as 1923, the motion picture had not yet been disciplined to reticence in reflecting ugly facts about the lives of the common people. In reviewing *The Little Church Around the Corner* (1923, Warner Bros.) in *The Moving Picture World,* Roger Ferri points out that: "Mine disasters have been frequent in the past few months and *it was to be expected* that some moving picture producer would . . . inject one into a production." But the disaster in this film is not "injected." It is an integral part of the story of a youth who becomes a minister hoping to use his office for the improvement of the miners' working conditions. His own father had been killed in a mine accident. He falls in love with the mine owner's daughter, is tempted by his rich associates to renounce the poverty-ridden people whence he sprung but, according to the reviewer, "a great strike and a mob in an ugly mood" bring him to see the error of his ways.

The inexperience of the movies' social commentators *circa* 1910 did not deter them even from satire, that tricky weapon which the mature film of today handles so diffidently. *The Egg Trust* (1910, Essanay), voicing indignation against the high cost of living, showed soldiers guarding hen-houses and escorting delivery trucks laden with precious eggs, and the president of the Egg Trust worshipping the image of a white hen on a pedestal.

From 1911 to 1916 there was a constant flow of films condemning slum owners, fake patent medicine manufacturers, unscrupulous insurance companies, sweatshop operators, food adulterators, and "the trusts" generally.

The Wedding Bell (1911, Edison); *The Awakening of John*

Bond (1911, Edison); and *The Atonement* (1911, Edison) were indictments of slum housing and landlords who profited therefrom.

The Price of Human Lives (1913, Edison); *Poison!* (1915, Kalem); *The White Terror* (1915, Imp) and similar films, gave short shrift to those who reaped fortunes from the sale of fraudulently advertised patent medicine. Perhaps the most outstanding of this group was *The Jungle* (1914, All Star) made from Upton Sinclair's book. Audiences received it with something of the excitement attendant on the opening of *The Grapes of Wrath.*

In a similar spirit of indignation and progressivism, the movies dealt with social and economic forces whose identities are suggested by such film titles as *The Money Kings* (1912, Vitagraph); *The Trust* (1912, Gaumont); *The Toll of Mammon* (1914, Excelsior); and *Money* (1915, World).

Probably the most unrestrained and prototypal specimen of the muckraking film was the 20-episode serial, *Graft* (1915, Universal). The plot was based on the bold and not too fantastic idea that various vested interests had pooled their power and perfidy to maneuver price increases, bribe public officials, prevent the organization of labor, and suppress public protests against such abuses.

The titles of many of these episodes are, in themselves, revealing: *The Tenement House Evil; The Traction Grab; The Harbor Transportation Trust; The Milk Battle; The Powder Trust and the War; The Patent Medicine Danger; The Insurance Swindlers; Grinding Down Life; Old King Coal; Pirates of Finance. Graft* was, in fact, a summary of the democratic tradition of the film from 1908 to 1917. Each of its episodes is representative of dozens of films made on a similar theme during these years.

The ideological climax of the series occurred in Episode Sixteen, *The Pirates of Finance.* The flavor of the film and the emotions it aroused are best suggested by this synopsis:

> Stone, head of the Mighty Money Trust, is preparing to create a panic in the money market to discredit Harding who is running for mayor on the Reform Political Party Ticket. [This was probably based on the Tammany fight against John

Purroy Mitchel and William J. Gaynor in New York City.]
Dorothy, reading a magazine, sees a cartoon of the money
monster crushing the people. Suddenly the figures become
animated: crowds of men toil in the sand, dressed in Egyptian
slave garments. Stone, as king, holds a club over their heads
and when one of the workers finds the precious Food Stone
and attempts to quit the struggle and enjoy it in the shade,
Stone goes to him, knocks him down with the club and takes
the stone away from him, tossing it on a great pile of stones he
has collected that way. A Stranger (Harding), comes along
and asks why they submit and they point to the club. He tells
them they have a much stronger weapon, the sword of the
Law. The slaves are too fearful or too stupid to use it, so the
Stranger raises it and does battle with the king. Knocked down
repeatedly, the stranger retires to examine his sword and
finds that a long chain, attached to the hilt, is held at its other
end by his adversary who deflects every blow of the sword by
pulling at the chain. The Stranger calls on the slaves to help
him detach the chain from the sword, and once this is
accomplished, the evil king is despatched, and the slaves are
freed.

The highly paid, sophisticated film writers of today would
dismiss so crude an allegory with the undignified dictum, "it
stinks" but to nickelodeon audiences in 1915 it had all the
savor of truth.

Prewar filmmakers recognized the antagonism between
labor and capital as the most elemental conflict of our times
and with a healthy, if somewhat naive dramaturgic instinct,
they proceeded to make drama of it. The attitude of the
nickelodeon film toward labor was conditioned in the first
place by the organization of a projectionists' union in
Chicago in 1908. *The Moving Picture World* for October 3,
1908, reports that the Chicago projectionists won a strike for
improved working conditions and the same issue reviews
The Power of Labor (1908, Selig), dealing with a successful
strike in an industrial plant. During the ensuing two years
there were numerous films dealing with strikes and labor
unions. Most of these tended to blame the bad judgment of
the workers and the malign influence of agitators for the
strikes they depicted, but virtually all of them established or
suggested the existence of some provocation on the part of

the employer. A transition toward the sympathetic treatment of labor was provided in *Tim Mahoney, The Scab* (1911, Vitagraph). The significance of the film was that it seemed to place an approximately correct valuation on the relations between a workingman and his union and that it conveyed quite clearly the ostracism in which a scab is held by his former comrades.

The Lockout (1911, Reliance) portrayed contemporary labor strife with such accuracy and pro-labor sympathy that *The Moving Picture World,* usually liberal in its judgments, was frightened enough to suggest that the National Board of Censorship should have prevented the release of the film. *Eyes That See Not* (1912, Rex) contrasted the luxury of a mill owner's home with the poverty of his workers. *The Triangle* (1912, Edison) was built around a purely economic plot whose moral was that employers could serve the common welfare by increasing the wages of their workmen and thus raising the general level of the nation's purchasing power. *Out of Darkness* (1915, Lasky) dealt with inhuman labor conditions in western canneries and *The Man With The Iron Heart* (1915, Selig) provided an unsympathetic portrayal of an industrialist who hires gunmen to break a strike. *The Bruiser* (1916, Mutual) is virtually a sermon against the dangers of company unionism and a warning against the manner in which employers use labor spies to wreck trade unions. *The Moving Picture World* deemed it "especially fruitful as propaganda on the labor side."

A natural transition from the intensely democratic mood of the nickelodeon to the complacent conservatism of the screen in the twenties and early thirties, was afforded by the World War. The slogan, "make the world safe for democracy" dovetailed perfectly with the movie mood of the preceding years. Democracy was precisely the right catchword to ensnare a people steeped in its tradition and hot in pursuit of its benefits, but there were at work, in the industry, changes which were making the motion picture less and less tenable as a channel for democratic expression.

Despite the fact that films were still housed in shabby nickel and dime theatres during the years preceding the Armistice, the industry was no longer in the handicraft stage.

Large-scale production had begun in New York, Philadelphia, Chicago and Los Angeles. Motion picture theatres like
Mitchell Mark's Strand and the Knickerbocker theatre were
beginning to invade Broadway in 1914, and to compete with
the legitimate drama in other cities. Otto Kahn of Kuhn, Loeb
and Company, William Randolph Hearst and other men of
substantial capital had become interested. The improved
quality of films was attracting a large middle class audience
to whom the frank progressivism of the contemporary screen
was rather distasteful. The war years redoubled the golden
flood which had been swelling the coffers of the biggest film
companies and by the time the Armistice was signed, the
movies had become big business. The familiar process by
which independent operators were being squeezed out and
control of the industry was being concentrated in relatively
few hands, was well under way. These considerations
affected not only the content of films, with which we are
mainly concerned here, but all its elements.

But even during 1917–18, when war incitement was
predominant on the screen, the critical spirit persisted. *The
Public Be Damned* (1917, Public Rights) offered an exposé
of food profiteering, and *Food Gamblers* (1917, Triangle)
was in a similar vein. *The Brass Check* (1918, Metro), having
no apparent connection with Upton Sinclair's book of a later
date, told the story of "the rubber trust's" efforts to defraud
the inventor of a synthetic rubber formula. *The Mother and
the Law* (1919, Griffith) suggested, in its sympathetic portrayal of poverty that the responsibility therefore rested with
capital. *The Woman God Sent* (1919, Selznick) struck boldly
at the evils of child labor. The film's wartime strictures
against food speculators and profiteers were entirely conso-
nant with war incitement. They served as a warning to those
who were profiting from the war that they must keep their
greed within respectable limits and they served, generally, to
preserve the illusion that democracy does not cease to
function in wartime.

Such productions, however, were not characteristic from
1917 to 1924. After the Armistice, war incitement gave way
to anti-labor incitement, in which the screen did its share.
Under the pressure of this vast counter-propaganda, the
propaganda of democracy, which had found ample scope

until 1917, was now temporarily overwhelmed, although not completely silenced. It sought refuge in themes of broad social import which were not directly touched by the political and economic controversies of the day.

Man-Woman-Marriage (1922, First National) dramatized the struggle of women for equal rights from primitive times to date. *The Four Horsemen of the Apocalypse* (1921, Metro) provided the screen's first normal, post-war reaction to the war. In 1922, the American Federation of Labor produced *The Contrast* which portrayed the efforts of striking coal miners to enlist railroad men in a sympathy strike. The film was banned in Kansas. *Main Street* (1923, Warners) contributed a defense of general progressivism at a period when defense was sorely needed. For the most part, however, the continuity of the democratic spirit was to be found in historical themes, particularly the winning of the west.

The ever-recurrent theme of the struggle against poverty was told in allegory by Josef Von Sternberg in *The Salvation Hunters* (1925, United Artists). In the lush period of the late twenties, however, there were few films that revealed any genuine sympathy for the people's aspirations or any comprehension of their underlying moods, save for occasional flashes like *The Crowd* (1928, MGM). Between 1928 and 1931, during the industrial and creative dislocation attendant on the transition to the sound film, nothing of any significance could be expected.

Once the talkies hit their stride, they found room, however, for serious-minded reconsideration of the war in such films as *The Case of Sergeant Grischa* (1930, RKO) and *All Quiet on the Western Front* (1930, Universal). The historic bonus march was sympathetically treated in *Washington Merry-Go-Round* (1932, Columbia). Earlier that year, *The Dark Horse* (1932, First National) gave satirical consideration to the manner in which political machines select Presidential candidates. Freed of Hays office restrictions during the years from 1931 to 1935, the screens of America would have been overrun with trenchant films on unemployment. Even as it was, one or two references to the matter managed to break through. Hollywood did not wholly ignore the depression, but soft-pedalled it. In the main, the West Coast tactic was to "laugh it off." The most desperate example of this approach, is probably Jimmy Durante's unforgettable line in *The Phantom President* (1932, Paramount), ". . . what's a depression? A depression is a hole. And what's a hole? Why, a hole is nuttin'!"

Among the more serious and accurate expressions of the popular mood during these years were *Broken Lullaby* (1932, Paramount); *Golden Harvest* (1933, Paramount) which portrayed a farm strike against foreclosures, *Wild Boys of the Road* (1933, First National) which dealt with the problem of the hundreds of thousands of migratory adolescents, disfranchised and brutalized by economic crisis, and *Gentlemen Are Born* (1934, First National) which treated a similar theme.

The inauguration of the New Deal gave the Hays Office, for the first time since its inception, an opportunity to align itself somewhere near the side of progressivism. It encouraged the making of numerous shorts in support of the President's recovery program, of which the most notable in some ways was *The Road is Open Again* (1933, Warner Bros.). By the end of President Roosevelt's first term there began to reappear some of the vigor with which the screen had reflected democratic mood and action in the prewar period. Made as outright propaganda for President Roosevelt's reelection, but receiving apparently poor distribution, *The President's Mystery* (1936, Republic) preached an undisguised sermon against the American Liberty League. Continuing this foresighted opposition to the mounting threat against American institutions and civil liberties was *Black Legion* (1936, Warner Bros.) and *Legion of Terror* (1936, Columbia).

Since 1936 there has been a growing consciousness that it is possible to broaden the channels of democratic thought on the screen. This promise has been realized in part by films like *Dead End* (1937, Goldwyn-United Artists); *The Story of Louis Pasteur* (1936, Warner Bros.); *The Life of Emile Zola* (1937, Warner Bros.); *A Man to Remember* (1938, RKO); *Blockade* (1938, Wagner-United Artists); *Fury* (1936, MGM); *Juarez* (1939, Warner Bros.); *Confessions of a Nazi Spy* (1939, Warner Bros.); *Let Freedom Ring* (1939, MGM); *"One-Third of a Nation"* (1939, Paramount); *Boy*

Slaves (1939, RKO); *When Tomorrow Comes* (1939, Universal); and *Mr. Smith Goes to Washington* (1939, Columbia).

It must not be assumed, however, that any of the examples offered here are absolute. On the contrary, the process by which propaganda generates counter-propaganda sometimes operates within a single film or even a single sequence. *Mr. Smith Goes to Washington* provides a praiseworthy exposure of the manner in which vested interests manipulate government. Certainly it partakes strongly of whatever democratic spirit there is in the American film. Nevertheless, it glorifies the "filibuster," a tactic whose function in recent times has been to levy blackmail on the democratic process. At the same time, its plot puts Congressional demands for relief in the mouths of the villains of the piece.

Even more damaging criticisms could be made of the melodramatic hokum in *Let Freedom Ring* and *"One-Third of a Nation,"* and of the inconclusive solution of the problem presented in *Boy Slaves*. It must be recalled, however, that no expression of democracy, on or off the screen, can operate with all the ideological elbow room it should have. The best instruments of propaganda are part and parcel of the *status quo*. Not only are they administered in defense of vested interests; they are themselves vested interests. Any criticism of the existing order which slips through these channels does so because press, radio and film, being commercial enterprises, cannot wholly ignore the moods of their customers. An additional factor is that these agencies, particularly the movies, are dependent on the possessors of certain creative talents. The artists are far more alert and eager to give dynamic expression to the moods and aspirations of their audiences than are their employers.

Sympathetic presentation of democratic attitudes sometimes occurs in films whose basic tendencies may be anti-democratic. This is particularly true of uninspired pictures whose plot, mood, setting, and characters are so stereotyped that the only lasting impression is made by sequences which deviate from the hackneyed pattern. An example that comes to mind in this connection is the largely objectionable *Pacific Liner* (1939, RKO) which portrays a struggle of weakling "agitators" in the stokehold of a cholera-infested ship, against a diamond-in-the-rough black-gang boss (Victor McLaglen) who rules them with a fist of iron and a heart of gold. From the welter of sociological and dramatic untruths afforded by this moth-eaten story, there emerges a flash of honest characterization; a Negro stoker is shown to be the physical and intellectual superior of his fellow shovelers.

It is evident from all the foregoing that there are quantitative and qualitative differences in the forms, intensities and opportunities of democratic expression on the screen before and after the First World War. The most vital of these differences is that the film industry, until 1917, consisted of independent freely competitive enterprises operating without the restrictive control of high finance, whereas after that point there was a rapid, intense concentration of industrial and financial control in the hands of relatively few companies.

One extraordinary labor film of the silent era needs to be added to Philip Sterling's dramatic survey. In 1913 an American (Studio) film titled simply Why, *reflected the mass movement against the trusts which split the Republican Party and elected a Democrat, Woodrow Wilson, to the Presidency in 1912, while winning nearly a million votes for Eugene Debs, the Socialist Party candidate, then an unprecedented achievement for a left party. The film dealt with such questions as "Why do we have children at hard labor?," "Why does capital sit easily at dinner with church and justice and the army while labor is outside starving?" (See Art Young's cartoons of that era.)*

The Moving Picture World *(May 31, 1913) summarized the plot of the film as follows:*

> *A wealthy hero takes a journey through the world and is struck by all the hardship of labor. When he discovers children at work on a treadmill he shoots their taskmaster who at once turns into a bag of gold, so that it is impossible to kill capital. Then he is invited to come to dinner with capital and while they are feasting, the laboring men revolt, demanding a seat at a table. The frightened capitalists rally around the generals as they shoot the people . . . who fall beside the food*

laden table. The climax comes with the burning of the Woolworth building and lower Manhattan by the workers, promulgating that what is theirs they can destroy.

The Moving Picture World *reviewer gave the film a high rating despite its anarchist ending: "It . . . will excite all who see it," he said. "It will get into their blood, especially if they are sensitive; and they will remember it. Yet we cannot say that the picture teaches anarchy."*

Efforts to locate a print of Why *have failed. Nor is there any record of where it was shown or of its impact on audiences. All that remains is this one review in the* World. *I should add that 1913 was also the year that William D. (Big Bill) Haywood was expelled from the Socialist Party Executive Committee for publicly expressing such extremist views as ". . . No Socialist can be a lawabiding citizen. When we come together and are of a common mind, and the purpose of our minds is to overthrow the capitalist system, we become conspirators then against the U.S. government. . . . I again want to justify direct action and sabotage. . . ." Ironically, among the New York intellectuals who defended Haywood as "dedicated to the organization of the unskilled, the poverty-stricken and forgotten workers" was the future stalwart defender of capitalism, Walter Lippman. (DP)*

5 SHOLEM ALEICHEM AND CHARLIE CHAPLIN

David Matis

IN 1914, AMERICA WAS ENRICHED by the creative activities of two immigrants, Sholem Aleichem and Charlie Chaplin. In that year Chaplin (who had come here in 1913 for a second time) began to strike roots in this country with his short film comedies. Each week a new Chaplin comedy appeared on the screen. In 1914, too, Sholem Aleichem, already well known and recognized through his greater and lesser humorous work as a classic writer in Yiddish literature, arrived in America for the second time.

Soon after his arrival here he continued his literary activities with his customary diligence. The popular and beloved Sholem Aleichem and the young, unknown Chaplin never met personally. Chaplin was always busy in faraway Hollywood, where with great difficulty he blazed a new trail for the film art in America and in the world. Sholem Aleichem, who settled in New York, did not surrender to his serious illness but continued until the last day of his life (May 13, 1916) to create new work and revise his older work. Sholem Aleichem was one of the few intellectuals in America as well as in Yiddish circles who helped to discover Chaplin.

At that time, most of the intellectuals in the United States, the "cream of society," looked down upon this new people's art form, the movies. It was especially difficult for them to

From *Jewish Currents* (October, 1959). Excerpted from David Matis, *The World of Charlie Chaplin,* published in Yiddish by YKUF. The translation is by Dr. F. Camenir. Reprinted by permission of *Jewish Currents.*

accept the success of the new star rising in the film world, Charlie Chaplin. Sholem Aleichem, however, never missed a single one of Chaplin's films, which were shown in the small theatres of Harlem and the Bronx where he lived. Furthermore, Sholem Aleichem began to consider himself Chaplin's personal friend and follower, who required defense and protection in time of need. The American Yiddish journalist, N. B. Linder, a constant visitor at Sholem Aleichem's home, relates the following significant incident.

"One evening there was a gathering of friends in Sholem Aleichem's house. Sholem Aleichem, who came late, probably from a Chaplin movie, began to speak with great enthusiasm of his new friend in this country, Chaplin. Among those present, there was a young man who considered himself a connoisseur of films, as he had studied this art in Germany. Sholem Aleichem's praise of Chaplin did not appeal to this young man. The following dialogue then ensued between them:

" 'Young Man—What, in particular, attracts you so in Chaplin? The way he sniffs like a dog smelling carrion?' (And the young man thereby imitated Chaplin's gesture of wiggling his mustache and turning up his nose.)

" 'Sholem Aleichem—No, that really isn't so nice.'

" 'Y. M.—(encouraged by his first victory) What then? The way he shrugs his shoulders or twirls his cane?' (And the Young Man tried to imitate Chaplin.)

" 'S. A.—That's also not so good.'

" 'Y. M.—Then what? The way he hops about on one leg? Or shoves his hat up and down his skull?' (And again, he imitated Chaplin.)

" 'S. A.—No, that's certainly nauseating.'

" 'Y. M.—If this is so, then what do you like so much in your Chaplin?'

" 'S. A.—You'll excuse me, young man. You didn't understand me. I was talking about the way *Chaplin* does all these things, and not the way *you* imitate *him*!' " (*Der Tog*—The Day, New York, April 2, 1939, quoted in *Dos Sholem Aleichem Buch*, N. Y., 1926, 1956.)

Sholem Aleichem's "personal friendship" with Chaplin was not accidental. His boundless enthusiasm for Chaplin's film comedies was basically the result of the mutual creative interests of both artists.

Both Sholem Aleichem and Charlie Chaplin, each through his own artistic medium, spotlighted in their work the folk figure, the little man. Sholem Aleichem and Charlie Chaplin found their cultural resources within the people; their work reflected the life of the people; and they both placed their enormous talents at the service of the broadest strata of the people. Furthermore, Sholem Aleichem and Chaplin identi- fied themselves fully with the wishes, thoughts and dreams of their heroes.

Sholem Aleichem speaks out through Tevye the dairy- man. The world of Charlie Chaplin is expressed through *The Tramp* (1915) and in all his prototypes from 1914 to date. During his first few years in this country (1914–1916), Chaplin produced about 50 light comedies. We may assume that Sholem Aleichem saw all or almost all of them. There is no doubt that Sholem Aleichem recognized in Chaplin's comedies his own Menahem Mendel, his own Tevye, his own Mottel Paisye the Cantor's son, his own "little man" from Boiberik, Kasrilovke and Yehupitz.

In these early Chaplin comedies, Sholem Aleichem recog- nized his own hero who could laugh and shed tears at one and the same time; who loved life but is smothered by its impact; who always dreams about a "little luck" in life and becomes bitter and disillusioned when the sweet dreams dissolve into nothing.

Chaplin's hero, who in the earlier years of his existence on the screen was steeped in primitive feelings of hate, bitter- ness and helplessness, became—in time—endowed with the spirit of humanism, just as were most of the Sholem Aleichem heroes, and became aware of the need to fight for a world without tears.

Nine years after Sholem Aleichem died, the Chaplin film comedy, *The Gold Rush,* made its appearance. This is strongly reminiscent—not only in name—of Sholem Alei- chem's *Gold Diggers.* In 1921, Chaplin's *The Kid* was produced, which brings to mind Sholem Aleichem's *Mottel Paisye.*

Sholem Aleichem and Charlie Chaplin had another quality in common. Both artists evidenced the greatest reverence for the language used by the common people. Sholem Aleichem wrote in Yiddish, although he could have written (and at one time did write) also in Russian and in Hebrew, because Yiddish was the people's language, denied and disdained by the wealthy, the assimilated, and the "power elite." Sholem Aleichem enriched the people's language and fought steadily against the nationalists and the assimilationists for its legitimate place.

Charlie Chaplin, too, from the screen, spoke a language of the common people, pantomime, which the "high and mighty" did not wish to acknowledge. Both artists, through their popular languages, brought laughter and joy to the suppressed and downtrodden members of society; both always stirred the imagination of the millions toward the possibility of achieving those goals of which Sholem Aleichem and Charlie Chaplin, together with their heroes, dreamed.

In his memoirs of Sholem Aleichem, Linder says, "Sholem Aleichem gives high praise to Chaplin's talents and his rare ability to express, in pantomime, the pathos of this tragicomic fop in all his unfortunate and mischievous behavior on the screen. Sholem Aleichem admires the whole concept of the Chaplin figure—his small mobile moustache; his big, shapeless shoes; his broad, long, and shabby trousers; his tight, greasy jacket; his faded little derby; his thin, crooked, little cane; his general attire; with his little jigging step, tripping over his own clumsy feet."

"This specific image," Sholem Aleichem said to his friend Linder, "is in itself a masterpiece, never yet created by any pen or any artist's brush." Because of his great admiration for Chaplin, and his own honorable modesty, Sholem Aleichem overlooked, at this moment, the fact that such a figure had already been produced by pen on paper, the pen of Sholem Aleichem himself, in his classic figures such as Tevye, Menahem Mendel and so on.

It is certainly a fact that, as far back as 1909, Sholem Aleichem in his romance *Wandering Star* created and immortalized a type who resembles strongly—in his entire personality, attire, behavior, and even in physical appearance—Chaplin's tramp of 1914.

Had Chaplin ever had the opportunity to meet Sholem

Aleichem personally, he would certainly have acknowledged such heroes as Tevye and Menahem Mendel to be blood relatives of his own "little man."

The creative accomplishments of Sholem Aleichem and Charlie Chaplin have stood the most stringent test of time. Chaplin's earliest film comedies are very popular now just as they were 40 years ago. Sholem Aleichem's works are, to this day, circulated in millions of copies and translated into many languages of the world.

The legend that Chaplin was Jewish persists despite all the hard evidence that he wasn't. As far back as 1923, the famous Anglo-Jewish novelist Israel Zangwill believed Chaplin was a Jew, and in an address before Jews at the Brooklyn Academy of Music berated the artist, saying he should be "ashamed of himself" for not admitting it (London Jewish Chronicle, Dec. 30, 1978). Perhaps he has never admitted it because it wasn't true. In fact, in his Autobiography *(1964), the comedian mentioned more than once that his mother was a regular churchgoer (Protestant) and recalled her "gentle restraining hand" one summer's day in church during Holy Communion when he drank a bit too much from the silver chalice containing "delicious grape juice." Chaplin also writes that his grandfather (on his mother's side) was an Irish cobbler who "came from County Cork," while his grandmother was "half gypsy." Little is known, really, about the "family tree" on his father's side, other than that his father was a music hall actor and a heavy drinker.*

It is true that Chaplin was often called a Jew, sometimes mistakenly, but most often insultingly, primarily because of his detestation of Nazism and fascism. One notes that in the early 1930's, the noted British screen writer Ivor Montagu called Chaplin's attention to a "filthy Nazi propaganda book of photographic portraits of Jews" titled Juden sehen dich an *(Jews are looking at you), which included Charlie's portrait with the caption, "Dieser ebenso langweilige wie widerwartige kleine Zappeljude" (This little Jewish tumbler, as disgusting as he is boring). This may have given Chaplin the idea for his 1940 classic,* The Great Dictator, *in which he played the dual role of Hynkel (Hitler) and the little Jewish barber. Montagu, who was very close to the artist, says that Chaplin "rigorously refused ever to deny publicly that he is a Jew. He says anyone who denies this in respect to himself plays into the hands of anti-Semites."*

It has also been suggested that some of the roles Chaplin played may have contributed to the myth that he was Jewish. There was a time in England—long before he had created the immortal Charlie, the tramp—when he was billed as a "Jewish comedian." It seems that everyone in those music-hall days was doing the "Jewish comedian" bit on the stage and Chaplin thought he should give it a whirl; he had thus gleefully accepted an invitation to give it a whirl in a theatre in the heart of the Jewish quarter of London, no less!

Charlie was literally driven off the stage, the artist recalled in his Autobiography. *"Although I was innocent of it," he said, "my comedy was most anti-Semitic, and my jokes were not only old ones but very poor, like my Jewish accent. . . . After the first couple of jokes the audience started throwing coins and orange peels and stamping their feet and booing. At first I was not conscious of what was going on. Then the horror of it filtered into my mind. I began to hurry and talk faster as the jeers, the razzberries and the throwing of coins and orange peels increased." This was Chaplin's first, and fortunately his last, appearance as a phony "Jewish comedian." (DP)*

6 THE IMPACT OF GRIFFITH'S *BIRTH OF A NATION* ON THE MODERN KU KLUX KLAN

Maxim Simcovitch

O VER THE YEARS, historians have linked David Wark Griffith's 1915 film, *The Birth of A Nation,* with the Modern Ku Klux Klan. Although statements and references have been made that the film "undoubtedly gave much stimulation to the use and growth of the Modern Ku Klux Klan,"[1] and that it "was a powerful force in aiding the revival of the Klan,"[2] little specific information has been gathered to support such claims. When historians conclude that "it is surely reasonable to link the revived Klan (1915) to the film,"[3] it prompts a film scholar to examine the film's development to the evolution and development of the organization.

In discussing the film's relation to the organization, two major questions will be concentrated upon: (1) How did the film assist in bringing about the development of the Modern Klan of 1915? (2) What were the circumstances and events surrounding the use of the film by the organization? Though one could never comprehend all the ways the organization exploited the film (due to the fact that many "Klaverns" or chapters existed throughout the nation), there is substantial information on the subject which illuminates the close

From the *Journal of Popular Film* (Vol. 1, No. 1, Winter, 1972). Reprinted by permission of *JPF&T, The Journal of Popular Film and Television.*

relationship that existed, and still exists, between the film and the Ku Klux Klan.

According to leading historians, the actual originator of the 1915 Modern Ku Klux Klan is William Joseph Simmons (the "Imperial Wizard" or head organizer of the revived order). On October 26, 1915, Simmons "decided to launch the movement"[4] and "to discuss the organization of the Ku Klux Klan"[5] with "personal" associates, and with "men from various fraternal orders."[6] Those at the meeting took a positive view of Simmons' idea of a revived order by voting to apply for a State charter. Though it was through interpersonal communication that Simmons persuaded thirty-four men to seek a charter for the order, the event that motivated Simmons was the scheduled Atlanta premiere of *The Birth of A Nation.*

> When an automobile accident laid him (Simmons) up in bed for three months he worked out all the details, which he duly copyrighted. It remained only to pick the time. In the fall of 1915, the right moment seemed at hand. With *The Birth of A Nation* scheduled to open in Atlanta, Simmons sprang into action.[7]

Simmons, aware of the film's premiere date in Atlanta, December 6, 1915, publicized the revived order ten days before the film arrived in the city. On November 25, 1915, Simmons and his followers met on Stone Mountain and "erected a fiery cross" to make the citizens of Atlanta aware of the revived organization, and at the same time, herald the coming of the film. As Simmons related in 1928,

> There was good reason, as I have said, for making Thanksgiving Day (November 25, 1915) the occasion for burning the fiery cross. Something was going to happen in town (Atlanta) the next week (the premiere of *The Birth of A Nation*) that would give the new order a tremendous popular boost.[8]

When *The Birth of A Nation* opened in Atlanta Simmons placed an "advertisement" beside the announcement of the film in the *Atlanta Constitution,* announcing the Ku Klux Klan's revival, purpose, and the need for members.

At this point, it is worth mentioning that, although Griffith has been accused of presenting pro-Klan "propaganda" by the film, in an interview in 1928 he stated that,

> If Simmons actually used *The Birth of A Nation* to raise membership in the Klan, as he says he did, running his Klan advertising simultaneously with advertising of the picture, I can see how many persons may have been confused. . . . I had no more idea that *The Birth of A Nation* might be used to revive the old Klan than I might have had that *Intolerance* (Griffith's 1916 film) would revive the ancient persecution of the Huguenots.[9]

When Simmons was interviewed in 1928 and asked "if there had been no film" could he have "pushed his new order forward as quickly as he did?" Simmons' reply was "no. . . . *The Birth of A Nation* helped the Klan tremendously."[10]

On December 4, 1915, the State of Georgia granted a "charter" for the "origination" of the Invisible Empire, Knights of the Ku Klux Klan. On December 6, 1915, two days following the Modern Klan's charter as a "fraternal" organization, *The Birth of A Nation* was opened to the public in the city of Atlanta. If the publicity and promotion for the film caused "prior expectations and excitement," surely the granting of a charter to the revived order, two days prior to the film's opening, probably heightened and added further to the excitement of both film and organization. Here one can see two complementary forces working simultaneously on the Southern mind—the expectations of *The Birth of A Nation* and the excitement of a revived Modern Klan. Taken from a sociological point-of-view, one could claim that "the film reinforced the romanticized image most Southerners held of the original Ku Kluxers."[11] The film can be said to have made the Southerners aware of the Modern Klan by bringing back the "fond" memories of the Old Reconstruction Klan of 1867. The revived Modern Klan of 1915 acted as a "purported tie" with the Old Klan to many Americans throughout the South, and later, the nation.

> Another factor . . . which has played an important part in preparing the soil for the growth of the new Klan, is the idealization of the Old Klan. Credit for this idealization belongs to Thomas Dixon and D. W. Griffith. *The Birth of A Nation* has

had a much greater influence than the *Clansman* (Dixon's novel of 1905), for the film has appealed to infinitely more people and has profited by the spontaneous emotions of the crowd.[12]

As was related by Richard Griffith in a letter to Seymour Stern on July 31, 1947, *"The Birth of A Nation* is a film embodiment of one of the several defense mechanisms which the South erected like bastions around its wounded psyche in the years after the defeat."[13]

Though one realizes that bits and pieces of information, thought, actions, and communication assisted in the evolution of the revived Klan, *The Birth of A Nation* seems to have played a major role in finally bringing the Klan to reality. Since both elements, *The Birth of A Nation* and the Klan, successfully "reacted upon each other," the rising Modern Klan adopted the film as a means for further recruitment and propaganda.

The picture *The Birth of A Nation* and the K.K.K. secret society . . . were sprouted from the same root. In subsequent years they reacted upon each other to the large profit of both. The film presented predigested dramatic experience and thrills. The society made the customers all actors in costumes.[14]

When the propaganda instrument, *The Birth of A Nation,* was presented in Atlanta, "on the night of the premiere," Simmons and his followers, "mounted and on foot, paraded down Peachtree Street and fired rifle salutes in front of the theatre."[15] Another means Simmons devised to "whip up excitement" for the Klan and the film, was to have a troop of horsemen dressed in the sheets of the Ku Klux Klan ride through towns on their hooded horses in advance of showings of the film.[16]

Although Simmons centered his organization around the film's presentation for propaganda, still other minute factors seeped in to assist with the spread of the Klan in the Southern regions. According to the *Chicago Examiner,* Southern States "distributed" various "bas relief plaques and souvenirs of Reconstruction Klansman, in Klan regalia of robe, mask and hood"[17] during the film's engagement. And when the film was presented in Southern theatres,

"Southern ushers . . . were garbed in Confederate uniform. In some states South of the Mason and Dixon Line . . . ushers were alternately dressed both in Confederate uniform and in the regalia of the Ku Klux Klan."[18] Here one sees two distinct instances of propaganda for the Klan: (1) Propaganda directly engendered by the organization itself (such as rifle salutes, parades, and troops of hooded horsemen at film showings), and (2) Propaganda produced through the presentation of the film (such as plaques, souvenirs, and ushers dressed in Confederate and Klan uniforms). The film acted as an influencing force throughout the South, for the dissemination of propaganda and publicity pertaining to the Modern Klan.

The showings and reshowings of The Birth of A Nation— beginning in 1915 and continuing into the twenties, until theatres in practically every town had run the film—helped to perpetuate the tradition of direct action, not only for Southerners, but for Americans throughout the country.[19]

While the organization's "personal copy" of The Birth of A Nation was being used for private (viewed by members only), recruiting, and social functions (speeches and rallies), the commercially revived showings in the early and mid-twenties were used for Klan propaganda. During the twenties, Northern, Midwestern, and Southern regions were experiencing new problems—"traditional orthodoxy doing battle against the new wave of the future."[20] Although "many interwoven factors (such as the redscare, immigration, and the "New Morality") produced . . . a peculiarly fertile seedbed for intolerance,"[21] one could consider two factors for the Klan's use of The Birth of A Nation: (1) When the "Negro troops began to come back from France an uneasiness ran through the black belt."[22] (2) Negro migration "northward precipitated race riots."[23] Whereas, in the late–teens, the Modern Klan was only a regional, Southern organization, during the twenties it advanced in force into the North and Middle West. Once again, the Klan recognized the advertising value of revived presentations of The Birth of A Nation "as part of Klan propaganda" on a national rather than regional level.[24]

During the organization's campaigns in 1921, the Robert E. Lee Klan No. 4 (Virginia) and Richmond Klan No. 1 (Virginia), sponsored "military training," "food baskets" for Christmas, made "donations" and "attended en masse a showing of *The Birth of A Nation.*"[25] To publicize its activities for recruitment, in 1922, the Luther I. Powell Klan chapter in Portland, Oregon, held "Lectures," staged "drills," gave "speeches" and "burned crosses," while at the same time, the Blue Mouse Theatre presented *The Birth of A Nation* for a return engagement. According to data at the time, by the summer of 1922, "Portland membership exceeded ten thousand."[26] When *The Birth of A Nation* was revived at the Selwyn and Capitol Theatres in New York City, members of the Ku Klux Klan were "seen cheering whenever a hooded and gowned figure appeared."[27]

Due to Klan growth and "riots" in various cities (protests against the film were made in Chicago on February 2, 1924, in Detroit on September 18, 1921, in Kansas on June 8, 1923, and New York City on May 7, 1921), *The Birth of A Nation* was "prohibited by the police" in different areas throughout the country. On December 2, 1922, there were demands that a revived "glorification" showing of *The Birth of A Nation* should be "prohibited" in New York City. At the time, a Reverend Oscar Haywood was accused of trying to increase membership in the Klan with the assistance of the film. Walter F. White, then Assistant Executive Secretary of the NAACP, wanted to uphold a "revocation" of the film since "it (was) a glorification of the Ku Klux Klan coming at a time when the Reverand [*sic*] Haywood has announced that a drive is on for an increased membership in the Klan."[28]

According to Klan testimony, in 1924, members of Klan No. 66 in Dallas, Texas, journeyed to cities for Klan celebrations, or usually attended "repeated engagements" of *The Birth of A Nation* at the Old Mill Theatre.[29] It was during the reissues and revivals of the film that the Klan celebrated the film's return engagements by "offering its literature, often gratis, and supplementary propaganda (e.g., circulars, flyers, handouts) to side-walk crowds and spectators, before and after the performances."[30]

In 1923-4, the U.S. Grant Klan of Chicago, Illinois, tried to "attract" new members in the organization. Not only did the organization sponsor pro-Klan plays (such as *The Invisible Empire*), but also, in February, 1924, brought new recruits to the Auditorium Theatre for a two-week engagement of *The Birth of A Nation.* According to the *Chicago Daily News,* "hundreds of Klansmen were in attendance."[31] And, according to film historian, Terry Ramsaye:

> Early in 1924, *The Birth of A Nation,* then nine years old, played in the great Auditorium Theatre in Chicago, surpassing any previous picture audience record for that house. The patronage of the Ku Klux Klan was credited with giving this run its extraordinary success.[32]

The organizers or opinion leaders of the Modern Klan were "fairly quick" to recognize the value of the film in their propaganda and recruitment activities. For example, in 1924, the Jackson, Mississippi, *Daily Clarion-Ledger* contained "a three-quarters page high endorsement" of *The Birth of A Nation* by the Jackson Klan, in which a Klan-leader wrote: "I feel sure that all good Americans in our city and surrounding territory, both men and women [,] will come to see this wonderful picture."[33]

Though *The Birth of A Nation* was revived at various times during the 1930's, 40's and 50's, Klan activity had subsided within the United States. While the Modern Klan of the late teens and twenties seemed to have centered their propaganda around *The Birth of A Nation* and interpersonal association, the Contemporary Klan (Robert M. Shelton's, United Klans of America, Knights of the Ku Klux Klan) has "a copy of the film *Birth of A Nation* and do use it occassionally [*sic*] for recruiting and when people wish to see it." However, the film is only one of the many ways the Contemporary Klan of today diffuses information to the public. For as was stated by Klan officials, "in most cases we find it not necessary."[34]

The means or methods in which the Contemporary Ku Klux Klan diffuses propaganda are interesting to note, since most of the diffusion elements or materials are associated with the media, particularly films. Not only does the Contemporary order diffuse data by *The Birth of A Nation,* interpersonal persuasion (through Klan lectures and speakers known as "Klokards"), opinion leaders (those in the hierarchy of the organization or group), and fieldworkers (who act as diffusion agents), but also through records, films, photographs, books, and magazines. According to various "Klaverns" or chapters, the films apt to be presented at recruiting drives or "rallies" are civil rights films (such as *Selma March* and *Anarchy USA*),[35] religious films (*Back To God*), and pro-Klan films (such as *While Brave Men Die* and *The Birth of A Nation*).[36]

One of the more important symbols of propaganda for the Modern, as well as Contemporary organization, is the use of the "rearing horse" brandishing the fiery cross. This symbol was incorporated from the publicity photograph for *The Birth of A Nation,* and is presently being used as the main insignia of the order. According to Seymour Sterns' study on the historical aspects of *The Birth of A Nation,*

> The figure of the Klansman on the rearing horse was used throughout the 1920's in advertisements and on billboards. But the mounted Klansman, brandishing the Fiery Cross, remained the emblem or insignia of the film until 1935, when it was replaced, because of mounting opposition to the new Klan, with a reproduction of one of the battle scenes.[37]

Finally, one could contend that both *The Birth of A Nation* and the Modern Ku Klux Klan reacted upon one another, and upon the social upheavals of the times. Both elements worked together to arouse the inner-most instincts, thoughts, and actions in man. Whereas the Modern Klan (1915) relied a great deal on the film as a major source of propaganda, the Contemporary Klan relies more on the numerous communicative elements that exist in our society. Though *The Birth of A Nation* has fallen from a major to a minor source of propaganda, nevertheless, throughout these many years, the film assisted with the evolution of the Modern Klan, flourished with the Klan in the 1920's, and still maintains a place among the Contemporary order.

NOTES

1. Bosley Crowther, "The Birth of *The Birth of A Nation,*" New York Times Magazine, February, 1965, p. 85.

2. Raymond A. Cook, "The Man Behind *The Birth of A Nation,*" The North Carolina Historical Review, XXXIX (October, 1962), p. 540.
3. William Pierce Randel, *The Ku Klux Klan: A Century of Infamy* (New York: Chilton Books, 1965), p. 180.
4. Robert L. Duffus, "Salesman of Hate: The Ku Klux Klan," *The World's Work,* XLVI (May, 1923), p. 32.
5. Charles C. Alexander, *The Ku Klux Klan In the Southwest* (Kentucky: University of Kentucky Press, 1965), p. 4.
6. David M. Chalmers, *Hooded Americanism* (Garden City, New York: Doubleday & Co., Inc., 1965), p. 29.
7. Chalmers, p. 29.
8. William G. Shepherd, "How I Put Over the Klan," *Collier's Magazine,* July 14, 1928, p. 34.
9. *Ibid.,* p. 35.
10. *Ibid.*
11. Alexander, p. 1.
12. Guy B. Johnson, "A Sociological Interpretation of the New Ku Klux Klan Movement," *The Journal of Social Forces,* I (May, 1923), p. 440.
13. Seymour Stern, "D. W. Griffith—*The Birth of A Nation:* Part I," *Film Culture,* XXXVI (Spring-Summer, 1965), 68.
14. Terry Ramsaye, *A Million & One Nights* (New York: Simon & Schuster, Inc., 1926), p. 638.
15. Stern, p. 80.
16. Crowther, p. 85.
17. Stern, p. 79.
18. *Ibid.,* p. 74.
19. Alexander, p. 18.
20. Milton Plesur, *The 1920's: Problems & Paradoxes* (Boston, Mass.: Allyn & Bacon, Inc., 1969), p. 8.
21. Paul L. Murphy, "Sources & Nature of Intolerance In the 1920's," *The Journal of American History,* LI (June, 1964), p. 76.
22. Robert L. Duffus, "How the KKK Sells Hate," *The World's Work,* XLVI (June, 1923), p. 178.
23. Plesur, p. 7.
24. John M. Mecklin, *The Ku Klux Klan: A Study of the American Mind* (New York: Russell & Russell, Inc., 1963), p. 71.
25. Kenneth T. Jackson, *The Ku Klux Klan In the City, 1915-1930* (New York: Oxford University Press, 1967), p. 81.
26. *Ibid.,* p. 200.
27. "A Problem Hard To Solve," *New York Times,* December 6, 1922, p. 18.
28. "Foes of Klan Fight *Birth of A Nation,*" *New York Times,* December 3, 1922, p. 5.
29. Jackson, p. 81.
30. Stern, p. 206.
31. *Chicago Daily News,* February 12, 1924, p. 12.
32. Ramsaye, p. 642.
33. Arnold S. Rice, *The Ku Klux Klan In American Politics* (Washington, D.C.: Public Affairs Press, 1962), p. 132.

34. A short informal letter to this writer—dated March 10, 1970—from the main headquarters of the United Klans of America located in Tuscaloosa, Alabama.

35. *The Fiery Cross Magazine,* III, April,1968., p. 31.

36. *The Fiery Cross Magazine,* IV, June, 1969, p. 12.

37. Stern, p. 202.

I had a hand in eliciting from Sergei Eisenstein the following statement on the D.W. Griffith film, published in the Soviet English–language journal, International Literature *(Nov.–Dec. 1940). It happened that early in 1940 I learned that Seymour Stern (a former close friend of mine) and his associates were planning to mark the 25th anniversary of the film with a well publicized showing in New York and were using Eisenstein's name to promote it, stating that he had hailed it as a major influence on his work in the mid–1920s. I and others involved with films knew of no evidence of this, and Stern and his group could produce none when challenged. When they refused to alter their publicity I wrote to Eisenstein in Moscow—he was then teaching at the Moscow State Film Institute—informing him of the matter. His reply, which I impatiently awaited for many months, finally came in October. It is printed below in full.*

To the Editors of International Literature

In connection with the revival on American screens of D.W. Griffith's Birth of a Nation, *certain shrewd businessmen, seeking to advertise the film, made assertions to the effect that I have praised it and have stated that in its time* Birth of a Nation *had greatly influenced my creative work.*

I emphatically protest against these assertions.

True, I have always given Griffith his due as an outstanding master of the bourgeois film. But this can in no way be applied to Birth of a Nation, *a film which is intrinsically alien and inimical to the ideals for which we are struggling. This film has never been shown here, and I saw it abroad, already after* Potemkin *had appeared, and therefore could have been in no way influenced by* Birth of a Nation.[1] *The disgraceful propaganda of racial hatred toward the colored people which permeates this film cannot be redeemed by the purely cinematographic effects of this production.*

As to the general problem of interrelation between the Soviet cinema and the "old man" of the American film, permit me to draw your attention to my extensive analysis of this problem, which will soon appear in a collection of studies devoted to the art of the cinema in Moscow (Goskino-izdat Editions).[2]

Professor S. Eisenstein

Moscow-Kratovo, October 15, 1940.

1. It was not The Birth of a Nation but Griffith's 1916 epic, Intolerance, that was a major influence on the work of Eisenstein and other Soviet filmmakers. See the article on the 60th anniversary of Intolerance below. (DP)
2. See Eisenstein's famous essay, "Dickens, Griffith and the Film Today," Film Form, edited by Jay Leyda.

7 THE SIXTIETH ANNIVERSARY OF GRIFFITH'S *INTOLERANCE*

David Platt

INTOLERANCE (1916) WAS D. W. GRIFFITH'S answer to the protests and picketlines organized by the young National Association for the Advancement of Colored People over the pernicious racism in his previous film, *The Birth of a Nation* (1915). That film's salute to the white-hooded Klansmen riding to lynch freed Negroes asserting their rights was rightfully condemned by notables like Lillian D. Wald, Jane Addams, Harvard's Charles E. Eliot and others, white and black. The film, said Oswald Garrison Villard, editor of *The Nation,* was "a deliberate attempt to humiliate 10 million American citizens and to portray them as nothing but beasts," a charge disputed today only by hardened racists and unreconstructed art-for-art-sake film aesthetes.

Griffith (1875–1948), son of "Roaring Jake" Griffith, a Confederate colonel, responded to these attacks with a rambling and unconvincing pamphlet *"The Rise and Fall of Free Speech in America"* castigating his critics for endangering freedom of the screen. No one takes this curiosity of literature seriously any more, but the movie *Intolerance,* which was the major part of his offensive against his detractors, is something else.

True, it is in many respects a continuation of Griffith's banal history and sociology. Floyd Dell, in his review in *The Masses* (Nov., 1916), was the first to note the irony in the idea of Griffith, the maker of the "hate-breeding" *The Birth of*

From *Jewish Currents* (December, 1976.) Reprinted by permission.

a Nation, "telling us to be tolerant." But beyond that, *Intolerance* towers as a work of pictorial and poetic beauty on the liberating theme of social justice and universal brotherhood—that is, for all but Blacks and Jews. One notes that there are no Blacks to be seen in the American episode of *Intolerance.* Apparently the director had said all that he wanted to say about Negroes in his previous epic. As for Jews—the victims of 20 centuries of the most barbaric form of racial hatred and intolerance—Griffith in his Judean segment chose to portray the alleged intolerance of Jews toward Jesus—but more about this later.

Griffith scoured world history—from ancient Babylonia to modern America—for material for his main theme. He built enormous sets with towers and walls big enough for an army to march around. He hired actors, horses and elephants by the thousands and built a private railroad to transport food and materials and provided special housing for them all. He shot miles and miles of film over a two-year period, then retired to the cutting-room to shape the mass into four parallel stories of intolerance through the centuries that shook the film world to its roots and opened up unimaginable new vistas of film art. In the finale, as Iris Barry pointed out, "history itself seems to pour like a cataract across the screen" as the director cuts back and forth with shattering effect from one story to the other, from the Persian armies of Cyrus advancing in great hordes on Belshazzar's Babylon to the signing of the death warrant of the Huguenots at the Catholic court and the bloody street fighting that followed on St. Bartholomew's Day; from Christ struggling toward Calvary to the break-neck auto race to save a frameup victim from the gallows.

To hold the four stories together the director used the recurring image of a mother rocking a cradle, a not too effective symbol suggested by Whitman's lines, "Out of the cradle endlessly rocking, uniter of here and hereafter." The screen title said: "Today as yesterday, endlessly rocking, ever bringing the same human passions, the same joys and sorrows."

But Griffith's undeniably vivid defense of human decency against the corruptive forces of society was in the end vitiated by his idea of intolerance as an unchanging evil that is the same for all times and places, and of course by his failure to deal with the two supreme examples of intolerance in history.

Of the four stories that make up the film, the Babylonian episode was by far the most spectacular and the one on which the director lavished without stint his phenomenal artistry, but intellectually the film is hollow. Its "fatal error," said one observant critic, was that in the great battle scenes "you didn't care which side won. It was just a great show."

Similarly, the medieval story of the slaughter of the Protestants by mobs unleashed by the Catholic royalists, described the violence and the horror in minute detail and with matchless art, but the meaning of St. Bartholomew's Day as a major chapter in the long struggle for religious freedom in France is hardly explored. Nevertheless, the continued effectiveness of the film is such that one would not want to risk showing it today in Northern Ireland.

The Judean story, widely acknowledged as the weakest of the lot, falsely portrays the Pharisees as the main antagonist of the gentle Jesus. Eric von Stroheim, soon to be cast in World War atrocity films as the "Hun you love to hate," portrayed one of these sinister Jewish characters in Griffith's film. Actually, the Pharisees represented the vast majority of the lower and middle classes of Jews in the time of Jesus and, after the destruction of Jerusalem, became the domi-nant force in the growth of Judaism. By picturing the Pharisees in conventional Christian fashion as "meddlers" intent on depriving the common people of their simple pleasures, and as "hypocrites" invariably on their knees giving thanks to the Lord "that I am better than other men," the film tended to reinforce the bigotry of the anti-Semites.

This was understood by the unnamed critic of the *N.Y. Evening Post* who wrote Sept. 6, 1916: "The story of Christ portrays the intolerance of the Jews for the teachings of the Master." Competent scholars agree that the stinging rebuke attributed to Jesus in *Luke* 11:44, "Scribes, Pharisees, hypocrites!," which the film repeats, is unjust and could not possibly have happened, as many of the views of the Pharisees were shared by Jesus, and much of Christianity has roots in pharisaic thinking. St. Paul himself was a Pharisee.

It is of extraordinary interest that in his Judean story Griffith was prevented by the fast action of a nationally known Jewish organization from committing a far more serious offense against the Jewish people. Several months before the film was due to be released, the Los Angeles chapter of the Anti-Defamation League of B'nai B'rith learned that Griffith intended to pin the blame for the crucifixion on the Jews and that for this dangerously provocative act he had gone to the ghetto in L.A. and "signed up all the Jews with long whiskers he could find." Remember, this was the era of the Mendel Beilis "blood libel" frame-up in Tsarist Russia, and still green in every Jew's memory was the tragic figure of Leo Frank, wrongfully sentenced in Atlanta for a crime he did not commit and lynched by anti-Semitic vigilantes in 1915. Understandably alarmed, a committee of ADL leaders met with Griffith to try to persuade him to remove these inflammatory and insulting scenes from his film. He refused.

On April 7, 1916 the amusement weekly *Variety* picked up the story that the group then brought the matter to the attention of notables like Jacob Schiff, Louis Brandeis, Louis Marshall and others, and in a short time the ADL leaders again called on Griffith, this time armed with "indisputable" proof that the crucifixion was the work of the Romans, not Jews. "They supplemented their proof," said *Variety,* with a "48 hour ultimatum to destroy that portion of the 'masterpiece' negative on penalty of a concerted national campaign of blacklisting and other pressure which powerful financial and industrial interests might bring to bear, which included the assertion that censors, governors of states and even the President would do all in their power to prevent the showing of the picture with the objectionable scenes." The story added: "confronted with such formidable antagonists, Griffith burned the negative with the scene in the presence of the committee and has retaken it, showing Roman soldiers nailing Christ to the cross."

B'nai B'rith News (May, 1916) confirmed that this was essentially what happened, but denied that Griffith was given a "48 hour ultimatum" or that threats of any kind were made or implied. An adjoining editorial spoke of the need for continued alertness against attempts to use the screen to inflame "the passions of the populace against the Jew for a crime supposedly committed by our ancestors." There is no record of any further Jewish protest against the film either before or after its release.

It is of course the modern story of *Intolerance,* with its remarkable scenes of hunger and social deprivation in the midst of inordinate wealth in industrial America in the years before World War I—and especially the militant strike scenes and their suppression by the militia—that commands attention today. The film showed unarmed factory workers striking against a 10% wage cut being shot down by company thugs as their families look on in horror. These scenes are intercut with shots of the factory owner sitting in splendor alone in his sumptuous quarters and telephoning the order to fire on the workers. There's something here close to the massacre in Ludlow, Colorado in 1914, when Rockefeller mine guards, aided by the state militia, burned a tent colony of striking miners and their families, killing 11 children and two women, one of whom gave birth to a posthumous child. John Reed wrote a classic piece of reportage on this tragedy that held Rockefeller and the coal barons responsible for the crime. Griffith based his film partly on the revelations of conditions in a chemical factory combine, whose owner, a prominent philanthropist, poured his firm's profits into charities while keeping his employees on starvation wages, and partly on newspaper reports of the sensational Steilow murder frameup that included the grim detail that the reprieve for the innocent man arrived just as the prison guards had slit his trouser leg for the electrode.

It was undoubtedly the modern story that made such a profound impression on Lenin and the young Soviet film-makers, Eisenstein, Pudovkin, Vertov and the rest when by an extraordinary stroke of luck a print of *Intolerance* eluded the blockade and found its way to Moscow in 1919.

For Lenin, Griffith's film, with its sweeping history, mass scenes of social struggle and eloquent pleading for justice and peace, not unlike what revolutionary Russia was then going through, must have stimulated the idea that films could be a powerful force for socialist progress. And from that moment on, wrote film historian Jay Leyda, "no Soviet film of importance made within the following 10 years was to be completely outside *Intolerance's* sphere of influence." Eisenstein, the· maker of *Potemkin* and *October,* whose film career began where Griffith left off, was to say later that "all that is best in the Soviet film has its origins in *Intolerance.*"

In the USA, Griffith's film had nowhere near the fantastic reception it got in the USSR. At the time of its release its pacifism conflicted with the growing spirit of war and it was widely banned. It also encountered sharp criticism for its excessively harsh treatment of the women "uplifters," "reformers," social workers, etc., almost all of whom were depicted contemptuously in the modern story as preying on the misfortunes of the poor. One particularly offensive title read: "When women cease to attract men they often turn to reform as a second choice." Reform women then were playing significant roles in the passage of child labor laws, workmen's compensation and state woman suffrage laws. Heywood Broun, in his review of *Intolerance* in the *N.Y. Tribune* Sept. 7, 1916, expressed his shock that anyone with Griffith's power should want to "go out of his way to attack such a useful institution, for instance, as the juvenile court, and whatever defects of organized charity it no way merits the abuse heaped upon it by *Intolerance.*"

The *Philadelphia North American* Dec. 30, 1916 called for a boycott of the film for similar reasons. The explosive social struggle theme of the first part of the modern story was defused, and diverted into safe channels by these scenes with the "uplifters," etc.

The adverse criticism of *Intolerance* and of *The Birth of a Nation* angered and unsettled Griffith and led to a steady decline in his artistic power. His films after 1916 continued to deal with major social and political questions: World War, postwar Germany, the French and American Revolutions, but the times were changing and he lacked the intellectual equipment to infuse these events with anything but outworn ideas. In 1917 he was persuaded to use his talent in the service of the warmakers. He made *Hearts of the World,* an elaborate piece of jingo war propaganda that shattered the pacifism that marked the closing scenes of *Intolerance.* In those scenes, after the title, "And perfect love shall bring peace forevermore," soldiers are shown laying down their weapons, flowers spring up where before there was a prison, happy children play in the sunshine.

Although many of his later films, such as *Broken Blossoms* (1919) and *Isn't Life Wonderful* (1924), were marked by flashes of social insight and art, never again was Griffith to attain the heights of *Intolerance*. "He had glimpsed the future," wrote John Howard Lawson, "but he could not go forward to the new territory that lay before him." The last two decades of his life in Hollywood were wasted, bitter, agonizing years for the great pioneer of film art. Griffith died July 23, 1948, a victim of, as well as a contributor to, the destructive social forces that, spearheaded by the House Un-American Activities Committee, were moving to drive from the industry hundreds of talented filmmakers who had dared to stand up for freedom of the screen. But his work, as Lawson points out, "continues to instruct all those who seek to carry forward the unfinished tasks which he had begun."

8 AMERICAN PROPAGANDA FILMS OF THE FIRST WORLD WAR

Anthony Slide

ALTHOUGH THE USE of propaganda films can be traced back as far as the Spanish-American War, it was not until the outbreak of the First World War in Europe that American political figures realized the value of the motion picture as a propaganda tool. Interestingly, it was the Vitagraph Company which produced those earliest of propaganda films from 1898, *Tearing down the Spanish Flag* and *The Battle of Manila Bay,* and it was one of the co-founders of the company, J. Stuart Blackton, who was the first to understand the potential of the motion picture for manipulating the minds and thoughts of Americans as they pondered what direction this country should take as the bloody conflict got underway in Europe.

J. Stuart Blackton was English-born—he became a naturalized American citizen in August 1915—and it has been suggested that his interest in producing films on preparedness, films urging America's entry into the war, was encouraged by the British Embassy in Washington, D.C. Although the suspicion remains, there is no evidence that the Embassy funneled money to the Vitagraph Company for the production of its propaganda features.

The first such feature, and the most important, was *The Battle Cry of Peace,* based on Hudson Maxim's book, *Defenseless America.* The latter was brought to Blackton's

This article was written especially for *Celluloid Power.*

attention by Theodore Roosevelt—the two were neighbors in exclusive Oyster Bay—who urged its filming, but would not appear in it for fear that such an appearance might be interpreted as a bid on his part for the 1916 Republican presidential nomination. Instead, *The Battle Cry of Peace* included cameo appearances by Admiral Dewey, Maxim, Major General Leonard Wood, and others, as well as a cast of players headed by Charles Richman and Norma Talmadge. The film, which unfortunately has not survived, was devastating in its depiction of an America unprepared for war and overrun by a Germanic-looking army, which pillages and rapes, and at the close leaves the Capitol in ruins.

At its premiere in New York on September 9, 1916, a celebrity-packed audience heard attacks on the song, "I Didn't Raise My Boy to Be a Soldier," and a letter from Roosevelt in which he urged that "the duty of military service should be as widespread as the right to vote." The Daughters of the American Revolution arranged for a special presentation of the film for Congress, but President Wilson declined to attend.

As a result in part not only of the continuing preparedness movement in the United States, but also because *The Battle Cry of Peace* was a commercial success, further films along similar lines were planned. Vitagraph released *Womanhood, the Glory of a Nation,* early in 1917, in which America was again invaded by thinly-disguised Germans. In 1916, the Fine Arts Company, with D.W. Griffith supervising, produced *The Flying Torpedo;* the Public Service Film Company was responsible for *Defense of a Nation:* and children were utilized by James A. Fitzpatrick in his production of *A World War in Kidland.*

Aside from the efforts of the Vitagraph Company, the most important feature on the subject of preparedness was written by Thomas Dixon, and titled *The Fall of a Nation*—obviously in counterpoint to *The Birth of a Nation,* for which he had provided the basic text. Released in 1916, with a score by Victor Herbert, the film urged a militant America. It ridiculed "pacifists" such as William Jennings Bryan and Henry Ford, and showed a feminist leader responsible for the downfall of the United States through her opposition to national defense.

(Dixon had an ongoing concern with the linkage between women's rights and socialism and found both abhorrent.) At the film's close, after this country is defeated, a loyalist legion of American women is founded, with its members seducing and killing their unsuspecting foreign escorts.

If women represented the spirit of war in *The Fall of a Nation,* they represent the means for peace in *Civilization,* on which the former is a basic attack. Produced by Thomas H. Ince and directed by Raymond B. West and Reginald Barker, *Civilization* depicts war as being the product of the business and military interests, with the women of the world belonging to a secret society dedicated to peace. Allegorical in content—the hero-inventor of a torpedo returns from the dead with the soul of Christ in his body—*Civilization* was first seen in New York on June 2, 1916, with a score by Victor Schertzinger. (It is curious that *The Battle Cry of Peace, The Fall of a Nation* and *Civilization* all received their premieres at the same theatre, the Criterion, known at one point as the Vitagraph.) For its general release, *Civilization* contained added footage of President Wilson endorsing the film's peace initiative. As an epic, it pales in comparison to D.W. Griffith's *Intolerance* (1916), which in its embracement of tolerance must be seen as anti-war, although it was never intended by its maker as a propaganda vehicle.

Blatant anti-German propaganda was offered by Mary Pickford in 1916 with *The Little American,* directed by Cecil B. DeMille, in which America's sweetheart is threatened with rape by a lecherous Hun. It paved the way for a score or more of virulent anti-German features produced after America's entry into the war. Only one American filmmaker had the courage or the foolhardiness to attack the British during this period; he was Robert Goldstein, whose previous claim to fame had been that he supplied the costumes for *The Birth of a Nation.* Goldstein wrote and produced *The Spirit of '76,* which utilized the backdrop of the American Revolution to present a lurid melodrama in which the British were decidedly the villains. He had the misfortune to open the film at Orchestra Hall, Chicago, in June 1917, some months after America's entry into the war. When the film reached Los Angeles in November 1917, it was seized by Federal agents and Goldstein was indicted on three counts of violation of the Espionage Act. Convicted, he was sentenced to ten years in prison, but he served only one, and by 1921 had his film again playing Chicago, where an enthusiastic audience hissed the British. *The Spirit of '76* has not survived, and as to its merit, one can only quote *The Moving Picture World* which commented that Goldstein's prison sentence should have been for an artistic crime and an offense against good taste and common sense.

The pro-German sentiment evident in many Irish-American communities was obviously something which concerned pro-British politicians. Following the hanging of Sir Roger Casement by the British, for his possible involvement in a plot concerning the Germans and Irish independence, the Vitagraph Company produced a fictionalized version of the affair titled *Whom the Gods Destroy.* Released in December 1916, the film told of an Irish patriot, Sir Denis Esmond, who is arrested as a traitor but pardoned by the British King. The production did little to appease Irish Americans. It was denounced as "slanderous and degrading" by the Friends of Irish Freedom of Boston, and rioting broke out at some theatres screening the feature.

With America's entry into the First World War, the use of films for propaganda purposes was officially recognized by the U.S. Government. On September 15, 1917, the United States Government Committee on Public Information: Division of Films was established. It produced a weekly newsreel, *The Official War Review,* as well as three feature-length propaganda documentaries, *Pershing's Crusaders* (1918), *America's Answer* (1918) and *Under Four Flags* (1919). An advisory board included such well-known directors as J. Searle Dawley, Maurice Tourneur, Edwin Carewe, Raoul Walsh, and Sidney Olcott. The Division, which also worked to ensure that German propaganda films were not screened in neutral countries, was disbanded by an Order of Congress on June 30, 1919.

The First World War was the occasion for the first major use of the cinema for propaganda. Within months of the war's close, the motion picture was again to be called in to use for even more insidious propaganda purposes. The

"Red Scare" was upon America, and during 1919 and 1920, nine features were released on that subject. A new and at times dangerous use had been found for the motion picture.

> *To preserve the appearance of neutrality and to show only pacifist intentions was still desirable; the mass desire for peace was strong and clearly expressed. In the Fall of 1914, for example,* Lay Down Your Arms, *a picture made by one of the regular producing firms, was shown to huge audiences everywhere by the Socialist Party. That a genuinely pacifist film could come out of one of the American studios is significant proof of the still uncoordinated forces in the industry.* New Theatre, *April 1935. (DP)*

9 CHAPLIN'S *SHOULDER ARMS* (THE MIRROR-CRACKING SEQUENCE)

Bela Balasz

In the following passage from his classic volume, *The Theory of Film,* Bela Balasz (1884–1949) cites the mirror-cracking sequence in the first reel of Chaplin's 1918 anti-war comedy as an outstanding example of the "subtle lyricism of the panorama shot."

CHARLIE IN THE bottom of a deep trench is standing with his comrades at the foot of the steps, waiting for the order to go over the top. The others are grim, motionless. Charlie is so frightened and trembles so much that in his clumsy fumbling he drops a little pocket mirror and it breaks. The men next to him see it and draw back from him in superstitious fear, as from one who had been marked for death by fate. Standing in a row in the narrow trench they cannot draw back very far, two short paces at most. But Charlie has understood why his neighbors drew back and looks after them like a man who has been abandoned by his friends in the hour of peril. The camera pans, following his sad and terrified gaze, and shows a greatly increased distance between Charlie and the other men. The panning is so slow, the camera takes such a long time in turning that the few feet seem an endless, empty desert. For what Charlie sees is a

From *The Theory of Film,* p. 142. Reprinted by permission of Dobson Books Limited, Durham, England.

great void between himself and his fellows, who have left him alone in his misfortune, an orphan left alone in the world. We have often seen the infinities of desert and ocean, of distant horizons dipping into space in other films, but never before, in films or in any other art, such solitude in so narrow a space. This is the subtle lyricism of the panorama shot.

When I read this brief passage by Balasz, whom I greatly admire as one of this century's foremost film theoreticians, I could not help wondering why I had failed to note this extraordinary bit of cinematography in the several times I had seen Shoulder Arms *over the years. And I don't think I am the only one. There doesn't seem to be any record anywhere that this aspect of Chaplin's artistry has ever been noted by others involved with films. Balasz is the lone exception. Most film critics or historians looking at* Shoulder Arms *invariably have their attention arrested by such creative comic scenes as Charlie's attempt to sleep in a flooded dugout by lowering his head in the water so as to rest it on a submerged pillow. Well recorded too is the scene in which the lonely, little soldier—the only one who had not received a single piece of mail from home—reads other people's letters over their forbidden shoulders with alternating moments of delight and despair. The nibbling of a piece of cheese from a mousetrap to show the wretchedness of his condition also never fails to draw laughter through tears, à la Sholem Aleichem; and who does not recall the Shakespearian comedy of Charlie, camouflaged as a tree, clubbing enemy soldiers one by one as they approach to uproot him for firewood. All this I remember well. I simply have no memory of the awesome sequence that Balasz described so brilliantly. I therefore had to see the film again. The Museum of Modern Art Film Study Center was kind enough to arrange a private showing for me within a few days.*

One can imagine my disappointment to find that what Balasz wrote had very little resemblance to what appeared in the film. Thinking that perhaps I had viewed a defective print I sent a transcript of Balasz's remarks to Timothy Lyons, Dean of the College of Fine and Performing Arts at

Youngstown (Ohio) State University and an experienced Chaplin scholar, and asked him to check his print of the film and give me his opinion. He did so within a few days as follows:

> After reading the disparity between Balasz's description of the sequence from Shoulder Arms I took a look at my print (from the 1959 release, as part of the The Chaplin Review). I did a shot analysis [see below] and as far as I can tell, this is the way this sequence has existed in every print I've seen.
>
> My tentative conclusion is that Balasz is simply wrong, his memory faulty; his Theory of Film compiles his writings back to 1922 and there's no way of knowing his source for the comments on Shoulder Arms. As I look at the progression of shots in this sequence, the rhythm seems totally contained in Chaplin's editing style; I simply cannot see this rhythm being disrupted presumably between shots 8 and 9. Besides this, Balasz is wrong that 'Charlie . . . drops a little pocket mirror and it breaks.' Further, there are few pans in Chaplin's work at this time, rarely a tracking shot, and when either of these is used it is to accommodate movement of a character or to shift focus from one character to another, never to realize a point-of-view expressive shot as Balasz describes. So, sorry to poke a bubble but I think Balasz has simply misremembered the sequence. No matter how many versions of this sequence may exist, the comic rhythm—it seems to me—simply precludes Balasz's description.

Timothy Lyons' Shot Analysis

SHOULDER ARMS
following "Bedtime" underwater sequence
TITLE: "Morning"
1. INT. MLS [medium-long-shot] dugout
   Charlie wakes up from his underwater slumber. He rubs his right foot to get the circulation going; mistakes Syd's foot as his own, concluding he's lost all feeling in his left foot.
2. EXT. LS [long-shot] trench
   A soldier rushes into the dugout.
3. INT. MLS dugout
   The soldier shouts to his comrades.
   TITLE: "Over the top in fifteen minutes!"
   As Charlie prepares to vacate the dugout, he collapses in the water.

4. *EXT. LS trench*
   Charlie appears from the dugout.
5. *EXT. MLS trench*
   The soldiers stand waiting.
6. *EXT. MLS trench*
   Charlie waits, near the "Broadway" sign. He reaches into his shirt to withdraw his dogtag.
   INSERT: The tag, in his hand, reads: "Identification No.13."
   He returns the tag and pulls a coin from his pocket, flips it onto his wrist, looks at it, then returns it to his pocket. Then he pulls a mirror from his chest pocket, studies his face, primps and straightens his hair, then returns it to his pocket.
7. *EXT. MS trench*
   A soldier studies his wristwatch.
   INSERT: clockface
8. *EXT. LS trench*
   Charlie stands in the middle foreground of the trench, resting on his rifle; he pounds on his chest to bolster his courage. As a soldier looks on, Charlie withdraws the mirror to find it broken in pieces. Others see this omen of bad luck and draw away.
9. *return to #7.*
10. *return to #8.*
   Charlie is determined to go over the top. He pushes others out of the way to mount the ladder, but the ladder collapses on him, allowing others to go over the top before him. Charlie pushes one soldier out of the way but, seeing a bomb explode nearby, he invites the soldier to precede him. Then, Charlie climbs the ladder as the sequence
   FADES OUT.

Later, I also asked two other distinguished film historians with a thorough knowledge of Chaplin's works—Kevin Brownlow and Lewis Jacobs—for their opinion of the disparity between what Balasz wrote and what was visible in Chaplin's film. Brownlow wrote:

> *I sympathize with you—it is a hazard of film history that writers describe a sequence decades after they've seen it, and reshoot it in their heads. I've done this myself, and when I looked back at the scene, find I'm completely wrong. It is*

almost impossible to remember precisely the way a sequence was shot—even people working with the film in front of them have been known to make crucial misunderstandings.

That is, however, the way it affected Balasz, and that is important.

I have seen virtually no outtakes on Shoulder Arms, *but Chaplin films do vary in detail from version to version. I doubt, however, that the Central European release would be so different.*

Lewis Jacobs wrote:

Your query about the Balasz description of the mirror-cracking incident in Shoulder Arms *was keenly appreciated. True, Chaplin wrote the sequence as it appears in the film; Balasz's memory of it was apparently quite different. My own feelings are for Balasz's 'false' memory, even if it didn't jibe with the reality of the scene. His comments were far deeper than Chaplin's conception.*

Agreed! Balasz's forte par excellence is film theory: his greatness is in his creative conception of cinematography, his lifelong effort to extend the boundaries of film art. True, he unwittingly improved on Chaplin's cinematography (thanks to his "false" memory, and I think we should all be grateful to him for doing it so beautifully). But Chaplin's genius lies in other areas of film art: his wonderful creation of Charlie, the Tramp; his revelation in almost all his films of poverty and hunger in the midst of riches, and of the idiocy of barbaric war. Remember Charlie's final goodbye to the blind flower seller in City Lights *after she has, with his help, had her sight restored and for a moment or two senses that the pitiful little guy before her is not the man of her dreams! It is one of the truly great moments of film art in our time.*

Remember also, that to Eisenstein, greatest of directors and a film theorist of the calibre of Balasz, the secret of Chaplin's art is in his ability "to see things most terrible, most pitiful, most tragic through the eyes of a laughing child." Eisenstein is reminded of this, he wrote in his celebrated essay, "Charlie, the Kid," by something he once read in Malraux's novel, Man's Fate, *about a group of Chinese children who are giggling at the sight of their mother slapping a man on a bed. They are laughing uncontrollably, he continued, although the slapped man is their father, and their mother is beating him because he has died and left them alone to face a future of hunger and homelessness.*

It is an interesting coincidence that the late film historian Jay Leyda (d. Feb. 15, 1988—what a great loss!) once noted in a footnote to "Charlie, the Kid" *(it appears in Eisenstein's* Film Essays *and a Lecture,* Princeton University Press *edition, 1982, which Leyda edited) that the passage as translated in the Penguin edition of Malraux's* Man's Fate *dealt with starving Russians, not Chinese. Leyda points out that Eisenstein's misquotation "may represent the way he recalled the passage." So with Balasz re the* Shoulder Arms *sequence. (DP)*

10 THE RED SCARE FILM CYCLE

Russell Campbell

A GROUP OF MOVIES which painted in lurid colors the threat posed to America by Bolshevism appeared between March 1919 and May 1920. This "Red Scare" cycle coincided with a period of nationwide labor militancy and government repression, and was unusually direct—for Hollywood—in its response to social unrest. Following the war a bitter series of strikes and lockouts had broken out, provoked by inflation and frustrations built up under wartime restraints. Socialist meetings and demonstrations—many expressing support for the October Revolution—were routed by police and returning servicemen. A bomb explosion in April 1919 led to the discovery of 35 other bombs in the mail, addressed to prominent businessmen, officials and legislators; more bomb attacks followed. The newly formed Communist Party and Communist Labor Party were actively recruiting. By November, about two million workers, notably in the steel and coal industries, were on strike, and Attorney-General Palmer conducted a series of raids, continuing until January 1920, in which thousands of socialists were rounded up and many deported.

The Red Scare movies acquired their special character through being part of a coordinated government-business campaign to stamp out socialism. Many left-wing newspapers and journals had been crushed, and de facto federal

Excerpted from "Nihilists and Bolsheviks: Revolutionary Russia in American Silent Film" by Russell Campbell, first published in *The Silent Picture* No. 19, 1974. Copyright 1974 by First Media Press. Reprinted by permission of the author.

censorship of films introduced under the provisions of the wartime Espionage Act. During the war the government had also produced movies of its own (one of these, aimed at stimulating Russian army recruiting, was directed by D. W. Griffith and apparently taken to Petrograd for exhibition in September 1917). After the Armistice the emphasis of government organs of repression shifted to labor issues, and *Variety* of November 29, 1918 reported that David K. Niles, chief of the motion picture section of the U.S. Department of Labor, had issued a letter to producers "with the belief in mind that the picture can instill destructive thoughts into the minds of the I.W.W. and Bolsheviki of this country, and also with the war now past and that the labor theme will be the next big thought of picture productions." Niles's letter urged the use of motion pictures "to stabilize labor and help bring about normal conditions," and offered his department's services in assisting members of the industry "who, being American citizens, are unwilling to produce anything for the screen that violates the policies of the Government." The approach Niles favored was what he termed "constructive education": "To portray the villain of a photoplay as a member of the I.W.W. or the Bolsheviki is positively harmful; while, portraying the hero as a strong, virile American, a believer of American institutions and ideals, will do much good." Niles was reported as saying "That while neither he nor the department wished to exercise a censorship over the making of films and their subsequent projections, he desired that the directors and producers would confer with him prior to starting productions based on Socialism, labor problems, etc."

The following month it was revealed that the Department of the Interior would "press agent"—via two million school-teachers—pictures it deemed desirable propaganda: "The campaign for the 100 per cent Americanization of the population," it was stated, "is to be conducted largely through the medium of films. . . . The Government officials are not looking for straight out educational material, but state that they prefer the romantic fiction tale."[1]

In January 1920 a joint committee of government officials and motion picture executives was formed "to combat Bolshevism and to teach Americanization through the medium of the picture." Members included Franklin K. Lane, Secretary of the Interior; Major R. W. Pulliam, Washington Chief of Police; and Adolph Zukor, Lewis J. Selznick, and William A. Brady. The Americanization Committee, as it was known, probably functioned more in a deterrent than a creative capacity, but it was directly responsible for at least one production, the two-reel *Land of Opportunity* (1920).

The eight or ten movies constituting the Red Scare cycle did not develop into a genre, but nevertheless shared characteristic features. The most typical plot, fusing patriotism and capitalism in accord with the official propaganda line, involved the subversion of honest Americans—working men or sincere idealists—by Bolshevik agents from Russia, followed by defeat of the foreigners and their ideology. A persistent contrast was drawn between the peaceful tactics of Americans and the disruptive violence of the Bolsheviks. Several films stressed the deceptive nature of radical propaganda (and of those who spread it)—perhaps to help expiate the favorable treatment motion pictures had accorded Russian revolutionary activity in the past. And repeatedly Bolshevism was shown to be at variance with such American virtues as love, compassion and sacrifice.

Subversion surfaced, for example, in *The Undercurrent* (1919), written and produced by Guy (*Over the Top*) Empey, who publicly endorsed deportation for radicals ("My motto for the Reds is S.O.S.—ship or shot"). The film demonstrated how "supposed agents of the Lenin-Trotsky regime . . . . begin to work their subtle propaganda into the hearts of loyalists, urging upon them the philosophy (?) of equality, etc., trying at last to sweep them into the vortex caused by their undercurrent maneuvering."[2] Empey himself plays an American soldier just returned from France: "Employed in the machine shop of the Loring steel mills he becomes the prey of Red agents who work secretly to undermine the industrial morale, with a hope of later overthrowing the government of the United States."

Dangerous Hours (1920) showed a socially concerned young university graduate deceived for a time into collaborating with a group of Bolsheviks, who are attempting to use a steel strike (here at a shipyard) to precipitate a national crisis. *Variety* commented: "This feature again depicts the picture warnings . . . of the scarlet red of terrorism as it affected the industrial element in certain sections of the United States, and brings home to an audience the moral that there are insidious forces ostensibly transported to America to sow the seed of discontent among the peaceful, toiling classes, whose wont it is to follow their occupations without complaining. . . ."

The Great Shadow (1920) also featured a shipyard strike: "A great shipbuilding plant is striving to ward off anarchistic propaganda, which is being forced into the union by Klimoff, leader of a band of Russian Reds. . . . The Reds want to plunge the country into a general strike." The Bolsheviks plan "to wreck the government and society by poisoning the mind of organized labor." "No effort is spared," stated a review, "to drive home the insidious method of Russian aliens disseminating the gospel of Bolshevism among labor organizations in this country."

Flatly denying Marxist theory, the Red Scare films contended that the interests of capital and labor could be harmoniously reconciled. *The Great Shadow* explicitly addressed the problem: "This picture is one showing the conflict of capital and labor since the war ended, as it has been fostered secretly by alien bolshevists. . . . As a solution of labor troubles, a plan for an armistice between capital and labor for one year is offered." A character in *Bolshevism On Trial* (*Shattered Dreams,* 1919) is a successful industrialist, or, as the title tells us:

> . . . a brain worker, whose inventions have
> —increased the comfort of his generation
> —created work for thousands of employees
> —brought wealth to himself.

The heroine of *Dangerous Hours* is a young woman who now manages the shipyard left to her by her father. "A sweet type of clean American womanhood," as a title describes her, she is on good terms with her workers, who go out on strike only on orders from their union. After the unsuccessful attempt of the Bolsheviks to disrupt negotiations, the men return to work and, we are informed, "peace and justice and fair play" triumph.

The measures employed by the Bolsheviks in *Dangerous Hours*—attempts to foment riots among striking workers and to blow up the building where a settlement is being reached—were typical of those imputed to radicals in the Red Scare films. Thus in *The Undercurrent* Red agents incite riots in the steel mills; in *The Great Shadow* they resort to incendiarism and sabotage; in *The Red Viper* (1919) they plot the assassination of a judge—and shoot the hero who saves the judge's life. *Boots* (1919) showed Bolshevik conspirators attempting to blow up King George V and President Wilson by placing a bomb "under the chamber where the great leaders of the Allies are to assemble to discuss peace terms."

The tactics of violence were traced to Russia. In *Lifting Shadows* (1920), for example, anti-Czarist revolutionist Serge Ostrowski levels the headquarters of his committee with a bomb blast when the building is raided by police, and in *Dangerous Hours* we are shown, in a sequence of sweeping flashback impressions, the "ghastly truth" of the Russian Revolution—firing squads, pillage, and rape (the last institutionalized by the "nationalization of women").

The Volcano (1919), a tale of conspiratorial violence perpetrated by a gang of Reds in Manhattan, went furthest in applying this formula to the current ferment in the United States. It included a documentary sequence of Governor Smith of New York signing the bill which prohibited the use of the red flag, and added "a little realistic touch" in the form of a "close-up on a list of names who were victims or intended victims of the recent nation-wide bomb plot scare." Governor Smith and Franklin D. Roosevelt, then Assistant Secretary of the Navy, officially endorsed the film, until protest against its anti-Semitism made it politic for them to retract. (The villain, Alexis Minsky, was a "gesticulating East Sider" with a "super-sized nose"; after the protest, he was captioned to explain, "I am not a Jew, I am a Bolshevik.")

Despite the advice of Niles, producers were clearly not about to forgo the melodramatic potential of the Bolshevik villain. The type is well represented by Herman Wolff (played by Leslie Stowe) in *Bolshevism on Trial,* which was based on a novel by the notoriously right-wing Thomas Dixon, author of *The Clansman.* Middle-aged, heavyset and beetle-browed, Wolff is introduced as a professional agitator with the title, "Wolff's type has emerged in every social revolution: the strong man who exploits the sincere ideals of less aggressive people, turning social discontent to his own advantage." His reading matter is seen to include, in addition to Marx, works by two prominent socialists of the time, Scott Nearing and John Spargo. Having engineered the founding of a utopian socialist colony on a Florida island (which he plans to use as a base for "world-wide operations"), Wolff bides his time while discontent rears its ugly head. Then, exploiting popular sentiment (the "socialists"object to working), he takes over control from deluded young idealist Captain Norman Worth (the October Revolution?) and proceeds to promulgate "the doctrines of Communism," promising his comrades they can "spread the Red Brotherhood over the world and come to power and riches." Religion is abolished. Marriage laws are suspended, whereupon Wolff savagely thrusts aside his wife and carries off the heroine by force. Dissent is silenced by terror. All would be lost were it not for the intervention of a contingent of U.S. Marines under the command of Norman's father (the industrialist), at which point it is revealed that Wolff is in fact the Russian Androvitch, and has been under surveillance for a year by the secret service. He is apprehended, and *Bolshevism on Trial* ends with the red flag being hauled down and the Stars and Stripes raised in its stead, to the acclamation of the crowd. (This finale stands on its head that of the 1905 *Mutiny on the Black Sea,* in which the sailors replace the Czarist flag with the red banner of revolution.)

Wolff/Androvitch is rivaled by Alexis Minsky; by Boris Blotchi, bulky, greasy and lecherous "agent from the New Russia," introduced as "one of the bloodiest butchers of the Revolution" (*Dangerous Hours*); and by *The Great Shadow's* Klimoff ("The filthy, repulsive appearance of the Russian alien characters as depicted in the picture cause one to shrink and shudder"). The only significant exceptions to this stereotype appear to be the Bolsheviks of *Boots,* the first film of the cycle (and set in England). These, the *New York Times* said, "seem to be well-bred folk of the upper middle class who have been driven to desperation by the shafts of George Bernard Shaw's satire. . . ." *Boots,* however, was at least partly a comedy.

Female Reds were not dyed-in-the-wool; for them, the possibility of redemption existed—though sometimes, as in *The Right to Happiness* (1919), the price was self-sacrifice. In that film, Sonia is "a fiery-tempered, cigarette-smoking Russian radical, who is sent to this country to spread the seeds of Bolshevism: a girl with a heart of gold, but carried away by impractical dreams. . . ." She encounters her sister, who has been brought up "the pampered daughter of a millionaire," when storming the girl's home "at the head of an angry mob." The crisis is resolved when "the big heart of the little revolutionist causes her to sacrifice herself for the wealthy girl, whose life is threatened"—thus illustrating, according to *Moving Picture World,* "the doctrine that love, understanding and sacrifice alone will make the world a better place to live in." Other female protagonists of this type include Yolanda Kosloff (*The Red Viper*), a bomb-plot conspirator who sees matters in a new light when her sweetheart becomes the victim of Red violence; and Vania Ostrowski (*Lifting Shadows*), who, though commissioned by her revolutionist father in Russia to flee with certain papers and start a campaign in America, "outwits the members of the Reds, with whose cause she has lost sympathy, and keeps them from obtaining the papers"—thereupon marrying a young American lawyer.

The Bolsheviks are invariably vanquished—rounded up by soldiers or police, captured by secret service agents, killed by one of their own number (in *The Undercurrent,* "one of the Reds—a woman—seeing that the law is about to checkmate her career, draws a revolver, kills her cringing associates and fires the lead into herself"), or, as in the spectacular *Dangerous Hours,* buried under the rubble of an explosion when one of their own bombs is hurled at them (distinguished by its viciousness, this film also celebrates a tar-and-feathering).

But wasn't any means justified in stamping out the Bolshevik menace? The vipers were ripe for extermination, the movies implied, and in life they were perhaps lucky to get away with deportation. After the last of Palmer's raids the

Red Scare cycle did not long survive, perhaps because the crisis had passed and authorities wished to take the mind of the populace off the subject. Exhibitors, steering clear of controversy, were becoming more circumspect. *Dangerous Hours* was cancelled at New York's 81st St. Theatre in April, 1920, the explanation given being that "the Bolshevism outlined in the film, while on the surface against the red element, was scoped in a manner that gave a back draught, with the feature left to be viewed either way, as a pacifier or antagonizer. Pictures of this nature being against the Keith policy, its exhibition was dropped."[3] Cinematic reflections on the Russian Revolution, whatever the reason, soon reverted to a more romantic and considerably tamer aspect of the matter: the lives of aristocrats forced to flee to the West.

NOTES

1. *Variety*, December 20, 1918.
2. Uncredited quotations are drawn from reviews and story synopses published in *Variety* and *Moving Picture World*.
3. *Variety*, April 16, 1920.

To Russell Campbell's informative article I should like to add the following three items:

1. *On February 11, 1919 Rep. Meyer London, a Socialist Party member, said in a speech on the floor of the U.S. Congress: "Mr. Chairman, the spectre of Bolshevism is haunting the world. Everybody—statesman, businessman, preacher, plutocrat, newspaper editor— keeps on warning the world that it is about to be destroyed by Bolshevism. . . . But the worst of it is that every movement, every new idea, every new suggestion, every new thought that is advanced, is immediately denounced as Bolshevism. It is not necessary to argue anymore with a man who advances a new idea; it is enough to say 'That is Bolshevism.' "*
2. *In his New Year's Diary of 1920, the 71-year-old maverick Democrat, Asst. U.S. Secretary of Labor, Louis*

Freeland Post, said: "There are signs of an overthrow of our government . . . going on under cover of a vigorous 'drive' against 'anarchism,' an 'anarchist' being almost anybody who objects to government of the people by tories and for financial interests." Epitomizing the attempt to stifle radical and liberal opinion, restrain the labor forces and give free reign to the Big Money was the Sacco-Vanzetti case which spanned the decade of the Harding and Coolidge Administrations. The "red scares" made easier the unrestrained looting of the national till, the high point of which was the Teapot Dome scandal.

3. *One notable film, Griffith's* Orphans of the Storm, *with the Gish sisters and Joseph Schildkraut, aided and abetted the 1920–21 witchhunt against liberals and radicals by portraying many of the French revolutionaries as having less humanity than the fallen aristocrats; and also by stating in the film's opening title that "We in the United States with a democratic government should beware lest we mistake traitors and fanatics for patriots, and replace law and order with anarchy and bolshevism." The massive strike wave in postwar industrial America was attributed in some of the films described by Campbell to "outside agitators" working for Lenin and the Bolsheviks. (DP)*

PART II

THE 1920s PROSPERITY ERA

"We in America," said Herbert Hoover in his inaugural address of January, 1929, "are nearer to the final triumph over poverty than ever before in the history of any land . . . the outlook for the world today is for the greatest era of commercial expansion in history." The United States, he said, had "reached a higher degree of comfort than ever existed before in the history of the world . . . in no nation are the fruits of accomplishment more secure."

Ten months later, in the last week of October 1929, the bottom dropped out of the stock market, leading to the most catastrophic economic crisis the country had ever seen.

11 A FILMOGRAPHY OF OSCAR MICHEAUX: AMERICA'S LEGENDARY BLACK FILMMAKER

Bernard L. Peterson, Jr.

(A completely revised version of an article which was first published as "The films of Oscar Micheaux: America's First Fabulous Black Filmmaker," in *Crisis,* April 1979, and is published here for the first time in its present form by permission of the author, who reserves all rights of republication.)

ALTHOUGH OSCAR MICHEAUX was not America's first black film producer as many published articles have asserted, he was undoubtedly the most prolific early black American filmmaker, and one of black cinema's most legendary figures.

Between 1918 and 1948 he wrote, produced and directed more than 40 feature films—more than any other American black filmmaker in history. He is credited with making the first

In the preparation of this article, the writer gratefully acknowledges the assistance of the library staff of the G. R. Little Library, Elizabeth City State University, Elizabeth City, North Carolina, and particularly the help of Mr. James B. Law, former Reference Librarian. Appreciation is also expressed to Mr. Hobson Thompson, Jr., Head Librarian of the Legler Branch of the Chicago Public Library, for furnishing photocopies of a number of articles on Micheaux, and for making the facilities of his library branch completely accessible to the writer.

full-length, all-black silent film produced by a black company, as well as the first full-length, all-black total sound film.

Prior to producing his first film, Micheaux had begun to launch a rather successful career as a novelist and publisher, and had written and self-published three autobiographical novels: *The Conquest* (more an autobiography than a novel, 1913), *The Forged Note* (1915), and *The Homesteader* (1917). The last two were published under his own imprint, Western Book Supply of Lincoln, Nebraska. Toward the end of his film career, and during the 1940s when he ceased making films altogether, he again turned to writing novels, and self-published *The Case of Mrs. Wingate* (1944), *The Wind from Nowhere* (1944), *The Story of Dorothy Stanfield* (1946), and *The Masquerade* (1948). Except for the last book, all of Micheaux's novels are at least partly autobiographical; and it is mainly from his books that we are able to deduce many of the otherwise unknown details of his colorful career.

Oscar Micheaux was born on January 2, 1884, in a small farming community near Metropolis, Illinois, which had been mainly settled by families of ex-slaves after the Civil War. His parents were Calvin and Belle (Willingham) Micheaux. From *The Conquest,* we learn that he was "the fourth son and fifth child of a family of thirteen." His father, despite his French-sounding name, came from Kentucky and was the son of a slave. By the time Oscar was born, his father owned eighty acres of land and was considered a rather well-to-do farmer, although he later experienced some financial reverses. His mother was a typical farm wife and a "shouting Methodist," who often got happy in church, much to Oscar's embarrassment. However, she "always declared emphatically that she wanted none of her sons to become lackeys."

In order "to give the children better educational facilities," the family moved from the farm to Metropolis, the nearby industrial river and factory town, where Oscar attended the woefully inadequate local colored school. His oldest sister became a teacher, his oldest brother became a dining car waiter for a Chicago railroad company, and his two other older brothers enlisted in the Army.

After a time the family moved back to the farm, where they continued to market their produce in Metropolis. Oscar, who did not enjoy farm work, was sent to town to do the marketing, and it was in this line of work that he acquired the art of salesmanship, aggressiveness, and ability to deal with people, which were to serve him well as a book publisher and filmmaker.

At the age of 17 Micheaux left Metropolis and worked at a number of odd jobs in various cities, finally visiting his brother in Chicago, where he eventually obtained a job as a Pullman porter. There he saved his money until he could purchase some land in South Dakota, where he sought to establish himself as a prosperous rancher and farmer. However, this dream was wrecked by a disastrous first marriage and by financial reversals brought about by mortgaging his homestead. In an attempt to recoup his losses, Micheaux turned to writing, and eventually completed and financed the printing of his most autobiographical novel, *The Conquest,* in which many of the details of his life up to his first marriage are delineated.

In one of his later books, *The Wind from Nowhere,* Micheaux presents a lengthy account of how he paid for the first 3,000 copies of *The Conquest,* with no actual cash in hand. Using the leading character of that book as a surrogate, he described how Martin Eden placed his order with the printer, and immediately went to work as a "high powered book agent," taking advance orders for the "3,000 copies at $2.00 per copy in less than three weeks." Since the printer demanded a certain amount in cash with the order, and a "guarantee of account for the balance," he went to a group of his prosperous friends (mostly other farmers), showing them that his advance orders totaled $6,000, and persuaded them to "put up the cash for him and [execute] the guarantee of account."

The Conquest apparently went through several printings, because in his second novel, *The Forged Note* (1915), which he subtitled "A Romance of the Darker Races," Micheaux dramatizes his attempts to sell his first book in the Deep South. In this and two subsequent novels, he introduces the character of Sidney Wyeth, who is the author's fictionalized surrogate. Wyeth appears as a novelist and book salesman in *The Forged Note,* and as a retired film producer in both *The Case of Mrs. Wingate* and *The Story of Dorothy*

Stanfield. He also appears as a lawyer and author in one of Micheaux's early films, *The Gunsaulus Mystery* (1921), the second of three films that Micheaux based on the Leo M. Frank murder-lynching case.

From *The Forged Note,* we can deduce how Micheaux (like his fictional counterpart, Sidney Wyeth) traveled by car from city to city, speaking at churches and schools, talking to leaders of fraternal lodges, civic groups, and social organizations; and going from house to house, peddling his books wherever he could. *The Forged Note* also shows how Micheaux was able to build a network of business and financial contacts throughout the South and Midwest which he could later use to launch and help finance his future film career.

His third book, *The Homesteader* (1917), is a rewritten version of *The Conquest,* carrying the story further forward in time, and introducing more fictitious plot details, including an interracial romance and a happy ending for his love life. The book was again rewritten in 1944 as *The Wind from Nowhere,* and further embellished with melodramatic situations designed to increase sales among both black and white readers.

The Conquest, The Homesteader, and *The Wind from Nowhere* all tell the story of Micheaux's life as a pioneer in South Dakota, combined with the interracial love story introduced in the second book and continued in the third. Although the characters in each book have different names, the basic plots are almost the same. A black man migrates from Illinois to the midwest where he becomes a prosperous farmer. He falls in love with a woman believed to be white, but does not marry her because of apparent racial barriers. He marries instead the daughter of a black minister, but the marriage fails because of the father's interference. He eventually marries his first love, after discovering that she is a mulatto.

The Case of Mrs. Wingate (1944) concerns an interracial romance between a white woman and a black barber. Married to a man too old for her, Mrs. Wingate later persuades the barber to become her chauffeur and lover. She finances his education at Harvard, where he obtains his Ph.D., and after the death of the husband, they marry and live in New York. The sub-plot of the novel concerns the exposé of a black Nazi spy ring by a Negro detective. *The Story of Dorothy Stanfield* (1946), a sequel to *The Case of Mrs. Wingate,* further develops both the interracial marriage and the detective element begun in the previous novel, and introduces a new sub-plot—the exposé of an insurance swindle. In both novels, Micheaux's surrogate character, Sidney Wyeth, is a retired film producer who has returned to his first career as a novelist. From Wyeth's discussions of his long and successful career as a producer, one can easily deduce many of the details of Micheaux's own film career. (However, these details will not be included in this short article.)

Micheaux's final book, *The Masquerade* (1947), has been dismissed by critics as a rewritten version of Charles W. Chesnutt's novel, *The House Behind the Cedars* (1905), which Micheaux had previously made into a film by the same title in 1923. *The Masquerade* was probably an expansion of Micheaux's film scenario, but does not give credit to Chesnutt as the original author.

How he became involved in filmmaking is one of the often-told anecdotes of Micheaux's career. Following the publication of *The Homesteader* in 1917, the Lincoln Motion Picture Company (the first all-black film company, established in 1916 by the actor Noble P. Johnson and his brother George P. Johnson) had tried to purchase the screen rights to Micheaux's novel. Micheaux agreed to sell the rights to the book—only if it were to be made into the first black full-length, eight-reel feature film, and if he were allowed to direct the picture. The Johnson Brothers, understandably, refused; but Micheaux (now determined to see his life story made into a film) set out to raise the necessary capital to form his own company, which became known as the Micheaux Film Corporation.

Micheaux's initial backing came from some of the contacts he had previously made while selling his books. Just how he went about learning the craft of movie-making is still not known. Since Leonard Galezio is listed as cameraman for *The Gunsaulus Mystery* (previously mentioned), it is conjectured that Micheaux originally learned the techniques by observation, trial, and error. Nevertheless, without prior experience or training, his first film was produced in 1919, and by 1948 he had written, produced and directed more than 40 films.

Micheaux promoted his films in almost the same way that he had promoted his books. Prior to making a film, and with only the scenarios or original novels in hand, he visited every city and town in the Midwest, East, and South that had a black movie house, or where a white theatre allowed Negroes to attend on a special night of the week, and persuaded the theatre managers to book his films in advance of filming. Among the major cities on his booking route, where he boasted that he could net from $150 to $500 per picture, were Cincinnati, St. Louis, Memphis, Chicago, Detroit, New Orleans, Atlanta, Baltimore, Washington D.C., Philadelphia, and New York. But there were numerous small towns in the South where he accepted considerably less than $100 per booking, and for a one-night stand in the Mississippi Delta, he was lucky to receive as much as $25. Still, it was reported that his income in 1920 was almost $50,000, and that he anticipated earning twice that amount in 1921.

The following filmography of Oscar Micheaux is neither complete nor definitive. Although it aims for both, it falls far short of the mark because of the limited information that can be located on most of his films. In spite of its shortcomings, however, this is probably the most comprehensive filmography of Oscar Micheaux that has been published up to the present time (1988). Hopefully it may serve a useful purpose in stimulating further interest and research on this significant film producer and in this most important area of black American history and culture.

THE FILMS OF OSCAR MICHEAUX,
1918–1948

Note: All the films listed below are 35mm films in black and white, produced by the Micheaux Film Corporation, directed by Oscar Micheaux, and based on scenarios written by Micheaux—unless otherwise indicated.

SILENT FILMS

The Homesteader (domestic melodrama, 8 reels, 1918). Adapted from Micheaux's novel by the same title (1917), which in turn was a rewritten version of his first autobiographical novel, *The Conquest* (1913). Significant as Micheaux's first film and the first full-length, all-black film by a black company. A fictionalized account of the author's life as a rancher in South Dakota, combined with an interracial love story and a story of domestic tragedy. Jean Baptiste, a young black man, has migrated from Chicago to the wilderness of South Dakota, in order to claim and develop a large tract of public land under the Homestead Act of 1862. There he becomes a prosperous rancher, and eventually falls in love with Agnes Stewart, the motherless daughter of a nearby white homesteader. Believing that he can never marry Agnes because of racial barriers, he returns to Chicago for a wife, and marries Orleans McCarthy, the daughter of a prominent black minister. This marriage proves to be disastrous, however, because of the dominance of Orleans father, his constant interference in their domestic affairs, and her complete submissiveness to her father's will. When the marriage finally collapses, Baptiste returns to his Dakota ranch, where he becomes reunited with his first love, and learns that he is now able to marry her because she is of part-black heritage. The film was shot in "the old Selig studio" in Chicago in 1918. Apparently it opened in Chicago in 1919, and received a New York State license on Sept. 20, 1922. Cast: Charles Lucas (Jean Baptiste), Iris Hall (Agnes Stewart, a mulatto, presumed to be white), Charles S. Moore (Jack Stewart, Agnes' father), William George (Agnes' white lover), Evelyn Preer (Orleans McCarthy), Vernon S. Duncan (The Reverend McCarthy, a black Chicago Minister), Inez Smith (Ethel McCarthy, Orleans' sister), and Trevy Woods (Glavis, Ethel's husband). See also: *The Exile* (1931), Micheaux's first total sound film, which is partly based on *The Homesteader;* and *The Betrayal* (1948), which is also based on Micheaux's autobiography.

Within Our Gates ("Photo-tragedy," 8 reels, later reduced to 7, 1919). According to the producer's publicity, it was "founded on the famous Leo M. Frank case as witnessed by the author of *The Homesteader* in 1914."* This is the first of three films that Micheaux based on the Frank case, which involved a young Jew who was lynched in Georgia for the alleged murder of a young white girl. Micheaux has treated the Frank case more explicitly in *The Gunsaulus Mystery,* described below. In *Within Our Gates,* the only aspect of the Frank case which Micheaux seems to focus on is that of an innocent man convicted of murder on the basis of circumstantial evidence. The film concerns the lynching of a black sharecropper, Jasper Landry, who is falsely accused, indicted, tried, and found guilty of the murder of Phillip Girdlestone, a wealthy white plantation owner for whom he worked. According to the producer's publicity:

> It was in late September, the cotton had been picked, ginned, baled and delivered, and Jasper Landry, a cropper, had prospered, clearing, according to a statement of account by his daughter, Sylvia, who had been off to school, $6,831.
>
> In the same community dwelt 'Eph,' the tattle-tale, whom the blacks called a 'white fo'kes' nigger,' a pest, making no effort toward his own betterment, but who made it his business to 'spread news.' [Eph goes] to Girdlestone, wealthy planter, aristocrat and owner of everything for miles around, telling him, among other things, that Landry was buying land, owned a mule, . . . was 'eddicatin' ' [his] children, and was therefore 'gettin' sma't.' 'Now dey,' said he, 'am keeping' books, and when he comes to settle, ain' gwine to take yo' figgers, but will be bringin' a bill!'
>
> Landry came 'bringing his bill.' Eph, secreted to 'peep' upon the mischief that he had caused, watched. There arose a dispute. Eph turned and saw Girdlestone falling to the floor mortally wounded—and Landry standing over him holding a smoking revolver.

---

*It is doubtful that Micheaux actually witnessed the Frank murder trial, although it is certainly possible. This is more probably an example of promotional "hype" or "puffing," which he often resorted to, in order to publicize his books and films. The Frank case was widely reported in the black press because it was the first recorded lynching of a Jew in America, and the first known case of a Southern white man to be judged guilty of murder on the testimony of a black man who was also circumstantially implicated in the crime. For more on the Frank case, see *The Gunsaulus Mystery,* below.

The film was produced in Chicago in 1919, under the title *Circumstantial Evidence.* Failing to receive a permit from the Chicago Board of Censors on first application, because of the controversial lynching scene and the belief that it might set off a second Chicago riot (the first one having occurred a year earlier), the title was changed and the film apparently reduced by one reel. It was given a second showing before a group of prominent black and white Chicago citizens, including the clergy and the Negro press, and as a result of opinions expressed after this showing, a permit was finally granted. Billed as "The Most Sensational Story on the Race Question Since Uncle Tom's Cabin," it premiered in Chicago at the Vendome Theatre in January 1920. Next it was shown in Detroit; and in August 1920, it opened at the Loyal Theatre in Omaha, Nebraska, after a two-month period of negotiations to obtain a permit in that city. Because of its controversial subject matter, it was banned by many theatres in the South, especially in Louisiana—on advice of the New Orleans Superintendent of Police. The cast featured Evelyn Preer (as the educated daughter of Jasper Landry), Lawrence Chenault, and Charles D. Lucas; with William Starks, Mattie Edwards, E. G. Tatum, Grant Edwards, and La Font Harris. See also: *The Gunsaulus Mystery* (1921), which also deals with the Leo M. Frank case.

The Brute (melodrama, 7 reels, 1920). About a beautiful woman caught in the clutches of a brutal, underworld gambling boss who constantly abuses her. This film featured a black boxer (played by boxer Sam Langford) as a symbol of black manhood in the Negro's struggle against lynching. Among the most sensational scenes in the film were the boxing sequences, the torrid love scenes, and scenes of low life in black dives and crapshooting joints. Also included were several scenes of racial violence, which caused the film to have difficulty in obtaining censor approval in Chicago where it was produced, for fear that it might contribute to race riots. The film was criticized by a number of black reviewers because its theme, in their opinion, did not contribute sufficiently to the moral uplifting of the race. It was shown in Omaha, Nebraska in November 1920; in New York City in December 1920; and in Chicago in April 1921. The cast featured Evelyn Preer (the young woman), A. B. Comathiere (the underworld gambling boss), Sam Langford (the boxing champion), Lawrence Chenault, and Susie Sutton (the young girl's Aunt Clara).

Symbol of the Unconquered (western melodrama, 7 reels, 1920). Also known as *The Wilderness Trail.* Described by *The Competitor* (Pittsburgh, January/February 1921, p. 61) as "A cautionary tale in opposition to 'passing,' " designed to teach "impressive lessons on the folly of color, both within and without the race." It tells the story of Evon Mason, a beautiful mulatto girl passing for white, who goes West, after her father's death, to claim some oil-bearing land that she has inherited. There she meets with trouble from a scoundrel named Drescola, who wishes to keep her from claiming her inheritance, and who uses the KKK and an Indian villain to try to drive her out of town. But Evon is protected by Hugh Van Allen, a Negro prospector, with whom she falls in love, and whose life she eventually saves. Opened in New York City and Pittsburgh, Pennsylvania in January 1921. Cast included Iris Hall (Evon Mason), Lawrence Chenault, Walker Thompson, E. G. Tatum, Jim Burris, Mattie Wilkes, and Leigh Whipper.

The Hypocrite (melodrama, 7 reels, 1921). Received a New York State license in June 1921, but apparently was not released as a separate film. It was reduced in length and wholly incorporated into his next film, *Deceit,* as a film-within-a-film. Cast included Evelyn Preer (Doris Rutledge); William E. Fountaine; Narman Johnson (Gregory Wainwright); Cornelius Watkins (Gregory Wainwright as a boy); Mrs. Irvin C. Miller (Mrs. Wainwright); Ira O. McGowan (Mr. Wainwright); William Patterson and Melton Henry (rescue party).

Deceit (melodrama [film-within-a-film], 6 reels, 1921). A dramatization of Micheaux's difficulties in gaining a permit from the Chicago Board of Censors for *Within Our Gates,* and possibly for *The Hypocrite.* The plot concerns film producer Alfred DuBois's efforts to gain approval of the board of censors for his film, *The Hyprocrite.* Approval of the film is opposed by a delegation of ministers, led by Reverend Christian B. Bentley, who succeed in having the picture rejected without having seen it. DuBois persists in having the film reviewed by a board of leading citizens and this framework allows for the showing of a condensed version of *The Hypocrite* as a film-within-a-film. In the end, *The Hypocrite* is vindicated and gains the censors' approval. Although production on *Deceit* was begun in June 1921 (immediately after the release of *The Hypocrite*), "at the Esste Studio in New York," it apparently did not open in New York until March 1, 1923, when it received a New York State license. The cast of *The Hypocrite* has been listed above. The external plot or framework involving the attempt to gain censor approval for the film included the following cast: Narman Johnson (Alfred DuBois, the film producer); Evelyn Preer (DuBois' secretary, Evalyn Bentley); Cleo Desmond (Charlotte Chesbro); A. B. Comathiere (Reverend Bentley); George Lucas; Mabel Young (Mrs. Levine); Mary Watkins and Vera Miles (teachers); Louis De Bulger (Mr. Chesbro); Louis Schooler (actor); Jerry Brown (actress); James Carey (banker); J. Coldwell, F. Sanfier, Jesse Billing, and Allen Dixon (preachers); Leonard Galezio, William Petterson, and Sadie Grey (censors).

The Gunsaulus Mystery (melodrama, 8 reels, 1921). (Also cited incorrectly as *The Gonzales Mystery*.) Micheaux's second of three films on the Leo M. Frank case, the first being *Within Our Gates* (1919) and the third, *Lem Hawkins' Confession* (1935), a remake of *The Gunsaulus Mystery* in sound. This film adheres more closely to the details of the Frank case than the other two films, except that Micheaux is more interested in vindicating the black man who is circumstantially implicated in the case than in the real victim, Leo Frank, a young Jew who was actually prosecuted and lynched, although his guilt was never legally proven. (The Frank case was concerned with the alleged murder of a young girl whose sexually assaulted body was discovered partially burned in a furnace in the cellar of a factory managed by Frank. It was established by testimony that the girl, who worked in the factory, had visited Frank alone on the previous afternoon to get her wages. It was alleged that

Frank raped her, murdered her, and intimidated a black janitor into helping him, unsuccessfully, to dispose of the body. After Frank was arrested, he reportedly tried to blame the crime completely on the janitor, who was finally exonerated.) The plot of the film is as follows: Arthur Gilpin, a young black janitor, is arrested and indicted for the murder of Myrtle Gunsaulus, a young girl whose body he discovered in the basement of the factory where he is employed. He is defended by Sidney Wyeth, a young black lawyer and author, who takes the case because he had once been in love with Gilpin's sister. During the course of the trial, suspicion is thrown from Gilpin to Arthur Brisbane, the general manager and foreman of the factory, and Wyeth succeeds in proving his client innocent of the crime. Wyeth then writes a book about the case, in which he reveals the true circumstances of the murder, which were never brought out at the trial. Premiered in New York on April 18, 1921, with Micheaux listed as producer-director-writer, and Leonard Galezio as photographer. Black cast members included Lawrence Chenault, Evelyn Preer, Edward R. ("Dick") Abrams, Louis De Bulger, Mattie Wilkes, Bessie Bearden, Ethel Williams, Edward Brown, Mabel Young, Hattie Christian, E. G. Tatum, and Ethel Waters (at the beginning of her film career). White cast members were George Russell, W. D. Sindle and Alex Kroll. See also *Lem Hawkins' Confession* (1935), a sound version of this film.

The Shadow (mystery-melodrama, 7 reels, 1921). Received a New York State license in October 1921.

The Dungeon (melodrama in the "Bluebeard" vein, 7 reels, 1922). Myrtle Downing, a beautiful young woman, is engaged to marry a young lawyer, Stephen Cameron. Before their marriage can take place, she is abducted by "Gyp" Lassiter, a known crook whose advances she has spurned. Gyp hires a hypnotist and drug fiend to gain control over Myrtle's mind, and forces her to marry him while she is in a drugged and hypnotic state. When Cameron learns that his fiancée has married a notorious criminal, he leaves town in a state of utter dejection and goes to Alaska to claim some land, on which he discovers a mine and "strikes it rich"—not, however, without some difficulty in fighting off a group of "claim-jumpers" who try to deprive him of his land. In the meantime, Myrtle, who has been kept a virtual prisoner since her marriage, learns that Gyp is a bigamist who has murdered eight previous wives, and also that he is running for Congress, with the backing of a criminal element which wishes to deprive blacks of valuable real estate, by forcing them to give up their homes in well-to-do-neighborhoods through a system of residential resegregation. In Alaska, Cameron receives news of Lassiter's political ambitions, including his plans to betray his own people, and he returns to his home town to oppose Lassiter by running for the same Congressional seat. When Myrtle makes an unsuccessful attempt to escape from Gyp's clutches, in order to save her life and expose him as a murderer and a crook, Gyp locks her in a dungeon where his previous wives have been killed, and attempts to murder her by asphyxiation. In the nick of time, Myrtle is saved by Cameron, who also kills Gyp. Released in New York on May 22, 1922. Cast included William E. Fountaine, Schingzie Howard, J. Kenneth Goodman, W. B. F. Crowell, Earle Browne Book, and Blanche Thompson. When the film was shown in Chicago, it was criticized by the *Chicago Defender* (July 9, 1922) for featuring only light-skinned ("almost white") actors, and for not being advertised as a "race production," in accordance with the custom of the time. The reviewer (D. Ireland Thomas) concluded that "Maybe [Micheaux] is after booking it in white theatres."

The Virgin of the Seminole (adventure melodrama, 7 reels, 1922). A drama of love and adventure set mainly in the Northwest. The hero is a black member of the Canadian mounted police. The film concerns his deeds of bravery, one of which was presumably the rescue of a girl of mixed ethnic heritage from the Indians, for which he receives a substantial reward and the love of the girl. Produced in 1922. Opened in New York on April 15, 1923. Cast included William E. Fountaine and Schingzie Howard.

The Ghost of Tolston's Manor (mystery melodrama, full length [presumably 7 reels], 1922). Produced in 1922.

Opened in New York in 1923. Cast: Andrew Bishop, Lawrence Chenault, Edna Morton, and Monte Hawley.

The House Behind the Cedars (melodrama, 9 reels, 1923). Film version of Charles W. Chesnutt's novel by the same title (1905), which was adapted by Micheaux and later published as his own novel, *The Masquerade* (1947). The original novel tells the story of Rena Walton, a beautiful mulatto girl passing for white, who is loved by two men: George Tryon, a white millionaire, and Frank Fowler, a black man, whose love she rejects. Micheaux apparently combined Chesnutt's story with features of the sensational Rhinelander case, involving the marriage of a woman of part-black heritage to Leonard Rhinelander, an heir to a huge fortune. Her racial identity was discovered less than a month after the marriage, and the family instituted an unsuccessful court suit to have it annulled. In Chesnutt's original story, George Tryon wishes to marry Rhena, but changes his mind when he discovers that she has Negro blood, and tries to persuade her, unsuccessfully, to become his mistress. In Micheaux's film, Rena becomes engaged to George and apparently manages to succeed in being accepted as white, but she fears that she may be eventually discovered, and voluntarily abandons her charade. She returns to Frank, who really loves her, and who in the meantime has risen to a position of power and respect in the community. Filmed in 1923 in Roanoke, Virginia, where extensive use was made of local talent as extras, including William "Big Bill" Crowell, a popular fraternal leader in Virginia. Was not released in New York until 1927 (although this date may have been a mistake for 1923). Cast included Shingzie Howard (Rena Walton), Lawrence Chenault (George Tryon), Douglas "C.D." Griffin (Frank Fowler), Andrew Bishop, and William Crowell.

Uncle Jasper's Will (melodrama, 6 reels, 1922). Original title: *Jasper Landry's Will.* Apparently a sequel to *Within Our Gates,* in which Jasper Landry, a sharecropper, is lynched for allegedly murdering a white planter. Opened in New York in 1922. Cast included William E. Fountaine and Schingzie Howard.

Birthright (drama, 10 reels, 1924). Adapted by Micheaux from Thomas S. Stribling's novel by the same title (1922). A black achievement film, combined with a story of unrequited love. It concerned the difficulties encountered by a young black man who returns to his Tennessee home after graduating from Harvard, determined to build a college for blacks. In his efforts, he encounters opposition and hostility not only from the prejudiced white Southerners who believe that blacks would be ruined by an education, but also from the members of the black community. Intertwined with the main plot is the story of one woman's hopeless love for the hero, whom she thinks is too good for her, because of his educational accomplishments and desire to improve himself and his race. Filmed on location in Roanoke, Virginia in 1922. Released in New York on February 1, 1924. Cast: J. Homer Tutt (Peter Siner), Evelyn Preer (Cissie Deldine), Salem Tutt Whitney (Tump Pack), Lawrence Chenault, and W. B. F. Crowell. The film was well-received and later was made into a talking version, also entitled *Birthright* (1939), cited below.

Body and Soul (melodrama, 5 reels, 1924). (Bears no relationship to the 1947 film of the same title, starring John Garfield and featuring black actor Canada Lee.) An exposé of black religious cult leaders, gamblers and bootleggers who exploit the black community. The film was made in two versions. The plot of the original version, according to the New York State licensing records, was as follows:

> The story of a man, minister of the gospel, whose habits and manners are anything but that of a good man. He associates with the proprietor of a notorious gambling house, extorts money from him, betrays a girl of his parish, forces her to steal from the Bible her mother's savings, forces the girl to leave home, and finally kills the girl's brother when he comes to his sister's protection.

In the second version, which was made to satisfy the censors, the minister (Paul Robeson) is shown to be playing a double role—that of a detective who is only posing as a sinful preacher in order to expose a ring of criminals.

Although the first version of this film was completed in 1924, Micheaux did not apply for a New York State license until November 9, 1925. This film is especially significant because it featured Paul Robeson in the cast, which also included Julia Theresa Russell and Mercedes Gilbert. Comedian Marshall ("Garbage") Rogers appeared as a saloon keeper.

(A) Son of Satan (melodrama, 6 or 7 reels, 1924). Presumably a re-release of *The Ghost of Tolston's Manor* (1922), since Captain Tolston appears as a character in this film. Having lost a bet or argument, a black man is obliged to spend the night in a haunted house. According to the New York State license records, "This picture is filled with scenes of drinking, carousing and shows masked men becoming intoxicated. It shows the playing of crap for money, a man [Captain Tolston] killing his wife by choking her, the killing of the leader of the hooded organization [KKK] and the killing of a cat by throwing a stone at it." Micheaux applied for a New York license on September 18, 1924. The film was presented in Chicago in January 1925, and received the qualified endorsement of D. Ireland Thomas, who reviewed it in the *Chicago Defender* (January 31, 1925):

> Some may not like the production because it shows up some of our race in their true colors. They might also protest against the language used. I do not endorse this particular part of the film myself, but I must admit that it is true. We have got to hand it to Oscar Micheaux when it comes to giving us the real stuff.

Thomas goes on to praise the "all-star cast," which includes Andrew S. Bishop, Lawrence Chenault, Emmett Anthony, Edna Morton, Monte Hawley, Shingzie Howard, Ida Anderson, and E. G. Tatum.

Marcus Garland (melodrama, feature length, 1925). Apparently based on the life and ideas of Marcus Garvey, father of the "back-to-Africa movement." Applied for a New York State license in 1925. Cast included Salem Tutt Whitney and Amy Birdsong.

The Conjure Woman (melodrama, feature length, 1926). Based on the Charles W. Chesnutt short story by the same title (1899). Applied for a New York State license in 1926. Cast included Evelyn Preer and Percy Verwayen.

The Devil's Disciple (melodrama, feature length, 1926). Apparently dealt with white slavery (compulsory prostitution) in New York City. Applied for a New York State license in 1926, on which it was classified as a comedy. Cast included Evelyn Preer and Lawrence Chenault.

The Spider's Web (melodrama, 7 reels, 1926). Based on a story, "The Policy Players," of unknown authorship and date. The story of Norma Shepard, a beautiful girl from New York City's Harlem community, who visits her aunt, Mary Austin, in a small Mississippi delta town. While there, she is forced to ward off the sexual advances of Ballinger, a well-to-do young white man, the son of a planter; but is saved by Elmer Harris, a Secret Service agent from Chicago who is in Mississippi investigating charges of peonage there. Norma takes her aunt back to Harlem, where the older woman becomes addicted to playing the numbers, and loses her life savings. Finally, her winning number comes up, but when she goes to the office of her numbers writer to collect, she finds him dead—and she is arrested on suspicion of murder. Again the situation is saved by Elmer Harris, who is called in to investigate the crime. He discovers the murderer, exonerates the aunt, and wins the love of Norma. Micheaux was granted a New York State license for this film on January 3, 1927. Cast included Lorenzo McLane, Evelyn Preer (Norma Shepard), Edward Thompson, Grace Smythe, Marshall Rogers, Henrietta Loveless, and Billy Gulfport.

The Broken Violin (melodrama, 7 reels, 1927). According to the New York State licensing records, this film was based on Micheaux's *House of Mystery,* presumably a novel which never materialized. It is the story of a beautiful Negro violin prodigy, Lilia Cooper, whose mother is a washerwoman and whose father is a drunkard. The film takes its title from an incident when the father loses his wages in a gambling game and comes home drunk, demanding money from his wife. When she refuses, he smashes Lilia's violin over the head of the mother. The father meets his just deserts after severely beating Lilia's brother, who comes to his mother's aid: he is killed by a passing truck. In spite of her poor and wretched family background, Lilia manages to achieve a successful musical career and find happiness in love. Received a New York State license in 1927. Cast: J. Homer Tutt, Ardell Dabney, Alice B. Russell, Ike Paul, Daisy Foster, Gertrude Snelson, Boots Hope, Ethel Smith, and W. Hill.

The Millionaire (melodrama, 7 reels, 1927). According to a publicity poster prepared by Micheaux (now in the Library of Congress), this film was advertised as "the screen version of [Micheaux's] own novel, *The Millionaire,*" which probably was never actually written, and certainly never published. It tells the story of Pelham Guitry, who made his fortune in South America, after 15 years of hard work. A gang of criminals try to swindle him out of his money by tricking him into marriage with Elia Wellington, who is in league with the crooks. Pelham, however, successfully evades the marriage trap, and also succeeds in reforming Elia. This film was apparently shot in Chicago, where one of the locations was the Plantation Cafe, whose patrons were also included in the film; and one of the actors was Robert S. Tatum, then editor of the *Chicago Defender* newspaper. Received a New York State license on December 10, 1927, and premiered in New York City on February 15, 1928, with Micheaux listed as producer-director-writer. Cast included Grace Smith, J. Lawrence Criner, Cleo Desmond, Lionel Monagas, William Edmonson, Vera Bracker, S. T. Jacks, and E. G. Tatum.

Dark Princess (presumed to be a feature-length melodrama, 1928). Listed as one of Micheaux's films in *Who's Who in Colored America* (1950), although no other reference has been located. Apparently based on, or suggested by, W. E. DuBois's novel by the same title (also 1920), although no relationship between the two can be definitely established. [That novel concerns a young Negro medical student, who, failing to secure a hospital internship in the U.S. because of racial discrimination, goes to Berlin, where he falls in love with an Indian princess.]

A Fool's Errand (presumed to be a feature-length melodrama, 1928). Listed as one of Micheaux's films in *Who's Who in Colored America* (1950), although no other reference has been located. Apparently based on, or suggested by Eulalie Spence's one-act play by the same title (1927), which won second prize at the National Little Theatre Tournament at the Frolic Theatre in New York, 1927. [In that play, a group of nosey neighbors assume that the daughter of a church member is pregnant, and try to force her into marriage.]

Thirty Years Later (melodrama, 7 reels, 1928). Based on Henry Francis Downing's *The Racial Tangle,* which in 1928 was scheduled to be produced as a play by the Quality Amusement Company, a stock company of the [New York] Lafayette Players. It tells the story of George Eldridge Van Paul, the mulatto son of a black mother and white father, who is brought up believing that he is white. During the course of the story, he falls in love with a black girl, Hester Morgan, who refuses his proposal of marriage on racial grounds. When told about his Negro blood, Van Paul becomes proud of his racial identity, and Hester finally accepts his proposal. This film received a New York State license on February 25, 1928, with Micheaux listed as director-writer. Cast included William Edmondson (George Eldridge Van Paul), A. B. Comathiere (Habisham Strutt), Mabel Kelly (Hester Morgan), Ardella Dabney (Clara Booker), Gertrude Snelson (Mrs. Van Paul), Barrington Carter, Arthur Ray, Ruth Williams, and Madame Robinson.

The Wages of Sin (melodrama, feature length, 1929). Adapted from a story entitled "Alias Jefferson Lee," of unknown authorship or source. About two brothers, one of sterling character, the other a reprobate. The good brother, Winston Le Jaune, a film producer, in compliance with his mother's dying wish that he take care of his brother, Jefferson Lee, agrees to give his brother a job in his film company. Soon after he begins working for the company,

Jefferson Lee begins spending large sums of money on women and parties, and it is soon discovered that he has stolen a sizable amount of the company's funds, pushing the company into financial difficulty, and forcing Winston to fire him. After Winston has begun to recover from his financial reverses, and in a moment of weakness, he rehires his brother, who now sets out in earnest to destroy the company, and almost succeeds, until an unexpected turn of events brings the story to a happy conclusion. Apparently filmed in Chicago, where it opened in 1928, but was closed by the Chicago censor board. Cast included Lorenzo Tucker, William A. Clayton, Jr., Bessie Gibbens, Gertrude Snelson, Ethel Smith, Alice Russell, Katherine Noisette, Sylvia Birdsong, and William Baker. See also next entry.

When Men Betray (melodrama, feature length, 1929). Believed to be a re-release of *Wages of Sin* (above), revised and retitled in order to satisfy the board of censors. Cast included Lorenzo Tucker, William Clayton, Jr., Bessie Gibbens, Gertrude Snelson, Ethel Smith, and Alice B. Russell.

Easy Street (melodrama, 5 reels, 1930). Granted a New York State license on August 1, 1930. Cast included Richard B. Harrison (best known for his portrayal of De Lawd in *The Green Pastures*) and Alice B. Russell (Mrs. Oscar Micheaux).

SOUND FILMS

A Daughter of the Congo (melodrama, 9 reels, 1930). Based on *The American Cavalryman: A Liberian Romance,* a novel of West Africa by Henry Francis Downing. Significant as Micheaux's first partly-sound film, with talking sequences and musical score. An African adventure story which concerned the brave efforts of a black cavalry officer, Captain Paul Dale, to rescue Lupelta, a beautiful mulatto girl (the daughter of a wealthy family) who had been abducted as a baby and brought up in the jungle by savages. After she becomes a grown woman, Lupelta is again abducted—by Arab slave hunters, while she is bathing in a brook. She is rescued by Captain Dale, who had been sent by the United States Army to the black republic of Monravia, in the Belgian Congo (actually Monrovia, Liberia), to operate a "constabulary" (i.e., a military police force). After Lupelta is rescued, "she is taken to a mission school," where, according to Micheaux's press book for this film, "she succumbs to learning readily and soon becomes the most popular maid of Monravia, in spite of the inclination very often, to revert to the wild life of the jungle from which she is rescued." According to the New York State license records, the first New York showing was on April 5, 1930. Cast: Joe Byrd (Whereaboo), Katherine Noisette (Lupelta), Wilhelmina Williams (Reesha), Clarence Redd (Lodango), Lorenzo Tucker (Captain Paul Dale), Roland Irving (Lieutenant Brown), Alice Russell (Miss Pattie), Charles Moore (John Calvert), Gertrude Snelson (John's sister), Percy Verwayen (Pidgly Muffy), Madame Robinson (Lobue), Salem Tutt Whitney (Kojo, President of the Republic), Willor Lee Guilford (Kulda), "Speedy" Wilson (Mwamba), Daisy Harding (singer), Rudolph Dawson (tap dancer). *The New York Amsterdam News* (April 16, 1930) criticized this film for "its persistent vaunting of intraracial [*sic*] color fetishism." According to reviewer Theophilus Lewis, "The scene is laid in a not so mythical republic in Africa. Half of the characters wear European clothes and are supposed to be civilized, while the other half wear their birthday suits and some feathers and are supposed to be savages. All of the noble characters are high yellows; all the ignoble ones are black."

The Exile (melodrama, with music and dance, 70 minutes, 1931). Partly based on the author's first film, *The Homesteader* (1918), which in turn was based on his novel by the same title (1917), combined with night club scenes featuring singing and dancing, to capitalize on the new medium of sound. Significant as the first all-talking picture by a black company. The story is concerned with a young man who is engaged to be married when his fiancée comes into possession of a large mansion, formerly owned by whites, on South Parkway Avenue in Chicago. In order to pay for its upkeep, she turns it into a cabaret combined with a house of ill repute; the young man breaks off his engagement when he discovers the truth. Disgusted with life in Chicago, he goes to the wilderness of South Dakota to establish a new life. There he claims and develops a large tract of land and becomes a successful rancher. He befriends and falls in love with a beautiful young woman whom he assumes to be white, and believes that he can never marry her because of racial barriers. However, it is later revealed that she is of part-Negro heritage, and the barrier to their future happiness is removed. The film was apparently made in New York City, using a number of singers, dancers, and musicians from the Cotton Club, Connie's Inn, the *Blackbirds,* Leonard Harper's Chorines, and Donald Heywood's Band. It premiered successfully in New York City in 1932; but when it opened in Pittsburgh, Pennsylvania—where the South Dakota scenes were probably filmed—it was closed midway through the showing by two censors who objected to what they presumed to be love scenes between a black man and a white woman. Cast included Stanley Murrell* (in the leading role), Eunice Brooks, Charles Moore, A. B. Comathiere, Carl Mahon, Lou Vernon, Katherine Noisette, Louis Cook, Ronald Holder, and George Randol.

Darktown Review (also known as *Darktown Scandals Revue,* feature length, 1931). Film version of a nightclub floor show, featuring musical producer Irvin C. Miller, who probably put the show together. Produced in 1931, in order to capitalize on the new medium of sound. Cast included Sara Martin, Maude Mills, the Club Alabam Stompers, the Dixie Jubilee Singers, and the Harlem Strutters.

Black Magic (musical revue, feature length, 1932). Another night club revue, as the film immediately above.

Ten Minutes to Live (gangster melodrama, feature length,

---

*Since *Stanley Murrell* was listed as *Stanleigh Morrell* in the credits for the original Broadway production of *The Green Pastures,* I assume that both Stanley and Stanleigh were used, and both Murrell and Morrell, in various sources. My spelling of Stanley Murrell was taken from the 1958 Ideal Pictures catalog, a page of which was reprinted in Donald Bogle's *Toms, Coons, Mulattoes, Mammies, and Bucks* (New York: Viking, 1973), p. 105.

1932). Cast included Lawrence Chenault, Willor Lee Guilford, and William Clayton, Jr.

Veiled Aristocrats (melodrama, feature length, 1932). Cast included Lorenzo Tucker and Barrington Guy.

The Girl from Chicago (crime melodrama, feature length, 1932). A remake of Micheaux's *The Spider's Web* (1926) in sound. Norma Shepard, a beautiful young woman from Chicago, receives a teaching appointment in Batesville, Mississippi, where she plans to live with her aunt, Mary Austin. At the same time, Alonzo Smith, a handsome young secret service agent, who has just returned from Scotland Yard to New York City, is assigned to a case in Batesville. Coincidentally, he also lodges with Norma's Aunt Mary. Norma and Alonzo become romantically involved, and he is able to save her from being sexually assaulted by Jeff Ballinger, a well-to-do young white man, who is arrested and sent to prison. Aunt Mary goes to New York, followed by Alonzo and Norma, where she becomes addicted to the playing of numbers and loses her life savings. When she is broke, she finally "hits" for $11,000, and rushes to her numbers broker, Gomez, to collect her winnings. She finds his dead body in front of his open safe. Mary grabs her rightful winnings and runs, but is soon arrested, tried, convicted, and sentenced to death for murder. Alonzo is assigned to the case, and succeeds in proving the aunt innocent and catching the real murderer. In the meantime, his romantic involvement with Norma has developed into true love, and the film ends happily for all three. Produced in 1932, with the following cast: Carl Mahon (Alonzo Smith), Starr Calloway (Norma Shepard), Eunice Brooks (Mary Austin), Grace Smith, Frank Wilson, Minta Cato, Juano Hernandez, Erwin Gary, John Everett, Alice B. Russell, Cherokee Thornton, Chick Evans, Bud Harris, and Alfred ("Slick") Chester. The Rhythm Rascals Orchestra also performed in this film.

The Phantom of Kenwood (mystery melodrama, feature length, 1933).

Ten Minutes to Kill (mystery melodrama, feature length, 1933). Presumably a sequel to *Ten Minutes to Live,* or the same film re-released under a modified title.

Harlem after Midnight (melodrama with music, feature length, 1934). According to the producer's press book, this film depicts "Gangdom in Action Again—but from a new angle—the Angle of the Kidnaper!" [*sic*]. It promised "An epidemic of high-yallers and sugar-cured browns straight from Harlem and sizzlin' hot!!" Apparently it focuses on both the seamy and exotic sides of Harlem night life, including cabaret and nightclub scenes, to capitalize on the new sound medium. Produced in 1934, with the following cast: Lorenzo Tucker, Dorothy Van Eagle, Bee Freeman, Alfred ("Slick") Chester, Rex Ingram, Lawrence Chenault, A. B. Comathiere, and Count Le Shine.

Lem Hawkins' Confession (crime melodrama, feature length, 1935). A remake of *The Gunsaulus Mystery* (1921) in sound. Henry Glory, a young law student and novelist, falls in love with Claudia Vance, three years prior to becoming a successful lawyer. At that time, he is told that she is a wicked woman, so he goes away, not realizing that the charges against Claudia are unfounded, because of mistaken identity. After Henry becomes a successful attorney, Claudia contacts him, asking him to defend her brother who has been charged with murder. Henry takes the case and successfully defends the brother after obtaining a confession from Lem Hawkins, a porter who apparently witnessed the crime. Henry finds that his opinion of Claudia's character is unfounded, and the two of them re-establish their romantic relationship on a true foundation for future happiness. Released in 1935 with the following cast: Clarence Brooks (Henry Glory), Dorothy Van Engle (Claudia Vance), Alex Lovejoy, Laura Bowman, Lionel Monagas, Eunice Wilson, Sandy Burns, Henrietta Loveless, Bee Freeman, Alice B. Russell, Andrew Bishop, Flournoy E. Miller, Clarence Williams (singer) and Eunice Wilson (singer).

Temptation (sex melodrama with music, feature length, 1936). In the manner of the seduction films of Cecil B.

De Mille, *Temptation* tells about the numerous underworld involvements (both professional and romantic) of a black model, and her difficulties in trying to escape from these tangled relationships in order to find a better life. According to the producer's press book, the cabaret sequences featured the following professional entertainers: the Pope Sisters, Bobby Hargreave's Kit Kat Club Orchestra, Lillian Fitzgerald, Raymond Kallund ("the roping fool"), Dot and Dash (tap dancers), the "Six Sizzlers" (performing orchestra), Taft Rice (entertainer), and other specialty acts and musical numbers. Produced in 1936, featuring Andrew S. Bishop, Ethel Moses, Lorenzo Tucker, Hilda Rogers, and "Slick" Chester.

Underworld (gangster thriller, feature length, 1936). Black version of the typical Hollywood gangster film of the prohibition years, in which a black college graduate becomes involved with the underworld of Chicago, where he has gone to live after graduation. Through association with the leading black racketeer and his sweetheart, he moves into a world of night clubs, gambling, prostitution, violence, alcohol, drugs, mobsters and low-life characters—all trappings of the typical gangster movie of the 1930s. Produced in 1936, and apparently opened in 1937. Cast included Oscar Polk (the gangster), Bee Freeman (his gun moll), Sol Johnson, Alfred "Slick" Chester, Ethel Moses, Larry Seymour, Lorenzo Tucker, and Angel Gabriel.

God's Stepchildren (melodrama, feature length [70 minutes], 1938). Concerned with the problem of "passing," in the manner of *Imitation of Life.* According to the catalog of Ideal Pictures (a black film distributor), *God's Stepchildren* was "From the story 'Naomi Negress,' of a baby that looks white." Naomi, a very fair-skinned Negro girl, is abandoned by her real mother and brought up by a foster mother who forces her to attend a black school. Deeply resentful, she invents a scandalous lie involving the sex life of one of her teachers, which results in her being expelled and placed in a convent, until she becomes of age. After leaving the convent, she falls in love with a white man who turns out to be her stepbrother. Forced then to marry a wealthy but dark-skinned farmer whom she finds repulsive, she abandons him and their child, and begins passing for white. She marries a white man who soon discovers her true race. Disgraced and full of guilt, she returns home and commits suicide. Produced in 1938, with the following cast: Alice B. Russell (Mrs. Saunders), Jacqueline Lewis (Naomi, as a child), Ethel Moses (her teacher), Gloria Press (Naomi, as a woman), Carman Newsome (Jimmy, presumably Naomi's step-brother), Alec Lovejoy (a gambler), Laura Bowman (Aunt Carrie), Sam Patterson (a banker), Charles Moore (Superintendent of Schools), Trixie Smith, Charles Thompson, Columbus Jackson, Consuelo Harris (muscle dancer), Sammy Gardiner and the Tyler Twins (tap dancers). The premiere was held at the RKO Regent Theatre in Harlem, but the film was closed after only two days and banned from all RKO Theatres because of some scenes that were deemed objectionable, such as the beating of Naomi by a white man who discovered that she had Negro blood.

Swing (musical, feature length, 1938). Apparently concerns the exciting experiences of a musician and faithless-lover, and his relationship with his trusting girlfriend, a cook, as they travel from Birmingham to Harlem, presumably visiting nightclubs and places of amusement along the way. Produced in 1938, with the following cast: Cora Green, Hazel Diaz, Carman Newsome, Dorothy Van Engle, Alec Lovejoy, and Amanda Randolph.

Birthright (drama, feature length, 1939). A remake of his successful 1924 silent film by the same title, which tells the story of Peter Siner, a black graduate of Harvard University, who tries to build a college for blacks in his Tennessee home town, and the difficulties that he encounters with both whites and blacks who oppose his plans. He falls in love with Cissie Dildine, who supports him in every way, but does not believe that she is socially or morally fit to be his wife. Produced in 1939, with the following cast: Alec Lovejoy, Laura Bowman, Ethel Moses, Carman Newsome, and George Vessey.

The Notorious Elinor Lee (melodrama, feature length, 1939). Described by *Time* (January 29, 1940) as "the story of

a double-crossing colored gun moll who gets properly shot."
Apparently Elinor Lee is assigned by her gangster friends to
seduce a great black boxing champion, in order that he can
be persuaded to throw an important fight, but changes her
mind when she gets to know him. This film was co-produced
by black aviator Col. Hubert Julian, known as the Black
Eagle. The world premiere was held in January 1940, and
was a gala occasion with all the usual Hollywood trappings—
searchlights, carpeted sidewalks, policemen, chauffeured
limousines, formal attire, and the arrival of black cinema's
most glamorous personalities. Cast included Edna Mae
Harris (Elinor Lee), Robert Earl Jones (the boxing champion), Carman Newsome, Gladys Williams, Ella Mae Waters, Sally Gooding, and Vera Burrelle.

Lying Lips (melodrama, feature length, 1939). The story of
Elsie Bellwood, a nightclub singer, who is convicted of
murdering her aunt, because she is the sole beneficiary of an
insurance policy which she (Elsie) had recently purchased.
The plot is concerned mainly with the efforts of two men,
Detective Benjamin Hadnott and Detective Wanzer, to find
the real killer and save Elsie from life imprisonment, to which
she has already been sentenced. The film was co-produced
in 1939 by Col. Hubert Julian, and featured many of the
same cast members who had appeared in *The Notorious
Elinor Lee* (above), including: Edna Mae Harris (Elsie Bel-
wood), Carman Newsome (Detective Benjamin Hadnott),
and James Earl Jones (Detective Wanzer).

The Betrayal (melodrama, feature length, 1948). Micheaux's last film. Based on his autobiographical novel, *The
Wind from Nowhere,* a rewritten version of *The Homesteader,* which had appeared both as a novel (in 1917) and
as a film (in 1918). It tells the story of Martin Eden (or, more
properly, of Micheaux himself) as a pioneer in South Dakota,
intermingled with the story of a disastrous marriage and an
interracial love story. (The plot is practically identical with
that of his first film, *The Homesteader,* except that the
characters' names have been changed.) Produced
independently by Micheaux, and billed as "the greatest
photoplay of all time," it was released by Astor Pictures and

was widely reviewed in the press when it premiered at the Mansfield Theatre in downtown New York. However, the film was poorly received and did not succeed at the box office. Cast featured Leroy Collins (as Martin Eden), Myra Standon, Verlie Cowan, Harris Gaines, Yvonne Machen, and Alice B. Russell. Other cast members: Lou Vernon, Edward Fraction, Jessie Johnson, William Byrd, Frances DeYoung, Arthur McCoo, Gladys Williams, Richard Lawrence, David Jones, Vernon B. Duncan, Curley Ellison, and Sue McBride.

This filmography of Oscar Micheaux, even in its incompleteness, reveals that he was undoubtedly the most prolific black filmmaker of his day, whose accomplishments must be regarded as phenomenal when one considers the limitations imposed by his lack of formal education and training, the lack of financial backing and large studio support; the inadequacy of equipment, facilities, personnel and resources; the difficulties of gaining censor approval and the denial of wide distribution and booking; and the general restrictions imposed by the racial climate of the times.

He is to be credited for his initiative, his aggressiveness, his ambition, and his success, in helping to open the doors for future black actors, producers, directors, screenwriters, and others who are now on the inside of the film industry.

Oscar Micheaux deserves to be called America's Most Legendary Black Filmmaker.

Prof. Petersen's exhaustively researched essay on the legendary black filmmaker Oscar Micheaux contributes an important missing chapter to American film history. It is of extraordinary interest that Micheaux made a silent film, Within Our Gates *(1919), with an all-black cast, based on the lynching of a Jew, Leo M. Frank, in 1915, and two other films on this subject later on; he did these three anti-lynching films many years before the release in 1937 of the outstanding Warner Bros. film* They Won't Forget, *also based on the Frank case. (See Lewis Jacobs' comment on the film in ch. 24) This film, directed by Mervyn Le Roy from a screenplay by Robert Rossen, is still in circulation; regrettably, the Micheaux films are long lost. The final outcome of the Frank case deserves a mention here. In its April 1986 issue,* Jewish Currents *reported:*

Leo Frank Pardoned but Not Exonerated by Georgia

Leo M. Frank got a measure of posthumous justice when the Georgia State Board of Pardons and Paroles March 11 issued a "pardon" that the N.Y. Times next day precisely headlined as "Georgia Pardons Victim/70 Years After Lynching."

On Dec. 22, 1983, that State Board had denied him a pardon that would exonerate Frank of the charges of murder of which he had been "convicted" in a trial staged in an atmosphere of such anti-Semitic hysteria that finally Gov. John Slaton commuted Frank's sentence to life imprisonment on Aug. 17, 1915. Whereupon a mob tore Frank out of prison and lynched him in Marietta, Ga., the second Jew to be lynched in the USA. In 1983, pardon was denied because supporters of Frank could not "prove his innocence"—when in fact he was never proved guilty in a fair trial. Now the State Board "pardons" Frank because Georgia failed to protect him from being lynched. This confession by the state of Georgia of its guilt in failing to protect him is accompanied by the statement that the pardon does not address the issue of Frank's innocence.

Even this "pardon," however, is a victory of sorts, obtained by the persistence of the local American Jewish Committee, Anti-Defamation League of B'nai B'rith and Jewish Federation of Atlanta, which refused to take the 1983 denial as the last word. History and informed opinion have already exonerated Leo M. Frank.   (D.P.)

12   THE REIGN OF THE DIRECTOR

Lewis Milestone

A SAPLING STOOD in the shadow of a mighty oak, so mighty that the appearance of the little sapling filled the oak with both pity and disgust.

A storm hit the forest. The oak proudly faced it, refusing to bend or even sway before it, but the little weak sapling bent to the ground with each blow of the wind. Such humility filled the mighty oak with disgust, and proudly, and more stubbornly than ever, he faced the fierce storm.

But when the storm had spent itself the sapling still stood as before. The mighty oak that had refused to sway and bend lay prone on the ground, torn out by the roots—dead.

I first arrived in Hollywood at the end of 1919. That and the subsequent three or four years can be called "the reign of the director"—a power supreme and absolute. D. W. Griffith! *Way Down East! Dream Street!* James Cruze! *Covered Wagon! Merton of the Movies!* Eric von Stroheim! *The Devil's Pass Key! Foolish Wives!* Rex Ingram! *Four Horsemen of the Apocalypse! Scaramouche!* Mickey Neilan! Another Neilan picture! What difference does it make who's in it or what the title is—it's a Neilan picture! Who can afford to miss it? The latest and the best in comedy, sophistication, speed. Another lesson in what the best motion picture can be like. Learn about inference, power of suggestion, subtlety; the most told in the shortest possible footage. *Why Get*

From *New Theatre and Film* (October 1937). Reprinted by permission of the author.

Married! Go and Get it! Fools First! Raymond Griffith is born—again Neilan!

And then came the storm. It started with a tiny gust of wind.

Irving Thalberg, the baby producer, the important general manager of the very unimportant Universal Manufacturing Company. And the first oak hit was von Stroheim, then directing *Merry-go-Round.*

The saplings (all unemployed at the time), Richard Wallace, W. K. Howard, Bill Wellman, and the writer of this piece, were sharing a borrowed dollar at Levy's Cafe. We sat through the lunch hour and long past it. The subject of conversation was (Hollywood forgive me!)—pictures.

"Let's start a rumor," said Wallace, "let's start a rumor that Irving Thalberg—you know, the little fellow at Universal— well, let's start a rumor that Irving Thalberg fired von Stroheim—took him off the picture."

When the laughter subsided we agreed that a more startling tale couldn't have been invented by Munchausen himself, and we promptly scattered to circulate the rumor. But Wallace must have been psychic. That evening Hollywood was shaken like no earthquake ever shook it. Newspaper headlines carried the startling news that Irving Thalberg fired von Stroheim—took him off the picture. At first we, the members of the conspiracy, thought it was the result of our own work, for no place in the world can you spread a rumor more quickly than in Hollywood (with the exception of an Army latrine). Imagine our surprise when we found out that we started the rumor simultaneously with the actual happening.

Well, that was the beginning of the storm and the end of the reign of the director, the mighty oak. The storm grew fiercer. Following the birth of the first producer, Irving Thalberg, came others, each adding to the ferocity of the storm, each outdoing the others in establishing his absolute power, and when the storm subsided there was no D.W. Griffith, no Cruze, no von Stroheim, no Ingram, no Neilan. These men knew only one way of working—the way of a director; select the story, have a hand in the writing of the story, cast it, cut it, etc. Deprived of that method, they couldn't function. They were forced to go and they went.

A come-back for a top-notch director is practically impossible. The reason is simple. To make a great picture a director needs the producer's absolute trust and confidence and a great deal of money, money to buy material, cast, etc. Once fallen into disfavor he gets none of those things, yet, because he had a great name once, the producer expects him to deliver a picture up to his old standard.

And, since I started this piece with a fable I suppose I should finish it with a moral, but I'm afraid I can't, for I have been both a sapling and an oak. What am I now? You'll have to wait until the next storm to get the answer.

"What am I now," Milestone asks in his prophetic little tale of the 1920s. The story of his case is not dissimilar to that of the other directors he mentions. Before becoming a victim of the storms that cut down such mighty oaks as Griffith, von Stroheim, Cruze and the others, the sapling Milestone (soon to mature as an oak) went on to direct All Quiet on the Western Front *(1930),* Front Page *(1931),* Of Mice and Men *(1939),* Edge of Darkness *(1943),* The Purple Heart *(1944),* A Walk in the Sun *(1945), and other films. Hardly anything of distinction under his name followed his being summoned in 1947 to appear before the House Committee on Un-American Activities. One of the original 19 Hollywood artists who received summonses, he was among the nine who, for one reason or another, were excused from testifying. Although not directly blacklisted, he felt the lash of the censor in the rapid decline in the quality of almost all Hollywood films. See the material on Blacklisting in the 1940s and 1950s elsewhere in this volume. (DP)*

13 PORTRAIT OF ASTA NIELSEN

Elsa Gress-Wright

THE FAMOUS FRENCH POET Apollinaire wrote during the great period of film actress Asta Nielsen: "She is everything! She is the drunkard's vision and the lonely man's dream. She looks like a young girl who is happy, and her eyes know things so delicate and untouchable that never a word of it shall pass her lips. She has the elan of an Yvette Guilbert, and the daintiness of a Japanese woman from the famous woodcuts of Utamaro. When hatred illuminates the eyes of Asta Nielsen, we clench our fists, and when she lifts her eyelids, it is the stars that light up."

These are no mean attributes to ascribe to an artist, and an artist, at that, in the latest arrival among the arts, which then was not yet recognized as art at all: the film. Film stars have not been spoken of like this before or after. But then, this was no ordinary star. The very concept "film star" had not been invented at that time, and had it been, it would not have even approximated *what* Asta Nielsen was and *who* she was and is.

For Asta Nielsen was something far more important and original and genuine than the leading diva of her time, as film stars were called during the adolescence of the film. She was, and at her advanced age of 88, still is, a great artistic personality, a gifted and lively person, and a creative force who above all helped shape the visual language of the new

---

The author of this essay, a distinguished playwright and musician, wrote it in Danish in February 1970 for a journal in Copenhagen, then translated it herself into English. It appears here with her permission.

art and give this language human contents. She was no product of a fashion or style, much less a symbol like the changing sex symbols of later decades. She was a primeval power. It was no coincidence that she spoke especially strongly and urgently to artists, poets and artistically engaged people. The best of them could not only admire her as a colleague, because they could evaluate her effort, they could also identify entirely and passionately with her, as Apollinaire did in the above quote, and as he had done ever since he saw her first film, *The Abyss,* in a small Parisian cinema in 1910 and described how he came under her spell: when he left the cinema, the world looked different, "her shadow lay over Paris."

Later she was praised in various keys by other artists abroad and even at home in Denmark, where her success was otherwise not officially accepted. The Nobel Prize-winning poet Johannes V. Jensen described her beauty in grandiose terms; the critic Georg Brandes called her a moss rose, because this flower has wholly special beauty, and never completely opens, but seems always to enclose some innermost, deep secret. The art historian R. Broby-Johansen tells how he, late in the twenties, full of resentment at what he had heard of the "affectation" of Asta Nielsen, went to see her in the Pabst film *Joyless Street,* and left a convert, deeply moved by her crystal clear, simple and anything but affected acting in the main scene of the film.

Affectation is, of course, an accusation easily leveled at any unusual personality or artist, and especially so in Denmark, where the fear of being "different" and of showing one's feelings reaches panical heights. It is not strange then, that an actress of Asta Nielsen's format was quickly given that label when she had attained international fame—just as her slightly younger famous compatriots, Karen Blixen (alias Isak Dinesen) and Carl Th. Dreyer, were given it during their lifetime. Nor is it strange, considering the manner in which Danes traditionally treat their important artists, that Asta Nielsen received no real recognition, beyond the circle of artists, while she worked as a film and stage actress, and that she was also not recognized duly in her other artistic functions: as the writer of the exuberantly rich autobiography, *The Silent Muse,* and as a pictorial artist. The delicate and sensitive and imaginative collages she has produced during her long, enforced retirement since she returned to Denmark in 1936 have been regarded as the harmless hobby of a peculiar old lady, although, as everything with which Asta Nielsen has occupied herself, they are artistically sure expressions of an indomitable artist's mind and an acute power of observation.

But the fact that Asta Nielsen's fate in her home country cannot be regarded as unexpected is in no way an excuse for the indifference, if not outright hostility with which she has met, nor for the fact, entirely incomprehensible to foreigners, that she has been unwanted by Danish stage and film for all these years, apart from a single half-hearted exception, where she appeared on stage in an unimportant play in the early fifties. The internationally known avant-garde director Tom O'Horgan, who met Asta Nielsen in 1967, could not get over his amazement that she was not constantly on TV, film and stage. "She is a glorious Grand Old Lady," he says in an interview in *Leonardo,* "as sharply observant and wryly self-aware as she can ever have been, and her eyes are terrific. You can just see what she did to people with them. In her time people did not speak of sex, but they knew it alright when they saw it, and she had lots of it, or rather of a poetic erotic radiance which nowadays is hard to come by, not because there is too much sex in the lively arts, but because there is not enough of the genuine article. And then she has got more personality than scores of successful actresses put together." And the curator of the film museum of the Museum of Modern Art in New York says she regards Asta Nielsen as one of the greatest cinematic forces ever.

If anyone were to believe that Asta Nielsen came easily by her triumphs, which included being the chosen pin-up for soldiers on both sides the frontier in the First World War, or that these triumphs have gone to her head, they would be dead wrong. She is the most truthful and incorruptible creature on earth, and these qualities have given her innumerable troubles in her career, but at the same time prevented her from becoming self-admiring in times of success, and self-pitying in times of neglect.

Furthermore, she was from the beginning hampered by the very peculiarities of appearances and mind which later made her famous. In the theater world at the turn of the century, when she made her appearance, she was found too "special," having too large eyes, too narrow lips, too deep a voice and whatever else can be imagined to reject an artist who permitted herself not to resemble the current ideal. The fact that she had struggled from childhood, through being hard of hearing, was a further obstruction in her way. But all difficulties and handicaps only enhanced her courage and her enormous vitality. In the film about her career which she made in 1968 she says that it was coincidence that led her into the film in 1910. She was dissatisfied at the way her abilities were badly used on stage, and followed the advice of director Urban Gad to try the new, exciting medium. She had no intentions of "improving the film," just of finding further outlet, and she had natural mimic gifts which could be used in the service of the silent muse.

Irrespective, however, of her planning, she not only managed to improve the medium, but to create a surprisingly rich visual form of expression, which was inimitable, being unique, but which put forth new standards and opened new perspectives for the young art. It was not the films in which she acted that had importance, but the fact that she was there. She has saved more bad films from oblivion than anyone, as she herself points out, but even though many of them can be seen at film museums and art cinemas, and even though they also occasionally have other values, it is *die Asta* whom you see and remember to the exclusion of practically everything else. Die Asta in a hundred guises, in elegant dresses, in rags and tags, as *grande dame,* and as demi-monde, as a proletarian, as a gypsy, as an artist, as a mother, as a mistress, as a man-eater (Lulu!), tormented, tormenting, roguish, exasperating, melancholy, dangerous, lazy, energetic, but above all as loving and suffering. There is hardly any type of role which she has not played, and there was no role stronger than she. But exactly because she remained herself and gave herself, she could convince and carry audiences with her in the most primitive films and the most hazardous and implausible situations.

It is impossible here to survey even cursorily die Asta's variegated career, which is described so vividly in her book *The Silent Muse.* Suffice it to mention a few naked data: born

1881, educated at the acting school of the Royal Theater in Copenhagen, worked in the theater 1902–1910, thereafter approximately 70 films, most of them made in Berlin. Home to Denmark 1936. The rest is silence about the artist Asta Nielsen, if not about the person, until in 1968 she created her own self-portrait, *Asta Nielsen,* after having rejected a young director's attempt at making a short on her.

This little film was made under poor conditions, for the Danish State Film Foundation, which has funds enough for such undertakings, found it fit to scrape and pinch on this film, which should have been made in color to give a full impression of the richly detailed and colorful home of Asta Nielsen with its Spanish Baroque furniture and objects d'art, draperies, tapestries and statues, but especially of her collages—and of herself. But even in its present skimpy form the film is a fine and moving picture of the aging artist who looks back at her career without bitterness, but with the consciousness that "fame is a word written in sand." And it contains cuts from her films that give an impression of her fantastic versatility and fantastic force of expression.

Among the many tragic glimpses in this artistic self-portrait is a comic section, where die Asta, then 32, plays a 14-year-old Lolita who is trying to make her uncle and threatens to drown herself because of his lack of understanding, a threat foiled, however, by the coldness of the water. That she played a flapper as an adult is, of course, no more strange than, for example, Dustin Hoffmann playing teenagers in his thirties, and her Lolita is still a fun little bitch in an otherwise heavy-handed Germanic comedy. In the midst of her suicidal project she begins to pick at a pimple she discovers on her knee, a completely genuine, completely observed touch. That Asta Nielsen includes it in her portrait, as "undignified" as it seems, and as misunderstood as it was by inexperienced young reviewers and audiences, proves her integrity. And integrity is the very essence of Asta Nielsen. It may not be fashionable at the moment. But it is durable, and something she has in common with most great artists.

Harry Alan Potamkin was the first American film critic to call attention to the artistry of Asta Nielsen, noting her appear-

ance in Von Gerlag's 1920 unique masterpiece, Vanina, that
was highly esteemed abroad but overlooked and neglected
in the U.S. "In it starred Asta Nielsen, to my mind the
greatest of film actresses," he wrote in Cinema (April 1930).
There are also two eloquent descriptions of her artistry on
pages 64–66 of the English edition of Bela Balasz's The
Theory of Film.

Elsa Gress, author of the above "Portrait of Asta Nielsen"
(written in 1970, a year after the death of the great actress),
added the following in a letter to me of October 31, 1987: "I
enclose a short play I did for TV on Asta in her old age. It was
paid for, but never produced, since the old actress who
seemed the only natural choice for Asta, died. There is now
a chance that the play will be done . . . . When Asta finally
succumbed, it was not to age—that could not wither
her—but to a fall with multiple complications. She lingered
for several months in a hospital, though lingered is hardly
the word, since she was very much awake and alive and
followed up on world affairs in papers and TV—until the day
when I came to see her, and she started talking of that
terrible catastrophe, that huge unsinkable ship going down,
all those people dead . . . and I realized she had finally left
the present and was back in 1912 with the news of the
Titanic. She died the next day.

"It is strange to have known and admired and worked
with those two giants of the film, Asta and Carl Dreyer. But I
am certainly glad I did know them." (DP)

14   VON STROHEIM AND REALISM

Jay Leyda

"THIS AUSTRIAN, sometime soldier and sometime everything—a wrapper of bundles at seven dollars a week, a bad singer in a German rathskeller, a flypaper salesman, a deputy sheriff, a track walker while learning to speak English in America, a dish-washer, a life-guard, a riding master, an 'extra' player in films—is one of the most dominating individuals in the screen world." Thus Jim Tully described Erich von Stroheim in 1926. He was then beginning *The Wedding March* for Paramount, his last important film. This and his other films suggest that he may have enjoyed a glamorous youth in Vienna, but his harsher American experiences are more responsible for the film often called "Stroheim's masterpiece of realism," *Greed.* At present von Stroheim is far from fame and masterpieces, acting in French and English films.

Von Stroheim gained his first film experience as actor, assistant director and art director under D. W. Griffith, graduating from extra-player to the role of the Pharisee in the Judean sequences of *Intolerance.* Later, when war-time films brought him into demand to play brutal Prussian officers, Griffith hired him to supervise military detail and to play yet another Prussian officer in *Hearts of the World.* Under this master he took lessons in realism and in artistic integrity as well as in film-making.

From Film Notes, Bulletin of the Museum of Modern Art, Vol. XVI, Nos. 2–3, Part 1, The Silent Film. Edited by Iris Barry. Copyright © 1949, The Museum of Modern Art, New York. All rights reserved. Reprinted by permission.

In 1919, von Stroheim convinced Carl Laemmle of Universal that an original story of his would make a successful film if he were allowed full supervision over its production. This film, *Blind Husbands,* in which von Stroheim also played the chief role, was released against the protests of Laemmle's advisers yet made enough money for Laemmle to confide another modestly financed film, *The Devil's Pass-Key* (1920) to von Stroheim. Then he was given unlimited funds to make *Foolish Wives* (1921). Universal widely publicized von Stroheim on the one hand as an actor, "the man you love to hate," and on the other as a director who spent almost legendary sums of money. *Foolish Wives,* which had cost $1,000,000 grossed only $800,000: the director was the first to be struck in an economy clean-up at Universal, and the unfinished but already costly film on which he was then working, *Merry-Go-Round,* was given to a thriftier director. Metro then invited him to make any subject he wished for them. At that time he wrote "it is possible to tell a great story in motion pictures in such a way that the spectator . . . will come to believe that what he is looking at is real . . . Even so Dickens and de Maupassant and Zola and Frank Norris catch and reflect life in their novels. There must be more of this realism on the screen. It is my humble ambition to furnish some of it. It is with that idea that I am producing Frank Norris's story, *McTeague.*"

GREED (1923–24)

Produced by Metro-Goldwyn-Mayer. Written and directed by Erich von Stroheim; adapted from *McTeague,* a novel by Frank Norris. Edited by June Mathis. Photography by Ben Reynolds, William Daniels, Ernest Schoedsack. Cast: Gibson Gowland as McTeague; Tempe Piggott as McTeague's mother; Jean Hersholt as Marcus; Zazu Pitts as Trina Sieppe; Chester Conklin as Trina's father; Sylvia Ashton as Trina's mother; Joan Standing as Selina; Austin Jewell as August; Oscar and Otto Gottell as the Sieppe twins; Dale Fuller as Maria. Acquired through the courtesy of Metro-Goldwyn-Mayer.

Eight years before, while von Stroheim was a movie extra, he had come upon this Norris novel and determined to make a film of it some day. (The novel was, at almost that same time, adapted for the screen, as *Life's Whirlpool* (1915) with Fania Marinoff and Holbrook Blinn.) When his chance came, von Stroheim insisted upon adapting the accumulative structure of the novel by including its every detail and "filming every scene against its original background and not against studio-made imitations, no matter how perfect they might be. In sharp contrast to the great majority of contemporary screen plays, not one single scene was produced or filmed in the studio!" (*Blue Book of the Screen,* ed. by Ruth Wing. Hollywood, 1924). What is more, *Greed* even in its shortened version gives evidence of being an utterly faithful transcription of the intent of the novel, as moralizing and clear in its purpose as the strongest of propaganda films. This purpose, to demonstrate the dehumanizing influence of money, is projected with all the richness of Norris's realistic technique.

Paul Rotha, in *The Film Till Now* (London, Jonathan Cape, 1930, p. 97) draws attention to the fine cinematic and psychological use made of significant details, related to the past with Griffith's *Broken Blossoms* and finding followers in von Sternberg and Pabst. The extraordinary detail of the character development often produced an intensity that dangerously approached caricature. The photography was by cameramen whom von Stroheim had coached through three earlier films of sharp reality. To the camera crew was also added a young newsreel cameraman, Ernest Schoedsack, who was afterwards to make the natural transition from the real backgrounds of San Francisco and the Mojave in *Greed* to the real backgrounds of the pioneering documentary films *Grass* and *Chang.*

The absence of any idealized character, the complete lack of any extenuating circumstances and the amount of time and money spent (whole houses and blocks were purchased for use as settings, walls were knocked out to make the lighting and photography of the interiors possible) created a film which discouraged and frightened its producers. Von

Stroheim reduced his finished cut print of thirty reels down to twenty reels, and proposed releasing the film in two parts, but *McTeague* was taken from him and given to June Mathis, who edited and cut it into a neatly structured story of ten reels, called *Greed,* in which version it is now shown here. Von Stroheim never saw *Greed.*

When it was released in America, the film was attacked both by idealists and by moralists as being unwholesome, and the public instinctively avoided it, making it probably the greatest box-office failure in American film history. Abroad it was almost as unpopular as in the United States, despite its exotic backgrounds, but it strongly attracted film critics and theorists upon whom it exerted as much influence as *The Cabinet of Dr. Caligari.* At a Berlin premiere *Greed* achieved fresh notoriety by causing a riot, created in part by von Stroheim's extreme unpopularity in Germany because of his war-time film-characterizations, and by an assumption on the part of the audience that the outmoded costumes indicated that the Americans were sending them an out-of-date picture.

The original *McTeague* was an experimental film in the truest sense of the word. Von Stroheim really attempted to extend the existing range of film expression and arrived at a more acid social reality than has been achieved since, outside of certain documentary films. Judging from stills of the complete film, he also went to the lengths of employing deliberately fantastic episodes to heighten the terrible reality of the rest of the film. Originally, gold tinting was used throughout for gold, gold teeth, brass beds, gilt frames and canary. The theme of money-gold-money was thus persistently reiterated throughout the whole. This tinting is absent from the present print, newly made from the negative which, despite all fantastic legends to the contrary, reposes safely in the archives of Metro-Goldwyn-Mayer.

15   BLOOD, SWEAT, TEARS

Judy Voccola

WORN HANDS held frayed weekly pay envelopes. The penciled amounts were $13.70, $10.60, $11.65.

It was a stark scene in a 1920s silent film made in Passaic showing the pay for 60 hours labor in the textile mills. The low pay was one of the reasons for a 1926 strike, which sparked the making of *The Passaic Strike*.

The movie, made to create sympathy for the strikers, has become a landmark in the history of the labor movement and the film-making industry.

The film is more than a cinema curiosity—its an accurate representation of the strike that can teach youths about the struggle for fair labor that many take for granted, said Mike Parsons, president of the Passaic County Central Labor Council.

Parsons, who is on the state Panel on Secondary Education, said students today are not prepared for the work place.

They do not know how hard it was for their predecessors to win such things as reasonable hours and paid holidays, he says. "They want everything at once."

Steve Krinsky, a professor of communications at Upsala College in East Orange, said the movie is unique. The film is an unusual combination of melodrama and documentary, Krinsky said.

The Passaic Strike, shown across the country to raise funds for the strikers and their families, was the forerunner of

From the *Herald & News,* Passaic, New Jersey (November 22, 1987). Reprinted by permission of North Jersey Newspapers.

films made by left-wing film-makers in the early 1930s to document the Depression. The group, called the Film and Photo League, showed their films in small theaters and to labor unions and local groups. Krinsky said.

In Seattle, *The Passaic Strike* was so successful that members of the Milk Wagon Drivers voted on assessment of 50 cents a member for the benefit of the Passaic strikers.

Krinsky said the movie is believed to be the first used by strikers to gain support.

The 13-month Passaic textile strike began Jan. 25, 1926, when employees walked out of Botany Worsted Mills.

The strike spread to eight mills, leaving 16,000 workers in Passaic, Garfield, Lodi, Clifton and Wallington idle. Before it was over, the strike cost both sides an estimated $15 million, with landlords and businessmen suffering along with the strikers.

Much of the movie focuses on groups of waving, smiling

The American Labor Museum Botto House National Landmark, Passaic, N.J.

workers and leaders gesturing wildly as they address crowds of strikers.

Some scenes appear to be staged, but the camera caught moments of real life.

Memorable scenes include police wading into a line of strikers and beating them with nightsticks, a mother defiantly pushing her baby carriage at the head of the strike line to prevent attack from onlookers, a line of strikers who had fought in World War I wearing their combat helmets as protection from police beatings.

Al Zwiazek of Clifton was 8 in 1926. His father and mother worked in the Forstmann-Huffmann Mill in Garfield, and he often joined the strike line before going to school.

He recalled scenes of violence similar to those in the movie, including one time when a woman trying to break the strike was repeatedly kicked and beaten by two male strikers.

In the movie a villainous-looking mill manager takes advantage of a 14-year-old female worker.

That part was melodrama, but it was based on fact, said Martha Stone Asher, a volunteer striker.

Asher, who lived in New York City at the time, spent the summer of 1926 in Passaic organizing activities for workers' children.

The strikers, barely able to support their families on their meager salaries, demanded a 10 percent wage increase, a 44-hour week and clean, safe conditions.

Work in the mills was heavy, the air humid and close, the machinery loud and reeking of oil. The tuberculosis rate was 100 percent above normal. Workers put in as many as 60 hours a week to increase their pay, which ranged between $10 and $12 weekly.

Discontent had been growing among the workers since October 1925, when the mills had announced a 10 percent wage cut. The owners blamed a poor selling year in 1925 and the low prices being paid for New England textile products. They said the New England factories also had reduced wages.

Everyone in the family worked, including mothers and 14-year-old children. The *Passaic Daily News* described the average woman mill worker as taking a night shift to be with her children during the day. After returning home from the mill, she usually slept for an hour before rising to care for her family and return to the mill at 7 p.m.

Among the labor leaders who came to Passaic to help was Albert Weisbord, a Harvard Law School graduate, communist and radical organizer. When it become apparent that anti-radical sentiment was preventing a settlement, Weisbord and his followers departed, leaving Gus Deak in charge. Deak, a mill worker, organized the United Front Committee of Passaic.

The strike ended in February 1927 with the 10 percent cut rescinded in some mills and reduced to 5 percent in others. But the workers did not get either the 10 percent increase or the 44-hour week. The mills agreed to recognize the unions, but the actual organization of such groups was not to occur in Passaic area mills until a decade later.

When the strike began, members of the Workers International Relief hired professional producers to document the struggle in an effort to create sympathy and financial support for the Passaic strikers. But after previewing the film, strikers rejected the Hollywood style melodrama, saying they wanted something showing the real conditions in Passaic.

The result was a seven-reel film that began with a fictional prologue and continued with a newsreel-style documentary. In the melodramatic prologue, however, the actors are genuine strikers and the background shows recognizable local sites. Krinsky said it is believed most of the movie was filmed locally.

Asher and Krinsky are searching for additional information about the film, which was salvaged from a Passaic basement in the 1950s. Two reels are missing, and little is known about who actually made the film. The film will be part of a 1926 strike commemoration project at the American Labor Museum in Passaic in 1988.

A POSTSCRIPT ON PASSAIC BY STEVE KRINSKY

The 1926 Passaic Textile Strike film is remarkable in many ways. Lost for many years, it has only recently been recovered and become available for viewing. Only five of its seven reels remain and it is still unclear who produced the film. The film itself is an odd combination of 1920s silent movie melodrama and documentary.

But the most important thing about this film is that it is probably the first effective use of film as an organizing tool within the labor movement. There were labor films prior to this, at least as early as 1913 when "an excellent program of labor moving pictures" (including footage of the 1913 Paterson Silk strike) ran in NYC. But none had the impact—and historical significance—of the Passaic Textile Strike film.

In 1926 and 1927, the film was seen by union members and supporters at dozens of screenings all across the country. It helped raise thousands of dollars to support the Passaic strike. It documented the strike from the workers' perspective, it helped energize the strikers themselves, it informed the public of the facts of the strike, and it promoted nationwide labor solidarity.

At first, two professional motion-picture producers from Boston were hired to make the film, but they were quickly replaced. One of the cameramen who replaced them was a 19-year-old named Sam Brody (1907–1987), who later went on to found the Film and Photo League. But, to this day, it is not clear who actually directed and edited the film.

Officials of the relief committee and strikers both worked on the film and it was not an amateur production. The film was part of a sophisticated media strategy to win public sympathy for the strike. Yet it is likely that neither the local relief committee nor International Workers Aid (who commissioned the film) were aware of the importance of this film.

It is assumed that the Boston producers were fired because they preferred to shoot staged melodrama instead of documentary. It is also likely that these producers were frightened by the intense police violence directed at the media. On March 4, 1926, the *New York Times* reported a police campaign to "get all the camera men." There are photos of news reporters with smashed cameras and newsreel cameramen in WWI helmets.

Despite these difficulties, Brody and others shot excellent documentary footage. The film shows powerful scenes of strikers marching through the streets of Passaic, shots of a police blockade of strike headquarters, huge rallies and speeches by local leaders and national political figures like Elizabeth Gurley Flynn and Norman Thomas. In one memorable scene—shot from a rooftop—the camera documents police attacks on a crowd of strikers.

The film is distributed by the Museum of Modern Art—donated, along with other films, by Tom Brandon (1910–1982). Even with two reels missing—and with the staged melodrama that opens the film—it remains an important document in the history of working people and the history of film. And it stands tall as a tribute to the power of media as an organizing tool.

(Sparked by renewed interest in the film, a committee of New Jersey labor activists, film historians, and others—under the auspices of the Botto House/American Labor Museum—is planning a conference in early 1989 to commemorate the strike. Led by Martha Stone Asher, a veteran of the strike, the group has been gathering oral histories from strike participants and preserving photographs and archival materials for an exhibit to coincide with the conference.)

Postscript on Sam Brody

In one of his last letters to me, Sam Brody (1907–1987) said he also had a hand in the 1929 Gastonia Strike film. Gastonia, North Carolina was the country's leading textile center and the home of the world's largest textile mill, the Loray Mill. On April 1, 1929, 80 percent of the Mill's 2,200 employees walked out under CP leadership. The end could be foreseen when an official of the Department of Labor charged that the strike—it was for more pay and shorter hours—was "a form of revolution."

Brody said he went down there with a 35mm Eyemo and DeVry, accompanied by a Daily Worker *reporter and a WIR representative. A National Guard unit, as the paper reported, sent in to protect the scabs, stood idly by as a mob of masked men broke into the union strike headquarters and destroyed the entire contents of a strike relief store. When the mob dispersed, the guardsmen arrested several strikers, charging them with destroying their own supplies in order to gain public sympathy. In the ensuing police and mob attacks on union meetings, the local police chief and folksinger Ella Mae Wiggins, were killed.*

There followed two trials and worldwide protests, including protests from Soviet mill workers. In the second trial the CP-led union was described by the prosecutor in his closing arguments to the jury as "fiends incarnate, stripped of their hoofs and horns." "They came into peaceful, contented Gastonia, with its flowers, birds and churches . . . sweeping like a cyclone and tornado to sink damnable fangs into the heart and lifeblood of my community," and he asked: "Do you believe in the flag of your country, floating in the breeze, kissing the sunlight, singing the song of freedom!"

In the end seven strikers were sentenced to from five to 20 years in jail. The feelings of the strikers were expressed by an old mountain preacher at the funeral service, saying: "I trust, O God, that those friends will go to a better place than this mill village . . . . Dear God, what would Jesus do if He were to come to Carolina?"

In nearby Marion, later that year, six mill workers were killed and 25 wounded when deputized strikebreakers opened fire at pickets fleeing from tear gas fumes. Though the Marion strike was organized by the United Textile Workers, affiliated with the AFL, the mill owners company president said he could see no difference between "this so-called conservative union and the communist union at Gastonia."

Brody was able to get some of this on film, before going on to play a major role in the formation of the Workers' Film and Photo League. Over the years he made a number of documentaries for the League and other groups; a few found their way to the Film Study Center of the Museum of Modern Art in New York; most were lost, among them his last film, a 27-minute documentary, The Roar of Many Waters, *made in 1965 for Lumière Films, Inc., then located in New York. According to Lumière's president, John Koenig, in a letter dated February 4, 1966, it won an award in the category of "General History" at the 1965 American Film Festival sponsored annually by the Educational Film Library Association (now the American Film & Video Association) for its presentation of "an historical background of current racial upheavals in the United States beginning with early African civilizations and cultures through slave trade, colonial period, the Civil War, Reconstruction, two World Wars and ending with the present-day conflict." Anyone with knowledge of the whereabouts of this film please contact the Museum of Modern Art Film Study Center. (DP)*

16 CARL DREYER'S *THE PASSION OF JEANNE D'ARC*

Harry Alan Potamkin

WE ARE ALWAYS WAITING in the cinema for the eventual film which will be the vindication of the major cinema devices. We are always waiting for the film down to essentials and yet conveying a profound human experience. For the craft of the movie, like the craft of any other art, is performance—of camera, of film, of player, of screen. (Mr. Alexander Bakshy has stated these four as the different cinema performances or movements, a fundamental statement). But as an art conclusive the cinema must find its source in experience and its final meaning in experience. Where is the motion picture—we are always asking—profound in its exploitation of performance, and profound in its transmission of experience? This query is the key to the importance of plot in the movie, not as detailed or episodic narrative but as subject-matter. The consideration of plot as narrative has been the cause and result of the movie's literalness (particularly in America) and the inability to include in the formation of the moving picture the inferences of the theme, much more important than the narrative. This inability has prevented a film so dramatically effective as Feyder's recent *Thérèse Raquin* (adapted from Zola's novel) from being a film of permanent importance.

In brief, we are always waiting for a film reduced but with

From *The Compound Cinema: The Film Writings of Harry Alan Potamkin*, Selected, Arranged and Edited by Lewis Jacobs (Teachers College Press, Columbia University). Reprinted by permission.

163

passionate human content. The purity of passionate apprehension. A film mindful of the plot as the subject-matter of
life. A film using the legitimate emphasis of the camera (or
other kino instruments) and realizing an experience of form
and content completely fused and fluid. We are always
waiting for the expression of a perspicacious knowledge of
the medium, and of the matter it is to convert into and by
means of itself. The American film has realized in its
literalness a pleasant but shallow ease of sequence. The
German has stressed, in the main, the device as virtuosity
rather than as an incorporate, revealing utility. The Swedish
film, like the notable *Atonement of Gösta Berling,* is a
rigorous life-exposition, but it has not fully grasped the
principle of the conversion of the subject-matter. The French
movie on the whole is too banal or too pretty or too frivolous
(without being lively) to merit our interest. Yet the film which
in this instance satisfies our anticipation is a French film. Its
achievement may be explained by the fact that its director is
a Dane, Carl Th. Dreyer. The film is *The Passion of Jeanne
d'Arc.*

   This profound and truly passionate motion picture concerns itself with the last day of Jeanne, the day of excruciat-
ing torment. The scenario is the combined work of the
director and Joseph Delteil, the dadaist who wrote the
prize-winning book on The Maid. It is, I hope, no libel of M.
Delteil to suspect that the disciplining will of the director (a
prime essential in the cinema industry today) kept the
narrative within the strenuous limits of reverence. Reverence
is a portion of the intensity of this film, an intensity to which
everything submits—the decor by Jean Victor-Hugo, the
photography by Maté, with its superb statement of personalities by the skin textures and moles. In total accord with this
intense and intensive exploitation of the subject-matter
(remember there is really no plot here, only the last moment—the queries, the betrayal, the final conflagration) is
the use of the succession of individual cine-photos. These
are not close-ups (there is no "closing-up" in the bland movie
way), not stills (for the angles and curves are lovely and
illuminating), but the bold concentration of individual faces
and figures in the active, critical, voracious eye of the
camera. This would suggest a static series of pictures, not

Mr. Bakshy's "dynamic sequence," rather the mere physical basis of filming than the aesthetic aspiration of the cinema. But it attests to Carl Dreyer's genius that the sequence is eminently fluid, dramatic, rhythmic. The succession has a definite time-order, a definite plastic arrangement in the time-order of exquisite curves (the performers exploited by the camera) and bodily angles, a definite utilization of the screen as the receptive instrument (advocated long ago by Mr. Bakshy, but very seldom realized), and a gradual almost unsuspected rise to the final mob explosion. There are diagonal curves of the moving performers, vertical inclines, a forehead above the lower frame boldly duplicating the moderated masses of the background.

There is no extraneous detail in the film. Not once does a detail fail to directly relate and contribute to the subject-matter. At one point, Jeanne sees the grave digger pull up a skull. Unnecessary? Obvious? There is a swift succession, almost staccato in its brevity, of a field of flowers. The previous detail becomes inevitable, poignant. In fact, the entire film has that virtue, that at any moment the detail on the screen validates what preceded it. This is rhythm, this is art. The beautiful flight of birds, as Jeanne is perishing, the mother suckling her child—the former might be a sentimentalism, the latter a surrealistic simplicism; but by the severe control of the director, they become terrible convictions of the world that would let one who loved free flight perish bound, and one who herself would suckle life burn at the stake. Creation against desolation!

The torment of the young peasant girl, "called Jeannette at home," convinced in her childishness and mysticism of her divine mission, becomes the emotional experience of the spectator. Her fears, persistent under the insistent examination, become heavy with the burden of the torment, become luminous with the momentary glamor and memory stirred by the queries. The heavy tear imparts to the spectator the sense of the days and months of anguish the girl has endured in her steadfastness to her inspiration. The luminous tear elucidates the girl's origins, her free fields, her home, and the momentum of the inspiration that has urged her into this betrayal. The tears of Falconetti, the portrayer of Jeanne, are not the tears of a Clara Bow, insipid, irritating, fraudulent. Her eyes enamored of God borrow no stage-pantomime, but with the grained skin and parched lips, the clipped hair, and chained walk, reveal the entire enterprise of God and land within the girl's body. Falconetti faithfully submits to the intensity of the unit, enters into it, and expresses it while she expresses Jeanne. She is the conception. She is the film. An identical loyalty is manifested by each of the accurately chosen, thoroughly participating cast. No specious prettiness, but hardiness, man in his physical variousness, man in his spiritual diversity serving the same master—Interest. The Interest of State, the Interest of God. Jeanne, serving God, alone of all has served herself, her systemic soul-and-body. She as the servant of herself becomes the everlasting, the others are left to weep upon the torment they have connived. The State alone (Warwick) remains unperturbed, save to halt the conflagration of Jeanne which threatens to burn down the power of England in Rouen. As no prologue was needed, no epilogue is asked for and no commentary from the distance of several centuries. How superior to Shaw's Joan! The inference all embodied in the unit-structure, not tagging along like loose threads, nor stressed like a moral to a fable. One fault alone disturbs the perfection of this grand film, a fault easily eliminated: there are too many captions, well written though they are. Fewer captions jotted in the staccato brevity of many of the images that pass almost before one sees them—these would have better suited the film's attitude, and not served to weaken (even if in the minutest degree, as the captions do at present) the demanding simplicity and rigorousness of this beautiful work.

The Passion of Jeanne d'Arc is an historical film, but not a costume film; an historical film that is contemporaneous in its universal references. *The Passion of Jeanne d'Arc* is a religious film, but not a santimonious film. Life, it urges, is transcendent. It is a transcendent film.

Elsa Gress, whose tribute to Asta Nielsen appears in Chapter 13, informs me that for the centennial of the birth of Carl Dreyer in 1989, she has written "The Ballad of Carl Dreyer" in collaboration with Tom O'Horgan of New York, and the chances are good that it will be produced by Danish State TV in English as well as Danish, and possibly shown on American TV "around the time of the actual centennial, early in 1989." The script, she writes, "is based on my own working with and talking to the old Dreyer through the last ten or 12 years of his life." Film scholars should note that a copy of the first draft (17 pages) of the Dreyer "Ballad" has been deposited at the Museum of Modern Art Film Study Center in New York, along with Elsa Gress' TV drama about Asta Nielsen and some of her other papers connected thereto. (DP)

17 A NEW LOOK AT EISENSTEIN'S *POTEMKIN*

Hector Currie

"**S**ERGEI EISENSTEIN'S *Battleship Potemkin* (1925) has deservedly been the subject of more *post facto* examination than any other film," is the considered judgment of Jay Leyda in *Kino: History of the Russian and Soviet Film* (1960). Yet, in the vast literature that has dealt with this landmark film from almost every conceivable angle, there is a paucity of material on its Jewish connection. Especially is there no awareness that the famous "slaughter on the Odessa steps" in June, 1905, was a screen transposition of an actual slaughter that October—of Jews—in the streets, shops, and homes of Odessa (30% Jewish).

Leyda supplies a possible answer to this enigma: "One of the curious effects of the film has been to replace the facts of the Potemkin mutiny with the film's artistic 'revision' of those events." He goes on to hint at the truth: "In actual fact . . . the Cossack slaughter occurred quite differently." Criticism has taken account of the fact that "no actual massacre [took place] on the Odessa steps" (Andrew Sinclair, *Potemkin,* 1968). Rather, as Yon Barna makes clear (*Eisenstein,* 1966): "The scene of the massacre on the Odessa steps—. . . often regarded as a true representation of the event—was based, according to Eisenstein himself, on other actual massacres." Critical notice was finally given to clearing up this widely held misconception by P. Adams Sitney (*The*

From *Jewish Currents* (January, 1988). Reprinted by permission of the author and publisher.

Essential Cinema, 1975): "[Eisenstein's] greatest liberty with historical truth was taken with the scene of the massacre which, although brutal enough—several thousand were killed—did not, for the most part, take place on the great staircase of Odessa."

Although the victims did not die on the steps, unaddressed is the question of who were slain. That they were Jewish is apparent from the headlines of the *N.Y. Times:*

MASSACRE OF JEWS CONTINUES: 5,000 REPORTED KILLED BY ODESSA MOB—PEOPLE SAY THEY WILL NOT LEAVE ONE JEW ALIVE

(Nov. 3, 1905)
ALL JEWS IN ODESSA REPORTED KILLED BY MOB

(Nov. 5, 1905)

There is reason to question the accuracy of the *Times* account of the pogrom. Historian Simon M. Dubnow, in *The History of the Jews in Russia and Poland* (Vol. 3, p. 129), reported as follows on the terror, which he called "the most terrible pogrom" in Russia's long history of anti-Semitism: "It lasted fully four days. The rioters were openly assisted by the police and troops, and were encouraged by the active support of city-governor Neidthart, and the criminal inactivity of the military governor, Kaulbars. The heroism displayed by the Jewish self-defense was strong enough to beat off the hooligans, but it was powerless to defeat the troops and police. Over 300 dead, thousands of wounded or crippled Jews, among them many who lost their minds from the horrors, 140 widows, 593 orphans, and more than 40,000 Jews materially ruined—such were the results of the battle which was fought against the Jews of Odessa during October 18–21."

Indeed, it had been pogroms that had driven Eisenstein's paternal grand-parents to give up their Jewish heritage.

That Eisenstein was conscious of this ineradicable heritage when he made *Potemkin* is evident from an entry in his cutting notes describing the victims of the Cossack onslaught (in Leon Moussinac, *Eisenstein*): "Old Jews." They were the victims. Further, one has only to recall the inciting incident on the quay, when the citizenry joined the (abortive) revolution of 1905, to appreciate the signal importance Eisenstein attached to the Jewish presence as prime victims of the carnage.

The critics have fully recognized the key line which touched off the revolutionary ardor in the crowd. Edward Murray (*Ten Classic Films*) writes: " . . . one well-dressed man persists in cynically sneering at the impassioned speakers. 'Down with the Jews!' he says. Close-up of a sailor's angry face. Shots of peasants and workers glaring at the well-dressed defender of the government. Suddenly the crowd attacks the man, beating him with their fists, driving him to the ground."

George Huaco (*The Sociology of Film Art,* 1965) confirms this: "A tall well-dressed man exclaims, 'Down with the Jews!'; the people strike him down. . . . In [this] brief anti-Semitic incident, Eisenstein seems to be suggesting that such an attitude was exclusively characteristic of the tsarist bourgeoisie (and alien to the peasants and workers). It has been eliminated from recent [after the bowdlerized 'official' version of 1950] Soviet copies of the film."

Such a moment Stanley J. Solomon (*The Classic Cinema,* 1973) notes as being one of "mass recognition of universal brotherhood . . ." "Brothers!"—the cry which is "heard" at the close of *Potemkin*—was also the cry of the Zionists. It was a cry which had its origin in—Odessa. Here, in 1882, was born the "Zionist particularism" which so inflamed Stalin. Here, in Odessa, Leon Pinsker, following the lead of Moses Hess (*Rome and Jerusalem,* 1862), who called for the establishment of a Zionist state in Palestine, had issued a proposal calling for Auto-Emancipation of the Jews. And here in Odessa were born the two earliest organizations on which Zionist aspirations centered: the Lovers of Zion (1884) and the Odessa Palestine Society (1890).

The official Soviet attitude toward Zionism can be gauged by the banning of Hebrew from the councils of higher learning in 1924. As Eric A. Goldman notes (*Visions, Images and Dreams, Yiddish Film Past and Present,* 1983): "in 1925 . . . Hebrew, [both as] a language and culture . . . came to be identified with 'reactionary clericalism' and 'Zionism.' . . . Hebrew . . . was no longer . . . acceptable . . . in the Soviet

Union." Further gleaning of the Soviet attitude toward Jews may be had from the contemptuous reference to Eisenstein by Sovkino's president, Konstantin Shvedchikov, in 1925 as "the nobleman of Jerusalem" (Jay Leyda, *Kino,* p. 197).

Yet Eisenstein did manage to insert this attack on anti-Semitism—destroying, quite literally, the perpetrator of the cry, "Down with the Jews!"—at the crucial turning point in his great epic.

Further evidence of his loyalty to the Jewish cause is to be found in his having gone to Odessa to make, conjointly with *Potemkin,* a screen adaptation of *Benia Krik,* an Isaac Babel Odessa story. He was much in the company of Babel as he prepared the shooting of *Potemkin.* And he kept his close friendship with Babel through the abortive *Bezhin Meadows* project, which Babel co-scripted. Later, Babel, as had Meyerhold, Eisenstein's teacher and mentor, was to "disappear." Eisenstein was to witness the decimation of the brilliant creative community of Jewish artists and poets. On this point, Mikhail Romm, another leading Russian Jewish director, was to write (*A Film Director Speaks Out,* Moscow, 1964, as cited by Herbert Marshall in *Masters of Soviet Cinema,* 1983): "dozens of our best theatre and movie people were declared 'cosmopolites without a fatherland' (i.e., 'Yid') . . . [Is] it possible to heal the wounds, to forget what one has suffered for so many years, when you are trampled on and covered with mud?"

Marshall goes on to note that "All the Soviet Jewish directors had to keep silent in order to survive, and this included all the leading directors: Grigori L. Roshal, Kozintsev and Leonid Trauberg, Ilya Trauberg, Zarkhi and Heifetz, Vertov, and Romm and Room." Abram Room's cry of despair echoes that uttered by Babel in his Odessa story, "How It Was Done in Odessa" (1924): "Wasn't it a mistake on God's part to settle Jews in Russia so they suffer as in hell?"

As noted, Eisenstein had intended to make a Babel story in tandem with *Potemkin.* And his cameraman, Edward Tisse, had worked on a film in Odessa that was to be released in the same year as *Potemkin,* 1925. It was a Yiddish comedy produced by the Yiddish Art Theater of Alexander Granovsky, starring Solomon Mikhoels, *Jewish*

Luck (Yidishe Glikn), a production for which Babel wrote the inter-titles developing Sholem Aleichem's "Menakhem Mendl Letters." Eric Goldman finds yet another "Jewish connection" for *Potemkin* in the film:

> Mendl finds . . . his list of brides . . . and tries his luck as a *shadkhn* (match-maker) . . . and dreams . . . he is outside Odessa's Grand Palace . . . preparing to export [the] brides to America.
> [The] dream sequence [was] shot on the steps of the Odessa harbor . . . [showing] a woman walking up the steps inter-cut with reaction shots of Menakhem Mendl watching her. Edward Tisse, who was chief cameraman . . . worked a year later with . . . Eisenstein on *Battleship Potemkin.* There is little doubt that the famous 'Odessa steps' sequence . . . was influenced by *[Jewish Luck].*

Goldman presents an illustration of Mendl (Mikhoels) standing before the famous steps. The case he makes is most convincing. But, as the world well knows, "Jewish luck" was running out in Russia. The shadow of the Stalinist repression, and oppression, was soon to fall over the creative genius of the Jewish minority.

Eisenstein felt its cold breath. Such a free spirit as his is sensitive to the drafts of prejudice. His great work is, as Moussinac described it so aptly, "a cry"—a cry for freedom, freedom for all who are oppressed.

For, in a deep sense, art shapes the energies of the human spirit. The energies of this greatest work of film art, *Potemkin,* are alive with the free spirit of the Jewish character. And Eisenstein, the greatest genius of motion pictures, in every vibrant frame gave us a graphic demonstration of that most endearing quality of the Jewish spirit, *hutzpa.* Truly, as long as light projects, his great film shall define the lineaments of man unbowed.

It interested me that Ivan Beshoff, the last survivor of the 1905 mutiny on the Battleship Potemkin died October 25, 1987 in Dublin, Ireland. He was 102 years old. His birth certificate gave his date of birth as 1885, contrary to

Beshoff's insistence that it was 1883, making him two years older (104) at death. Knowing that British film historian Kevin Brownlow once taped an interview with Beshoff in Dublin I passed this information on to him in case he had not seen the obituary in the New York Times. *He wrote back: "... I did indeed film an interview with Beshoff—and a wild experience it was. He was only around 99 then, but he got drunk on the vodka I'd taken him and when he saw the TV crew, he mutinied all over again. But we got a few rolls of film, although it was all pretty incoherent."*

Beshoff, who was born near the Black Sea port of Odessa, started out as a student of chemistry, but gave it up to join the Tsar's navy, serving in the engine room of the Potemkin at the time of the mutiny. Later, to avoid arrest by tsarist authorities, he fled Russia through Turkey to London and thence to Ireland, where he settled in 1913. After the 1917 Russian Revolution he worked for a Soviet oil distribution company and was twice arrested as a "Soviet spy," but eventually, the Times *noted, he became a "beloved figure in the Irish community." At the end of World War II Beshoff opened a fish and chips shop in Dublin. His sons "opened branches elsewhere in the city."*

Living and working in Moscow in 1934, Eisenstein learned that Nazi Propaganda Minister Joseph Goebbels had praised his 1925 film, The Battleship Potemkin, *in a speech to a gathering of Nazi filmmakers. Goebbels went so far as to draw a handsome sketch of what he termed the "creative potentiality" of the German cinema, based on the principles of "national socialism" (Nazism). Eisenstein sat down and penned a classic statement against the idea that great art could come through supporting and defending Murder Incorporated (this was shortly after the Nazis torched the Reichstag, attributing the arson to a pathetic tool named Van der Lubbe). Following are some excerpts from Eisenstein's celebrated essay (reprinted courtesy of Jay Leyda [DP]).*

> *... truth and National Socialism are a contradiction in terms. He who follows truth cannot follow the path of National Socialism. He who is for truth, is against you!*
> *How dare you speak of life at all, you who with axe and*

machine-gun are bringing death and exile to everything live and worthwhile in your country? Slaughtering the best sons of the German workingclass and scattering like ashes throughout the world those who are the pride of German science and the culture of the world?

How dare you call upon your film organization to portray life truthfully without demanding of it first of all to portray to the world the thousands languishing and maltreated in the catacombs of your prisons, the torture chambers of your fortresses?

In the voice of the good shepherd, you thus pursue your oration:

'. . . if only I receive the conviction that behind any film there lies honest, artistic endeavor, I shall foster and defend it by every means . . .' (Same Goebbels speech)

You are lying, Mr. Goebbels.

You know only too well that an honest and artistic film could only be one which would expose to its full depth the hell in which Germany has been plunged by national-Socialism.

You would hardly encourage such a film!

Real German film art is that which would call upon the revolutionary masses of Germany to fight you.

For that, real courage and daring are certainly necessary.

Because despite all the sweet tunes of your speeches, you keep your art and culture in the same iron fetters as the thousands of your prisoners in the hundreds of your concentration camps.

And works of art are not born as you imagine them.

We, for example, know and some of our work has proved besides, that works that deserve that title do, have done, and will do so only by virtue of the fact that, through the medium of the creative artist, is expressed the clearly formulated determined striving of the class . . .

And the better the work of art, the better has the artist succeeded in understanding, in feeling and in transmuting this creative striving of the masses themselves.

You do not view thus class and masses.

As you say: '. . . Every People is what is made out of it . . . .' And there can be found idiots who applaud you at this point of your speech.

Just wait a little. The working-class will make its own correction of this, if one may call it such, conception, Mr. Demiurge of Divine Power.

Then you will learn who is the real force of history.

You will learn then who makes whom, and what will be done with you and . . . out of you.

War, it is said, gives birth to heroes.

Mountains, it is said, give birth to mice.

But no Goebbels, aspiring to give birth to a New Germany, like Athena, from his head, is capable of giving birth to a great National Socialist cinema!

Strain as you may, you cannot create a national-Socialist realism!

For in that lying mongrel there would be as much real truth and realism as there is in National-Socialist . . . Socialism.

Get back to your drums, Master Drummer-in-Chief!

Stop disporting yourself with ritual pipings on the magic flute of National Socialist realism in the cinema.

Stop imitating your idol Frederick the Great and on his own flute, too.

Just stay at your more congenial instrument—the axe.

Don't waste your time to no purpose.

It's not much longer that you'll be able to wield that axe.

So go it while the going's good!

Burn books.

Burn the Reichstag.

But don't imagine that a parade-ground art reared on all this filth will ever be able to burn with its voice the hearts of men.

18 KING VIDOR'S *THE CROWD*

Kevin Brownlow

DESPITE MY AFFECTION for Hollywood silent films, I can't credit them with much concern for the vital issues of the day. Admittedly, entertainment for its own sake can be valuable, but there's enough of the puritan in me to demand something more. And that's one reason I love *The Crowd*. When a film of enormous social significance succeeds in being immensely entertaining, then as far as I'm concerned the director has achieved near-perfection.

The Crowd is one of the most eloquent of all silent pictures. It came out just before the Depression—and yet it might have been made in the thick of it, so poignant is its picture of unemployment. It is surprising that it reached the public at all, for it broke all the rules of Hollywood. You weren't supposed to show the casual use of liquor, during Prohibition. You weren't supposed to suggest that work, the great dignifier, could be boring. You weren't supposed to show a young man's nerves on his wedding night, or a wife telling her husband she's pregnant. And you weren't supposed to show that failure and poverty could exist in the Land of Opportunity.

Opportunity is all that Johnny Sims needs. Johnny is the hero of the film (and he is no hero). He grows up with faith in the American Dream: he is going to be somebody big. But life follows its usual rut: he marries, has two children and an $8 raise. He writes advertising slogans in his spare time. One

From *The Observer* (London), October 26, 1980. Reprinted by permission of the author.

wins a prize, but leads to tragedy. His small daughter is hit by a truck as she runs to see the present he has bought with the prize money. John goes to pieces; he loses job after job and considers suicide, but fails even in that. His wife decides to leave him, but when he gets a meagre job she decides *not* to go—just yet. They celebrate at a vaudeville show, and forget their troubles by laughing with the crowd.

That's all it is; *The Crowd* is practically plotless. And yet each incident is so brilliantly directed and acted that the film blazes to life. One's heart leaps with recognition at the behaviour of the characters. John, and his wife, Mary, are getting up one morning in their poky little flat. The lavatory cistern goes wrong. "Why didn't you tell me this was busted?" asks John. The bathroom door has always been defective, but he adds this to his catalogue of her crimes. "You've got this on the blink, too."

At breakfast, he stares at her, witheringly. "Your hair looks like Kelcy's cat." She adjusts it and tries to continue eating, but his remarks wear her down and she leaves the table. "I'm getting sick and tired of you always criticizing me." "Forget it, Mary, I'll overlook your faults." His heavy humor merely inflames her, and he becomes more annoyed himself. He reaches for a milk bottle; as he opens it the milk squirts him full in the face. He turns on her again. "Why can't you tell me when things are full?"

Most directors would be satisfied to leave the scene there, but where most directors stop, the director of this film, King Vidor, is just beginning. Mary has taken all she can from John and declares that she's leaving. John seems glad. "Take it from me," he says, as he storms out. "Marriage isn't a word—it's a sentence." The door slams. Mary stares after him, full of self-pity and remorse. Vidor holds the shot of her without interruption, and it is one of the most brilliant examples of pure film acting I have ever seen. Mary begins to cry; what *is* she going to do? Where will she go? As if for security, she clutches her arms across her stomach, and this gesture reminds her of something terribly important. We can see the realisation flash across her face; she forgot to tell him!

After an angonising delay, she runs to the window, and calls out. John stands in the street, unwilling to return, but she gently persuades him. The only title in this part of the scene occurs when John runs upstairs and stands before her: "I didn't get a chance to tell you." She pulls him closer, and does up one of his coat buttons. We can lip read her saying she is pregnant, but there is no title. John's mood changes; he slowly embraces her; then becomes ridiculously considerate, sitting her down, putting the milk in her coffee, carefully wiping the plates. "From now on, I'm going to treat you differently, dearest." He goes to the door, and in contrast to the last time he left, he keeps popping back, grinning and miming the forthcoming event by cradling his hat.

The shots are simple, yet full of emotional power; Vidor treats his characters so lovingly, and with such understanding, that one cannot help but share his feelings. In a way, it's odd that this portrait of failure should have such uncanny intensity, for it was created by a man for whom the American dream came true. Vidor had made MGM's biggest money-maker, *The Big Parade* (1925), and it was thanks to this success that he was able to make *The Crowd* with the large budget it needed. Impressed by the German experiments, Vidor was able to weave into the picture moments of technical bravura—the camera travelling up the front of a skyscraper, and moving into a vast office, where acres of desks attest to the deadly routine of John's working life. I doubt if there is another film in cinema history combining the stunning artifice of the German film with documentary scenes snatched in the streets.

A scene that has these elements—one I've never forgotten—occurs when the daughter lies in a coma, after the road accident. Mary's family sits round the bed; her brother is cracking peanuts, and John gently gestures to him to soften the noise. He asks the mother to stop sniffling. Outside, a paper-boy yells the headlines; John goes to the window, holds his finger to his lips. Fire engines thunder down the street. John goes out to try and stop the sirens. Hundreds of people chase after the fire, and John is glimpsed, battling against the crowd, pleading for quiet. A cop pushes him back. "Get inside! The world can't stop just because your baby's sick."

The extraordinary thing about this tragic film is how funny

it is—it's as funny as it's sad. A superb scene showing the family on an apparently lonely beach opens with John, strumming on his ukulele, singing "I'm so alone." A change of angle reveals the crowds that surround them. An elderly man is trying to get some rest. "In one ear I got it sand," he protests, "in the other, I got it you and your zither." Junior jumps up and down and Mary, preoccupied with cooking on a tiny camp fire, tells John to take him to the toilet. A large post has to do for Junior and the baby girl—John strumming on his ukulele all the while. Junior then starts a new game running round and round the fire, kicking sand on the cake. Mary cuts her hand, yells at Junior, who steps on the cake—and the coffee pot falls in the fire. "Hey," says John, still idiotically strumming his ukulele, "your fire's out." Mary explodes; this is no fun for her—she's doing the same things she does at home.

"Don't crab, dear. Everything will be all right when my ship comes in."

"Your ship? A worm must be towing it from the North Pole."

Despite everything, John *does* have a brainwave—he thinks up the slogan which wins him the prize. Advertising is a constant theme throughout the film, in a way it rules John's life. When we first see him in his new job, he is surreptitiously writing slogans. In the subway, returning from a Coney Island date, the sign "You Furnish the Girl, We Furnish the Home" gives him the idea of marriage. He mocks a sandwich-board man he sees from the bus: "The poor sap! And I bet his father thought he'd be President." But that, with grim irony, is how John ends up—a human advertisement.

MGM had not expected such strong stuff, and they insisted Vidor end the film with a scene in which John becomes wealthy from his advertising slogans. Vidor was horrified, and fought this as long as he could—shooting and previewing no less than seven endings. His inspired idea was the one that survives in all the existing prints. But the front office had their ending sent out as well, to give the exhibitors a choice.

Vidor's ending shows the little family rocking with laughter at a vaudeville show; the clowns are dressed like John, in his advertising costume. John doesn't notice. He spots his slogan in the programme, and cannot resist sharing his delight with his neighbour. They shake hands, and with that gesture, John is accepted back into society. The camera pulls back and back until the little family is swallowed by the crowd.

For a film of social importance, it was significant that Vidor paid such tribute, in his last scene, to the value of pure entertainment.

Two Other Views

Harry Alan Potamkin: *"The theme of Vidor's* The Crowd *was enormous: ineffectual man, doomed by prophecy, caught within the indifference or hostility of the mass. But the vast scope of such a theme is immediately reduced to a trite duplication of the irony-and-pity, human interest feuilleton. Not human experience, but human interest. . . . It is the theme that would have justified the opening of the film with the colossal structures of New York (an introduction by now a banality)."* Potamkin faults the director for not seeing that the scenarist, John V. A. Weaver, was unequal to the task of developing such a profound theme to the fullest. *(*Close Up, *May, 1929).*

John Howard Lawson: *" . . . almost the only American attempt to convey the dominant mood of frustration in a direct statement. It tells us simply that human beings are lonely and helpless, and can find no contact with the masses that surround them."* Yet Lawson cannot resist comparing the crowds in Vidor's film unfavorably with the crowds *"united by a common aspiration"* in the films of Eisenstein and Pudovkin. Vidor's crowd was *"everyman's enemy." (*Film, the Creative Process, *1964).*

I prefer the way Brownlow handles this pre-Depression social theme with its poignant criticism of the deteriorating American Dream. (DP)

19 PUDOVKIN'S *STORM OVER ASIA* AND GRIFFITH'S *LINCOLN*

Harry Alan Potamkin

I N THE FIRST CHAPTER of the history of the art of the motion picture, the name of David Wark Griffith will be important. He was the first to suspect the scope of the new medium, and, although the new devices he introduced were conceived by him solely as expedience, they have been utilized by other succeeding directors as experiences. These directors are mainly the Soviet artists. The American movie has not extended in the least the work of Griffith and his early contemporaries. Pudovkin, among the Soviet directors, has developed the early American film to its ultimate. *Storm Over Asia* is the culmination of the romantic technique of the Griffith-Western period. As a culmination or perfection of the primitive film it is a reflection upon the inertia of the American movie. As a perfection of the film of muscular impact, it is still unsuited in method to the profound material of the Soviet kino.

I first saw *Storm Over Asia,* intact, in Amsterdam. I have seen it three times since. My reaction has been always the same. An exciting film, which beats any American audience film. It makes the boasted dramatic technique of America appear a schoolboy's exercise. Griffith's *Lincoln,* in comparison with it, is a mooning idyll. Yet both Pudovkin and Griffith suffer commonly from a sentimentalism which expresses

From *The Compound Cinema: The Film Writings of Harry Alan Potamkin* (Teachers College Press, Columbia University). © 1977. Reprinted by permission.

itself in bad "figures of speech" and oversimplification. The theme in Pudovkin's film is tremendous: imperialism. In Griffith's film it is trivial: the Lincoln of the least of the epigrams—a Lincoln that any child beyond the fifth grade in school would disown. Pudovkin, like every Soviet director, had a social theme to convert into a dramatic instance. Griffith had a sentimental figure out of a fairy tale. In the particularization of the theme, the film itself, Pudovkin selected frequent symbols below the level of the theme, and stressed too ardently the personalities and their narrative, so that very often the theme—the implication of the narrative— is not perceivable in the occurrences. That is one reason the film, while possessing strength, physical strength, lacks poignancy, penetration. *China Express,* in contrast, while not grand, remains a more poignant, permanently appealing, film upon imperialism.

In Griffith we see what Pudovkin might have been in America 1910–30. In Pudovkin we see what Griffith might have been in the U.S.S.R. Griffith, possessing social sympathies, expressed these in platitudes on "tolerance" and "free speech," and read his American history in the terms of *The Clansman* (the Ku Klux Klan and the Confederacy, in whose army his father—Colonel Jacob Wark Griffith—was), and in the terms of the crudest Lincoln myths. His films in the past have been innocuous idylls and grandiose panoramas, allowing his distinction for his instincts of composition. *Lincoln* has everything of the sentimentally idyllic, and nothing of the grandiose. It is an unintelligent Drinkwater chronicle-play on the screen, despite Stephen Vincent Benét's hand in the scenario (why "despite"?). The fact that it draws tears is rather against it than for it. The pathos of a tremendous social occurrence should not be refined or lachrymose, but revealing. The social occurrence seldom gets a chance here. Slogans of spurious manufacture explain the motivations of the Civil War.

The legend of a people may offer as much substance for revelation as the actual unmythical source. But such revelation demands a critical understanding which alone assures a surpassing of the elementary myth. Griffith possesses no critical penetration. The nostalgia of a dessicate aristocracy seeps through the film: in the silly pretense with music to toleration of the black (what an hypocrisy after *The Birth of A Nation*); in the tiresome reiteration of the virtues of the protagonists—Lee especially, etc. Griffith, still bound to the conceptions of refinement and good taste (a tradition set by him by now noxious in the American movie), thwarted a player of more eloquent talents, Walter Huston. And the innovator of the silent film contributes nothing to the improvement of the garrulous. The simple-minded spectator will carry away with him an amiable sentiment toward North and South, emancipation and slavery, and the Union forever! The close, with Lincoln's monument, is a palpable bid for patriotism. Who says the American movie is against propaganda?

A last tribute: to Soviet photography in *Storm Over Asia,* as against the sickening "artisticalness" of the Menzies-Struss collaboration in *Lincoln.* To the authentic types (they become prototypes) in *Storm Over Asia* as against the dubious histrionics of *Lincoln* (notice Abe Lincoln's lip-rouge). The selection of types among non-professionals has taught the Soviet director to select the authentic even among professionals.

These two films call forth speculations upon the nature of propaganda, which coincides with the nature of art. *Storm Over Asia* asks: "How much immediate impact, how much after-effect? Cannot what drives in too forcefully, just as easily drive out? Is not propaganda the accumulation of what is implied?" *Lincoln* says: "The less critical the propaganda, the less valid art it demands."

PART III

SOCIAL AWAKENING—THE 1930s

20 EISENSTEIN IN PARIS IN 1930: AN EYEWITNESS REPORT

Samuel Brody

IT WAS NINE O'CLOCK in the evening. In a small lecture hall at the Sorbonne University in Paris, nearly two thousand people are crowded together to witness a private showing of *The General Line,* and hear S. M. Eisenstein lecture on the "Principles of the New Russian Film." The occasion is given under the auspices of a group of austere academicians ponderously named, *Groupe d'Etudes Philosophiques et Scientifiques pour l'Examen des Tendances Nouvelles.*

The atmosphere is severe. Many learned men of France have been heard in this same room before. The problems of Intuition and Kantian Transcendentalism as well as other burning questions of the day have time and again been discussed here by copiously bewhiskered professors before bored young students of the University. In a few minutes our beloved Eisenstein will be sitting on this same platform. We have never seen him before, but *Potemkin* still lives in our minds and the tempered-steel quality of *Ten Days* has not been forgotten.

Eisenstein appears on the platform. The atmosphere of respectable behaviour is immediately broken as his wide smile announces a friend, a comrade. Loud applause. But he

This account by Brody of Eisenstein's lecture, "Principles of the New Russian Cinema," given at the Paris Sorbonne on February 17, 1930, is reprinted from the British film journal *Close Up* (Vol. VI, No. 4, April 1930), by permission of the author.

does not seem to like that and he motions the audience to stop.

In the meantime, something has happened. Whispers in the audience. The chairman announces that the Parisian police has forbidden the showing of *The General Line.* Faintly he mutters a few words about ". . . hindering the spread of knowledge . . . shameful . . . liberty." No one is satisfied, and the audience starts a demonstration that lasts for fifteen minutes. Eisenstein seems to be pleased with all this. The prohibition of the film has been a powerful boomerang. No Russian film that I have seen has ever succeeded in arousing so much bitterness against the powers that be as was evident in the crowd that night.

The commotion subsides and the speaker is introduced. He does not "lecture" nor read from a prepared paper. His French is slightly tight, but his accent flawless and delivery fluent. The words he cannot remember he describes with characteristic gestures that *everybody* understands.

"I am sorry that you cannot see my film . . . . This makes my task much harder, as I will have to make up for what you cannot see with my limited French. When I am thru speaking you may throw questions at me and I will try to answer. A sort of friendly ping-pong game. But I beg you not to ask me the whereabouts of General Koutepov or what salary I earn in the USSR, for if you do I am certain that my replies will not satisfy you."

And thus, after he has won the confidence of everyone in the audience, Eisenstein proceeds to a broad outline of his subject. He begins by drawing a clear differentiation between the conception of the film in the Soviet Union and in the capitalist countries. The destruction of the rotten dramatic trilogy and the raising of the film to an educational and cultural level, he says, was the first task of the Russian directors after the Revolution. He tells of the concrete problems which confront the Soviet movie in regard to the education and political enlightenment of the formerly oppressed national minorities; the establishment in Moscow and Leningrad of the first cinema universities in the world for the purpose of training permanent scientific and artistic cadres.

"We are working to draw broad masses into the production

of our films. Criticisms of our work by the workers and peasants is most valuable to us. Indeed, only their needs and opinions are important, as we are working with and for them. They discuss the value of scenarios in their factory committees and are quite frequently very critical of our work. In the Soviet Union the director and his cameramen play a comparatively secondary role. They are only called in when the ideological importance of a certain theme for a film has been decided upon by those for whom the film is produced."

Eisenstein then gives a brief résumé of the Russian directors' achievements in the technical sphere of the movies.

"The importance of our method lies in the fact that we have discovered how to force the spectator to think in a certain direction. By mounting our films in a way scientifically calculated to create a given impression on an audience, we have developed a powerful weapon for the propagation of the ideas upon which our new social systems is based.

"We have discarded the professional actor for 'the man in the street.' We are convinced that this has brought us a step nearer to life. When we require an old man in a film, the actor who rehearses three days before he can play the part can never do it so well as a real old man who has been rehearsing for say—sixty years. This method has its difficulties, of course, but so far it has proven its advantages over the old way."

This does not all sound like music to many highly-paid movie actors in the audience, but in Eisenstein's case, "first came the deed," and those who have seen his films acted by real sailors, real workers and on authentic locales, are well convinced that the proof of the pudding is in the eating.

Cinedialectic. The making of Marx's *Capital* into a film. The cinema of the future!

A lot has been said and written recently about Eisenstein's so-called "new principle of the film." Distorted translations of his articles and vague interpretations of his new theory have appeared in the press. The author now speaks for himself.

"My new conception of the film is based on the idea that the intellectual and emotional processes which so far have been conceived of as existing independently of each other— art versus science—and forming an antithesis heretofore never united, can be brought together to form a synthesis on the basis of *cinedialectic,* a process that only the cinema can achieve. A spectator can be made to *feel-and-think* what he sees on the screen. The scientific formula can be given the emotional quality of a poem. And whether my ideas on this matter are right or wrong, I am at present working in this direction. I will attempt to film *Capital* so that the humble worker or peasant can understand it."

Our scepticism means but little, for we are before a man who has succeeded in making people weep at the sight of a milk-separator in *The General Line.* Moreover, the organization of human feeling on the basis of a correct *understanding* of reality is nothing new to the Marxian. Incidentally, the famous French physiologist, Claude Bernard, had the same problem in mind when he said more than sixty years ago, "Can we speak of a peremptory contradiction between science and art, between sentiment and reason? I do not believe in the possibility of this contradiction."

Eisenstein is making a concrete approach to this problem which is obviously not an academic one. As he tells us, it was born out of the necessity to teach economics to workers and peasants.

"If we succeed, it will have been Russia's great contribution to the general history of the arts."

And in conclusion:

"Our cinema has developed in the midst of the Dictatorship of the Proletariat. Its birth and development cannot be dissociated from the great aim of our country, the building of socialism."

The lecture is over and Eisenstein calls for questions. Sound? Stereoscopy? Colour? The speaker is bombarded with questions from all sides. Some are bitter and unfriendly, but Eisenstein never weakens.

An actor shouts: "Will the speaker please tell me whether it is possible for an actor who is an individualist in his art and in his philosophy, to exist in the Soviet Union?"

Eisenstein: "Stay here young man, you will find Parisian soil much more fertile than ours!"

In answering questions on sound, the speaker again expounds what he and his co-workers had to say a few months ago in the official statement issued by them.

"Every fact optically perceived has its corresponding value in sound. As far as I know, only the Japanese Kabouki Theatre has employed sound-sight in this way. For example, while an actor is *seen* committing hari-haki on the stage, the tearing of silk is *heard* offstage. The Mickey Mouse sound cartoons have also come very close to this method. It is the only justification for sound in the movies. The present usage which establishes a naturalistic coincidence of image and sound is nonsense."

Eisenstein believes that in the near future the black-and-white film will disappear to be replaced by the colour film, of which he says, he has seen some fine examples.

"There will remain only a few isolated enthusiasts who will crusade against the colour film in the name of the black-and-white principle."

He further emphasizes that none of the recent discoveries in the cinema, (colour, stereoscopy, wide film, etc.) will create revolutionary changes. He understands, above all, the commercial significance of all these innovations.

And so Eisenstein leaves us amidst a tremendous acclaim.

We have not seen *The General Line,* but two hours in presence of its genial creator have been ample compensation to us.

The greatest movie director in the Soviet Union is at present working in the Tobis Sound Studios at Epinay, near Paris, where he is experimenting with a German sound system. This in the midst of a conspiracy of silence on the part of the French movie press and an active boycott by the official cinema circles of Paris.

Out of over two hundred people present at a dinner tendered in honour of Eisenstein and his assistants by the Friends of the Soviet Union, not a single soul from the French movie world was present.

I cannot help agreeing with Leon Moussinac on this matter: "Jealousy and envy are one of the forms of the petty-bourgeois mind. Cowardice is a form of decadence."

A Farmers Movie Circuit, set up by the United Farmers League and the Workers and Farmers Cooperative Unity

Alliance, has made it possible for some 80 towns and villages in Minnesota, North Dakota, South Dakota, Wisconsin and part of Michigan, some of which do not have movie theatres, to see Soviet and other workers' films (16mm silent and sound), in churches, town halls, small theatres and barns. Among the films shown to farmers, whose recent strikes and anti-eviction struggles have stirred the nation, are Eisenstein's Potemkin, *Pudovkin's* Mother *and Ermler's* A Fragment of an Empire. (New Theatre, *August 1934 [DP]*).

21 MANIFESTO ON ¡QUE VIVA MÉXICO! (1934)

Editors, *Experimental Cinema*

> The notion of anyone doing the montage of Eisenstein's film except Eisenstein himself is outrageous to all the canons of Art. No economic situation justifies such an aesthetic crime.
>
> —*Waldo Frank*

> Of the grandeur of the undamaged original *(The Last Supper)* we can only guess . . . dreadful restorations were made by heavy-handed meddlers; some inbecile Dominican monks cut a door through the lower central part; Napoleon's dragoons stabled their horses in the refectory and threw their boots at Judas Iscariot; more restorations and more disfigurements. . . .
>
> —*Thomas Craven, Men of Art*

TO OUR READERS

LAST YEAR, a great deal of space was devoted to a film entitled *¡Que Viva México!,* which S. M. Eisenstein, the

---

The Scenario of *¡Que Viva México!* by Eisenstein and Alexandroff, as well as the Manifesto by the Editors of *Experimental Cinema* on *Thunder Over Mexico,* a falsification of the Scenario, are reprinted by permission from *Experimental Cinema,* No. 5, 1934.

renowned Soviet director was making at that time. There were two articles on the film, one of them an authorized interpretation by Agustín Aragón Leiva, Eisenstein's special assistant throughout the production. In addition, there were ten pages of still reproductions, which, to quote Laurence Stallings, gave a "foretaste" of the film. The editors of *Experimental Cinema* were more than merely enthusiastic about it: they had been given a copy of the scenario by Eisenstein himself and they were convinced that *¡Que Viva México!* would materialize, as no film had ever done, the highest principles of the cinema as a fine art.

There is now being released on the world market a movie called *Thunder Over Mexico,* which is what it is: a fragmentary and entirely conventional version of Eisenstein's original majestic conception. The story behind this commercialized version is without doubt the greatest tragedy in the history of films and one of the saddest in the history of art. It represents the latest instance of a film director, in this case a genius of the first rank, forfeiting a masterpiece in a hopeless struggle against sordid commercial interests.

We decry this illegitimate version of *¡Que Viva México!* and denounce it for what it is,—a mere vulgarization of Eisenstein's original conception put forth in his name in order to capitalize on his renown as a creative artist. We denounce the cutting of *¡Que Viva México!* by professional Hollywood cutters as an unmitigated mockery of Eisenstein's intention. We denounce *Thunder Over Mexico* as a cheap debasement of *¡Que Viva México!*

As all students of the cinema are aware, Eisenstein edits ("mounts") his own films. Contrary to the methods generally employed by professional directors in Hollywood, Eisenstein gives final form to the film in the cutting-room. The very essence of his creative genius, and of his oft-quoted theory of the cinema, consists in the editing of the separate shots after all the scenes have been photographed. Virtually every film director of note has testified, time and again, to the revolutionary consequences of Eisenstein's montage technique on the modern cinema, and every student of the cinema knows how impossible it is for anyone except Eisenstein to edit his pictures.

Thunder Over Mexico has not been edited by Eisenstein

and yet is being exploited as his achievement. The editing of *Thunder Over Mexico* is not Eisenstein montage.

Out of approximately 200,000 feet of film shot by Eisenstein in Mexico, a picture of some 7,000 feet cut according to convential Hollywood standards, has been produced,—an emasculated fragment of Eisenstein's original scenario which provided for *six* interrelated episodes, in which were included a dramatic prologue depicting the life of ancient Yucatan and an epilogue foreshadowing the destinies of the Mexican people. What has happened to this material?

Eisenstein's original prologue, which was intended to trace the sources and primitive manifestations of Mexican culture, thus projecting the most vital cutural forms among the Aztecs, Toltecs and the Mayans, has been converted into a pseudo-travelogue.

Worse than this is the fate of Eisenstein's original epilogue, which was intended to establish the timeless continuity of types from ancient Yucatan to modern Mexico, and which was meant to anticipate the revolutionary urge dormant in the descendants of those ancient races. Under the guidance of Eisenstein's backers, who have never from the start shown a due consciousness of what the film is all about, the epilogue has now been converted into a cheerful ballyhoo about "a new Mexico," *with definite fascist implications.*

The remaining mass of material, consisting of more than 180,000 feet, is in danger of being sold piecemeal to commercial film concerns.

Thus, Eisenstein's great vision of the Mexican ethos, which he had intended to present in the form of a "film symphony," has been destroyed. Of the original conception, as revealed in the scenario and in Eisenstein's correspondence with the editors of *Experimental Cinema,* nothing remains in the commercialized version except the photography, which no amount of mediocre cutting could destroy. As feared by Eisenstein's friends and admirers, the scenario, written in the form of a prose poem, merely confused the professional Hollywood cutters. The original *meaning* of the film has been perverted by reduction of the whole to a single unconnected romantic story which the backers of the picture are offering to please popular taste. The result is *Thunder Over Mexico:* a "Best-Picture-of-the-Year," Hollywood special, but in the annals of true art, the saddest miscarriage on record of a high and glorious enterprise.

For more than a year Eisenstein's friends and admirers in the United States have been appealing to his backers, represented by Upton Sinclair, to save the picture and to preserve it so that eventually Eisenstein might edit it. A campaign was even launched to raise $100,000 to purchase the material for Eisenstein. Finally, a Committee for Eisenstein's Mexican Film was formed, consisting of the editors of *Experimental Cinema* and including Waldo Frank, Lincoln Kirstein, Agustín Aragón Leiva and J. M. Valdes-Rodriguez. All these efforts, however, were unsuccessful. It is now too late to stop the release of *Thunder Over Mexico.*

But there is one alternative left to those who wish to save the original negative of *¡Que Viva México!:* the pressure of world-wide appeal to the conscience of the backers may induce them to realize the gravity of the situation and give the film to Eisenstein.

The purpose of this manifesto, therefore, is two-fold: (1) to orient and forewarn public taste on the eve of the arrival of a much misrepresented product, *Thunder Over Mexico;* and (2) to incite public opinion to bring pressure to bear upon the backers in a last effort to save the complete negative, both cut and uncut, for Eisenstein.

22 ¡QUE VIVA MÉXICO! ORIGINAL SCENARIO

S. M. Eisenstein *and* G. V. Alexandroff

The story of this film is unusual. Four novels framed by prologue and epilogue, unified in conception and spirit, creating its entity. Different in content. Different in location. Different in landscape, people, customs. Opposite in rhythm and form, they create a vast and multicolored film-symphony about Mexico. Six Mexican folk-songs accompany these novels, which themselves are but songs, legends, tales from different parts of Mexico brought together in one united cinema show.

PROLOGUE

Time in the prologue is eternity. It might be today. It might as well be twenty years ago. Might be a thousand.

For the dwellers of Yucatan, land of ruins and huge pyramids, have still conserved, in feature and forms, the character of their ancestors, the great race of the ancient Mayas. Stones—Gods—Men—Act in the prologue. In time remote . . .

In the land of Yucatan, among heathen temples, holy cities and majestic pyramids. In the realms of death, where the past still prevails over the present, there the starting-point of our film is laid.

Reprinted by permission from *Experimental Cinema,* No. 5, 1934.

197

As a symbol of recalling the past, as a farewell rite to the ancient Maya civilization, a weird funeral ceremony is held.

In this ceremony idols of the heathen temples, masks of the gods, phantoms of the past, take part.

In the corresponding grouping of the stone images, the masks, the bas-reliefs and the living people, the immobile act of the funeral is displayed.

The people bear resemblance to the stone images, for those images represent the faces of their ancestors.

The people seem turned to stone over the grave of the deceased in the same poses, the same expressions of face, as those portrayed on the ancient stone carvings.

A variety of groups that seem turned to stone, and of monuments of antiquity—the component parts of the symbolic funerals—appear in a shifting procession on the screen.

And only the quaint rhythm of the drums of the Yucatan music, and the high-pitched maya song, accompany this immobile procession.

Thus ends the prologue—overture to the cinematographic symphony, the meaning of which shall be revealed in the contents of the four following stories and of the Finale at the end of these.

FIRST NOVEL: *SANDUNGA*

Tropical Tehuantepec. The Isthmus between Pacific and Atlantic oceans. Near the borders of Guatemala. Time is unknown in Tehuantepec. Time runs slowly under the dreamy weaving of palms and costumes, and customs do not change for years and years.

PERSONS:

1. Concepción, an Indian girl.
2. Abundio, her *novio* (fiancé).
3. His Mother.
4. Tehuanas (Tehuantepec girls).
5. Population of Tehuantepec in festivals, ceremonies and a popular wedding.

SANDUNGA

The rising sun sends its irresistible call to life. Its all-pervading rays penetrate into the darkest of the tropical forest, and, with the sun and the sound of the gentle morning breeze of the ocean, the denizens of the Mexican tropical land awaken.

Flocks of screaming parrots flutter noisily among the palm branches waking up the monkeys, who close their ears in anger and run down to the river.

On their course these startle the solemn pelicans off the shore sands, and then they plunge, grumbling loudly, into the waves to fish floating bananas and cocoanuts.

From the deep of the river crabs, turtles, and sluggish alligators crawl up to the shore to bask their century-old bodies in the sun.

Indian maids are bathing in the river; they lie on the sandy, shallow bottom of the river and sing a song.

Slow as an old-time waltz, sensual as a Danzon, and happy as their own dreams—an Oaxaca song—the "Sandunga."

Another group of girls in tanned little boats glide slowly by in the bright surface of the river, indulging in the luxury of idleness and the warm kisses of the sunbeams.

A cascade of jet black shining hair drying in the sun denotes a third group of girls seated by the trunks of the nearby palm-trees.

Proud and majestic, like a fairy queen in her natural maiden beauty, is among them a girl by the name of Concepción.

Under the caress of the waves of her hair she lets herself float into dream-land. A wreath of flowers crowns her brow. While listening to the song of her chums she closes her eyes, and in her imagination gold takes the place of flowers.

A necklace of golden coins, adorned with rough pearls strung on threads of golden chains, is glimmering on her breast.

A golden necklace—this is the object of all her dreams; this is the dream of all the Tehuanas—the Tehuantepec girls.

From tender childhood a girl begins to work, saving painstakingly every nickel, every penny, in order that at the age of sixteen or eighteen she may have the golden necklace.

The necklace—that is a fortune, it is an estate. The necklace is the future dowry.

And the bigger, the more expensive it is, the happier future, marital life.

That is why the dreams of Concepión are so passionate; that is why the visions floating before her mind's eye are so colorful.

Handsome youths alternate with the necklace dreams.

Youthful beauty blossoms on the screen. . . .

The dreamy song of the girls wafts over the dreamy voluptuous tropics. . . .

Oh, . . . we have let ourselves drift so deeply into dreams, that we have not even noticed how the girls got to work, when they went over to the market place, exhibited their wares: oranges, bananas, pineapples, flowers, pots, fish, and other merchandise for sale. The Tehuantepec market-place is an interesting sight. If you will look in this corrner you may think yourself in India.

On turning to the other side you will find it like Bagdad because of the big earthenware pots surrounding its youthful vendor.

In still another place it looks like the South Seas. However, there are also spots that look like nothing else on earth, for four-eyed fishes are sold only in Tehuantepec.

As soon as a girl sells some trifle, as soon as she receives the few cents in payment, she immediately begins to think of the necklace, begins to count the gold coins she still has to earn.

Thus, coin by coin, the necklace is built, enhanced, but, alas, it is still short one—the bigger, central coin.

So figured Concepción, she needed only one, just one more coin to win the right to happiness!

Business, however, is slow in the quiet, lazy tropical market.

Concepción goes on dreaming about this last coin, while the song, the song that stands for happiness with Tehuantepec girls, continues to float in the air.

But at last the bananas are sold, those bananas that were to bring in the money for completion of the necklace. And as the customer pays Concepción, she says: "May your necklace bring you luck!"

The happy Concepción tightly grips the long wished-for coin in her hand.

THE BALL

The most beautiful that the tropical forest can yield, flowers, banana-trees, palm-leaves, fruits, adorn the walls of the dance hall.

The most elegantly dressed of the Tehuana girls are seen there. The dance hall is the only place where a youth and a girl may meet, where they can confide to each other the secret of the heart!

In the brilliance of her best dress and the high pitch of her feelings she casts aside the silk veil of her shawl to draw the eyes of all youths and maidens and keep them spellbound upon the splendor of her beauty and her new golden necklace.

After the dance, when Concepción withdraws with her beloved to a retired corner, Abundio proposes to her. And now:

THE PROPOSAL

Behold Concepción trembling, pensive, frightened. And here the author speaks!

—Why Concepción, isn't this what you came for? Is it not what you expected? Is it not what you longed for? In reply to the voice of the author Concepción smiles, nods her head in assent. But! The Bridegroom's Mother is a practical woman! She sends her women to the bride's house to take stock of the dowry and make sure that all is right. That there are enough petticoats in the trousseau. That the gold coins in the necklace are plentiful.

Experienced old women, nearly centenarians who had taken hands in the marriages of three generations come to Concepción's home. They examine all her outfit, feel the velvet, smell the silk, count the gold coins in the necklace and subject them to the tooth-test to make sure of the purity of the gold.

Stirred to the depths of her soul Concepción laughs with joy and happiness. The venerable women then pronounce judgment:

All is perfectly right! So, traditional rites begin.

Concepción's friends bring her presents: A cow dressed up in a masquerade costume; goats with bow ties around their necks; they are carrying on their shoulders many hens, turkeys, little pigs and other gifts and in a quaint procession are advancing toward the bride's home.

In compliance with a tradition centuries old they bring her pure bee's-wax candles fantastically decorated.

Middle-aged women are busy in the elaborated preparation of typical and delicious dishes for the indispensable, peculiar banquet.

Entire Tehuantepec is stirred up by this event.

All the girls are wearing the fairy regional costumes and wait for the newly-wedded near the church.

Under the sound of the wedding bells the procession carrying palm branches goes to the house of the young couple.

And when left by themselves, Concepción coyly allows her husband to take off her pride—the golden necklace.

Grandma runs out on the balcony and loudly announces to the expectant Tehuantepecans that Concepción—the girl, has become Concepción the woman.

Sky rockets soar up high; fire-works crack, all the young girl friends of Concepción turn their fairy head-gear inside out, like a flock of bih-birds all spreading out their wings, and they dance and sing!

THE SANDUNGA

The Sandunga that always sings in the air whenever happiness comes—either in dreams or in reality. While throughout the tropical forest under the peaceful fragrance of the palm-trees life pursues its habitual daily course.

The old apes rock their offspring to sleep. Parrots teach their young to scream. Pelicans bring fish for their little ones in their pouches. Time passes, new flowers bloom. Concepción the woman is now a happy mother.

Thus the story of Concepción comes to an end, with the portraying of happy, contented parents and a laughing boy. With the sun setting beyond the Ocean. With the peaceful lyric-song of dreaming beautiful girls. Ends the romance of tropical Tehuantepec.

SECOND NOVEL: *MAGUEY*

The action of this story develops through the endless fields of maguey in the Llanos de Apam and the ancient Hacienda de Tetlapayac, State of Hidalgo. Llanos de Apam are the foremost "pulque"-producing section of Mexico.

Time of the action, beginning of this century under the social conditions of Porfirio Diáz's dictatorship.

PERSONS

1. Sebastián, indian peon
2. María, his bride
3. Joaquín, her father
4. Ana, her mother
5. The hacendado
6. Sara, his daughter
7. Don Julio, her cousin
8. Don Nicolás, the administrator
9. Melesio, his *mozo*
10. Señor Balderas, a guest
11. Felix
12. Luciano—peons, friends of Sebastián
13. Valerio
14. *Charros, mozos,* guests and peons

MAGUEY

Aggressiveness, virility, arrogance and austerity characterize this novel. As the North Pole differs from the Equator, so unlike to dreamy Tehuantepec are the famous "Llanos de Apam." So different their people, customs, ways and mode of living.

At the foot of the high volcanoes, at an altitude of ten thousand feet, on this desert land grows the big cactus plant—the Maguey.

With their mouths they suck the juice of this cactus plant to make the Indian drink known as "pulque."

White, like milk—a gift of the gods, according to legend and belief, this strongest intoxicator drowns sorrows, inflames passions and makes pistols fly out of their holsters.

Feudal estates, former monasteries of the Spanish conquerors, stand like unapproachable fortresses amidst the vast seas of cactus groves.

Long before dawn, long before the snowy peaks of the volcanoes are lit up by the first rays of the sun, over the high walls of the massive farmhouse come the sad, slow tunes of a song. "El Alabado" the peons call this song. They sing it every morning before they get to work.

It is a hymn in which they pray to the Holy Virgin to help them on the newly dawning day. When the high snowy peaks of the mountains begin to glitter under the rising sun the gates of the fortress-like farm-house are opened and, ending their song, the peons tightly wrapped in their serapes and holding their big sombreros in their hands, pour out into the cactus fields to suck in the juice of the maguey with long, especially fitted calabashs.

On the screen you shall see the astonishingly original process of pulque production—which originated hundreds of years ago and has not changed up to the epoch of this story.

Later, when the fog has cleared away, when the sun has warmed the earth, the servants of the landlord's household get up and begin preparations for the evening, for on this day the annual feast of the hacienda is to be celebrated.

The *charros* put on their best costumes in honor of the guests and they exhibit boastfully their remarkable horses.

Meantime, in the maguey field, where the peon Sebastián is working, a meeting takes place. María's parents bring their daughter to hand her over to her fiancé.

According to tradition, Sebastián will have to take his bride to the owner of the hacienda as homage.

But the *charros* who are guarding the landlord's house won't let Sebastián in, so he has to remain in the front yard.

On the terrace the landlord, in the company of a group of his nearest friends, are having drinks—and their spirits are rising.

The hacendado receives María; he is a good-natured old man; he fumbles in his vest pocket for a few pesos as a gift to the bride.

But at this moment an old-fashioned carriage drawn by six mules comes speeding along. The old man's daughter, Sara, has arrived.

She has brought her cousin with her and has broken in upon the group on the veranda in a storm of laughter and gaiety.

She flies into her father's arms. And all their friends drink a toast to her health. María is forgotten.

Sebastián gets restless, while waiting in the front yard. His sweetheart is slow in coming back to him and the explosive laughter on the veranda sounds suspicious.

The forgotten, frightened, inexperienced María is awaiting her luck. Bad luck appears in the shape of a coarse, drunken guest with a big mustache.

Availing himself of the fact that the company is too absorbed with drinking and merry-making, he seizes María from behind a door and drags her into a remote room.

One of the servants, a close friend of Sebastián, witnesses this scene and runs with all his might to the yard with his startling news.

The Indian blood of Sebastián dictates his further course of action. He rushes up the veranda knocking the guards off their feet, he breaks in like a storm among the merry guests. . . . He demands María, his bride.

A fight starts at once, but is brought just as quickly to an end, for slim are the chances of Sebastián alone against all the assemblage. Sebastián is sent rolling down the stairs for his insolence and effrontery.

A door opens and the intoxicated villain appears before the excited group. Distraught, weeping, María slips by stealthily behind his back.

The tenseness of the situation is aggravated. But the hacendado is a good-natured old man. He does not want to mortify his guests, he does not want to spoil the feast. To distract the people he issues orders to start the music, the fireworks and the games.

María is put under lock till next morning, pending the hearing of the case. In the rattle of the music, the excitement of the games and intoxication of hilarity, the sad incident is forgotten.

The brighter the fireworks blaze, the more violent wrath rages within Sebastián's heart. Vengeance germinates in his mind. Vengeance begets conspiracy. Three of his comrades pledge themselves to help him get revenge.

In an auspicious moment they direct the blazing sky-rockets into hay-stacks. The flames spread like wild fire.

While the assemblage is panic-stricken, Sebastián and his associates provide themselves with arms and cartridges out of the landlord's supplies and make an attempt to release María from confinement. But the guards fire back and the conspirators are forced to flee.

Under cover of night the fugitives evade persecution. Morning overtakes them in a forest on the slope of a mountain.

Vending their way towards the mountain pass across the ridges, they plod laboriously through the thickest of the fairy-woods. The *charros,* however, on their fine horses, accompanied by the indomitable Sara and her cousin, make the pass first and intercept the fugitives.

Cross-firing breaks out in the tangle of the nopalwood. Sara, fascinated by the shooting, incessantly makes attempts to rush forward and her cousin has to keep her back at a distance from the whizzing bullets by sheer force.

Sara kills one of the peons and pays with her life for her daring.

A bullet finds its way to her heart through the watch she is so fond of. The mechanism of the broken watch trembles under the shots and slowly stops its movement.

Sara's cousin puts her body across his saddle and carries her away from the field of battle.

The shooting breaks out anew with increased violence.

The fugitives are retreating into the maguey fields.

In the stronghold of a huge cactus, three of them seek refuge.

The hissing bullets pierce the succulent leaves of the maguey plant and the juice, like tears, trickles down its trunk.

The cartridges are exhausted.

The peons make an attempt to flee.

The agile *charros* fling their lazos around the fugitives and hold them captives.

All torn, tottering Sebastián and two of his surviving friends are brought in upon the scene of Sara's funeral.

Eye for an eye . . . they pay with their lives for their daring.

Among the magueys, where Sebastián had worked and loved, he finds his tragic end. . . .

Beyond the great snow-white summits of the volcanoes the sun is sinking. The day is dying.

The large gates of the estate are closing.

María is set at liberty and goes looking for the body of Sebastián amidst the maguey plants.

Her appearance startles the buzzards and they fly away.

While over the high walls of the estate float the sounds of wailing.

A mournful, drawn-out wailing—the Indian farewell to the setting sun.

María finds the remains of her beloved, of him who was to become her husband, who had raised his arm in her defense . . . she sobs convulsively over his dead body.

Beyond the tall walls of the hacienda the peons are singing their vesper song just as plaintive, as mournful as their morning Alabado.

THIRD NOVEL: *THE FIESTA*

Time of the action—same as *Maguey*—that is—prior to the Revolution of 1910.

Action includes scenery of all the most beautiful spots of Spanish colonial style and influence in Art, buildings and people in Mexico.

(Mexico City, Xochimilco, Merida, Taxco, Puebla, Cholula, etc.)

The atmosphere of this part is of pure Spanish character.

PERSONS

1. Baronita, picador and first lover
2. The Matador (played by champion matador David Liceaga)
3. Señora Calderón, one of the queens at the bull-fight
4. Señor Calderón, her husband
5. Hundreds of ritual dancers, *danzantes* in front of the Basílica de Guadalupe
6. Crowds of pilgrims and penitents
7. Crowds enjoying the bull-fight and the floating gardens of the Mexican Venice—Xochimilco

THE FIESTA

Weirdness, Romance and Glamour constitute the make-up of the third novel.

Like the Spanish colonial *barroco*—works the stone into fanciful lace—work on the wire-ribbon of columns and church-altars. Thus the complex designs, the elaborate composition of this episode.

All the beauty that the Spaniards have brought with them into Mexican life appears in this part of the picture.

Spanish Architecture, costumes, bull-fights, romantic love, southern jealousy, treachery, facility at drawing the gun, manifest themselves in this story.

In old pre-revolutionary Mexico the annual holiday in worship of the holy Virgin of Guadalupe is taking place.

Hence the abundance of merry-go-rounds, shows, flowers, the multitudes of people. Pilgrims from all parts of the country are coming to the feast.

Dancers of ritual dances are getting their fantastic costumes and masks ready.

The bishops and archbishops are donning their gorgeous feature robes.

The girls who are destined to appear as queens of the bull-fights are putting on their expensive combs and mantillas in a tremor of vanity.

And finally the heroes of this tale, the famous matadors,

are getting dressed for the performance on the veranda of a Spanish patio, amid the tinkling of guitars and the sound of militant songs of the ring.

The best of the matadors is enacted by David Liceaga, the most renowned matador of Mexico and "champion" of the "golden ear."

In front of a peir-glass, swelling with the selfconsciousness of their importance and grandeur, the matadors are putting on their gold and silk embroidered costumes.

More than the others, wriggles in front of the mirror, (the most concerned about his personal appearance) the care-free picador, the lazy Don Juan Baronita.

He is mindful of every detail, for an encounter more hazardous than the bull-fight awaits him.

He has a date with another man's wife! Having dressed, the matadors drive to the chapel of the Holy Virgin, the patron of their dangerous art.

Having knelt before her altar, whispered to her his prayer, and begged her benediction, the best of the great matadors drive over to the quiet home of his mother to bid her—

Good Bye!

May be for the last time—

And on the plaza a multitude of some sixty-thousand people, amid hand-clapping, shouts its impatience. The orchestra in gayful tunes begins to play the opening official march and the matadors make their appearance in the arena.

During the parade the picador Baronita appears in full splendor, mounted on his white horse, and throws a stealthy glance in the direction where the queens are seated.

The belles of the city in expensive lace under the refreshing breeze of fans, and open coquetry, are filling the "Royal" box seats.

Baronita manages to locate the queen of his inflamed heart and give her his "killing" glance.

And as in the traditional "Carmen" the eyes of the matadors meet the dark eyes of the beautiful queens and as a tradition dictates, this glance kindles the flame of valor in the matadors' eyes.

The sixty thousand attendants release an Ah! of wonder the moment the bull runs out into the ring. The very famous David Liceaga displays all the beauty and elegance of the art of the matador.

Full of grace and valor he dances his "dance" on the margin of death and triumph.

He does not stir from his place even when the bull's horns come within a hair's breadth of his body; he does not tremble, but smiles serene, and to top it all he pets the sharp horns of the animal and this provokes an endless savage outburst of delight from the crowd.

But the bull, enraged by the teasing of Leceaga knocks down the horse of the infatuated Baronita.

And he is forced disgracefully to jump the enclosure under the roars of derisive laughter from the crowd.

Notwithstanding all this, his love remains true to him,—she gives him the high sign of the feasibility of their rendezvous.

In the meantime, in the town square, fairs and market-places, a crowd of many thousands are contemplating the ritual ceremonial dances of Indians dressed up in gilded brocade, ostrich feathers and huge masks.

Under the peals of the ancient Spanish church bells, under the sound of music and the rolling of beating drums, the thunder of exploding sky rockets, the feast flourishes. Under the roar of the exalted crowd, at the other place, the killed bull is taken away from the grounds.

A maelstrom of hats and unabating ovations accompany the triumphant exit of the valiant matador.

Baronita has now met his "queen." Wrapped up in one cloak, the pair of lovers make their way through the narrow Spanish alleys to the landing of the boats adorned with flowers.

Their boat sails by the floating gardens along the dream-land canals of Xochimilco, the so-called Venetia of Mexico.

In the shade of an awning under the sound of guitars and marimbas the pair of lovers will forget their troubles.

But trouble does not forget them.

The wife catches sight of her husband; the pair hide behind the curtain and a swift change of their course saves them from a tragic look.

The husband is furious, he is raving, because he can find no trace of his wife. A mad pursuit among the moving maze of flower-covered floating temples of love . . . .

The boat of the amorous pair passes under his very nose and disappears among hundreds of other festively adorned boats.

In a retired nook of a remote canal the "Ship of Love" lands. Baronita conducts his forbidden love to the summit of a mountain, to a big stone crucifix, where they watch the sunset and exchange kisses.

In their moment of utmost bliss they are surprised by the husband. He draws his Spanish fancy-made pistol. He is ready to discharge it. And by pure miracle Baronita escapes the avenging hand . . .

The final song of the great feast ends the day.

Happy, romantic, is the finale of the story about this ancient and beautiful Spanish holiday.

FOURTH NOVEL: SOLDADERA

The background of this story is the tumultuous canvas of uninterrupted movements of armies, battles and military trains which followed the revolution of 1910 until peace and the new order of modern Mexico were established.

Deserts, woods, mountains and the Pacific Coast at Acapulco, and Cuautla, Morelos, are the landscapes of this story.

PERSONS

1. Pancha, the woman who follows the soldier—the *soldadera.*
2. Juan, Pancha's soldier.
3. The sentinel, Pancha's second soldier.
4. Pancha's child.
5. The army in march and fight.
6. Hundreds of soldaderas, wives of the soldiers, following the armies.

SOLDADERA

Yells, shouts, general havoc seems to reign in the small Mexican village.

At first one gets bewildered, one cannot understand what is going on—women are catching hens, pigs, turkeys; women are hastily seizing tortillas and chile in the houses.

Women wrangling, fighting, shouting at each other . . . .

What is up?

These are soldiers' wives, soldaderas, forerunners of the army, who have invaded the village.

Those are the soldaderas getting provisions to feed their weary husbands.

One of them is Pancha; a machine-gun ribbon hangs across her shoulder, a big sack containing household utensils weighs heavily on her back . . . .

Having caught a chicken and voiced her snappish retort to the protests of its owner, she finds a convenient place for the day quarters.

The soldaderas are breaking camp by the bridge on the bank of the river, they are getting their brimstones—*metates*—out of their sacks, are husking corn, kindling fires, and the clapping of their palms, patting tortillas, into shape, seem to announce peace.

A little girl is crying and to console her, the mother, for lack of candy, gives her a cartridge.

The child sucks at the dum-dum bullet and rejoices over the glistening toy.

The weary army enters the village and the soldiers in ravenous anticipation inhale the smoke of the bonfires.

Clarions sound the call to rest.

Artillery soldiers release the donkeys and mules from the dust-covered machine-gun carriages; the women are looking for their men.

Pancha finds her soldier, Juan.

She treats him to a roast chicken and hot tortillas.

Supper over, Juan rests his head in Pancha's lap and hums the tune the guitars are playing.

"Adelita" is the name of the song and this song is the *leitmotif* of the *Soldadera*.

When overcome by exhaustion he falls asleep and his stentorian snoring joins in the general snoring chorus of sleeping soldiers.

Pancha washes his shirt—and cleans his gun.

At dawn, while the echo of the desert still reverberates with the soldiers' snoring, Pancha places five or six cartridges in Juan's gun and puts the gun by his side.

She packs her household belongings in her big sack and lifting it to her back she joins the crowd of women setting out on their endless pilgrimage.

Faint under their heavy loads, trying to calm the crying children, munching the tortillas left over from breakfast, the crowd of women runs along the dusty, deserted road.

Suddenly the loud voice of the author calls to Pancha:

—Say, Soldadera. . . .

Pancha stops, turns her head toward the camera first, she just stares; then, pointing her finger to her breast, she inquires silently: "Did he call her?" The Voice, again:

"Where art thou going, woman?"

She turns pensive, smiles enigmatically, shrugs her shoulders, as if ignorant of what to answer, parts her hands in the broad gesture women are apt to make when saying:

—"Who knows?" ("¿Quién sabe . . .?")

She is borne onwards by the strong current of women and gets lost in the big moving mass of humanity and in the dust that veils everything from the human eye.

Machine-guns are roaring.

The clatter of cavalry is heard.

A battle is raging.

Juan is fighting like all the rest of the soldiers.

He discharges his gun.

Shouts: *"Ora . . . arriba . . . adelante"* . . . .

Rushes into attack amidst bursting shells.

Under the cars of a freight train the soldaderas are praying for their fighting men.

They have suspended their Santos—the holy images of their dearest devotion—from the car wheel and placed their little votive lamps on the springs of the car axle.

The machine guns are silent.

The shooting abates.

The soldiers' shouts are no longer heard.

The soldaderas go to the head of the train, to the engine, and hence they look in direction of the ending battle.

The soldaderas rush up to meet them, scrutinize their faces.

Question . . . ! "Have you seen mine?"

The excited Pancha is looking for Juan.

Here they bring him wounded.

Pancha runs up to him.

Uncovers his face . . .

No, that is not he . . .

The soldaderas bandage up wounds, treat them to the best of their knowledge. Apply tortillas to the wounds and fasten them with willow fibres.

Juan is safe and sound but worn out, and he must get into the car of his troop for the officers and engines are blowing the whistles for departure.

Having seen him board the train, Pancha gets on the engine platform.

The angry voice of the sentinel calls to her.

"What have you there under your shawl?"

And lifting her rebozo, Pancha answers quietly:

"Who knows, señor, it may be a girl or it may be a boy . . ."

The troops start off noisily. In the packed cars the soldiers are singing "Adelita." And on the roofs, the soldaderas with their kitchens and children are squatted like crows.

They have kindled bonfires on the iron roofs and the patting of palms making tortillas seems to compete with the rattling of the car wheels.

The military train vanishes into the dark of night.

At daybreak the soot-covered stoker leaps from car to car of the train in motion—jumps among the wandering women and children.

On one of the cars he drops flat on his belly and shouts through the open door . . .

In answer to his call Juan, aided by his comrades, climbs up to the roof.

The rattling of the train drowns the words of the message the stoker has brought to Juan.

They run fast to the engine, frightening the sprawled

women and on reaching their destination, they climb to the front platform.

Under the clothes hung out in the lanterns to dry, under soldiers' underwear waved by the wind, near the blazing bonfire, Pancha is sitting with her newborn baby.

And the same cross-guard seated close by, near a machine-gun, asks Pancha:

"—It is a girl or a boy?"

Among the mountains in the clouds, puffing with effort on the steep stretches of the road, the military train is advancing.

Another battle . . . !

Again the racket of machine-guns . . .

Again the soldaderas are awaiting the returning wounded soldiers . . .

This time Juan does not come back.

And when the fight is over amidst its smoking ruins Pancha finds the body of her husband . . .

She gathers a pile of rocks, makes him a primitive tombstone, weaves him a cross of reeds . . .

She takes his gun, his carriage belt, his baby, and follows the slowly advancing, tired army.

Her legs can hardly support her body, heavy under the burden of grief and weariness.

And then the same cross soldier walks up to her and takes the baby from her.

Pancha leans on the strong arm of her new husband in order not to fall and not to lag behind the army.

"Adelita" is the tune the tired bands are playing, falsely and out of rhythm.

The army has prepared for an attack, but the people from the city come up and explain.

The civil war is over.

Revolution has triumphed.

There is no need now of Mexicans fighting Mexicans.

The brass-band discovers a new source of strength that enables it to play "Adelita" stoutly, solemnly and triumphantly.

Like peals of thunder roll the triumphant shouts above the heads of the soldiers.

The armies are fraternizing.

One might decipher on the banner—the last word of its device.

Towards Revolution.

Towards a New Life . . . says the voice of the author.

Toward a New Life! . . .

EPILOGUE

Time and location—modern Mexico.

Mexico of today on the ways of peace, prosperity and civilization.

Factories, railroads, harbors with enormous boats; Chapultepac, castle, parks, museums, schools, sporting-grounds.

The people of today.

Leaders of the country.

Generals.

Engineers.

Aviators.

Builders of new Mexico.

and

Children—the future people of future Mexico.

The work of factories.

The hissing of aero-propellers.

The whistles of work-plants.

Modern . . . Civilized . . . Industrial Mexico appears on the screen.

Highways, dams, railways . . .

The bustle of a big city.

New machinery.

New houses.

New people.

Aviators.

Chauffeurs.

Engineers.

Officers.

Technicians.

Students.

Agriculture experts.

And the nation's leaders, the president, generals, secretaries of state departments. Life, activity, work of new, energetic people . . . but if you look closer, you will behold in the land and in the cities the same faces.

Faces that bear close resemblance to those who held funeral of antiquity in Yucatán, those who danced in Tehuantepec; those who sang the "Alabado" behind the tall walls, those who danced in queer costumes around the temples, those who fought and died in the battles of revolution.

The same faces—
but different people.
A different country,
A new, civilized nation.
But, what is that?
After the bustle of factory machines.
After the parading of modern troops.
After the president's speeches and the generals' commands—
Death comes along dancing!
Not just one, but many deaths; many skulls, skeletons . . .
What is that?
That is the Carnival pageant.
The most original, traditional pageant, "Calavera," death day.

This is a remarkable Mexican day, when Mexicans recall the past and show their contempt of death.

The film began with the realm of death.

With victory of life over death, over the influences of the past, the film ends.

Life brims from under the cardboard skeletons, life gushes forth, and death retreats, fades away.

A gay little Indian carefully removes his deathmask and smiles a contagious smile—he impersonates the new growing Mexico.

The late Sam Brody (1907–87) translated this hitherto unpublished letter written by Eisenstein in French in July 1934 to Victoria Ocampo, the famous Argentine writer and editor of the literary journal Sur. *It is a poignant cry by the great Soviet filmmaker over the destruction of his epic,* ¡Que Viva México! *Film historian Jay Leyda (1910–88) gave it to*

Brody to translate, along with others, but apparently the project it was intended for never materialized. The latter, knowing of my great interest in anything concerning Eisenstein's Mexican film, sent it to me to use as I saw fit. With it was a letter stating: "Yes, of course, you have my permission to use one or all the letters. I understand translations of original material are the copyrightable property of the translator. So go to it."

The 1936 film that Eisenstein refers to in his letter to Ocampo was the ill-fated, never produced, Bezhin Meadow. *His next fully completed and released film would be the celebrated* Alexander Nevsky. *See Leyda's* Kino: A History of the Russian and Soviet Film, *as well as Leyda's editions of Eisenstein's* Film Form *and* Film Sense.

Very dear friend!

I was delighted to receive your atlantic [sic—S. B.] postcard and all the more so to learn of your intention to come to Moscow. Malraux and Ehrenburg are here and it is good for all foreigners to come and see our extraordinary country. We do not have any "wild blacks" ("fauves noirs")—but there are other things that are remarkable. My entire Mexican adventure ended in total disaster, as you probably already know. The photography (and it is very beautiful) is all that remains—but the entire composition, montage, etc. are completely destroyed by the imbeciles who contrived it. As well as the total epic conception. I so loved Mexico and I find it painful not to be able to express it in this film which is destroyed . . . . I hope you will discern where Eisenstein ends and Hollywood idiocy begins! This whole affair has broken my heart to the point where I have become disgusted with cinema and have not made a film since. Instead I have worked on a big theoretical opus which will be finished in a month. It is in part the lectures and lessons I gave at the Moscow Cinematographic University. This fall, for the sake of a change, I will probably do a theatre production and shall return to films only in January/February 1936. I hope that by then my heart will be without scars!

I would very much like to see you in Moscow and a trip across our country will prove very interesting for you.

I await to hear from you and remain very affectionately yours,

Cordialamente [Written in Spanish—S. B.]
S. M. Eisenstein

I-VII-1934

I wait impatiently to hear from you!

British filmmaker Ivor Montagu (d. 1985), who was associated with Eisenstein throughout his sojourn in Hollywood, wrote the following on ¡Que Viva México! as an "Afterthought" in his 1971 volume, With Eisenstein in Hollywood, published by International Publishers, Inc., New York. It is reprinted by permission. (DP)

I do not write about it now to rehash old battles, but to do justice to all. Sergei Mikhailich is gone. Sinclair is a very old man now—passion must be spent. I know the principals. I talked with others. I received letters; to understand the situation is to have compassion. Sinclair dealt harshly with Eisenstein, but he thought that Eisenstein had wronged him. Sinclair accused Eisenstein of impracticality, megalomania, deceit. None of these charges was justified, but Sinclair's motives had been pure and it was inevitable that he should mistakenly think they were. . . . Eisenstein in Mexico did not shoot wastefully or impracticably or unnecessarily. This was an entirely false impression of Sinclair's based on his own innocence and lack of experience. In fact Eisenstein shot economically, as the surviving material shows. . . . The fact is that the total cost of the enterprise was less than Gaumont-British—the firm I was working for at about this time—spent on the Flaherty documentary, Man of Aran. . . .

23 ALL QUIET ON THE WESTERN FRONT AND CABIN IN THE COTTON: REVIEWS

Alexander Bakshy

ACCORDING TO one of Bernard Shaw's pet theories the stage in the matter of ideas is usually ten years behind literature. It would be difficult to say how far behind the movies are, for as a rule they care precious little about ideas. But there is one exception. Let the idea attract public interest, let the book in which it has found expression be a best-seller, and no expense will keep the film companies from producing the book as a movie as quickly as they can get the rights. During the past year the Great War was the most popular subject in literature, and for once, to refute Bernard Shaw, also on the stage; and so *All Quiet on the Western Front,* as well as *Journey's End,* has already found its way on to the screen. Need it be added that both cost tremendous sums to produce (it is said, two million in the case of *All Quiet*), and that both have been unprecedented box-office successes?

There can be little doubt that Remarque's *All Quiet* is not a great literary masterpiece. At least this was the conclusion that I arrived at after I had found that nearly every page of the book required a special focusing of imagination in order to bring out in clear relief the episodes and facts that stud the author's guileless and inarticulate prose. Nevertheless, there is no denying the interest and importance of the story as a human document. No book had spoken so coura-

---

All Quiet on the Western Front (June 11, 1930) and *Cabin in the Cotton* (October 26, 1932) are reprinted by permission from *The Nation.*

geously and, granting the necessary effort of mental readjustment, so vividly of the sheer horror of war—of man's relapse into bestiality with its frenzy of fear and rage, of his physical suffering and moral prostration. It is just as such a document that *All Quiet* emerges in a film of the same name (Central)—a terrifying document that reveals the carnage of war with staggering force. Battle scenes have been represented in many a picture, but *All Quiet* surpasses them all in the stark horror and madness of the business of fighting. Although the picture is not devoid of gentler moods, and is sprinkled generously with captivating humor, the predominant impression is that of life in the raw, of existence stripped of all adornments and bared to the bone. For this reason the total effect produced is not so much the tragedy of war as its callous bestiality. One is staggered, and shaken, and almost ready to sob, but one is not really thrilled. It is probably because of the elemental quality of its material that *All Quiet* is not so good a drama as *Journey's End;* but its appeal is more immediate, and technically it is a superior piece of cinematic craftsmanship, for which achievement Mr. Milestone, who directed the picture, deserves unstinted praise.

CABIN IN THE COTTON

This Warner Bros. film (directed by Michael Curtiz) was one of the first Hollywood films to show the plight of the Negro tenant farmers and the poor Whites of the South. A foreword stated that the picture did not take sides but the conclusion clearly favored the landowners. (DP)

There is no need to dwell at length on the main theme of the picture—the fierce struggle between the tenants and the planters in the cotton-growing South. The general facts are familiar enough—ceaseless toil and squalor on the one side, ruthless exploitation and a life of ease and luxury on the other. But if the facts are not new, their presentation on the screen without any glossing over of their disturbing social significance is something to be decidedly grateful for. Here is a corner of human life simmering with passions and hatreds that now and again burst into flames of wholesale destruction: to have it brought home to one's mind is to gain a new and valuable experience.

It is not that the film is faultless even as a social document. It makes a feeble attempt to suggest that the conflicting interests of the tenants and planters might be reconciled by some amicable arrangement on the basis of cooperative enterprise. But this is obviously a concession which the author of the scenario, Paul Green, had to make to his producers to absolve them from taking sides in a social conflict. One may wonder why a film-producing company should feel constrained to disclaim any intention of approving or disapproving the implicit message of a story it produces, as Warner Brothers do in this case by a special introductory statement from the screen. After all, the public is not particularly interested in the opinions of the producing companies. But such is the anomaly of the film industry. A film is not merely sponsored by a producing company, as a play would be, but is actually written and directed under the constant supervision of its producers. Under the Hollywood system it will be a long time before the author and the director are free to say just what they want to say and in the way they want to say it.

24 *I AM A FUGITIVE FROM A CHAIN GANG* AND *THEY WON'T FORGET*

Lewis Jacobs

OTHER CONTEMPORARY DIRECTORS, no less commercially proficient and who occasionally also produce arresting pictures, are Mervyn LeRoy, Lewis Milestone, William Dieterle, Michael Curtiz, Rowland Brown, William Wyler, William Wellman, William K. Howard, W. S. Van Dyke, Gregory La Cava, Frank Borzage, George Cukor, and Sidney Franklin.

Mervyn LeRoy, one of the most prolific, turns out films swiftly and competently. He has a vigorous style that deals only in essentials, and this style, when it works on material of real import as in *Little Caesar* (1931), *I Am a Fugitive from a Chain Gang* (1932), and *They Won't Forget* (1937), shows strength and conviction. *Little Caesar* was a tight, well-knit portrait of an egomaniac, bleakly realistic. Its straightforward, economic cutting, with each sequence growing out of a particular detail, provided an organizational unity that only a first-rate craftsman could achieve. Excellent in its feeling for pace (dialogue was kept terse, images were cut to the essentials) and sharp in characterization (Edward G. Robinson has ever since been tagged as a gangster), the film was one of the best of the gangster cycle, making LeRoy's reputation as well as its leading performer's.

I Am a Fugitive had the same succinct quality: it spoke simply and to the point. Its scenes of brutality, the road

---

Excerpted from *The Rise of the American Film,* first published in 1939. Reprinted by permission of the author.

gangs, the escape of the convicts, the sterling character work by Muni, were all notable. There was, too, its unforgettable last shot, in which Muni in the half-darkness, replying to his sweetheart's question "How do you live?", hisses, "I steal!" and then recedes into blackness. The film's deep social message, its unrelenting singleness of purpose, its elimination of all comic concessions, and the general high tenor of its exposé made it a genuinely moving production and established LeRoy as a genuine talent.

They Won't Forget was even more forthright. A grim and scathing portrayal of prejudice, intolerance, and mob fury in the deep South, its story progresses with a newsreel objectivity that gives its incidents the reality if not the intensity of Lang's *Fury*. The depiction of Redwine, the terrified Negro janitor who discovers the body of the murdered girl in the school's elevator shaft, is one of the few instances in American films in which the fear and oppression that fill the life of the Southern Negro is strikingly told.

Other outstanding touches are the concluding scenes. Hale, the framed victim, is being rushed by train from the lynch mob in the Southern city to a place of safety. But a lynch posse board the train, overpower Hale's guards, and drag him to their waiting cronies. As he shrieks for help, another train speeds by, its rumble and roar drowning out Hale's cries.

This kidnapping scene is followed by one in which symbolism is used most expressively. The shot reveals a mailbag suspended from a crosstree beside the railroad tracks. At the moment of the lynching of Hale, a train roars by, emitting an unearthly shriek as a steel hook extended from the mail car catches the mail sack and whirls it away. So the unseen horrible deed is summed up far more tellingly than would be possible in an actual scene of lynching. Such imaginative touches reveal LeRoy at his best.

25 JOHN FORD'S *THE INFORMER* (1934)

Roger Manvell

JOHN FORD'S CAREER as a film director began early in the silent period, but his name as one of the foremost artists of the American cinema was made by his association with the scriptwriter, Dudley Nichols, when they made *The Informer* together in 1935. Lewis Jacobs, in *The Rise of the American Film,* states that Ford was in a strong position as a commercial director when after five years' pressure he managed to persuade the studios to let him make this film. Jacobs writes:

> Instead of salary Ford took a percentage of the profits. The production is said to have cost $218,000, a relatively small sum; $5,000 was paid for the rights to Liam O'Flaherty's novel. The picture took only three weeks to shoot, and Ford declared it was the easiest he ever made. And no wonder: he says he dreamed of the film for five years. [p. 480]

The Informer is an example of the near-perfect union of theme and structure. It has complete simplicity, unspoiled by deviations and sub-plots. Each episode is short, a constructive contribution to the carrying forward of the action from its beginning (the temptation, leading up to the betrayal of Frankie by his friend, Gypo, the brainless giant), through its middle (the foolish behavior of Gypo deprived of the leadership of the man he has betrayed, leading up to his arrest and trial by the Rebel organisation) to its end (the flight of Gypo

From the British Film Institute, *Records of the Film,* London, No. 11, April 15, 1948. Reprinted by permission of the author.

from earthly justice and the moments that lead up to his death before the altar where Frankie's mother forgives him). The unities are observed, of action, of place (the back streets that harbour the Rebels) and of time (the action is completed over-night, from dusk to dawn). The inevitability of *The Informer* makes it one of the rare tragedies so far created for the screen.

The film begins with the great figure of Gypo in the narrow streets, lamplit and misty. The street-sets are of the barest economy, their effect of realism achieved by a few details, their atmosphere created by the highlights from the lamp-posts and doorways. With no word of dialogue until well into the first reel, the feeling of the film is created by the poster offering the £20 reward for information about Frankie McPhillip, a poster which Gypo tears down but which, blown by the wind, haunts him, clinging to his feet as he listens to the street-tenor singing "Rose of Tralee," blowing on until it brings us to the feet of Katie, Gypo's girlfriend for whom he eventually betrays Frankie in order to buy them both a passage to the States. It is then that the first word is spoken by Katie, "Gypo—," like a wail, the trailing note of it caught up by the music, lonely, full of pleading. But the wind blows the poster on until it is eventually burnt before Gypo's staring eyes in the Rebel Commandant's hide-out. The close lamp-lit streets and archways, the steps and courts and alleys, the bright bar–rooms, the fish-and-chip shop and other refuges from the bleak pavements are a major part of this film, as they were of Fritz Lang's *M* made before it and Carol Reed's *Odd Man Out* made since.

Wherever he can, Ford uses visual methods of building tension. Gypo in an agony of fear after the betrayal suddenly finds himself throttling a man outside the police-station. But the man is blind and crazy. Nevertheless at the later trial scene, the camera creeps round the witnesses and comes to rest on this same mad empty face. Gypo, in funds with the reward money, enters a bar; the few people in the bar leave it just at the moment Gypo shows his cash, unconsciously ostracising him. Gypo after the death of Frankie goes to visit the dead man's mother in an agonised attempt to appear innocent. He is already drunk, and he blunders in upon the assembled family and mourners. The women are chanting, and the great dark body of Gypo sits in the foreground like a shroud over the scene. He bursts out "I'm sorry for your trouble, Mrs. McPhillip." The wake suddenly stops: they stare at him; he jumps up; the accusing coins drop on the floor from his pocket, and the rest of the scene is the tension of exchanged glances of suspicion. This method of timed glances shows the reactions of Commandant Gallagher and his lieutenants to Gypo as the portrait of Frankie on the poster burns in the grate. So, too, the visual rather than the aural method is used when the young Rebels draw the cuts to see who is to shoot the imprisoned Gypo. No one wants to do it, least of all the man who draws the cut for the job. The heads of his companions withdraw out of the frame of the picture; then the hand offering the last cut withdraws. The executioner is left alone, isolated with the symbol of his task.

Nevertheless, the film is rich in dialogue scenes where Victor McLaglen is seen at his best. Here the emphasis shifts from the symbolic, carefully selected visual touches just described to words and actions of complete realism and conviction. Outstanding scenes include Gypo drunk and garrulous with recriminations against Frankie's betrayer when he is summoned before the Rebel Commandant, Gypo more drunk and treating everyone in the street to fish-and-chips, Gypo in the middle of the night visiting a brothel with a buddy anxious that the cash should be spent to his advantage, the trial of Gypo, and the scene in Katie's small bedroom after his escape when he lies down like a child in front of the fire to sleep off his exhaustion. The scenes are human and right and apt; they are vigorous, crazily energetic, drunken or touching, according to the moment and the mood. They are scripting as a film should be scripted, and they are most notably directed and acted, often with the barest simplicity.

If there is a weakness in the film it comes towards the end in the scene when Katie comes to plead for Gypo's life with Gallagher, who is in love with Frankie's sister. Here the dialogue seems to leave aside what would have been said in order to dramatise the sentiment of the situation. Similarly after Gypo has been shot at close range, he manages to stagger to the Church, drag himself inside and reach the altar before which Frankie's mother is kneeling. Although this end is right in terms of theme, for Gypo above all things needs to feel forgiveness from both man and God before he dies, the playing of this scene is in the exaggerated style of melo-drama, and therefore is out of keeping with the treatment of the film, as a whole.

Nevertheless, *The Informer* remains one of the outstand-ing achievements of the American screen. It bears all the marks of the artistic conviction which led Ford and those associated with him to bargain with the studio authorities to be allowed to make it, and to achieve these results with such sure economy of effort on the floor. Victor McLaglen gives a performance which remains vivid in the memory, like having met a man briefly whom one cannot somehow forget. Gypo commits an evil of the worst kind; he spends the night following in drunkenness and boasting and yet he never ceases to command sympathy as a man incapable of responsibility for what he does. His tragedy is a sheer inability to understand; he is a fool who blunders into wisdom at the expense of his life. There are many such people in the world. *The Informer* has the universality which belongs to tragedy.

See New Theatre *magazine (April 1936) for Emanuel Eisenberg's interview with John Ford in which, among other things, the director talks about the compromises he had to make with the studio before he could shoot* The Informer. *(DP)*

26 PAUL STRAND'S MEXICAN FILM
REDES (1935)

Robert Stebbins

THE EMERGENCE OF THE FILM *Redes (Nets)* from the welter of world film production is an event of incommensurable importance. Not only is *Redes* the first full-length film made in America on a working class theme, embodying the aspirations of the great masses of men but it is moreover extraordinarily beautiful and moving as few films in our experience have been.

We saw *Redes* in the usual tiny, bare projection room, in its original Spanish, a language unfamiliar to us. Nevertheless, in spite of these handicaps and the unfavorable advance reports of acquaintances who had prevued the film on the coast, our wonder at what was unfolding before us increased from moment to moment. The old thrill one gets when present at the "beginning" of things was there, but more than that was the joy that *Redes* should have risen so high above the tyranny of circumstance that usually dooms "beginnings" to mediocrity.

Redes was produced in Mexico. The project, under the supervision of Paul Strand, was initiated by Carlos Chavez, the Mexican composer and conductor, when he was chief of the Department of Fine Arts in the Secretariat of Education in 1933. Full credits for the production follow: Production (save for synchronization of the sound): Paul Strand; story: Paul

From *New Theatre* (November, 1936). Reprinted by permission of Edna O. Meyers. Robert Stebbins was the pseudonym of Sidney Meyers (d. 1969). *Redes* is also known to audiences in the U.S. as *The Wave*.

229

Strand assisted by Velasquez Chavez; screen treatment: Henwar Rodakiewicz; direction: Fred Zinneman assisted by Gomez Muriel; photography: Paul Strand; edited by Gunther von Fritsch; music by Sylvestre Revueltas; stills by Ned Scott.

The setting of *Redes* is Alvarado, a fishing village on the Gulf of Vera Cruz.

There, in the midst of strangulating poverty the fishermen make an heroic pilgrimage from abject, suicidal resignation to conscious full-statured protest against their lot. As the film opens we see a village exhausted by inanition and poverty. There has been no catch for months. Miro, one of the fishermen, has lost a child because he has been unable to afford medical attention. The child is buried. Miro, himself, takes a spade from the hands of the gravedigger and throws earth on the coffin in a last self-imposed agony. He speaks for the first time in the film to say, "It isn't right—it isn't just for a man's child to die because he has no money to cure it." Miro is lead away by his companions. After an interval of time, fishermen rush into the village telling that a school of fish has entered their waters.

Then follows the fish hunt, frenzied yet grave, surely among the greatest single sequences in the history of films. The men take their catch to a nearby city. The local dealer, a wealthy padrone, gives them a meagre handful of pesos in return. The men stand overwhelmed with shame and misery. But Miro, already embittered by the death of his child, is aroused to action. He calls a meeting at which some of the men decide not to sell unless they receive higher prices. But not all of them are persuaded. A group under the leadership of Miro's friend, Miguel, hold that action against the dealer can only lead to further disaster. They attempt to scab. There is a struggle. A politician, Juan Garcia Sanchez, hating Miro for his influence over the men, and currying the favor of the padrone, takes advantage of the tumult and shoots Miro, wounding him fatally. At the sound of the shot the battle ends. Miro's followers take him to his home. The others are confounded by the event and slowly perceive the folly of their dissension and the consequences of their cowardice. They return to Miro to find him dead. Miguel through the death of Miro has quickly come to realize the need for unity. He speaks the funeral oration over the body of his dead friend.

Miro is placed on a boat on a stretcher of oars. The fishermen row back toward the city. Other crews gather; two boats become many. As the film ends we see a phalanx of ships which suggest the power of the waves as they rise higher and higher, rushing in to break on the shore.

Here we have a story of utmost simplicity, told directly, with almost a complete absence of symbolic digression.

I tried to think of the people who had made *Redes* and chiefly of Paul Strand who had conceived and guided it to completion. I thought of Paul Strand's still photographs, perhaps the most beautiful created in our time. It seemed strange. How could a man who had spent most of his life arresting the fugitive nobility of real things, whose photographs arouse such elusive ideas and feelings in the onlooker, how could this man give voice so completely and unerringly to the forthright statements of *Redes?* And the answer came—there was no essential difference between the stills and the film. From his earliest works, like the blind woman in Stieglitz's magazine, Camera Work, to *Redes,* Strand has spoken of one thing predominantly—the dignity of human life and of the things man has made that reflect his image. But in addition, *Redes* was under the necessity of pointing to those relationships that stand in the way of man's rightful assumption of a desirable and dignified life. Hence the difference in approach. But the substance is the same.

Strand moved toward this simplicity with conscious deliberation. In the course of a statement prepared for the Secretariat of Education of Mexico, he declared: "We assume that these pictures are not being made for subtle and sophisticated people or even very sensitive minds accustomed to follow the intricacies of esthetic nuance. On the contrary, we assume that these films are being made for a great majority of rather simple people to whom elementary facts should be presented in a direct and unequivocal way; a way that might even bore more complicated sensibilities, though we believe otherwise. We feel that almost a certain crudeness of statement is necessary to achieve the purposes of these films." Yet, despite this foreknowledge, there is in *Redes* not the slightest trace of condescension or the quaint archaism that results from the self-conscious turning of a sophisticate to simpler modes. This we can only attribute to Strand's complete belief in what he was saying. The dialogue of the film, for example, strikes the ear with the true ring of authenticity.

In the weighing scene:

Miro: We sure got a haul this time.

Fogonero: If it keeps up this way I'll hitch up with Elena.

Antonio: Which is more of a fool, a man or a fish?

Yi–yi: Who knows? You're asking me?

Miguel: Any man who lets a woman hook him—

Fogonero: How well yours caught you.

Or later:

Miguel: There's no use griping—the sharks always eat the robalo.

Miro: Yes—but don't forget—we are not fish.

But after the vigor of much of the dialogue has been noted one must always return to the visual expressiveness of the film. In a conversation with Mr. Strand some time ago he conveyed his surprise that so few films were visually beautiful, particularly since the film was a visual medium. He pointed out that even so majestic a work as Dovjenko's *Frontier* was photographically indifferent; that seldom did the photography begin to approach the heights of Dovjenko's conception. *Redes* makes it easy for one to agree with him about *Frontier.*

In thinking over *Redes,* two films inevitably come to mind—Flaherty's *Man of Aran* and Eisenstein's unfortunate *Thunder Over Mexico.* This, not only because both films possess great photographic beauty but because Strand has admitted the influence of Flaherty and of the Russian school. As early as 1933, however, Strand pointed out certain shortcomings in Flaherty's aesthetic. Talking of *Nanook of the North* and *Moana,* he said: ". . . It was necessary for Flaherty to more or less reconstruct the past since all these people are already undergoing changes from the contacts of so–called Western civilization. And unless Flaherty widens the scope of his work this dramatic theme of elemental struggle for survival would seem to be a limited one." In other words, the true enemies of man were the manmade social and economic relationships. These were the things you had to struggle against. Undoubtedly, Flaherty, by taking himself off to the Arctic, the South Sea Islands or the Island of Aran, was in his way, expressing dissatisfaction with modern life. But in so doing he was utilizing symbols that no longer obtain today, symbols that men couldn't believe in. As a consequence, *Man of Aran* was merely *picturesque.*

In *Redes* Strand turned his back on the purely picturesque. To quote further from his letter to the Secretariat of Education: ". . . In a world in which human exploitation is so general it seems to me a further exploitation of people, however picturesque, different and interesting to us they may appear, to merely make use of them as *material."* True, Mr. Strand was himself, as he admitted, in a not altogether impregnable position, but he was confident of defending himself. "As to the criticism that the people will know and always accept the injustice of their lot, this one does not know. It is well to remember that new generations are being born and that children may have other feelings and ideas from those of their parents." As in the phrase of Andre Malraux, the artist "has created an illusion of conquest for the reader."

Thunder Over Mexico, mutilated in America by blind and unknowing hands, is certainly not to be thought of as the work of Eisenstein. Therefore it is only possible photographically to compare *Thunder Over Mexico* with *Redes.* On that score Strand is more human, simple, closer to the people than Eisenstein's photographer Tisse. Perhaps, the gigantic scale on which *Thunder Over Mexico* was conceived militated against complete success. Thesis and antithesis run through every frame. Not only did Tisse have to show the Mexicans as they are today but he also had to point out that they came of an ancient race of great cultural achievements, a race brought to a point just short of annihilation by imperialist oppression.

Whether *Redes* will or can be followed by films of a similar nature is open to question. In times like these, with great numbers of men blind to their true interests, perhaps a more oblique introduction of progressive thought is necessary in films—the greater use of melodramas like *The General Died at Dawn* and *Fury,* social comedies like *Mr. Deeds Goes to Town.* Yet it is difficult to believe that so complete an affirmation of a man's faith as *Redes,* so rich an intimation of a more desirable world will fail to move audiences wherever it is shown.

27 FRITZ LANG AND *FURY* (1936)

Robert Stebbins

IN 1929, IT WAS POSSIBLE for Paul Rotha, the eminent British movie-historian and *documentaire,* to say of Fritz Lang: "One regrets his entire lack of filmic detail, of the play of human emotions, of the intimacy which is so peculiar a property of the film." But that was some five years before *M,* and seven before *Fury!*

When Mr. Rotha penned those words, Fritz Lang, already in his forties, had won wide acclaim for *The Spy, Siegfried,* and *Metropolis,* his only film besides *Fury* to be widely distributed in America. As a general rule, most artists at forty have their greatest achievements behind them. Fritz Lang's art, however, has been a consistently unfolding, ripening phenomenon, both in human and filmic terms. Today we see him at the height of his powers confronted with the strong probability that soon there will be no place for him to work. At the present writing it appears that Metro-Goldwyn-Mayer does not intend renewing Lang's contract. We wonder if it can be because *Fury* will make their remaining films look so childish, so hopelessly redundant? What is more to the point, is that the man's integrity must have proved extremely trying to the Hollywood producers.

Integrity, honesty of purpose, lies at the foundation of the entire conflict between Lang and MGM or any true artist and Hollywood. For *Fury,* with all its limitations, is among the

From *New Theatre* (July, 1936). Reprinted by permission of Edna O. Meyers. Robert Stebbins was the pseudonym of filmmaker and critic Sidney Meyers (d. 1969).

The Memphis Press

LYNCHING PARTY ON WAY TO ARK. TO PASS THRU MEMPHIS

Mob Holds Negro
Invitations Issued
For Lynch Part

MOB MEMBER LAUGHS AT PROBE

Officers Won't Act, He Says, Declaring Negro Positively Identified

BLACK LEGION SAYS 6,000,000 ARE MEMBERS

All of America Knew of Lynching in Advance

BLACK LEGION KILLER NAMES DOZEN IN PLOT

THE 14th AMENDMENT SAYS—

FURY: A lynching occurs in the United States on an average of every three days. Over 5,000 men and women, most of them Negroes, have been lynched in this country since 1882. There have been very few convictions because it is always in such crimes. Ku Klux Klansmen, Vigilantes, leaderless mobs and again taken the law into their own hands. Twenty per cent as is shown in Fury, to cover up recently. Black Legion naires, have time and again wished to put out of sex crimes. Shoemaker and Taylor, and the lynching fever murdering anyone are accused of organizers trade unionists. The hysterical out- the victims are accused of the Michigan trade to stop such hysterical out- the Tampa murders of Michigan must be done in Fury. Because State and Black Legion and something depicted in the covering up of lynching is spreading, so unfortunately are often a party to the anti-lynch action lies in the fili- bursts as that comments are often of any effective legislation has been delayed by the Wagner-Costigan Municipal Government of including Borah, against has been postponed until the next perpetrators. But Congressional Borah, for lynching is nothing less than Government of Senators, therefore been We call upon our readers to butstering bill. Action has be passed. We call upon our anti-lynching bill. Action must a national disgrace. that they support the session of Congress and a national representatives that they demand of their Congressional representatives —THE EDITORS.

most honest, forthright films to emerge from a Hollywood cutting-room. Here you will find no sly prurient preface to concupiscence, no Graustarkian pipedream of which Bartolomeo Vanzetti once said ". . . these romances that distort truth and realities; provoke, cultivate and embellish all the morbid emotions, confusions, ignorances, prejudices and horrors; and purposely and skillfully pervert the hearts and still more the minds . . ."

True, Vanzetti's keen and fiery mind would have immediately seized upon the compromises in *Fury*. He'd have pointed out that the second half of the film almost renders invalid its object by shifting the emphasis of guilt from the lynchers to vengeful Joe Wilson (Spencer Tracy); that by contrast with the ingrown, embittered maniacal creature Joe becomes—(he even pulls a gun on his brothers and threatens to kill them if they don't go through with his plans)—the lynchers are portrayed sympathetically. Katherine (Sylvia Sidney), Joe's sweetheart, pleads for them: "You might as well kill me too and do a good job of it. Twenty-two, twenty-three, twenty-five, what's the difference? . . . Oh Joe! a mob doesn't think, doesn't know what it's doing." Vanzetti would have pointed out that the institution of lynching has an economic and racial background that is necessary to a complete understanding of the problem and that the film was faulty for the want of it. He'd have proceeded to point out that almost eighty percent of the lynched are Negroes. And lastly, he'd scorn the likelihood of the innocent, dead or alive, receiving legal justice. In his own words, "There is venom in my heart, and fire in my brain, because I see the real things so clearly, to utterly realize what a tragic laughing stock our case and fate are."

Apart from these weaknesses, in all probability compromises demanded by the box-office experts and not of Lang's making, *Fury* is the most forceful indictment of lynch justice ever projected on a screen. In fact, with the exception of certain sequences in *M*, *Fury* is entirely without parallel. Not that lynching hasn't figured in films before! The Westerns crawl with them. But in every case—*Frisco Kid, Barbary Coast*—the vigilante is upheld as a noble example, a cow-punching Cincinnatus come to rescue Rome from the alien invader.

To accomplish his ends, Lang has lavished a stupendous fund of illuminating detail on the film. The scenic recreations under the art direction of Cedric Gibbons, William Horning and Edwin B. Wells are extraordinarily effective. The recent revival of *Taxi,* with its fine realistic interiors, made me realize how much Hollywood has lost in exchange for the gold and ivory of the penthouse period. Unlike the sets and appointments in *Taxi,* however, the scenic reconstructions of *Fury* not only convince but even add to a comprehension of the principals, and at times, actually advance the story. When Joe embraces Katherine underneath the "El" the pillars, though almost wavering in the darkness, in their rigidity express the loneliness and heartbreak of the lover's impending separation. When Joe returns to his incredibly untidy apartment you sense at once Joe's life with his brothers and understand the great attraction that Katherine, with her neat schoolteacher orderliness, has for him. There are too many instances of Lang's remarkable grip on realistic detail, both scenic and directorial, to include within the limited scope of this piece. Suffice it to mention the moving solitariness of Joe in the business man's lunch with the Negro bartender and the raucous radio; and that masterpiece of fidelity, the facade of the County jail.

The brilliant use of the newsreels in the court room is another case in point. Lang originally hit on the idea in *Liliom.* You will remember that in the Lang production of the play Liliom goes to heaven. There the good Lord, instead of reading Liliom a list of his misdemeanours from the book of books, shows him a news reel of his mortal life. But what was a pleasant device in *Liliom,* in *Fury* takes on a cogency and moral force that is terrifying. The tremendous contrast between the piteous woman on trial for her life and the insane caricature of herself she sees on the screen, murderously whirling the firebrand around her head, is a warning to all who take to the rope or torch for the destruction of a fellow human.

The chief glory of the film, however, is the thrillingly dissected and synthesized lynching perpetrated by the brutalized and excitement-starved lower middle-class shopkeepers aided and abetted by the chamber of commerce in close collaboration with the gangsters, hoodlums and strikebreakers of the town. From Joe's arrest by the slow-witted "Bugs" Meyers, who later is unobtrusively shown nabbing flies on the wall while Joe is questioned by the Sheriff to that unforgettable moment when Katherine staggers into the square of Strand to find the entire town hypnotized by Joe's supposed funeral pyre, Lang has given us a memorable example of film making at its apogee.

Felicitations for splendid performances are due the entire cast, are due Norman Krasna for his superb screen original (how he ever got it past the front office is nothing short of a miracle), and Bartlett Cormack for his work with Lang on the screen-play. Bartlett Cormack, however, although a screen librettist of undeniable talent, in his propensity to break out in a voluntary rash of red-baiting, shows unfortunate promise of becoming the Zioncheck of the writers' colony. A week after the preview of *Fury* he inserted the following advertisement in the Hollywood Reporter:

> Bartlett Cormack* wrote the screen play of *Fury,* a dramatization of some "cells" of the United States, rather than of the United Front, and is proud of it, as a good job, and of its studio** and its bosses, i.e. captains of entrenched greed, for having made it with enthusiasm, and without squeamishness or stint.
>
> * Member Sons American Revolution.
> ** Metro-Goldwyn-Mayer.

Assuming that MGM's decision to go through with *Fury* had nothing to do with the unprofitable and sulphurous egg they laid, called *Riffraff*—assuming that MGM got the idea all by itself, totally unaffected by the constant hammering of liberals against the fascist proclivities of the producers, even then, it is too early for Bartlett Cormack to crow. The latest indications, if we are to judge from Douglas W. Churchill's article in the *New York Times* of June 14th, are that MGM never wanted to make the film and even today considers it a mistake. If Mr. Cormack will permit I should like to quote one last time from the letters of Vanzetti. Somehow *Fury* brings Vanzetti inevitably to mind. His letter of May 25th, 1927, to

Mrs. Sarah Root Adams, mentions a note a friend once sent him in which she describes the treatment she is taking for her broken arm. ". . . My arm's bone refused to heal again for quite long time, then the Doctor recurred to electricity, apply it to my fracture and I recuperated quickly and well. *How sorry I am to think that this same force which healed me may be applied to you.*" I venture to state that for every film that will heal suffering mankind, there will be 20 to slay the Saccos and Vanzettis. I am afraid MGM is not yet on the side of the angels.

28 SURVIVAL LIST: FILMS OF THE GREAT DEPRESSION

Tom Brandon

MOST OF THESE TITLES have been rediscovered by Brandon and some have been restored under his supervision by Leo Seltzer, who was photographer/editor on many of them. Abbreviations and Sources (of availability for examination by film scholars or for rental) are listed at the end of the filmography.

Film and Photo League, except No. 11 and 12 which are by Nykino.

1. *Workers Newsreel: Unemployed Special*
1930–32. Producer (pr): Workers' Film and Photo League; Photographers (ph): Robert Del Ducca, Leo Seltzer, with one section from commercial newsreels; b/w, 10 min. Silent. PS/MPC.
   A record of the historic mass demonstration of the unemployed on March 1930, in Union Square for government action on immediate relief and jobs. This protest meeting—in response to a call by the Trade Union Unity League and the Communist Party—was met with police violence.

2. *Halsted Street*
1934. pr: Chicago Film and Photo League; ph; C. O. Nelson; b/w, 12 min. Silent. PS/MPC/FS/AIC.

From *Film Library Quarterly,* Vol. 12, Nos. 2/3, 1979. Reprinted by permission. The late Mr. Brandon (d. 1982) was guest editor of this special American Labor Film issue.

How the people looked and went about their lives in the crucial Great Depression year of 1934 in Chicago as seen in many revealing glimpses of the varied ethnic groupings (Scandinavians, Slavs, Germans, Italians, Jews, etc.) from the suburban end to the crowded downtown beginning of Halsted Street.

3. *The Ford Massacre (Detroit Workers's News Special)* 1932. pr: Detroit Film and Photo League; ph: Joseph P. Hudyma (Dearborn), Jack Auringer, John Herd, Robert Del Ducca; ed: Joseph P. Hudyma, Lester Balog; b/w, 8 min. Silent. PS/MPC.

The only newsreel coverage of the historic mass march in downtown Detroit on February 4, 1932, against the policies of Hoover, and the armed attack by Dearborn police and Ford guards on unemployed auto workers at the gates of the River Rouge plant. Shows the march and assembly in Cadillac square of thousands of hungry but determined men and women, black and white, who petitioned for relief.

The Ford Massacre should be compared with the same kind of ambush at the notorious 1938 Memorial Day massacre at "Little Steel" in Chicago, where Paramount News covered a great deal, but *suppressed* its newsreel in the immediate aftermath of the events until the public clamored for release.

4. *The National Hunger March, 1931* 1931. pr: Workers' Film and Photo League; ph: Sam Brody, Robert Del Ducca, Kita Kamura, Leo Seltzer, Alfredo Valente, others; b/w, one reel. Silent. (This version is a condensation of the original.) PS/MPC.

The surviving film record of the first massive protest against the federal government's and industry's failure to adopt programs to alleviate the starvation and deprivation of 12,000,000 unemployed men, women and youth.

This short surviving version shows glimpses of many of the major aspects: the columns going to Detroit, Cleveland, St. Louis, Indianapolis, Pittsburgh, Providence, New Haven, Hartford, New York City; street collections; and in Washington, the leaders Dunn, Hawkins and Benjamin going into the Capitol. Above all, the film captures memorable images of the people going through the towns en route to Washington.

5. *The Bonus March*
1932. pr: Film and Photo League; ph & ed: Leo Seltzer; b/w, 20 min. Silent. PS/MPC.

A documentary film based on newsreel coverage of the ex-servicemen's national demonstration in Washington, D.C. in the early summer of 1932 and the U.S. Army's victory in driving and burning them out—on orders from President Hoover—in support of the National Economy League's (industrialists and military "economizers") position against the vets.

This film shows the encampment, the Army's assault (led by General MacArthur) on the vets, the burning out, and the retreat to Johnstown, Pa.

6. *Hunger: The National Hunger March to Washington, 1932.*
Pr: Workers' Film and Photo League; ph: Sam Brody, Robert Del Ducca, Leo Hurwitz, C. O. Nelson, Leo Seltzer; b/w, 24 min. Silent speed. The present release version is the first and last reel of the revised four-reel film.

It is a graphic account of the purpose, program and organization of the historic National March in December, 1932, a mass action which responded to the call of the National Unemployed Councils after regional and national conferences.

The film effectively captures some of the reality of the lives of the unemployed; the work of the Unemployed Councils and the supportive groups; the movement of the Northeast columns; the police opposition in Boston and in the trap on New York Avenue in Washington (a close-up of the confrontation there); and the march down Pennsylvania Avenue to assembly at the Capitol.

7. *America Today*
1932–34. pr: Film and Photo League; ph & ed: Leo Seltzer; b/w, 10 min. Silent.

A news review of mass actions in the streets in the critical Great Depression years of 1932–34, filmed and edited from the working class point of view. This issue shows New York police violently attacking protestors of the arrival of the first Special Emissary from Nazi Germany.

The second half, "The World in Review," shows, in full,

scenes filmed by commercial companies which were suppressed entirely or cut and distorted in release. United Front political strike in France in 1933 against the threat of dictatorship, a confrontation of 150,000 workers in Paris in opposition to French fascism; complete coverage of a gas and gun attack by a sheriff and his deputized goons on the Steel Workers Industrial Union in Ambridge, Pa.; and a Wisconsin Farmers' milk strike for fair prices.

This film was one of the *America Today* series which grew out of the *Workers Newsreel* series.

8. *Conditions in Los Angeles, 1932*
Pr: L. A. Film and Photo League; D, ph: Louis Siminow; b/w, 12min. Silent. PS/MPC.

Contrasts between poor and rich as seen in streets, housing, neighborhoods, jobless and leisure class.

9. *Century of Progress*
1933. pr: NY and SF Film and Photo League; ph: mainly Lester Balog; b/w, one reel. Silent. PS/MPC.

Contrasts the boasts of progress displayed in the Chicago Worlds Fair with the reality of the unemployed in various sections of the U.S.

10. *The Great Depression (Chicago)*
1934. pr: Chicago Film and Photo League; d, sc & ed: Maurice Bailen; ph: John Freitag; b/w, 9 min. Silent. PS/AIC.

This low-budget independent documentary provides memorable social history of the people and events of 1934 in Chicago: the life of the poor and the rich; the streets and the homes; the united protest actions, with Mother Ella Bloor, Heywood Broun, Lucie Parsons (widow of a Haymarket martyr), Norman Thomas and John L. Spivak.

11. *Pie in the Sky*
1934. p: NYKino (N. Y.) d (evolved by) Elia Kazan, Molly Day Thatcher, Irving Lerner, Ralph Steiner; ph: Ralph Steiner; cast: Kagan, Koolish, Russell Collins, Will Lee, others of the Group Theatre. b/w, 14 min. Silent. PS/MPCR/MAL FS/MA.

An improvised satirical and farcical treatment of unemployed who have become drifters and their futile quest for aid from the church—the theme of the old Wobbly song. More of interest as a notable experiment in filmmaking than as social history, *Pie in the Sky* is very funny today as an anarchistic comedy.

Ralph Steiner's photographic style in this film is memorable.

THE RISE OF THE C.I.O.: SECOND HALF OF THE THIRTIES

12. *The World Today*
1935. NYKino. b/w, 20 min. Sound. (1)*Sunnyside;* d: Michael Gordon; ph: Ralph Steiner and Willard Van Dyke. (2)*Black Legion;* ph: Ralph Steiner; PS/MPC.

A dramatic documentary re-enactment of two topical events: *Sunnyside* showed the fight against the mortgage companies by residents of New York's lower middle-class suburb, Sunnyside, Long Island; *Black Legion* was a stark depiction of the activities of the Black Legion in Michigan and the murder of a WPA worker, Poole, by Black Legion killer Dean. The script for *Sunnyside* was written with the help of the dispossessed home-owners who re-enacted their own fight for the camera; *Black Legion* was performed by professional actors and some amateurs, in simulated newsreel style.

13. *Millions of Us*
1934–35. pr: American Labor Films, Inc., Hollywood; *Co-D:* Slavko Vorkapich; b/w, 17 min. Sound. PS/MPC.

The story of millions of unemployed in the soup kitchens and breadline days vs. the millions still working, personalized in the drama of a young man driven by hunger to become a scab, and whose experiences lead him to recognize his common interests with the strikers and to be converted to trade unionism.

14. *People of the Cumberland*
1938. pr: Frontier Films; d: Sidney Meyers and Jay Leyda; assts: Elia Kazan (on location) and William Watts; ph: Ralph Steiner; sc & ed: Helen Van Dongen; b/w, 18 min. Sound. MPC FS/MA.

When Frontier Films made this first of its productions to be filmed on American soil, its popularity gave widespread publicity to the struggle of poor whites living in the bad lands—the Cumberland mountaineers—to build unions and fight for their rights with the help of the Highlander Folk School. A combination of documentary and reenacted dramatization.

15. *Men and Dust*
1940. pr: Lee and Sheldon Dick for Dial Films; b/w, 17 min. Sound. PS/MPC FS/MA.

An expose, based on the findings of the Tri-State Survey Committee, of the appalling health conditions and survival problems of the workers in the zinc and lead mining areas at the junction of Kansas, Missouri and Oklahoma. It shows the fight led by Mine, Mill and Smelter Workers Union to improve the efforts of mine owners to eliminate silicosis, tuberculosis and lead poisoning.

16. *United Action for Victory*
1939. pr: UAW and FF sound track; d and ph by Michael Martini; b/w, 33 min. Sound. FS/LC R/UAW.

17. *Native Land*
1939–1941. pr: Frontier Films. Full credits and annotation available direct from distributor. b/w, 84 min. Sound. PS & R/RAF FS/MA.

Based on the Senate (La Follette) Civil Liberties Committee's findings of the violations of civil liberties and civil rights by industry in the thirties, this powerful film was the most ambitious and most significant independent feature production of the period. It combines six dramatized sections on an inter-linked documentary background to reveal the ongoing struggle for the rights of workers and farmers, black and white, men and women.

THE FIGHT AGAINST INTERNATIONAL FASCISM
AND JAPANESE IMPERIALISM (THE SPANISH CIVIL WAR
AND THE INVASION OF CHINA)

18. *Heart of Spain*
1936–37. FF pr: Herbert Kline and Geza Karpathi; ph: Karpathi; sc/ed: Paul Strand and Leo T. Hurwitz; comm: Ben Maddow, with Kline; b/w, 28 min. Sound. FS/MA.

From a mass of material documented under shell-fire along the Madrid front by Herbert Kline and Geza Karpathi, Frontier Films made a memorable record of the U.S. and Canadian volunteer services under Dr. Norman Bethune.

19. *Stop Japan*
1935–36. pr: Tom Brandon/Garrison Films; d/ph/ed: Leo Seltzer; b/w, 20 min. Silent. PS/MPC.

Among the earliest Western (possibly the first) films to depict the invasion of China by Japan and the struggle for a free China.

20. *China Strikes Back*
1937. pr: Frontier Films; ph (Shensi Province): Harry Dunham; sc/ed/sd/mus arr: Jay Leyda, Irving Lerner, Ben Maddow, Sidney Meyers; b/w, 24 min. Sound. FS/MA.

An eye-opening first account on film of the Chinese Communists in their fortress province of Shensi in the Northwest after the Long March. Close-up coverage of the Chinese Eighth Route Army, its training, guerrilla tactics, political program, and relations with the peasants; leader Mao Tse-tung and Chu-Teh and others; and its efforts toward uniting all China against the Japanese invaders.

21. *The Spanish Earth*
1937. pr: Contemporary Historians; d: Joris Ivens; sc: Joris Ivens, John Dos Passos, Lillian Hellman, Ernest Hemingway, Archibald MacLeish; ph: John Ferno, Ivens; ed: Helen Van Dongen; comm (written and spoken by): Ernest Hemingway; b/w, 54 min. Sound. PS/R/ABM FS/MA.

An outstanding screen story of the issues behind the Civil War in Spain, dramatizing the effect of the Fascist uprising and invasion on the ordinary citizen.

22. *Return to Life*
1939. pr-FF coop-Medical Bureau and the North American Committee to Aid Spanish Democracy; d: Henri Cartier-Bresson; b/w, 10 min. Sound. FS/MA.

Filmed in Spain by the French director Henri Cartier-Bresson and cameraman Jacques Lemare, edited in part in

Paris and New York, with a sound track completely made in New York this U.S. documentary of the Spanish Civil War followed *People of the Cumberland* a year later in Frontier Films' output. It showed the behind-the-lines services of volunteer American and Canadian doctors and nurses of the International Medical Aid to the Loyalists.

ORGANIZED LABOR AND FARMERS IN THE POST WAR FORTIES

23. *For the Record*
1946. pr: Thomas J. Brandon for Public Affairs Films, Inc.; d: Julian Roffman; sc & ed: Sidney Meyers; b/w, 20 min. Sound. PS/MPC FS/MA.

A look at volatile labor-management relations in 1945–46 from the standpoint of the embattled strikers. When inflation and the removal of OPA ceilings forced labor to ask for higher wages to meet the rising cost of living, and employers refused, the rank and file of the unions, supporting their leaders, went out on strike in the steel, electrical, rubber, auto, and other industries: the biggest strikes in 50 years.

24. *Deadline for Action (Excerpt)*
1946. sp. UE-CIO w/d Carl Marzani; pr: Union Films, b/w, 5 min. Sound. PS/MPC.

An animation film treatment of transnational corporations in the electrical industry from the trade union point of view. An excerpt showing charts and animation. *Not a complete Film.*

25. *Dollar Patriots (Excerpt)*
1946. Produced and directed by Carl Marzani for Union Films, sponsored by the United Electrical Workers Union of America (UE), then of the CIO. b/w, 10 min. Sound. PS/MPC.

Some of the explosive animation work conceived by economist and author Marzani which exposed the "patriotic" war profiteers who exploited their work force before, during and after World War II. *Not a complete film.*

26. *Seed for Tomorrow*
1946. pr: Thomas J. Brandon for Public Affairs Films, Inc.; d: Julian Roffman; sc: John Grierson and Stuart Legg; ed: Sidney Meyers; spon: National Farmers Union; b/w, 20 min. Sound. PS/MPC FS/MA.

Deals with some of the major issues of American farmers, rooted in the experience of members of the National Farmers Union. A typical small farmer, squeezed by mortgages, debts, the high cost of materials, and the pressure of big farm monopolies, has his profits drained off by truckers, processors, and packagers. It is a dramatized social documentary made on farm locations from a scenario and dialogue written anonymously by Stuart Legg and John Grierson.

27. *Hands*
1934. p/od: Pathe, for WPA; d/ph: Ralph Steiner and Willard Van Dyke; b/w, 11 min. Silent. MPC/PS & FS/NA.

A documentary of images which dramatize the paid work of the WPA: the passage of a government check from the earner into the business world, shown entirely through shots of hands.

U.S. Film Service
These U.S. Film Service releases are well-known and are widely available in many rental libraries. Only the titles are listed here; for descriptions and prices write to PS or regional and local film libraries that have them. PS/NAVC & BH FS/NA.
The Plow That Broke The Plains
The River
Power And The Land
The Fight For Life

FOUNDATION AND SOCIAL AGENCY SPONSORED REFORM FILMS

28. *The City*
1939. pr: American Documentary Films, Inc.; sp: American Institute of Planners and the Carnegie Corp.; d: Willard Van Dyke, Ralph Steiner; sc: Henwar Rodakiewicz from an

outline by Pare Lorentz; comm: Lewis Mumford; b/w, 44 min. Sound. PS & R/MAL FS/MA.

Classic documentary on the need for city planning.

29. *Valley Town*

1940. pr: EFI, NYU and DFP; sp: Alfred P. Sloan Foundation; d: Willard Van Dyke; b/w, 27 min. Sound. PS & R/NYU FS/MA.

The problem, human consequence, economic waste and a partial solution of technological unemployment in a small Pennsylvania steelmill town.

30. *And So They Live*

1940. pr: EFI, NYU (coop) Univ. of Kentucky; spon: Alfred P. Sloan Foundation; d/sc: John Ferno, Julian Roffman; b/w, 25 min. Sound. PS & R/NYU.

An indictment of an outdated school in a grimly poor Kentucky community where the curriculum is irrelevant to the mountain people's daily struggle with hunger and want.

This film and *The Children Must Learn,* were intended to document related educational experiments on whether a functional type of education in the schools will eventually raise the level of living in the communities. Neither the experiments nor the film probed the questions concerning structural changes in society.

31. *The Children Must Learn*

1940. pr: Educational Film Institute of N. Y. U. and Documentary Film Productions, Inc.; sp: Alfred P. Sloan Foundation; d: Willard Van Dyke; b/w, 17 min. Sound. PS & R/NYU.

32. *Machine: Master or Slave?*

1941. pr: Educational Film Institute; NYU; d: Walter Neibuhr; b/w, 17 min. Sound. PS & R/NYU.

Managerial point of view on problems raised by technological advances.

33. *A Place to Live.*

1941. pr: Irving Lerner, Documentary Film Prod. Inc.; dir. Irving Lerner; sc: Muriel Rukeyser; b/w, 18 min. Sound. PS & R/ABM FS/MA.

Based on a survey by the Phila. Housing Association (sponsor), this film took housing problems out of the realm of remote social ills and statistics and personalized both by focusing on one slum area and one slum mother and her sons.

Civil Liberties, Civil Rights, Political Prisoners

34. *The Strange Case of Tom Mooney*
1933. An independent production; introduction on screen by Theodore Dreiser; b/w, 15 min. Sound. FS/MPC.
  On the false arrest of Tom Mooney, leader of a 1916 strike of San Francisco streetcar workers, and Warren K. Billings, another young labor organizer, in connection with the bombing of a Preparedness Day parade.

35. *Strange Victory*
1948. pr: Barnet L. Rosset Jr. for Target Films, Inc.; sc/d/ed: Leo Hurwitz; b/w, 72 min. Sound.
  On the postwar social paradox: ours was "a strange victory, with the ideas of the loser (Hitler) still active in the land of the winner."

36. *White Flood*
1940. pr: Frontier Films; ph: William C. Field, Sherman Pratt; b/w, 20 min. Sound. FS/MA.
  Poetic study of the life history of a glacier, from its birthplace in the mountains to the day when it floats into the ocean. Frontier Films' only non-social documentary.

Sources

ABM: Audio Brandon MacMillan, 34 Macquesten Pkway., S. Mt. Vernon, N. Y. 10550.
AIC: Film Center, Art Institute, Chicago, Ill. 60611.
BH; Blackhawk Films, Davenport, Iowa 52808.
LC: Library of Congress, Motion Picture Section, Washington, D.C. 20541.
MA: Museum of Modern Art, Film Study Center, 11 W. 53rd St. N. Y. 10019.

MAL: Museum of Modern Art, Circulating Film Library, same
address.

MPC: Motion Picture Center, Inc. 80 E. 11 St. New York,
N.Y. 10003.

NA: National Archives, Audio Visual Archives Div., Washington, D.C. 20409.

NAC; National Audio Visual Center, Order Section, Washington, D.C. 20409.

NYU: New York University Film Library, 26 Washington Pl.
New York, N. Y. 10003.

RAF: Radim Films Inc., 1034 Lake St. Oak Park, Ill. 60301.

29 DOCUMENTING THE DEPRESSION OF THE 1930s: THE WORK OF THE FILM AND PHOTO LEAGUE

Leo Seltzer

THIS ARTICLE IS REPRINTED from the Film Library Quarterly *(Vol. 13, No. 1, 1980). It was written in response to a lengthy essay in the same issue by Roy Rosenzweig which raised controversial questions about the documentary films of the Great Depression turned out by the Film and Photo League. Among other things, Rosenzweig charged, (wrongly, I think) that because League cameramen were so closely involved with Communist Party causes, their films "provide an incomplete portrait of workingclass life." Thus, "The thousands of unemployed workers who organized under the leadership of other radical groups such as the Socialists and Musteites are largely absent from FPL films. More importantly, FPL films provide little insight into the consciousness and behavior of the millions of unemployed workers who did not participate in any formal protests." In printing Seltzer's response, William Sloane, editor of the* Film Library Quarterly *(it ceased publication in 1986), wanted it understood that the journal was not "attempting to second-guess Rosenzweig's fine scholarship but simply to throw some additional light on the period and to present the attitude of one of the principal filmmakers who lived through the events of the thirties."*

Leo Seltzer, now 77, is internationally known for his documentaries of the Great Depression. Since 1931 he has made over sixty films and has won many awards, including an Academy Award for Best Documentary (First Steps,

New York City: Harlem demonstration against lynching. Photo by Leo Seltzer, © 1977.

*1948). He has taught film at Brooklyn College of the City
University of New York and at other schools and colleges.
He is president of Leo Seltzer Associates, Inc. in New York
and served as Cinema-Biographer to the White House
under President Kennedy. During the war years he served
with the U.S. Army as First Lieutenant in the Signal Corps.
As Film Production Officer, he directed many training and
public information films and was second unit director with
John Huston on* Shades of Gray, *a film on the treatment of
war-related emotional problems. This film was produced for
the Army Medical Corps and later released publicly as* Let
There Be Light. *Seltzer also served in Germany as Officer in
Charge of the Film and Equipment Depot for the European
Theatre of Operations. His copyrighted article below is
reprinted with his permission. (DP)*

Having lived through the great depression of the 1930s
and been actively involved at the time in the production of
social-documentary films depicting and interpreting that era,
I have always been interested in the literature of the period
as a counterpoint to my personal experience. It is somewhat
discouraging to find that much of the historical and critical
writing of the social, political and cultural activities of the
early 1930s is often incomplete or inaccurate.

It was the policy of President Hoover and his administration to play down and even deny the existence of the 1930s
depression. 1932 was an election year and the government
wanted to avoid involvement in the economic crisis. It also
refused to accept any responsibility to alleviate the widespread unemployment and starvation that eventually affected almost half of the people in the United States. The
media: newspapers, newsreels and radio, for the most part,
conformed to this policy and either suppressed or distorted
news of the depression. Workers in one city or industry had
no way of knowing what was happening in other areas, and
many felt that their unemployment was the result of some
personal failure. The impact of the depression of the 1930s
was felt for ten years until 1939, when America's industries
were revitalized in preparation for World War II.

There is a deadly similarity between the depression of the

1930s and our present recession with its constant overhanging threat of war. This may be the reason for the growing public and academic interest in that decade, in the search for historical fact and insight in the hope that they may point the way to some alternative, constructive solution to our present crisis.

Contemporary historians and students of American studies are keenly aware of the lack of definitive factual information about the great depression of the 1930s. There is even a greater void in the record of activities of the various social, cultural and political organizations that were dedicated to counteracting and correcting the demoralizing impact of that economic depression. Writers who choose to exploit the growing interest in the 1930s have a special responsibility to uncover new facts and to clarify our historic knowledge and insight. Unfortunately, much of the contemporary writing about the work and organization of the Film and Photo League and other radical film production groups of the 1930s is usually a rephrasing of the discrepancies and misinformation of earlier writers. Instead of engaging in independent research and interviewing survivors of the 1930s to uncover fresh information, writers often embellish and further confuse the facts with imaginative concepts. Historic fact is not enhanced by improvisation.

It is unfortunate that these same deficiencies are evident in the article by Roy Rosenzweig. . . . Instead of presenting new information or insight, he further confuses historical fact by introducing the abstract supposition that the Film and Photo League represented only those workers affiliated with Communist organizations.

Rather than critically analyze Roy Rosenzweig's article point by point, I think it would better serve the readers of *Film Library Quarterly* and the more serious students and writers of documentary film history if I described the organization and work of the Film and Photo League from my own point of view as an active member of that group from 1931 to 1935. This presentation, I believe, will adequately fill the voids and clarify the confusing and contradictory statements. It will also clearly refute his concept that the Film and Photo League neglected the uncommitted and non-Communist worker.

The Film and Photo League began in 1931 as one of the

informational-cultural units of the Workers International Relief. The WIR was established by workers to supply food,
clothing and medical care to strikers and unemployed
workers. It was a workers Red Cross. Under the auspices of
the WIR there were organized groups of actors, musicians,
dancers, artists, writers, photographers and filmmakers. The
actors and dancers entertained and dramatized the struggle
against unemployment, low wages and discrimination. The
artists and writers made picket signs and wrote leaflets. The
photographers and filmmakers documented the struggles of
the workers and unemployed. We showed our films in
meetings halls and at strike headquarters, often to the same
people we had photographed at demonstrations and on
picket lines. There were Film and Photo League branches in
other cities besides New York: in Detroit, Chicago, Los
Angeles and San Francisco, and we were able to compile
and show films of worker's activities in different parts of the
country. I took some of our films to the Pennsylvania coal
fields and showed them on a sheet stretched between trees
to miners who had been out on strike for two years. On
another occasion, with a projector improvised to run off an
automobile battery, I went through the middle west with
Sidney Howard, the playwright, showing Film and Photo
League films to farmers in their homes and in rural school-
houses. Often these films and the photographs we made
were the only source of information about the depression for
many workers and farmers throughout the country. This
combination of filming and screening was our day-to-day
activity.

In the early 1930s the production of documentary films,
and the production of any films outside of Hollywood, was an
uncommon occurrence in the United States. Raw stock and
35mm equipment were expensive, especially when figured
in depression dollars, and there was little opportunity for
training or involvement in professional filmmaking.

The romantic aura and practical potential of the film
attracted many members to the Film and Photo League;
people with a variety of motives. Some were primarily
interested in establishing theoretical guidelines for social-
documentary films. Others hoped that through the League
they could gain experience in fiction filmmaking and thereby

gain entre into the commercial film industry. A few others were interested in active and direct involvement in the daily activities and struggles of the unemployed. My motivation for joining the Film and Photo League was somewhat intuitive; to fulfill an innate need for real experience and for direct involvement in a vital activity. Filmmaking also fulfilled my dual interest in art and technology. Between 1931 and 1935, in association with Lester Balog and Robert DelDuca, I made many of the films produced under the auspices of the Film and Photo League. We were the production unit that was involved in the day-to-day filming, editing and screening of social-documentary films and newsreels that recorded and interpreted the background and struggles of the great depression. I was the live-in filmmaker and often slept on the editing table wrapped in the sheet we used as a projection screen. I found myself totally involved in the process of making films. The Film and Photo League was the original film collective and we produced the first social-documentary films that were made in America. For me it was a challenging and totally gratifying experience. My only concern at the time was how long it would last. My fulfillment was not shared by many other members of the League. Some were more concerned with establishing a theory that would certify the birth and define the continued existence of this new genre we had developed: the social-documentary film. Other members were more interested in the acted film and were involved in speaking and writing about what they thought the Film and Photo League ought to do. In their search for satisfaction some of these members left the League and set up other film groups such as Nykino and Frontier Films where they could experiment with dramatic and enacted films.

The documentary films and newsreels produced by the Film and Photo League were photographed on 35mm nitrate film. Many of the films were destroyed in a film vault fire in the 1940s. Others were lost or had disintegrated due to the chemically unstable nature of nitrate film. Much of the present written history of the Film and Photo League was derived from statements other than those who were continuously making and screening films under the auspices of the Film and Photo League.

I have recently restored six of the original Film and Photo League productions from fragments located by Tom Brandon in various government archives and private collections. (The restored films are: *Workers Newsreel-Unemployment; Hunger March 1931; Detroit Workers News-Ford Massacre 1932; America Today 1932–34; Hunger March 1932; Bonus March to Washington 1932.*) After viewing these films, Mr. Rosenzweig concludes, and I quote him, "films of the Film and Photo League provide an incomplete portrait of working class life . . . FPL films provide little insight into the consciousness and behavior of the millions of the unemployed workers who did not participate in any formal protests." The fact is that the League was neither dedicated, equipped or financially able to record this broad general image of the American working class. The six restored films represent less than 5% of the League's total production. Though quite typical, they hardly indicate the broad range of subject matter that was recorded by our cameras. We filmed and photographed the breadlines, the Hoovervilles, evictions, longshoremen, taxi drivers, ex-servicemen and others in their daily existence and activities. On several occasions we rented a small theatre and showed our films to the general public. In none of these occasions did we ask our subjects or audiences to certify their affiliation with any organization before we photographed them or let them view our films. In fact, our films often stimulated the organization of unaffiliated workers.

Insofar as many of us were also unemployed workers, the active members of the Film and Photo League participated in as well as recorded the struggle against economic and social oppression.

It is a historical fact, recognized even by Mr. Rosenzweig, that most of the militant and mass actions: the demonstrations, picket lines and hunger marches of the early thirties, were organized by Communist affiliated organizations. In our early films we probably were partial to filming such events which were involved with movement and sometimes violence. Most of us were inexperienced and unsophisticated in the technical and creative aspects of documentary filmmaking, and a shot of a mass picket line or of police attacking a demonstration could make an impact without the need for more sophisticated cinematic interpretation. It was simply a matter of recording the action. As we developed our skills of filming and editing, we learned to move the camera and to film from various points of view; close-ups, high shots and low angles. We discovered the elements of editing; of creating visual tension, continuity, counterpoint and rhythm with documentary film material that was not based on narrative or dramatic acting. We learned to construct film sequences that were visually interesting and informative even though there was little inherent movement or action or dramatic continuity in the subject matter. We were then better able to record and interpret the more passive aspects of our environment and the conditions of the depression. We were able to show in our films not only what was happening but also why and how as, well as the feelings of the people who were involved.

We were stimulated not only by our direct involvement in the vital activities of the 1930s but also in our pioneering experiments and discoveries in the development of the syntax and structure of the social-documentary film. It is unlikely that the opportunities for fulfillment and creative exploration could have existed had we been restricted to filming only the organized or Communist affiliated activities.

Is it true that the Film and Photo League and its successors neglected the uncommitted and non-communist worker during the Great Depression? Bill Moyer didn't think so when in his TV series, A Walk Through the 20th Century, *he lauded the work of Seltzer and his colleagues in the 1930s. In one segment of his series, titled* The Reel World of News, *Moyer commented on the lack of reality in the commercial newsreel of the 1930s that were circulated throughout Depression America by Fox, Hearst, Paramount and the other Hollywood companies. He compared "those unrealistic and irrelevant films of beauty pageants and marathon dancers with the realistic films produced by the Film and Photo League," Seltzer wrote me recently. Moyer saw that the films produced by the League were among the only ones that spread the news of what was really going on. As if to underscore his remarks, Seltzer points out that in those times when he first showed his films to miners in Pennsylvania and to farmers in the Midwest, many viewers were made aware for the first time that the Depression was nationwide, not just a local aberration.*

I fully support Seltzer's view that the films turned out by the Film and Photo League "were effective beyond all doubt." But what a pity that the lack of funds prevented more widespread coverage, especially of the more neglected or forgotten areas of Depression America. The few films that have survived, of the many that were made, represent a priceless heritage that should be protected and defended against narrow criticism. (DP)

30 ONE MAN'S VOYAGE: IDEAS AND FILMS IN THE 1930s

Leo Hurwitz

I DON'T KNOW that I can give anything like a complete picture of the films of the thirties and the forces running through them. I am not a scholar, but a film maker. My experiences with talk and writing on events I have lived through tell me that most reconstructions of even the recent past have a large admixture of fantasy, self-justification, and the distortions of neatness and summary. Nor do they often take into account the simple fact that this past *was* present, and therefore shared the complexities and the search for simple truth that is characteristic of the current present. Much as I would like to take the time and mental wrestling to come up with a full, meaningful picture of the period, I have to forego the role of historian.

What can I do? I am an entity with continuity. I was a struggling film maker then. I am a struggling film maker now. (To make a film is to struggle.) I was moved then by certain key feelings and ideas: That art is fundamentally an extraction from experience, shaping the data of experience into an organic object that has a double life—a life of its own and an active interpenetration with the process of experience. That art/film relates to experience in wide and deep ways—not only in a sensory way but in feeling, in ideas, in meanings—in taking a thrust from the passions of life and sending thrusts into the channels of living, sometimes in crystallizing out

From *Cinema Journal,* University of Iowa (Vol. 15, No. 1, Fall 1975). Reprinted by permission of the author.

prime empathies and life-purposes. That a man, an artist, does not live alone any more than a tree docs: he is an integral part of the continuum of nature, the continuum of society, with its satisfactions, distortions, and cruelties, its struggles for human solutions. His life is bound with other men and women, nor can he help reaching for or blocking the solution of social problems. That film as a medium is unique in many ways: its relative newness, which offers the excitement of finding untried ways of expressing things; its capacity to make a *direct* route into the minds and feelings of the audience; its sense of immediacy and contemporaneity. That because of these qualities there exits the danger of what I call film chauvinism: film viewed as an art to displace all others, making poetry, painting, dancing, drama, etc., irrelevant rather than being one of many ways of stating oneself to oneself and to others, of extracting permanences from the flowing evanescence of experience. That art/film can speak truth or falsehood.

These are some of the ideas that moved me then and equally move me now. So perhaps the best thing I can do here is to try to give a feeling of the time and its work as it filtered through me and my aims as a film maker.

Let us step into 1930—the year I graduated from Harvard. The years before were the years of the post-war and then the Coolidge years of "prosperity." Prosperity hadn't touched me personally. I had worked and scholarshipped my way through college. My father, an immigrant of the turn of the century, was of a non-materialistic, idealistic, humanistic bent, and had not hooked into the mobile upwardness of business. My head was full of all kinds of marvellous things. I had heard the sorrowful prophecy of T. S. Eliot that the world was going to end not with a bang but with a whimper. I had listened to the more passionate, choiring strings of Hart Crane's "Bridge," promising a prophetic meaning to the American experience. I had steeped my eyes in the works of Cezanne, Picasso, El Greco, Van Gogh, Blake, Goya, Rembrandt, the medieval Christs suffering for all of us, of and not of the Christian tradition. I had discovered the photographs of Brady, Atget, Stieglitz, and Strand. Mencken and Lewis had put the empty babbitry of the booboisie down, as President Coolidge wore his many different hats, including Indian headdresses. He and Hoover promised an eternal era of American prosperity with more and more cars and electric toasters. The new power of advertising and public relations was still a joke to the literati. One toothpaste covered the landscape with the vital information that it comes out like a ribbon, lies flat on the brush. Another product promised relief from that specifically modern plague, B. O.—and always in parentheses (body odor). In general there was a guerrilla war between the world of art and intellect and the world of politics and business, with the guerrillas winning the war on the battlefields of books, painting, and music, and the establishment so impervious that it did not know it was being attacked. After all, the *Dial,* the *Little Review,* Stravinsky's and Schoenberg's music, the books of Hemingway, Mumford, Brooks, Frank, etc., commanded few divisions. But the *Saturday Evening Post* and the Hearst papers commanded legions in the millions. Nobody even thought of "coopting" anything or anybody, yet. The cultural rebels were outside the pale.

True, during these years, there were echoes of the savage repression of political dissent that followed World War I. One had heard of socialist legislators in New York being deprived of their elective offices, of round-ups and deportations of political agitators by Attorney General A. Mitchell Palmer. That happened in the early twenties. But later in the twenties (during the calm era of "prosperity") the two gentle anarchists, Sacco and Vanzetti, were executed. Tom Mooney was still in jail. These were judicial victims of the hysteria of a previous era. But through this whole period, there were great if remote dangers. The BOLSHEVIKS were lying in wait, characterized in political cartoons across the country as the man with long splayed whiskers carrying a round bomb the size of a balloon. Somehow the country's prosperity needed to be safeguarded from him.

I had been a student of Alfred North Whitehead at college. He himself was what he called William James, a "darling genius." His ideas penetrated all the avenues of sensibility and thought in me: especially the idea that reality is a process, that change is the heart of all experience and all ideas. All the static fixations of previous education were called into question. Somehow I fused together this aspect of

the ideas of Marx, Freud, Whitehead, and what I knew of
Einstein; they all seemed powerfully relevant to understanding the world about me as I was emerging from adolescence,
my first adolescence.

During these years I was in love with the movies. Not many
thought of this medium as an art or a potential art. It was
entertainment on a mass scale, a thriving business. It was in
the process of replacing vaudeville as the less-than-
respectable mind-circus for the masses. True, Gilbert
Seldes added it to the muses' domain in his Seven Lively
Arts, but America went to the movies as to a more engrossing juggler or acrobat. And it is quite true that most movies
were vapid public dreams, extraordinarily engrossing in their
hypnotic hold. Hollywood was perfecting the skills of mass
hypnosis. One of the great exceptions to this dreamy
wasteland for me was the work of Charlie Chaplin, which I
had seen from earliest childhood. Here I found bright humor,
beautiful fantasies of power for the powerless, the constant
surprise of imaginative pantomime, and somehow a deeply
human connection, a relevance to what one lived through
day by day. It was a different dimension for the movies. And
when one saw some films by Eisenstein, Dovzhenko,
Dreyer, Pabst, Lang, Pudovkin, the promise of the film
medium became enlarged for me beyond its power for
emptying out the head and replacing one's own fantasies
with public concoctions of violence, riches, power, speed,
and sexual fulfillment.

From all of this it is not hard to see that when the stock
market crashed in 1929, when The New York Times reported
suicides falling into the streets from Wall Street's financial
towers, I did not take it personally. My family held no financial
paper; prosperity was more of a headline than a reality to me
and I was familiar with Marx's predictions of cyclical depres-
sions under capitalism.

2

I left Cambridge in June of 1930, graduated into the
soon-to-be-felt depression. Late in my sophomore year, I
had decided film was for me. The long-held idea of becoming
a physician had evaporated. (Though underneath there may

have been an emotional connection between the idea of "healer" in the drive to be a doctor and the idea of "healer" in the new commitment to becoming a film maker . . . subtle and deep-lying . . . understandable to me now but not then.) I felt what I was *into* in college was a good preparation for making films: steepage in poetry and literature, the stuff of the Fogg and Boston museums, the mind-stimulation of philosophy and psychology, my inner skepticism of the shibboleths of the social environment, the "withness" of my eyes in all my comings and goings, the free music that was available—and movies at the Harvard Square theater, its screen sometimes pelted with eggs and tomatoes by local students, a criticism frequently justified, if not decorous. Among my fellow students there was no one I knew of who shared my interest. My friends were on their way to being writers, ballet producers, painters, scientists, lawyers, curators, bond salesmen, etc.; to them, working in films did not seem an acceptable way of life.

In the middle of my junior year, I got the notion that I needed some specific and technical training in film. Since I knew of no schools or courses in the field, I wrote—with sublime innocence —to the one man in America I wanted to apprentice myself to: Chaplin. His protectors, as I learned later, did not consider the letter of a student a practical enough matter; and after watching the mail for a few weeks I gave up the idea. I stayed where I was, assuming that the accretions of experience were my best preparations. At about this time, I got hold of Pudovkin's book, *Film Technique,* published in England. I had been struggling with discovering the language of film in the darkness of the movie theaters, extracting what I could of visible techniques from the fast flow of image and story. I got to counting the length of shots in seconds to discover the relation of cutting of rhythm, but mostly to break down the flow of the film into its parts. This was much easier to do in a bad film than in a good or a slick film. So for some films I stayed twice or came back a second time, or purposely came in in the middle so as to avoid the hypnotic pile-up of involvement.

Pudovkin's book came at me like an illumination. Here was something immediately relevant. It made clear what I was trying to get at in the desperate struggles to hold onto the fluid images on the screen, it enabled me to see the world about me as film images and put them together in my head. The germinal idea was that an image, a piece of film, was not a finality in itself, but that it took on its precise meaning and feeling only in a context, in active interaction with the shot or shots that preceded and followed it. Wow! I could now—walking, sitting in class, reading a novel —translate my experiences into imagined sequences of film images. I could work on films without camera, studio, or cutting room. And furthermore I could relate this inner secret of films to much else I had been involved in. For the idea of film strips acting on each other to transmute meaning was not so different from the impact of words on each other in a poem or what brushstrokes of different color do to each other in an impressionist painting. Also I was reading in Gestalt psychology at the time. Its idea that the experiencing of the whole is primary (the perception of the discrete parts secondary) conformed to my own experience and illuminated the Pudovkin-Kuleshov idea. Further, Whitehead's idea of "organism" also related closely: that the whole is more than the sum of its parts, a product of the inter-relatedness.

The four years at Cambridge came to an end, and I headed back to New York to discover how I could join film. There seemed to be two ways of doing it. One was to continue my self-teaching. The other was to get into the film industry. This latter I half-tried. I offered my inexperience to Merian Cooper and Ernest Schoedsack, who had made a quite beautiful documentary called *Grass,* and who were planning another expedition to the hunting wilds of Africa. I tried the shorts and feature industry in New York (Paramount had a working studio in Flushing). But apart from the difficulty of being a novice, there was a major disruption in the industry. The vast expenditure on sound equipment had put most of the large producer-distributors into the hands of the banks who had financed the capitalization. Also there was a depression on; people were staying away from the box office, even though admission to neighborhood theaters was, if memory serves, about a quarter. I say I only half-tried because I felt that the division of production into specialists of the various crafts was the way to mechanicalize the art of film making, to depersonalize it. I was after a full experience in the related crafts of camera, story, editing, sound, directing, since it appeared to me an organic film could come only from their functional relatedness. I was concerned that if I got slotted into an apprentice job, I might learn that craft well enough over the years, but be blocked from getting experience in other crafts. In any case the option was academic; there were no jobs.

When I say there were no jobs in the film business, you will have to expand the picture to the millions of recently unemployed. Shortly after I graduated there were 10, 12, 14, 16 million people without jobs—suddenly shaken loose from the much publicized "permanent prosperity" of America. The breadlines grew day by day. An army of apple sellers—recently carpenters, garment workers, sailors, storekeepers—appeared on street corners and in front of every subway station. Homeless men (where were the women? crowded into the rooms of relatives?) built shanty towns in Central Park and on the edges of the city. Shelter was pieced together from scraps of wood and tin. Food was gathered from the wastes of butcher and vegetable and bakery shops. In all of New York's seasons this Hooverville life was in the open air. But there were respectable voices, bureaucratic voices, that said these Hoovervilles were unsightly, they endangered the health of the community. So in the end, without the government undertaking to meet these needs (except by some piddling emergency relief), the Hoovervilles were bulldozed level, the men scattered. These were only some of the visible evidences of socially created misery, socially ignored. You can interpolate the unseen: the problems of food on the table, the monthly rent, shoes and clothes, the daily anxiety about getting a job, or holding one.

Being young and supple, having friends and relatives to share with, my own situation was not as rough. There were meals consisting of peanut butter without bread, eaten on a rooftop watching the New York skyline. And greasy-spoon-restaurant dinners; one hot dog, one danish, one coffee, 15¢. I shared an apartment with a poet friend. He earned an occasional freelance buck by doing posters for stores; I earned an occasional buck by doing photo portraits and other odd activities. Our apartment was open house to friends who needed to flop. The attitudes of sharing were not too different from those of young people today who have dropped into some version of communal living. (Only then we were listening to the records of Fats Waller, Duke Ellington, Count Basie, Bessie Smith, Benny Goodman, Paul Robeson, etc.)

The road I took into film was outside the film industry. It involved, on a practical level, borrowing still camera equipment and making photographs, buying in a pawnshop a Sept motion picture camera capable of shooting a cartridge of 17 (35mm) feet at 16 frames per second (17 seconds' worth of film in one load) and starting to make a film with this camera using short ends. It involved writing: ideas for short films, a feature script based on *Alice in Wonderland.* It involved of course seeing films, seeing more films, and trying to learn the language, to imagine what might be. The world of film, as distinct from the world of job-possibility, seemed very open. It involved reading *Close-Up,* an English avant garde publication which was interested in film more as an art. Writing about films and working as an assistant editor for *Creative Art.* Writing book reviews. All of this was an education in film making.

With it went associations with others who shared my passionate interest. The first of these was Jay Leyda, recently come to New York from Dayton, Ohio. He had a folder of poem-scenarios, and he was making a lyric film called *Bronx Morning.* Paul Strand I met while laying out an article on his work for *Creative Art* magazine. I was bowled over by his photographs; he was good enough to lend me a lens for a newly acquired view camera. Ralph Steiner gave me some concise and valuable lessons in still photography. Competitiveness was not an important aspect of the relationships of people interested in film. We shared what we knew. We felt tied by a kinship of meaning and aim. Underneath was the latent feeling that we and unknown cohorts were preparing to storm the citadel of commercialized, meretricious, and dehumanized art. If "storming the citadel" is too romantic a metaphor, then at least we felt we were preparing to break through the narrow frontiers of the dominant attitudes toward film.

What were these attitudes? As an art whose primary purpose was the production of commodities for massive sale, film was severely limited in (a) its subject matter, (b) the forms and techniques it explored, and (c) the relationships of the makers to their product. Factory production had for the most part substituted mechanical, committee judgment for the organic flow from the artist's experience through his skills and invention to the final shape of the product. The forms utilized were the forms that worked in the market. The occasional invention was tested only against its money-making power. The basic forms were the feature and shorts. The feature was a long short story. The shorts were comedies, newsreels, animated cartoons, travelogues—largely stereotyped. Any experiential stuff not containable in these well-tried forms was excluded, exiled to the other arts. The subject matter was based on the surrogate fulfillment of the simple wish. If workers were crowded into incommodious cities and towns or coal mines and steel mills, the movies gave them public dreams of the freedom of western plains, mountains, and deserts. If living was tight and massively ordered, what could break through these oppressive barriers better than the bank robber, the horse-riding gunman, the cool gangster—the man who determined his own fate with the tools of violence. Beautiful clothes, women, and men in palatial sets were the dream inoculations against the daily grinding of life. The formula of boy-wants-girl through the plot's obstructions to boy-gets-girl became the screen meta-phor, the dream-wish answer to all problems. Come to the movies and we'll lay out your dream for you.[1] The well-nurtured passivity of the audience—hypnotized, narcotized, tickled, masssaged, siren-serenaded—was the desired re-sult. It created the addiction of movie-going, the cycle of box office intake.

3

The depression was going on, deepening day by day. My feelings about the art of the movies were inevitably affected. This social crisis—which began in the headlines with the bottom dropping out of the stock market, with bank failures, with suicides of speculators—became an enveloping phe-nomenon, seeping into the bones. For a while the words of President Herbert Hoover comforted some: Prosperity is right around the corner. But the happy future was receding. Piled furniture on the streets more frequently met the eye. The skilled tailor-uncle, always jolly and confident, became silent to hide his distress. People used empty storefronts to set up organizations of the unemployed. Demands began to be heard: work relief, unemployment insurance, social security. There was some marching with placards to City Hall. There were "penny sales" of bankrupt farms in which the neighbors kept bankers from taking them over. All of which was unusual and unAmerican. The veterans of World War I marched to Washington and camped in tents and shanties, demanding that their promised bonuses be paid for their war service. General Douglas MacArthur cleared them out with tear gas, setting flames to their temporary city.

What happens when you put your hand in your pocket, and you can count there your total savings—and you don't know how the contents of the pocket are going to be renewed? What happens is that it stirs the mind. Rumblings in the belly become rumblings in the head. Moreover, your life is revealed not as the private thing it seemed before. It is connected with others who share your problems. The people-continuum began to be restored. One began to be aware that it was always there, though fractured by daily pressures, by such social shibboleths as individual enterprise, dog-eat-dog, another day another dollar, new world of opportunity, a man's poverty is his own fault, a man's property is his own doing.

Thousands of people, among them artists, were confronted with a suddenly clear contradiction. This America we were living in—with factories, farms, and technical skills—had the capability of feeding, clothing, sheltering everyone with adequate security. At that very moment people were widely hungry, insecure. Their labor was being wasted. In the early thirties the radical dislocations of the world led people to face the dislocations in the structure of society. There was something wrong—deeply wrong.

A lot of people became radicalized. (Radical: meaning the root of things.) I was one of them. This did not happen in one fell swoop. The daily questionings made one add up what lay unrelated in corners of the mind: a system of society was helpless in respect to the human havoc it created; its prime concern was money and property, not people. The government responded at a snail's pace to human needs, with resistance even to massive and unusual pressures. We were forced to go beyond the daily detail to central forces, to try to grasp something of the whole. At a time when all "isms"—socialism, collectivism, communism—were suspect and unAmerican, one had to ask whether that other "ism," capitalism, was a viable form of social living. And clearly it was not for huge numbers of people. Marx, Engels, Lenin, Debs, DuBois, Frederick Douglass—men whose works were not even of serious interest to scholars in the previous decade—became relevant again. To interpret what one saw and lived through day by day, it became necessary to study again, to study the reality around one and the ideas with which to grasp hold of this reality.[2]

As one went to the movies there was little that reflected what was happening to people, to their bodies and minds. Occasionally a newsreel shot of an unemployment demonstration or the bonus march, always with a protective commentary to take the meaning out of the event. Once in a while a breadline, an apple seller—so handled to extract its sentimentality, to dissociate it from causation. Mostly the newsreels had the usual "news dictated" events: Babe Ruth hitting a home run, a flooding storm in the Florida keys, the launching of a battleship, a beauty contest, and the like. The feature films ran on as before, though at this time they were wrestling with the static and talky qualities which had come in with sound. Boy was still winning girl, still in rich surroundings; the cattle rustler was still being mean, the steel safe still being fingered by deft gloved hands, the gangster still getting a belly full of lead... What I remember of this period that had connection was the early Marx Brothers comedies with their zany put-down of respectability and arbitrary social order.

I had heard of the Film and Photo League, an organization interested in reflecting the content of events which did not show up in the commercial media. Its point of view: the commercial media were basically propagandistic, intended to lull, to stifle articulate need and protest. Ordinary people could use film and photography with more relevance and purpose than the professionals. The League chiefly covered news events, filling in where the newsreel did not go.

Because it was not interested in converting news into spectacular entertainment but rather in revealing the reality, with the purpose of arousing people to action, the Film and Photo League began to deal with events in what might be called essay form rather than as dissociated fragments of camera-recording, the conventional form of the newsreel. There was at this time no such thing as documentary studies of current events in America, although we had seen exciting documentary films from the Soviet Union and pre-Hitler Germany. I joined the League and was soon involved in photographing the Hunger March in the spring of 1932, and then, in very few days, editing the footage into a four-reel film called *Hunger 1932.*

The work of the Film and Photo League was crude. But it had energy derived from a real sense of purpose, from doing something needed and new, from a personal identification with subject matter. When homeless men were photographed in doorways or on park benches, feeling guided the viewfinder. The world had to be shown what its eyes were turned away from. When an anti-Nazi demonstration was covered on the Brooklyn docks, the cameraman was daringly close to the mounted cops who were dragging demonstrators by their coat collars and running them down the street. This was an image with a felt point of view: the fine efficient brutality of the police-horsemen, an identification with people trying to express their anger at the arrival of the first Nazi envoy to America.

It had happened before and would happen again. People not professionally trained in films would be seized by the potency of the medium, would apply to it a passionate purpose and thereby bring to it something new, something electric. The great mystique of craft was being dissipated. You didn't have to apprentice yourself for years to people with guarded secrets in order to become a cameraman, editor, or director. With desire and zest one could learn the learnable—by practice, by study, by having ideas in one's head, feelings that demanded to be expressed. By working with others.

The Film and Photo League was what was called a "mass organization," made up of a variety of dues-paying members. Film work was assigned on the basis of someone volunteering to do it. By and large this brought out those with the greatest interest and the greatest capacity. But the organization was loose, and over the long run there was insufficient accumulation of skill, insufficient continuity of production, insufficient exploration of the medium. So we organized classes to teach ourselves elements of camerawork, lighting, image-thinking, editing. We were our own teachers, there being among us individuals with different amounts of experience in various areas. The class sessions were improvised and experimental. At the same time, with bits of money donated by such people as Sidney Howard, the playwright, and used for buying film stock and processing, some of us continued to make short films. There was no money to pay the film makers. I made a film on the Scottsboro Case. Nine young blacks had been rounded up on a freight train and falsely prosecuted for rape; it was one of the early and celebrated cases dramatizing racism. I made a film called *Sweet Land of Liberty* on the harassment of dissenters. The commercial film companies barely touched these themes (when they did, it was without insight or with distortion). But there were individuals in the management who made available to us relevant stock footage at little cost. It turned out that the newsreel companies had remarkable footage shot by their cameramen which never saw the light of the silver screen.

After a while it became clear to some that we needed something more focused and more concentrated if this seed of revolutionary film was to grow. The core of talented and vitally interested people needed continuity of study and production—to develop as film makers—to make films of greater impact and depth. This kind of pressure was felt also in the other arts, and it met with sectarian resistance: We're trying to build a people's film, theater, dance; you can't introduce elitism, a professional isolation. We tried to make the point that an art takes deep involvement, continual search, as well as an identification with the living needs of people.

In the end a group of us, unable to convince the executive committee that such a development was feasible within the League, formed a transitional small organization called Nykino; the "Ny" stood for New York. We gathered to us

some newcomers—a musician, a poet, a publicity man, a
bookseller, a social worker—all eager to move into the
extraordinary medium of film—proceeding again to study
and to make films, with new energy and, as we hoped, on a
new artistic level. I was the only paid member of the group:
$15 per week, equal to the salary I had been earning as film
and managing editor of *New Theatre Magazine*. The others
had outside jobs or were on work-relief. We earned money
for my salary and for our film work by doing still photographs
for *Harpers Bazaar* and other publications. One of the group
had a grant from a small foundation to make experimental
films. He had shot footage for several of these, was stuck on
their structuring. With relish I edited and completed them:
Harbor Scenes, Quarry, Pie in the Sky.

4

All this was going on in the years 1931 to 1935: What was
going on in the world?

In the U.S., Roosevelt had been elected in a massive
rejection of the Hoover do-nothing policy; Roosevelt responded with action to ameliorate economic conditions.
Work-relief programs, legislation to stabilize the banks, laws
recognizing the right of labor to organize, aid to farmers,
pump-priming of the economy. Internationally, fascism was
becoming a monumental danger, with Hitler coming to power
in Germany—the third, most efficient fascist state. For those
who could see it—any many could not —the Nazi solution to
the crisis of capitalism threatened cataclysm for the world.

Radical political thinking became international. The events
at home and the events of the world were clearly interrelated. My own deep involvement in politics meant that I
focused on the development of a film form that would reflect
the content of our lives—films that would affect people in
their view of themselves, of the world. You can call this
propaganda, so long as you don't equate propaganda for this
with propaganda for that, so long as you evaluate the "this"
and the "that" in terms of human value and experiential
content. I had not lost my interest in the fiction film, but I was
preoccupied with the documentary. (The term was new, and
never satisfactory.)

We had seen films in the documentary/realistic tradition from the Soviet Union—films by Dziga Vertov, Dovzhenko, Eisenstein, Pudovkin, Barnet . . . we had seen *Turksib* and others. We also began to see films from England: *North Sea, Night Mail.* I found the Russian films eloquent and the British films pale, though well-formed.

The difference had to do with the passion in the interior that spoke through the filmic devices. The Russians were treating climactic human content with deep concern. The English were using their content in the service of creating a new film form, loving the textural values of real places and faces, solving problems of structure and the use of sound. It was the difference between Goya and Gainsborough (maybe Hogarth), between Orozco and Raoul Dufy. Unlike the Russians, whom they learned from, the English were not letting their minds and hearts move into the deeper layers of their experience. The Russians were turning over a world—inner and outer.

We were moving on our own tack, considering neither as archetype, but more stimulated by the Russians. I was fascinated by the mosaic character of film, by the capacity of documentary film to extract fragments out of the matrix of a visual-sound reality, then to weave these fragments into a form very different from the reality but capable of rendering the meaning and feeling of the real event. From this point of view, the documentary film was anything but a document. It did not "document" reality at all. Its tiny documents in the form of shots and sounds bore the same relation to the film as the small pieces of colored stone and glass to the mosaic mural, the brush-strokes to the painting, the individual words and phrases to the novel. The stuff was document, but the construction was invented, a time-collage. And it was clear that the question of *truth or lie* lay not in the stuff you were using but in the thoughts, responsibility, empathy of the film maker and his capacity to shape a form which could tell . . . how much of the truth? This responsibility and empathy were not different from the truth or lie of the fiction film or any other art.

And so I got to hate the word documentary (though I never devised a better), and later hated with even more vehemence the words cinéma vérité to describe films that had little vérité to them. In the thirties, documentary was a dirty word for a long while. Distributors looked at you with the expression: Who needs it? That was mild. In some quarters it was equivalent to "red." After a while it became respectable, even commercial.

Another aspect of the documentary film that interested me was the problem of structure. If you thought of a documentary as a journalistic form, as being about something, a report on something, then you used the structure of the event as the basic form, or you constructed it like a news story or essay with words to swing you along from topic to topic. And you could hop it up with the voice of God like "The March of Time." You could hop it up with fast cutting and sensational events. You could hop it up by saving your most spectacular sequence to the end. But in any case, the basic connection was the *"and"* connection: this happened "and" then that, this idea "and" then that.

But if you wanted to create an experience with your film, an experience in itself which could move people or stir them to ideas and action, then the journalistic form with its primary "and" connectives was very limited. What was needed was a principle of growth, enabling the film to grow out of its parts into a whole, much as a plot functions in a fiction film. One needed in the documentary film an equivalent of plot, with connectives of "but," "against," "despite," "growing into." The key to this, we found, was that a sequence had not merely to describe or relate but to create a *need* in the audience, as in a fiction film, by identification with the characters, a feeling of want or anxiety is created in the audience. Then one could look at the structure of a film and design it—with image and word and sound —as a chain of interactive needs progressing toward a resolution. If you were handling ideas, then your ideas would also have to be woven into this progression of needs.

5

During the Nykino period, which was a time of production and study and a preparation for more intensive production, Joris Ivens came from Holland with his films, among them *New Earth.* His point of view about film and about the conditions of our world were similar to our own. A friendship grew. His longer experience, his persistent devotion to holding the line as an independent film maker, was an important stimulation to us in our struggle, a stimulation toward setting up the conditions for full-time production of independent films in America.

During this period, Paul Strand came back from Mexico, having completed *The Wave*. When he heard what we were up to, he joined us with enthusiasm, putting aside for some years his single-minded devotion to still photography. This set the basis for a long and rewarding collaboration between us. Also during this period, Pare Lorentz had made arrangements for a film on the dust bowl with the Resettlement Administration. He approached us to prepare an outline for the film, which we did. In 1935, Strand, Steiner, and I set out for Wyoming, Montana, and Texas to photograph it. This became the first of Lorentz' series of remarkable, independent films: *The Plow That Broke the Plains*. In our script thinking on this film, we had our first full opportunity to put into practice the ideas we had been germinating: the translation of meanings into images, the fusion of images into sequence-wholes, the dramatic structuring of a documentary film on the basis of a chain of needs into a time-growing totality. We wanted our films to possess at the same time a progression of emotion and a close and true relationship to the events and their causes, direct and submerged.

When we returned from the west, we set to moving Nykino into a new stage: an independent production company with day-to-day continuity and with a full-time staff. We had the interest of artists, writers, trade union people, people in the city government, etc. There was a strong interest in the "new film," and a strong community among intellectuals, progressive and "left"—a strong enthusiasm for an emerging culture, opening up stereotyped forms, digging into the content of living experience, pulling up the blinds of isolated art-oriented art, making real connections with people. Artists and writers and others joined our launching—as advisers, supporters—from John Dos Passos to Lillian Hellman, Joseph Freeman, Harold Clurman, Ben Shahn, Archibald Macleish, and others.

We formed Frontier Films. Frontier Films was a non-profit company devoted to making films that touched the realities of American life, and subjects relevant to these realities. We wanted to make films outside the current market, where film was a commodity whose primary intention was to make a profit. We thought of films as a medium of conveying experience and insight. We proposed, in the process, to enlarge and deepen the expressive values and techniques of the art. We were young and confident. The confidence arose from two things: the existing constriction of the medium which asked for new ideas, and the generating power imbedded in having something important to say, deeply felt and deeply needed. Our underlying belief was that the penetration of real experience and a substratum of real feelings were prime energies for art.

Nevertheless, it would be necessary to have money for rent, for raw stock and processing, for production expenses, cutting rooms, screenings, and a subsistence level for the staff. Thirty-five dollars a week, applied equally regardless of different responsibilities and efforts, was what we paid ourselves, but many weeks went by without salary. We raised money primarily from richer individuals, who felt what we were doing was important and who could take advantage of tax deductions, and also by undertaking to make sponsored films which said what we wanted to say. Our own unpaid work-time—and the minimally paid work of actors, composers, and others who wanted to work with us—was the chief contributor to our financing.

Distribution was something we would have to break through. In the theaters there was block-booking and therefore control by the major production companies. Independent films, especially in a new form and with social content, didn't have a chance in the national circuits. The 16mm market was far more limited than it is today. We counted on an expansion of the 16mm market to the new and vital trade unions, clubs, church groups, progressive organizations, and perhaps some colleges. We hoped also to build up an independent theatrical distribution based on independently owned neighborhood theaters, in areas where a demand for our films could be stimulated. We were aware that we were tackling a vastly difficult job; we were prepared to struggle.

We began to open up these fields, but our larger objective was never achieved.

In addition to Paul Strand, Ralph Steiner, and myself, the basic production group included Lionel Berman, Sidney Meyers, Irving Lerner, Willard Van Dyke, Jay Leyda, David Wolff, and later, Arnold Perl. Steiner and Van Dyke dropped away early. Others like Michael Gordon, Elia Kazan, Ricky Leacock, Herbert Kline, Henri Bresson, Marc Blitzstein, Paul Robeson, Hans Eisler, Howard da Sylva, Art Smith, etc., worked with us on specific projects.

Some of our films, the main ones, were: *The World Today* (two episodes, *Sunnyside* and *Black Legion*), *Heart of Spain, People of the Cumberland, China Strikes Back, Return to Life, White Flood, Native Land.* They were not even in their qualities, but they did pioneer a new film form. They were truly independent, nonconformist. They were bold in subject matter and treatment. They provided a key stimulus to a growing generation of film makers on the fringes of the film industry in the growing "documentary" field and in Hollywood. They were responsive to important aspects of the human experience and the underlying forces of the time.

There isn't space to tell about each of these films. The final production, *Native Land,* was the longest one and had the fullest production. It introduced a new feature form weaving together enacted stories and documentary episodes. The function of the technique was to bring together seemingly unrelated events into the real coherence they possessed and so dramatize underlying forces and conflict. It added up in practice the years of study and experiment in film.

There were no computers or electronic memory banks in these years from 1931 to 1941 (when Frontier Films was disbanded because of the war), but this activity did earn for some of us labels of "reds," "fellow-travellers," "premature anti-fascists," and it did earn the watchful eye of Congressional and state committees eager to ferret out the practice of inalienable rights; it did set the hunters of the FBI to compiling dossiers. It put former colleagues in the position where they could scare a film project in their direction by dropping the rumor that so-and-so was a red. It did provide material for blacklists before, during, and after the McCarthy period.

Nevertheless for me this was a great school of struggle and film making. It set important vectors for my life: to enjoy the struggle for worth, to be oneself (at the same time as one is responsive to other people's needs), to shoulder off the pressures to conform, to find one's own sense of truth. It gave me a deep-lying conviction that social and individual predicaments are amenable to solution—that the changes and contradictions we live through can go beyond despair and alienation. And it confirmed my feeling that I belonged in the conspiracy of art (against socially dictated modes of perception, feeling, thinking), which is part of the larger and continuing conspiracy to be human.

NOTES

1. The dream-wish is still the most frequent manipulative device of commercial advertising on TV. The thing—the purchasable thing—pain killer, deodorant, detergent, savings account, antacid, car, etc.—is the answer to all of life's need. And what we used to call the conversion ending is still the prime determinant of all those little movies whose purpose is to get you to buy all those little things, without which life is impossible. We still go for it; we still suffer it. And as far as the big movies are concerned, with their tendency to reverse the simple dream-wish into the negation of dream-hope—maybe it's really the same thing in a complicated way. So that when you hit the street (the street which, before you saw the movie, was filled with terror and despair) it is now a welcome place compared to the tortures and terrors you experienced empathically in the movie. As Freud said, the dream holds its complex contradictory secrets.
2. While writing, I have been thinking about why people become radical and stay radical, or on the other hand why their thoughts and feelings disappear from their lives. Your life moves along on its own track. Your connections with family and a few others are sufficient. Then out of the pressure of circumstances and ideas, your life becomes more widely connected. You understand you are inextricably threaded into your environment. (The fish suddenly understands that it needs the sea to live and breathe.) The self is connected to others known and unknown. Why does the environment create the conditions of rich and poor? Why wars? Why oppression of less developed peoples? Why are the prisons so brutalized and filled with the poor, the blacks, the Puerto Ricans? Why, when the adequate means of living are socially feasible, are so many people deprived? There seems to be an earthquake fault in social relationships. The you put your finger on it: as in other historic eras (where it is easier to see) economic and social relationships have

been outlived but they are fought for and persisted in by people who have the property, power, and privilege.

Well, now you have "dangerous thoughts" in your head. The FBI, your neighbor, the UnAmerican Activities Committee, your colleagues, the newspaper, radio, TV may label them "red." But the empathy you have discovered, your connection with others, is real, to be denied at the risk of losing much of your humanity. You may find your comrades not exactly as selfless as you thought. You may commit yourself to specific loyalties without adequate information, on the basis of your general push and understanding. But you hold on to what you know.

Now the pressures against nonconformity pile up. Along with success, with a good job, do you break the link of empathy, neutralize your ideas and feelings, because there is privilege to protect or to gain? In my short lifetime, I have seen many who did this, including good friends, when the pressure of blacklists, FBI, and committee harassment piled up. For them, the judgment that "I was wrong or misled in my estimate of Stalin or the local political line" became an excuse to erase the feeling of human community, a device to cease the continual search for new answers, as change shifts the facts of living again and again. What is sad in this, as I look back, is the defection from self.

31   JORIS IVENS' *SPANISH EARTH* (1937)

Otis Ferguson

TOP PLACE IN IMPORTANCE for the week goes to the set of pictures [*Spanish Earth*] Joris Ivens brought back from Madrid area and has finally got edited, scored for music, and ready to go. His camera was in the fields, the rocking streets of the city, behind redoubts and with the tanks, sometimes in the advancing front line. He got as much of it as he could under such difficulties, sizing up not only perspective, sufficiency of lighting, the best points of shelter and focus, sizing up as well how each thing would fit with his idea. Then he took what he had and worked out his idea through it.

There are two simple themes: the suffering and dogged purposefulness of war for the cause: and the bulk and onward motion of the cause itself—the earth and its rightful function and what the chance to use and irrigate it will bring forth for men to eat, and how they will not be denied now at last even if they have to die for it. The film opens on the husbandry of the countryside, the look and meaning of the land. A spoken comment rushes in here to assume the unestablished, its faulty cuing presently demonstrated by the ease with which the film brings about the contrast in its own terms. Over the loaves of bread from the ovens, the war posters look down, and over the ordered fields and fruit trees the sound of firing comes to end the first sequence, the explosions growing louder, still unseen.

From Robert Wilson's *The Film Criticism of Otis Ferguson* © 1971. Published by Temple University. Reprinted by permission of Temple University Press.

Then the defense of Madrid, the ravages within the city, the fighting itself, rifle and machine-gun fire from the gaunt shells of buildings, field-pieces in the orchard, citizens lined up to drill and become soldiers, soldiers lined up for attack or for soup, scattered in sleep or sniping positions or over newspapers. In the trenches as in the city life goes on, precarious but familiar, a strange world of death and strenuous doing, yet somehow the same, people clinging to their songs and houses, and in the fields there is yeoman work on the ditches and rude aqueducts: much of the old machine is down or silent but the life processes go on and a new machinery must be set up. And over all this, the strangeness itself becomes a part of routine, the heightened tempo of trucks hammering up with soldiers, the big planes out of the cloud somewhere, and the air full of plaster dust, stretchers, and ambulances by the door.

Though the camera never seems to get near enough the business end of things to catch the fearful symbol of the enemy or telltale thinning of the line (one figure falls; for the rest we get a particular group, the scream of a shell on the sound-track, and cut to a stock explosion), the picture is definitely on the side of the harsh truth, for there are plenty of close-ups of violent death after the fact, and the comment is beautifully explicit on the price men will pay—that advance in echelons of six, the six becoming five and the four three, and this is the way they go into action, not with trumpets. Yet one of the most convincing things about it is its abstention from bombast and sloganism.

Much of the carrying power in understatement should be credited to Ernest Hemingway's commentary. His voice doesn't come over too well, and what with his suggestion of some overrehearsed WNEW announcer in an embarrassment it isn't vintage Hemingway; but with his knowledge and quiet statements of the odds against survival, that feeling for the people of Spain which comes from his heart, the combination of experience and intuition directing your attention quietly to the mortal truth you might well have missed in the frame, there could hardly be a better choice.

But the rest of the credit goes to Ivens and his unquenchable feeling for the life of people, at war or at work. He might have found a way around the sort of scene where "natural" people are not natural at all but stiff and uneasy, and he skimped a little. But what he has brought back is convincing as the real thing, sparing neither cause nor effect, talking straightly as a man should talk. There are beautiful shots of ruin against the sky, and of the rise of native hills under it. There are no razzmatazz of angles, trick dissolves, symbols as such. He has saved for the last the advance that took the bridge and the running comment of symbol-in-fact represented by the completion of the business that loosed the water over the parched waiting land—but the whole film has been built up toward these two things, not just around them as spectacle. And though it is not a great film, it has been made so that somehow the power and meaning of its subject matter are there to feed the imagination of those who have any.

It isn't so much in the outward drama of the attack, the rattling trucks and tanks, breastworks and machine-gun placements and range-finders. These things are here but subordinated to a purpose, which is recorded in this camera simply because it is there in Ivens' and Hemingway's people—the serene grim cast of feature or carriage of the body, the fine figure of a man who comes up to address his brigade or parliamentary body. Men for the most part whose clouds of doubt and petty worry have burned off before a confident power imposing its symmetry from within. Relaxed, haggard, or plain dirty, one after another is seen on the screen going through his heavy job as though in very token of the fact that a million or ten thousand or even fifty such cannot be wrong. There is no need for vilification and babble of glory here; showing the Spanish land and the people related to it, the film does not have to raise its voice to be undeniable, its report a plain testimonial to the way men can be lifted clear beyond themselves by the conception of and full response to the epic demand of their time.

32 FIFTY YEARS OF POLITICAL FILMMAKING: AN INTERVIEW WITH JORIS IVENS

Deborah Shaffer

JORIS IVENS HAS BEEN MAKING documentary films for over fifty years and his political commitment has led him to make films in countries throughout the world, including the Soviet Union *(Komsomol)*, the U.S. *(The Power and the Land)*, Spain *(Spanish Earth)*, Australia *(Indonesia Calling)*, Poland *(Peace Will Win)*, East Germany *(Song of the Rivers)*, France *(Far from Vietnam)*, Italy *(Italy Is Not a Poor Country)*, Cuba *(An Armed People)*, Chile *(A Valparaiso)*, Vietnam *(The 17th Parallel)*, Laos *(The People and Their Guns)*, and China *(How Yukong Moved the Mountains)*, amongst others. At the time of this interview, Ivens, at the age of 85, was making plans for a new documentary to be shot in Italy.

Deborah Shaffer, who conducted this interview with Ivens last year at his Paris apartment, is herself a filmmaker with a special interest in political documentaries, having directed such films as *The Wobblies* (co-directed with Stewart Bird), *Nicaragua: Report from the Front,* and, most recently, *Witness to War: An American Doctor in El Salvador.*

Cinéaste: You've been making your kind of films, documentaries about real people and real places, for close to fifty years.
Joris Ivens: Fifty-two, to be precise.

From *Cinéaste* (Vol. 14, No. 1, Spring, 1985). Reprinted by permission of the editors.

Cinéaste: The question is, how do you manage to support your productions year after year? It must have meant tremendous sacrifices, because there's rarely been money for this kind of film.

Ivens: Well, if you want to stay independent and work freely you have to make certain sacrifices, but you can't generalize and say where the money is coming from because each film is different. Take, for example, 1936 in Spain, when General Franco attacked the Republic. He was supported by Hitler and Mussolini, and it was the beginning of the Second World War for us. We saw it coming. So, at that moment, all over the world, an anti-fascist feeling arose, and it was in this stream of anti-fascist feeling—as you maybe experienced a stream of anti-Vietnam war feeling—in this stream of history one finds possibilities. I hadn't been long in the U.S., but we got a group of well-known people together, like Lillian Hellman and Archibald MacLeish, and asked for contributions. When we had $2,000 I bought film stock, asked the cameraman I had worked with before [John Ferno—ed.] to

Joris Ivens. Photo by Larry Bogdanow.

come along, and off we went. We took a great risk, but we knew that people would support us and send more money. The whole film at that time cost about $18,000 for fifty minutes in black and white.

Cinéaste: That was a lot of money at that time.
Ivens: Yes, but the film was still cheap. We didn't take any salaries—myself, John Ferno, Lillian Hellman, the musician Virgil Thompson, Hemingway, the editor Helen Van Dongen—because it was a film for a cause. We worked for the same reasons as the boys in the Lincoln Brigade. That's very rare, but I use it as an extreme example. Then I returned to the United States and had no money or work anymore. Through Pare Lorentz, who knew my work, I was offered a commission to do a film for the rural electrification program. Because it was for the government, certain things had to be in it and certain things left out. So one really doesn't have free will and is rather limited, but well paid.

Later, when I was back in Europe, there were real commissioned films. There was a man called Mattei in Italy who was the head of the state gas and petroleum industry which was fighting against a kind of American monopoly. It was kind of state capitalism, advanced state capitalism if you like, and he asked me to do a film about it. He told me what they wanted, but because I already had a certain reputation they allowed me some freedom. I said I wanted to do it mostly in a documentary form, but with some fantasy, and not plain propaganda.

Usually when a young filmmaker has to take commissions they are very limited. They practically tell you what to do, and if you have any imagination or do anything experimental they say, "Oh no, that's not it." But when I began the form for industrials was not nearly so well established. When I made the film for Philips Radio, which was well paid, I made enough to live on for six months and make the film *Borinage,* because I lived very simply and had no family. After *Borinage,* I had nothing. Happily I was invited to go back to the Soviet Union and do a film there. So, there are always periods where you have practically no work, where you can't plan and have no security because there's no regular salary. When I made *La Seine a recontré Paris,* the whole group received a small regular salary which provided a kind of security. But sometimes, for instance in a war, it's quite different. When you go to a place like Vietnam, you risk your life—not for sensation, not to make money. We did it because we thought someone had to bring out the truth as we see it, that these people had the right to fight against American aggression. So there you have part of the answer—ideology helps you to make the difficult films, and even to face the risks you have to take in your life.

Cinéaste: But weren't there times when you felt like giving it up, and saying this is too hard?
Ivens: Well, yes, but still I never gave up. If I had been in a worse situation, I would have given up because I'm not 100 percent a hero, you know. But because I also had the stimulus of an ideological point of view, aside from a purely personal, artistic one, it kept me going. If you make a film about Spain, or about a liberation movement in China, you have something to say, and also a great responsibility, to the people you film and to the millions of other people who will see it. That maybe helped me sometimes to overcome the tiredness, the feeling that it's too difficult. I always had something I could work for. It's more difficult now for the independent filmmaker. I'm not even talking about the militant filmmaker, or the political filmmaker, but the independent filmmaker. In a sense, we're small artisans in a big industry.

When we want to work, we always need money—ten minutes of film is already $10,000. If you're a painter with an idea, boom!, with $50 for paint you can begin with no risk. But filmmakers need an immediate investment, so it makes us different from other artists. We have the same needs for expression as dancers, painters or musicians, but we also have more difficulties. It's not because we *want* money, but our means of expression requires it. So, when you ask me how I got through all these things, at certain times it was easier, sometimes more difficult, sometimes I went without work. I was very sad in Hollywood at one point. I had returned there after the Spanish Civil War, and I had some friends, but no work. In a center of 50,000 people working on their own films, I was unemployed, and it was difficult for me. I thought,

"What the hell, I'll take another job . . . become a sailor or something, because I like sailing." That's one of the hardest problems facing filmmakers today, how to keep going from film to film, and how far to go in compromising—compromising in an ideological and in an artistic sense.

Cinéaste: Did you ever have to compromise?

Ivens: Certainly, in several films. Sometimes the compromise is that you don't really want to make a film, but you do it because you have to eat. Sometimes you have to compromise in the film itself. When I made the film for Philips Radio in 1933, I said that I wanted liberty and they said, "OK within the factory itself, but you can't go out and show how the workers live at home." I had to think about it, but I said OK. I was young and I had to work. It was the first time I could use sound, so it gave me an opportunity to learn something. But I didn't compromise in the sense that I didn't do at all what they wanted in the factory. They wanted to show how wonderful and technically advanced it was, but I showed the conveyor belts and what it means to a worker to be there for eight hours like machines. In principle, you should try not to compromise. When they said they wanted to show the triumph of Philips and how it was the most wonderful factory in the world, I said, "No, I don't think you are, and I can't do it, even if you pay me." But sometimes when a young man has a family and kids, he can't be too tough. But in my life I saw that if you begin to compromise on your philosophy or what you believe in, then you're headed in a dangerous direction.

Cinéaste: Were there also conflicts between your work as a film artist and your ideology as a political filmmaker?

Ivens: First of all, I'm not always a 'political filmmaker,' as people have labeled me. I always tried to stay out of party politics. When I make a film it's from a freer perspective of Marxism—the fight for liberty, for the right of people, big ideological ideas made concrete in one place. Sometimes I make films that are not political at all, like *Le Mistral,* a film about the wind in Southern France. When I showed it, some people on the left said, "Yes, but what's the political sense of it?" I said, "Whatever you like, the wind can be the revolution, or love for your wife, or anything." In my life there have been two forces that motivated me—the artistic, the professional, and the other is the ideological motivation, the understanding that a certain film is necessary at a certain moment. I never would have gone to Spain in '36 if there hadn't been a war. It wouldn't have occurred to me. I was happy to be in the States. But suddenly you have to give everything up and you go. It becomes part of your life, and the best films for me are when they overlap each other.

Cinéaste: Are there also compromises between art and politics?
Ivens: Yes, sometimes a film can be too political. Take, for instance, the first film I made in Vietnam. *Le Ciel, La Terre.* It's a short film where I wanted to wave the flag and say, "Look at these courageous, heroic people who are fighting there." Then, when I came back and showed it—because I always follow my films with the public—they said, "Yes, it's all very well, but how do they live? What does it mean? Are they heroic every day?" I said, "No, maybe on some days not at all, and other days they're heroic without knowing it." They said, "Why don't you show that?" So then I made *The 17th Parallel.*

Another important factor in the documentary is that you must have complete mutual confidence between the people that you film and yourself. You can't just arrive with a camera and film on the first day. Sometimes I spend a week where I don't even use the camera, and just get to know people. Have a whiskey together, make friends, and then begin to film. The quality that is always admired in my films is that the people are always alive, always real, and not self-conscious in front of the camera. That's because they know *why* I'm making the film, and that I'm not making money on their backs. When you get to know them you have the same worries, or, in a war, the same risks. Then you get a film that has great quality.

It's a more difficult way to work. When I filmed the Parkinsons in Ohio in 1940 for *Power and the Land,* I lived with the family for three months. In the beginning I stayed in town, and it wasn't working well. After four days the farmer said, "Dutchy, it's better that you live in our house, because then you can make it better." Then, you see, I was happy. In the end, you're more worried about his crop, and he's worried about the film [laughs]. That's very extreme, but it's real.

Cinéaste: Within each film, were there times when you felt that one scene was maybe more beautiful, but you felt you had to choose another because of the information in it?
Ivens: In that case, I'm not in favor of being 100 percent perfectionist, especially not in a formal sense. There are some filmmakers who are such perfectionists that if they didn't get a scene right the first time, they'll do the whole thing over, state it. I think that's false. You have to be so *keen* doing the work that you do the best you can, but if you didn't get everything because of the sunlight, or you're counting on something and the people don't show up, then you have to compromise in terms of content and form. You have to try as an artist to find the means to express what you want to say, but not to worry afterwards that it could have been better. If you're that much of a perfectionist, it's difficult, and you don't make many films.

Once you're in the editing room with what's been filmed, you have nothing more to do with the reality outside. You have in that room your material, and that's your reality. It's like a sculptor who cuts a stone to make a head. If he cuts a piece where the nose should be, he's lost, but the stone is what he has to work on. So you shouldn't think, "Oh, but in reality I should have done this." No 'should have done,' because then you're lost. You have to be clever during the shooting period, and have a unit that is with you. If you've done the best you can do, then don't worry. After the shooting, there's nothing more to do. Your new reality is the filmed material, and *that* you have to shape.

Cinéaste: Do you think that any one stage of the process is more critical than another, say between pre-production and shooting and editing?
Ivens: No. I think every stage is important. If you make a mistake in the original conception, you can never correct it in brilliant shooting, for example. You can perhaps fool your public and yourself for a time, but not in the long run. Of course, it also depends on your talent. Many people are more talented

in shooting, or editing, but that's the wonderful thing about our work. It's not an individual art, like painting or poetry. It's an art that, I wouldn't call it collective, but it involves a group or a team. A collective is something different.

When we did the film about Laos, *The People and Their Guns,* we tried, with the ideas of '68, to make it a collective, with ten people around the cutting table discussing and then voting where to make the cut [chuckles]. It's interesting to do once in your life. In China I learned a lot about what collective work really is. It doesn't mean a false democracy, or voting on everything, or that the majority is always right. It is more that everybody should bring his utmost potentiality to the film, but at a certain moment decisions have to be made by one person. Of course, that person has to have the confidence of everyone else. I myself went too far in thinking of this as a collective art, and that everyone could do everything and have his say and it would work. But I don't like the kind of filmmaking where one person is a genius and knows everything and everyone has to follow him. I don't like to work like that. I think of it more as a soccer team, where the left forward is as important as the goalkeeper, and they all contribute. A good documentary director has to be a person who brings the team together.

Cinéaste: How big a group do you usually work with?
Ivens: In general there's a nucleus of six or seven, plus translators for another language. But it can even be done by two.

Cinéaste: That's very small compared to Hollywood or television.
Ivens: Yes, but you don't want to disturb people in their daily lives. When I want to make something very intimate with a family, there are only three of us in the room. We never use a clapboard or anything like that, just taps on the shoulder, so people hardly know that they're being filmed.

Cinéaste: Do you work with the same group from project to project?
Ivens: No, that hasn't been possible, partly because I have worked in so many countries—Cuba, Chile, Africa, and France, for example—always one after the other.

Cinéaste: What is the current state of financing for documentary films?

Ivens: In France right now it's very difficult to find financing, as it is in every country. In Europe we don't have a system of private foundations as you do. Here it's usually the state that gives an advance against the later income of the film. That's the only way to start a project, but it gives you a little bit. Then a producer comes in and raises a little more, and with that you can begin. It's good that people can get this help, but the state, of course, has committees that must look at all the submissions, and they are not always film people, so they don't always make the right decisions. But in general it works in France, for both fiction and documentary films.

The other possibility in these countries is television, which, if it hasn't exactly killed the documentary, has made it very difficult for them. Why? Because television is really the means of communicating facts, of daily reporting the surface truth—who, where, what, why—and that's all. And they do very well at it, it's highly developed. But with documentaries it's very difficult, because they have no real sense for it, I don't know why. So, when young people come in with a proposal for a documentary, firstly they cannot be too controversial, and, secondly, they don't get any real facilities. If you ask for a shooting ratio of ten-to-one, they're used to working at four-to-one, or three-to-one. Even the director knows that they can't finance a really good documentary! Another example—say you had gone to Lebanon during the recent fighting there, and had made a good documentary. They wouldn't accept it today. They would say that's not news anymore, we've already done enough on it. Your film could show a deeper truth, the background of the conflict, and a broader view, but they'll say, "Sorry." Television has limited enormously the possibilities of documentary filmmaking.

Cinéaste: How have your films changed from the earlier documentaries to now?

Ivens: One of the biggest changes was with the film *Borinage.* Before that I made *Rain, The Bridge,* and *The Breakers,* films without much content. I'm speaking not only of social content, but also human relations. They were esthetic films, very beautiful, and I learned my craft, but after four years I saw that it was a dead-end street. I could have done more rain, more bridges, even bigger bridges, but it would have been a change in quantity, not quality. I saw that content, especially in the documentary film, had to mean social content. That social content, in a stronger situation, becomes political content, and, in an even stronger situation, becomes militant.

Cinéaste: What are some of the further differences between, say, *Power and the Land* and *Yukong?*
Ivens: There are enormous differences. First, there are technical changes like direct, synch sound which makes it possible to be more eloquent. Then there's color film. Also, in getting older, the political aspects of my work became even more human, closer to reality. It's not because of age directly, but because of experience. Before I was much more limited, much more at the stage of manifesto. Some of the things we wrote at Filmliga were idiotic.

Now there will be enormous changes with the new developments in video. Eventually film won't even be made on film anymore. It'll be another material, maybe on videotape or a laser plate. I don't think it's more than fifteen or twenty years off. But still the most important thing is the integrity of the artist. I don't care if he works in 8mm or 70mm. The measurement is not his skill, or better cameras—it's in his head, in his heart, in his soul. The artist has a responsibility, not only in how he expresses himself, but in what he says. People assume that they're being told the truth, so you have to be honest. From then on it can be deepened, but this fundamental truthfulness is the key.

Cinéaste: What is your relationship with the people you film?
Ivens: There is a triangular relationship between the filmmaker, the people you're going to film, and the audience. The people who see your film should have confidence in you, you should have confidence in the people you film, and the people you film should have confidence in you. If this triangular relationship is honest and good, you'll be all right. It's a very simple thing, but it illustrates well the filmmaker's responsibility, because when you talk about El Salvador or Guatemala, you're talking about the life and death of people, of a nation, of liberty. You'd better be damned sure on your

feet because you're going to tell this story to millions of people. *Yukong* has been seen by 150 million people. There was a time when I counted my public in thousands, then tens of thousands, then hundreds of thousands. You can't let it weigh too heavily on your shoulders, but you must be aware of it. The more important your theme, and the higher your aim, the greater is your responsibility toward the audience. If you're just doing a love story, that's already eternal and the public knows about it. It was established thousands of years before the birth of cinema, so you don't have work within this triangle. But if you're making films about liberty, decency, equality, the rights of people—these are big themes and not every artist can handle them.

There's another aspect which is important in doing these kinds of films. You can never say that you didn't pay enough attention to the technical aspects. You absolutely have to use the best means available. If not, you give the people who are against you ammunition. That's why *Spanish Earth* was so effective in helping the Spanish cause, because it had this artistic quality. You have to touch people not just with tricks and eloquence, but you yourself have to be very emotionally touched by it. Then, as an artist, you have to put your brains, your heart, everything to work to say it in the most penetrating way. It's the essential unity of content and form. You shouldn't just make a technically perfect film with no content.

Cinéaste: Were you ever tempted to work more in fiction films as opposed to documentary?
Ivens: Yes, because for certain themes I think fiction is more effective. Some themes are especially appropriate for documentary and other themes are more appropriate for fiction.

Cinéaste: But did you ever personally feel that you wanted to work more in fiction?
Ivens: Yes, but I was immediately aware that it would involve a lot of money and compromises. In the very beginning, after *Rain*, I made a fiction film in Holland called *The Breakers,* so I have a feeling for it. But I saw that there were so many people already making fiction and I *love* making documentaries. It's in my character. I love to work in the field. I don't like the four walls of a studio. Other people do—I remember that

whenever Rene Clair, for example, needed to shoot in the street, he was very nervous.

For most people documentary is still a kind of transition period, which is OK, too, because you can't make a real living from documentary films. But in many ways your life is much richer working in documentaries. Each film has its own history and you become involved. Some people don't want to be involved, they just want to make love stories.

Cinéaste: I would like to see documentaries continue to grow. I think there's still a lot of room for the form to develop. *Ivens:* Yes, but we barely have time to make films, so it's very difficult to experiment, especially for younger people. But I agree. Take, for example, the question of memory as it's used in fiction films. There are all kinds of devices, flashbacks and so on, which create emotion. In documentaries it's very stiff and mechanical. There should be other ways, more like in real life where we're constantly remembering. It could be done in a visual sense, to have the memories coming in and out so the screen is alive. Fiction has been better able to capture the subtlety of psychological things and personal affections. We have to find the documentary translation of that. We are like poets. Poetry can outdo a novel by saying something precisely and concisely, by condensing things. The power of poetry should play a larger part in our work.

Filming reality is copying it, but you have to go further than that, into art. I don't know if I've succeeded, but I still worry about it. Think about the genius of Dante, who in a poem could describe a battle scene as it looked from the air. When I was in a fighter plane during the war, it looked just as he had described it. How he did it, God knows, but he did in his imagination. So you shouldn't be afraid to ask your imagination to do more than you think you can.

The Museum of Modern Art in New York and other film institutions in other parts of the country scheduled special showings of Joris Ivens' documentary films to coincide with his 90th birthday, November 18, 1988. (DP)

33   THE GOOD FIGHT: THE ABRAHAM LINCOLN BRIGADE IN THE SPANISH CIVIL WAR

Gary Crowdus

Produced and directed by Noel Buckner, Mary Dore, and Sam Sills; narrated by Studs Terkel; cinematography by Stephen Lighthill, Peter Rosen, Joe Vitagliano and Renner Wunderlich; edited by Noel Buckner; music by Wendy Blackstone and Bernardo Palombo. Color, 98 minutes. Distributed by First Run Features, 153 Waverly Place, NYC 10014.

IN RECENT YEARS, American independent filmmakers have produced a remarkable series of oral history documentaries and have thereby played an important role in bringing to light neglected chapters of American history. Providing a dramatic framework for their personal accounts of historical events, these films have focused on specific aspects of feminist, labor, ethnic, and radical political history that for decades have been suppressed or ignored in official versions of American history. Films such as *Union Maids, With Babies and Banners, Free Voice of Labor, Rosie the*

Reprinted by permission from *Cinéaste* (Vol. XIII, No. 4, 1984).

Riveter, The Wobblies, and *Seeing Red,* to name just the best known, have not only helped to set some historical records straight, but have also revealed the rich heritage of experience from which younger generations of activists can learn.

One of the most recent oral history documentaries, *The Good Fight,* about American volunteers in the Spanish Civil War, is an example of the genre at its best, bringing history vividly to life and making it meaningful and relevant for contemporary viewers. From 1936 to 1938, some 3200 Americans in the Abraham Lincoln Brigade joined 37,000 other volunteers from over fifty countries in the International Brigades which fought on the side of the Spanish Republic against an uprising led by General Francisco Franco. Because Franco was aided by the fascist armies of Hitler and Mussolini, the conflict generated worldwide political controversy, and, as a testing ground for German military armaments and tactics, it eventually paved the way for World War II. In recounting these events, filmmakers Noel Buckner, Mary Dore, and Sam Sills use the by now traditional elements of the oral history documentary, interweaving archival footage, contemporary interviews, graphics and newspaper clippings, period music and songs, and excerpts from contemporaneous Hollywood and independent films, all tied together by a terse narration spoken by Studs Terkel.

While *The Good Fight* clearly aims to celebrate the heroic actions of a group of men and women little known today outside leftist circles, the filmmakers have also tried to temper the romanticism inherent in their subject by making, as they describe it in the accompanying interview, a "heroic anti-war movie." They have succeeded admirably on both counts. *The Good Fight* is an emotionally stirring, dramatically compelling account of a momentous historical event, and, at the same time, a sobering, no-nonsense view of human suffering and death in war.

Early sequences of the film attempt to provide some basic historical context and definitions, tracing the growth of political radicalism during the Great Depression and showing how the support of the Popular Front government in Spain against a fascist assault became a rallying point for the American left. After a roughly chronological account of the Spanish conflict, with a focus on American involvement, from the arrival of the first volunteers in late '36 to the withdrawal of the International Brigades in late '38, *The Good Fight* then shows how the Lincoln Brigade veterans were subjected to decades of redbaiting harassment by the U.S. Government, from the difficulties the vets encountered in trying to enlist during World War II, when they were labelled as "premature anti-fascists," through the Mc-Carthyite witchhunts of the Fifties.

The heart of the film consists of contemporary interviews with eleven Americans—eight men and three women—a colorful and remarkably articulate group, many of whom, now in their 60s and 70s, remain politically active today. Bill McCarthy, who proudly proclaims his working class roots, and Dave Thompson, who comes from an upper class family, both explain the same process of growing political commitment which ultimately led to their decisions to go to Spain. Bill Bailey, a former seaman with a gravelly-voiced, Hell's Kitchen accent, is one of the film's greatest raconteurs, and provides some of the film's funniest and most expressive anecdotes, including a hilarious account of how he and his friend, "Low-life" McCormack, ripped a Nazi flag from a German ship docked in New York harbor. In one of the film's more reflective moments, Abe Osheroff, a former carpenter, explains how the fact that they lost their "good fight" can be seen as a disquieting metaphor for the human condition. Evelyn Hutchins recalls how she had to overcome the sexism of Communist Party bureaucrats before being al-lowed to go to Spain as an ambulance driver. Tom Page describes how, as a young black man, Spain for him represented the first time in his life he was treated with dignity as a human being. Ed Balchowsky, who lost an arm in Spain, offers most of his testimony by pounding away with his remaining arm at an old upright piano and singing a series of rousing wartime songs. Milt Wolff, a Brooklyn youth who at the age of 23 became a Commander of the Abraham Lincoln Brigade, describes carefully concocting a story to keep his mother from knowing what he was doing in Spain and how his cover story was blown when his photo, showing him in military uniform, appeared one day on the front page of *The Jewish Daily Forward.* Salaria Kea and Ruth

Davidow, who served as nurses in Spain, describe the grueling ·conditions under which they worked, including a virtually nonstop schedule and a perpetual shortage of medical supplies. Steven Nelson, a respected CP organizer, describes his role as a political commissar in Spain.

In keeping with the film's anti-war perspective, many of the interviews emphasize the volunteers' sudden and shocking introduction to the brutal realities of warfare. Most of those who fought in the Abraham Lincoln Brigade were youngsters with no prior military experience—indeed, many of them had never even handled a firearm before—and they received virtually no military training in Spain. Abe Osheroff movingly describes their constant fear of injury or death, the inescapable human reality that, no matter how much political commitment or ideological fervor, one's body simply did not want to go into battle. Bill Bailey recounts the trauma of seeing the horribly mutilated bodies of his friends strewn about the battlefield.

Perhaps the best example of the film's consistent refusal to indulge in conventionally romanticized notions of battlefield heroics is its sole account of the Lincoln Brigade's participation in the battles at Quinto and Belchite, which were among the Brigade's few real military successes. Bill McCarthy recounts how he was hurled against a wall by an explosion. Picking himself up, he proceeded to walk, his ears ringing and his body trembling the entire time, all the way back to the International Brigades headquarters in Barcelona where he announced that, "The battle is over with and *I'm* over with." The film's sobering views of warfare convey great credibility, of course, precisely because they are expressed by battle-hardened veterans.

Although the accounts of these combat veterans echo those of other veterans of other wars at other times and in other places, the Abraham Lincoln Brigade was not a conventional military force—it was a political army. They were not draftees, but volunteers motivated by everything from purely humanitarian sentiment to anti-fascist politics or international class solidarity. The International Brigades were organized and largely administered in Spain by the Comintern, and the majority of the Lincoln Brigade volunteers were Communist Party members. (The frankness and

ease with which the film's interviewees discuss CP involvement in the events is a significant indication of how much this
documentary genre—and perhaps our national political environment—has developed from just eight years ago when the
filmmakers of *Union Maids,* one of the first of the oral history
documentaries, deliberately avoided all references to the
Socialist or Communist Party affiliations of its interviewees
out of a fear of redbaiting.) In addition to the traditional
hierarchies of military discipline, therefore, the International
Brigades utilized a system of political commissars to interpret the politics of the war, to explain to the troops the
reasons why they were being asked to risk their lives. Abe
Osheroff readily acknowledges that the political commissar
was an accepted fact of life in Spain. If you were lucky, he
was a decent human being, but, if you weren't, he was likely
to be "a son of a bitch who insisted on explaining *everything*
in political terms."

The Good Fight makes it abundantly clear that soldiers
who were daily risking their lives in combat had little stomach
for political rhetoric or inspirational speeches from Party
bureaucrats who periodically visited the front. Abe Osheroff
delights in singing a few verses from some of the humorously
irreverent songs with which CP head Earl Browder was
regaled during one of his visits, and recalls Browder's
outraged response to this flagrant display of "demoraliza-
tion." Bill Bailey offers several amusing anecdotes about the
Lincolns' resistance to the attempted enforcement of traditional military discipline, such as the saluting of officers. It is
this look at the more complex human reality obscured
beneath layers of romantically glorified and politically ortho-
dox Party histories and journalistic accounts that is one of
the film's greatest virtues and most refreshing qualities.

Some critics have nevertheless complained that, in this
regard, *The Good Fight* hasn't been critical enough. The
more politically knowledgeable or opinionated the viewer, of
course, the more such a viewer brings his or her own political
agenda to a historical documentary. A number of critics, both
from within and outside the left, have chided the filmmakers
for not dealing more critically with the role of the Soviet-
controlled Comintern in Spain, and in particular with the
Soviet repression of anarchist and Trotskyist forces, that

"civil war within the civil war" popularized in George Orwell's *Homage to Catalonia.* Without wanting to be apologists for the Soviet role in these events, the filmmakers have explained that the film makes only a passing reference to this issue because their specific subject is not the Spanish Civil War overall but the Abraham Lincoln Brigade in particular, and in their interviews it became clear that the veterans were not involved in, and at the time were largely unaware of, these events. As even Orwell himself notes in *Homage to Catalonia:*

> One of the most horrible features of war is that all the war propaganda, all the screaming and lies and hatred, comes invariably from people who are not fighting. The P.S.U.C. militiamen whom I knew in the line, the Communists from the International Brigades whom I met from time to time, never called me a Trotskyist or a traitor . . . The people who wrote pamphlets against us and vilified us in the newspapers all remained safe at home, or at worst in the newspaper offices of Valencia, hundreds of miles from the bullets and mud.

Whether the veterans interviewed in *The Good Fight* were unaware of the Stalinist repression, or were simply unwilling to discuss what little they did know, the filmmakers acknowledge that they did wrestle with the dilemma before finally conceding that this issue, despite its politically controversial nature, was simply not of central importance to their story. It should also be obvious that it would have been difficult, if not impossible, and certainly inadvisable, for the filmmakers to have doggedly pursued this line of inquiry if they realistically expected to maintain access to and the sympathy of the interviewees who were crucial to their cinematic account of this history. (The political difficulties involved in interviewing former or present Communist Party members, even for sympathetic New Left historians, have been best explained in the Afterword to *The Inquisition in Hollywood: Politics in the Film Community, 1930–1950,* by Larry Ceplair and Steven Englund.)

Those who criticize oral history documentaries such as *The Good Fight* for failing to provide a level of comprehensiveness or sophisticated, in-depth analysis comparable to that found in books really miss the point. Documentary films, much less narrative films, are by the very nature of the medium incapable of matching the historical complexity or detail found in written histories. On the other hand, the printed page cannot rival the motion picture in conveying the immediacy of historical events, in directly communicating the look, the sound, even the emotional quality of history in the making. The oral history interview, in particular, in which the viewer becomes a privileged witness to first person accounts of history, enables us to hear a peculiar inflection in the voice, a catch of emotion in the throat, a heartfelt sigh, or to glimpse a moistness in the eyes, a particularly telling use of the hands, or a revealing facial expression, and can thereby communicate a more palpable and human, even a more meaningful, sense of history than any amount of reading. To paraphrase H. L. Mencken, one emotionally moving anecdote is worth ten thousand footnotes.

Despite its automatic appeal to a specialized left audience, then, the real purpose and greatest value (even for the left) of a film such as *The Good Fight* is in popularizing its historical subject, in introducing it to a general audience, rather than in trying to address fine points of historical interpretation or political controversy of concern primarily to academics or activists. It is precisely its success in capturing the human side of history that makes *The Good Fight* such an important film. At its best—for example, during Bill Bailey's moving account of his personal response to the rise of fascism in Germany, or Evelyn Hutchins's description of the powerful emotions generated by helping other people—*The Good Fight* transcends the specifics of its historical subject and enables even an apolitical viewer to understand better the meaning of political commitment and how it can transform one's life. This point is emphasized in the film's concluding montage which shows veterans of the Abraham Lincoln Brigade participating in political demonstrations throughout the last three decades. In thus indicating how the veterans have continued their "good fight" right up to the present day, the film ultimately becomes a portrait of a group of American radicals who have remained true to their political ideals.

This unusually engaging historical documentary thus also serves as a moving tribute to a remarkable group of men and women. By making their heroism understandable in human terms, *The Good Fight* also encourages the belief that it is a trait which each of us, at our best, would possess.

The following is excerpted from Dan Georgakas's article "Malpractice in the Radical Documentary" (Cinéaste, Vol. 16, Nos. 1–2, 1987–88). His thesis is that, although "American radical documentary has enjoyed a twenty-year renaissance unprecedented in quantity, quality and variety, [this] very success has tended to obscure the uneven development of the genre. Excellent cinematic strategies have come to coexist with highly questionable ones, and repetition has transformed procedures that were innovative when introduced into mannerisms and visual cliches." Of the Lincoln Brigaders' film The Good Fight, *he writes: (DP)*

Hidden or misrepresented history is also perpetuated by unasked questions. The Good Fight *is a surprising culprit in this regard. The film is quite candid in dealing with the role of the Communist Party in organizing the Abraham Lincoln Brigade and even deals with internal tensions rarely touched on. What is not discussed is how the Lincolns felt about the military suppression of other left wing military units such as those of the anarchists and the anti-Stalinist POUM (Workers Party of Marxist Unification). The filmmakers report that their interviewees told them that at the time they were unaware of these events. Whether or not that's true, in a summary film made some fifty years later, the vets ought to have some comments on what may be the most controversial aspect of the Spanish Civil War. We need not assume the vets will express guilt. A number of Lincolns have stated elsewhere that the suppression of what they term leftist extremists was essential. Among those holding that view, some would see that suppression as tragic necessity, others as courageous foresight.*

The internecine warfare issue is not a matter of sectarian hairsplitting. How an individual responds offers insight into the kind of world he or she thought the Lincolns were fighting to create. Avoidance of the issue keeps a fine film from being truly unique and even profound. Critics have sometimes confused the issue by faulting the filmmakers for not dealing with the whole scope of the conflict when their announced focus was a study of the Lincoln Brigade only.

34 JEAN RENOIR'S *GRAND ILLUSION*

Otis Ferguson

O F ALL THE WAR FILMS there has been up to now only one which was made with something like the dignity and terror the subject demands, and it was made eight years ago in Hollywood by Lewis Milestone, from the book *All Quiet on the Western Front.* Now there is one to put beside it, a nearly prophetic story for these days made by Jean Renoir and showing in New York at the Filmarte Theatre: *Grand Illusion.* There aren't any trenches in it, for it is a story like *The Enormous Room,* more serious-seeming if not so beautiful. It is about what happens to people—three French captives in particular, and the German commandant, and later the young German widow—in country behind the German lines; finally of the escape of two of the men.

And while this war drags on there are echoes through the story of another, in the relationships among the commandant of the fort and three Frenchmen: gentleman, bourgeois, and Jew. The German is more stiff in his courteous contempt; the French gentleman seems to have no bitterness against the democratic idea but maintains as a part of nature the reserve that baffles his comrades. And when he dies (he created the diversion that allowed the other two to escape) he represents for this story the end of a world, the only "escape" possible for his class.

The picture is filled out with these complexities, which lie

From Robert Wilson's *The Film Criticism of Otis Ferguson,* ©1971. Published by Temple University. Reprinted by permission of Temple University Press.

between the crude black-and-white of enemy and friend, between simple ideals and difficult reality. Soldiers and sick to death of it, they come up with delight to the lifting roll of men marching in formation. Safe for the first time and knowing that "freedom" means going back to be shot at, they scheme, dig, and suffer for it, to regain their dignity and hear people talk like home folks. There is nothing to live for any longer, except to live—which becomes the main business of a strange, twisted world.

In all this there is a rare compassion shown—for the broken commandant in his gloomy stone fort and for the men in their degrees of hopelessness and dirt. Surely one of the most moving expositions in the film is the flare-up between Gabin and the Jew, the blunt words and misery, and the bond of common suffering still too strong to break; and then the idyll in the German cottage, so easy a thing to go astray on, but done beautifully with little scraps of French and German, a cow, and oddments of food. The acting is as fine as the picture deserves: Erich von Stroheim, Jean Gabin, Pierre Fresnay, Dalio, the first two especially giving the thing its basis in believable life, but all contributing: in a fairly extensive supporting cast I cannot recall even a walk-on that was not easy and right. The only weak points are in its structure as a film.

Renoir has not learned how to indicate shifts in time, and the result is that you jump from sickness to health, from today to tomorrow to Christmas, even, with the abrupt jar of scenes in a play but without so much as a curtain fall. Its moments of feeling are never squeezed limp, but there is a rhythm to be discovered in any kind of feeling and Renoir doesn't always have it. He is apt to leave an emotion before you have finished with it—sometimes where even a casual dissolve would have allowed the last three beats, four, five, six, to raise it to the proper intensity. Or he will cut flatly from one level of emotion to another without that transitional strip as necessary as the modulation between keys in the line of music.

Nobody wants a good thing muddied up with the heavy symbolism of special-effects men; and the length of the film is about right as it is. But the way could have been made smoother at the expense of some of those bits that a moment's reflection will show to have been tossed in without thought for true dramatic purpose. The man suffocating in the tunnel was effective but perfunctory; the rifle shot after the two had crossed the border was false suspense; the effect of the soldier in woman's clothes was pertinent but unskillfully done. Perhaps a few others.

If such considerations were pure fussy arithmetic we could laugh at them. But the truth is that in the special liquid form of pictures, an audience confused even for a moment (where are they now? how long has this been going on?) is an audience losing altitude and that much heavier to get back up. A little more art (always as opposed to artifice or the arty) could have heightened the beauty and truth of this film, which already has as much as we've seen anywhere this year.

35 WILLIAM DIETERLE'S *BLOCKADE*

Alvah Bessie

FROM *The Great Train Robbery* to *The True Glory* every
major manifestation of our time has found itself reflected
on our screens. The first World War, the boom and the
depression, the New Deal and the rise of fascist terrorism,
then World War II, the nature of our allies and our enemies—
all achieved important statement in many films, whatever
their shortcomings. During the recent war itself, the underground struggle in France, Belgium, Holland, Norway, even
Germany was given recognition—and generally romanticized. But one major issue of our time was stinted: the issue
of Republican Spain.

It will be seven years in February since that Republic was
drowned in the blood of its heroic people; and today it is
anticlimactic to remind people that World War II started on
the Iberian Peninsula. Yet in those seven years the Spanish
reflection we have seen in our theaters has been no more
than a ghost of the actuality. What was—and is—important
about Spain never appeared; superficial aspects alone were
revealed. We will examine the reasons for this, but let us first
examine the exact nature and extent of that reflection.

Two films alone achieved a contemporaneous Spanish
setting: Blockade (the earliest) and *For Whom the Bell Tolls*
(the most successful from a boxoffice standpoint). Other
films that touched upon the subject, touched it in a gingerly
fashion—or a purely meretricious. Two films alone offered a

From *The Screen Writer* (January 1946). ©1945 The Screen Writer.
Reprinted by permission of the author.

Spanish Republican hero: Blockade and Confidential Agent (and the hero's activities here were confined to England). In three other films the hero was a man who had fought in Spain presumably in the ranks of the International Brigades: *Casablanca* (an American); *Watch on the Rhine* (a German); *The Fallen Sparrow* (an American). But in two of these (*Casablanca* and *Sparrow*) the hero's Spanish activities were important only as timid and belated tribute to the men of fifty-four nations who fought beside the Spanish people in the opening battle of World War II.

Whereas the hero of *Watch on the Rhine* (derived from Lillian Hellman's play) was a professional antifascist who "works at it," the hero of *Casablanca* ran a dive and pursued Ingrid Bergman; and in *Sparrow* the hero ran after three women and pursued a vendetta that was both personally ludicrous and historically absurd.

Now these six films constitute the major cinematic treatment of the Spanish struggle, a struggle whose crucial nature is becoming daily more apparent, and whose effects continue into the present and the future. It is said that Spain was mentioned in several other films whose scripts could not be examined for the purposes of this paper; among them *Arise, My Love* and *The Last Train to Madrid*. In *A Yank on the Burma Road* there is a pilot who actually flew for General Franco, and he is properly characterized as flying—when he is captured—for the Japanese. (Incidentally, the reason this pilot gives for being on the wrong side of the democratic struggle is the same given by Humphrey Bogart in *Casablanca* for fighting on the right side: "They paid me well.")

Since Hollywood is invariably a lap or two behind the rest of the world in its understanding of contemporary events, it is not surprising that one major studio spent a great deal of time and money preparing a film to glorify the "heroic defenders" of the Alcazar. It nearly achieved production and release before the heroic resistance of the fascists in the Toledo fortress was explained . . . by the natural reluctance of the Spanish Republicans to murdering their own wives and children—held as hostages in the Alcazar by its heroic defenders. (That this time-lapse in understanding still exists in Hollywood was evidenced by the production and release of such a film as *Chetniks,* which glorified Yugoslavia's traitors and totally ignored the real resistance forces under Tito, now the leader of the Yugoslav Republic.)

The meat, however, of whatever was or was not said about Spain by our American film industry appears in *Blockade, For Whom the Bell Tolls* and *Confidential Agent.* As such, they deserve more than casual examination. Nor is it intended here to disparage the appearance on the American screen of a hero (however trivial his subsequent activities) who once "fought in Spain" for the Republic. His mere appearance was important, for it meant that Hollywood (i.e., generally our writers) was aware that such a hero had become respectable; that it was an honor, worthy of applause, for a man to have fought in Spain on the side of the people. But let us examine the two films that achieved a Spanish locale—and the second that presented a Spanish hero, and confined him to England.

Blockade was released in 1938. It was written by John Howard Lawson, produced by Walter Wanger and directed by William Dieterle. Appearing, as it did, during the last year of the struggle itself, its importance cannot be under-rated, whatever may be felt about its actual achievement, cinematically or historically. The Americans who were fighting in Spain were heartened to learn that such a film had been produced; and that a struggle around it was in progress back home. If, when they saw it, they were disappointed, who can blame them?

For the hero of *Blockade* was a completely apolitical young man in a nation of people who thoroughly understood why they were fighting. The conventional pattern of the story—the democratic hero in love with the wavering daughter of a stated reactionary, naturally limited both the scope and action of the film. It was even more limited, however, by what was not said about the struggle itself. For only two aspects of the war were mentioned: the bombing of civilians and the blockade of the country.

While the film recognized that there were reactionary forces at work in Spain, their representatives (the heroine's father and the hero's rival) as well as the girl herself, are foreigners. No identification is ever made of the internal enemy (the Army, the industrialists, the landlords and the hierarchy). No connection is ever made between the heavies of the piece and the real heavies—Nazi Germany and Fascist Italy. In fact they are not even mentioned. Nor is any identification made of the contending sides in the so-called civil war. A war starts (Why?); the hero decides to fight (Whom?) because "this is my valley . . . this is our earth . . . let's fight for it." The entire film was therefore a compromise and a specie of appeasement, understandable in a period when appeasement was the major policy of democracy. Those who saw the film and understood the issues were gratified to find even so diluted a recognition of Spain's martyrdom, and they echoed the hero's cry: "Where is the conscience of mankind?" But it is doubtful that the average movie-goer found anything more in the film than confusion and veiled references to a struggle whose aims were never revealed.

With *Confidential Agent* (written by Robert Buckner from a novel by Graham Greene) the only other film with a Spanish Republican hero, the audience had the perspective of time and all that has been learned since 1939, to help it. Here again is the personal melodrama of a democratic hero in love with the wavering daughter of a stated reactionary. The scrapes he gets into when followed to England by fascist agents endear the hero to the heroine and provide her with her first allegiance. And with the failure of his apocryphal mission—to secretly purchase coal for the Republic and thus keep it out of the hands of the enemy—she returns to Spain with him because, "I cannot be faithful to people I cannot see."

Despite its shortcomings as history, as melodrama, as play of character, as cinema—*Confidential Agent* must be appreciated for its hero; for the explicit identification of its villains; for its revelation of the nature of businessmen who "have no politics" and will sell to either side depending on the size of the profit; for its sympathetic presentation of the Republican cause; for its prefiguration (by hindsight) of the fact that appeasement of fascism in Spain could lead to a fascist attack on Britain. But again, the issues of the war are omitted: Why were Germany and Italy invading Spain? What were the Republic and its people fighting for? What against?

Nor will you find these issues either stated or implied in *For Whom the Bell Tolls,* the one successful box-office film about

Spain, just as Hemingway's novel was the one successful box-office novel. If anything, Bell provides the greatest distortions of them all and its justification for these distortions (if such is possible) can be based only on the fact that it is a faithful transcription of a novel that—whatever its intentions—is objectively anti-Loyalist.

A great controversy raged about this film even before it was released. Rumors were current that it had been submitted to the Franco Embassy for approval. These rumors were denied. A spokesman for Paramount protested that the film "really isn't about anything." Its director, Sam Wood, insisted that it took no sides in what he chose to call a battle between Communism and Fascism; that it merely showed the horrors of civil war between brothers, and had no political implications whatsoever.

Now quite aside from the fact that Bell was enormously boring—with its endless sleeping-bag sequences—it provided a curious mixture of fact and fantasy (largely derived from the novel, again). People familiar with Spain found many nostalgic echoes of the country in the careful reproduction of exteriors. At least one character, magnificently played by Katina Paxinou, echoes what is known about the dignity, the love for life and the heroism of the Spanish people. (She was the best character in the book as well.)

If you can discount the fact that with the exception of the hero and heroine, all the people in the film had green faces, other attributes of these characters are worthy of attention. All the major characters of the guerrilla band were "for the Republic." But what the Republic was, not one of them seemed to know or care. One is an old man who does not like to kill fascists—but will do it "for the Republic." The leader of the guerrillas is a practicing anarchist, a coward and a drunkard who does not scruple at murdering his own people if he needs an extra horse to insure his safety. One is a Gipsy, charming, a liar, a thief, unstable and untrustworthy. One is a boy who parrots the Republican slogans with no understanding of their meaning. Minor characters are brave soldiers for an unstated cause that seems hopelessly bogged down in confusion, inefficiency and Soviet influence (the fascist lie, perpetrated again).

The most vivid sequence in the film—as well as in the

book—was a sequence of Spanish Republican atrocity. The fact that such incidents were practically non-existent and that atrocity was and is a world-wide fascist policy found no reflection either in the book or in the film. Maria says she was raped and tortured by the fascists; but the audience sees the democratic people of Spain (portrayed as mobsters of a most repulsive type) take inhuman vengeance on their tyrants.

So again, the end result of the film—so far as any audience's understanding of what is being shown is concerned—is a Hearst magazine love story played against a background of a war whose causes, issues and world significance are never revealed. No one could learn from any of these films what most of us have learned since 1939: that the war in Spain was the first organized attack of the Fascist International upon the democratic peoples of the world. No one could learn that the traitors of Spain had combined with the Axis to destroy the first successful attempt to achieve in Spain—in the 20th Century—what our own people achieved in the 18th. No one could have learned that what the Republic was doing—and which incurred the implacable wrath of its owning class and wrought its destruction—was the extension of economic and political democracy, for the first time in Spain's history, to its total population.

In seeking an explanation for these phenomena of silence, distortion, lying and betrayal, we need not go outside our own country, for the same forces are still at work today. What strangled Spain was the greatest weapon the Axis ever devised—the weapon of the "Red Menace." The fear of Communism—which in its most important aspects is not the fear of Communism at all but the fear and hatred of popular democracy—destroyed the Spanish Republic in 1939. In 1921 it had destroyed the possibilities of democracy in Italy; in 1933 it destroyed the development of democracy in Germany. In 1940 it destroyed France. Nazi Germany, its chief proponent, utilized this weapon to such fine effect that it was able to destroy all of Europe and almost conquer the world before the governments of the great democracies were moved to the unity of action that in 1936 would have saved Spain and probably prevented World War II.

We have—or rather, we should have learned a bitter

lesson from this. Yet a mass production industry, such as ours, still feels that it must avoid the "controversial." It cannot afford to step on the toes of the powers that be. (It is in fact, one of the powers that be and would not willingly step on its own toes.) If this seems questionable, how else explain the simple fact that no American motion picture has ever attempted seriously or honestly to evaluate in terms of human character, the contribution made to our society by its organized labor movement? With their families the thirteen million trade-unionists of America constitute a sizeable portion of our population. With the unorganized millions who work for wages (and their families) labor constitutes a majority of all Americans. One could reasonably expect, therefore, to see that majority, its problems, aspirations, organizations and human relationships reflected on the screen.

So far as Spain itself is concerned, it is significant that more of its actuality, its historic importance, will be found in the orientation films made by our armed services during the war, than will be found in any fiction film. The *Why We Fight* series did not have to make a profit for its producers; its audience was special—and it was being prepared for battle. It was a matter of life or death for America that this special audience understand something of what was happening in the world, and why it had been taken out of civilian life and given rifles, machine-guns, tanks and airplanes.

Today, when there is a nation-wide—and world-wide— campaign on foot to break diplomatic and commercial relations with fascist Spain, it is gratifying to learn that Constancia de la Mora's autobiography, *In Place of Splendour,* is being prepared for production. Whether it will achieve production (and distribution) is another question. But the story of this distinguished woman is a natural screenplay—it is the stuff of life. Born into one of the most wealthy and "traditional" of Spanish aristocratic families, de la Mora found her allegiance shifting. She abandoned her class to take her place, during the war, on the side of the workers, peasants and intellectuals of Spain, and against her own family. And there is a magnificent love story too, that might conceivably make palatable to those who control production (and ideas) the statement of certain other facts of life. At the Writers Congress held at UCLA in 1943, there was a seminar on The Nature of the Enemy. At this seminar Dudley Nichols, who wrote the screenplay of *For Whom the Bell Tolls,* delivered an important paper. During the discussion that followed, Mr. Nichols was asked a question from the floor. The question and its answer will follow, for they might possibly serve as symbol of, and clue to, the frustration many screenwriters feel periodically when their best attempts to make sense of life (on paper) find themselves edited out of existence.

Someone asked, "Mr. Nichols, who prevented you from naming the fascists in *For Whom the Bell Tolls?"*

The chairman said, "You need not answer that, Mr. Nichols."

But Mr. Nichols grinned, and replied, "I can answer that in two words: the fascists."

This laconic reply, while offering no specific identification of the source, gave further recognition to the existence of a subtle and pervasive anti-democratic influence on the content of films. This influence is real and all the more subversive because it is sanctified by long usage. It may be found not only in films, but in newspapers, radio commentary, schoolbooks, magazines, advertising, publicity, novels, public lectures and Congressional oratory.

But in respect to films alone—what else are we talking about than the existence of this reactionary influence when we cynically admit that the vast majority of our films reflect a dream world that has no validity in terms of the lives most people live? It is contended here that if that life is to be truly, deeply and honestly reflected, the truth about people must be fought for—both within the motion picture industry and outside it. For it is just as possible (and just as deadly) to blockade ideas as nations.

36 JOHN FORD'S *THE GRAPES OF WRATH*

Edwin Locke

MR. MARTIN QUIGLEY and various other spokesmen of the *movie business* will continue to demand that the commercial screen be reserved exclusively for the presentation of elegant untruths, gilded dreams, and badly refracted memories. Mr. Quigley has proved many times that social, religious, political, or economic problems are not fit subjects for the motion picture. He insists that American audiences, for whom he presumingly speaks, want nothing for their money but entertainment, undefined. But he is not fooling the men who put *The Grapes of Wrath* on the screen. He is not fooling the producers and working people of the industry, nor Twentieth Century-Fox, nor the Chase National Bank. He is not fooling anybody, because audiences who have never heard of Mr. Quigley are crowding the box offices and breaking into spontaneous applause after each screening of the picture.

Hollywood knows that a good deal of box-office turnout can be bought with heavy investment in stars, publicity, and production, as in *Gone With the Wind;* but it also knows that no investment can purchase the little restless movements of an audience building up a static charge of excitement and appreciation which finally breaks out in crackles and little thunder of applause. The reactionaries of the *movie business* who have fastened themselves to the production of motion pictures, like shark suckers to their host, would seem

Reprinted from *Films: A Quarterly* (Spring, 1940).

to be in the position of having to revise their concept of the audience or to enlarge their definition of what constitutes entertainment. They may prefer to believe that those who remained in their seats to applaud *The Grapes of Wrath* were Leftists of one sort or another. Unfortunately, that belief leads to the unpleasant conclusion that the American audience is lefter than they think. The critics too would seem to be bidding for honorable mention by Mr. Dies.

A great picture has been produced and the verbal flares and bombshells of the critics have not been touched off altogether without occasion. The realization that motion picture history has been made is calling forth audible appreciation from the usually silent tiers of watchful darkness. The crowds—typical crowds of clerks, homebodies, casuals, and intellectuals—are deeply impressed by the outcome of what looks like singular intrepidity on the part of Mr. Darryl Zanuck.

The motives compelling Mr. Zanuck to buy *The Grapes of Wrath* and to produce from it a motion picture that loses none of the sincerity and power of the book have been widely speculated upon. Those who have been wondering forget that he is still a good businessman. Although *The Grapes of Wrath* is his finest, it is not his first venture into sociological themes. He has been quick in perceiving and exploiting the current interest of the public, whether it be directed toward gangsters, chain gangs, or Oklahoma migrants. He may be also possessed of information which leads him to believe that audiences are a little tired of the usual vast and stupid antics of Hollywood. But whatever his motives, he cannot be denied courage and vision for his part in bringing John Steinbeck's novel, artistically intact, to the screen.

The filming of *The Grapes of Wrath* took more than a decision to be faithful to the book. Producer, director, cameraman, actors, all were confronted by new material which demanded that they discard some of the comfortable certainties of the average Hollywood production and learn how to bring something of the quality of real people to the screen. Meanwhile, the watchful and belligerent gaze of Steinbeck was upon them.

Nunnally Johnson has used his disposition and ability to think in terms of people to make an excellent script from the novel. He has articulated the main episodes of the book into a straight line of action so that the gain in power and simplicity offsets a good deal of the loss in perspective. In his handling of the dialogue he has used the same discriminating selection, almost always going to the book for his lines, but not hesitating to transpose lines among the characters where the purposes of the film seem better served by the changes. For the most part the dialogue has the ring of the people's language, and he has made John Ford's task a little easier by holding long speeches to a minimum. After wondering why Johnson's script treated hardly at all of the destruction of the land, which was so effective and necessary a prelude to the book and regretting that the woolly lines about how the people go on and on are handed to Ma to end the picture, there is nothing to cavil with.

None of the gains made by Johnson have been lost in John Ford's direction. There is no hesitation, no milling around on film. That the master of dark milieu and driven men has a powerful way of putting people on film is a matter of record in *The Informer, Lost Patrol,* and *Stagecoach.* Ford's work in *Grapes of Wrath* is outstanding again in terms of people. His sense of the value of a face, of a voice, of a posture, of clothing, has served him well in his excellent casting of the supporting players: the truckdrivers, migrants, deputies, and vigilantes. And Ford has done more than to choose good examples of real people. He has come upon something that could never have been discovered in the studios: a realization of the highly developed awareness which the common people of the world have of one another.

He has used the knowledge in the memorable scenes of the picture: in the lunchroom where Pa Joad buys a loaf of bread; in the first migrant camp entered by the Joads, where we get a full and immediate understanding of their plight, not only from the wretched tents and paste-board hovels and the litter, but also from the apathetic curiosity of the miserable squatters as silent notice of the new arrival runs intuitively through the camp, attracted by Ma's stew, gather to beg silently, realizing the needlessness of words; in the masterful scene of the dance in the government camp where the direction measures up to Steinbeck's full meaning by a brilliant handling of mass and detail that would have been impossible if Ford had not understood the innate decency and joy of life and goodness which bloom in the lowliest people with the slightest encouragement.

It is a pity that Ford's sense of environment has not come through as well as his sense of people. The opening of the picture is greatly weakened because he has given us no feeling of the country or of the people's background. Where are the vast stretches of the dust bowl and the tiny houses as lonely as ships at sea? Where is the dust? It is hard to believe that Ford has ever seen *The Plow That Broke the Plains.* It is baffling to hear that a camera crew was sent into Oklahoma along Route 66; certainly but a few feet of their film was used. It is regrettable that the Joads were snatched across the beautiful and terrifying expanses of the country in a few pans and process shots; we could justly have expected more. We could have expected more of what it is like to be tractored off the land, more than the knocking over of a prop house by a Caterpillar roaming at large, more than a hackneyed montage of clanking monsters in abstract maneuvers. We might have had all these things, and a richer picture, if Ford had followed a little further the documentary technique that is now being talked about in connection with his work.

Like Ford, Gregg Toland, director of photography, has a long record of fine work. The excellence of his photography in *Grapes of Wrath* cannot be appreciated fully without realizing what it means to a Hollywood cameraman to be denied the use of most of his cozy little studio tricks: backlighting, baby spots, gauzes, and diffusion: and to be called upon as well to shoot players without make-up. Toland has worked the hard way and has distinguished himself by the naturalness of lighting throughout most of the film. His work is beautiful, once or twice too beautiful, too reminiscent of *Wuthering Heights.* There are beautiful skies in Oklahoma and westward, but they are not the skies Toland has given us.

The work of director, writer, and cameraman could have been considerably enhanced by a good musical score. Alfred Newman has provided little more than a fitful accompaniment by dragging two undistinguished come-all-ye's thinly through the picture. Oscar Levant has written that for some reason or other two government pictures he has seen have been unique in their intelligent use of music. Mr. Newman, as well as Mr. Levant, might look more closely into that reason.

The casting of *The Grapes of Wrath* strikes a good average somewhere between the fine choice of Henry Fonda as Tom Joad and the unhappy selection of Charley Grapewin as Grampa. Fonda, in playing Tom, knows what the story is about and what he is about in relation to it. He gives a fine performance throughout, and one of his finest bits is the scene in which he chases the hungry kids from the stewpot, using an apologetic gruffness to cover his sympathy and the unpleasant logic of his common sense. Jane Darwell, as Ma Joad, seems a less fortunate choice. Although she plays intelligently, no amount of experience or artistry could make her look like a woman of the Oklahoma people. A lean, stringy rawhide woman would have been excellent for the part, or a woman heavy with unhealthy flesh, but never a firm, plump, shiny woman like Darwell's Ma, who defies wearing down even after a catastrophe and the long trek from Sallisaw County to Fresno. John Carradine makes a good Casy except for several times in the opening scenes where he looks like a Zombie. Dorris Bowdon makes of Rosasharn a shy, sweet girl, entirely passive in character and not very convincingly pregnant despite help from the family in pointing out her condition. John Qualen's Muley is excellently fey. Russell Simpson's bewildered and ineffectual Pa is adequate. Grampa and Granma are a silly pair of japes. The superb casting of the supporting players has already been remarked.

Hollywood has given us in the past a fine series of frontier epics: the great American romance of a people hacking its way westward through forests and redskins, the quiet courage of pioneers in wagon trains lurching along the Santa Fe trail surrounded by a big still rim of hostile eyes that might close in at any moment in a grotesque carrousel dealing death by gunshot and arrow. But not before *The Grapes of Wrath* has it given us a picture that totalled, in human values, some of the results of our drive to the frontier. The cost of making a grabbag of our country, while it has provided stirring subject matter for the art of Pare Lorentz in *The Plow*

That Broke the Plains and *The River,* has never before been reckoned by Hollywood. Now, in one brave leap, the industry has caught up with at least one phase of our current economic history. By touching on some of the results of land speculation, submarginal farming, agricultural mechanization, and the California latifundia, *The Grapes of Wrath* has set a precedent for contemporary and historical honesty in movie-making. It has dramatized and memorialized one wretched section of the victims of American history. No succeeding picture can alter or erase the gaunt, hungry image of the tractored-out farmer menaced in his struggle to keep alive no longer by Indians, but by starvation.

> *The big fellows is workin' their farms with tractors an' day labor . . .*
> *The peoples is walking the road, looking for places.*

That is one of our twentieth-century psalms, the words of an Oklahoman, recorded in the field by the photographer Dorothea Lange, the wisest and most compassionate observer at work in our country, whose book, *An American Exodus,* is the result of her study of migratory workers up and down the country since 1934. Those words are a simple summary of *The Grapes of Wrath,* and the proof of the picture's greatness lies in the fact that it is as simple, as dignified, and as moving as the statement of one of the people.

Mr. Quigley, referred to at the outset of this review, has been brooding forebodingly over the consequences to the screen of the production of *The Grapes of Wrath.* What they may be he does not state, but it is unlikely that they will be unpleasant to any but members of the Old Guard of the *movie business.* How much longer audiences will continue to gape at the usual run of vapid and distant dreams when they can have, if they support them, beautiful and stirring accounts of reality like *The Grapes of Wrath* is still a matter for speculation. The public reaction toward *The Grapes of Wrath* will give the answer. The steady decline in attendance at the movies, traceable mainly to boredom with the average Hollywood product, offers some encouragement. If Hollywood persists in squandering most of its energies of talent and wealth in making pictures considered good enough for the audience by the *movie business,* it will sooner or later run up against the fact that there are not enough Shirley Temple devotees left in this country to go around. If *The Grapes of Wrath* achieves the success it deserves, perhaps some elementary calculations will be made by the producers of bad pictures. Perhaps Mr. Quigley will permit the audience to enlarge the scope of its desires.

Those who expect that the major result of *The Grapes of Wrath* will be some sort of change in Hollywood's attitude toward what it does would seem to be more realistic than those who expect something in the way of a social upheaval close upon the run of the picture. Most people already feel that something should be done about the migratory workers. The picture will undoubtedly make more converts to the idea of government-owned and -operated camps for the dispossessed. Few will derive from the picture—and it is the picture's fault, not theirs—that the plight of the people they pity is the result of a land tragedy, a terrible blunder of our civilization for which all of us will eventually suffer if more strenuous and rational efforts of correction are not quickly made. The picture may stir up bad blood in the more backward parts of the country among those who fear its message, but it is unlikely that the reaction will be violent or widespread. There is no chance, as some people seem to think, that those who consider themselves as badly off as the Joads will arise with clenched fists after seeing *The Grapes of Wrath.* After all, the picture has two endings. The spirit of burning revolt in Tom Joad is overlaid by the final smugness of the incredible Ma. Her ultimate realization that *we* are the people, that *we* will go on even if *they* bash in *our* heads with sawed-off bats and cuesticks, that *we,* the meek, shall inherit the earth, may put comforting and proud thoughts into the heads of the wretched, but like many other middle-class philosophies, hers are not the words which move men, except in the endless and overgrown paths of acceptance.

Of all of John Ford's films made up to 1939, Eisenstein preferred Young Mr. Lincoln, *not* The Informer, Stagecoach, Grapes of Wrath *or any of the others, as the film that he would wish, most of all, to have made. (Henry Fonda played the title role.) Eisenstein went on to tell why he loved it so. It has, he said, a "quality, a wonderful quality, a quality that every work of art must have—an astonishing harmony of all its commonest parts, a really amazing harmony as a whole." Although the film's story is limited to Lincoln's youth, he added, Fonda nevertheless managed to convey much more than this one episode from Lincoln's legal practice. "Behind these visible events," said the Soviet director, "can be sensed the universal pathos with which Lincoln burned—as head and leader of the American people, elected President at the most critical moment of U.S. history. . . ." Eisenstein had seen the film on the eve of World War II and was "immediately enthralled" by the "perfection of its harmony and the rare skill with which it employed all the expressive means at its disposal." Read his entire extraordinary article in Jay Leyda's 1982 edition of Eisenstein's* Film Essays and a Lecture *(Princeton University Press Paperback). (DP)*

37 FOUR MILLION DOLLARS WORTH OF WIND: DAVID SELZNICK'S *GONE WITH THE WIND*

Albert Maltz

WHEN THE TECHNICOLOR has faded, and the drama has been boiled down, *Gone With the Wind* sums itself up into this and nothing else: a Bourbon's history of the Civil War, a slaver's version of his own "tragic" defeat. The story is contrived so as to capture sympathy for the heroic, cultured slave-owners who were ruined by that buzzard Sherman and blasted out of existence by that Yankee marauder Abe Lincoln. The story is definitely not told to show what these heroic land-owners were really fighting for—that they were fighting to maintain the most unholy, the most evil, the most brutalized system of society man has known! No, the stench of slavery does not intrude into the glamorous portrait of the O'Hara's, and the sweat and pain of four million human beings, bought and sold like cattle, whipped, exploited, and kept in bondage *by force of arms only,* does not intrude to spoil the rosy technicolor of this David Selznick super-epic. But despite the fine acting, the fine direction, the theatrical excitement, it remains what it is at the core, the story of Judas wrapped in pink cellophane, the heartbreak of Judas stirringly told—*but with the crucifixion of Jesus very carefully omitted.*

Poor Abe Lincoln must be uneasy in his grave these days! We shudder to think of the mighty strong language he will use if he ever meets up with David Selznick. Because the

From *Equality* (February 1940). Reprinted by permission of the author.

sins of *Gone With the Wind*—and they are sins and nothing less—are not only those of omission. They reside in the picture by deliberate, premeditated commission as well. This is no case where the producer or anyone else can plead ignorance. We may be sure that every last detail of the costumes of the period was investigated, checked and rechecked. There are no errors there. It is merely history that Hollywood has not bothered to verify. And let no one plead in extenuation that a film cannot tell everything, that a story cannot be history. No one condemns *Gone With the Wind* because it does not tell the "whole" story of the Civil War. We must condemn it because it tells a certain kind of history, a phony history, because every premise of the film and the totality of its impressions make for untruth, slander, and perversion from the first moment to the last.

All of history could be rewritten this way. We could tell the tragic story of Marie Antoinette with the enslaved peasants of France as the mass villain. We could concoct a fine film about the American Revolution in which we wept to see Tories driven from their homes, as they were; to see how the coarse soldiers of that brigand George Washington broke the heart of that gentleman and scholar, Cornwallis, as they did. Of course the people on the wrong side of history suffer! Of course the Southern aristocrats suffered when they were wounded, and suffered like nobody's business when they could no longer maintain themselves by the enslavement of other human beings. But to dramatize these sufferings without reference to cause and effect, to make the slaver a tragic hero and the liberator of slaves a villain, that does not make a historical film, it makes a historical lie!

Nowhere is this more revealing than in the handling of the Negro characters in the film. The slaves are shown as of one of two kinds: either faithful retainers who love nothing better than their state of slavery, or else as comic and hysterical, moronic and "simple as a child." What is the truth? The truth is that the attractive Southern aristocrats who are the main characters of *Gone With the Wind* lost their fight because their own Negro slaves fought tooth and nail with the Union armies throughout the Civil War! From its beginnings, slavery in our country was maintained only by the use of repressive law, by the whip, the shackle, the gun. And when the war came every Union general had two fists—his own soldiers and the slaves behind the Confederate lines. By 1862 the state of North Carolina was losing one million dollars worth of slaves every week. Where were these "docile, slavery-loving, comic" slaves going? They were going with the wind all right, they were going north. Despite one white overseer for every fifteen slaves, despite patrols in every district, despite the fact that tens of thousands of Confederate soldiers never saw front line action because they had to be kept at home to keep down insurrection, these slaves were breaking for freedom, gaining freedom, winning the right to fight in the Union armies! And they fought! They fought so well and so hard and so bravely and in such numbers *that the central political question of the Confederacy in the last two years of its existence was whether or not to free its slaves in the hope of getting them to fight in the Southern armies.*

But this is not part of the history that *Gone With the Wind* has chosen to tell. The army of Sherman is not shown as an army of emancipation, but as a locust plague of brutes trampling on the fair South.

The Negro organizations of this country have reacted as they should have to this mint julep slaver's film. They have declared a boycott against it. In this they have already been joined by trade unions, by many liberal and progressive organizations. This is just what is needed. It's splendid. We live at a time when civil liberties, when the rights of minorities, are being threatened, slandered, attacked and misrepresented on all fronts. We who believe with real sincerity in civil liberty, we who give more than lip service to the idea of equality, must fight back! And this means on all fronts. Or else we shall be naïve fools, too careless of our own security to be worthy of liberty.

Gone With the Wind failed to win the New York Film Critics Circle Best Film of 1939 Award; it was won, by a vote of 13 to 3, by Wuthering Heights. *This editor, then a member of the Circle, was among the 10 who were not persuaded by the three reviewers of the* Daily News, *headed by Kate Cameron, that bigotry, no matter how well done, deserved*

enshrinement. The verdict infuriated John Chapman, entertainment editor of the News, *who blasted the Critics Circle decision as "intellectually immature." To the contrary, never before 1939, nor in the 50 years since, has the New York Film Critics Circle rendered a more mature judgment.*
Reviewing David Selznick's hit movie Duel in the Sun (Daily Worker), I wrote: "It is a degrading film. Not since Gone With the Wind, *which also came out of the House of Selznick, have we seen such a display of chauvinism toward colored people." Calling the movie a harbinger of the growth of fascist thinking in Hollywood, I attacked the way Jennifer Jones, playing a part-Indian, was degraded and called "Papoose," "Half-Breed Squaw," "Bob-Tailed Half-Breed," "Minnehaha," "Tamale," "Pocahontas," and similar epithets. "The chauvinism in* Duel in the Sun, *extends to the Negro maid played by Butterfly McQueen, who evokes laughter every time she opens her mouth to speak. Jennifer Jones was doomed to die in the end because the Production Code forbade Charles Bickford, Joseph Cotten, and Gregory Peck, all of whom lusted after her, to marry her." (DP)*

38 HOW THE SCREEN WRITERS FORMED A UNION IN 1933

Lester Cole

TOWARD THE END OF MAY, 1975, some young filmmakers from Boston came to Hollywood. They were shooting a documentary feature film about the blacklist in Hollywood during the dark decade of the late '40s and early '50s. Among others, they visited Roy M. Brewer in his office at the International Alliance of Theatrical Stage Employees (IATSE), the controlling craft union in the film industry. They wanted to interview him on film; he was a key figure in those days. He declined. A pity. Brewer, a union piecard and ambitious red-baiter, rose to his greatest heights in those days as Lord High Executioner of the blacklist. The Producers Association had made him the clearance man; it was to him the stool-pigeons and penitents came pleading for their jobs. The price was to "purge" themselves by going before the un-American Activities Committee and name names and disavow all unclean thoughts and associations of the past.

In the course of refusing to appear in the film Brewer intimated it was part of the ongoing Red Conspiracy, and stated that this had started in Hollywood decades before, when in 1933 the Communist Party had sent out a well-known playwright to organize the Screen Writers Guild. This was vicious nonsense, of course. Communists don't create unions; far more often union struggle creates communists. As for the creation of the Screen Writers Guild in 1933, I am

This memoir of the Screen Writers Guild by one of its founders was written for *Celluloid Power* in 1976.

one of the few still around who was among the nine original organizers. I remember it well.

Early in 1933, almost immediately after his Inauguration, Franklin Roosevelt took a drastic measure in an attempt to stem the rising tide of misery and desperation rising everywhere from the depression. He ordered a one-week bank holiday to prevent an imminent run on the banks, many of which had already closed their doors. Under the edict no deposits could be withdrawn; during this time the government and the banks would retreat and consolidate their lines.

The effect of the nationwide depression was minimal on the film industry. With the advent of talking pictures a few years before, it was a novelty that drew millions of people into theaters seeking solace and escape from their reality. Famous Broadway actors like the Barrymores were lured to films, well-known playwrights and top newspaper men were brought out at fabulous salaries; new life had been injected into a decadent environment.

Production companies are not in business merely to make money; their goal is to make *more* money. And this bank holiday seemed to offer such an opportunity. A day or two after it was announced, the Producers called meetings in every studio of writers, directors and actors. At these meetings the panic button was pushed, anti-unionism was pounded with flags unfurled in patriotic fervor. At Paramount Studios, everyone—stars, directors and writers (I was one of them, newly arrived)—was called to a meeting in a large projection room. There we listened to an impassioned appeal by Emmanuel Cohen, then a Vice-president. After reminding us that in this grave crisis Paramount and the Nation were worth saving, he outlined his plan for salvation. Because unions of carpenters, electricians, prop men and other technicians held the studios in the tyrannical grip of union contracts, their wages could not be cut, contracts could not be broken and the studios had no alternative, if they were to survive, but to ask our assistance. He was confident we would respond affirmatively to a fifty percent cut in salary, which would be instituted industry wide. That was it.

I remember people coming out of the projection room into the bright sunlight stunned and blinking. I came out with a writer, Brian Marlow, veteran of the Dramatist's Guild strike on Broadway some years before. "What chutzpah!" this Irishman howled, and we both laughed as we instantly understood what had to be done. We needed what the carpenters, electricians, grips and prop men had—a trade union. Back to our offices, where we started calling writers, both at Paramount and at other studios. That night nine of us met, discussed the situation. It became clear there were many serious grievances beside this proposed outrage. We drew up a statement of principles and a call for a meeting of all screen writers. Its first paragraph read:

> For the purpose of discussing the betterment of conditions under which writers work in Hollywood the following motion picture writers met on February 3rd, 1933: Kubec Glasmon, Courtney Terrett, Brian Marlow, Lester Cole, Samson Raphaelson, John Howard Lawson, Edwin Justus Mayer, Louis Weitzenkorn, John Bright, Bertram Block.

The document then outlined the need for a powerful organization to combat the proposed wage cut and the intolerable conditions under which the writers worked. The grievances were many: arbitrary changes in material written, abuses of credit on the screen and in advertising, a demand for a system of royalty payments such as playwrights received, rather than salaries, and many others.

Within two weeks more than four hundred writers joined and formed the Screen Writers Guild. Immediately an opposing union was formed at MGM under the guidance of Irving Thalberg, then head of the studio. It was called the Screen Playwrights. Instantly recognized and given a contract, this company union became the opponent of the SWG in 1937 when NLRB elections were held. The SWG won. It took three more years and a strike threat to get a contract.

With the attempt to enforce a fifty percent cut, with abuses to writers' material and their credits, with indignities that were insufferable, creative men and women for the first time formed a trade union. It wasn't the Communist Party, as Roy Brewer charged, that organized the film writers, it was the Motion Picture Producers Association.

39 PROFESSOR MAMLOCK AND OTHER SOVIET ANTI-NAZI FILMS

David Platt

FILM HISTORIAN JAY LEYDA who studied with Soviet director Sergei Eisenstein in Moscow during the 1930s, once observed that at the height of the Stalin terror in 1937–38, "in this darkest period of suspicions, informers, arrests, disappearances, some of the most lasting and hopeful Soviet films appeared." (*Kino, History of the Russian and Soviet Film,* MacMillan, 1960.)

Among such "most lasting and hopeful films" were three of the world's most powerful anti-Hitler films: *Professor Mamlock* (1938), *The Oppenheim Family* (1939), and *Concentration Camp* (originally called *Swamp Soldiers,* 1939). Eisenstein's *Alexander Nevsky* (1937), although it dealt with medieval Russia's struggle against the invading Teutonic Knights (Germans), also belongs in this group. All were made at the height of the world struggle against Hitler Fascism and prior to the signing of the Soviet-German Non-Aggression Pact of August 23, 1939. All were taken out of circulation by the Soviet authorities when the Pact was signed and were not shown again until after the Nazi invasion of the Soviet Union on June 22, 1941.

The best of the anti-nazi films was *Professor Mamlock,* an adaptation of Friedrich Wolf's anti-Nazi play, brilliantly directed by Adolf Minkin and Herbert Rappoport, and acted by Sergei Mezhinsky as an assimilated German Jewish surgeon who is vilely persecuted by the Nazis. When the Hitler regime comes to power Mamlock is deeply distressed that his son has decided to join the Communist underground. The

331

professor is under the illusion that he himself is immune from attack because of his professional position and distinguished war record. In the end he is shot to death while proclaiming his love for the Germany of Beethoven and Goethe. In the film's most famous scene Mamlock endures with great dignity the jeers and insults of a crowd of stormtroopers as he is paraded through the streets wearing his surgeon's uniform on which is inscribed a yellow star with the word "Jude."

It is an interesting coincidence that around the time this Soviet film was being shown in Europe and the USA, John Howard Lawson, the noted dramatist and screenwriter then in Hollywood, had completed a film script on a similar theme about the Nazi persecution of a Jewish doctor, and William Dieterle (director of Life of Zola and Story of Pasteur) had been assigned to direct it. Everything was all set to go: the sets had been built, the cast selected, the camera crews were ready to move. Then suddenly, the producer, Walter Wanger, pulled the film out of production. He had just received word that if he went through with his plan to make an anti-Hitler film the banks would cut off his funds.

It would be quite a while before a Hollywood film would dare to mention that Jews were being persecuted in Hitler's Germany.

The year 1939 also saw the release of the much acclaimed Soviet film version of Leon Feuchtwanger's novel, The Oppenheim Family, which dealt with the ups and downs of a German Jewish family before and after the Nazis burned the Reichstag. The great Yiddish actor Solomon Michoels had an important role in The Oppenheim Family.

It is worth noting that when this Soviet film was submitted to the Chicago Board of Censors in June 1939 it was rejected on the ground that it "exposes to contempt, derision and obloquy a class of German citizens (i.e., the Nazis)." The record also shows that in December 1938, the same Chicago Censors banned Professor Mamlock as "purely Jewish and Communist propaganda against Germany and Hitler and might incite to riot." Protests against the Chicago bans eventually compelled the authorities to release both films to the theatre.

In the 1939 Soviet film Concentration Camp, S. Mezhinsky,

the actor who played Professor Mamlock, was cast as a Jewish pharmacist who is beaten up by Hitler's brown-shirted thugs for refusing to inform on his comrades in the underground. A bit later he is seen in a concentration camp digging in a ditch and having to endure a Nazi guard's litany of vicious anti-Semitic insults.

A frightening incident in connection with the showing of this film in New York deserves to be mentioned here. At the point in the film where the Jewish people are being flayed as inferior to Germans, a loud explosion is heard—an explosion many times louder than a pistol shot.

The explosion is not in the film but in the theatre where it is being shown. It was the explosion of a tear-gas bomb thrown, as it turned out, by Yorkville Nazis. The *Daily Worker* of May 10, 1939 gave an account of this act of terror. It is an eyewitness report by novelist Benjamin Appel who was in the theatre—the Thalia Theatre on 95th Street, just off Broadway—viewing the film when it happened. And, apparently, Appel knew what to do as soon as the "faint sweetish smell of tear gas" crept into his nostrils. "Stay where you are," he shouted to the screaming, baffled and amazed audience, "Move to the doors," and in response to his calming voice, all filed out into the street, many with tears pouring down their cheeks, and handkerchiefs shooting out of hundreds of pockets. Once safely outdoors, nobody went home; they milled around the theatre, talking about what happened, who did it, and how to prevent its recurrence.

As Appel pointed out, "This movie about fascist horror is being continued on the sidewalks of New York City, as if all of us have suddenly become extras in a mass play," and he goes on to describe the commotion caused by the appearance of police cars with their shrieking sirens, along with an ambulance from a nearby hospital, other honking cars, detectives, reporters, and scores of curious passersby. He particularly notes the crowd's skepticism of the police theory (a position they later abandoned) that "labor troubles of some kind" were involved here, but "minds and hearts know better." Still, there was one "thin man in a shabby blue suit" who muttered something about all strikers being 'reds' and should be deported, and "Jews shouldn't go to Russian movies." In the end there's general agreement with a young college student that if America is to remain free, "we must all unite—Jew and Christian—to see that no concentration camps come to this country."

That film showing took place in May, 1939. By the end of August or the middle of September it would no longer be available for showing anywhere in the world for nearly two years, and this would hold true for all the other powerful Soviet anti-Nazi films released before the Pact. *Professor Mamlock* was withdrawn from the New York World's Fair within a week of the signing of the Pact by Molotov and Ribbentrop. Its next showing in New York would be on June 25, 1941—three days after the Nazi invasion of the Soviet Union.

A MEMORABLE DOCUMENT

In December, 1938 the Hollywood film colony issued an extraordinary document against Nazism and anti-Semitism; it was signed by 56 topflight actors, directors, writers and producers. The document, dated December, 1938 and entitled *Declaration of Democratic Independence,* was published in the form of the American Declaration of Independence of July 4, 1776. There were 56 signers representing the film colony because that was the exact number of signers of the original Declaration in '76. Paul Muni, Edward G. Robinson, Bette Davis, Myrna Loy, Joan Crawford, Groucho Marx, Henry Fonda, George Arliss and Rosalind Russell were among them.

This little known Declaration petitioned the President, the Congress and the People of the United States to sever all economic and trade relations with Nazi Germany for its "wanton persecution of defenseless minorities," its enslavement of labor, its "strident contempt" for the democratic way of life, its brazen proclamation that it intends to continue to "loot, pillage, inflict torture and commit murder."

Its publication was the start of a sweeping campaign to obtain 20 million signatures as one aspect of the movie colony's response to the Nazi persecution of Jews. In the previous month (November 1938), Hitler's stormtroopers had launched their coordinated attack on the Jewish community in Germany. These were the "Kristallnacht" pogroms, as they came to be known, of November 10, 1938—a night of infamy in which every synagogue in the Third Reich was destroyed, along with thousands of Jewish stores and shops, and some 30,000 Jews were rounded up and sent to concentration camps. Leni Riefenstahl, Hitler's top movie propagandist, was visiting Hollywood in the Fall of that year in what turned out to be an unsuccessful effort of this "Ribbentrop in Skirts," as she was dubbed, to sell her fascist films to the American people. The entire film industry, with very few dishonorable exceptions, boycotted the unwelcome visitor. "There is no room in Hollywood for Leni Riefenstahl," said an effective and widely circulated statement of the Hollywood Anti-Nazi League, expressing the views of all decent Americans, "in this moment when hundreds of thousands of our brethren await certain death. Close your doors to all Nazi agents" (*New York Times*, Nov. 30, 1938).

AN EXCERPT FROM THE DECLARATION

This, then, was the background of the film colony's "Declaration," which said:

> On July 4, 1776, the people of our country threw off the yoke of tyranny and called upon the world to witness their Declaration of Independence. Men of free spirit, they proclaimed their belief in man's inalienable right to Life, Liberty and the Pursuit of Happiness. Since that time . . . whenever challenged, we have reaffirmed our faith in these rights. . . . We accuse the leaders of Nazi Germany, as a ruler was accused in 1776, of a design to reduce the world under absolute despotism. . . . They deny the rights of man. They destroy Freedom of Speech, Freedom of Worship, Freedom of the Press, and the Right to Peaceful Assembly. They wantonly persecute defenseless minorities; they imprison ministers of all religions; they enslave labor; they victimize their own citizenry . . . and brazenly proclaim that this victimization has only begun; in the name of the state they loot, pillage, inflict torture and commit murder. . . . This our conscience will permit no longer. . . .
>
> THEREFORE, we, the undersigned, respectfully petition the President, the Congress of the United States to make such

executive orders . . . to the end that all economic connections between the USA and Germany be totally severed, until such time as Germany is willing to re-enter the family of nations, in accordance with humane principles of international law and universal freedom.

Other signers included Melvyn Douglas, Walter Wanger, Harry M. Warner, John Ford, Gale Sondergaard, Herbert Biberman, Donald Ogden Stewart, Nunnally Johnson, Ira Gershwin, Helen Gahagan (Douglas), and Frank Tuttle.

What happened to the Declaration, to the 56 signers and the film industry as a whole in the ensuing decade of World War II, the Holocaust, Cold War, McCarthyite witchhunting and blacklisting, is told in the ensuing pages of this volume.

40   DZIGA VERTOV'S *THREE SONGS OF LENIN*

Jay Leyda

THE FIRST EXCITING FILM EXPERIENCE after getting back to Moscow in September was the new film of my temporary boss, Vertov. After three years of anxiety and hesitation and false starts, he had produced his greatest film, *Three Songs of Lenin*—and for once no one was left unmoved. His original idea of a film about Lenin had grown into a film about the effect of Lenin's life and teaching, and this led him to show this effect on some who had changed most—the women of central Asia. From the mass of folklore born from the revolution, Vertov found his vehicle in three anonymous songs of Uzbekistan, "folk-songs" about Lenin. For those women, as expressed in their songs, Lenin meant freedom, his death a dreadful blow, and his teachings the basis of their future life. These three subjects shape the structure of the film.

The film opens with the first song, "My face was in a prison black . . ." a song about women, imprisoned in the terrifying black horse-hair "veils" of the past. This part of the film is heavy with the weight of oppression, the chains of tradition that burdened the women of the Asian colonies of Tsarist Russia; the section ends in brightness and hope. The second song, about the death of Lenin, achieves an emo-

From "Witnessed Years," in Jay Leyda's 1960 volume, *KINO: A History of the Russian and Soviet Film*. Third edition copyright © 1983 by Princeton University Press. Reprinted by permission of the author and of Princeton University Press.

tional impact seldom realized in the film medium. "We loved him. . . ." Afterwards one wonders how the suffering was conveyed. ". . . we never looked upon his face, we never heard his voice, but he loved us like a father—no, more than that, for no father ever did for his children what Ilyich did for us." The third song opens with the triumphant chords of "In a great stone city," expanding into a glowing lyricism that Vertov's work, alongside its proclaimed factuality, had always hinted. The dependence on songs (later done into English by W.H. Auden) also determined the emotional tone of the film, a new tone not so much for Vertov, but for the international documentary film form.

Even before 1918, when Vertov entered the cinema in a professional capacity, he had dreamed of making an art of the sights and sounds of the world around him, arranging harmonies and dissonances out of these realities. It is interesting that, working as a poet when a boy, he became interested in films for their *partial* realization of his dream. His first use of the sound-film, almost a miraculous answer to that dream, was still linked to "pure" documentation, in *Enthusiasm*. It was in his second sound-film that the boy-poet, Vertov, was recalled. Vertov's former "absolute" dependence upon montage of otherwise untouched material had developed into a wish for more concrete images than the pure document can ever accomplish, but without discarding his long experience with archive material and with the untouched document. *Three Songs of Lenin* contains a quantity of archive material, moulded so deftly into the whole that it ascends beyond its specific historic source. It is really remarkable how the same footage brings such different results in the hands of Shub and Vertov. An example of the latter's lyrical method occurs in the second song where newsreel material of Lenin's funeral is juxtaposed to a series of faces, of many times and places, flooded with sorrow, creating a passage of genuine tragic beauty. There is a use of the untouched document in the third song when three spontaneous speeches are recorded. The strength of these uses of archive and untouched materials lies in Vertov's experience. He knew how far the pure document can be useful, because he had advanced beyond it.

Leyda wrote that after reading New York reviews of Vertov's Three Songs of Lenin, the leading trade weekly, Motion Picture Herald, edited by Martin Quigley, published three frightened pages, beginning:

The American screen, already burdened quite with its own sins and faced with endless problems of political regulation, taxation and general bedevilment of all sorts, now unwittingly adds entanglement in the web of propaganda woven in Moscow in the cause of chaos and the Third Internationale.

The Hearst Press developed this campaign; after Motion Picture Herald's survey, published February 23, 1935, "Soviet Pictures Showing in 152 Theatres in US," a commendably factual account (in four pages), the Hearst American (March 6, 1935) described the "multi-armed Octopus in Moscow" to its readers:

The avowed purpose is the complete annihilation of the United States of America and its democratic institutions and the substitution of the dictatorship of the proletariat, the complete destruction of personal liberty, and, finally, as a matter of course, the transference of the national law-making body from Washington to Moscow.[!]

The latest propagandist move in this attempt of Russia to conquer America is in the field of the motion picture.

And now, 53 years later, there's Mikhail Gorbachev's Glasnost, which, if we are to believe Jesse Helms and Norman Podhoretz, hastens our physical and cultural demise. (DP)

PART IV

WAR, POST-WAR, AND McCARTHYISM

41 CHAPLIN'S *THE GREAT DICTATOR*

Herman G. Weinberg

The Great Dictator (U.S. 1940). Written and directed by Charles Chaplin. Photography by Karl Struss, Rollie Totheroh. Design: J. Russell Spencer. With Charles Chaplin, Paulette Goddard, Jack Oakie, Reginald Gardiner, Henry Daniell, Billy Gilbert, Grace Hale, Carter De Haven, Maurice Moscovitch.

THE GREAT DICTATOR begins and ends on a note of terror. Starkly, it opens on that fateful morning of November 11, 1918, somewhere on the western front. The earth shakes with paroxysm, coughs, strangles, and vomits its gorge as the screaming shells plow into it, burst and send the hot iron shrapnel flying in all directions from the roseate irises of foul black and red, like poisonous flowers laughing hysterically in their death agony, rising slowly in putrescent grandeur, infecting the sweet, cool morning air with its gangrenous vapor. (Elsewhere, the knife-glitter of the surgery ward, the torn flesh on the beds of pain, cotton soaked in ether, the clotted blood, twisted faces and mingled stink of sweat, tetanus, and carbolic acid.) Behind the cold, gray opening of *The Great Dictator,* etched sketchily in charcoal blacks and whites of a gun here, a bursting shell there, and men scurrying like rats in a trench all around, is Latzko's *Men in*

From Herman G. Weinberg's collection of his writings in *Saint Cinema* (November 1940). Reprinted by permission of the author.

War and the hatred of war of the artist who begins here to make his plea for universal brotherhood.

When the camera swings swiftly by "Big Bertha," the obscene product of a diseased imagination, a little man, cog number "x" in the horrendous war machine now got out of control, stands ready to pull the lever-cord that will send a shell hurtling seventy miles to Paris on the Cathedral of Notre Dame. What an achievement! What a thing is man, indeed! But the little man by the big gun is Charlie Chaplin and so with an exquisite pas de seul he pulls the lever-cord and the shell spits out of the gun to land on a nearby outhouse, with a boom and a splintering crash, and a "pshaw!" with a disappointed snap of the fingers from Chaplin. From this moment on Chaplin ridicules war. The spectator's horror has turned to bitter laughter. Chaplin struggles with a hand grenade that has fallen down his sleeve into the recesses of his uniform. "Take the pin out, count ten and throw it!" he was warned. But with the pin out it is now sputtering somewhere in his clothing. Frantically he tears at his uniform as the precious seconds tick off, locates it, tosses it quickly away and it explodes. With a sigh of relief, he faints. This is not war as the dictators teach it to their youth.

So Chaplin begins *The Great Dictator* by reviling war and showing his contempt for it as a thing of vast and horrible imbecility.

Wounded, he spends the next fifteen years in a hospital, emerging to find his fatherland held in thrall by a dictator heading a political party that has terrorized an entire nation into whimpering submission. He returns to his little barber shop, to take up life where he left it, but the street has now become a ghetto and the other Jews live in constant fear of the storm troopers. It seems that Jews have become the special butt of the new regime and his first encounter with storm troops who paint "Jew" over his shop windows leads to a fight and a realization that something terrible has happened while he has been away.

Then we see what it is that has happened. Before a great throng, against banners with their ridiculous arbitrary insignia (Chaplin humorously substitutes the double-cross for the swastika), the great dictator himself. Again, Chaplin—the dictator, who had the misfortune to look like the little Jewish barber. (None of the reviewers of the film have commented on the beautiful logic of this resemblance in Chaplin's scenario; how it is borne out in real life that the world's most hated figure is indicted by the world's most loved figure.) Then follows a devastating parody of Hitler having a seizure, in other words, giving a speech. The psychopathic sobbings, breast-beating, contemptuous exhortations for sacrifice which the fatherland demands and all the assorted razzle-dazzle and pure, unadulterated sheep-dip, have been scrambled by Chaplin into such a towering edifice of hilarious nonsense that at his conclusion, when the great dictator has shouted himself dry, Chaplin makes his final crushing comment on the whole paranoiac performance. The dictator gulps down a drink of water and then . . . but perhaps you had better see for yourself how deliciously Chaplin puts across one of the things he thinks is the matter with Hitler. ("My speech makes as much sense as his do," commented Chaplin recently.) Subsequently, there is another bit with the dictator again having shrieked himself hoarse, raising the glass of water spontaneously to his ear, but, suddenly realizing that what he regarded up to now as his *Sitzfleisch* was really only a hole in the ground, brings the glass down to his mouth. (But if you think Chaplin lets it go at that, you just don't know Chaplin, nor, for that matter, do you know the very funny story of the lunatic and the Queen of the Netherlands that refugees brought over in recent weeks. If you know the story, you'll know what I mean when you see this episode in the film.)

"Originality and truth are to be found only in details," said Stendhal. If I dwell on the details of Chaplin's great fresco, it is only because in them truth is revealed in all its splendid incandescence; in these seemingly insignificant details are Chaplin's sharpest observations and, by far, his greatest originality. Such as, following upon an auto-erotic tête-à-tête with his minister of propaganda who envisions for him a beautiful blonde Aryan world ruled by a brunette dictator whom this race of supermen and superwomen would worship as a god, the great dictator leaps in ecstasy across the room and up a drapery, where he remains, for a moment poised and transfigured. In what way is this merciless observation of Chaplin's different essentially from the mystic of Berchtesgaden, perched in his armoured aviary on a high crag of the Bavarian Alps, there brooding on the Gotterdammerung he has unleashed on the world? ("I hear a beating of wings!" said Herod. "I do not wish to hear it! It is an omen of death!" Oscar Wilde would have understood Hitler, as Freud did. But the beating of wings is the R.A.F. and they understand him, too, as do now even his former appeasers and as soon everyone will understand him.)

The dictator slides down the drapery, he is alone. He approaches a terrestial globe, lifts it—and flings it rapturously into the air. A beatific smile plays upon his mouth. Against soft, shimmering music out of Wagner by way of a good Aryan pogrom, the great dictator does a bubble dance with the terrestial globe. The *morbidezza* of this scene, the profundity with which Chaplin, with shocking suddenness, has realized the essence, not only of his own film, but of what is happening to the world today because of the aberration of one man, is apocalyptic. It is not only the most intense lyrical moment that Chaplin has ever touched, but one has really to go back to Shakespeare and Goethe to find passages that will equal it in its febrile glow.

The rest of the film's story, of how the little Jewish barber, after a series of misadventures, comes to be mistaken for the "Furore" and is called upon to speak before a massed throng come to "celebrate" the fall of Austria, is too well known by now to need detailing here. The critical boys and girls of the metropolitan press have had their field day with this passionate summing up by Chaplin of how he feels about the spectacle of humanity being kicked around. But Chaplin, himself, has answered his critics better than I, or anyone, could do. "May I not be excused in pleading for a better world? . . . It was a very difficult thing to do. It would have been much easier to have the barber and Hannah disappear over the horizon, off to the promised land against the glowing sunset. But there is no promised land for the oppressed people of the world. There is no place over the horizon to which they can go for sanctuary. They must stand and we must stand."

Listen to the closing words of Chaplin in *The Great Dictator,* that bitter six-minute speech in which he says, "I should like to help every one, if possible, Jew, Gentile, black man, white. We all want to help one another. Human beings are like that. We want to live by each other's happiness. . . . In the 17th Chapter of St. Luke it is written: 'The Kingdom of God is within man'—not in one man nor a group of men, but in all men. You, the people, have the power to make this life free and beautiful, to make this life a wonderful adventure. . . .' " Listen to these words and then contemplate the crowning irony of the National Legion of Decency's statement that they are not recommending *The Great Dictator* for children because; "Unrelated to plot or characterization, Chaplin utters a seemingly gratuitous and personal remark suggesting his disbelief in God. In view of the star's following, this utterance in its possible harmful effect on audiences is deplored." (Hannah, played by Paulette Goddard, asks the barber if he believes in God, and the barber thinks for a moment and begins, "Well . . ." but she interrupts him and goes on to tell him an incident apropos.)

I say here and now that every child in America should see *The Great Dictator,* that God is not the special concern (nor the private property) of the National Legion of Decency, that Chaplin's God is as good as theirs, that the god-head in man is a more real God than the detached Being that any individual or group of individuals can summon according to what axe he has to grind. Why did the Legion of Decency make no statement about the godlessness and bestiality of the Nazi film, *Feldzug in Polen,* which played for two months to packed and cheering houses in the German quarter of New York? What kind of "decency" is that?

In the Talmud it is written that there are things on earth which make even the angels in Heaven weep.

Do a bit of scratching of a critic of Chaplin's six-minute Speech in The Great Dictator *and find a hater of his fourteen-minute oration, "On the Battlefields of Russia Democracy Will Live Or Die." Chaplin delivered his Oration over the telephone July 22, 1942 from Hollywood to a giant rally at Madison Square Park, New York, "in support of President Roosevelt for the immediate opening of a second front to hasten the final victory over Hitler and the Axis." This great rally of 60,000 trade unionists and members of civic, fraternal, veteran, community and church organizations was sponsored by no fewer than 250 unions affiliated with the Greater New York CIO. A reprint of the speech, issued in massive thousands of copies by the Council of the CIO, noted that "the great crowd, previously warned not to interrupt with applause, hushed and strained for every word" as the artist made his persuasive plea to open a second front. Chaplin's speeches—and the thunderous rallies—aroused the nation. It was not difficult, he said in his* Autobiography, *"to ignite the sympathy of all America for a second front." The Red Army had just won a smashing victory at Stalingrad. Not everybody was pleased, however, with the way things were going. As a result of his stand Chaplin's social life "gradually receded." The invitations to spend weekends in "opulent country houses" stopped, he revealed. (DP)*

42 ORSON WELLES' *CITIZEN KANE*

Cedric Belfrage

A PPARENTLY *Citizen Kane* is not, after all, destined to go down in history as the great Hollywood myth. The press has seen it, with highballs, caviar, canapes and soft music to follow—and never were these traditional cushioners of a flop's fall so superfluous. It is not difficult to imagine the tremendous forces that have been at grips behind the scenes to decide whether it should be shown or shelved. On the one hand, a picture which the people of America will pay millions of dollars to see. On the other, the might and majesty and profits of dark yellow journalism—exposed by *Kane* so effectively, because so humanly and with such inspired craftsmanship.

There has never—and I speak as one who has attended thousands of them—been a more exciting press show. For on that screen the slaves, the houris and the camp-followers of the press lords saw some of the truth told about what enslaves, degrades and makes prostitutes of them. And at the same time they saw the whole spangled pyramid of Hollywood movie conventions, which they have had to support with their bodies in their advertisement-controlled "criticism," toppled over and left in ruins by the heroic Orson Welles and his Mercury Theater nobodies.

Heaven knows what lies or evasions many of them had to go back to their offices and write about the picture's theme—for it is very much one of those assignments in

---

From *The Clipper*, Los Angeles literary journal (May, 1941). Reprinted by permission of the author.

which, as ·we delicately phrase it, "questions of policy" are involved. But never mind. The people are going to see *Citizen Kane,* and not one of them will *be quite the same person after seeing it as he was before.* It is as profoundly moving an experience as only this extraordinary and hitherto unexplored medium of sound-cinema can afford in two hours. You leave it with regret, wishing you could see it all through again, feeling all of your old belief in the medium restored, all of your shattered illusions made whole. You become dizzy trying to recall all the good things in it, the excellencies of different kinds—lighting, composition, direction, dialogue, acting, make up, music and sound, editing and construction—which are present simultaneously at almost any moment in the picture. You realize how rusty your faculties for apprehending all the qualities of a motion picture have become, through long experience of striving to find even one good quality at a time.

Certainly it represents a revolution, and a major one, in Hollywood's approach to cinema. Trying to find in my critical memories any Hollywood celluloid that gave me a comparative emotional and artistic experience, I could only think of Chaplin's *Woman of Paris.* One recalls how the techniques used in that picture turned the studios upside down and inside out. Remember Edna Purviance waiting for the train which was to take her away from her home and her lover to Paris. She stood quite still, filling the screen, looking straight ahead of her just over the camera. The train was never shown except by shadows from its lights which passed, gradually slowing to a halt, over her face—then she walked toward the camera and out of the picture. Remember how the fact that she was being kept by Menjou in the Paris flat was shown simply by Menjou going to a drawer and taking a handkerchief—then a close-up of a collar dropping out. Simple and obvious, perhaps—but something nobody had ever done before; as exciting as the cross-cut simultaneous-action chase was in its day, and for the same reason, it was a use of the medium in an authentic way, giving it the dignity of being a medium different from the stage or any other, able to do things the others cannot do. Only the movie could in a few seconds emphasize that collar and what it meant, and so tell a whole story with it.

Since then sound has come. And one can fairly say that, if possibly there are a hundred uses of sound authentic and appropriate to the sound-film medium, at most one or two have been exploited by Hollywood. Perhaps of all the delectable flavors that linger on the palate after seeing *Kane,* the use of sound is strongest. Welles brings to the movie studio a mastery of sound technique in the radio medium, yet that mastery is such that it adapts itself to cinema with effortlessness and discrimination. The scene that everyone will be speaking about—that will be to sound-film what Chaplin's train scene was to silent-film—is the breakfast-table sequence between Kane and his first wife. The whole story of that marriage is told while they sit at the table. There are perhaps five or six lapses of time during the sequences, each one necessitating a change of costume, make-up and position by the two characters. But the dialogue runs straight on without a break, from the first scene where Kane speaks lovingly to his wife, to the last where the wife silently picks up and is hidden behind a copy of the rival paper to Kane's.

Without seeing the picture again it is only possible to touch on what it has. In sound invention Welles seems inexhaustible. He varies it constantly and shatters at every turn the complacency of the critical hack, who never quite recovers from the effect of the first two or three minutes: the main title in silence, then the use of music with the death scene of Kane, then the sudden plunge into gaudy newsreel tempo as accompaniment to the "March of Time" film-within-a-film showing the legendary Kane's life in headlines. An essay or two could be written about the "March of Time" sequence alone. The scenes of Kane's earlier life are scratched as if the film were taken from newsreel archives, and a camera of early days has presumably been used, exposing fewer frames to the second than the cameras of today. The effect of the "real thing" is quite startling.

But the script, the approach to and treatment of the material, is a revolution in itself. It does everything that cannot, must not be done according to Hollywood's dreary 'box-office' conventions. The story of a man's life begins with his death: he speaks a single word which all by itself gives every foot that follows pace and suspense. His story is unfolded through the efforts of a "March of Time" scout to discover the significance of this deathbed word: the strange word "Rosebud." You cannot possibly guess the answer, and the investigator never finds it, though Welles gives it to the audience in the final scene of all. The worst 'crime' of the script—its most fascinating and praiseworthy feature—is that it not only darts about in time from Kane's boyhood to his old age, back to his heyday as a newspaper publisher, back again to his first day on his first paper, on again suddenly to his political and personal decay; not only that, but that it shows the same events several times over. But as each time they are seen through the eyes of a different person, the repetitions do more to build the whole structure of the character and his environment than new scenes could do. Here we are really in the cinema medium, in that and nothing else. What other mediums could show so forcefully that truth is not merely objective, but subjective also and at the same time? Not even the novel.

And what all this does is to make Kane the most three-dimensional human being who ever walked and talked on the screen—I would almost say the only one. Welles does not merely show us one aspect of the man and pound on it. He comes not to praise nor to indict Kane, but to reveal him, as he is and as others see him. The result is that profound pity is stirred up in the audience, and the indictment is not of a man but of environments and social and economic factors which make him what he becomes. The Hollywood axiom that men are born good or bad, and that wrongs and tragedies occur because Mr. Bad temporarily triumphs over Mr. Good, is shown up for the infantile and completely shopworn thing it is.

The implications of *Citizen Kane* for Hollywood and its future products can hardly be estimated at this time. A big man in the studios who was among those privileged to see *Kane* soon after it was finished, is said to have declared that not Hearst, but the top writers and sound men and cameramen and other experts had reason to be scared silly by what the picture revealed. He meant that *Kane* showed them all up as incompetents who need to go back to school to learn the first principles of the medium.

I do not share his concern for these people. Certainly,

Hollywood has an extra-large quota of those phonies in high places who infest every sphere from politics to waterproof roofing. Anything in the way of showing them up and kicking them around that *Kane* can do will be a service to art and mankind. But by no means all of the craftsmen who have not been doing the things *Kane* does are "shown up" by *Kane*. The reason they have not done these things is not that they cannot do them but that they have not been allowed to do them.

Imagine, just for example, a regular Hollywood writer of even the most eminent class daring to submit to his producer a script like *Kane's*! Imagine a make-up man daring to allow real sweat and agony to disorder the hair and face of the heroine as she comes out of a stupor after taking poison! Imagine a set designer putting the characters under real ceilings only a foot or two above their heads! Imagine a cameraman placing his lights so that almost half the time the faces are in shadow! Preposterous! Throw them out!

Yet does any film-goer really think that only Orson Welles and his staff are *capable* of such things? He need not think so. To say that there are in Hollywood a score of cameramen, a score of writers, a score of sound experts, a score of make-up artists—all equal to Orson's men in their own field—is probably to underestimate. For years they have been hoping and trying for a chance to show their skill and originality, but always the film salesman, speaking through the producer, has had the last word; and the film salesman is one trained in not seeing the wood for the trees. Those who are honest in Hollywood know that the regular craftsman, who earns his salary in studios year in and year out, is not allowed to show originality save within the tiny limits that the box-office tradition has laid down. Only when it is a best-selling novel does Hollywood make a *Grapes of Wrath*. And only an Orson Welles or a Chaplin, whose names cast a spell of magic even over the sales force and who are quite independent financially, can break the spells that bind the rank and file to formula. The slaves and houris of Hollywood are like the slaves and houris of Kane's empire, except that the chains of some of them are made of platinum. Yet when a Welles does come along and break the spell, and the box-office tune changes, the effect is like the big scene in *The Sleeping Beauty.* Suddenly tongues begin to talk, brains to operate, everything to move again.

It is just about certain that we shall now see another of Hollywood's copy-cat orgies, with whole films in which nobody's face is ever seen at all, time sequence is mixed up like a Christmas pudding, and every time lapse is shown by continuous dialogue over changing pictures of the same people. But with that, there will also be the release of a whole storehouse of original invention and craft skill which has been bottled up.

None of this is intended as any detraction from the stature of Orson Welles. Hollywood has no score, no dozen, of Welles'. Probably it has only one. He is bigger than any of them, or he could not have put *Citizen Kane* across. He would, I believe, be the first to admit that the things that seem miraculous in *Kane* could, taken individually, have been equalled by many other craftsmen in the departments concerned. But the unique quality he has is the ability to lead and to coordinate the skilled work of others. He does not try to tell the specialists on his staff how to play their own game, but recognizes the skill of each, and gives it full expression within a disciplined and ordered framework which can display it at its best. That, at least, is the impression *Kane* gives me. It is the work of many artists and yet, with and above that, the work of one, as great works of art in any medium have always been up to now. It is correctly described as "By Orson Welles"—not "produced" or "directed" or "from a story" by Welles, but *by* him. And because it is all *by* him, because of his conception and coordination of the work, his collaborators on camera and art direction and sound and all the rest shine more brightly.

He is the biggest man in Hollywood today. And he is the Prince Charming whose bold, smacking kiss on the brow of a bewitched art puts us all in his debt.

Ralph Waldo Emerson said: "The scholar or critic defending the cause of slavery, of arbitrary government, of monopoly, of the oppressor, is a traitor to his profession. He is not company for clean people."

Big business corruption is the central theme of such powerful novels and plays as: Mark Twain's Gilded Age, Dreiser's Sister Carrie and The Financier, Upton Sinclair's The Jungle, Frank Norris' The Octopus, Jack London's Iron Heel, William Dean Howell's Rise of Silas Lapham, Edward Bellamy's Looking Backward, Steinbeck's Grapes of Wrath, Mike Gold's Jews Without Money, Arthur Miller's All My Sons, Lillian Hellman's Little Foxes and Sherwood Anderson's Poor White. Jean-Paul Sartre once said "that there can be no great work of literature which does not contribute to the liberation of man and surely this must hold true of film as well." (DP)

43 WORLD WAR II AND THE AMERICAN FILM

Lewis Jacobs

IN THE RUSH to translate the shock of war into stories of dynamic action—to serve both the national purpose and entertainment—stock patterns and formulas became the rule. The preponderance of shoddy plots, the similarity of situation and action stirred up protests in trade papers and from exhibitors who told Hollywood that the public was fed up with war films. By the spring of 1943, the rising agitation had stampeded many producers into scheduling programs heavy with musicals and other frivolous films, advertised as having absolutely nothing to do with war.

Hostile to the wishful complacency of his colleagues, Harry M. Warner, president of Warner Brothers Pictures, Inc., denounced any abandonment of war movies. "A small group of entertainment appeasers are trying to keep the truth from audiences," he declared.[1] Bosley Crowther, who reported the executive's concern over the urgent need of war films, held much the same opinion. "The public is not tired of war's realities, but of woefully cheap make-believe," he wrote. "What we want in our war films is honest expression of national resolve and a clear indication of realities unadorned with Hollywood hoop-la."[2]

Excerpted from *Cinema Journal* (Winter 1967–8) by permission of the author.

THE DOCUMENTARY INFLUENCE

Lowell Mellett, chief of the Office of War Information's Bureau of Motion Pictures, deplored the emphasis that film-makers had laid on the melodramatic aspects of the conflict, without conveying what the war was all about, or what it meant "for a great democracy to commit itself to war." He told the National Board of Review of Motion Pictures: "Somehow it is almost impossible to feel the war here in America where we seem to be safe. We are still in a state that makes it necessary for us to keep telling ourselves that it is true, that it is real, that we are part of it."[3]

Mellett's dissatisfaction with war films led to the army's deciding to show Hollywood its own viewpoint and thinking on war by giving the film capital the same indoctrination it administered to soldiers. In a series of evening screenings, conducted for producers, directors, writers and the press, the army showed a program of orientation films and documentaries, among which were the *Why We Fight* series. These included *The Prelude To War, The Nazis Strike, Divide and Conquer, The Battle of Britain* and *The Battle of Russia*. (*Battle of China* and *War Comes to America* were still in production.) Individually and as a series these military films were sharp and quick in impact, penetrating in persuasiveness. They were imbued with a clarity of meaning seldom approached by Hollywood, and set a challenging standard for studio-made products.

The *Why We Fight* series was produced under the supervision of Lieutenant-Colonel Frank Capra with the assistance of skilled Hollywood as well as documentary film craftsmen. The events leading to the war, the battle scenes, the intensities of combat were all treated on a very high level. There were no heroics, no romantic conceptions of war, and these pictures in their vividness and technical proficiency and in their doctrine of total war—accepted both by the fascist countries and the democracies—were a powerful embodiment of the War Department's concern for "interpretation of the causes of war, the evidence on which the interpretation is based, and the events which combined to produce the present state of conflict."

The Capra series was made in the belief that if a man

knows his enemy, the reasons for war, and why he is fighting, he will make a better soldier. Similar viewpoints and ideas were expressed in related informational and educational films, produced by the War Department, Army Pictorial Services, the AAF First Motion Picture Unit, the U.S. Navy, the U.S. Marine Corps, and the OWI in cooperation with the British Ministry of Information. Among the best were William Wyler's *Memphis Bell* (1944), John Ford's *Battle of Midway* (1944), *The Battle For the Marianas* (1944), John Huston's *The Battle For San Pietro* and *Let There Be Light* (1945), *Fury In the Pacific* (1945), and *The True Glory* (1945) directed by Carol Reed and Garson Kanin. All were striking studies of men preparing for, engaging in, or suffering from combat. Their intense, intimate, authentic tone, like the *Why We Fight* pictures, had an enormous effect on film-makers, inspiring them with a constant urge to make their own war pictures more genuine and meaningful.

Imbued with a new spirit, indoctrinated Hollywood responded more authoritatively to the need for weightier themes and to the demands of the democratic ethos. Pictures dealing with the nature of the enemy became marked by a deepening of the sociological and psychological issues. From stock portrayals of the enemy as a buffoon, a sentimentalist, a coward or a brutal gangster (in such pictures as *To Be or Not To Be, The Devil With Hitler, Once Upon a Honeymoon* and *Margin For Error*) a handful of subsequent pictures focused on revealing the enemy's disregard of moral precepts and ethical sensibilities, his calculated cruelty, his cunning, and his actual strength. *Keeper of the Flame* (1943) warned against Fascists in America, who masqueraded under Americanism but were plotting to destroy democracy. *Hitler's Children* (1943) revealed the training and indoctrination of German youth scientifically subjected to Nazi ideology. *Watch on the Rhine* (1943) dramatized the struggle for power in an American household in Washington between an anti-Fascist and a Fascist and its central conflict was the strategy of ideologies. A somewhat similar struggle informed *Tomorrow the World* (1944). Here a well-meaning American family was caught between its own liberal principles and the cynicism of Nazi-trained youth. *The Hitler Gang* (1944) portrayed the brutal nature of the Nazi leaders and their ruthless methods of achieving power.

One of the more ambitious and controversial films was Hitchcock's *Lifeboat* (1944). Here was an effort to create an allegory of world shipwreck, in which a deliberate attempt was made to give a more realistic complexion to the strengths and weaknesses of those responsible for the debacle, and to examine, at the same time, varieties of democratic egalitarianism.

The entire action of the picture takes place in a drifting lifeboat containing a group of eight Americans, survivors of a torpedoed freighter, and a Nazi commander, whose U-boat gunned down the freighter before it was itself hit and destroyed. The survivors seemed deliberately chosen to serve the ideological as well as the dramatic needs of the plot. Among them are a millionaire shipbuilder with all the virtues and vices of capitalism, a cynical lady journalist who believes in nothing, a religious Negro steward who loves all humanity, an engineer with liberal views, and the cold-blooded, arrogant U-boat commander. Each of these particular people takes his own particular view of their situation and brings to bear his own kind and degree of moral courage. The Nazi functions as a point of reference in relation to which the other types fix their moral attitudes. Together the occupants form an adroit microcosm of the two warring societies.

Lifeboat posed the problem of survival when social patterns begin to collapse, and when men (or nations) can only survive if they have strength and resourcefulness. In the life and death conditions that prevailed, the Nazi captain was deliberately portrayed as a resolute and cunning figure because, Hitchcock declared, "In the analogue of war, he *was* the victor at the time."[4] He manipulated the Americans' weakness for his own purpose. He was more competent and showed more skill and initiative. He was the only one who knew anything about sailing. He knew where he was heading for, could take command, plan for survival, and even cope with disastrous emergencies—in this case the amputation of the gangrenous leg on one of the crew members from the freighter.

By comparison, the other survivors "representing the

democracies, hadn't gotten together yet, hadn't summoned their strength."[5] They seemed weak, poorly prepared to cope with their dangerous situation, and couldn't act as a group. Not until they discovered the Nazi's treachery were they able to act as one and oppose him. They learned that he had been secretly navigating the boat toward a Nazi supply ship, using a compass he had concealed from them; that he had stolen a bottle of water for himself while they were suffering from thirst; that his apparently superhuman strength had come from food tablets and energy pills; and finally, that he had drowned a member of their group, who had surprised him at his trickery. Outraged, and in a burst of common fury, they collectively beat the Nazi to death. Afterwards, still united and determined in purpose, they fish together.

The picture ends in a kind of allegorical epilogue. The survivors, having drifted in sight of a Nazi supply ship, prepare to die as it attempts to run them down, when, from beyond the horizon, comes a volley of fire, and the Nazi boat is destroyed. As the Americans begin planning their rescue, a Nazi sailor from the sunken supply ship attempts to climb into their lifeboat, precipitating a quarrel over whether to save the German or not. The sailor suddenly confronts them with a gun. The others respond by a group attack and take the weapon away from the Nazi. The last scene leaves them quarreling over whether any German can ever again be trusted or should be treated humanely.

Made at a crucial period in the war, at a time when many people were calling for a second front and the danger of German rocket and missile attacks from the French coast was imminent, *Lifeboat* was a grim reminder against underestimating the resourcefulness and power of the enemy.

ALLIES AND ACTUALITIES

Hollywood also deepened its treatment of the theme in many pictures coming under the classification of "our brothers in arms." These were mainly inside stories of the conquered people in Nazi-occupied Europe. In the past only surface reference had been made to any conflicts raging within individual characters, the films being largely stories of escape, intrigue and espionage. Seldom had any attention been paid to making the background real or saying anything about how the occupation affected the ordinary citizen. Now such pictures not only began to probe deeper into their characters, but also to argue the political aspects of fascism in addition to its barbarism, and to dramatize the craving and need of human beings resisting Nazification for freedom. Beneath the exterior melodrama of underground plots, sabotage schemes and commando raids, the best of them tried to convey the reason some men resist and fight on moral grounds, and others don't.

The Moon is Down, This Land is Mine, Hangmen Also Die, The Commandos, Edge of Darkness, Cross of Lorraine, Song of Russia and North Star—a vintage crop from 1943—were grim and brutal stories of destruction, torture, heroic resistance and death. But they also tried to get underneath the externals of their action and to probe the feelings of individuals, to examine the conflicts between truth and hypocrisy, good will and selfishness. The enemy was called by name—fascism. American and Allied nationals were shown fighting together in plots that graphically illustrated the possibility of victory over the "invincible" enemy, once questions of conscience had been resolved in the determination to win for a just cause.

One of the most outstanding pictures in this category, and one whose story was not set in occupied territory was Mission to Moscow (1943). The picture followed the book of the same name by our former Ambassador to Russia, Joseph E. Davies, and made use of confidential reports to the State Department, selections from the Ambassador's diaries, and official correspondence during his two-year mission in the Soviet Union. Its purpose was clearly to speak out against anti-Soviet prejudice and isolationist feeling in the United States with the object of promoting good will for America's ally.

Mission to Moscow had no plot or story line in the usual sense. It attempted to be a documentary of living history. Its events, presented more or less chronologically, began in 1936 at the Geneva Conference when Haile Selassie appealed for action against Italian aggression, and continued up to the time of Roosevelt's appointment of lawyer Davies to Moscow in 1937, where he was instructed to get the facts about the famous purge trials, and to assess Russia's strength and her attitude toward war or peace in Europe. Every important character in the picture was a counterpart of a real person on the stage of world events. Real names were used—Roosevelt, Churchill, Stalin, Litvinov, Trotsky and others. These roles were enacted by performers chosen for their likeness to the real person, with the exception of Ambassador Davies, who was portrayed by Walter Huston.

The realism given by such casting was reinforced by an introduction featuring Davies himself, who said: "There was so much prejudice and misunderstanding of the Soviet Union, in which I partly shared, that I felt it my duty to tell the truth as I saw it, for such value as it might have. . . ." Thereafter the picture loosely followed the approach of the book, recreating pictorially the diary and journal entries, plus numerous official reports, in an effort to present a strong case for the Russian system and its rulers. The Ambassador was shown touring Russian factories, both civilian and military, standing with the political elite at a May Day spectacle, attending an exhibition of Russian Army maneuvers, and conferring with Stalin about a united stand by the democracies against Hitler's aggressions. The Ambassador's wife and daughter were also pictured with Russian friends and with women in business and industry.

Among sequences arousing dispute (such as those criticising the Chamberlain government and the Congressional isolationists) by far the most controversial was the film's visual re-enactment of the famed Bukharin-Radik trials of 1937. Using what Davies reported to be the actual transcripts of the trials and the defendants' confessions of guilt, the picture followed the Stalinist contention that Trotsky and the men on trial had conspired with Germany and Japan to sabotage Russia's defenses, partition the country, and take over the government.

The picture's missionary zeal to approve the famous Moscow purge trials and to celebrate a country "long maligned and disgracefully minimized in our press and cinema"[6] evoked a sharp storm of debate. Divergent opinions evaluating the film ranged from "an epoch making film for America"[7] to: "The film is anti-British, anti-Congress, anti-Democratic and anti-truth."[8] One group of sixty-six distinguished and prominent commentators, including Anne O'Hare McCormick, Dorothy Thompson, Sidney Hook, Eugene Lyons and W. E. Woodward, took strong exception to the film and sided with the comment expressed by John Haynes Holmes: "As history it is a lie, as propaganda it is a scandal of the first order."[9] Another group of equally prominent Americans representing all fields of endeavor, among whom were Representative John M. Coffee, Senator Claude Pepper, Walter Duranty, Theodore Dreiser, Fritz Mahler and more than two hundred others, issued a signed statement denouncing the attacks as a "distinct disservice to the cause of American-Soviet unity during the war and afterward." *Mission to Moscow,* they declared, "is more than a motion picture; it is a gesture of international friendship made at the most crucial period of American history with the highly laudable and important object of promoting trust instead of distrust in the Soviet Union."

By the end of America's second year of involvement in the war, films about the "fighting forces" began to disassociate themselves from their romantic military heritage. In this period just prior to the invasion of Europe and the Allied advances in the Pacific, any focus on the romantic involvements of soldiers faded, and the enemy was treated with much less compassion. The typically chauvinistic values and verities of military romanticism and flag-waving, which had commonly inspired and molded war pictures, became increasingly rarer. G.I. audiences had pointed out the obvious phoniness of settings and surroundings in many combat films. Books by war correspondents and soldier novelists made a mockery of scenes that showed soldiers preoccupied by trivial anxieties and sentimental aspirations, or that showed the "beautiful" death of the fighting men. Documentaries by the armed services and newsreels by the Signal Corps had by now painfully familiarized film-makers with the truth and conviction of combat and violent death. Shaped by the dynamic interaction between America's grinding military advances and the rendering of deeper war-like images, the screen reached out for the heart and essence of war's reality. Movies began to serialize the butchery and profanity of war, its soberness and attrition, the fighting man's dignity, his acts of conscience and personal decision, his fulfillment in group responsibility. In every section of the globe, on all battlefronts, on bomber fields, in merchant ships, in submarines, in the skies, jungles, beaches and prisoner-of-war camps, the camera became an articulate and penetrating witness to the pain, bitterness, and horror or war. *Bataan* (1943), *With the Marines at Tarawa* (1944), *Guadacanal Diary* (1944), *The Battle for the Marianas* (1944), *Attack: Invasion of New Britain* (1944), truthfully projected the dirty business of fighting. These pictures were imbued with conviction and unavoidable horror. They documented unflinchingly the desperate involvement of men in close quarters with each other, the shattering muteness of men before the anonymity of death, and the bewildering sense of war's toll and waste.

INDIVIDUALISM AND IDEALISM

Among films that were preoccupied with the deep emotional crisis and individual agony of the average Joe, anxiously examining his own conscience, were *Action in the North Atlantic* (1943), *Destination Tokyo* (1943), *Sahara* (1944), *Air Force* (1944), *A Walk in the Sun* (1945), *The Story of G.I. Joe* (1945), and *The Purple Heart* (1945). They showed the perilous journey of a bomber or convoy bringing its lethal cargo safely through Axis flak or "wolf-packs" to its destination, the enforced quiet of an improvised hospital bed, the tension and tribulation of a march through enemy-controlled sectors, the humbled faces of men in prison compounds, the obstinate doggedness of prisoners refusing to divulge information to their brutal captors, and the fury and turbulence of actual combat itself. But there were vivid flashes and undercurrents of the human obsessions and depravities that war evoked. In the best of these films, there was implicit a rationale that attempted to define the moral consequences of the fighting and dying.

At the same time, the retreat from the war film as a glorified poster involved also the condemnation of old assumptions. To express the imperatives of an ideological and global war demanded scripts with characters coming from every economic level and representing almost every racial strain in American society. The ethnic composition of soldier groups was stressed, and they invariably included a Jew, a Negro, an Irishman, an Italian, a Pole or Swede—a choice obviously meant to present a microcosm of America. This kind of national collective hero, who wanted the Axis destroyed and a good society created, clearly sprang from the liberal social attitudes of the Thirties that questioned prejudice and social injustice and focused attention on those wronged or victimized by society. Unfortunately, the recognition of democratic and humane conceptions often was not in itself sufficient to convert psychological and sociological truths into imaginative truth.

While combat films had developed greater realism, those movies dealing with the home front applied the salve of humor to ease the pain of innumerable petty annoyances, anxieties, and other more profound changes in American life. Comedies and farces proved enormously helpful in alleviating the irritations of well-fed Americans whose menus were curtailed by food rationing, their mobility restricted by gasoline rationing, their jobs and wages frozen, and their income taxes and living costs raised. *Hail the Conquering Hero* (1944), *The Miracle of Morgan's Creek (1944), and See Here Private Hargrove* (1944) were among the best of a sundry output of farces, which, with irrepressible impudence, extravagant action and wild travesty, mocked some of the cherished notions and practices of a public now caught up in the frenzy of war-time living. The tongue-in-cheek sentiment and racy humor of *The More the Merrier* (1943) and *Princess O'Rourke* (1943) distinguished them from dozens of less successful films that mocked the irksome tribulations of a people who had to put up with seemingly endless scarcities and inconveniences and had to stand in line for almost everything.

Also intended to ease the uncertainties and anxieties of a home-front public were a number of pictures that attempted to pay tribute to the radiance of faith and to satisfy the craving for spiritual sustenance. The expert blending of comedy with religious virtue in *Going My Way* (1944), and the more sober pieties of *Song of Bernadette* (1944) set a trend for soothing the apathy and despair of mixed peoples held together by common sacrifices and common anguish.

A picture that was tradition-breaking and quite different from those made to fulfill the government's wartime demands appeared some months after the Allied invasion of Europe when the final phase of the war was already under way. *Wilson* (1944) paid homage to a man who tried to prevent a second world war, but it had a sharp relevance to the current war's end and to the impending Grand Alliance. The film was less a biography of a wartime President than an effort to show how politics relate to war and peace, and a reminder that the very war in which the world was then involved need not have happened but for the failure of others to recognize and act upon Woodrow Wilson's plan for world peace.

The story of *Wilson* was the dignified record of a champion of democracy. From the introduction of Woodrow Wilson at a football game in 1909 as president of Princeton to the closing scenes of his death as President of the United States in 1921, the film characterized him as a crusading American dedicated to democratic principles. He was presented not as the politician, the President, or the war-time Commander-in-Chief, but as the singular idealist.

The War Department banned the picture under Title V of Senator Taft's Soldier's Vote Act which forbade the distribution to the troops of any material "containing political argument or political propaganda of any kind designed or calculated to affect the result of any election." Hollywood saw the action as a serious threat to freedom of the screen and was preparing "to mobilize for broad action" when the ban was suddenly removed and Congress "set about repealing the censorship section of Taft's Act."[10]

Film reviewers also reacted strongly. James Agee wrote: "Pictures like *Wilson* have little if anything to do with mature serious cinema as such, and those who think of *Wilson* as a mature film are not in the least concerned with its liveliness or deadness as a work of art; they are excited because serious ideas are being used on the screen."[11] Bosley Crowther asked "whether this is not truly a picture with an importance far beyond the theater, a film with the impulse to action of a popular battle cry?"[12] Then he went on to add:

". . . The fact is too plain for disputation that there is heady special pleading in this film—special pleading for an international ideal envisioning permanent peace."

In the array of pictures dealing with the war and world events, *Wilson* stood out for its pervasive idealism. It appeared as victory neared in both the Pacific and European theaters, and when allied leaders were soon to meet in San Francisco to establish the United Nations and give increasing attention to shaping the post-war world. The picture's pro-international sentiment and its implied warning against repeating the foreign policy mistakes of the last world war gave it a residual influence, the impact of which could not be readily measured.

By 1945 the rising tide of Allied victories and the prospect of a sudden termination of the war shifted producers' interest away from war pictures. Martial subjects in production were hurried to a desperate conclusion. Those in planning stages were quickly abandoned. On the assumption that movies with men in uniform would become "box-office poison" after V-Day, there was a wild scramble for post-war themes as Hollywood beat all other industries to reconversion.

Energized by the demands of war, the motion picture during these war years gained point, purpose and direction. They provided entertainment to those hammering out the weapons of war as well as to those fighting the battles. They furthered the military effort by conveying information about war and increased the public's awareness of what was going on. Their real opportunity came in emotionalizing the war situation. This led to an exposure of the nature of the enemy and his assaulting ideology, a more realistic treatment of Allied efforts, and a more dignified portrayal of the fighting men. In dramatizing the stories of conquered countries and attempting to tell what Americans and their allies were fighting for, the screen psychologically and materially met the crisis persuasively and with an urgent sense of its obligations.

Of the more than seventeen hundred features made during this period, more than five hundred were directly concerned with some aspect of fascism and war. A good many were trite and superficial, aimed to keep civilian and military morale high and satisfy the home front about

American and Allied struggles "out there." Others were of another sort—opportunistic responses to the need of the moment—either earnest or patriotically stimulating. Yet buried in this vast serialization of evolving history were a small number of notable films that sharply reflected the varied aspects of war and heightened our understanding of it at that moment. The best of these broke through the barriers of propaganda and entertainment to penetrate the truth of the terror and insanity let loose by fascism and by war itself.

NOTES

1. *New York Times,* May 23, 1943.
2. *Ibid.*
3. Reported by *New York Times,* November 11, 1942.
4. Peter Bogdanovich, *The Cinema of Alfred Hitchcock,* page 25.
5. *Ibid.*
6. From a letter by Clifford Odets, *News Republic,* June 14, 1943.
7. From the text of a statement by 266 leading Americans denouncing disruptive attacks on the picture.
8. From a letter by John Dewey and reported by *The Hollywood Reporter,* June 2, 1943.
9. *Hollywood Reporter,* June 8, 1943.
10. *Los Angeles News,* July 21, 1944.
11. *Nation,* August 19, 1944.
12. *New York Times,* September 10, 1944.

Writers War Board on Mission to Moscow *(June 1943): "We are aware that the picture does a valuable service for a trusted ally, but we feel that the deepest principle of human liberty is involved—the necessity of telling the public the truth. The true case for Russia is excellent. It is not necessary for Hollywood to falsify facts to make it slightly better." (Signed): Rex Stout, Chairman, F. P. Adams, Pearl S. Buck, Carl Carmer, Clifton Fadiman, Paul Gallico, Oscar Hammerstein, J. P. Marquard, William L. Shirer. (DP)*

44 THE SCREEN AND THE HOLOCAUST

Herbert G. Luft

SINCE WAR'S END, the tragedy of European Jewry has received only marginal expression on the screen. Our brethren across the ocean, alive or dead, have remained anonymous victims of Nazi oppression in an indifferent world. Those who had known, forgot conveniently or buried their awareness in the depth of their subconscious.

If we exclude such Eastern European films as *The Long Road, The Last Stop* and *Kapo,* the first feature examining in detail on the plight of concentration camp inmates, is the current epic, *The Hiding Place,* reflecting the struggle for survival within the confines of the notorious Ravensbrueck installation for women. The texture of life behind the barbed wire has been caught with nightmarish intensity in the film produced by a Hollywood company [headed by William F. Brown] in conjunction with Billy Graham's Evangelistic Association; yet, there is one major fault with the story! The Dutch Jews of *The Hiding Place* are depicted throughout as cowards or fools, with hardly any one of them displaying courage or an inkling of dignity. They cause so-called innocent, Christians to be arrested while they hide out and eventually escape. Dutch Christians in this overly sentimental yarn feel no hatred for their oppressors and willingly sacrifice themselves to the glory of their Lord Jesus, be-

From *Davka* Magazine (Fall 1975), quarterly published by the Los Angeles Hillel Council. Reprinted by permission of the author and publisher.

cause it is reasoned that there is no redemption without the forgiveness of sin. Yet, in reality no Christian was ever put to death in a German concentration camp for his or her religious beliefs, with the exception of Jehovah's Witnesses, who were regarded by the Nazis as social outcasts. When I came to the U.S.A. from war-torn Europe, after having gone through a winter at Dachau and a year of bombing raids in England, I was quite dismayed to find that the American cinema regarded the menace of Hitlerism as something hilariously funny.

I objected to the slant of the Academy Award-winning film, *Woman of the Year* (Katharine Hepburn) of 1942, because the sophisticated George Stevens comedy applauded splendid isolationism. Business as usual was the slogan before Pearl Harbor, and it didn't change much later for those who stayed home. The slapstick approach to the rape of Poland in Ernst Lubitsch's *To Be or Not To Be* was quite shocking to me (though the picture was beautifully directed, with Jack Benny and Carole Lombard portraying a famed theatrical couple in Warsaw). But the story itself belittled the greatest tragedy in human history. I was appalled by the silliness of *The Hitler Gang* (1944), an epic dealing with the rise to power of the most tyrannical regime the world has ever seen. Directed by the late John Farrow, who had no knowledge of the subject matter, *The Hitler Gang* starred comedian Bobby Watson as the unlamented "Fuehrer," a grotesquely absurd con man surrounded by an assortment of cheap little thugs.

Most of the so-called, well-meant anti-Nazi films of the war-time period reduced the hierarchy of the party, the German military, and key members of the industrial empire to small-time cartoon characters, and by sketching the aggressors as stupid, inefficient imbeciles, their victims became exceedingly small and insignificant. Of all movies dealing at that time with the Hitler regime in humorous terms, I could endorse only one. Charles Chaplin's *The Great Dictator* was made with guts and satirical bite while also revealing deep compassion for the victims of racial and nationalistic insanity.

There were other films made in Hollywood during World War II dealing seriously with the growing menace of Nazism, but those pictures referred to the Jewish problem only incidentally, if at all. The earliest forewarning of an emerging threat to civilization was Anatole Litvak's *Confession of a Nazi Spy,* (the Warner Bros. picture of 1939, with Francis Lederer and Edward G. Robinson), which caused all Warner films to be banned throughout the Reich on orders of Dr. Goebbels. Next came the revealing MGM epic, *The Mortal Storm* of 1940. Two pictures of 1943 vintage, Warners' *Edge of Darkness* and Twentieth Century-Fox's *The Moon Is Down* dealt forcefully with the invasion of Norway. Sam Goldwyn's *The North Star* (also 1943) dealt with the Russian peasant resistance against the German aggressors.

A highly refined cinema emerged in Germany during the Weimar Republic period (1919–1933), with technical innovations which spread from Berlin to London, Paris and Hollywood. This was part of a renaissance of art and culture that coincided with a resurgence of moral values and an unsurpassed uplifting of the spirit expressed in novels, dramatic plays and in the stage productions of Max Reinhardt, Leopold Jessner and Erwin Piscator. The Golden Era of the German screen was inspired to some extent by the creative talent of Jews, many of them of Austrian, Hungarian, Czech and Polish origin. Both authors of the first literary film, *Caligari,* Carl Mayer and Hans Janowitz were Jewish, as were the avant-garde picture's producer, Erich Pommer and director Robert Wiene. Pommer was also at the helm of *The Last Laugh* (UFA), 1923, written by Carl Mayer.

Fritz Lang was at the helm of *M,* a psychological study of a child-killer (portrayed by Peter Lorre). He then directed *The Last Will of Dr. Mabuse* (sequel to the original two-part picture made in 1922), an account of gang violence in Berlin that fore-shadowed the rise of Nazism and ultimately was banned upon completion and the negative destroyed after the Hitler takeover. Both *M* and *Mabuse* were produced under the "Nero" label by New York-born Seymour Nebenzal, perhaps Germany's most influential producer before the onslaught of Nazism. He was noted for a series of courageous films such as *Westfront 1918,* a stirring anti-war epic (1929); *The Three Penny Opera,* a subtle attack on corrupt government (from the stage musical by Kurt Weill and Bertolt Brecht, 1930); *Comradeship,* a semi-documentary recreating the disaster at Courriere that unified French and German coal miners in the rescue efforts (1931). All the great films of the most creative period of German cinema, directed by Murnau, Lang, Dupont, Oswald, Pabst and Lubitsch dealt with utter violence and the obsessive thoughts of death, as if the artists had a premonition of sinister currents still latent in the general population.

The high technical quality of the German film industry was maintained in the film studios of Berlin and Munich, but with Hitler's rise to power in 1933, the screen was gradually perverted to a tool of Dr. Goebbels' propaganda ministry. Goebbels had studied the Russian method of mass persuasion in the media and followed the example of Vladimir Ilyich Lenin, father of the Soviet revolution, to fuse the moving image projected onto the screen into a three-dimensional weapon and throw unstable minds into an abyss of hatred and prejudice. S. M. Eisenstein's *Potemkin* gave Goebbels the impetus to ignite racial hatred through staccato images on the screen with close-ups and weird sound effects accentuating the "ugly" qualities of those he was scheming to ridicule.

To "clean up" the studios, actors, writers and directors of "aryan" origin, who were not tainted with democratic ideals and social views, were lured into the Nazi fold by promises of titles, decorations, money, and women. At first, the program of Hitler's cinema stressed the unity of the people and the purity of race in such films as *Bluetendes Deutschland, Der Judas von Tirol* and *Fluechtlinge;* then came the filmic account of the Nazi struggle against the Weimar Republic with *Horst Wessel* and *Hitlerjunge Quex;* patriotic themes were expressed in the World War I U-boat drama, *Morgenrot;* the plight of the peasants during the years of the republic in *Unter der Schwarzen Flagge* and a number of similar features. At the beginning of the Second World War, top pictures of UFA and Terra, both financed by the German government, became pointedly anti-Semitic. There was a perversion of history in *The Rothschilds* (1940); and in the hypnotic spell of *Jud Suess,* a 1940 hateful version of Lion Feuchtwanger's classic novel, which had been filmed with dignity in England in 1933 with Conrad Veidt in the title role. *Heimkehr* (1941) dealt with the demands to accommodate German minorities in foreign lands, i.e., to incorporate such countries into the Greater Reich. *Ohm Krueger* (1941) was a distorted account of the Boer War designed to create hatred against the British.

Leni Riefenstahl, the capricious woman director, chose to glorify the Nazi regime as early as 1933 with a cinematic account of the Party Congress staged annually at Nuremberg, where millions of Germans gathered to show their allegiance to their "Fuehrer." Her first documentary, *Der Sieg des Glaubens* (Victory of Faith) was followed in autumn of 1934 with a feature-length epic, *Triumph des Willens* (Triumph of the Will), which netted her a German State Prize, a Film-of-the-Nation citation and a Gold Medal at the Venice Film Festival. If we look at *Triumph of the Will* today, we would be shocked by the hysterical outbursts of devotion accorded the Hitler regime by the multitude of onlookers, with more than one million brown and blackshirted SS men marching through the town of Nuremberg in a goose-stepping parade lasting many hours. Undesirable elements such as Jews, Gypsies, Jehovah's Witnesses, socialists, communists, democrats and monarchists had been herded into concentration camps such as Dachau, Buchenwald, Sachsenhausen, and the vast Oranienburg police prison since 1933.

When Leni Riefenstahl visited Hollywood, at the invitation of Walt Disney on the eve of World War II, she told an unreceptive gathering of film producers that the atrocity reports were *greuelpropaganda* of irresponsible journalists. While Jews were being beaten up and starved to death in concentration camps (extermination centers were not yet operative), Miss Riefenstahl concerned herself with filming the nordic beauty display of the Olympic contest in a tribute to the human body and the spirit of man.

Her filmic work which added to the normalcy of life in the Third Reich, where trains were on time and the sport events well timed, actually accelerated the impending mass murder, because it helped to convince the leaders of Germany that no one cared to stop their policy of genocide. In 1944, when Auschwitz worked at high speed to process millions of bodies in record time, Leni Riefenstahl busied herself with a new feature film, *Tiefland,* from the opera by Eugen D'Albert, glorifying the "honest" nature of mountain people who refuse to come down to the "immorality" of city life. While filming in Germany, Spain, and finally in the Tyrolian Alps, she was caught by the U.S. 7th Army at Kitzbuehl after the German surrender in 1945.

The worst of the German films during the Hitler period was the documentary feature, *Der Ewige Jude* (The Eternal Jew), in which Eastern European Jewish ghetto inmates, starved and ill-clothed, forbidden to wash and shave, were photographed in their misery and presented as a "sub-human" species in contrast to healthy, well-nourished German guards. *Der Ewige Jude* was put together so cunningly that the enraged public went out from the theatre onto the street ready to massacre the "unclean" foreign element.

Throughout the twelve years of the Third Reich, motion pictures played a very important part in setting up the climate for pogroms. When the order for the "Final Solution of the Jewish Question" was adapted at the Wannsee Conference in January of 1942, the bulk of the people were already conditioned to the mass extermination, implemented during the same year without any protest. The propaganda ministry was right in that images on the screen could trigger the basest instincts in man.

Not only the obviously tendentious films were helping the Nazi war machine, but the hundreds of light entertainment features produced from 1933 to 1945 were just as important because they created a sense of normalcy among the German people that induced them to overlook the horrifying crimes then committed in their names. Viewing their favorites in humorous or heroic roles or romantically involved with the opposite sex reinforced the public morale.

Films became so important to the propaganda ministry that the highest priority was accorded to the manufacture and transportation of motion picture equipment. None of the screen, stage and radio stars of the Reich were called to serve in the armed forces in World War II though fourteen-year-old boys had been drafted for home front duty to guard and defend the beleaguered cities. When the Allies marched into Berlin, motion pictures were in the making at the Neubabelsberg studios. Emil Jannings and his director, Hans Steinhoff, were at Barandov near Prague leisurely grinding away at movie-making when the American Third Army made the surprise move into Czechoslovakia. Surrender didn't bring any resurgence of artistic and moral values to the German theater and cinema. Since there was no feeling of guilt, no remorse for the crimes committed against humanity, there could be no redemption. The writers of the new Reich touched only shallow surface problems, when they were not busy feeling sorry for themselves and their mistreated and misunderstood people.

Die Moerder Sind Unter Uns (The Murderers Among Us), produced in the Russian Zone, was the first picture made by the Germans after World War II. The title led us to believe that the story would deal with a sense of awakening within the people. But we were wrong to believe that there would be any admission of collective guilt. In *The Murderers Among Us* the hospital doctor simply says, "It was the war." Crimes against humanity, though attacked in spots, are somehow justified in the final analysis. Mass murder, if it actually took place, (and the doubt is being planted in the minds of the people) was forced upon the regime by the cold necessity of war.

Though the spirit of the German film pioneers had died with the establishment of human death factories, there were a few productions of social concern made in that early post-war period. Gerhard Lamprecht, who had become a champion of the underprivileged with his *Zille* films of the early 1930's, now dealt with the re-education of German youth in *Irgendwo in Berlin* (Somewhere in Berlin).

Werner Klinger shot *Razia* (Raid) in the Johannisthal studios and in the slums of Berlin, a non-political study of the underworld. Out of the chaos emerged a rather superficial impulse for a renewal of literary values in the theatre and on the screen. *Film Without Title,* produced and directed by Helmut Kaeutner under British license in the Bavaria Studios, was concerned with the petty problems of the war's aftermath and afflicted us with miserable pleas for sympathy. It ignored the mere existence of enslaved foreign workers to focus on kindhearted farm folk eager to feed bombed-out refugees in an attempt to tell us that we must have been dreaming when we talk about atrocities.

Ehe im Schatten (Marriage in the Shadow), made in the

Russian zone of Berlin in 1947, the most mature film of the period, traces the tragic fate of German actor Joachim Gottschalk, one of the stars of the Berlin stage, who committed suicide with his Jewish wife when life became unbearable for both in Nazi Germany. Written and directed by Kurt Maetzig, the story treatment of the book by Hans Schweikart remained evasive; the producers were careful not to offend the "better" feelings of the Germans and not to confess too much to foreign movie-goers. Deportations are shamefacedly discussed, but it is never admitted that it meant gas chambers and human slaughterhouses. The great manhunt of November 10th, 1938, and the subsequent shipment of 100,000 Jews to concentration camps throughout Germany is shrugged off in one line, and a beautifully diffused dissolve takes us through five years of mass murder.

Affaire Blum (The Blum Affair) unfolds on the screen an actual case of injustice which occurred in Magdeburg in 1926 where an anti-Semitic middle class society is accused of condemning and convicting an innocent man whose only crime is his Jewish origin.

The late G. W. Pabst who had guided outstanding German films before Hitler rose to power, including those for "Nero" Pictures, but later prostituted his talent for the Nazi regime, tried to redeem himself with *Der Prozess* (The Trial), a film dealing with the factual case of a ritual murder trial in the Hungarian village of Tinza-Eszler in the 1880's. The film made in 1948 was a strong appeal for racial understanding. It starred Ernst Deutsch who had spent the war years in America.

In 1955, G. W. Pabst produced a monumental picture which he made in Austria, *The Last Ten Days,* from the account of Justice M. A. Musmanno and a story by Erich Marie Remarque, dealing with the final days of Adolf Hitler in the bunker of the chancellery of Berlin. Unfortunately, *The Last Ten Days* demanded sympathy for the doomed citizenry of the capital, but rarely touched upon the crimes committed against humanity which lead to the punishment. It shows a madman sacrificing non-existing divisions, and the tender concern of his officers for their families and for the women and children of their fellow Berliners in the bombed-out metropolis.

For sentimental reasons, the children of Dr. Goebbels are dragged into the picture shouting in unison, "Uncle Adolf"; yet, the same Uncle Adolf who loved children so much was responsible for the slaughter of two million Jewish babies.

Pabst turned once more to the period of Hitler with his picture, *Es Geschah am 20, Juli* (It happened on the 20th of July) dealing with the Stauffenberg-Witzleben attack on the life of Hitler in 1944. Though the film was to show that the German people wanted to get rid of Hitler at that late moment in history, it actually convinced the viewer that the generals were quarreling with him only because he was losing their war.

The new-wave epoch of West German films fizzled out in the 1950's and there were only two more pictures worth mentioning in this connection, Wolf Thiele's *Rosemarie* (with Nadja Tiller) focusing on the corruption and sexual perversion among the military and German industrialists in postwar Deutschland, and Kurt Hoffmann's satirical *Wunderkinder* (Aren't We Wonderful), a cavalcade of Germany, from the beginning of Hitler, through defeat into the new economic miracle of recovery (*Wirtschaftswunder*) to the resurgence of Nazism and anti-Semitism. The picture was brought to America by the late I. G. Goldsmith, Austrian pioneer filmmaker, but in spite of an extensive campaign to interest the public, and especially the Jewish people, in viewing this strengthened new Germany, no one was interested in the past. This was ten years ago.

With German film producers in Berlin, Hamburg, Wiesbaden and Munich turning their minds towards pornography, the Eastern German studio in Neubabelsberg, now labeled Defa, continued to make films dealing with classical themes and the near past.

In Hollywood during the years immediately following World War II it became fashionable for film companies to turn their cameras towards the rubble of Berlin for some fascinatingly macabre effects. None of the films made in the aftermath cut through to the core of the tragedy that few could comprehend.

There were four pictures of the 1947/48 vintage I shall

discuss here: Billy Wilder's *A Foreign Affair,* Jacques Tourneur's *Berlin Express,* Mitchell Leisen's *Golden Earrings,* and Lewis Allen's *Sealed Verdict.* Wilder who had contributed to the World War II variety of anti-Nazi films his *Five Graves to Cairo,* an adventure yarn dealing with the North African campaign (in which Erich von Stroheim appeared as a stereotyped, stonefaced Marshal Rommel), came back from Germany in 1948 with his screen comedy *A Foreign Affair,* which was hailed by almost everyone here and selected by *Look* as the year's best in 1949. The story was slick and smart; it had a cleverly constructed plot, sparkling dialogue, a lavish production, and featured a number of beautiful women, headed by Marlene Dietrich. Behind the romantic facade of *A Foreign Affair* was the state of mind of a people, the revenge-thirsty mind of fanatics who drew the curtain over their own crimes and blamed misfortune on the harsh hand of the Allies. Audiences from Maine to Oregon cried their hearts out for the poor Germans who had suffered so much. The screen showed us the stone jungle of devastation, but not one word told us why Berlin had to be bombed to force the Nazis into submission. We didn't think it was funny that complacent *fräuleins,* as early as 1948, were ruling the destiny of American officers while a vast blackmarket existed under the very eyes of the occupation forces. Others found *A Foreign Affair* hilarious entertainment. In fact it is frivolous and obscene.

Berlin Express, also shot in Germany in its entirety, was an attempt to treat the Nazis within the framework of a gangster story, with heroes and heavies, and finishing with a wild cops and robber chase. *Sealed Verdict,* a Hollywood product, dealt with the guilt of war criminals, but the novel by Lionel Shapiro and the screenplay by Mr. Latimer remained evasive though excerpts from the chief prosecutor at the Nuremberg War Crime trials are being recited, pointing to the consequences of the crimes, namely the death of 20 million of our fellow men and the devastation of a whole continent. Aside from the pointed remarks, we are confused by a sheer endless stream of dogmatic dialogue. Two Jewish characters are inserted into the soap opera; Ludwig Donath, a man who lives in the past, and Norbert Schiller as a distorted caricature of a D.P.

From Swiss producer Lazar Wechsler (1948) came one of the few remarkable films dealing with the effect of the Holocaust on those children who miraculously survived. The picture was *The Search,* directed by Fred Zinnemann and starring the late Montgomery Clift. Zinnemann was able to create moments of unbearable anxiety among the homeless orphans who thought they were herded into a van to be gassed, as had been their parents, sisters, and brothers. Only gradually, the little ones learn to believe in the humanity of others, especially of those in the American army and the Red Cross who had come to help.

As previously noted, most of the Hollywood films remained on the sidelines of the Jewish suffering when touching upon the war and aftermath. There was Otto Preminger's *Exodus,* which showed the effect of Nazi prisons on a meagre group of survivors arriving in Israel. Sidney Lumet's, *The Pawnbroker,* illustrated the past in a series of staccato flashbacks— subliminal remembrances of years behind the barbed wire. Stanley Kramer's *The Juggler* sketches the plight of one who escaped the physical torture of the camps but remained sick and confused. Kirk Douglas portrays the human wreck who only gradually manages to rejoin the society of man. Luchino Visconti's *The Damned* cuts through to those responsible for the emergence of a Hitler, the industrialists of the Ruhr, in this case the Krupp family. As a native of Essen I learned a great deal from the film about those who had ruled my home town in a "benevolent" spirit for three hundred years.

It has been told that the late David O. Selznick planned to produce a multi-million dollar picture from the novel *The Wall* by John Hersey, one of the great documents coming out of World War II, published in 1950. The book is based on the truth about the ghetto uprising in Warsaw and would illustrate the sacrifice of many of our brethren. *The Wall* was transposed to the stage with George C. Scott portraying the leading character on Broadway. Yet, Selznick, we were told, was asked by those high up in our government to abstain from making the film because it could endanger our good relations with Germany. Another venture, the filming of William L. Shirer's *The Rise and Fall of the Third Reich* by John Houseman was shelved and later abandoned. A Hitler picture was assembled from actual footage and edited by the eminent documentary director Paul Rotha in England, but never shown in this country. Erwin Leiser, a Swedish citizen now residing in Switzerland compiled a documentary feature entitled *The Third Reich* which was shown at the San Francisco Film Festival of 1960 but received no general release in America.

One monumental television film (six-hour running time) shown on two evenings last year, comes closer to the truth of the Jewish plight under the Nazis than anything we have previously viewed—except perhaps some Eastern European pictures. It is Leon Uris' *QB VII* transposed to the screen by Edward Anhalt and directed by Tom Gries. At the Pinewood Studios in Iver Heath, Bucks, I watched filmization of the courtroom sequence in which the screen becomes the tribunal of world conscience. It is in the exchange of questions and answers by defense attorney (Anthony Quayle) and witness (Dame Edith Evans) that the core of the Nazi policy in regard to the Jewish minority of Europe is thoroughly exposed.

The Odessa File by British novelist Frederich Forsyth emerged on the screen as an adventure story with a *Hamlet* twist in which the young German journalist (portrayed by Jon Voight) pursues extermination camp commander SS Captain Eduard Roschmann (Maximilian Schell) not for the mass murders he has committed but to bring him to justice for the shooting of his own father.

The Man in the Glass Booth, the Ely Landau presentation of the controversial Robert Shaw play, already muddled on the stage became even more confused with the screen treatment by Edward Anhalt, normally one of our best craftsmen. Arthur Hiller's direction reduced the drama to a farce and Maximilian Schell portrayed the central character as a clown.

Schell has also produced and directed a motion picture of his own in 1973, *The Pedestrian,* on locations in Germany and Israel, in which he transposed a tragedy of immense scope into visual terms and explored the collective guilt of the Germans during the occupation of Greece where the inhabitants of a whole village were senselessly massacred. Though the Greek sequence was photographed in Israel, the story doesn't deal with the Jewish problem.

Currently planned in England is the filming of young British author Anthony Masters' stirring *The Summer That Bled,* the biography of Hannah Senesh, which Nigel Marsh will produce on actual locations in Hungary and Israel.

In spite of the indifference of official French circles to the plight for survival and the future of the State of Israel, there have been four important motion pictures to come out of France during the last year dealing with the fate of the Jews under the Nazi occupation.

Les Violins du Bal, Gouchets de Louvre and *Lacombe, Lucienne* not only tell us that Jews were singled out among the French for deportation by the Germans, but also point at the French collaborationists and uniformed fascists who aided and abetted their country's enemy for personal gain. Of course, there are also a few French citizens on the screen who go out of their way to help, but the majority of those depicted in the strongly phrased films are either traitors to their own country or indifferent to the plight of the Jews.

Claude Lelouche's *Tout en Vie* is a cavalcade of a French-Jewish family from the beginning of World War I to the present day, dealing with three generations of Parisiennes. Lelouche (in his mid-thirties today) is Jewish and grew up in a concentration camp. Perhaps, this is the reason that one of his main characters, portrayed by Charles Dener, is seen for one short scene in a Nazi camp during World War II, just before the hour of liberation. But the farcical contents of the picture overshadow the reference to Jewish sufferings.

Finally, I wish to turn to a personal experience which had a profound influence on my own career in the cinema. In a sealed prison train enroute to the concentration camp of Dachau in November of 1938, I listened by chance to the chat of two men hidden from view who deliberately detached themselves from reality to discuss, seemingly irrationally, the merits of Frank Borzage's film, *Seventh Heaven.* They weighed the silent version in which Oscar-winning Janet Gaynor shared star-billing with Charles Farrell against the talkie of the 1930's with Simone Simon, James Stewart and the late Mady Christians. The subject matter had no relevance to them directly, yet, the two were moving towards an uncertain destination where all of us expected the worst to happen. The discussion took them into the realm of fantasy and for a moment made them forget their fears and anxieties.

Marcel Proust has stated that completely unrelated physical and physiological events, a certain smell, touch or texture can trigger memories into action. Such excursions into the hidden chambers of the past are not unlike staccato images from films of bygone days. In order to maintain my equilibrium, I pushed names, locales and tragic events from my earlier life into the subconscious, yet vividly remember movies I had seen thirty and forty years ago. I remember the films not with nostalgia, but rather with a sense of reality. Perhaps no other medium in the field of arts and mass communication has made such an impact on as many people at the same time as have those strips of celluloid projected onto a screen; photographs moving along at ninety feet a minute to create the illusion of life.

Hollywood Anti-Nazi News, *December 5, 1936, published a copy of a leaflet distributed by U.S. Nazis aimed especially at Hollywood stars and producers. It read: (DP)*

"HEIL! HEIL"
All Germans and Aryans of Pure Nordic Blood!
We have the Jews on the run!
Let us keep up the good work!
Do not attend any theatre showing pictures with any of these Jews or Jew lovers:
Claudette Colbert is married to a Jew.
Norma Shearer was married to a Jew.
Margaret Sullavan was married to a Jew.
Eddie Cantor is a Jew.
Al Jolson is a Jew.
Sylvia Sidney is a Jew.
Ruby Keeler is married to a Jew.
Ricardo Cortez is a Jew.

45 THE SIGN OF THE BOSS: CECIL De MILLE, UNION BUSTER

Ring Lardner, Jr.

DISCUSSING HIS FAMOUS BATTLE against the American Federation of Radio Artists last March, Cecil B. De Mille declared that "there has been built up in this country an unelected government which is superseding in power and authority the elected government. And a dissenting voice raised against this unelected but all-encompassing power is condemned to obliteration."

Eight months later, it appears that Mr. De Mille was speaking with a rare and unwarranted pessimism. Far from obliterated, he is being provided with an increasing number of platforms from which to raise his voice to ever-mounting heights of indignation against the forces which have joined in persecuting him. Lecture audiences and newspaper columns have been available to him in impressive quantities, though admittedly his following is not as general as it was when he was promoting such less controversial causes as the divinity of the Savior and the infallibility of the Northwest Mounted Police. Yet in spite of this encouraging trend, De Mille, ever the farsighted showman, has insured himself against the day when even chambers of commerce and executives' clubs may tire of hearing paraphrases of the same speech by organizing his own permanent audience in the form of the De Mille Foundation for Political Freedom. This potential mass force in American life is carefully

From *The Screen Writer* (November 1945). ©1945 The Screen Writer. Reprinted by permission of the author.

constituted so that, in the words of its principal founder, it cannot be "taken over by subversive groups." All policy and action are determined by its self-perpetuating board of directors, yet every rank-and-file member is assured his political freedom to read and listen to whatever pronouncement Mr. De Mille is moved to make on the state of the nation.

It is provocative to consider briefly the hot debate which must have preceded the selection of the De Mille Foundation for Political Freedom as the name for this grass-roots movement. Any conscientious publicist would take pause before choosing the precise inspirational title for a group dedicated, again in the words of Mr. De Mille, to "an issue between all liberty-loving citizens and a few unscrupulous men who are trying to gather into their own hands . . . the power of the people."

Fortunately, one of this magazine's highly-paid secret operatives lay concealed in a mass of floral tributes at the very hour when De Mille and his associates were determining the proper name for the national uprising they had volunteered to lead. His notes are incomplete, since he was eventually drowned by the tears of joy which accompanied the final selection, but he did manage to record for posterity some of the names which were proposed and rejected before the ultimate inspiration. Among them were "The Washington-Jefferson-Lincoln-Hoover Foundation for Political Freedom," which was turned down as too cumbersome; "The American League for the 100% American Defense of Americanism," which was regarded as too gaudy; "The Employers Protective Association," dismissed because of a previous copyright; and "Millions for the Defense of Property, Not One Cent for Tribute to Labor," which some partisans considered too long and others too direct. Finally a spokesman who seemed familiar to the chair was recognized and started to suggest "The De Mille . . ." The rest of his words were lost in pandemonium and were only recovered during a later search of that region.

But, significant as the choice of name was in terms of popular appeal, the basic issues which lay behind the whole revolutionary surge are still more so. And we cannot completely grasp its urgency unless the particular degree of discrimination which inspired this particular movement is brought into consideration. The average patriotic American would not be roused to vehemence by some union regulation which deprived an exploited janitor's assistant, let us say, of the right to assemble garbage for a salary of eighteen dollars a week. The man can be relieved of an unpleasant job and placed, without much sacrifice in income, on unemployment insurance or whatever form of relief is devised to meet the current crisis. His family is hardly worse off than before.

The situation of Mr. De Mille is drastically different. Here we have the case of a man who was being paid two thousand dollars a week for producing the Lux Radio Theatre. In order to gauge the extent of loss to him when AFRA ruled him off the air, we must consider the nature of his duties on the program according to the unassailable theory that the more money he was paid per hour, the greater his sacrifice. It happens that the role of "producer" in this type of radio show is actually that of a master of ceremonies. Whereas the other actors were called on to rehearse on Fridays and Saturdays, De Mille's first rehearsal was on Sunday, when he saw for the first time the lines assigned to him. Then on Mondays he had a second rehearsal just before going on the air, and finally the program itself, on which his task was to read the opening and closing remarks.

Of course, this bald statement of the facts fails to take into account the tension which must have gripped him on every program because of the fact that the listening public was under the impression he was choosing and guiding the dramatizations which were presented under his aegis. That he was conscious of this responsibility is amply proved by his conduct during those broadcasts. Having no authority whatsoever over the program, he was compelled to act as a man who did. And there is no doubt that De Mille lived the part. After he had read his own lines, he would pace up and down in front of the studio audience, making notations in his copy of the script, underlining certain speeches and checking off scenes as they were played. The precise function of these labors is not entirely clear; presumably he was providing against the day when the show, having run out of material, would have to do the same scripts over again and someone might happen to ask him what he had thought of the first performance.

In addition to this chore, he would frequently take out his pocket watch, check it with his wrist watch and then with the studio clock. Up until the day he was fired, no one connected with the Lux Radio Theatre ever raised the suspicion that De Mille was not fully aware what time it was at any given moment during the program.

The rehearsals consumed an hour apiece and the show itself brought De Mille's working time up to a total of three hours weekly. He was thus receiving something over eleven dollars a minute for the job which he sacrificed by refusing to pay the one dollar special assessment which AFRA levied on its members in August, 1944 to combat Proposition Number Twelve, the open shop amendment, on the California state ballot. There is no other recorded martyrdom in history which cost its hero such an impressive cash total.

One would expect in view of this fact that De Mille would be acutely aware of the precise issue he was championing, but strangely enough his voluminous speeches and writings on the subject reveal him to be under a totally false impression in this regard. Always a quick reader, he appears to have misunderstood the text of the notice sent him by his union, which was a simple request for one of his reputed eight million dollars to be used in protecting the union's existence against a measure designed to make it and all other labor organizations powerless. But the way De Mille read it, the notice covered much more ground. As he has since reported, it began with an arbitrary demand for "a proxy which would give the leaders of that union the use of my free rights as a voter." On top of that, it went on to announce a program of "intimidation and coercion" in which AFRA's leaders proposed "to gather into their own hands . . . the power of the people—just as it was gathered in Germany and Italy." Finally, it wound up with a violent denunciation of the United States Constitution, the Magna Carta and the Mayflower Compact.

Naturally, De Mille was outraged, so much so that he was unable to give the letter a second reading to see what it actually said. Nor have all the subsequent attempts by friends and well-wishers been able to clarify the matter for him. One of the most patient and painstaking of these was made by Judge Emmet Wilson of the Los Angeles Superior Court. Deciding the case in favor of AFRA, he reminded De Mille that when he joined the union he had agreed to all the provisions of its bylaws, whereby the union had a clear right to make assessments to fight or support legislation.

"No right of suffrage or of discussion was interfered with," the judge assured the complaining trade unionist. "No member was coerced in his voting by the action of his organization. He could have voted one way while his share of the organization's money was being used in support of the opposite." Most people thought this definitive statement solved the problem, but the plaintiff was unimpressed.

It would be unfair, however, to assume that he stands entirely alone in the matter. Among De Mille's supporters is no less an authority on democratic unionism than the *Saturday Evening Post,* which, in an editorial last February struck at the very heart of the issue as follows: "If the question had been the use of funds already in the union treasury, the determination of the majority of the members would have to stand. But Mr. De Mille was resisting an extra assessment specifically for the purpose of fighting a measure which he favored. The common man will make a distinction." Unfortunately, this strategy ended in failure. All nine of those *Post* readers who regard themselves as common men sat down to a session of distinction-making which lasted well into March, but this particular one has yet to be cracked, either by them or the *Post.*

Ever since the first stirrings of the labor movement a century and a half ago, it has been a fascinating subject for students of human nature to speculate on the motivations and circumstances which have driven a few laboring men to desert their own class and align themselves with the owners. So today even those people who do not take the De Mille Foundation for Political Freedom seriously (the figure in this country alone is close to 140 million) find it interesting to consider what it was that impelled Cecil De Mille, an apparently passive, dues-paying member of AFRA, to join battle from the camp of the enemy against his confreres.

A study of the man's history, both before and after he

joined the working class, furnishes many significant clues. It is our purpose here merely to call attention to a few of them which seem especially relevant and perhaps thus stimulate the reader to determine his own answer to the question.

Cecil Blount De Mille, Knight of the Holy Sepulchre and holder of the distinguished service medal of the United Daughters of the Confederacy, is a descendant of one Anthony deMil, who came to this country from Holland in 1658. Many men are inclined to forget the traditions and standards which are handed down to them from their forbears, to lose sight, amid the pressures of present-day life, of the responsibilities that go with honored lineage. But De Mille is deeply conscious of his heritage. In May, 1940, on hearing the news of the beginning of the German western offensive, he is reported (by John Durant in the *Saturday Evening Post*) to have exclaimed: "He has invaded the Hague! That's where my ancestors and their descendants have lived for 800 years. All our records will now be lost."

His first profession was acting, and most people who have worked with him feel that he still devotes about sixteen hours of the waking day to that craft. Some of his most memorable performances have been given at story conferences, where he is apt to convey his suggestions to the writer by acting out entire scenes which would be ludicrously theatrical if they ever appeared on the screen. Some of them have.

During the preparation and making of a picture he imagines himself to be living in the period with which it deals. Sometimes he almost seems to believe that he himself is the leading character in the story, and his conversation and behavior become those of, say Wild Bill Hickok or Moses. When he made *The Crusades,* he assumed the role of Richard the Lionhearted, and the correspondents whom he invited in droves for three successive nights to watch him conduct the siege of Acre, agreed that there probably was never in all history such a flamboyantly gallant, dictatorial and tireless military commander. During the *King of Kings,* the atmosphere on the set was so holy that many of the actors, who were among other things forbidden to smoke while in costume, toyed with the notion of putting De Mille up for crucifixion. He himself was so carried away by the sanctimonious tone of the proceedings that, while normally a quick-tempered and impious man, he refrained from swearing throughout the production, even on the day the zebras ran away. On the morning he started shooting he summoned clerics of every religion and sect obtainable in Los Angeles, including a Mohammedan and a Shintoist, to say prayers for the success of the picture. One would suppose that some of these men of various gods might have had reservations about how their particular interests were involved in the project, but there is no record of any of them resisting De Mille's blandishments.

His insatiable desire for publicity, which seems to go far beyond the normal dictates of good business, is another reflection of the same side of his character. The two main points of emphasis in most of what has been written about him—his use of bathtub scenes and his costumes on the set—are deliberately fostered by De Mille himself, though he never admits as much in so many words, even to his press agents. A typical working costume, incidentally, consists of tan, high-laced field boots, dark riding breeches, a pastel green jacket with vest to match and a dark green shirt. As an added adornment he is likely to wear some sort of matching jewelry, perhaps a stickpin and cufflinks. There is thus an obvious relation between De Mille and the comic strip conception of a Hollywood director, though which is based on which we leave to other researchers.

His own compulsion to act and to dominate the scene has always had an unfortunate effect on the performers who are hired for that purpose in his pictures. In spite of the frequent publicity claim that he has been a "star-maker," many people in Hollywood believe he has killed more careers than he has created; even quite good actors are unable to emerge from a De Mille picture with anything better than an imitation of the way De Mille himself would play the part. It is interesting to note that, despite their tremendous box office success, no De Mille picture has ever won an Academy award, either for production, direction, acting or writing.

It is characteristic of De Mille that he has never permitted himself to be bothered by the consistent lack of acclaim accorded his work by his fellow artists in the industry and by the more intellectual of the nation's film critics. Such reactions are amply outweighed by the double satisfaction of enormous profits and an undaunted faith in his own estimation of himself as a man of extreme refinement, good taste and spirituality. His criteria in these matters are simple: he compares his present pictures with his past ones. Thus when he was preparing *The Crusades* in 1935, he announced: "Everything in this picture will be authentic, as it was in *Cleopatra.* Yet fools will write to me and say I am taking liberties with history." And in 1940, when the Catholic Sodality of Our Lady expressed alarm about a then contemplated venture to be called *The Queen of Queens,* he replied, in terms obviously intended to give them complete reassurance: "We are approaching the hallowed story . . . with a deep sense of responsibility and with the same spiritual and artistic thrill that impelled the making of *The King of Kings.*" On a more mundane level he once dismissed the misgivings of an associate with the statement: "What is hokum to you, to me and the vast American public is Heart." In this connection he is frank to admit that in his entire career he has only run across three men with any real dramatic sense. They are David Belasco, with whom his father used to collaborate, William De Mille, his brother, and himself.

Another possible source of his present defection from the ranks of the proletariat may lie in the living habits to which has become attached during the thirty-year period of this success. At one time content with a single mansion on De Mille Drive, he long ago purchased the adjoining Charles Chaplin house and connected the two with a glass-enclosed passage. The adjunct now serves as a library, a museum and as an office for his considerable interests outside the picture field. It is there that, when not engaged in shooting a picture, he spends the morning, first reading a specially prepared digest of the contents of the day's newspapers and then taking up his ramified affairs with the help of two secretaries and a business manager.

But it is at Paradise Ranch, his 1200-acre refuge in the Sierras, that De Mille is most in his element. There, far from the enforced glamor of life in the film capital and the necessity of keeping up the front demanded by his place in the world, he can be himself. Of late the war curtailed his famous weekends at this mountain retreat, but the memory of them is still fresh in many a Hollywood mind.

In addition to the main ranch house the non-commercial portion of the place consists of a rustic rock cottage, which serves as De Mille's own personal living quarters, and nine guest houses. Women guests are requested to bring evening clothes, men only the trousers of theirs. To complete his costume each male guest finds in his closet a choice of three Russian shirts, red, white and black, and of a gold or a silver chain to adorn it. Only one guest, a well-known playwright and screenwriter, is reported as ever having refused to subscribe to this masquerade, and he was shortly thereafter dismissed from De Mille's employ.

Cocktails are decreed at 7:30. Shortly after the guests are assembled in the big house, the host makes his appearance, clad in the same simple garb as the rest of the men, with no added embellishments to mark his station other than a pearl-handled revolver, an alpenstock and a cape. The last of these, incidentally, is a garment to which he attaches a special importance; his only recorded definitive summary of the histrionic art is the statement: "Any actor who can't wear a cape is no actor."

Saturday nights at the ranch bring an additional ceremony at cocktail time. A valet carries in a three-tiered basket lined with crumpled black velvet and full of costume jewelry, Hawaiian perfume, nylon stockings, gloves and similar gifts. Women are permitted to examine these items before dinner but forbidden to touch any of them. Just before eating, they gather at the billiard table and roll the balls according to a prescribed set of rules to determine the order in which they may choose their gifts. Later, when dinner is over, each takes her turn at examining the display more closely and experimenting with possible selections before a try-on mirror, while the others stand by watching and hoping their own choices won't be taken before their turns come. De Mille, who makes a hobby of collecting jewels, has been known to toss in a pigeon blood ruby or other unset gem worth far more than the whole basket and revel in the fact that no one chose it over the more gaudily presented items. It seems to put women in their proper perspective for him.

Still another clue to the De Mille rebellion is the fact that the nature of his career has long since brought him into contact with elements of neither a proletarian nor an artistic character. When he first came to Hollywood thirty years ago, he could not secure financing from the local bank and went instead to a struggling institution downtown called the Bank of Italy, later to become the Bank of America with Cecil De Mille as vice-president in charge of motion picture financing. As his fortune grew to its presently estimated eight million dollars, he undertook other sidelines which have included an epsom salts mine, a stock brokerage, an herb tea firm, an airline, a chain of grocery stores, various apartment houses and restaurants and some of the most profitable real estate holdings in Los Angeles. Along with these ventures he found time to interest himself in California politics and was a delegate to the Republican National Conventions in 1936 and 1944. His bitterness against President Roosevelt was in no way diminished by the extremes to which the latter went to furnish him all possible cooperation in the making of *The Story of Dr. Wassell.* When the $25,000 salary ceiling was an issue, De Mille put up a poster against it on his office door, and he once referred to a close associate who favored Roosevelt as "the only traitor in my midst."

It is interesting that it was the Screen Actors Guild, a sister organization of De Mille's own AFRA, that first gave him pause about the unqualified benefits of trade unionism. De Mille had always been famous for his lavish use of extras in his pictures, though he himself was wont to abjure the use of the word. It was his custom, before directing a mob scene to address the players as follows: "Ladies and gentlemen, I want you to know that when you work for me, you are not extras. You are actors." In pursuance of this policy he made it a fetish that there never be mere crowd noises in the background, but that each person called on to make a sound, no matter how distant from the mike, be given a specific written line, of which the director always kept a vest pocket full.

This practice was generally regarded as a pleasant whim among those close to De Mille, and indeed there were some who felt it to be the best possible utilization of the master's passion for writing dialogue. Then the Guild came into being and proposed a minimum of twenty-five dollars a day for all speaking parts. De Mille, whose basic principle of labor relations has always been that anyone should be willing to cut his salary in half in exchange for the intangible compensations of working for De Mille, was hurt, deeply, by the innovation.

It may be that this last item is the most significant one on the list. One can easily imagine how that act of ingratitude may have affected his enthusiasm at the time he was called on to join another branch of the same international. One is even tempted to speculate that he never was a very ardent member of his union, which would lead, in turn, to the hypothesis that his famous gesture was designed not only to free himself from his own frustration but to strike a shattering blow against all the organizations which lure innocent workers into bondage. One would be inclined to support such a theory if one attached much importance to his growing tendency, as noted by his associates, to speak of all unions in antagonistic terms. But it is specifically refuted by his calmer and more reasoned statements from public platforms, in which he invariably assures his audience that his present campaign is actually designed to preserve honest unionism.

It is not the principal aim of this piece, however, to pass judgments or to apportion the precise significance of the various clues we have cited. It would amply fulfill our purpose if we have merely suggested that there are extenuating considerations and deep-lying roots beneath even the most seemingly hotheaded insurrections against the established order.

One final thing remains to be said in order to clear De Mille of the charges of insincerity which have been leveled at him from many directions. These have all taken the form of questioning whether his foundation is actually devoted to its declared cause of political freedom. On that score at least, even such a cursory analysis as this can reach a categorical conclusion. What the De Mille Foundation defends is every workingman's right to independence from any united stand of his co-workers, or, in broader terms, the superior authority of the individual over the organized group. Clearly then, the foundation stands for exactly what it says it does, for that is the purest and most extreme of all philosophies of political freedom. Its formal name is anarchism and it was the creed of such distinguished men as Zeno of Citium, William Godwin, Proudhon and Bakunin. It has even numbered among its advocates a prince, Kropotkin, and a count, Tolstoy. But in all its long and curious history no one ever expected it to show up on De Mille Drive.

46   CHAPLIN AMONG THE IMMORTALS

Jean Renoir

> Man is interested in only one thing: man.
>
> —Pascal

LAST NIGHT, I had a strange dream. I was sitting at my dining room table carving a leg-of-mutton. I went at it in the French manner, which is to slice it in length. In that way, you get a great variety of cuts. Those who like it well done are served first. You wait till you get closer to the bone, for those who prefer it rarer. My guests had been lost in a sort of fog, but as I asked each one how he liked his meat, they suddenly came into a very sharp focus, and I recognized them as people I admire and like. The couples of *The Best Years of Our Lives* were right there at my table, smiling amiably at me. I served them, and they ate with robust appetite. Next to them were the priest and the pregnant woman of *Open City,* a bit more reserved but no less cordial. At the end of the table, the loving pair of *Brief Encounter* were holding hands. This abandon was proof that they felt themselves among friends, and I was gratified by it. As I was about to proceed to the beautiful courtesan of *Children of Paradise,* the doorbell rang.

I went to open the door and found myself facing a

From *The Screen Writer,* (July 1947). ©1945 The Screen Writer. Reprinted by permission of the author. *Mr. Renoir wrote this article in French and translated it into English with the assistance of Harold Salemson.*

gentleman of distinguished appearance. Offhand, he reminded me vaguely of someone I knew well, a little old tramp
who had made the whole world laugh. But I quickly understood that the resemblance was merely physical. Even
under the rich fur coat of a goldmine owner, the other one
had remained a bit of a gutter-snipe. It was obvious that he
would never completely get rid of his lowdown ways.
Whereas this one, on the other hand, was most certainly the
scion of a "good family." His parents had taught him proper
table manners, and when and how to kiss a lady's hand. He
had breeding. And all of his person gave off that impression
of suppressed passions, of hidden secrets, which is the
earmark of the bourgeoisie in our old Western civilizations.

I introduced myself. With exquisite politeness which be-
spoke his old provincial background and his prep-school
education, he told me his name was Verdoux. Then he
placed his hat and cane on a chair, flicked a speck of dust
from his jacket, adjusted his cuffs, and headed for the dining
room. Immediately, the others edged closer together to
make room for him. They seemed happy to see him.
Obviously, they were all members of the same social world.

After dinner, we went outdoors. But word of the presence
of my famous guests had spread, and the street was
crowded with people. When we walked down the porch
steps, the public enthusiasm burst out. Everyone wanted to
shake their hands, there was a terrific crush, the autograph-
seekers were at work. Suddenly, a very dry lady, wearing an
aggressive little hat, recognized Monsieur Verdoux and
pointed a finger at him. And, strangely, the enthusiasm
turned into fury. They rushed at him, raising their fists. I tried
to understand, and kept asking the same question over and
over again: "What did he do? What did he do? . . ." But I
could not hear the answers, for everyone was speaking at
once and the caning the poor man was taking made a
deafening racket. So deafening, in fact, that I awoke with a
start and had to close my window, which a sudden stormy
wind was violently banging back and forth.

I don't believe that the people who attacked Chaplin so
sharply over his latest film did so for personal or political
reasons. In America we haven't yet reached that stage. I
think rather that the trouble is their panic terror before total

change, before a particularly long step forward in the evolution of an artist.

This is not the first time such a thing has happened, nor will it be the last. Molière was a victim of the same kind of misunderstanding. And the Hollywood commentators who have been unable to recognize the qualities of *Monsieur Verdoux* are in very good company, indeed. Molière's detractors had names no less important than La Bruyère, Fénelon, Vauvenargues, Sherer. They said he wrote badly. They criticized him for his barbarism, his jargon, his artificial phrasing, his improper usage, his incorrect wording, his mountains of metaphors, his boring repetitions, his inorganic style. "Molière," said Sherer, "is as bad a writer as one can be."

This animosity on the part of certain self-appointed intellectuals is not the only point of resemblance between the careers of Molière and Chaplin.

In his early stages, the former achieved great success by simply following the traditions of the Italian Comedy. His characters bore the familiar names and costumes, their predicaments were those to which the public was accustomed. Only, beneath Sganarelle's makeup and behind Scapin's somersaults, the author injected a rarer element, a little human truth. But on the surface, there was not too much of an apparent change. When the action slowed down, a solid laying-on with a stick was always good for a laugh. The sentimental side was taken care of with formulae no different, except for the author's masterful touch, from those used elsewhere in the same period: a noble young gentleman falls in love with a scullerymaid and his family will have none of her. But, in the end, it all works out. It is revealed that the ingénue was really a well-born maiden who, as a baby, had been carried off by pirates.

Chaplin, to begin with, simply followed the traditions of the then most popular form in the world, English farce. His feet foul him up on the stairs and his hands get entangled in flypaper. The sentimental side in his films is represented by babies left on doorsteps, streetgirls mistreated by life, or other carryovers from the good old mellers. In spite of that, he never falls into the worst vulgarity of our time, phony bathetic goodness. And beneath his character's flour-face, as well as behind the fake beards of his companions, we rapidly discern real men of flesh and blood. As he grows, like Molière, he introduces into the conventional framework, which he has made his very own through the vigor of his talent, the elements of a sharper and sharper observation of humanity, of a more and more bitter social satire. Nevertheless, since the appearances remain the same, no one is shocked, no one protests.

One day, Molière decided to give up the form which had brought him his success,and he wrote *The School for Wives.* Accusations were heaped upon him. He was called a mountebank. People became irritated with him because he was director, actor and writer all at the same time.

One day, Chaplin wrote *Monsieur Verdoux.* He turned his back on the outward forms to which he had accustomed his public. There was a great hue and cry of indignation, he was dragged through the mud.

After *The School for Wives,* instead of giving in, Molière went on hitting harder and harder. His next play was *Tartuffe,* which impaled phony religion and bigotry.

What will Chaplin's next film be?

I think it is unnecessary to explain why I like the Chaplin of the old school, since everyone seems to share that taste. It is even probable that some of the attackers of his present film must have written glowing tributes to *The Gold Rush* or *The Kid.* I would like, however, to present a few of the reasons which, to me, made the showing of *Monsieur Verdoux* a pure delight.

Like everybody else, I have my own ideas about what is conventionally called Art. I firmly believe that since the end of the period in which the great cathedrals were built, since the all-pervading faith which was to bring forth our modern world is no longer present to give artists the strength to lose themselves in an immense paean to the glory of God, there can be quality to human expression only if it is individual. Even in case of collaboration, the work is valuable only insofar as the personality of each of the authors remains perceptible to the audience. Now, in this film, that presence is, to me, as clear as that of a painter in his canvas or of a composer in his symphony.

Moreover, every man matures, his knowledge of life

increases, and his creations must develop at the same time he does. If we do not admit these truths in our profession, we might as well admit right now that it is an industry no different than the rest, and that we make films like efficiency experts supervise the production of iceboxes or shaving cream. And let's stop priding ourselves on being artists, and claiming that we're carrying forward the grand old traditions.

It is agreed, some will say, that Chaplin has created a highly personal work, and we admit that he had undergone a natural artistic transformation. We only feel that he has done all this in a wrong direction. And they add that the greatest crime of *Monsieur Verdoux* was the killing-off of the beloved little vagabond who had been such a charmer. His creator should not only have kept him alive but depended on him in his search for a new form of expression. I cannot share this opinion.

In giving up the rundown shoes, the old derby hat and willowy cane of the raggedy little guy whose pathetic hangdog look used to melt our hearts, Chaplin has gone deliberately into a world that is more dangerous, because it is closer to the one we live in. His new character, with neatly-pressed trousers, impeccably-knotted tie, well-dressed and no longer able to appeal to our pity, does not belong in those good old situations, outlined in strong broad strokes, where the rich trample the poor in so obvious a manner that even the most childish audience can immediately grasp the moral of the story. Before, we could imagine that the adventures of the little tramp took place in some world that belonged exclusively to the movies, that they were a sort of fairy tale.

With *Monsieur Verdoux,* such misapprehension is no longer possible. This one really takes place in our time, and the problems faced on the screen are really our own. By thus giving up a formula which afforded him full security, and undertaking squarely the critique of the society in which he himself lives, a dangerous job if ever there was one, the author raises our craft to the level of the great classical expressions of the human mind, and strengthens our hope of being able to look upon it more and more as an art.

Let me add a purely personal note here: Having given up the powerful weapon which was the defenselessness of his old character, Chaplin had to look for another to be used by his latest creation. The weapon he chose is one that appeals particularly to the Frenchman in me, steeped as he is in the 18th Century: paradoxical logic.

I understand perfectly the misgivings of certain conformists minds before this method which seems to belong to a bygone aristocratic era. I hope they will forgive a devoted reader of the works of Diderot, Voltaire and Beaumarchais for the pleasure he found in *Monsieur Verdoux.*

Moreover, even when it is not thus spiced with paradoxical logic, genius often has something shocking about it, something subversive, some of the characteristics of a Cassandra. That is because it has better vision than ordinary mortals, and the commonsensical truths that it sees still strike the rest of us as something akin to madness.

Another reason for liking *Monsieur Verdoux;* I love to be amused at the movies, and this film made me laugh until my tears flowed like wine.

I believe I see growing up about me a certain taste for collective accomplishments, the anonymousness of which is a tribute to the adoration of new deities. Let me mention at random some of these false idols: public opinion polls, organization, technics. These are but the saints of a dangerous god that some are trying to substitute for the God of our childhood. This new divinity is called Scientific Progress. Like any self-respecting God, he tries to attract us with his miracles. For how else can one describe electricity, anaesthesia or atomic fission? But I am very leery of this newcomer. I am afraid that, in exchange for the refrigerators and the television sets that he will distribute so generously, he may try to deprive us of a part of our spiritual heritage.

In other times, every object was a work of art, in that it was a reflection of the one who made it. The humblest early American sideboard is the creation of one given woodworker, and not of any other. This personal touch was present in everything, in houses, in clothes, in food.

When I was young, in my village in Burgundy, when we drank a glass of wine, we could say: That comes from the Terre à Pot vineyard up over the hill behind the little pine wood, or from the Sarment Fountain, or from some other specific spot. Some bottles left on your tongue the silex taste of their vines, others were like velvet and you knew they came from a lush green valley with plenty of moisture. Closing your eyes, you could see a certain greyish hill, with its twisted little oaks and the imprints of the boars' feet which had been found there last fall after the harvest. And later the young girls bending under the weight of their baskets full of luscious grapes. Especially, you recalled the wrinkled face of the vintner who had devoted his life to the culture of that difficult soil.

All the manifestations of life took on a profound meaning, because men had left their mark upon them. You felt that you were in the center of an immense prayer sent heavenward by all of the workers, with their plows, their hammers, their needles, or even simply their brains. Today we live in a desert of anonymity. The wines are blended. The nickel-plated tubing in my bathroom, the hardwood of my floor, the fence around my garden, all bring to mind for me only the uniform purr of the machines that turned them out.

There are still a few places where we can seek a refuge. A painter can still speak to us of himself in his canvases, as a chef can in his culinary creations. That is probably why we are ready to pay fortunes for a good picture or for a good meal. And then there is also this film craft of ours, which will remain one of the great expressions of human personality if we are able to retain our artisans' spirit, which fortunately is still very much alive. That spirit is Chaplin's, down to the tips of his toenails. One feels it in a certain decent way he has of going into a scene, in the almost peasant-like thriftiness of his sets, in his wariness of technique for technique's sake, in his respect for the personalities of actors,and in that internal richness which makes us feel that each character just has too much to say.

Monsieur Verdoux will some day go into history along with the creations of artists who have contributed to the building of our civilization. He will have his place alongside the pottery of Urbino and the paintings of the French Impressionists, between a tale by Mark Twain and a minuet by Lulli. And during that time, the films which are so highly endowed with money, with technique and with publicity, the ones that enchant his detractors, will find their way God knows where, let us say into oblivion, along with the expensive mahogany chairs mass-produced in the beautiful nickel-plated factories.

47   *THE BEST YEARS OF OUR LIVES*

Abraham Polonsky

> N'est-ce pas parce que nous cultivons la brume?
>
> —Mallarmé

The Best Years of Our Lives, RKO, 1946. Director, William Wyler. Screenplay, Robert E. Sherwood. Based on the novel *Glory for Me* by Mackinlay Kantor. Photography, Gregg Toland. Musical score, Hugo Friedhofer. A Samuel Goldwyn production.

ABOUT THIS TIME each year, the Academy Awards remind us of the fictional odds and ends produced in the Hollywood studios. I suppose everyone will agree that *The Best Years of Our Lives* stands above its competitors as life itself dominates our fictions.

We are offered a view of three veterans from different social classes adjusting themselves to modern times in Boone City, America. It is a pattern of reality as Wyler and Sherwood see it, the life that touches their imagination with truth, with warmth, with communication. The social environment of former Captain Fred Derry is treated reluctantly and without a true perspective, but if Wyler and Sherwood knew

From *Hollywood Quarterly,* Vol. 2, No. 3, November 1947. ©1947 by The Regents of the University of California. Reprinted by permission of The Regents and of the author.

better, like their most sympathetic protagonist, the banker Al Stephenson, they realize that some version of the Boone City bank is in control of the film industry. Author and director bowed and passed. Nevertheless, the area of human character which the *Best Years* makes available to its audience is a landmark in the fog of escapism, meretricious violence, and the gimmick plot attitude of the usual movie. It becomes very clear that an artist who happens to bring even a tag of daily experience into the studio is making an immense contribution to the screen. The *Best Years* indicates for every director and writer that the struggle for content, for social reality, no matter how limited the point of view, is a necessary atmosphere for growth in the American film.

As the plot goes, three veterans meet by accident and return to their city in the same place. Each goes home and is welcomed: one to the rich emotional sympathy of an upper-class family; one to an earnest but narrow white-collar house; and one to a poor man's broken home and a slut of a wife. Al Stephenson is a hit-the-beach sergeant, and, oddly enough, a banker. Homer Parrish is an enlisted man from the Navy, now equipped with hands in the form of two hooks. Fred Derry, the poor boy, is the Air Force captain, formerly a soda jerk. Director and writer were intensely interested in these three men, but the same understanding was not brought to bear on their special problems. Homer, the petty bourgeois, has a girl whom he loves and who loves him. She wants to marry him, but Homer is self-conscious about his hooks, resentful of pity. Wilma, in a slow and lovely scene, faces up to the broken flesh; Homer is rescued from himself; and we are left happily aware of their happiness, recalling a previous scene in which the government pension puts an economic base under their marriage. Fred Derry comes from "across the tracks" (we even hear the trains); his father is a drunk, his stepmother anomalous, his wife less so. Fred is forced back behind the soda fountain, loses his job with a punch, his wife to another man, and ex-G.I., and decides to leave town. His wife is going to divorce him because he can't make money, and finally he is magically offered a position as a laborer, which he accepts. Al Stephenson, the banker, has a "wonderful" wife and two of the "finest" children in the world. He gets a bigger job in his "old" bank, this time as a vice-president in charge of G.I. loans. Unable to grant such loans without collateral, Al gets drunk (evidently the forms of courage in the economic system need different stimuli than in combat) and makes a speech in which he beautifully points out that the soldier asked no collateral for his final sacrifices in the war. Al doesn't lose his job, and the final scene, although unresolved, is not unhappy.

These three unrelated plots are bound together with some wire left over from a million movies: the poor boy, having found himself, gets the daughter of the well-to-do veteran. Homer stays with us because his uncle owns a bar, in which some of the scenes are played.

It is obvious enough that we are here faced with the general stereotypes of the film industry and popular fiction. The original novel by Mackinlay Kantor is even more run-of-the-mill, and the Wyler-Sherwood changes move the story progressively toward realism. In Kantor's story, Al leaves the bank to become a small-time farmer and Fred narrowly escapes becoming a bank robber. The film's drive toward truth is evident in every sequence. There is immense patience for detail and emotional texture, especially in the homecoming scenes of Al and Homer, where the inventive commentary on human behavior is enormous. A passion for insight smashes the stereotypes, around the edges. The lesson for directors and writers is evident: writing for the movies is writing under censorship. The censorship forces stereotypes of motive and environment on the creators, and the problem is to press enough concrete experience into the mold to make imagination live.

Unfortunately, in the *Best Years,* as in most social-problem fiction, the artist falls into the trap of trying to find local solutions in existence for the social conflicts, instead of solving them in feeling. This is, of course, the industry's demand for happy endings. Now the truth of the matter is that veterans have been sold out *en masse* by society. The picture exposes the fraud of America's promises to its soldiers, the promises of businessmen and cheap publicists. We all remember the refrigerators that became planes and flew off to the lonely beaches and mud; we all remember the girls who waited at home and the jobs that would be there. The new world was articulate in the newspaper editorials.

The soldiers would take care of the fighting, and the powers-that-be would take care of the peace and prosperity. In the *Best Years,* fakery is laid bare, but the plot forces easy solutions on its creators. Fascism is solved with a punch; a bad marriage by the easy disappearance of a wife; the profound emotional adjustment of a handless veteran by a fine girl; the itchy conscience of a banker by too many drinks. The future is not to be predicted out of such formulas.

Despite the fact that the Hollywood fog which hangs over modern life as portrayed in film is cleared from time to time, the basic stereotype holds constantly. Where the economics of life make naked the terror of a return to a bad old world, the southern California mist moves in and obscures the truth. This is why the crux of the story lies at the point where the veteran's problem is most mental, least rude and real. Al, the banker, has a bad conscience about the abandoned ordinary veteran. What happens to these "buddies" bothers him, and this intellectual approach is both sound and useful. But a story which has a Fred Derry who must meet the brutal indifference of society, solve it, or be destroyed, seems suddenly oddly accented when the story point of view is that of the man least involved, Al Stephenson.

I suspect that Wyler and Sherwood are not really emotionally conscious of the Derrys, the majority of veterans. People of the kind the author and director best understand, with whom their sympathies lie, are good people like the Stephensons. So it follows that the only family in the story with size, roundness, dignity, beauty, sympathy, and passion, is the family of the good banker. For Derry the environment of action has been specialized to mere plot, built for violent contrast, and localized in the inability of the poor boy who made a little easy dough flying a bomber to adjust himself to his former economic status. The concentration of human virtue in the least affected of the social strata lends a certain lopsidedness to the understanding of veterans' adjustment.

Two scenes most sharply indicate the attitude.

One is Al's daughter accusing her parents of being smug with happiness, of not understanding Fred's desperate plight of joblessness, a broken marriage, of general reorientation. The daughter tells her parents that they have escaped the

basic conflicts of the times in a decent standard of living, a
good job, and a honeymoon in the South of France. Smug
self-pity replies that mama and papa have had their emotional ups and downs, that sometimes mama didn't like papa
and vice versa. The girl is defeated and cries. This is
blindness.

The other scene is a wonderful metaphor. Captain Fred
Derry, the junked bombardier, walks in the graveyard of the
air fleet, seen first from his point of view. The camera lifts
until at last he is small and abandoned in what seems an
endless pattern of power nailed down to uselessness,
objects chosen for oblivion. A whole society has poured forth
its strength to create these marvelous machines, and a
whole society has combined power to train this former soda
clerk to the machine. Now, both (the film tells us) are not
needed. Finally, Derry climbs aboard a motorless bomber,
sits in its nose, in the dust, in the sun, staring through the
dirty plastic into the sky. The camera, returning to the
outside, catches up in music the noise of the gunning motors,
then advances head-on toward the bomber, and from a low
angle imaginatively lifts the plane into the clouds. Inside
again, the music roaring like motors, Derry relives the terror,
the individual destiny of combat—then the junkman appears,
the bombardier is chased from his plane.

A life and a society are supposed to be summed up in this,
one of the ultimate scenes of the film. Here for a moment the
plot became almost identified with reality. Here the plastic
values of the different arts merged as in some fabulous aria;
and then, as always, the Hollywood fog moved in, obscuring
what we have just seen and almost realized. Derry gets a job
from the junkman, takes off his jacket, and we are all
enormously relieved to know that the intense experience of
the last few minutes has meant just nothing at all.

The movies just seem to find it impossible to deal with
people who work for their living in factories and on farms.
This submerged majority of the public is left inarticulate by
the artists, covered with a fog which occasionally breaks to
reveal a Capra pixie. Greatness was possible for the *Best
Years,* but this meant examining Fred Derry where society
hurts hardest. It was not done.

Technically, the picture is free from the nervous cutting for mechanical pace so holy in Hollywood, and close-ups do not pop in to fill dramatic vacuums. There is no excess of moving shots having the aesthetic value of vertigo. The style of shooting is round, built about the people in relation to one another, held in the shot to let the story come through.

Within its imposed limits and compromises the film is an enormous success, something like the war itself, which has invigorated many a European country and stirred vast colonial peoples, while here at home we have returned to cynicism from our betters, sharpened social conflicts, and a mood of vulgar despair among the artists.

William Wyler said in 1948 at the beginning of the witchhunting mania: "I wouldn't be allowed to make The Best Years of Our Lives *in Hollywood today. That is directly the result of the activities of the Un-American Activities Committee. They are making decent people afraid to express their opinions. They are creating fear in Hollywood. Fear will result in self-censorship. Self-censorship will paralyze the screen. In the last analysis, you will suffer. You will be deprived of entertainment which stimulates you, and you will be given a diet of pictures which conform to arbitrary standards of Americanism. I hope to make many more pictures as popular, as meaningful and as successful at the box office as* The Best Years of Our Lives." (Hollywood On Trial—The Story of the Ten Who Were Indicted, *by Gordon Kahn, 1948).*

The Best Years of Our Lives *turned out to be Wyler's last important film. His previous outstanding films included* These Three *(1936),* Dead End *(1937),* Wuthering Heights *(1939),* The Letter *(1940),* The Little Foxes *(1941). (DP)*

48 SOME OF MY WORST FRIENDS: MOTION PICTURES AND ANTI-SEMITISM

Adrian Scott

1

A T THIS WRITING, *Crossfire* has just completed six weeks at the Rivoli Theatre in New York, and is continuing to run. Business has been splendid, even boff, in the big city. The picture has been seen in a few resort towns on the Atlantic seaboard. Reports from there are incomplete but aggregate grosses on the first day had the picture running $150 behind *The Hucksters,* which is the most boff of the pictures currently running. This means, I gather, that the box office is not as pessimistic about *Crossfire* as some people are.

From the very beginning *Crossfire* has been the victim of a strong minority pessimism. It would be easy to say that its source was anti-Semitic, which in part it was. But chiefly it stemmed from sources that had genuine anxiety about the project and thought it would be better left alone. Pictures should be made on the subject, the sources said, but not *Crossfire.* Others among the minority said *Crossfire* should be done differently. Still others: If it were done badly, it would cause more anti-Semitism. Still others: If it were done well, it would be those smart Jews in Hollywood at work, and this, too, would not have the effect of abating but rather increasing anti-Semitism.

This is the partial, bewildering context of *Crossfire's* inception; the whole of it is monumental.

From *The Screen Writer* (October 1947). ©1945 The Screen Writer. Reprinted by permission of the author.

The first rumbling of an anti-Semitic nature came to us when the project was first announced. A troubled few had difficulty assigning the right motives to the making and to the makers of *Crossfire*. Eddie Dmytryk was labeled a Jew. It was said that I was a Jew, too, a fact which I had managed to conceal for many years but which now came out since I was involved in the project. Of John Paxton, who wrote the screen play, it was noted by someone who read the script that he couldn't possibly have been this brilliant about anti-Semitism unless he himself was an anti-Semite. Finally, it was said categorically that the whole bunch at RKO involved in this project were Jews.

We were not accorded the professional's right of evaluating the contemporary scene or the right of feeling compassion for our fellow men. Nor were we accorded a fundamental Hollywood right of considering ourselves fairly good business men for attempting to make a good picture with a new and vital theme. These, incidentally, were our motives. They haven't changed. We continue to like them.

Since the picture's release the original pessimism has taken some new forms but mostly the old forms remain intact. Naturally, it was very rewarding to find majority opinion behind the film's content, praising the fact that it was done, deploring the fact that it was necessary to be done. But minority opinion has let out a loud wail, placing its attack in the context of that indefatigable cliche that Hollywood has not grown up. The specific attack is confining itself to certain issues in the picture.

Minority opinion attaches itself to what it considers a formidable weakness in content, not quality. In most cases the picture gets a grudgingly proffered "A" in quality. This minority view seems less an opinion—even a complex opinion—than it does a fascinating and tortuous obscurity. But despite this, and despite its irrelevance, it is well and articulately done. It is, therefore, considerably more dangerous.

Here it is.

Crossfire, the argument goes, concerns itself with "lunatic fringe" anti-Semitism (which it primarily does). But, because it deals with lunatic fringe anti-Semitism, it separates itself from majority anti-Semitic practice. Because it separates itself from majority anti-Semitic practice, the film is not about you and me.

The argument shifts and proceeds: The "you and me" kind of anti-Semitism is chiefly the social discrimination variety—the kind which keeps Jews out of a club or a hotel or a camp, which says the Jews own the motion picture industry, which they clearly do not. And this "you and me" kind, it is argued, since it has to do with the kind of anti-Semitism practiced by most Americans, is the kind one ought to make a picture about.

Because *Crossfire* does not deal with this variety of anti-Semitism, the film is not only *not* about you and me but it is, moreover, not valid and not true.

Crossfire is not valid and not true because (1) lunatic anti-Semitism either does not exist or it does exist but it is not important; or (2) it is important but it doesn't happen as it does in *Crossfire*; or (3) if it does happen, the picture's attack is nevertheless too confined, it is not a definitive picture of anti-Semitism: therefore, it will not promote understanding of anti-Semitism; or (4) the anti-Semite, Monty, in *Crossfire,* for a variety of obscure reasons, will be considered the hero—audiences will sympathize with him, identify themselves with him. As a result the pictures will have the opposite effect of the one intended.

It would be stupid to deny the charge—and it has become a charge—about the "you and me" business. It should be freely admitted at the outset: *Crossfire* is not about you and me. When work was started some two years ago, it was purposely designed *not* to be about you and me. Its attack was limited and confined; its story was limited and confined, as is the story of almost any theatrical experience. To attempt to do a definitive study of anti-Semitism in one picture is a fool's errand. It is proper material for pamphlets and books. But even in these media it is doubtful if definitiveness is possible. Look at the literature which has investigated anti-Semitism. Find, if you can, a one-volume definitive analysis.

Most of the minority charges against *Crossfire* probably dismiss themselves, crumbling with their own faulty and insubstantial structure. But the charge that the lunatic fringe anti-Semitism of *Crossfire* is invalid and untrue is just silly enough to be picked up by groups which engage wilfully in anti-Semitism. For this reason it should be answered.

Lunatic fringe anti-Semitism is important, dangerously and terribly important. It was important in Hitler's Reich and in Czarist Russia, and in most of the countries of Europe at some time. The social discrimination variety is important, too; so is every minor or major practice which goes to make up the whole hateful body of anti-Semitic practice. And anyone who attempts to estimate which kind of anti-Semitism is most important or which kind should have the most emphasis announces an incomplete understanding of anti-Semitism.

Monty, the anti-Semite in *Crossfire*, exists. This very night he is roaming the streets of Queens, N.Y., looking for a Jew to beat up. He has already beaten up many. He has associates. They are looking to prove their superiority by kicking around someone they consider decidedly inferior. They want a scapegoat for their own insecurity and maladjustment. They are ignorant and organized. They hoot and howl with fanatic energy at the Messianic raving of Gerald L. K. Smith. They are the storm troopers of tomorrow. If this country were depressed enough to fall victim to a Leader, these men would qualify brilliantly for the chieftains of American Buchenwalds and Dachaus.

Such a group, organized and disciplined, a significant section of native American fascists, is a threat to the Jews, and to the entire population. It is depressing at this point in our history to find it necessary to say that.

It is also depressing, after the experience of *Crossfire*, to hear the fancies which are currently being distributed about *Gentleman's Agreement.* This is again a minority opinion, as in the case of *Crossfire*. And it is something which the makers of *Gentleman's Agreement* will face and undoubtedly answer.

The lunatic fringe charge, of course, is not made against *Gentleman's Agreement.* The charge here is that *Gentleman's Agreement* has a dubious device; that, while the book has some fine things to say about anti-Semitism, the point of departure is unsound.

You may have heard it. It goes like this: *Gentleman's Agreement* has a great angle—a slick, glib and familiar angle—but it does not truthfully correspond with experience. The protagonist, Green, who pretends to be a Jew, is not really going through what a Jew goes through. Thus, the picture will have a sense of not happening, or at best, happening in vacuum. The end result will be special—as special as the problem it poses—and, therefore, not effective against total anti-Semitism.

This is an interesting deviation from the criticism of *Crossfire.* Remember, *Crossfire* did not correspond with majority anti-Semitic practice? Well, *Gentleman's Agreement* does. But even though *Gentleman's Agreement* has selected the proper kind of anti-Semitism to attack, it's no good because the *method* of attack is no good!

Discussions of anti-Semitism on this level are weird and unreal. They are debates in limbo. Nobody really cares how they come out. But they are important, recklessly important, for they throw off anti-Semitic particles to be used and to be expanded in the whole body of anti-Semitic practice.

The plain, simple fact is that the device of *Gentleman's Agreement* is brilliant for its purpose. To describe sharply the villainy of anti-Semitism, a man is persecuted and depraved simply because he says he is a Jew. If it is a trick, it is a Swiftian trick. It, furthermore, lends itself to a savage and ruthless exposition of anti-Semitism.

2

During the preparation of *Crossfire* we had no notion what the specific effect of the picture would be on the anti-Semitic and non-anti-Semitic population. There was no possible way of gauging this except by making a picture and finding out what happened. The full potential impact of a motion picture cannot be completely determined by its script, nor is it possible to survey scientifically the effect of the final product. Anti-Semitism is slippery and takes many forms. A picture could affect one form and not another.

We hoped the effect would be enormous. We weren't so sanguine as to expect the picture would, in one fell swoop, eradicate anti-Semitism. But we did know that public discussion and lively debate have a valuable place in a democratic society. The air could be cleared. The problem could be more clearly visualized. We hoped for this, for more clarity.

Although we rejected the minority disturbance, we nevertheless wondered about it. We wondered, for example, if it had reached our fellow professionals, and if not, would they have the minority reservation without having experienced minority influence.

We decided to ask and to ask further what was their opinion of the possible effect of the picture. We hoped it would be like ours. It wouldn't prove anything scientifically, but it would describe an attitude—whether that attitude was favorably inclined toward this project and others like it; whether that attitude properly stimulated would be the beneficiary of further attitudes and further action against anti-Semitism. We simply wanted to know the effect—any kind of effect—on professionals and we could get this simply by asking.

A poll was conducted. The specific question of "effect" was asked and one other: Is it possible to end anti-Semitism in America? This latter produced some lively results. The questionees freely spoke their minds. Here are the answers:

Answer Number One. Number One thought the effect of pictures dealing with anti-Semitism would be enormous. They would be applauded by the country as a whole, by legislators, educators, churches, etc. He was quite certain that on people of good will who were unconscious of their own anti-Semitic practice the effect would be positive; i.e., in the future they would resist anti-Semitic impulses and be wary of anti-Semitic practice in others. He felt the pictures would have no effect on the practicing anti-Semite, the semi-fascist, who would conclude that these pictures were all Jewish inspired. He thought that anti-Semitism could be ended in America if all the media of communication lent themselves to the project. The project would need the endless cooperation of radio, newspapers, motion pictures, educators and school systems. He added ruefully that although it could be done, it probably wouldn't simply because the media themselves would develop insuperable obstacles to their ever getting together. They would not consider it their job fundamentally. It would belong to somebody else.

Answer Number Two. Number Two was uncertain as to what the effect of pictures exposing anti-Semitism would be. Undoubtedly, on some people there would be a salutary effect but he wondered how permanent the effect would be. Attacking ·aspects of anti-Semitism in pictures would certainly neutralize to a great extent those aspects but wouldn't anti-Semitism find new ways of exploiting itself? Wouldn't it rise in new forms? Wouldn't it transfer itself to other minorities, the Negroes, for example? He hadn't really thought enough about it, but despite his hesitancies he felt that the fact that pictures were being made was a great stride forward. He thought anti-Semitism and all minority prejudice could be removed from the American scene by proper educational methods but he would not attempt to guess how long this would take.

Answer Number Three. Number Three couldn't estimate or guess at the effect of the pictures being made but he was proud they were being made. Proud of the industry and himself (he was working in one of the pictures). He didn't know how long it would take but he knew it could be done, citing himself as an example. Until he was 28 years old he was anti-Semitic himself. Not active and not vicious. When he first came to New York from a small Nebraska town, he'd never to his knowledge met a Jew. There weren't any in his town and yet the town was anti-Semitic. During a time he was out of work in New York, he roamed the city—in the slums, middle class and wealthy areas. Particularly in the slums his anti-Semitism was confirmed. He would see dirty people, fat, sloppy. His simple standard of judgment was that he wouldn't like to be invited into these peoples' houses to sit at their table. The thought revolted him. These were Jews. In later years, when his perspective had changed, he confessed to himself that he never knew for certain whether these "dirty, sloppy people" were Jews. They could have been anything: Irish, Polish, Hungarians, or what they actually were, Americans. His real hate was for poverty and the dirt and filth that accompany it. He hated the wrong things; he hated the people instead of the conditions that made people that way. Today he says, "If the seed of anti-Semitism could be removed from me, it can be removed from anybody—when educated properly."

Answer Number Four. Number four felt that the pictures being made were a drop in a bucket. No more. To be really effective, a national campaign of education was necessary, including the help of motion pictures, newspapers, radio, publishers, legislators, congressmen, senators, presidents, school systems and the whole American people. That they could ever get together was an idea which should be properly patronized. But if they did, and stayed together, the demise of anti-Semitism could be estimated as a certainty in a very short time.

Answer Number Five. Number Five applauded the pictures being made. He was not interested as a professional in the specific effect of these pictures—he knew it would be good. He didn't know how widespread the effect would be. He felt the violent anti-Semite would ignore and actively campaign against the pictures. He felt that even certain people of good will, unconscious of their anti-Semitic prejudice, ignorant of the full meaning of anti-Semitism, would pick on the pictures and try very hard to find something wrong with them. But all this was irrelevant. What was important was that the most effective voice in the country had the guts to stand up and say anti-Semitism was wrong. Not only was it education for the people but it was education for the professional. Here was a precedent which excites and stimulates the professional to examine his own work. As a good citizen, he wanted anti-Semitism to end. Anti-Semitism, or any minority prejudice, was the tool of the semi-fascist and the fascist, something to use against the country as a whole, and against him and his family. It was a machine by which democracy could be liquidated. He was certain that anti-Semitism could be ended. He didn't care how long it took, so long as something in a big way was done to combat it.

Answer Number Six. This man was an executive in the industry. He couldn't determine the effect of the pictures. But he was convinced that this was a proper step and he hoped the pictures would make a lot of money, for, he argued, this would guarantee that many people would see them. But whether money was made or not was not of first importance. Whether the pictures were big successes, moderate successes or miserable failures was not of first importance. The importance was the public service. The industry occasionally should make pictures, he felt, with the objective of servicing democratic institutions. He considered prejudice of any kind anti-democratic. If the pictures fail, they should be written off and made available to anyone or any organization that wanted to show them.

Answer Number Seven. This man was a veteran. He thought it was possible to neutralize anti-Semitism and having been abroad in Germany he thought we damn well better had. Anti-Semitism in pre-Hitler Germany was far less extensive than it is here now. He was appalled when he came home from the war at the extent to which we have continued to underestimate minority prejudice. We have learned some lessons from the war, he thought, but we have not learned enough. We have failed to understand that with existing prejudices against the Jews and the Negroes and other minorities, it would be simple—so very simple—for an American Fuehrer to whip this country into a violent and ghastly hatred as a step toward the eventual destruction of our democratic institutions. In depression, which our most conservative economists agree is coming, the soil for demagoguery grows rich and fertile. The minority becomes the scapegoat and the scapegoat the smoke screen for anti-democratic activity. In this context, anyone who subscribes to full democratic practice is expendable.

These are some of the answers. There were more, about twenty in all but there isn't enough space to report them.

On the whole the experiment, however unscientific it might seem to Mr. Gallup, was successful. A majority approved the pictures, were pleased that the subject was being aired in frank terms, agreed that the techniques so far developed for battling anti-Semitism have proved miserable failures.

One opinion was violent on the subject of the frail intellectual who would snipe and pick and submit his own anxiety as proof that these pictures will cause more anti-Semitism—whose real position when examined closely would prevent pictures on anti-Semitism from being made at all.

Everyone realized it was a gigantic job to neutralize anti-Semitism but that perhaps as a result of these pictures, activity would be hastened. But there was no absolute, positive guarantee that this would be done. It seemed rather that the only positive guarantee was that anti-Semitism would continue.

This is true. Anti-Semitism will continue. The pictures, when they have been released nationally and have completed their runs, will certainly have the effect of abating somewhat the virulence of anti-Semitism. But at best the effect is temporary. These pictures are no permanent cure. For a year or perhaps five years they will be shown and used, but in the end, they cannot be counted on to handle the job of servicing a nation riddled with prejudice. There is no proof that any program, legislative or educational, now in work is large enough in scope to defend successfully our people against prejudice of whatever kind.

Although the poll confirmed our hopes about *Crossfire,* it brought to the foreground a new and grave concern: The motion picture industry had lifted the lid on a controversy on a national scale; it would hardly accrue to its credit to allow that controversy to be debated or aired superficially.

Medicine would not put a highly infectious patient in a fine hospital bed and deny him the use of penicillin. Motion pictures cannot make two or five or even ten films and announce their responsibility has been discharged. If the industry believes, and not simply pays lip service to the notion that American life guarantees freedom from prejudice, as the pictures on anti-Semitism will say directly or indirectly, then clearly there is a responsibility facing the industry.

The responsibility, very simply, is to implement the job already started.

In the course of conducting the poll, a number of gifted people said they were available for use in combating minority prejudice. This was enough encouragement to ask other people among our actors, directors, producers and writers if they would be willing to give their services to making pictures on anti-Semitism and minority prejudice.

No one refused.

They agreed to make time if they were busy. They were all stimulated by the prospect and not a few pointed out a precedent exists. No studio in the business made a penny on pictures produced for the Army or Navy during wartime. True, this was a national crisis, but as someone pointed out, there is a crisis among minorities. When any minority is abused, degraded or deprived of earning a living, this constitutes a crisis for the entire nation.

The broad program is yet to be devised. But suppose it went something like this:

The program of pictures would be shorts—documentaries, if you prefer that word—made by some of the industry's finest craftsmen. Individually, they would deal with one aspect of anti-minority practice. They would be designed for the consumption of all age groups. For the very young, obviously a cartoon. For college groups, a more mature analysis. One picture could possibly lay low the infamous "Christ killer" legend. Another could treat with anti-Semitism among the Negroes. Several could be devoted to the historical aspects of anti-Semitism. And so on, until the whole body of anti-Semitism is exposed.

These pictures would be made with the assistance of experts—psychologists, social workers, effective fighters against race and minority prejudice.

They would be made available free of charge to anyone who requested them. To social organizations, to school systems, to labor organizations, to colleges, to motion picture exhibitors, etc., etc.

Twenty shorts would be enough to start the program, enough to service the country for five years, say. A production expert figures, with services donated by those who can afford it, the pictures should cost less than $10,000 apiece. My very poor arithmetic makes the price per day for five years about one hundred dollars.

If this job is done, if these pictures are made, the nation will be given the machinery by which a large scale operation can be instituted. Everyone applauds the yearly campaigns of good will organizations to combat prejudice; but these good will organizations do not have enough weapons. One week, every year, is not enough time to devote to the destruction of prejudice. Doctors would go mad if they were permitted to work only one week on the cure for polio or cancer. We would still have no cure for syphilis if Ehrlich assigned one week a year to find his specific. It's a full-time job. To destroy a mass prejudice, a mass instrument is necessary. A motion picture program is the start. But a big start.

Clearly, we have the facilities in this country democratically mobilized to work effectively for the destruction of anti-Semitism or any minority prejudice. Tragedy will befall us if as a result of the program spontaneously combusting nothing is done to follow it up. The time will be ripe a few months hence for action. A certain conditioning in public thinking will have taken place. The challenge of action will then face us.

Some of my worst friends are those who ignore or refuse the challenge.

Shortly after Adrian Scott's article appeared in The Screen Writer *he received a subpoena to appear before the House Un-American Activities Committee. As one of the Hollywood Ten who appeared before that body in October, 1947 as an unfriendly witness, Scott was forthwith fired by RKO and blacklisted by all the major Hollywood studios, together with* Crossfire's *director, Edward Dmytryk (also of the Hollywood Ten), and John Paxton, author of the screenplay. See the article on the* Hollywood Witchhunt of 1947 *that follows for further material on this subject. (DP)*

49 THE HOLLYWOOD WITCHHUNT OF 1947: A THIRTIETH ANNIVERSARY

David Platt

"**I** HAVE NOW IN MY POSSESSION complete and indubitable proof . . . an officially authenticated list of names, ages, places of nativity, professions, etc. of the officers and members of a Society of Illuminati . . . instituted in Virginia by the Grand Orient of France." —From the writings of the New England Congregationalist Minister Jedidiah Morse in 1790. Quoted in *The Great Fear* by David Caute (1978). In a style all too familiar to students of McCarthy, Morse assailed "the myth of the secret order of Illuminati . . . fanned by John Robison's Proofs of a Conspiracy, a conspiracy apparently dedicated to the overthrow not only of all governments but also of Christianity itself." Morse's activities contributed to the passage by the Federalists in 1798 of the Alien and Sedition Acts.

The decline of Hollywood as a world film center stems from the House Un-American Activities Committee (HUAC) witch hunt of 1947 that sent 10 noted screen artists to prison and ousted from the industry several hundred others, representing the bulk of its most talented and socially aware writers, actors and directors. Blacklisted or otherwise effectively silenced were artists who, under the impact of the "New Deal," the great CIO organizing drives and the anti-fascist struggles of the depression and war decades, made some of the finest and most influential films in our

From *Jewish Currents* (December 1977). © 1977. Reprinted by permission.

history: Films that protested hunger and illiteracy, Jew-baiting, Negro-baiting, union-hating, profiteering, lynching, war and fascism. Films in the democratic tradition that sought to reflect, however imperfectly, the times we live in, and sometimes dared to urge social change. Films such as *The Grapes of Wrath, The Great Dictator, Blockade, Cross-fire, I Am a Fugitive from a Chain Gang, Wild Boys of the Road, Fury, Zola, Watch on the Rhine, Monsieur Verdoux,* in contrast to the mounds of Busby Berkeley—Shirley Temple—Andy Hardy musicals and comedies.

The origins of the HUAC assault are related to the powerful social awakening in the country in the 1930s. The mass struggles of those times left their mark not only on film content but on the Hollywood film community as a whole. One form that it took was an upsurge of support by leading film personalities for such causes as Tom Mooney, Scottsboro, Angelo Herndon, the fight against Hitler fascism, the defense of Loyalist Spain. Witch-hunted out of the industry were the people who had helped organize and liberalize the screen guilds and unions; who had founded the Hollywood Anti-Nazi League and built it into an organization powerful enough to shut almost every door in the face of Leni Riefenstahl, maker of the Nazi propaganda film *Triumph of the Will,* when she visited the studios in 1938 as an emissary of Hitler shortly after the Crystal Night pogroms, which wrecked every synagogue in the Third Reich and sent 30,000 Jews to Dachau and other death camps.

Part of HUAC's indictment of the "Hollywood Ten" was that they were premature anti-fascists, believers in detente, obsessed with labor and civil rights problems, and somehow also managed to be elected to leading posts in the Screen Writers Guild, the Hollywood Writers Congress and the Hollywood Writers Mobilization. So "subversive" was this Mobilization during the war that it was given the responsibility of writing 120 documentaries and short subjects and preparing 1,069 radio scripts for the armed forces and war agencies. The 1947 witch hunt was deeply tainted with race hate. "Hollywood Ten" member Sam Ornitz noted that HUAC had subpoenaed the author, director and producer of *Crossfire,* an outstanding film against anti-Semitism. Adrian Scott, the film's producer, challenged the Un-Americans to deny they were engaged in an attempt to destroy screen artists who had made unstereotyped films about Jews, Blacks and other minorities and had actively worked against rightists like Gerald L. K. Smith and the Klan. In that heralded 1942 HUAC "October" in Washington the Committee put on the stand what John Howard Lawson called an assortment of "stool-pigeons, neurotics, publicity-seeking clowns, Gestapo agents, paid informers, and a few ignorant and frightened Hollywood artists," claiming they had evidence of "communism" in the industry. How fragile was this evidence, so reminiscent of 17th-century Salem, was suggested by the remarks of friendly witness Adolphe Menjou, the "haberdasher's gentleman," as Lillian Hellman once dubbed him, and self-proclaimed "expert" on "Marxism, Fabian Socialism, Communism, Stalinism and its probable effects on the American people, if they ever gain power here." Menjou testified as to his belief that "under certain circumstances a Communistic director . . . writer or actor, even if he were under orders from the head of the studio not to inject Communism or un-Americanism or subversion into pictures could easily subvert that order, under the proper circumstances, by a look, by an inflection, by a change in the voice." And he thought it could be easily done, though "I have never seen it done, but I think it could be done." It turned out that Menjou's idea of un-Americanism was listening to and applauding Paul Robeson.

Perhaps a more realistic picture of the forces driving to rid the movies of its "trouble-makers" was the appearance as a friendly witness for HUAC of Jack L. Warner, boss of the studio that once prided itself on being able to "combine good citizenship with good entertainment," a noble idea that ended abruptly in Oct., 1945, near the end of the 33-week-long Hollywood studio strike that shook the citadels of film finance. In that strike Warner's goons, headed by one "Brass Knuckles" Blayney Matthews, a character straight out of a Riefenstahl film, used tire chains, tear gas and high pressure fire hoses against the picketlines of the company's striking employes, flinging men and women to the ground, beating, clubbing and injuring many.

"Publicly and privately," wrote Gordon Kahn in his 1948 volume, *Hollywood on Trial,* "J. L. Warner declared he was through making motion pictures about 'the little man.' It can be said that he has kept his word." Now, before HUAC, he was taking a stand against the "ideological termites . . . breeding subversive germs in dark corners," by which he meant the actors, writers and directors who had brought distinction to his company over a 15-year stretch with such films about "the little man" as *Gentlemen Are Born, Juarez, Destination Tokyo* and *Action in the North Atlantic.* In the "Time of the Toad," as Dalton Trumbo observed, there's a rush to deny all in one's tradition that's clean and to exalt all that is vile, and what could be viler than such heralds of "Toad" time endorsed by Warner as "loyalty oaths, the compulsory revelation of faith and the secret police." These and similar maladies of the spirit infected every aspect of our culture as the Cold War gathered steam, but the ferocity of HUAC's attacks on the movie industry surpassed anything the country had yet seen. Consider the state of the nation that brought the Hollywood witches' brew to the smoking point: The Hitler regime had been smashed by the Grand Alliance though the fuehrer's barbaric ideas continued to march on. The Holocaust was over, though Jews the world over vowed never to forget, never to forgive the planned extermination of a people. Roosevelt had died, but his successor in the White House was unable or unwilling to stop his foes from sabotaging the labor and social advances of the past 12 years. "Quietly," said a National Association of Manufacturers report July 7, 1945, "the new president [Truman] is removing the New Deal element from high authority and replacing it with men recognized as Democrats in the sense this word was used before 1932."

The age of the atom had opened and with it paranoic fear of Soviet intentions as well as fear of the growing power of organized labor here. Two years after V-day some 200 anti-labor bills were pending in Congress, with many states enacting legislation aimed at weakening the labor movement. Redbaiting of the CIO as "Moscow-controlled," and of liberals and radicals, organizations and persons, was unrelenting, particularly in the election campaigns of 1946–48, in which the Republicans captured most of the governorships and both houses of Congress. The mood of the country was reflected in public apathy to the rightist attacks on Chaplin and his film *Monsieur Verdoux* (1947), a masterly social satire and indictment of war that contributed to his being locked out of the U.S. after his film was locked out of the theatres.

The ultra-right, after a long spell underground during the war years, was on the prowl again with its vicious racism and had resumed shooting at one of its favorite targets: "Jewish Hollywood," the "Reds' chief base of operations," charges originally made in 1939 by Fritz Kuhn, fuehrer of the German American Bund, at the time Warner's *Confessions of a Nazi Spy* was released. Kuhn's public "demand" for the "thorough cleansing of the Hollywood film industry of all alien, subversive elements," was picked up by all sorts of pro-Nazi rags here and abroad. In the fall of 1940, one G. Allison Phelps, a Bund supporter, appeared with an anti-Semitic pamphlet, *An American's History of Hollywood—The Tower of Babel,* that reiterated the charge that aliens (meaning Jews, of course) and "Reds" had grabbed control of the movies and, to prove it, he appended a list of screen personalities with Jewish names: Izzie Itzkowitz (Eddie Cantor), David Daniel Kamirsky (Danny Kaye), Melvyn Hesselberg (Melvyn Douglas), etc.

Actually this was a Nazi German's, not an American's, history of Hollywood, since, as Michael Sayers and Albert E. Kahn noted in their 1942 volume, *Sabotage: The Secret War Against America,* "an almost identical list of names" had appeared Jan. 12, 1940, eight months earlier, in the official Nazi propaganda newsletter, *Welt Dienst (World Service)* under the title, "Judaized Hollywood." Suffice it to say that shortly thereafter this Nazi propaganda was reprinted in Silver Shirt mobster William Dudley Pelley's publication, *Liberation,* as "Who's Who in Hollywood—Find the Gentile," and in *Social Justice,* organ of Father Charles E. Coughlin's Christian Front stormtroopers, and other such journals.

After the war it fell to Christian Nationalist leader Gerald L. K. Smith to continue the work of Fritz Kuhn and Father Coughlin, and, beginning in 1945, he devoted issue after issue of his *The Cross and the Flag* to articles like "Rape of America by Hollywood," coupled with demands for a Congressional investigation of the industry. Eventually, this inflammatory material became the basis for HUAC's 1947

Hollywood indictments. Smith had the key to the front door of HUAC through Rep. John E. Rankin, the ranking Democrat on the Committee and the most obnoxious racist and anti-Semite ever to hold a seat in Congress. There can be no disputing Smith's claim that "We take credit, we Christian Nationalists, for the recent investigation into Hollywood" (*The Cross and the Flag,* Jan., 1948). It was his West Coast campaign that "turned the trick," he said, and it probably did. The fact is that Smith and his followers collected thousands of signatures on a petition—it was "over 150 ft. long" and "we carried it to Washington and delivered it to the house . . . and displayed it and unrolled it until it went up one aisle and down the other and around Mr. Rankin's shoulders and up another aisle." An inspiring picture that apparently did convince all but a tiny handful of honorable public servants like Vito Marcantonio and Emanuel Celler of New York that the time had come to give HUAC the power to rule or ruin the movies. Never before had the far right been able to achieve a victory such as this, carrying out the dream of the German American Bund to wreck "Judaized Hollywood."

It is interesting that before Pearl Harbor, all attempts of the ultras to get a probe of the industry going failed. In 1941 when America First Senators Robert Rice Reynolds, Gerald P. Nye and Bennett Champ Clark prodded the Senate to adopt Resolution No. 152 authorizing an investigation of Hollywood as a "center of war propaganda," the campaign blew up in their faces when the heads of the industry stood firm. Wendell Willkie, retained as spokesman for the studios, led the counter-attack that exposed the Senate Committee's attempt to censor anti-Nazi films like *The Great Dictator* and Warner's *Confessions of a Nazi Spy,* while saying nothing about the Nazi-made war films circulating in U.S. cities: UFA's *Sieg im Westen (Victory in the West)* for example. The investigation was dropped. In 1947, however, the aims of the Cold War required a different outcome. This time the probe succeeded far beyond the wildest hopes of its promoters.

The witch hunters, after almost taking the count, were able to squash the counter-attack, led by the Committee for the First Amendment set up by leading film personalities to defend the subpoenaed artists. But before going down to defeat the movie colony's democratic core made a magnifi-

cent, though brief, stand for freedom of the screen. Led by
such actors as Humphrey Bogart, Lauren Bacall, Danny
Kaye, Gene Kelly and Paul Henreid, a large Hollywood
contingent flew to Washington with one idea in mind—to stop
HUAC. In Rankin's hunting grounds they made two sensational radio broadcasts (directed by Norman Corwin) that
brought home to Americans the facts about HUAC's brutal
violations of human and constitutional rights.

While there they succeeded in persuading leading people
in the other arts and sciences to join them. Soon they saw
their small Hollywood Committee grow into a National
Committee of One Thousand, headed by such notables as
Albert Einstein, Dr. Harlow Shapley, Helen Keller, Van Wyck
Brooks, Archibald MacLeish and Rabbi Stephen S. Wise,
and supported by such prestigious institutions as the National Institute of Arts and Letters and the Authors League of
America, Inc., comprising the Authors, Dramatists, Radio
Writers and Screen Writers Guilds. But this promising
movement of the arts and sciences in defense of freedom of
expression, betrayed from within and without by cold warriors and informers, collapsed within a few months. Its
collapse was hastened by the fact that by 1947 the policies
and practices of HUAC and the U.S. government had
"become identical," as Albert Kahn was to note in his 1950
book, *High Treason.*

Whereas in Roosevelt's time there were occasions when
Justice Department officials would blast HUAC as "anti-
democratic" and "itself bordering on the subversive," after
his death, Attorney General Tom Clark was informing HUAC
members that "We, in the Department . . . are laboring in
neighboring vineyards . . . We have the same purpose in
view. The program of this Committee . . . can render real
service to the American people."

The Hollywood-inspired Committee for the First Amendment was unable to hold out against the combined pressures
of HUAC and the government, both involved in Cold War with
the Soviets, and especially against the pressure of the
industry's financial overlords who saw their profits going
down the drain as the ultra-right made good its threats to
boycott their theatres. It was now left to the "Hollywood Ten"

to carry on the fight against HUAC and McCarthyism, which they did courageously throughout the '50's.

The American movie is still suffering from the effects of that decade-long ban on "dangerous thoughts" that brought the film industry down to the lowest levels of its history. And though the witch hunt ended around the time of the Montgomery bus boycott that launched the great Black people's movement and inspired the student rebellions and the anti-war movement of the 1960s, the blacklisting of ideas, if not of persons, goes on.

Offensive screen portrayals of Blacks, Jews and other minorities have increased, it would seem, in inverse ratio to the growth of concern for one's ethnic identity and culture. With some exceptions the major studios, in this era of blockbuster escapism, shy away from grappling with the great issues that face us all. HUAC, of course, has been abolished and that is good, but the exposures of the Watergate conspiracy and particularly what was not exposed in depth reveal that the forces capable of creating HUACS, witch hunts and blacklists are alive and well and living comfortably in our midst. What is required is the involvement of all Americans with questions of social justice, peace and social progress that were the concern of the "Hollywood Ten."

EXCERPTS FROM STATEMENTS BY THE "HOLLYWOOD TEN" BEFORE THE UN-AMERICAN COMMITTEE IN WASHINGTON, OCTOBER 20, 1947

Alvah Bessie: "If this investigation is permitted to achieve its immediate objective it will not hesitate to move on from the motion-picture industry it has emasculated to the throttling of the press, the radio, the theater and the book publishers of America."

Herbert Biberman: "It is because I have been an active citizen that I am here. . . . I am here because I love, believe in, respect and have unlimited faith in my fellow citizens. I have been brought here because I believe they will constantly achieve a richer social and economic life under the Constitution, which will eliminate prejudice and inequality in spite of the efforts of this Committee to prevent it."

Lester Cole: "HUAC is out to accomplish one thing and one thing only, as far as the American motion picture industry is concerned . . . to sow fear of blacklists; to intimidate management, to destroy democratic guilds and unions by interference in their internal affairs, and through their destruction bring chaos and strife."

Edward Dmytryk: "The dark periods in our history have been those in which our freedoms have been suppressed, to however small a degree. Some of that darkness exists into the present day in the continued suppression of certain minorities. In my last few years in Hollywood, I have devoted myself, through pictures such as *Crossfire,* to a fight against these racial suppressions and prejudices. My work speaks for itself. I believe that it speaks clearly enough so that the people of the country and this Committee which has no right to inquire into my politics or my thinking, can still judge my thoughts and my beliefs by my work, and by my work alone." (Edward Dmytryk changed his views in 1951 while in prison, cooperated with HUAC by naming names, and was removed from the blacklist.)

Ring Lardner Jr.: "What I am most concerned about is the ultimate result that might come from a successful fulfillment of your purpose. . . . The really important effect would be that the producers themselves would lose control over their pictures and that the same shackling of education, labor, radio and newspapers would follow."

John Howard Lawson: "If I can be destroyed no American is safe. . . . Let no one think that this is an idle or thoughtless statement. This is the course that the Un-American Activities Committee has charted. Millions of Americans who may as yet be unconscious of what may be in store for them will find that the warning I speak today is literally fulfilled."

Albert Maltz: ". . . here is the other reason why I and others have been commanded to appear before the Committee—

our ideas. In common with many Americans, I supported the New Deal. In common with many Americans I supported, against Mr. Thomas and Mr. Rankin, the anti-lynching bill. . . . I signed petitions for these measures, joined organizations that advocate them, contributed money, sometimes spoke from public platforms, and I will continue to do so."

Samuel Ornitz: "I wish to address this Committee as a Jew, because one of its leading members is the outstanding anti-Semite in the Congress and revels in that fact. I refer to John E. Rankin. I refer to this evil because it has been responsible for the systematic and ruthless slaughter of six million of my people. . . . I am struck forcibly by the fact that this Committee has subpoenaed the three men who made *Crossfire,* a powerful attack on anti-Semitism."

Adrian Scott: "Many times in their films (the subpoenaed witnesses) have presented the Jew and the Negro (and other minorities as well) in unstereotyped terms. . . . These men oppose and actively work against Gerald L. K. Smith and the Ku Klux Klan."

Dalton Trumbo: "Already the gentlemen of this Committee . . . have produced in this capital city a political atmosphere which is acrid with fear and repression; a community in which anti-Semitism finds safe refuge behind secret tests of loyalty; a city in which no union leader can trust his telephone . . . a city in which men and women who dissent even slightly from the orthodoxy you seek to impose speak with confidence only in moving cars and in the open air."

THE FRONT

The Front (1977) is one of a number of recent films, TV dramas and books that have begun seriously to explore the blacklist mania, a particularly loathsome offshoot of the red scare decade of 1947–57. The blacklist served as a warning to everybody in the entertainment media that if they wanted to hold on to their jobs they had to keep their mouths shut and not become involved in social justice or peace causes. That ten Hollywood artists were condemned to prison terms and hundreds of others were driven out of the industry for defending their democratic right to hold unpopular political opinions tells much about the ferocity of the witchhunt and also that it was courageously opposed by many.

The Front, which was written, directed and acted by blacklisted artists, is a funny, angry and often deeply moving indictment of that infamous era that saw the rise and fall of J. Parnell Thomas, the chairman of the House Un-American Activities Committee (HUAC), who later was convicted and jailed for stealing government funds. Tricky Dick Nixon also got his start with HUAC and went on to become the first U.S. President to plead "I am not a crook," and just barely to escape going to prison for capital offenses against the American people. The road to Watergate was paved, one could say, with the broken careers and lives of premature enemies of Nixonism.

One of the more striking aspects of *The Front* is that Communists and sympathizers are portrayed as decent human beings who are victims of unjust persecution, rather than, as in the past, as "red menaces" with horns and bombs. It is also made clear that many of the victims are Jewish, but that some spineless Jews in key posts acquiesced in the orgy of recrimination and deceit. The blacklisting of large numbers of Jews had to do with their involvement as actors, producers, writers and directors in a very large proportion of the progressive social, anti-fascist and anti-racist films and plays of the 1930s, '40s and '50s, as well as with their active participation in similarly large numbers in the major struggles of those decades.

The incidents in *The Front* take place in 1953—the year Ethel and Julius Rosenberg were legally lynched. Zero Mostel brilliantly portrays Hecky Brown (Brownstein), a desperately troubled Jewish actor with a growing family and debts to match, who is blacklisted because his FBI file showed he is politically suspect. Hecky's crime is that years ago he marched in a May Day parade, signed a petition for loyalist Spain, contributed to Russian War Relief. On the latter, Hecky quietly reminds his accuser, "I thought we were on the same side."

The implication here is that Hecky's loyalty would never

have come into question and he would not have made the blacklist if the record showed he had burned a cross on a black man's lawn or had donated money to Father Charles E. Coughlin, the poison-tongued rabblerouser and anti-Semitic publisher of the pro-nazi weekly *Social Justice.* One simply does not persecute or punish aggressive racists or fascists.

Some of the film's most powerful moments are connected with the hounding and destruction of Hecky, as the black-listers attempt to get the actor to "clear" his record by informing on his fellow artists. "Tell me what to do, I'll do it," he exclaims. "I'll send a letter that I was duped." "Not enough," is the reply. "It must come from the heart," and the inquisitor adds, "it's an honor to be a spy for freedom," "Freedom Information Service" is the name of this vigilante outfit that promotes informing on one's fellowmen for private gain as an act of patriotism. F.I.S. is modelled after such blacklisting agencies as "Counterattack" and "Aware, Inc.," which ravaged and savaged the entertainment industry in the 1940's and '50's, and their files encompassed far more than Communists and Communist sympathizers. "Stars for Stevenson," supporters of Democratic presidential candidate Adlai Stevenson, were blacklisted after being fingered by "Counterattack."

In the end Hecky decides that death is preferable to dishonor. The FBI, characteristically, is shown taking pictures of everybody at the funeral, to add to its "enemies" list.

Woody Allen gives a vigorous new twist to his familiar role of a perennial "loser" by playing to perfection the part of Howard Prince, a meek bar-and-grill cashier and part-time bookie who, as a front for blacklisted writers, becomes the toast of the Madison Avenue cocktail set, as well as the subject of discussion at Americanism meetings. Eventually when he too becomes blacklisted for associating with suspicious characters who meet in a Jewish restaurant, and is brought before HUAC, he throws the hearing room into an uproar and achieves a moment or two of dignity by suddenly breaking off his dialogue with the committee and telling them in no uncertain four letter words what they could do to themselves.

Some of Allen's encounters with studio executives also have a sharp satirical edge, such as the scene in which he is persuaded to delete from a script on the Holocaust a reference to Jews going to their death in a gas chamber, because the sponsors, a gas company, objected that it would hurt their image. Surely, argues TV producer Phil Sussman (Herschel Bernardi), a firing squad could be substituted. "After all, the Nazis killed Jews that way too." Another comic vignette tells of a blacklisted actor with no political record insisting that he should be "cleared" because he has been confused with a man with a similar name, which happened to be true. On being told that the "clearance" agency can only help those who are prepared to make a clean breast of things, he pleads, "I haven't done anything so how can I confess." "Well, then," is the reply, "I'm sorry, we can't do anything for you."

The makers of *The Front* drew on their own personal experiences and that of others during the McCarthy era for the Woody Allen role. It is no secret that Walter Bernstein and two other blacklisted writers produced under pseudonyms most of the famous CBS series *You Are There,* which often dealt with such significant themes as book-burnings, witch-hunts, miscarriages of justice and frameups in other times. Such is the lunacy of blacklisting that even some of the pseudonyms were blacklisted when occasionally the real identities of the authors became known, but this of course did not prevent them from writing and producing CBS scripts under other *nom de plumes.* In Hollywood, it is well known that the blacklisted writing team of Michael Wilson and the late Dalton Trumbo achieved something of a record by turning out a complete script every five weeks over an 18 months stretch under fictitious names, and several of them won Academy Awards.

It is interesting that Frank Sinatra's singing voice is heard in the early part of the film in something called "When We Were Young At Heart." I take this to be an oblique comment on two actions by Sinatra in regard to McCarthyism and the blacklist. In 1947, at the beginning of the witch-hunt, which he opposed, he stated: "Once they get the movies throttled, how long will it be before the committee goes to work on freedom of the air . . . Are they gonna scare us into silence? I wonder." He accurately predicted the widespread fear that would grip the industry throughout the next decade, and eventually silence him too. In 1960, when Sinatra sought to break the blacklist by hiring Albert Maltz to write the screenplay for *The Execution of Private Slovik,* he was unable to withstand the enormous pressure brought to bear against him by the Hearst press, the American Legion and others and was forced to fire the blacklisted writer.

If *The Front* could be criticized for anything, it should be for the weak newsreel prologue that is supposed to indicate something of the social and political atmosphere in the country that contributed to the ugliness. It doesn't really. There are, to be sure, shots of the Korean war, the Rosenbergs, air-raid shelters, shots of MacArthur, Truman, the Eisenhowers, DiMaggio and Marilyn Monroe and not much else and no really incisive comment on the little that is shown. I am aware that no one film could possibly tell the whole story of that dreadful period, but certainly the introduction to a film as significant as this should, perhaps, have made it clear that the red scare was a smoke-screen, that the witchhunt was really aimed against the CIO and the New Deal's "20 years of treason," that this was a time of loyalty boards, loyalty oaths, Smith, McCarran and Taft-Hartley indictments. West German rearmament was in the air, Nazi nuclear scientists were being let into the U.S. under strict orders of secrecy, and last, but far from least, re-emerging from under the overturned rocks were the crawling things that, until Pearl Harbor, as former Special Assistant to the U.S. Attorney General, O. John Rogge said, "damned democracy . . . applauded every Axis triumph, echoed every Nazi propaganda tune" and now were back again, more powerful than ever, spreading mindless anti-communism, racism and anti-Semitism, and receiving boundless support in high places. In short, the major peril was the threat of fascism, not communism, as Rogge said shortly after he was fired from the Justice Department for revealing the Nazi connections of a large number of powerful U.S. industrialists and congressmen, among others. (In *Fact,* Feb. 3 and 10, 1947.)

These were some of the factors that brought about McCarthyism and blacklisting and they are being wilfully covered up in the redbaiting attacks on *The Front* by such as Hilton Kramer of the *New York Times.*

Kramer insists he will not listen to anyone condemning the blacklist unless he first condemns Stalin. In other words, as Hofstra Law Prof. Leon Friedman points out, "one must take a loyalty oath of anti-communism before criticizing injustice in the U.S." (Letter, *New York Times,* Nov. 7, 1976.) Isn't what Kramer is saying precisely what McCarthyism was all about? The issue then, as now, was the constitutional right to one's private beliefs, even beliefs so dogmatic and so blind that it took some of us years to realize the full extent of the Stalinist horror.

The message of *The Front* is that people were pilloried not for what they did but for what they thought and believed, and it is a miracle that Walter Bernstein and Martin Ritt were able to persuade Columbia Pictures to make the film. Several other studios turned it down.

In a 1975 interview Mostel recalled that when he testified before HUAC in 1955 he "held up his right hand wiggling five fingers" to indicate that he was taking the Fifth. Also, in answering the committee's question, "What studio were you employed at?" he shot back, "18th Century Fox." "Do you want that remark to stand?" the chairman sternly asked him. "No, change it to '19th Century Fox.' " (New York Times, *Dec. 7, 1975).*

LILLIAN HELLMAN'S SCATHING MEMOIR

Scoundrel Time, by Lillian Hellman. Introduction by Garry Wills. Little, Brown, Boston, 1976, 155 pages, $7.95.

Lillian Hellman took the Fifth Amendment in her appearance as an unfriendly witness before the House Un-American Activities Committee (HUAC) May 21, 1952, following their rejection of her letter (reprinted in this scintillating memoir of the scoundrels, "toads" and informers of those times) that she would agree to answer questions about herself but not about others.

In words that still retain their crisp eloquence, she stated: "I am not willing, now or in the future, to bring bad trouble to people who, in my past association with them, were completely innocent of any talk or any action that was disloyal or subversive. I do not like subversion or disloyalty in any form and if I had ever seen any I would have considered it my duty to have reported it to the proper authorities. But to hurt innocent people whom I knew many years ago in order to save myself, is, to me, inhuman and indecent and dishonorable. I cannot and will not cut my conscience to fit this year's fashions."

Ms. Hellman escaped the jail sentence for contempt that she had expected and feared but she suffered other consequences of her courageous stand. And though her book fails to give credit to any of the hundreds of unfriendly witnesses who preceded her, such as Paul Robeson and the Hollywood Ten, it is obvious that what they had done eased her path. It is a measure of Ms. Hellman's integrity and decency that she turned down her lawyer Joseph Rauh's proposal that it would be useful, as a way of showing the "independence of her past," to point out to HUAC and to the press that the "CP, sometimes through the *Daily Worker,* sometimes in other publications," had attacked her, and she cited "the nonsense about *Watch on the Rhine.* The play, opening before the Soviet Union was invaded . . . was reviewed as warmongering. The movie, opening after the . . . war . . . was wonderful." Ms. Hellman objected to Rauh's idea on grounds that she could be charged with "playing the enemy's game" at a time when Communist Party leaders were under fire.

To set the record straight, the Hellman play was, despite some criticism, warmly applauded in the *Daily Worker* April 4, 1941 as a "poignant drama of anti-fascist struggle" and a "first-rate theatre piece." Looking back on it, I find this appraisal interesting in view of the party's position, during the period of the Soviet-German Pact and up to the Nazi invasion of the USSR June 22, 1941, that the war was imperialist on both sides. The review in *New Masses* April 15, 1941, however, as the book says, ripped the play as pro-war. Some years later Albert Maltz stirred up a hornet's nest when, in a controversial article in *New Masses* Feb. 12, 1946, he sought to use this mischievous review, among other things, to hit the vulgar notion that a work of art could be created out of the changing slogans of some official committee. But Mr. Wills's account of this episode in his introductory essay is inaccurate and nasty.

Ms. Hellman's *Watch on the Rhine* survives as one of the glories of the American theatre. Its author went on to write other significant plays, but her film career was cut short in 1947—nearly five years *before* her HUAC appearance. Her being blacklisted stemmed from her opposition, along with hundreds of other writers and artists, to the *first* witchhunt by HUAC in Oct., 1947 against the film industry, and from her refusal to sign a Hollywood loyalty oath. In those earlier times, as the book notes, the idea that Hollywood films contained "Communist propaganda" was ridiculed in the press and on the air. Typical of the idiocies of the time was HUAC's example of "Communism" as a performance of *Othello* at liberal Antioch College with a Black woman portraying Desdemona, and right-wing novelist Ayn Rand's assertion that MGM's wartime anti-Nazi film, *Song of Russia,* was propaganda for communism because it showed "smiling" Russians, "a stock (Kremlin) propaganda trick."

But what about the Communist trick of showing "sullen" workers? Mrs. Lela Rogers, mother of Ginger, insisted before HUAC that the Clifford Odets film, *None But the Lonely Heart,* about the Welsh miners, was "communistic." The story, she quoted a review as saying, "pitched in a low key, is moody and somber in the Russian manner." There's no record that Odets agreed with this estimate of his film when he testified as a friendly witness before HUAC May 20, 1952, the day before Ms. Hellman appeared.

In her book, she tells of having had dinner with Odets a few weeks before, in the course of which suddenly, he "pounded on the table so hard that his wineglass spilled and he yelled, 'Well, I can tell you what I am going to do before those bastards on the Committee. I am going to show them the face of a radical man.' " One can only surmise that in the interim he found he could not face the ruin of his film career, and Ms. Hellman adds: ". . . the loss of a swimming pool, a tennis court . . . future deprivation, were powerful threats to many people, and the heads of studios knew it and played heavy with it."

Ms. Hellman's vivid recollection of her own ordeal provides a refreshing contrast with those who abased themselves. She tells of getting an offer from Columbia Pictures of a million-dollar "dream" contract to write and produce four films, any story she liked, with full control over the material, "unheard of in those days and even now . . . seldom granted." The only hitch was that she would have had to sign a paper swearing to stear clear of a certain kind of politics. This came to be known as the "American Legion" oath and was supinely agreed to by the top executives and producers, concerned over the possible decline of their properties under the combined assaults of HUAC, the bankers and their lawyers, the Legionaires and others. Ms. Hellman's refusal to bow to this demand marked her as a trouble-maker and ended her Hollywood career. Eventually her name emerged as one of the 162 persons named as "Communists" by Martin Berkeley, a screenwriter turned informer. Berkeley's list contained the names of Communists, of course, but included were many more non-communists, people who had at one time or another also been touched by democratic and anti-fascist causes. Ms. Hellman writes that her own political education began in the early 1930s with her discovery of what Hitler was up to when she visited Bonn, "intending to enroll at the university," and it was then "for the first time in my life I thought about being a Jew." What frightened her was not only anti-Semitism but the "boasts of hopeful conquerors, the sounds of war" from people her own age.

After the war, HUAC became interested in her mainly because of her intimate relationship with Dashiell Hammett, who had served a term in prison for refusing to divulge the names of contributors to the Civil Rights Congress Bail Fund. They also had their eye on her because of her sponsorship of the Cultural and Scientific Conference for World Peace held at the New York Waldorf Astoria early in 1949. In preparation for that much maligned event, she had gone to the USSR at the request of the State Department and, as we learn from Mr. Wills, "she helped arrange for artists and scholars to meet and discuss what would later (when a new line came in) be called detente."

Scoundrel Time reminds us that it was in this setting that Dimitri Shostakovich and other Soviet artists were "in the name of freedom" harrassed and insulted for not being free. Leading the attackers were none other than the same "anti-Communist" intellectuals that, 30 years later, are still trying to heat up the Cold War by opposing detente. Ms.

Hellman reserves her real scorn for the "hollow men" of *Commentary* and *Partisan Review* who, through the years, hypocritically protested the repression of dissidents in the socialist lands but were silent when McCarthy, Nixon and company were flailing and ruining the lives of "Communists, near-Communists and nowhere near-Communists." Some of these literary cold warriors later openly joined with rightists in CIA-funded anti-Communist organizations, and Ms. Hellman does not for one moment let them forget that their "capers" led straight to Vietnam, Nixon and Watergate. Such people, she writes, "would have a right to say that I, and many like me, took too long to see what was going on in the Soviet Union. But whatever our mistakes, I do not believe we did our country any harm. And I think they did. They went to too many respectable conferences that turned out not to be under respectable auspices, contributed to and published too many CIA magazines. . . . None of them, as far as I know, has yet found it a part of conscience to admit that their Cold War anti-Communism was perverted, possibly against their wishes, into the Vietnam War and then into the reign of Nixon, their unwanted but inevitable leader."

If the pillars of the CIA-tainted "Cultural Freedom Committee"—McCarthy's and Nixon's helpers—are busy sniping at Lillian Hellman's book the reasons are obvious.

The Editor's reviews of *The Front* and *Scoundrel Time* are reprinted by permission from the February and May 1977 issues of *Jewish Currents*.

50 ELIA KAZAN AND *VIVA ZAPATA!*

John Howard Lawson

THE APPEARANCE OF *Viva Zapata!* early in 1952 has caused the usual controversy, and more than the usual confusion, concerning Hollywood's ability to deal honestly with important social themes. In this case, there can be no question that the theme is significant. The film portrays the revolutionary movement of the peasants of Mexico led by Emiliano Zapata in the second decade of the 20th century. Zapata is one of the great figures in the history of Mexico, and of the Americas. The most farsighted and consistent leader of the Mexican revolution, he created a tradition that is still a vital force in the culture and political life of the Western Hemisphere.

The picture has been hailed as an honest and sympathetic portrait of Zapata, and as a powerful presentation of the peasant struggle for land and liberty. Some progressives, while noting that the film has weaknesses, have greeted it as a generally positive achievement; a contribution to our understanding of the spirit and strength of a people's movement.

If the applause is merited, *Viva Zapata!* is an astonishing phenomenon disproving what we have said about Hollywood and showing that we have done the motion picture industry a grave injustice. The agrarian revolt led by Zapata was essentially anti-imperialist, and the events have far-reaching present-day implications. If the struggle is presented with

---

From *Masses & Mainstream* (August 1952). Reprinted by permission of the author.

sympathy and respect, it means that the film monopolists have defied the official foreign policy of the United States government. While the rulers of our country burn Korean villages, aid the suppression of peasant movements in Indo-China and Malaya, support anti-democratic regimes in all parts of the world and increase the heavy burdens imposed on the people of Latin America by Yankee imperialism, Hollywood asserts the peasants' right to land and liberty and honors the struggle of oppressed peoples!

Critical appraisal of *Viva Zapata!* must be based upon the film itself, the cinematic images and sound-track which project its structure and meaning as a work of art. But in examining the picture, it is essential to consider a number of pertinent facts which have a bearing on the finished work—the circumstances of its production, the plans and purposes of its makers, its place in the social and political pattern of Hollywood production.

Viva Zapata! was written by John Steinbeck, directed by Elia Kazan, produced by Darryl Zanuck for Twentieth Century-Fox. I have not seen any statements by Steinbeck or Zanuck concerning the film, but the director has stated his views with unusual frankness, in two letters to the *Saturday Review* and in testimony before the House Committee on Un-American Activities. The first of Kazan's communications appeared in the *Saturday Review* of April 5, 1952. Five days later, he appeared as an informer before the House Committee. (Hollywood methods of production place major responsibility on the director. It therefore seems proper to place major emphasis on Kazan's viewpoint toward the picture, and his explanation of his own work. Kazan's statements make frequent mention of Steinbeck and indicate that the writer and the director were in complete agreement. Both, of course, were accountable to Zanuck, who acted as the direct representative of the corporation.)

We are accustomed by this time to the dreary spectacle of frightened men and women, who lie and supplicate and repent, denying all that is decent and progressive in their professional and personal lives in order to secure absolution from the ignorant politicians who have become the arbiters of culture in the United States. But Kazan seemed determined to outdo other informers, both in treachery to his friends and in personal abasement.

In addition to supplying the committee with names, Kazan offered an affidavit in which he provided "a list of my entire professional career as a director, all the plays I have done and the films I have made." (Decent citizens have warned that it is the committee's purpose to establish total control of the artist's life and professional activity. In an earlier chapter, I have cited the statement of the Council of the Authors League of America in 1947, denouncing the committee's attempt to censor "the whole corpus of a man's work, past and future.")

Kazan gave the inquisitors the whole corpus of his work, twenty-five plays and films, each accompanied by a craven note of apology—"No politics" . . . "not political" . . . "shows the exact opposite of the Communist libels on America" . . . "again, it is opposite to the picture which Communists present of Americans" . . . "not political" . . . "almost everybody liked this except the Communists," etc., *ad nauseam.*

Kazan's conduct is of some interest as a case-history of moral degradation. But we are less concerned with his personal infamy than with the cultural and social pattern of which it is a part. *Viva Zapata!* cannot be divorced from Kazan's testimony before the Un-Americans. The director emphasizes the connection. His affidavit says: "This is an anti-Communist picture. Please see my article on political aspects of this picture in the *Saturday Review* of April 5, which I forwarded to your investigator, Mr. Nixon." (Official transcript of Hearings, April 10, 1952.) (Not only does the artist submit his work to the Congressional Gestapo; his comments on the work are slanted for their approval, and submitted with due reverence.)

Let us examine Kazan's evidence, laid before the enemies of democracy as proof that *Viva Zapata!* has no democratic taint.

Kazan begins his letter to the *Saturday Review* with a comment on "the political tensions that bore down on us—John Steinbeck and Darryl Zanuck and me—as we thought about and shaped a historical picture." The tensions, according to Kazan, related to one point in Zapata's career:

What fascinated us about Zapata was one nakedly dramatic act. In the moment of victory, he turned his back on power. In that moment, in the capital with his ragged troops, Zapata could have made himself president, dictator, caudillo. Instead, abruptly, and without explanation, he rode back to his village. . . . We felt this act of renunciation was the high point in our story and the key to Zapata himself.

In the first place, we must ask whether this situation is historically accurate? In the second place, why was the incident selected as the crux of Zapata's story?

The act of renunciation which fascinated Kazan and Steinbeck, not to mention Zanuck, is an irresponsible fabrication. There is no mystery, and no hint of renunciation, in Zapata's departure from the capital. He could not hold power because the forces arrayed against him were too strong. Among these forces was the military might of the United States, which threatened Zapata with full-scale armed intervention.

Carleton Beals writes that the Kazan-Steinbeck theory of Zapata's renunciation of power is an "absurd concept . . . Zapata committed no such gross betrayal of his followers . . . . He was in a trap with powerful armies closing in on him. . . . Zapata was outnumbered ten to one and when he rode out of the National Palace that last time, rifle fire and artillery were already shaking Mexico City" (*Saturday Review*, May 24, 1952).

In answer to Beals, Kazan says that the research conducted for the picture "was extensive," but "I never did hear the version Mr. Beals tells." (Kazan's answer appears in the same issue of the *Saturday Review*, May 24, 1952.) This is an alarming commentary on techniques of film research. Kazan could not have picked up any reputable history of the period without finding that Zapata's position in Mexico City was threatened by Carranza's army to the east, Gonzales' troops to the south; the far more modern and well-equipped army of Obregon, backed by the White House, stood at Puebla within striking distance of the capital.

Kazan and Steinbeck, and their modest co-worker, Zanuck, were blind to historical facts because the facts did not fit their political purpose. The essence of Zapata's life is summarized by Frank Tannenbaum, a bourgeois scholar whose books on the Mexican Revolution must be known to Kazan: "From the day he rose in rebellion to the day he was killed, he never surrendered, never was defeated, never stopped fighting." (*Peace by Revolution,* New York, 1933.) It is the real Zapata, the unconquerable hero of the revolution, whose grave in southern Mexico is a sacred shrine to the people of his country.

The makers of *Viva Zapata!* wanted a hero who surrenders. "In a moment of decision," according to Kazan, "this taciturn, untaught leader, must have felt, freshly and deeply, the impact of the ancient law: power corrupts. And he refused power."

Underlying this phony philosophy, which Carleton Beals describes as "eye-wash," lies the hard core of the film's political meaning. Every struggle for human rights involves the question of power. If power is an absolute source of corruption, if it must be renounced by every honest leader, the people are doomed to eternal submission. The "ancient law," presented as the central theme of *Viva Zapata!*, denies any possibility of the rational use of power for democratic and socially constructive ends.

At a time when colonial peoples are throwing off the yoke of poverty and oppression, it is not possible to deny that these great popular movements exist. It is possible, however, to deal sympathetically with the "futility" of revolt, to lament the "inevitable betrayal" of the revolution by those leaders who demand fundamental changes in the system of exploitation. This service to imperialism occupies the lives of whole regiments of scholars in the fields of sociology, political economy and history.

Hollywood selects a moment of Mexican history for its lesson in the futility of people's movements. The choice is not accidental. Careful, and conscious, political analysis determined the selection of the time and the place. The period is sufficiently distant to avoid any direct allusion to contemporary events. The plight of the farm workers of Morelos is similar, in many respects, to the plight of colonial populations. We cannot miss the historical parallel, but the role of the United States imperialism is not so obvious in the

Mexican conflict as in more recent events is Asia and other parts of the world.

It is a gross distortion of history to ignore the fact that the peasant movement led by Zapata was part of a national uprising which was chiefly directed against the imperial power of the United States. But the film presents Mexico as a land of corrupt generals and politicians, acknowledging no obligation to any foreign power. The demand for land on the part of the poverty-stricken Indians and Mestizos of Morelos is treated as a separate and isolated struggle, humanly justified, but doomed from the start because the peasants are too ignorant or innocent to seize and hold state power.

White chauvinism, contempt for the darker peoples of the world, is inherent in this conception. The directorial treatment, the lighting, setting, costumes and movement of the actors, are all designed to reinforce the impression that the people of Morelos are "picturesque," artistically attractive, but totally incapable of effective organized action. Zapata's brother is shown as a drunken lout. The characterization of Zapata deprives him of the intellectual stature he unquestionably possessed. The author of the Plan of Ayala, the program of land reform and national unity which is one of the great documents of the history of the Americas, is played by Marlon Brando as a man who is not only culturally, but politically, illiterate. The actor employs the crude tricks and mannerisms which he used a few months earlier to depict the brutally inhuman "worker" in *A Streetcar Named Desire*.

Answering Beals' criticism, Kazan exposes his chauvinistic contempt for the Mexican peasants and for Zapata as their representative. He quotes a letter from a lady, in which the lady asserts that the real reason for Zapata's retreat from the capital "was the typewriters":

> He conquered the city, vanquished rivals, contenders, occupied government offices, and there faced modern equipment for the manipulation of law and order. He did not know how to go on. The rows and rows of typewriters decided his retreat.

Kazan observes: "Still another version! And just human enough to have truth in it." To be sure, Kazan does not blame Zapata for his "fear of typewriters." He loves him for it. The "simple" peasant is a saint, if only he will bow to the "ancient law" that power corrupts—conveniently leaving power in the hands of those who exploit and starve the peasants. Like all authoritarian concepts, this theory of power is mystical and irrational. Kazan shares, or pretends to share, his protagonist's mystical belief that power can never be used rationally or democratically. The anti-intellectualism of the film is embodied in the symbolic figure of the man who "'loves only logic," "the man with the typewriter," an incongruous individual who wanders through the story like a lost soul, having nothing to do with the action.

He serves solely as an example of a "real revolutionist." He is close to Zapata in the peasant's rise to power, but turns against him after his "renunciation." If my eyes did not deceive me, he appears in later scenes in a sort of "commissar's" uniform. He displays his affection for logic by urging everyone who will listen to him to burn and destroy. We are fortunate in having the director's explanation of this character's function:

> There is such a thing as a Communist mentality. We created a figure of this complexion in Fernando, whom the audience identify as 'the man with the typewriter.' He typifies the men who use the just grievances of the people for their own ends, who shift and twist their course, betray any friend or principle or promise to get power and keep it.

It may be argued that Kazan is merely introducing a "harmless" touch of anti-Communism, seeking to clear himself by muttering the penitential words which he also used in his appearance before the Un-American Committee. But in the film, as in the proceedings of the committee, the idiocies of Red-baiting provide ideological excuses for the betrayal of democracy. Fernando is an utterly ridiculous figure in *Viva Zapata!* Carleton Beals asks: "Why introduce this absurd stereotype utterly devoid of Mexican savor? . . . The phony papier-mâché Fernando seems unwarranted even by box-office considerations."

It is true that there is no artistic or dramatic reason for Fernando's presence; the lack of invention or skill in the use of the character is appalling. But the *political* reason for his presence is inescapable; political necessity made it impossible for the author and director to dispense with the character, but the same necessity made it impossible for the character to speak rationally or to play any understandable part in the action. Fernando is just as witless as the anti-Communist he personifies.

Fernando's function is directly related to Zapata's "renunciation." There must be a conflict—or a least the shadow of a conflict—between the hero's abandonment of power and another course of action. The alternative cannot be a real struggle for the land, because the film's social philosophy holds that the struggle is self-defeating and destructive. Yet it is not sufficient to counterpoise the aspirations of the peasants to the corruption of politics-as-usual, because this makes a fool out of Zapata and exposes the moral rottenness of his "renunciation." His choice must be between the existing corruption and something worse, which will eventuate if he continues to lead the people. Something worse is socialism or communism, or any genuine change in class relationships and control of the state.

This, of course, is the purpose of all anti-Communist propaganda. Kazan would appear to be an absolute fool in renouncing his liberal past before the Un-American Committee, if he could not claim that he is avoiding *something worse* by yielding to the badgering of the corrupt politicians. The stale clichés of Red-baiting were used long before the Soviet Union was born, long before the great pioneering work of Marx and Engels, to discredit any struggle for the rights of the oppressed and disinherited.

The lies of anti-Communism are anti-democratic in the most fundamental sense. Their whole purpose is to deny the people's right to organize and act, or to take any action for the common good. Red-baiting is the most direct expression of the class-interest of the class in power. It calls for absolute control over the thinking, and over the trade unions and organizations, of the people, on the ground that the people are incapable of judgment or discretion, and that only the class in power can be trusted to use its authority with some degree of moderation.

In *Viva Zapata!* anti-Communism is offered as the excuse for re-writing the recent history of Mexico. According to

Kazan, "No Communist, no totalitarian, ever refused power. . . . By showing that Zapata did this, we spoiled a poster figure that the Communists have been at some pains to create." It is of no concern to Kazan that the "poster figure" he discards is known and loved by the people of the land.

He tells us, with the arrogance of the imperialist, that he and Steinbeck were warned in advance that the Mexican people would regard their film as a violation of their history and traditions. The director and writer gave a preliminary script to "two men who are prominent in the Mexican film industry. . . . They came back with an attack that left us reeling. The script was impossible!" The Mexican film workers found it inaccurate in many respects, "But above all, they attacked with sarcastic fury our emphasis on his refusal to take power."

Kazan and Steinbeck "smelled the Party line." Their suspicion, Kazan informs us, was confirmed two years later "by a rabid attack on the picture in the *Daily Worker.*"

We need not comment on Kazan's reasoning that the similarity of opinion between two men in the Mexican film industry and a review in the *Daily Worker* reveals "the Party line." We are accustomed to hearing the same fantasies from the McCarthyites and from stoolpigeon witnesses in the McCarran hearings and Smith Act trials.

Some of the more astute reviewers of the commercial press have noted that *Viva Zapata!* is a defense of the status quo. Otis L. Guernsey, Jr., writes in the *New York Herald Tribune* (February 17, 1952) that the social problem is handled "as though Zapata's chief contribution to Mexican freedom had been a negative one." According to Guernsey, it is only after Zapata takes "to the hills in disgust at the corrupting influence of power" that he "comprehends the real issue with which his society is faced. . . . Peace and stability, Zapata finds, cannot be won by replacing a bad leader with a good one (even himself); it can be won only when each individual is able to take his own responsibility, when there is no longer a need for any leader at all."

Admirers of the film have said that it ends affirmatively, stressing the people's love of Zapata and their feeling that the cause he represented is unconquerable. But the film hero is the man who denies struggle and forswears power.

The *Herald Tribune* critic notes the real point of the conclusion: "The obvious goal—land reform—is as far off as it ever was." Furthermore, Guernsey sees that the characterization of Zapata is designed to reinforce the political lesson:

> The over-lapping values of bloody banditry and historical meaning are carried out in Brando's portrayal of the brooding Zapata. He is the slow fuse attached to the heavy powder-charge, a grim-looking, mustachioed fellow with dirt on his skin and simple conceptions of justice and violence in his mind. Like most Brando performances, Zapata is heavily underlined with animal traits. . . .

The cinema Zapata is a saintly animal, always torn between the brutal impulses of his class and his desire to avoid conflict. He dreams of peace, "a time of rest and kindness." But he is quick to renounce the hope, asking: "Can good come from a bad act? From so much violence?"

It is significant that Zapata's final parting from his wife, when he rides into the trap that brings his death, is a scene of stupid physical violence. She clings to his horse, and he throws her off so roughly that she almost falls under the animal's feet. It is a fitting climax to a relationship totally lacking in dignity or depth of feeling.

The scene has a vital place in the thematic development. Zapata has not wholly renounced power. He is still seeking guns and allies to continue the fight. Therefore, it is necessary to show him in a violent mood, rejecting his wife's love, exhibiting the brutal side of his nature. His spectacular death fulfills the theme of renunciation. He must die because he is unable to hold to the "good life" which the makers of the film prescribe for the repentant leader.

Kazan speaks of the people of Morelos as "the proudest and most independent in all Mexico. Their bearing is proof of the kind of man who led them out of bondage and did not betray them. I think it is also witness to the relationship of two things not usually coupled: politics and human dignity."

In a sense, this is the most revealing passage in the director's *apologia*. Ignoring the present poverty of the Morelos peasants, Kazan speaks of their having been "led out of bondage." Zapata did not betray them, as he apparently would have done if he had led them to victory against

their oppressors. As long as they accept hunger and renounce struggle, Kazan is pleased to grant them their
dignity. This is the significance of the relationship between
politics and human dignity as the director sees it: the
peasant's pride is personal, inward, unrelated to political and
economic reality—except in the fundamental fact, the "ancient law," that he can retain dignity only by eschewing
politics.

Kazan elucidates his meaning more fully in his testimony
before the Un-American Committee. He performs an act of
renunciation, subtly connected with the meretricious "renunciation" which he imposes on the celluloid Zapata. Kazan
renounces political struggle, denies even the right to conduct
struggle or hold opinions. Just as his false Zapata abandons
land-reform to avoid any suspicion of Communism, Kazan
discards all pretense of personal or artistic independence in
order to retain whatever shreds of "dignity" the Committee
will grant him.

Kazan's testimony has its moments of cruel comedy. The
contradiction in the cultural informer's position—his pretense
of speaking for freedom while he grovels before the inquisitors—is so intense that the witnesses seem slightly de-
mented, as frantic to abandon sense and reason as if the
wrack and the wheel awaited them in the ante-room. Kazan's
affidavit dismisses the political activity of his adult years with
these words: "My connections with these front organizations
were so slight and so transitory that I am forced to rely on a
listing of these prepared for me after research by my
employer, Twentieth Century-Fox."

Kazan attains epic irony in describing his reasons for
quitting the Communist Party in 1936. Going back over
nearly twenty years to crawl and apologize and admit errors
to the committee, Kazan explains his withdrawal from the
party: "The last straw came when I was invited to go through
a typical Communist scene of crawling and apologizing and
admitting the error of my ways."

Statements of this sort are required by the committee. One
may assume that the Congressmen, the witness, and
everybody present know that the statement is false. If Kazan
had gone through any such experience in 1936, his views
and activities during the following years would have been

affected by it; he would have spoken against Communism; he would have questioned the desirability of unified action of Communists, progressives and liberals. His artistic career would have followed a different course, both in the Group Theatre and in his later career as a director.

The Un-American Committee is not interested in the reliability, or even in the common sense, of the testimony offered by its victims. It has its political purpose, determined by the general strategy of the fascist drive. Gilbert W. Gabriel points out that Kazan "came pretty close to giving the impression that a connection with the late Group Theatre had been next door to inevitable partnership in a Communist cultural plot." Gabriel is kind enough to say that this seemed contrary to the witness' intentions. But Kazan's intentions were obviously dictated by the committee, and the impression given about the Group Theatre was the heart of his testimony: it reflected the committee's main objective in turning its spotlight on the theatre.

Fifteen years ago, the Group was a lively organization of young artists reflecting to some degree the hopeful temper, social sensitivity and democratic conscience of the militant Thirties. Kazan's attack on the Group is designed to undermine the elements of courage and integrity which the stage retains as a heritage of the days of the Group and the Theatre Union and the Federal Theatre.

Gabriel emphasizes the disastrous effect of Kazan's testimony on the nations's drama: "It may all be supposed to save our country, but it's sure hell on the theatre." Commenting on the testimony of Odets and other witnesses who followed Kazan and shared his ignominy, Gabriel observes that Lillian Hellman, "alone, of this fresh batch of theatrical witnesses, has done the theatre no disservice and lost none of its respect" (*The Nation*, June 28, 1952).

The disservice is not only to theatrical art, and to the witness' fellow-craftsmen. The creative vitality that enriched the drama in the Roosevelt years was part of a great current of social change. It was a decade of the growing unity of popular forces, the gradual emergence of a democratic coalition in which Communists played an honorable part. One of the main objectives of the fascist drive in the United States is the destruction of this recent heritage, which cannot be accomplished without going back into our national past to destroy or distort its historical roots in earlier struggles and traditions.

The contempt for the Bill of Rights which Kazan exhibited before the Un-American Committee is one with the mockery of the aspirations of the Mexican people in *Viva Zapata!*

Screenwriter Lester Cole of the Hollywood Ten once revealed that in 1947, before Kazan and Steinbeck made their film, he had been assigned, as an employee of MGM, to adapt a book they had owned for many years on the life of Zapata. According to Stephanie Allen's interview with him in World Magazine, *June 7, 1975, Cole researched the script in Mexico, and the Mexican government was so pleased with the detailed treatment submitted by Cole, together with the producer's suggestion that two of Mexico's leading filmmakers, Gabriel Figueroa and Indio Fernandez, should play major roles in the production, that they volunteered $1.5 million in services if it were filmed in Mexico. (The picture's budget was $3 million.) At the same time, said Cole, the script was read by Eddie Mannix of MGM, an ex-security cop at Palisades Amusement Park in New Jersey. "He screamed when he read it, calling it out-and-out Communist propaganda that would be made at MGM over his dead body." But that was before word came from Mexico of the million and a half dollar offer. "It was astonishing," said Cole, how this changed Mannix's point of view. It suddenly occurred to him, as he put it, that "Jesus Christ was a Communist and there was a hell of a profit in this."*

Everything was ready to roll when the House Un-American Activities Committee's subpoena for Cole arrived. "It was one thing to do a story about Zapata by a nondescript screen writer, but one so charged with being a Communist made it look like a revolutionary plot," and that scared MGM. So the script was quickly sold to Twentieth Century-Fox, along with the $1.5 million Mexican offer. "When Kazan and Steinbeck finished the alterations of the script and sent it to Mexico for their approval, there was such outrage that the Mexican government told them not *only would they not give any money for this production, but they would not permit them to shoot it in Mexico.'' The film, finally, was shot in Arizona. Later, when it was shown in Mexico, audiences threw tomatoes and rocks at the screen, forcing it to be withdrawn there, Cole told Ms. Allen.*

Lester Cole passed away August 15, 1985. But he left behind an enviable record of service in many just causes, and his autobiography, Hollywood Red, *which we highly recommend. (DP)*

51   *OLIVER TWIST* AND ANTI-SEMITISM

Morris U. Schappes

A S I WALKED OUT of an afternoon performance of *Oliver Twist* at the Park Avenue Theater in New York, with a sizable part of the audience consisting of school children, I felt sickened and revolted by the almost grotesque anti-Semitism. Yet others defended the film.

There was the gentle 22-year-old lad, now nine years in our country, whose own father had been murdered by the Nazis, and who argued with me on a street corner that *Oliver Twist* was a classic that could do no harm, and that Fagin was presented as simply an isolated, individual, bad Jew, and what was the danger in that? In fact, the pickets outside the theater, he said, were doing more harm to the Jews than Fagin. . . . Then there was the university student in a large city in upstate New York who sought me out to protest that Nathaniel Buchwald's review (*Jewish Life,* September) was just hysterical: the United States was not Germany and Fagin had not been identified in the film with any Jewish religious or ceremonial objects, so the effect could not be anti-Semitic. . . .

If such persons see Fagin but are blind to the menace of the film, one reason is that they seem to be unaware of the climate of increasing anti-Semitism in which we are living. Let us just rehearse some *representative* facts taken only from the period when *Oliver Twist* began to be shown in this country.

From *Jewish Life* (November, 1951). © 1951 by *Jewish Currents.* Reprinted by permission of the author.

June 14, in Houston, Texas, General MacArthur raised the anti-Semitic slogan, "the Cross and the Flag." July 14, Walter Winchell's syndicated column, commenting on the arrest of 17 victims of the Smith Act, made this anti-Semitic contrast: "The U.S. Marshals, all clean-cut people, looked like Americans should. . . . Betty Gannett, one of the arrested Reds, is actually named Rifka Yarashevsky." In mid-July, in Cicero, Ill., the riot to prevent a Negro couple from moving into the city was marked by the cry to drive the Jews out of it. July 29, in Detroit, a plane twice dropped leaflets showing beak-nosed caricatures of Jews and calling on "Americans" to drive them out of the country.

In August, Bill Hendrix, Grand Dragon of the Florida Ku Klux Klan, announced his candidacy for Governor on a platform that would include driving the Jews from Miami Beach. August 6, near Poughkeepsie, N. Y. (not far from Peekskill), anti-Semites wrecked the 15-room house of a Zionist youth center training farmers for Israel. Late in August, KKK speakers in South Carolina denounced Zionism, Anna Rosenberg and Jews in general. About this time, stickers were seen in the Bronx subways with anti-Semitic attacks on Julius and Ethel Rosenberg. In rural Colorado, 28 percent of those asked the question agreed that Jews "naturally tend to be dishonest so that they can make money."

In September, anti-Semitic pamphlets were being distributed in Ogunquit, Kennebunk, Biddeford and Old Orchard Beach, Maine. In Northampton, Mass. the B'nai Israel synagogue was desecrated, dollar signs being scrawled over some pictures and rude crucifixion scenes daubed on walls.

In Cleveland, a Jewish center was broken into and wrecked. From Santa Ana, Calif., Robert H. Williams, a hooligan red-baiter, sent thousands of anti-Semitic pamphlets through the mails urging that Jews be arrested and congregated in areas where our high command expects atomic bombs to fall, denouncing Eisenhower as a Jew and a front for the "Zionists." The Alsops in their syndicated column thought it necessary to look into such a sewer as Williams because they say "very bluntly that the sewers are threatening to well up into our public life."

It is this sewage that has poisoned the minds already of millions of people in our country. The false-face of the greedy, ruthless Jew is stamped on the minds of millions. It does not need much to provoke anti-Semitic actions. I remember the well-dressed hoodlums on Eighth Avenue deriding the May Day parade, and wearing "Jewish-noses" on their beaks, and I saw the shops later where such merchandise is sold. And in the East German Democratic Republic, when underground nazis went in for fascist propaganda, they considered it sufficient for their purpose to manufacture just such anti-Semitic masks as Streicher had popularized among the German people. Such masks, without comment or explanation, are anti-Semitic propaganda.

In our own country, this image, this mask has flourished so far only in the underworld of anti-Semitic propaganda. Now Fagin, who is that mask embodied, is being shown in "respectable" theaters, to the general American public, to school-children who have been advised to go not only by the May Quinns but also by teachers influenced by the "aesthetes" who write movie reviews for the general American press. The sewer has backed right up into the movie theaters.

Fagin is the most horrible image of fiendish inhumanity to cross the screen in 30 years. It is not only the outer features: the nose (and how the camera focuses on that nose, from all angles, but usually in profile!), the huge beard, the way he plays with his beard, the hopping gait, the large flat-brimmed hat, the kaftan, the shawl, the hand-gestures, the accent (not Yiddish), thick, lisping, guttural. These outer features fuse with a moral degeneracy that not only leads to the kidnapping of children to be trained as thieves, but to the murder of Nancy by Bill Sikes.

There are those who argue that Sikes is a villain and a murderer, and Sikes is an Englishman, so why is not *Oliver Twist* as much anti-English as it is anti-Semitic? But Sikes is a mindless, crude brute who is incited to the murder by Fagin's plots and lies; and to counter Sikes there is the lovely English family that rescues Oliver from Fagin. Not only is Fagin the master-mind and organizer of thievery, villainy and murder; he is also the arch-hypocrite. As the police, backed by a huge crowd, are about to rush upon Fagin after battering down the door to his hideout, Fagin draws himself up and calls out, "What right have you to butcher me?" On the basis of what has come before, the audience is supposed to know quite well why Fagin should be "butchered"; and are not these audiences being cunningly prepared for more butchery of Fagins, of Jews?

The deliberate anti-Semitism of the producer and director of *Oliver Twist* is unmistakable. "Faithfulness to a classic" is a faithless defense. As shown in *Jewish Life* last month, Dickens himself later realized the anti-Semitic effect of his portrayal, and in a half-hearted, bumbling, ineffective way tried to make amends. Had the producer and director wished to be really true to Dickens's own later understanding of the situation, they could easily have stripped Fagin not only of the appellation, "Jew" (which they had), but of *all* his other external features. Fagin, or a villain by even another name, since the name itself is a common Jewish name, could have been presented as an English rogue; his degeneracy and wickedness would not have helped turn millions into anti-English genocides. Considering all the stupid liberties with "classics" that are common in the industry, one can hardly believe that it was sheer devotion to the original text, despite Dickens's own partial repudiation of it, that motivated the producer to make the film, and the American censors to approve it.

52 THE CASE OF THE INVISIBLE FORCE: IMAGES OF THE NEGRO IN HOLLYWOOD FILMS

Lorraine Hansberry

IMAGINE TEN THOUSAND PEOPLE pour into a city square in Johannesburg, South Africa. Their faces are resolute and angry. The loudspeakers around the square sound out the mighty voice of Paul Robeson. Leaders of the people mount the platforms and they say that the black and brown peoples of South Africa are sick unto death of the oppression. They say that from this date forward—May 7, 1951—they will disobey all laws which seek to impose a fifth-class citizenship on them. In the days that follow, the newspapers of the world report that the jails of South Africa are being filled with a determined people, black South Africans, Indians and Colored People. It is as if a people have lifted their fists as one and shouted out for all the world to hear—"Freedom now!"

And then, here in the United States, you go into a movie to see *Cry the Beloved Country*. And what makes up this tale? There are long speeches about faith and goodness and forgiveness and morality wound around the story of a young South African who accidentally murders a white man in the process of burglarizing his house. After this, the balance of the story is spent showing how the pious father (Canada

Lee) of the young African grieves that his son has done this thing. It finally reaches such a pitch that he falls on his knees before the father of the dead white man and begs forgiveness. *He,* the black man, falls on *his* knees, on *his* African earth, to ask the white man's forgiveness.

Incidental to the story, the camera picks up some revealing scenes of the living conditions of the Africans. You see poverty and misery of the most hideous description possible. You see workers on their way to the mines, miners who constitute some of the most exploited people on the face of the earth. *And in the whole movie there is not one word of protest.* Not one hint of dissatisfaction, hatred or movements for change. Indeed, the only angry words are between black men. The young priest (Sidney Poitier) spends his religious wrath on an uncle of the young man, who seeks to keep him from punishment. There is, according to this film, no wrath against the Malan government or the international financiers who have turned that beautiful country into a fascistic nightmare of oppression.

In the past couple of years, since the outbreak of the Korean War, the film capital has come up with more than ten such films on the "Negro problem," but as yet not one has made the remotest effort to say *why* there is a problem. If anything, the rich indulgence in the individual "psychoses" of white and Negro characters has sought only to confuse the reasons.

It is as if Hollywood had at last, at the expense of Black America, achieved the Great American Mystery: *The Case of the Invisible Force* behind the oppression of the Negro people.

Let's take a look at this phenomenon in the current crop of "Negro interest" films. When these films first began to be advertised there were glimmers of hope among black people that at last Hollywood, after its long, disgraceful history of anti-Negro films from *Birth of a Nation* through *Gone with the Wind,* its racist hiring policies and openly stated "taboo" on films about Negroes, was going to give some forthright treatment to our struggles. The "New Wave," as the industry proclaimed these films, was ballyhooed across the land as "honest portrayals" . . . that "hit home" . . . and "pull no punches." And so we went in great numbers to see the first: *Home of the Brave.* And this is what we saw:

A Negro soldier on duty in the South Pacific is almost called an anti-Negro name by a white buddy. This incident, along with the death of his friend, stuns him into a paralysis. He is cured by an Army psychiatrist, who tells him that it is all in his mind. That he is "just like everyone else." He returns to the United States, and pals up with a white ex-G. I. who wants to go into business with him in a fine demonstration of Negro-white fraternity, on which the movie ends. And when the black hero suggests that a partnership with himself would not be easy because of racism in this country, the white man's answer is to lift an empty sleeve and say that *he too* knows something of this kind of a problem.

This, then, is the equation with the Negro oppressed—a one-armed white man.

Leaving the theatre, a black person reflects on what has been said: "Your oppression is in your minds. All you have to do is take your *fifteen millions* to mental therapists and just let them convince you!"

So here again, in new "enlightened" guise, is the old answer to our charges and protests: Take that "chip" off your shoulder. *The source and the root of Negro oppression lies in the persecution complex of the Negro.* Does not every individual have a problem of some kind? Here, for instance, is a *white* man without an arm, and he is a decent fellow, but must we crusade for him? Must we organize meetings and organizations and protests about his one-armedness? Racism is a problem of perception and attitude. Why make such a big issue of it?

This, in short, is the infamous outrage of an answer given to black people who say: "But we are not discriminated against because of our individual personalities or habits. For three hundred years in this unfriendly land we have been *collectively* brutalized, enslaved, cheated of dignity, wages, life and everything but hope itself. A Negro is usually lynched by people who have never known him—or her. Those who refuse to hire Negroes, refuse to hire *Negroes,* not individuals. Any equation of the Negro question with the individual problems of whites is therefore senseless. The legislation in the Congress that permits and encourages the Klan and the Poll Tax (and they must be considered 'encouraged' until they are outlawed) is not discriminating against a Negro here and there, but SOME FIFTEEN MILLION BLACK FOLK. The *whole* Negro people!"

We charge this of the *white rulers* of this country, and today because the colored peoples of the world hold the balance of power and are conscious that they do, our protests sound all over the world and make it difficult and awkward for the transporters of State Department hypocrisy, *so that the agencies responsible must find a new lie to quiet and confuse the struggle.* Hence the fable of *Home of the Brave:* the same fable that is elaborated and taught in our college classrooms, printed in great volumes by dead-serious "scholars," and which now surfaces in the slick new movie scripts of the New Wave. The new lie of 1951 that is to replace the outmoded open claim of "inferiority" that went with chattel slavery: the Myth of the Invisible Force, inexplicable, indefinable, internalized, which says, in effect, to the Negro people: "Your feelings, your deep protests, your great organizations of struggle, your angry eyes, your mighty songs of protest . . . indeed your raised fists across the land, are really, in spite of all we have done to you (lynchings in the night, Harlem and Southside ghettoes, empty ice-boxes, the hurt in the faces of your children, your gouged and bloody eyes)—these are nothing more, nothing more than . . . persecution complexes!"

So, leaving the theatre, we know that once again in history our hope has been betrayed. And we almost "expect" *Pinky,* which comes next in the story of:

A fair-skinned young Negro woman who "passes" for white while going to nursing school in the North, where she meets a young white doctor. Doc wants to marry her until he follows her South and learns her secret. He becomes discouraged when she refuses to give up her identity as a Negro, just to marry him. The insults in the film pile up. We meet "Aunt Dicey," Pinky's grandmother, complete in bandana, who just "loves old Miss Em" who has exploited her all her life. And then there are the scenes of the razor-toting Negro woman, and the "shiftless, good-for-nothing, lying" Hollywood stock character of a black man.

Finally, the story ends with a great act in a courtroom, in which justice is awarded *to the Negro* over whites—in the Deep South! This is the supreme insult. Hollywood is making a mockery of one of the most terrible facts of Southern life, where a Negro's chance in the courts is not any shade removed from his "chance" before a howling lynch mob. But *Pinky* has no time to confront this truth . . . or indict a system which causes people to "pass" in order to get training, or jobs, or to marry. Rather, the sympathy is aimed at the white supremacist suitor, prepared to marry Pinky if she will move with him to distant Denver where no one knows them and they can lead a "normal" (white) life, but who just can't bring himself to marry her *as is.* The possibility doesn't even occur to him.

As in *Home of the Brave,* there are aspects of even this film that show that Hollywood has felt the pressure of the insistent demands of the Negro people for honest representation: the near-rape scene of the Negro woman, the cheating of Negroes in the local store, and a few other things. But this just doesn't outweigh the final feeling *Pinky* leaves, which is, first of all, of Hollywood's absurd preoccupation with the "passing" theme—certainly a topic mighty low in importance among the Negro people themselves. The fact is that Hollywood hasn't really moved too far since *Imitation of Life,* which never stirred up love for the movie industry among Negroes either. Indeed, in a sense it has moved backwards, inasmuch as in the earlier film the similar role assigned to white actress Jeanne Crain in *Pinky* was at least given to Freddi Washington, a Negro. This is not minor since, if Hollywood really wanted to do a theme close to the hearts of the Negro people and of *real* importance, it would do something on the great question of unemployment, felt so deeply within the ranks of America's most oppressed. And which certainly includes our artists, actors, dancers and musicians.

A third film, *Intruder in the Dust,* presents us with Lucas Beauchamps, a proud, dignified Negro who is almost lynched. The big to-do of the film deals with the inability of a young white Southerner to make his inherent urge toward justice compatible with the white supremacy around him. The result is that he gets a lawyer for Beauchamps, who, according to this fantasy, is freed because *the evidence is in his favor.* So while the lynch mob goes quietly away, Lucas Beauchamps walks away from the jailhouse, unmolested, in the Mississippi dust.

This movie beyond all others shows Hollywood's role as a deliberate one: daring to suggest that a lynch mob has a conscience, that it stands about patiently and orderly waiting to see if it will be just or unjust to lynch a Negro; indeed, the action suggests that if Beauchamps had been guilty, then . . . *a lynching might have been justified.* Nowhere in the film is there any identification of the real organizers of the usual lynching mobs, the highly organized terrorists: the Ku Klux Klan and the local sheriffs and deputies. Nor of the "legal" bodies that commit, protect and encourage terroristic attacks on the Negro people both in the North and in the South. (Witness the police at Cicero, Illinois, Peekskill, New York, and Columbia, Tennessee; witness the sheriffs in Opelousa, Louisiana, and—most bitterly recent—Groveland, Florida. And witness all over the South the open and free functioning of the Ku Klux Klan.) Instead, according to *Intruder in the Dust,* the lynch mob is a *spontaneous* uprising of working-class whites—a case of momentary mass possession. It is the highly educated middle-class gentlefolk in the courts who are the friendly, persevering allies of black folk. For, as the "liberal" white Southern attorney informs us, the Negro is "our conscience"—modern for "the white man's burden." Invisible Force Meets Noblesse Oblige!

And so by the time the fourth movie is released we know what to expect. We know it is no accident that the consecutive messages of these first films have been: (1) Negroes have no special problem; (2) There is justice in the South; (3) Negroes are still "the white man's burden."

Then comes *Lost Boundaries,* and things get really ridiculous: A Negro doctor's family "lives a lie" (the whole family is "passing") for several years. They are "found out" and promptly ostracized by an indignant town. Until, that is, the local Protestant minister delivers a kindly sermon one Sunday morning on tolerance and the whole town forgives *them.* The end. And the fourth point obviously is: *Negroes should not deceive white people.*

The *Lost Boundaries* story would also have us believe that

the thing that drives Negroes to pass is not oppression by white America at all. The one act of prejudice shown against the ambitious, young, light-skinned Negro doctor is *from his own people.* What an ugly lie. Seekers of truth have but to walk into a Negro institution anywhere in America and find Negroes of every hue teaching, administering and learning. In a Negro hospital not only fair-skinned Negroes but white doctors are to be found. In fact if there were any element of importance to be shown in the question of Negroes discriminating against Negroes it would be the precise opposite of that depicted: it is *blackness* that has been made despised in America and not the other way around.

But it is ridiculous and sinister to make a thematic problem of discrimination among Negroes while the real enemies of the Negro people, the white ruling class of this country, are ignored. It is this point which makes *Lost Boundaries* the most fiercely dangerous of all, for within its story *is an attack, clear and sharp, directed against the very unity of the Negro people.*

America might simply laugh at this farce of an attempt if the lives and happiness of such a large percentage of her people were not involved. Indeed, if *her whole people* were not involved. But in any case, after *Lost Boundaries* we know that a Second, and a Third, "New Wave" will follow inevitably, and we are not misled. Three recent examples:

Bright Victory. This is the simple story of a blind white G. I. who unwittingly insults his best buddy (James Edwards) before he finds out that he is black. He goes through a mild period of white supremacist shock and then decides he likes the guy anyhow. Again there is nothing wrong with the message except that it, too, fails to say that "prejudice" is anything more than individual intolerance. A case of the Invisible Force quietly at work.

Red Ball Express. This is perhaps the best of the lot in that it does bring to the screen the heroic record—in the face of segregation and incredible racist obstacles—of the Negro Quartermaster units in World War II. Yet even so, the Invisible Force Returns, relentless:

A Negro G. I. (Sidney Poitier) doesn't like it when a white soldier makes cracks about minstrel shows and resents his presence on a chow line. When the Lieutenant (Jeff Chandler) breaks up a fight between them, he too gains the sensitive man's animosity. Finally, a Negro hero is blown to bits trying to show his comrades a safe route through a mine field and is given a genuinely moving burial by the outfit. The Lieutenant is the most deeply affected by the death, and the "sensitive" Negro realizes that he had him all wrong, the Lieutenant is really an impartial decent guy. The point of it all seems to be to show the Negro soldier how wrong he is to assume that every white man is against him. It is striking, too, that the other Negro soldiers in the film never particularly associate their feelings with Poitier's; he seems to be the only one who resents the slurs. *Is it really such a rare Negro who resents second-class citizenship?*

What makes white soldiers hate Negro soldiers? What is it in the experience of Negro soldiers that makes them expect this and hate back? Could it be discrimination and jim crow, the terror and violence practiced against them since birth? Of course not, says Hollywood. It's psychological: the Invisible Force!

Finally, there is *Lydia Bailey*. Here we have a mixture of killing and hatred and bitter words in exotic Haiti. There is a romance of a young white couple running through the story for some reason or other, and somewhere in between it all, it is not too easy to find the Haitian revolution—and impossible to find out *why it was fought!* Toussaint L'Ouverture himself is incidental to the love affair of course. And all who don't know, *before* they go to see the film, that slavery is hell on earth, won't be convinced there was any need for the Haitian people to make one of the greatest thrusts for freedom in modern history. And so the Mystery goes on.

There is, of course, the "this-is-a-step-forward" crowd which insists that "first things must come first," and "you have to start somewhere." But if any white American thinks I exaggerate, he should go to the nearest theatre in a Negro community where such a film is being shown, and see just how it is received. He would find bitter laughter and at other times passionate, collective anger, not at all in the places where the movie-makers have intended. For the Negro audiences are, after all, the *real* critics and experts on the question, and precisely not the hired press agents of the multi-billion-dollar movie-producing studios.

The fact is, however, that the arts like everything else in America are subject to the operations of big business. It is a simple matter to see that those who have turned the motion picture industry into one of America's major big profit industries are bound to have a common eye with those who extract four and half billions of dollars per year in profit from the exploitation of the Negro people.

From all this, two questions arise. First, if the owners of the movie industry are so all-powerful, isn't the situation hopeless? Indeed not. While it is true that they can buy up the movies and all other means of propaganda, they cannot buy up either history or the spirit of oppressed peoples.

We shall continue to surround them with truth and the power of truth. We shall continue to insist that their writers stop writing *around* history, stop writing *around* life. We shall demand, for instance, if Haiti is the subject, that they show the brutal inhumanity of French overseers and plantation owners, the inhumanity that caused the Haitian people to drive the armies of Bonaparte into the sea and change the whole subsequent history of half a hemisphere. That they show the *real* experiences of that American black man who after years of job refusals, slander, insult and violence finally shows up on their screens as the overly "sensitive" Negro.

A second question: What is it exactly that we Negroes want to see on the screen? The answer is simple—*reality*. We want to see films about people who live and work like everybody else, but who currently must battle fierce oppression to do so. We want to see films about lynchings that *did* come off—or that *can be stopped* by the mass strength of black and white all over the country. Or about job-hunting when you are black; or house-hunting or school-hunting. About restaurants, hotels, theatres that do not admit. We want an end to the evasions of the Invisible Force so that all the world can see who our oppressors are and what lies at the root of their evil.

And lastly, we want employment for our young writers and actors who can best give expression to our sorrow, songs and laughter, to our blues and our poetry—and the authentic drama of our lives.

Clearly, as long as the sources of Negro oppression remain unidentified, it is a simple matter to show the whole thing as a matter of mass delusion and individual psychosis. But once Hollywood is forced to deal with our *real* problems—and to hire black writers and directors committed to making films that *will have meaning* and that truly do begin the task of reclaiming our past and confronting our present— then it will answer its own vicious projections of the "future," symbolically laid out for us in the latest New Wave title: *No Way Out!*

In that progression, the ultimate reality is that three hundred years of resistance to oppression have given us a mighty song to sing, and the powerful strains of that melody will no longer yield—in art or in history—to the obfuscating mystifications of the Invisible Force.

For a stimulating discussion of the 1985 controversial Steven Spielberg film, The Color Purple—*which gives the reactions of both the Black feminist critics who defend it and the Black male reviewers who vehemently denounce it— see Jacqueline Bobo's well-researched essay in* Jump Cut, *No. 33, February, 1988. (Address: P. O. Box 865, Berkeley, CA 94701.) (DP)*

53 THE UNITED STATES VS. CHARLIE CHAPLIN

Timothy J. Lyons

IN OCTOBER OF 1952, a month after Charles Chaplin and his family boarded the *Queen Elizabeth* in New York for a trip to England, the U.S. Federal Bureau of Investigation issued a massive internal report citing almost forty years of investigative interest in the comedian, including his political associations as well as his off-screen love affairs. One copy was sent to Attorney General James P. McGranery, who had announced, on September 20, that the British-born Chaplin would not be readmitted to the United States without a hearing before Immigration officials; the attorney general characterized Chaplin as an "unsavory character" who had made statements and committed actions "indicating a leering, sneering attitude toward the country whose hospitality has enriched him."

Not only was the FBI interested in Chaplin, but also Army and Navy Intelligence, the Internal Revenue Service, the Central Intelligence Agency, the Department of State, and even the U.S. Postal Service. Today, more than fifteen thousand pages of governmental memos and reports on Chaplin are still in existence, some of these recently released through the Freedom of Information Act. Thousands more have been destroyed or are being withheld.

The October 1952 FBI summary report took 125 pages to specify government allegations against Charles Chaplin, but

From *American Film* (September 1984), publication of the American Film Institute. Reprinted by permission of the editor and publisher.

it didn't fully chronicle the intense and continued surveillance of the celebrity during his forty-year residence in the country. Chaplin first came under the scrutiny of military intelligence in 1919 because of his financial contributions to Max Eastman's radical publication, the *Liberator*. Three years later, the FBI raided a convention of the American Communist Party in Bridgman, Michigan, and discovered correspondence and files linking Chaplin to the "Parlor Bolsheviki," a wealthy California clique cavorting with the likes of Socialist Upton Sinclair and labor leader William Z. Foster.

For the next three decades, Chaplin figured prominently in the government's scrutiny of financial support for labor dissidents and the Soviet cause, from those whom the government labeled "pre-mature anti-Fascists." Listed as a sponsor of numerous Popular Front organizations during the late thirties, Chaplin openly incurred the wrath of the political Right when in October 1942 he advocated the opening of a "Second Front" in support of the Russians.

Nine months after he made a speech in New York in favor of this strategy, Chaplin found himself embroiled in an FBI investigation that was initially sparked by the notorious paternity suit filed against him by actress Joan Barry. Chaplin was indicted for violating the White Slave Traffic Act of 1910 (he paid for Barry's round-trip transportation to New York at the time of his speechmaking) and with conspiring to violate Barry's civil liberties. These two charges were to be handled in separate trials. The FBI, in its investigation, made use of such eager informants as gossip columnists Hedda Hopper and Florabel Muir, and enlisted some close associates and friends of Chaplin's. The Bureau even obtained inside information from an attorney involved in the paternity suit. During the year of investigation (until Chaplin's acquittal in April 1944), FBI agents compiled more than three thousand pages of reports and interviews, including indications that Chaplin had ordered two abortions for Barry, twice conspired with the Beverly Hills Police Department to run Barry out of town, and engaged in black-market dealings. They were even convinced that Chaplin had discovered a way to change his blood type for the tests that proved conclusively he was not the father of Barry's child, Carol Ann.

Agent H. Frank Angell and his associates had also

provided U.S. attorney Charles H. Carr with substantial information about the erratic and unstable character of Joan Barry, the chief witness for the prosecution. According to the FBI, Barry, born Mary Louise Gribble, had used almost a dozen different aliases, and traveled throughout the country leaving bills and disappointed suitors behind, not the least of whom was financier J. Paul Getty. At the beginning of the investigation, J. Edgar Hoover was fully supportive, scrawling notes on reports, encouraging his aides to vigorously pursue the case. But after Chaplin's acquittal, even the sanguinary director of the FBI had to conclude that the investigation had been an embarrassment to the all-important image of the Bureau. Nevertheless, despite pressure from Hoover and Associate Attorney General Tom Clark (acting for Attorney General Francis Biddle), Carr strenuously pursued the case, balking at dropping the conspiracy charges even after Chaplin had been found innocent of being a white-slave trafficker.

During the Barry affair, FBI agents worked closely with Internal Revenue Service and Immigration personnel to coordinate whatever information was available regarding Chaplin's character and personal affairs. The goal was obvious. In a memo dated January 8, 1944, top Hoover aide Alex Rosen reported a telephone conversation with the Los Angeles special agent in charge, R. B. Hood: "We discussed the possibility of [Chaplin's] being deported after the war and Mr. Hood advised he thought there was an excellent chance for this." When all charges against Chaplin were dropped in federal court, Bureau agents stepped up their efforts to compile evidence linking him to what was called the international Communist conspiracy.

Two professional informants aided them. On June 21, 1950, Louis F. Budenz—the former managing editor of the Communist *Daily Worker* newspaper, who had broken with the party five years earlier—told a New York FBI agent that in 1936, Chaplin was "the equivalent of a member of the Party." Budenz also claimed that in the early forties, party officials discouraged Chaplin from applying for U.S. citizenship, "since it would raise the whole question of his being an alien, an attack on his personal life, and all sorts of things that might lead to his deportation." Finally, Budenz reported that the *Daily Worker* was ordered by party officials to run an editorial supporting Chaplin's "private morals" because "we had to defend the integrity of Chaplin, a Communist artist." These allegations appeared in the 1952 FBI report.

The other major informant quoted in the report was Paul Crouch, a Communist Party functionary from 1925 until 1942, who told Immigration officials that Chaplin "was a member-at-large of the Communist Party." He said that Chaplin was "temperamental but loyal" to the party and that "to protect him and to protect the best interests of the Party," officials had decided "he should remain a member-at-large and not be affiliated with the Party units being set up in Hollywood."

Although agents were convinced of Chaplin's financial support of party front organizations, the testimony of Budenz and Crouch was the only concrete evidence they had to link Chaplin to party membership. None of the further reports citing the allegations of Budenz and Crouch reflected the serious questions later raised about their credibility.

Probably the most influential document in the 1952 FBI report was an interview with Chaplin conducted four years earlier by Immigration investigators. Reprinted in full in numerous FBI reports from 1948 to 1955, the interview offered what could best be called the government's bill of particulars against Chaplin, along with the comedian's responses to these charges.

For the Immigration investigators, Chaplin's associations with various organizations deemed Communist fronts were of prime importance. They hammered away at such groups as an Actors Guild ("I think I have to belong to an Actors Guild in order to work," Chaplin responded), the New Workers Party ("I am sure I am not a member of anything"), "A Soviet America to Come," the Russian-American Society for Medical Aid to Russia, the National Council of American-Soviet Friendship ("I think, yes, maybe, yes . . . it was one of those things that perhaps went on during the war"), Russian War Relief, and the Artists' Front to Win the War. Immigration officials also stressed allegations that Chaplin had been a guest numerous times at the Russian consulate in Los Angeles ("I think I have been [there] one time. . . . I remember practically the whole of Hollywood there").

The Immigration officials interrogated Chaplin about his

associations: labor leader Harry Bridges ("I think I met him once"); composer Hanns Eisler ("I met him socially through other people"); Eugene Dennis, Leon Josephson, and Gerhardt Eisler, on trial as alleged Communist Party leaders ("We wanted to see justice done in the proper way. That's all"). For the FBI, other associations indicated Chaplin's subversiveness: Leon Feuchtwanger ("In August 1952, informant of known reliability advised that [Chaplin] was personally acquainted with Feuchtwanger, [who] claims to be a leftist, but it is believed that he is a top man in the Communist circle"); novelist Theodore Dreiser, *Life* editor Richard Lauterbach (who, according to Budenz, was a Communist); Lubomir Linhart ("a known Communist and director of the Czechoslovakian film industry"); and others figuring in leftist activities in Hollywood.

Star-struck Immigration officials were also intensely interested in the guests Chaplin entertained at home. They did remember to ask him whether members of the Russian consulate had visited his home, to which Chaplin replied, "I don't recall. You see, we get a lot of people. I entertain lots of these consulates, ambassadors, and Chinese and so forth. They all come up here, you know, because I am pretty much of an international figure, but not much."

During the interview, Chaplin was of little assistance as Immigration agents tried to determine which organizations received money from the comedian:

Q: In 1922 or '23, did you make a large donation to the Communist Party?
A: I did not.
Q: Have you ever made any donations to the Communist Party?
A: I am sure, never, not to my—I am sure.
Q: Hedda Hopper, Hollywood columnist, in her column December 27, 1943, stated, "From things I have learned, Charlie Chaplin contributed $25,000 to the Communist cause and $100 to the Red Cross." What have you to say about that, Mr. Chaplin?
A: That is a complete lie. . . . We make our yearly thing to the Red Cross and have done so throughout the years. Same thing with the buying of war bonds and everything. I bought half a million dollars' worth of war bonds.

It was Chaplin's Second Front speech in New York, during October of 1942, that received close attention during the Immigration interview:

> Q: Mr. Chaplin, were you honorary chairman of a cultural meeting held at Carnegie Hall, New York City, October 16, 1942?
> A: I spoke there, yes.
> Q: You were the honorary chairman, then, of this meeting?
> A: I don't remember. I know that they requested and wanted to know if I would speak on that occasion. I think Orson Welles was the chairman. I wasn't the chairman at all, and I was to speak.
> Q: And, now, during that address—or rather at the commencement of the address—did you preface your remarks by saying: "Dear Comrades. Yes. I mean Comrades"?
> A: Yes.
> Q: And just what did you mean to imply with the salutation?
> A: I mean to imply—there were obviously some Russians in the audience and as we were all together in the Allied cause and fighting for democracy and that they were our comrades and I was very proud to be able to refer to them as comrades. We were all in one cause.
> Q: Did it have any significance that you were and considered yourself a follower of the Communist line?
> A: No.
> Q: Or a member of the Communist Party?
> A: It had a certain wit. It got a big laugh, and there was at that time a pervading sort of feeling that the Russians were very strange bedfellows.

For Chaplin, the accusations against him rested on the speeches he had given in 1942:

> This all emanates from the—all this sort of association of Communist attached to me emanates from the fact that I was called up during the war to make a speech and deputize for Mr. [Joseph] Davies, who was the [former] ambassador to Russia, and he was to speak in San Francisco. He was taken suddenly ill with laryngitis, and at the last moment they called me up and asked me if I would go there for [the] rally and so forth and get money for the Russia thing, charity or whatever it was. I went down there the last moment. I made a speech. I felt very emotional about the whole thing, and the news was

coming through that they were at Stalingrad and so forth and all this business, they had fought and died a great deal, and I made a talk, a eulogy of Russia and the Russian people, and then, from there they said, "Good work," and it was the thing to do, and we wanted unity, and there seemed to be other forces trying to divide us at that time, and the thing I always spoke and in all my speeches I said, "We want [everyone from capitalist] Thomas Lamont to [labor leader] Harry Bridges, we want that same unity, we have to win this war." I mean that is the whole thing.

Crucial, especially to Immigration authorities, was the status of Chaplin as a resident alien:

Q: As a matter of fact, Mr. Chaplin, you are not a citizen of the United States, are you?
A: I am not.
Q: Have you ever applied for citizenship in this country?
A: I have never applied; from the time I was nineteen, I have always had a sense of internationalism and I feel that it is coming closer every day, for the United Nations and for One World as Mr.—what's his name that died.
Q: Is that the reason you have never applied for citizenship in the United States?
A: Yes. I consider myself as much a citizen of America as anybody else and my great love has always been here in this country. I have been here thirty, thirty-five years. My children and everybody is as much a part of my—at the same time I don't feel I am allied to any one particular country. I feel I am a citizen of the world.

For Chaplin, the citizenship issue was one raised by the press. "They don't like anybody that speaks frankly, the press. I despise the press and they have always lied about me. It isn't true what the press said. Seventy-five percent of my revenue comes from Europe, you see, and this country enjoys one hundred percent of its taxation."

Throughout the interview, questions always returned to Chaplin's sentiments about communism and its relationship to American life. At one point, Chaplin commented:

Frankly, I don't know anything about the Communist way of life. I must say that, but I must say this, I don't see why we can't have peace with Russia. Their way of life—I am not interested in their ideology, I assure you. I assure you. I don't know whether you believe me or not, but I am not. I am interested to the point where—they say they want peace, and I don't see why we can't have peace here. I don't see why we can't have trade relationship and ameliorate matters and so forth and avoid a world war.

Asked if he had anything to add before the interview concluded, Chaplin reiterated much of the sentiment his answers had tried to express:

> I don't deny the fact that I spoke and eulogized and extolled Russia, because I felt it was a necessary thing to do, because I personally believe and honestly believed they were doing a splendid job and I believe if it hadn't been for Russia we might have had these Nazis over here and I firmly believe that and I don't see any reason for any antagonism now against Russia. . . . I don't like war and I don't like revolution. I don't like anything overthrown. If the status quo of anything is all right let it go. In my sense of being a liberal, I just want to see things function in harmony. I want to see everybody pretty well, happy, and satisfied.

Thus concluded Charles Chaplin's lengthy interview with Immigration officials.

Military intelligence, also interested in Chaplin, pursued the same lines of investigation as the FBI and Immigration. A major part of the Army Intelligence reports stemmed from the surveillance activities of a group of retired officers located in San Diego, with contacts throughout the country. Headed by Major General Ralph Van Deman, this group cataloged Communist newspapers like the *People's World* and the *Daily Worker,* compiled a massive file index with cross-references by name, subject, and location; and were generally vigilant in supplying their findings to the FBI, the U.S. Fifth Army Command, and other agencies, as well as to the American Legion.

Probably the most striking episode of surveillance appeared in a 1948 report from Navy Intelligence that linked Chaplin to the sale of surplus tanks to the Zionist Haganah forces in Palestine. According to the navy, Chaplin was mentioned in a conversation by Service Airways personnel as someone who "had to be consulted on both the financial aspect and the general advisability of the proposed acquisition" of thirty-six surplus tanks from a storage depot in Barstow, California. Other prominent personalities mentioned as sponsors of this project were Walter Winchell and Bernard M. Baruch. Plans were to load the tanks onto barges and "get them to Palestine somehow." Navy Intelligence agents commented deadpan that: "The inference was that this would be a clandestine export; but no explanation was made as to how thirty-six armored tanks could be moved surreptitiously."

Throughout the months following the 1952 FBI report, Bureau agents worked closely with Immigration personnel to arrange interviews with informants from the FBI investigation, in preparation for Chaplin's hearing before the Immigration authorities on his return to this country. Even after Chaplin surrendered his reentry permit in April 1953, agents continued their detective work, including the posting of "appropriate look-out notices [at border stations] . . . to guard against Chaplin's reentry." Not until August 1953 did FBI officials in Washington authorize the cancellation of Chaplin's Security Index Card.

Surveillance of Chaplin continued after the comedian had settled in Switzerland, where the FBI and the State Department monitored his mail and noted the visitors to Manoir de Ban in Corsier-sur-Vevey, Chaplin's lakeside villa. Agents were particularly alarmed by a Swedish newspaper report in February 1954 that Chaplin planned to adopt the orphaned children of suspected spies Ethel and Julius Rosenberg. Chaplin's characterization of this as "without foundation and absolutely ridiculous" was noted in the New York field-office report, which was subsequently stamped: "Do Not Destroy—Pending Litigation."

In October 1957, Chaplin again came to the attention of the FBI, this time in a memo from A. H. Belmont to L. V. Boardman, Hoover aides who ranked high in command. Chaplin was no longer a "Security Risk": His file now read, "Central Research Matter." Belmont cited the release of Chaplin's *A King in New York* and warned that American Communists are creating "an issue for propaganda exploitation." For Belmont, the three concerns of such a campaign were: "(1) The State Department could be put on the spot. Either a move by State to prevent importation of the film or a hands-off policy could subject it to criticism. Any criticism of State would inure to Communist benefit as a discrediting of the United States Government. (2) A successful campaign would provide wide, effective distribution in this country of the malicious Communist propaganda the movie contains. (3) An unsuccessful campaign to import the film would, nevertheless, be beneficial to Communists. It would provide an issue of freedom of expression around which Communists could attract a sizable following with the rallying cry 'suppression.' " Belmont recommended that these matters be brought to the personal attention of J. Edgar Hoover.

When Chaplin received an honorary degree from Oxford University in 1962 (along with U.S. secretary of state Dean Rusk and others), newspapers in America editorialized that the time had come to welcome Chaplin back to the United States. Hoover responded to such sentiments by requesting "a concise summary memorandum" on Chaplin from the Bureau's considerable files. A few days later, Hoover aide Clyde Tolson ordered this summary sent to former attorney general James P. McGranery, then a federal judge in New York City. McGranery had complained that he was receiving unfair blame for barring Chaplin from the country.

In 1967, Immigration officials received an application from Chaplin for "temporary admission to the United States." Reviewing the Department of State's previous determination that Chaplin was ineligible to receive a visa, based on political and moral charges, Immigration officials decided "that the denial of a visa sought for the above purpose would seriously mar the image of the United States throughout the world, particularly in Western Europe, and that his world-wide renown as an artist would undoubtedly make the matter a 'cause celebre' with the U.S. portrayed as vindictive and fearful. . . ." In view of this, Immigration approved the application for Chaplin to attend the premiere of his new film, *A Countess From Hong Kong,* in the United States. However, Chaplin canceled his trip without ever picking up the temporary visa.

Five years later, Chaplin returned for tributes in New York and Los Angeles. Neither Immigration nor the FBI sought to bar his reentry. But even after Chaplin's death on Christmas Eve 1977, the Bureau continued to monitor the comedian, in particular the events surrounding the theft of his body from a Swiss graveyard; at one point agents entertained the notion of enlisting the aid of a psychic in Portland, Maine, to assist in tracking down the grave robbers.

Samuel Goldwyn, the producer, has often been ridiculed for his "malopopisms" but in my mind he will always be associated with the time in London when he berated Attorney General McGranery for locking Chaplin out of the USA after his film, Monsieur Verdoux, *was locked out of the theatres. "If they don't like me defending him," Goldwyn said angrily, "well, they can stop me from re-entering America too." Even Mary Pickford, a stalwart Republican, regarded the McGranery move as "beneath the dignity of the great USA." (DP)*

54 BREAKING GROUND: THE MAKING OF *SALT OF THE EARTH*

Paul Jarrico *and* Herbert J. Biberman

I

WHEN OUR COMPANY WAS FORMED two years ago, we were agreed that our films must be based in actuality. Therefore, we were entering an arena of art to which we as craftsmen brought little experience and in which we found little precedent to guide us. It was clear that the best guarantee of artful realism lay not in fictions invented by us but in stories drawn from the living experience of people long ignored by Hollywood—the working men and women of America.

And so we searched for stories that would reflect the true stature of union men and women. We dug into material dealing with minority peoples, because we believed that where greater struggle is necessary, greater genius is developed. We looked for material that might record something of the dynamic quality women are bringing to our social scene.

Salt of the Earth, originally the third project on our schedule, seemed the best embodiment of the elements for which we had been striving. A true account of the miners of the Southwest and their families, predominantly Mexican-Americans, begged to be told without the hackneyed melodramatics which so often destroy honesty in the name of excitement. It was not the many abuses and hardships

From *The California Quarterly* (1953). Reprinted by permission.

suffered by these people that loomed so significantly out of the material—it was their humanity, their courage and accomplishment. We decided that these Americans, at once typical and exceptional, could best be realized on the screen by the simplest story form of motion picture: a love story of two mature and decent people.

Michael Wilson, author of the story, had come to know these New Mexico miners during a long and bitter strike they waged against a powerful zinc company in 1951 and 1952. The story idea was born out of his first visit there, and he then wrote an extended outline, or, in movie parlance, a treatment of the story. Mr. Wilson returned to the mining community with this treatment, where it was read, discussed and criticized by a score of miners and their wives. With this guidance in authenticity he proceeded to write the first draft screenplay. When it was completed, again we followed the procedure of group discussion and collective, constructive criticism. By rough estimate, no less than four hundred people had read, or heard a reading of, the screenplay by the time we commenced production.

Perhaps it was our determination that the people in this film be life-size that led to our second decision. We asked the miners and their families to play themselves rather than be enacted by others.

These decisions brought the writer, director, crew and cast face to face with intricate problems of realistic form and content. How could we by-pass the pitfall of naturalism—a mere surface record of actual events—and emerge with an imaginative work of art that was still true in detail? How could we best blend the social authenticity of documentary form with the personal authenticity of dramatic form? What range of characterization should be given individual roles whose enactment would be undertaken by non-professionals? How could we capture the quality of speech of these bi-lingual people and yet make the picture completely intelligible to an average English-speaking audience? How could we make the amazing heroism of these people not only stirring, but *believable* and *inevitable*?

This last problem was particularly important to us, because only if we solved it could our picture help engender in an audience a belief in its own capacities, a confidence that what these people had done could be done again. We hoped that our film might become a cultural stimulus to other trade unions and minority groups, and convince them that they could tell their own stories through the medium of film. High hopes! And vast problems. Certainly we cannot boast of having solved all these aesthetic questions. But we do think we have broken new ground. If our film can illuminate the truth that the lives and struggles of ordinary people are the richest untapped source of contemporary American art, and if it can demonstrate that such films can be made by these people themselves, then it will have achieved a basic purpose.

II

It is against this background of intention and dedication that the attacks upon this picture during the course of production must be seen. We had been shooting *Salt of the Earth* since January 20th, Inauguration Day. The production was sponsored by the International Union of Mine, Mill and Smelter Workers, and our cast included hundreds of its members and their families. Even after a storm of hysterical publicity burst over us, thousands of our neighbors and associates in the Silver City area assumed we had a right to be there.

A false assumption, said Congressman Donald Jackson. On February 24th, this California Representative delivered a speech in the halls of Congress, in which he said:

> . . . Mr. Speaker, I have received reports of the sequences filmed to date . . . This picture is deliberately designed to inflame racial hatreds . . . [It] is a new weapon for Russia. For instance, in one sequence, two deputy sheriffs arrest a meek American miner of Mexican descent and proceed to pistol whip the miner's very young son. [They] also imported two auto carloads of colored people for the purpose of shooting a scene depicting mob violence.

As a direct result of Congressman Jackson's speech, our leading lady was arrested, members of our cast and crew were physically assaulted, and a vigilante committee warned us to leave "within twelve hours or be carried out in black boxes." We defied the deadline, demanding and receiving the protection of the New Mexico State police, and finished our work on March 6th. After we did depart, however, and the protective police as well, the attacks on our Mine-Mill brothers and sisters continued. Two union halls were set afire, one of them burning to the ground. Also razed by arson was the home of a union leader, Floyd Bostock, who had played a role in the film. His three young children narrowly escaped the flames.

Without reading the script, or asking to, without seeing the film, or waiting to, an incendiary Congressman had spoken.

His fury can be understood only if one recognizes how unprecedented it was for manual workers and cultural workers of our country to collaborate, and what promise for a more truly democratic future such a collaboration holds. In organizing for independent production, we had one basic aim: to place the talents of the blacklisted (both those who had worked in films and those who had never been given the opportunity) at the service of ordinary people. There were indeed Negroes in this production: an assistant to the director, an assistant cameraman and two technicians—all in categories of work never available to Negroes in Hollywood.

Simon Lazarus, a respected motion picture exhibitor, had formed Independent Productions Corporation to back us. Money was borrowed from liberal Americans, it being understood that none of us who wrote, directed or produced the film would receive any remuneration until the loans were repaid.

In the wake of the Silver City storm, Mr. Lazarus was himself hailed before the Un-American Activities Committee and asked to divulge who the backers were. He refused to answer personal questions and thus could not be forced to inform on others. He did, however, volunteer to tell the Committee what our film was about. But the investigators were not interested. They did not want to investigate, but to prejudge and censor.

The efforts to prevent *Salt of the Earth* from being made

began long before the spectacular assaults in Silver City, and continued long after our location shooting was completed.

Consider, as a pre-production problem, a crew. In Hollywood, most motion picture technicians belong to the International Alliance of Theatrical and Stage Employees (AFL). West coast head of the IATSE is Roy M. Brewer, who inherited his protectorate over Hollywood labor from two gangsters, William Bioff and George E. Browne. A zealous adherent of Congressional witch-hunters, Brewer has understood that his civic responsibility to enforce the blacklist goes far beyond his trade union responsibility to see that his men get jobs. That, no doubt, is why he refused to let us hire an IATSE crew. As a trade paper reported it later:

> Simon Lazarus, named as prexy of the company approached Roy M. Brewer, the chairman of the AFL Film Council, about nine months ago, seeking assurance from him that he could make a motion picture using the 'Unfriendly Ten.' Brewer yesterday recalled he flatly told Lazarus he would prevent such a project in every legal way possible.—*Daily Variety,* February 25, 1953

"Legal" was an afterthought. What Brewer said was that he would see us in hell first.

We gathered a union crew despite Roy Brewer. Some were members of his own IATSE. Some had been expelled from the IATSE for opposing Brewer's rule. Three were Negroes, denied membership in the IATSE because of its Jim Crow policies. Every member of our crew carried a union card.

As for post-production problems, the would-be censors of the picture have tried to sabotage it in every way. They have demanded that all laboratories close their doors to us, warned technicians not to help us—lest they find themselves blacklisted. Failing here, we expect they will extend their intimidation to film exhibitors when the picture is ready for release. Meanwhile Congressman Jackson has been needling the Departments of State and Commerce to find some obscure statute which might forbid the export of this picture. No such statute exists, but we would be naive to think that the legality of our endeavor will give the bigots pause.

III

Will the film be shown? We have no illusions about the fight that lies ahead. Of this we are certain—the harassment will continue, and we will need many allies to defeat the censors and saboteurs. Naturally, the degree of support we eventually get will depend on the end product—the finished film. If trade unionists someday discover that this picture is the first feature film ever made in this country which is of labor, by labor and for labor; if minority peoples come to see in it a film that does not tolerate minorities but celebrates their greatness; if men and women together find in it some new recognition of the worth and dignity of a working class woman—then this audience, these judges, will find ways of overcoming the harassment.

But to reach these judges, we must first get past the *prejudgers.* To reach these eventual allies, we need immediate allies—for whether the people are to praise this film or damn it, they must first have the right to see it. That is why we appeal to everyone who is morally concerned with free communication to help provide the atmosphere and the place in which *Salt of the Earth* can be shown and judged on its own merits.

Blacklisted screenwriter Michael Wilson (1915–1978) wrote the script of Salt of the Earth. Although corporate Hollywood, as the Guardian's Los Angeles bureau noted, April 26, 1978, successfully prevented its commercial distribution in the USA for many years (between 1953 and 1963), it was Wilson's brilliant scenario about a strike struggle of Mexican-American zinc workers, in which the "key to victory" was a fight against racism and male supremacy, that ultimately catapulted the film to worldwide fame. Today, Salt of the Earth is widely acknowledged as an American film classic, one that celebrates, beyond anything in the past, the greatness of minorities. But it is not the only Wilson screenplay that shook up the commercial film industry during the McCarthy era.

Wilson also authored the script of the 1956 Allied Artists/ William Wyler-directed film, Friendly Persuasion, which has also earned its place in film history, and not only because it *stands as the only major Hollywood film ever released without a credit line to the screen writer. Wilson's name was rubbed out by the producer in 1957 when his script for Friendly Persuasion, written in 1947, was nominated for an Academy Award. In frightened anticipation of the nomination, the Academy of Motion Picture Arts and Sciences adopted a special bylaw (rescinded two years later following protests) barring an award to any screen artist whose name was on a blacklist. (New York Times, April 9, 1978). The producer thereupon sought to credit others for work on the screenplay. But when Wilson appealed to the Writers Guild, and a panel set up to arbitrate the dispute decided unanimously in his favor, Allied Artists chose to credit no one for the screenplay.*

President Reagan added a bit of excitement to this wondrous tale in June, 1988 when he surprised everyone by hailing Friendly Persuasion as an "American Classic" during his Kremlin dinner toast to Gorbachev, saying that this story about a Quaker colony's struggle with problems of war, pacifism, patriotism and love of peace, was an example of what the Summit was all about. It was a very good choice for the occasion. Understandingly, Reagan did not inform his hosts that it was scripted by a blacklisted writer. Perhaps he didn't know, or simply "forgot to remember" that untidy bit of film history which he himself contributed to, when as President of the Screen Actors Guild he doubled as an enforcer of the blacklist. As The Nation pointed out editorially in its June 11, 1988 issue, ". . . Here was Reagan in the heart of the 'evil empire' lecturing his hosts on human rights yet never acknowledging that the suppression of American dissidents in Hollywood in the fifties launched him on the political career that enabled him to go to Moscow and deplore the suppression of Soviet dissidents in the eighties." (DP)

55   *SALT OF THE EARTH*

Peter Morris

I T TOOK COURAGE TO MAKE such a film as *Salt of the Earth* in 1953. This was the heyday of McCarthy and the film makers who produced it were blacklisted in Hollywood. The union which sponsored it had been expelled from the CIO in 1950 for alleged Communist domination. The film itself dealt with so-called "sensitive" issues: racial inequality, the labor-capital conflict and the struggle by women for equal rights with men. Given the hysterical "Red scare" mood of the times, it is hardly surprising that it met unprecedented hostility in North America, accusations of "Communist propaganda" and effective boycott of its theatrical release. Pauline Kael described it as "extremely shrewd propaganda for the urgent business of the USSR." Representative Donald Jackson, Republican from California, spent twenty minutes in Congress attacking the film, declaring his intention to "do everything in my power to prevent it being shown at home or abroad." Members of the Projectionists' Union were forbidden to run the film. However, in total contrast, *Salt of the Earth* was a great success in France. *Cahiers du cinéma* described it as "by far the best film made in the USA in the past ten years." Others hailed it as a "human document" and it received an award for the Best Film Exhibited in 1955.

Quite simply, *Salt of the Earth* depicts the struggle for equality by Mexican-American zinc workers and their

This formerly unpublished essay, written in 1976, appears here by permission of the author. © 1990 by Peter Morris.

wives—the men for equality of working and living conditions with white "Anglo" miners and the women for equality with men. The story was derived, broadly, from the events of the 1951–52 strike by members of Local 890, International Union of Mine, Mill and Smelter Workers against Empire Zinc of Silver City, New Mexico. Responsible for initiating and guiding its production were four one-time Hollywood film makers, now blacklisted after being pilloried by the House Un-American Activities Committee: Herbert Biberman, Paul Jarrico, Michael Wilson and Sol Kaplan. The film's director and prime mover, Herbert Biberman, had been one of the founders of the Screen Directors' Guild. He was one of the original "Hollywood Ten" who served a jail sentence in 1950 for "contempt of Congress" and has been described by Alvah Bessie, another of the Hollywood Ten, as "a man who would die in pieces for what he believes." Michael Wilson, scriptwriter, had won a 1951 Oscar for his script for A Place in the Sun and was later one of the first to break through the blacklist when he wrote Friendly Persuasion and The Bridge on the River Kwai. Paul Jarrico, producer, had written the scripts for Song of Russia (one of HUAC's favourite hates and a film Louis B. Mayer later attempted to destroy) and Zinnemann's Oscar-winning The Search.

But though these men were responsible for the principal creative thrust behind Salt of the Earth, it was very much a cooperative production that grew out of the events and the people themselves. Michael Wilson wrote the story only after several visits to the strike-bound area. And by the time actual shooting began no less than four hundred people had read, or heard a reading of, the screenplay. Juan Chacon, the Union Local's president in real life and in the film, said that a production committee had "the responsibility of ensuring that our picture ran true to life from start to finish. Salt of the Earth was not intended as a documentary record of that particular strike but . . . it is a true account of our people's lives and struggles." Only five professional actors were used—and only one of those played a Mexican-American role. All other parts were played by actual miners and their wives. Among the professional actors were blacklisted Will Geer, who played the Sheriff in characteristically sinister fashion, and

Rosaura Revueltas, an actress of great fame in her native Mexico, who played the wife of the Union president. The story is simple enough. The Mexican-American miners working for the Delaware Zinc Corporation in Zinc Town bitterly resent the company's policy of discrimination which results in the "Anglo" miners being provided with better wages and working conditions. Inadequate safety precautions in the mine lead to an accident and the miners decide to strike for equality with the "Anglos." Despite bitter opposition from their husbands, the miners' wives set up a Ladies Auxiliary to add their demands for plumbing in the huts on company premises to the strikers' grievances. Esperanza, the wife of the Union president, Ramon, leads the women and Ramon particularly resents his wife's independent action. The company refuses to negotiate and gets a court injunction to prevent the miners from picketing. To save the strike, the women take over the picket line and hold it despite taunts, tear gas and violence. The leaders of the women—including Esperanza, who is pregnant—are arrested and thrown in jail. But they make such a nuisance of themselves that the authorities are glad to release them. Esperanza immediately calls a meeting of the women and she and Ramon quarrel bitterly over her "independence." Further attempts are made to break the strike. Ramon is savagely beaten. Company officials refuse to send the company doctor when Esperanza's baby is born. Later, police arrive with an eviction order but are driven away by the presence of a sullen, angry crowd of miners. However, other unions come to the support of the strikers with gifts of money and food and, finally, the company is forced to capitulate.

It is a rough, tough story which draws the lines of battle sharply and brooks no quarter. Its theme is clear: the miners' (and the wives') refusal to compromise their principles leads to final victory. But this simple, humanistic conviction (one hardly exclusive to Communism) fomented an hysterical opposition during the production that is unprecedented in American cinema. There was initial difficulty to forming a technical crew because the SMPTE refused to let its members work on the film. Howard Hughes, then head of RKO, led a campaign to block its production and release. The FBI brought their own, rather special, kinds of pressure to bear. Rosaura Revueltas was detained at the border and later deported to Mexico for illegally entering the United States. When exterior scenes were being filmed in Silver City, the townspeople threatened to send the "subversive" movie makers out of town in "little black boxes." The camera crew was assaulted by fifty men. Juan Chacon was personally attacked twice. The state police patrolled the streets, ostensibly to maintain order. One had to be not only brave in spirit to make such a film during the McCarthy era, one had to have physical courage too.

Similar repressions continued after the film was completed. Projectionists were ordered not to show it under pain of expulsion from their union. Finally, a total boycott was imposed by all "right-thinking" organizations, a boycott led by Hollywood itself. After brief runs in New York and Toronto, *Salt of the Earth* disappeared from the theatrical circuits and surfaced occasionally only in film societies and quasi-secret union showings. Perhaps the bitterest attacks on the film came from those who considered themselves the staunchest liberals—as if to prove that, though liberal, they were not tainted by the Marxist brush. Pauline Kael's reactions are typical of many. Condemning it as a "popular front morality play," she castigated its "pedagogical tone, so reminiscent of the thirties," and indirectly supported the blacklist by avoiding naming Biberman and his colleagues whom she described only as "fellow travellers." In a benighted piece of self-deception she claimed that "socially, economically and legally the United States has been expiating its sins against minorities in record time" and wondered why the film makers did not present "a look at the life of the integrated as well as the un-integrated minorities." She concluded the film was "ridiculously and patently false," nothing less than gross propaganda. Perhaps surprisingly, the important theme of women's liberation totally escaped her.

Salt of the Earth is not, indeed, a "balanced" film. It is unequivocal. It is concerned not with presenting both sides of the issue but only with the way the miners themselves saw the situation. Biberman and his colleagues were well aware that all art (particularly a commercialized art like the movies) is ideologically conditioned, that the Hollywood cinema had inevitably reflected the ideology of those who controlled it economically. They wanted to ensure that the people who had never had a voice should be given it. As Biberman and Jarrico said: "We have tried to picture a minority from its own point of view. We have tried to picture women as the heroic equal of men. . . . If the film can illuminate the truth that the lives and struggles of ordinary people are the richest source of contemporary American art, and if it can demonstrate that such films can be made only with the help of the people themselves, then it will have achieved its basic purpose."

Viewed recently, *Salt of the Earth* has lost none of its original power. In fact, it seems stronger, particularly when compared to more modern films (such as those of Costa-Gavras) which have used political commitment as a publicity gimmick. Its honesty, integrity and sincerity are still beyond criticism, but what seemed like a certain Manichaeism in its theme twenty years ago has softened in the light of later events and no longer appears quite so schematic. John Howard Lawson has noted that *Salt of the Earth* has been honored for its integrity but has not yet received its due recognition as a work of art. He is right. Most film histories—with the notable exception of the French—simply ignore it. Yet its lean and angry air remains emotionally affective. The avoidance of studio sets and make-up and the use of the people themselves to act out their own lives helps create an always authentic and persuasive portrait of a situation both particular and general. Its stark visual style presents unforgettable images: the cold comfort of the homes, the cheerless atmosphere of the surrounding countryside, the poignant faces of the children. Rosaura Revueltas gives an intensely moving performance but it is the non-professionals, the miners themselves, who are most memorable; they are more convincing than trained actors could ever be. Juan Chacon, in particular, is unforgettable.

In all this there is more than a hint of the influence of Italian neo-realism. And in fact, in both theme and style, *Salt of the Earth* could be described as the first—if not the only—American film to participate in the neo-realist movement. If it did not exactly herald a new spring for American cinema (as

Rome, Open City had for the Italian) it did influence some film makers and encouraged them (as John Howard Lawson noted) "to deepen the content of their work."

The dramatic pivot of the film is the meeting of the women and the fierce quarrel between Ramon and Esperanza over her "independence." And, indeed, much of the film's continuing power stems from the struggle by the women for equality with the men who consider them capable of no more than looking after their homes and children. Ramon, too, must learn that the women's struggle for their own liberation is as necessary and worthy as that he and his colleagues are waging. In 1953, this theme was consistently ignored by the critics; now it gives the film an almost fashionable air. But in this theme—as in the miners' struggle for their rights—there is reflected a personal gesture of faith by Herbert Biberman: the necessity of maintaining one's principles despite the most savage opposition. *Salt of the Earth,* humanistic, political and compassionate though it is, in the end is also a personal film, a film by a man who would "die in pieces for his beliefs."

56   "DO NOT FORGIVE THEM, FOR THEY KNOW WHAT THEY DO"

Gale Sondergaard

I HAVE BEEN A WORKING ACTRESS practically all my life—if you will permit me not to count the first eighteen years—and the last two. I have views on many subjects—I have convictions—political convictions, but I am basically an actress.

If you were to ask me what kind of time 1938 was—as compared with 1950—I might not remember the political events, but I would remember that in 1938 I played the wife of Alfred Dreyfus in the picture *The Life of Emile Zola.* And I would think of the year 1938 as a time in which we were allowed to make a picture dealing with a great champion of social justice like Emile Zola—of an unbending victim of military arrogance and bigotry like Alfred Dreyfus. And I would conclude that there was vitality in a time in which an actress could play a courageous and embattled wife of a courageous and embattled man upon the screen.

Today I bring the same emotion and the same imagination to the same role—only now it is played upon a very real stage—and I am playing the role today, not for a living, not for an Academy Award—but for the preservation of my family, even as Mrs. Dreyfus.

I chose to play Mrs. Dreyfus. I enjoyed playing her. I did not choose to play this role today, and I do not enjoy it. But

Address delivered at a rally in Hollywood, April 21, 1950. Reprinted by permission of the author.

having to play it, I will play it with all the initiative and tenacity
and effectiveness I can command.

At Zola's funeral you will remember that Anatole France
(played in the film so beautifully by Morris Carnovsky) said of
Zola that he was a moment in the conscience of mankind. I
do not hesitate to say that long after the name of Eric
Johnston, collaborator with Parnell Thomas and Senator
Mundt in forging implements of mental slavery for our
country, has ceased to be remembered even as a name—
long after the quiet ones in our community, who fear to
interrupt the stultification of our medium, have withered into
the oblivion they deserve—The Ten men of Hollywood will
be known as part of the conscience of the American artist in
a very black cultural moment in American history. And I
believe that all the rest of us will be remembered as we stand
forth—and only if we stand forth—to save the conscience of
our community and our profession from the censor, the bigot
and the coward.

I believe these men, "these beloved Ten" as they were
named by Rabbi Franklin Cohn at a Passover ceremony in
which I participated, have cut their names into the real rock
upon which this community stands. Censors and bigots may
use their temporary power to remove these men from us for
a time—but they cannot erase their contribution to the dignity
and decency of our medium and our community.

I still find it difficult to believe that these men may actually
be taken forcibly from us. But I have come to understand that
I had better believe it. The uglier the fact, the less can we
afford to ignore it. If this shameful thing happens—then I will
say of those who caused it—*do not forgive them—for they
know what they do.*

I confess to fear of the callous and the arrogant who
walk—who run across our land today. But I have an even
greater fear—that by inaction we deliver this lovely land and
its people into their hands—the hands of thieves, inquisitors
and non-interfering courts.

As a wife, a mother, an actress, a citizen—as the daughter
of Danish parents who came here to build more liberty—as
the daughter-in-law of my husband's Russian-Jewish parents who came here to build more liberty—as an American
who reverences the great moments of American conscience

and humanity—I accept my present role with conviction that none of us is alone—that the forces do exist which can prevent our America from being taken away from us and frozen into the ugly image of the year 1950. Yes, I believe more fearlessly than I fear.

Do you nod your heads and say to yourselves, "all that is wishful thinking—I don't blame her but let's face it—she's whistling into the wind?"

Then you are wrong—

I recall a story of a young antifascist thrown before a Nazi firing squad. He looked at the assassins before him and laughed—not with bravado but because he couldn't help it. "You think you are killing something when you shoot me," he said. "You are wrong. You are giving birth to a hundred who will take my place." He opened his shirt and called to them "Shoot and destroy yourselves."

He was not wrong. I am not wrong. The fight for our men of Hollywood is a fight against the cultural, social and political assassins in our time. And we—who have gathered together to participate in only one stage of that fight may well cry out our warning: *Take these men from us and you will further expose and destroy yourselves!*

57 LETTERS ON THE HOLLYWOOD BLACKLIST

Dalton Trumbo

1. LETTER TO WILLIAM FAULKNER

Los Angeles, California
January 24, 1957

Dear Mr. Faulkner:

In the autumn of 1947, after a series of hearings by the House Committee on Un-American Activities, a blacklist was established in the American motion picture industry. During the nine years that have ensued over three hundred writers, directors, actors, musicians, artists, and technicians have been driven from their profession and denied passports that would enable them to work in other countries.

Those who remain in motion pictures work under the surveillance of private pressure groups, a permanent Hollywood representative of the Committee, and a system of clearances which certify them to be patriotic American artists. The blacklist, once thought to be a temporary reflection of troubled times, has become institutionalized. Motion pictures, policed and censored by Federal authority, have become official art.

Will you, as an American writer whose work has been transferred to the screen—perhaps by some of those same persons in whose behalf I make this request—send me a statement condemning the Hollywood blacklist? And will you permit me to release your statement to the press as I see fit in still another effort to destroy this hateful business before it overwhelms us altogether?*

Sincerely,

Dalton Trumbo

2. EXCERPT OF LETTER TO SAM SILLEN

The Screen Writers' Guild achieved recognition during the great struggles of the thirties.** It was precisely during this period that motion pictures underwent a sharp decline in the use of reactionary themes, in the slander of minority groups and in general vilification of organized labor. The organized writers of Hollywood contributed very greatly to this improvement, but it would be a mistake to assume that they accomplished it alone. Their rising prestige—and with it their rising influence over the content of films—corresponded to the great upsurge of the CIO, the general organizational advance of workers all over the country, the developing struggle against fascism and the confirmation of labor rights by federal legislation. Hollywood writers, by participating in

---

*The same letter was sent to A. B. Guthrie, Ernest Hemingway, William Saroyan, John Steinbeck, Thornton Wilder, and Tennessee Williams. Trumbo did not receive a single reply.

**Trumbo refers to the 1936 conflict between the Screen Writers' Guild and the Screen Playwrights, Inc. The studios in violent opposition to the liberal Guild formed the Playwrights, a company union, recognized by the producers as the representative body of all screen writers in spite of the fact that the Screen Playwrights numbered approximately one hundred in contrast to the six or seven hundred members of the Screen Writers' Guild. Unable to withstand the power of the producers, the ranks of the Guild dwindled to some thirty members, of which Trumbo was one. As has already been mentioned, the Guild later reformed and regained its former influence.

the general struggle for social advancement, achieved greater effectiveness for their art as a weapon. They achieved it not as talented Galahads jousting individually, but as organized industrial workers.

A second forward move in screen content came with the war. Here again it was the tremendous mass pressure of the anti-fascist masses of the world, the direct intervention of the federal government through the OWI [Office of War Information] and affiliated agencies, and the formation by writers themselves of the Hollywood Writers' Mobilization, which caused motion pictures—temporarily at least—to give voice to the democratic aspirations of the great coalition. Without the war, without the tremendous upsurge of anti-fascist feeling that came with it, no writer—even the most talented— would have had the opportunities then made available to him to affect so decisively the social content of the screen.

Many of Hollywood's war films were superficial, uncritical and frankly opportunistic. A few were deeply searching in their implications and in their contribution to the morale of the embattled democracies. Symbols of racial, political, economic and religious prejudice practically vanished from the screen. But something else, something significant, also happened: sustained by the tremendous anti-fascist feelings of the great masses of people, a few motion pictures went over to the offensive. In such films as *Confessions of a Nazi Spy, Joe Smith, American, Watch on the Rhine, Sahara, The Great Dictator* and *Action in the North Atlantic,* screen writers took the point of view that it was much more desirable and honorable and dramatic to attack evil than simply to refrain from evil. A fundamental change of viewpoint was involved in this process; and since it occurred under the impact of one historical phase of the war against fascism, there is no reason to believe that it cannot develop and deepen in the succeeding phase of that same war.

3. Excerpt of Letter to Edward Stevens

Of the original 19 witnesses who were called before the first committee hearings in 1947, there were some who were not Communists, and some who had never been Communists. It is also my recollection of these hearings that when they became nasty and most violative of individual rights, Mr. N[ixon] absented himself from them, and it was generally taken as evidence of his disesteem for the chairman's methods.

As for the present day, eleven years later, I doubt that there are five members of the Communist Party left in all of Hollywood. Most blacklistees have been out of the party for years. Some of them have become conservatives, some have become democrats, and some have maintained a generally socialist point of view. But to the last man they cannot in conscience admit the right of any legislative committee to judge their loyalty. Beyond this, they view a forced confession of former guilt or stupidity as no different in principle from the public confessions that have characterized Russian justice, or the brainwashing that is charged to the Chinese. For this reason, and this reason only, scores of them have kept silent and suffered the consequences.

I do think there are very very strong arguments against the blacklist in terms of the industry's present need and its international relations—and I have taken the liberty of setting down a few notes, in a style which I hope is cool enough and detached enough that they might be left in the possession of Mr. N[ixon] without compromising the person who turned them over to him. I do hope he [the "friend"] can at least see them before he takes off.

Best,

Sam*

ENGLAND

A number of blacklisted Hollywood persons migrated to London, where British motion picture unions intervened in their behalf for the procurement of residential status and work permits. Prominent members of the British film industry

---

*Sam Jackson was Trumbo's favorite pseudonym during the *Spartacus* project.

cooperated in finding jobs for them, and openly expressed sympathy for them. Inherent in such sympathy was a thinly veiled anti-American attitude which the existence of an American blacklist permitted them to disseminate. Certain specific cases have been widely publicized:

1. Carl Foreman. Foreman was blacklisted five or six years ago after having written such films as *The Champion* and *High Noon.* He moved to London, where he worked steadily under various pseudonyms in the British film industry. His true identity and the reasons for his residence in England were known and widely commented on. He worked directly with leading British film personalities. His connection with *Bridge on the River Kwai,* one of the most successful American-produced films in recent years, has been the subject of much comment in the British press. As lately as May 15 of this year it occasioned an article in *The Reporter,* an American magazine published in New York City.

2. Donald Ogden Stewart. One of the most prominent of American screenwriters, Stewart also took up residence in London after being blacklisted. Like Foreman, he has won wide acceptance in film and theatrical circles there. He has worked openly with the British industry, although the problem of American release compelled him to use pseudonyms. He presently has a successful play running in the West End under his own name. The British press has not failed to point out that he is a man who cannot use his name in his native America.

There are numerous other blacklisted Americans working in British films, theatre and television; wherever an American motion picture personality goes in London he is subject to politely satirical remarks about his blacklisting homeland. . . .

FRANCE

Jules Dassin. A blacklisted director, Dassin took up residence in Paris. There, under his own name, he directed an immensely successful film entitled *Rififi.* In addition to making everyone associated with it rich, the film won numerous European prizes, as have subsequent Dassin productions. He has become an ornament to the world of the

French cinema, and his films are regarded as representative not of American but of French art and culture.

Rififi enjoyed great success even in the United States, with Dassin's name prominently on the screen. American producers who saw the film were made uncomfortably aware of a talent which produced both profits and honors for the French film industry, yet which could not be used in the American. The Dassin case is regularly cited in French intellectual circles as a criticism of American democracy.

Michael Wilson. Wilson is the blacklisted author of the Academy winning film, *A Place in the Sun,* and of the more recent *Friendly Persuasion.* Having been blacklisted in the early fifties, his name was removed from the latter film. Meanwhile, he had taken up residence in Paris. When *Friendly Persuasion* was honored at the Cannes festival, Wilson's authorship of the film and his lack of credit for it drew scathing and overtly anti-American notices from the French press. At a formal ball in Paris honoring festival winners, Wilson was given a place in the central box, where he was deliberately seated beside Europe's most widely publicized actress.

The enormous success of *Bridge on the River Kwai,* and the gossip in international film circles that its script was written by two blacklisted Americans (Foreman and Wilson) burst into the open during the 1958 Academy award season. For a full week the American blacklist was front page news in metropolitan newspapers throughout Europe, as well as in America, where the film editor of *The Los Angeles Times* took occasion to devote a good deal of space to the matter. Wilson made no comment to the press in Paris, and is understood to have foiled a scheme by friendly French journalists to reveal the truth of the matter. . . .*

ITALY

The most important film producers in Italy are now availing themselves of blacklisted American writing talent. This is

---

*Michael Wilson's most recent film was *Planet of the Apes,* written under his own name. The film was enormously successful.

perfectly open, and occasions a good deal of cynical comment in Italian intellectual circles. It was commonly known throughout the Italian industry that *Summertime,* an English production filmed in Venice which won numerous European prizes, was written by Donald Ogden Stewart, although other names appeared on it.

LATIN-AMERICA

Blacklisted American talent has now become integrated into the Mexican film industry. Many Mexican films are financed by the government itself, and officials are perfectly aware of the past histories of those Americans whom they employ. Two Mexican films involving blacklisted American talent have won high honors for Mexico in various European film festivals. Mexican film circles openly deride the United States for its blacklist of film personalities, and the derision fortifies Mexican nationalism at the expense of Mexican-American friendship.

One of the most successful American films ever released in Latin America was *The Brave One,* which dealt with a Mexican boy and a fighting bull. In Mexico City the crowds on its first day were so great that the pressure of people waiting for the theatre to open broke down the glass doors [leading into] the lobby. In Caracas the film broke all existing records, with the exception of one film starring Cantinflas several years ago. It was exuberantly praised by critics throughout South America as a warm and friendly portrayal of Mexican life.

Yet its reception was clouded by the world-wide publicity given to the fact that when the Academy voted an award to its author, one Robert Rich, no one could be found to claim the honor. Press speculation that the missing Robert Rich was in fact a blacklisted writer led reporters in Los Angeles, New York, Mexico City, London and Paris to a series of inquiring interviews with blacklisted persons resident in each city, and their interviews received world coverage.

The unfortunate part of the blacklist is that it arouses adverse feelings in every country among the very persons who have direct access to the press and public opinion, persons who because of their profession actually create public opinion. Thus a correspondent for *Excelsior* in Mexico City, mocking what he called American "cultural values" wrote that the vulgar content of most American films, in contrast to that of *The Brave One,* should be attributed to the fact that in Hollywood ". . . the talent of writing a political oath is more demanded than a talent of writing thoughtful films." The Paris edition of the New York *Herald Tribune* reprinted an editorial which originally appeared in the Louisville *Courier-Journal.* . . .* This kind of press is always bad.

THE MOTION PICTURE ACADEMY

During the 1957 award ceremonies, the Academy was ridiculed throughout the world because Michael Wilson's name was removed from *Friendly Persuasion,* and because the unknown Robert Rich would not come forward to accept his award for *The Brave One.* In 1958 scandal again gathered about the award given to Pierre Bouille for the screenplay of *Bridge on the River Kwai,* since it was internationally accepted that Foreman and Wilson had actually written the script. The reaction in Paris, where M. Bouille is highly regarded, was particularly unfortunate. There is no assurance that similar disasters will not attend future Academy presentations.

Academy night is probably the most widely publicized cultural event in the world. It is also uniquely American. A situation that brings it into disrepute year after year is greatly damaging to American prestige. The blacklist, which other nations use as an excuse for anti-American propaganda, is not good for the Academy, nor for the troubled American motion picture industry, nor for our government, which detractors of America invariably blame for it.

The existence of the blacklist also jeopardizes the possibility of holding an international film festival in this country. In addition to the fact that there is a certain reticence on the part of European artists to compete for honors in a country where all artists are not permitted an equal chance to compete,

---

*Trumbo attached copies of the reference articles to his notes.

there is the further possibility that winning films may turn up with no visible authors, and that this will increasingly publicize the blacklist, thus destroying every advantage the festival could have brought to the country, and opening the American film industry to further caustic comment from abroad.

THE AMERICAN MOTION PICTURE INDUSTRY

The industry has for three long years been in a state of economic crisis. Its public relations throughout the world are a matter of first importance to it. Hollywood cannot exist without its world market. The films which it sends out to the world are, or ought to be, ambassadors of American good will toward the world. Yet its own blacklisting casts doubt upon its good intentions. Its necessary dealings with European producers and studios are greatly complicated by the blacklist. It is constantly plagued abroad by the embarrassing question of whether American democracy is for all or just for some. On the other hand, it is engaged in a bitter struggle with the film industries of other nations for a fair share of the world market. Under such circumstances it is unfortunate that many of the most successful foreign films presently competing with it for that market are now written or directed by blacklisted persons whose talents may not be used by the American industry that first discovered and developed them.

PART V

THE 1960s AND 1970s

58   STANLEY KUBRICK'S *DR. STRANGELOVE* (1964)

David Platt

TWO EXTREMELY IMPORTANT and popular Hollywood films, both dealing with aspects of survival in the nuclear age, are in effect restoring a measure of confidence in a shaky film industry.

Stanley Kubrick's *Dr. Strangelove or: How I Learned to Stop Worrying and Love the Bomb* brilliantly satirizes the idiocy of the arms race.

John Frankenheimer's *Seven Days in May* is a chilling story of a Pentagon plot, in 1974, to overthrow the U.S. government and tear up the nuclear disarmament pact just signed by Washington and Moscow.

Both films are extraordinarily frank about the monumental lunacy of the military mind. Both indicate that this insanity is rooted in the crackpot ideas of the right wing which infect the U.S. military machine.

In *Seven Days in May* no less a personage than the chairman of the Joint Chiefs of Staff, the nation's highest ranking military officer, is shown working with rightist groups for the destruction of constitutional and democratic government. Gen. Scott, minus Burt Lancaster's good looks, appears to be modelled after Gen. Walker. He also recalls Admiral Radford, a former chairman of the Joint Chiefs, who once told a congressional committee that "Red China had to be destroyed even if it required a 50 year war." He failed to add, "and 50 million dead Americans." One of Gen. Scott's

From *Jewish Currents* (May, 1964) ©. Reprinted by permission.

closest pals in treason is an officer identified as "an out-and-out fascist."

In *Dr. Strangelove,* a psychotic U.S. air force general (he believes the Birchers' propaganda that the communists are poisoning the country's lakes, rivers and sea with fluorides, thus sapping and contaminating "all our natural bodily fluids"), orders his airborne nuclear bombers not to return from their test flight but to proceed eastward and destroy the USSR.

The suspense and the satire derive from the knowledge that the Russians have a doomsday bomb set to go off automatically when Soviet soil is violated, from the frenzied efforts to call the planes back before doomsday begins, from the frantic phone calls to Moscow to explain that the flight was unauthorized and to express regret, and last but not least from the massive stupidity of the brass.

George Scott, one of America's most creative actors, portrays a fun-loving, trigger-happy, communist hating general that is the concentrated essence of military folly. One of the three roles played by the versatile Peter Sellers is a Pentagon weapons specialist, an ex-Nazi who cannot resist raising his withered right hand, shaped like an iron claw, in a menacing Hitler salute. Slim Pickens is a Texas Confederate flag-waving super-patriot. The pilot of one of the death ships, he solemnly assures his mixed crew that when the bomb is dropped they can all expect decorations "regardless of race, color or creed."

The impact of this grim humor is quite terrifying at times because we know that in real life panic buttons have been pressed when nothing more significant than a flock of geese has crossed the radar screens. Much of the satire in *Dr. Stranglove* is in the vein of Swift's "A Modest Proposal for Preventing the Children of the Poor of Ireland from Being a Burden," in which the great writer revealed the terrible suffering in Ireland by ironically suggesting that the poor should bring up children for no other purpose than to be killed and eaten. Not since Chaplin's *The Great Dictator* have we had such incisive criticism of the makers of war, and such deep laughter at their expense.

Lewis Mumford, in a letter to the *New York Times* March 1 rightly hailed *Dr. Strangelove* as the "first break in the cold war trance that has so long held our country in its rigid group," but in other influential quarters the film has been under violent attack. Chalmers Roberts, National Editor of the *Washington Post,* whose column, according to *Variety* Feb. 26, is "a favorite repository of State Department leaks," condemned the film as capable of causing the U.S. "as much harm as many a coup or revolution." "No communist," he said, "could dream of a more effective anti-American film to spread abroad than this one. U.S. officials, including the President, had better take a look at this one to see its effect on the national interest."

The national interest seems to be pretty well protected at the box office, where house records of long standing are being broken by audiences which undoubtedly share the opinion of Loudon Wainwright in *Life* magazine March 13 that *Dr. Strangelove* "is a brilliant and edifying, even a moral movie."

Similar adverse criticism has hit *Seven Days in May.* It is interesting that the late John F. Kennedy liked the Knebel-Bailey book and warmly cooperated with the film producers when they sought his help in shooting scenes inside and around the White House, but the Defense Department, wrote Knebel in *Look* magazine Nov. 19, "turned a frosty eye on the venture. Frankenheimer and company were denied permission to visit the office of Gen. Maxwell Taylor, chairman of the Joint Chiefs of Staff, unless the script were submitted to the Defense Department for consideration." Frankenheimer refused.

Kennedy apparently understood what the book and film were trying to convey to the country. As the co-architect of the historic nuclear test ban treaty he was well aware of the powerful opposition in military circles to the treaty and to a general weakening of Cold War tensions.

The appearance of both *Seven Days in May* and *Dr. Strangelove* within a few weeks of each other reflects growing public awareness that questions of war or peace are too important to be left to the generals and that disarmament is a matter of life or death in our time. It is therefore unfortunate that *Seven Days* ends on a sour note. When the planned coup is nipped in the bud, the whole thing is hushed up. No arrests. No trial. Not a word to the press that a

Pentagon clique with right wing support tried to impose a military dictatorship on the country. No attempt is made to arouse the people against the threat to their independence. The President (Fredric March) asks only that the traitors turn in their uniforms. The enemy, he declares weakly, is not the generals, but the nuclear age, which leads some people to do strange things—such as trying to overthrow the government? Or atom-bombing Russia?

See Mike Felker's review of Kubrick's 1987 film, Full Metal Jacket *in* Jump Cut *(No. 33, February 1988). Felker, a Vietnam Vet who writes about films, says that the first 45 minutes dealing with the cruelty of marine basic training "should be mandatory viewing for every young person thinking of joining the armed forces. It accurately previews the 'world of shit' they will enter." The rest of the film, he writes, doesn't quite live up to the first part, and we agree. (DP)*

59 LORRAINE HANSBERRY'S *A RAISIN IN THE SUN*

Arthur Knight

SIEGFRIED KRACAUER, in his new, basic *Theory of Film* (Oxford, 1960), makes a point that might well alarm cinematic purists, but has long needed not merely clarification but statement. A film, Kracauer says, "may acquire a cinematic quality provided its technical execution testifies to a sense of the medium." He promply adds, quite properly, that such a film is less cinematic than one devoted to camera reality, which is the very essence of motion pictures. But the recognition that technique can impart a sense of film to even a theatre-based work is something that few estheticians have been able to grasp or willing to admit. They are all too prone to dismiss all adaptations as "canned plays," and by so doing deny to the medium a vast area of human experience.

In all fairness, it must be admitted that in most instances they are right. Plays are generally brought to the screen with a literalness, an adherence to theatre staging, that transforms them into monstrosities. Movie audiences watch in a stupor as characters mouth their lines and make their gestures to a static, inflexible lens. Directors, more concerned with performance than with the camera, permit shots to run for minutes on end without change of position, relationships, or visual accents. The motion picture medium, robbed of its dynamics, degenerates into a mere reproduc-

From *Saturday Review* (March 25, 1961). Reprinted by permission of the author.

tion of another art form—and a decidely inferior reproduction at that.

But it is the exceptions that the estheticians are unprepared for, those pictures that, despite their stage origins, achieve a cinematic validity with precious little alteration. Such an exception is the David Susskind-Philip Rose production of Lorraine Hansberry's *A Raisin in the Sun.* As directed by Daniel Petrie, and performed by Sidney Poitier, Claudia McNeil, Ruby Dee, and most of the play's Broadway cast, it transcends the limitations of its single set and its three-act construction. And this is achieved not by opening out the play (although three new scenes carry the action beyond the four walls of the Youngers' shabby flat), but rather by playing each shot for its full dramatic weight and intensity, and by permitting the camera to probe each scene for the utmost revelation of character and milieu. Petrie's camera is constantly on the prowl, stalking his people or receding before them, cutting now to one face or another for a reaction or a word of protest. And somehow, despite the restrictive, even oppressive setting, Miss Hansberry's fine play comes glowingly alive.

To film *Raisin*, Mr. Petrie—another of the young talents developed by television–worked largely with "master shots." But with an important difference. Where most "masters" tend to be rather static long shots that cover all the action in a given scene, Petrie will start in close on a dialogue between two players, hold tight on them as they move about the room, then open out only when additional characters enter into the action. There is, in other words, considerable camera mobility to begin with. To this are added the accents of close-ups, inserts, cut-aways–framentary glimpses that afford sudden insights into the emotions of everyone involved in the scene or that assert, in Kracauer's favorite phrase, the "physical reality" of the scene itself.

Actually, it was with the performers in mind that Petrie developed this technique. Realiizing that his picture would stand or fall on the quality of the acting, that performances would have to override what was, in Miss Hansberry's adaptation of her own play, essentially an uncinematic script, he went for long takes in which his actors could build the momentum of a scene. The main effort was to draw from each member of the company his peak performance. And in this, he has succeeded beyond belief. Sidney Poitier, always a splendid actor, rises to new heights as the tormented, ambitious Walter Lee who, at the play's finale, "comes into his manhood." With never a false move, he projects all the pride, the hurt, the frustration, and, ultimately, the dignity of a race-conscious Negro. His is one of the few fully realized character portraits ever to come onto celluloid, and one of the most moving. Scarcely less affecting is Claudia McNeil's mother role, although her work is more studied, less spontaneous—and, it might be added, less demanding. Her physical demeanor alone suggests the tower of strength that she represents in the Younger household, while the writing builds such sympathy for her that only a novice could destroy the part completely. And Miss McNeil, who has played the role ever since it opened on Broadway, is clearly no novice. Ruby Dee, on the other hand, brings a quiet beauty and great charm to the more complex (and not so fully developed) role of Walter Lee's pregnant, pragmatic wife. Ivan Dixon is enormously effective as a young African student smitten with Walter Lee's sister; and John Fiedler, the only white in the cast, neatly manages to keep this side of caricature his subtle delineation of a Good Neighbor emmisary delegated to keep Negroes from becoming good neighbors in a white neighborhood.

Despite all this, however, it is still Miss Hansberry's play that makes this an important and memorable movie. Here, for the first time, is the new Negro on the screen. Not a Negro fighting for his rights against the intolerance or injustices of society; but an entire family that has become aware of, and is determined to combat, racial discrimination in a supposedly democratic land. Walter Lee is summoned by his employer over a loudspeaker system. His wife must work in kitchens. His mother learns that rents in the white neighborhoods are lower than in the Negro ghettos. His sister, who wants to be a doctor, must fight for her education. Naturally, there is bitterness here. But there is also hope—the hope for a better life, the hope for a better world.

Nor, praise be, are the Youngers depicted as paragons of

all the virtues. Walter Lee lies and cheats for the money that, he hopes, will set him up in the liquor business. He bickers with his wife, his sister, his son. The wife would prefer an abortion to bearing a loveless child. The sister turns on Walter Lee with animal ferocity when she learns that the money she had counted on to see her through medical school is gone. But through it all seeps an awareness that these people, essentially so decent, have been warped and distorted by a lack of money, a lack of job opportunities, a lack of proper housing, a lack of equality as human beings. It is their humanness that shines through this film; and one feels, as it closes, that he has been wrenched away from people he has come to know, and admire, and perhaps even to love.

A Raisin in the Sun is not a perfect film. By its very nature, it could never be. The first half-hour, before the characters and situations begin to grow, seems excessively talky, and one becomes uncomfortably aware of the dangerous compromise between stage and screen. But thanks to Mr. Petrie, thanks to Miss Hansberry, thanks to a modest but marvelously apposite score by Laurence Rosenthal, and above all, thanks to incandescent performances from the entire cast, the picture rises above its limitations to become even more affecting and effective than the play on which it was based. Perhaps the final thanks should go to David Susskind for daring to bring to the screen so controversial a theme while it still is controversial.

60 FILMMAKERS DISCOVER "NEW" NATIVE AMERICANS

Kyle Steenland *and* John Trimbur

IN SEARCH OF ART AND PROFIT American filmmakers have turned recently to "Indian" movies, movies that attempt to reverse the traditional Hollywood view of Indians as evil, cunning savages who treacherously refused the generous and disinterested help offered by white civilization. The appeal of recasting the American Indian shows in the popularity of films like *Little Big Man, Man Called Horse,* and *Tell Them Willie Boy Is Here*—all obvious improvements over such traditional fare as *Stagecoach* and the whole battery of "cavalry-to-the-rescue" films. But Hollywood's discovery of the "real" Indian is only partial and one-sided; various filmmakers' attempts to find an accurate version of the American Indian get distorted in their inability to see past the inherited mythologies of the American West.

Making the Indians into heroes and reversing the traditional good-guy bad-guy roles does not clarify the conflict between two cultures at widely separated points of historical development, an epochal drama that continues to resound throughout the world. Instead, these movies serve the traditional mythology of the American West as the stage where larger-than-life heroes and demi-gods act out the romantic ideals the tradition demands. Though the camera's focus has shifted from the white conquerer to the Indian victim and his suffering and nobility, we are not shown that

From *Red Buffalo,* a Journal of American Studies (Summer 1971). Reprinted by permission of the authors.

WAR PARTY

What do Indians think of their Hollywood image? Using the tomahawk to show relative merit, here are the results of an informal poll of young Indians. One tomahawk denotes fair to good, two tomahawks poor, three terrible, and four—a massacre.

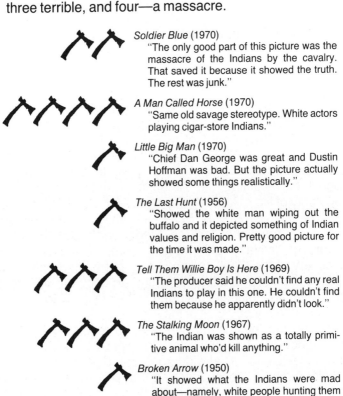

Soldier Blue (1970)
"The only good part of this picture was the massacre of the Indians by the cavalry. That saved it because it showed the truth. The rest was junk."

A Man Called Horse (1970)
"Same old savage stereotype. White actors playing cigar-store Indians."

Little Big Man (1970)
"Chief Dan George was great and Dustin Hoffman was bad. But the picture actually showed some things realistically."

The Last Hunt (1956)
"Showed the white man wiping out the buffalo and it depicted something of Indian values and religion. Pretty good picture for the time it was made."

Tell Them Willie Boy Is Here (1969)
"The producer said he couldn't find any real Indians to play in this one. He couldn't find them because he apparently didn't look."

The Stalking Moon (1967)
"The Indian was shown as a totally primitive animal who'd kill anything."

Broken Arrow (1950)
"It showed what the Indians were mad about—namely, white people hunting them for scalps."

Flap (Original title: *Nobody Loves a Drunken Indian* 1970)
"This picture makes a joke of Indian rights. We don't mind a laugh at ourselves but this picture made us look like idiots."

From the May 1971 issue of *Akwesasne Notes,* published by The White Roots of Peace, Mohawk Nation.

what is at stake is the geo-political claims of the American empire and the future of capitalism in North America. The new "Indian" movie recognizes that a certain moral failure is inherent in this conflict but represents it as a tragedy for which the audience feels but a vague, undefined guilt. Such renditions of "national quiet" only obscure the past by dishing up its carnage and violence without explaining the system that led to the horror and inhumanity. The viewer's genuinely felt moral concern cannot, at least through these movies, uncover the sources of moral failure, and the tragic past takes on a fatalistic inevitability. And the viewer is left to direct the guilt inward, as these movies identify *all* Americans with the crimes of the past. Such anguished national self-examination, as it varies between the self-righteous and the self-destructive, cannot substitute, as it is made to do by ruling class ideologues, for social action that can come to grips with the conflicts of the past and deal with their persistent patterns in the present.

There has always been an undercurrent of sympathy toward Indians in American films. Movies like *Broken Arrow* and *Apache Attack* through John Ford's *Cheyenne Autumn* show Indians as good guys betrayed by conniving government bureaucrats and greedy miners and cattlemen. These movies have much in common with *Tell Them Willie Boy Is Here,* but also with any western. As a genre the western relies on a pattern of moral simplicity with the good guy fighting forces which are stacked against him. The good guy has only himself to count on; it's up to him to find the courage and summon the initiative to attain a final moral victory in the face of overwhelming odds. In the mountains and on the desert or prairie, preferably photographed in the gorgeous sunset hues of technicolor, the good guy is the apotheosis of the American self-made man.

Indians as good guys become the same kind of individual hero as Alan Ladd in *Shane* or Gary Cooper in *High Noon.* They become the stars of movies with the same dramatic formula—like Geronimo in *Apache Attack* or *Willie Boy Is Here.* The triumphing (or tragic) individual as hero makes it difficult to portray the conflict of cultures that lay beneath the actions of brave (or cowardly) men. Geronimo, for example, cannot be understood apart from the collective life of the

Chiricahua Apaches. He is not an individual trying to find his identity or make a life for himself, cut off from his tribe and its struggle against the encroachment of white civilization. But the star system Hollywood needs for good box-office spotlights its heroes in isolation, reinforcing the American ideology of individualism. Heroes and villains clash in Hollywood, not the cultures and classes of history.

All the movies under consideration are examples of the star system. *A Man Called Horse* gives Richard Harris top billing and, as a movie that tries to show Indians accurately and sympathetically, still sees the white man as the most important figure and the focus of the viewer's emotional sympathy. In the end the movie glorifies the white man's mind; Richard Harris not only survives his captivity among the Sioux but becomes the best Indian in the tribe, leaving with the adulation of his former captors. The movie advertised as the first Hollywood film to portray Indians accurately (down to the last ethnographic detail) ends as an homage to Western intellect.

The ambition of *Little Big Man* is to be more than a remake of the stereotyped Hollywood western. The director, Arthur Penn, sets out in an attempt to come to grips with the history and mythology of the Battle of the Little Big Horn, Custer's last stand. The history is accurate inasmuch as it depicts Custer as an egotistical fool who discounted totally the fighting ability of the Sioux. And the movie seeks to replace the good-guy bad-guy mythology with a picture of Indian life and culture that shows Indians coming from a distinct society and yet one that can be understood. Penn's direction of Dan George as a Cheyenne chief is a serious attempt to make Indian values and wisdom accessible. In this sense *Little Big Man* represents a qualitative improvement over most movies about Indians.

In addition the film treats cultures in conflict more seriously than previous movies; Penn here is trying to make a movie to explain the genocidal assault on the American Indian. The movie's flaw is not in intention but in tone: Penn finds history too insane to be depicted realistically. Instead, Penn seems to want to show us the absurdity of the campaigns against the Indians. But the black humor Penn uses to string the movie together is neither funny nor chilling enough.

In Penn's earlier movies—*Left-handed Gun, Bonnie and Clyde* and *Alice's Restaurant*—he dealt successfully with gunfighters, outlaws, hippies and others on the fringe of American mainstream. Penn was able in these films to separate the real people from the cultural myths and give the appearance that he had found the real Billy the Kid and the real Clyde Barrow behind their images in the media, the ballads and the dime novels. Because the cultural myths were isolated from the lives they were supposed to depict, the myths themselves seemed like hollow forms. In this way Penn could display them as artifacts and ultimately explode them.

In *Little Big Man,* however, dealing with the myths of another culture, Penn's manipulation of images is not so sure-handed. His use of Indian myth gets no deeper than the level of rhetorical slogans. That the "human beings"—the Cheyenne—believed that all the things of the world were alive, while the white man believed them all to be dead, is a fine critical comparison of the two cultures, but Penn cannot see that such beliefs are rooted in the actual social life of the Indian tribes. So, when Dan George goes to the mountain top and delivers his magnificent death speech and lies down to die, Penn cannot relate this as an Indian's way of dealing with the natural event of death but undercuts the scene by turning it into a joke. The Indian rituals expressing the continuity of life and death were sources of power and understanding for the tribesmen, but Penn represents them as superstitions, treats them humorously and ends with his Indians as nothing more than fantasies.

Penn's history-as-fantasy gives us a portrait of Custer as merely crazy, enacting his personal fantasies rather than serving as an extreme agent of expanding capitalism. And the core of the history of the Battle of the Little Big Horn, where the largest number of Plains Indians ever gathered fought in defense of their land and way of life, is lost in the fantasy spinning.

So far no movies exist which capture accurately Indian history or culture, the real drama of tribal peoples trying to comprehend the white invaders in North America. It is difficult therefore to imagine what such a movie would look like. The problem, however, is not a narrow aesthetic one but broadly one of historical imagination. What needs to be shown is not only the ruthless elimination of precapitalist tribal societies by the expanding American empire but also the social life internal to the tribes as their world views stretch to include the fact of this strange and relentless white man.

One other film on this subject deserves a comment. Is there really any difference (except in technique) between the 1916 William S. Hart silent film, The Aryan, *and the 1956 John Ford/John Wayne "Western,"* The Searchers, *which drew "rave" critical notices wherever it was shown, although, as it seemed to me, Frank Nugent's screenplay was little more than a re-statement in sound of the "Code of the Aryan Race" as enunciated in the opening subtitle of* The Aryan *which read: "Our women shall be guarded," and "a man of the white race may forget much—friends, duty, honor, but this he will not, he cannot forget."*

In The Searchers, *John Wayne sets out to avenge the murder of his brother's family by Comanches. At the end of his long and relentless pursuit of the Indians he finds that his kidnapped niece has been turned into a squaw, and sexually dishonored. That leads into the main theme: the evil of miscegenation. Obviously, the only way that Ford and his screenwriter could make this point credible to American audiences is to falsely portray the Comanches as a group of maniacal killers and rapists, and then have the lean, tough ex-Confederate Texan Indian fighter Wayne rescue the violated girl from the clutches of the lustful Indian with whom she has been living throughout the years of her captivity. And so, in the final reel, as Wayne tenderly embraces his long-lost niece after venting his rage on her, it is understood that now she will be free to pick up the threads of her life in safety in the civilized world. True or false? False. Because the film is based on a celebrated 19th-century frontier case dealt with by Alan Lemay in his novel, also titled* The Searchers; *in both cases the abducted white girl enjoyed her life among Native Americans and refused to be rescued. Years later when she was liberated against her will and her adopted tribe was annihilated, including the Kiowan she loved, she died of grief. (DP)*

61 THE DEFIANCE IN *THE DEFIANT ONES*

Gordon Hitchens

ACTOR-WRITER NEDRICK YOUNG and Harold Jacob Smith collaborated on the screenplay of *The Defiant Ones,* made in 1958, but Young was obliged to use a pseudonym, "Nathan E. Douglas," due to the Hollywood blacklist. In vengeful humor, producer-director Stanley Kramer cast the two writers as drivers of the truck that transports prisoners, including stars Sidney Poitier and Tony Curtis. In the sequence that opens the film, under the credits, the names "Nathan E. Douglas" and Harold Jacob Smith are superimposed over the faces of the writers. Insiders in Hollywood, of course, recognized Young as "Douglas." A nice ironical thrust at the blacklisters, one of those Hollywood sick jokes.

Honors and praise for *The Defiant Ones* poured in. Ken Englund, President of the Screen Writers Branch of the Writers Guild of America, West, on February 16, 1959, wrote: "Dear Mr. Douglas: It is my pleasure and duty to inform you that your fellow screen writers have nominated *The Defiant Ones* as the Best-Written American Drama of 1958. . . ." Englund concluded by inviting "Douglas" to make his dinner reservations for the awards ceremony at the Moulin Rouge in Hollywood.

A moral problem for "Douglas" and Young was exposing

From *Film Culture,* Nos. 50–51, Fall & Winter 1970 issue. This was a special double-issue on Hollywood Blacklisting, guest-edited by Gordon Hitchens. His article is reprinted by permission of *Film Culture's* editor-in-chief, Jonas Mekas.

the device of the pseudonym, which could mean the end of writing assignments, and also the film industry's chastisement of producers able to show some courage. Section F, Article 8, of the By-Laws of the Academy of Motion Picture Arts and Sciences, later rescinded, expressed the film industry's attitude toward such blacklisted film artists as Young:

> Any person who, before any duly constituted Federal legislative committee or body, shall have admitted that he is a member of the Communist Party, (and has not since publicly renounced the party) or who shall have refused to answer whether or not he is, or was, a member of the Communist Party, or who shall have refused to respond to a subpoena to appear before such a committee or body, shall be ineligible for any Academy Award so long as he persists in such refusal.

Section F, Article 8 of the Academy's By-Laws was one of many devices by which the film industry disciplined its employees. This regulation was totally political and had no reference of any kind to art or the aesthetics of film. Yet, curiously, the President of the Academy at that time, George Stevens, has been quoted by radio-station KPOL, Los Angeles, as saying: "The Academy is only interested in making its awards on the basis of merit."

The success of *The Defiant Ones* contributed to the atrophy of the blacklist. Within months, the film had earned a barrel of awards, foreign and domestic. It was making money, and the stardom of the two leads was secured. *The Defiant Ones* settled down in cinema history as a pioneering effort at humanitarian idealism and improved race-relations within that old decadent dream-factory, Hollywood Fabulous Follywood. The film is now praised by some critics as the first to star a Black, the first to dramatize persuasively that friendship can transcend the prejudice inculcated by society.

Bosley Crowther in *The New York Times* on February 1, 1959, discussed *The Defiant Ones* doubtfully. With Harold Jacob Smith, co-scenarist of the film, Ned Young wrote the following letter to Crowther on February 3, using his real name:

> In reference to the ending of the picture, *The Defiant Ones,* as being "uncertain and ambiguous":

Our simple thesis is that from common struggle toward common goal, man realizes his interdependence with other men. The realization of "brotherhood" is in itself a goal of the first importance. It follows, therefore, that the thematic resolution of the film occurs with the acts of mutual sacrifice performed by the two men and it could not depend upon the "triumph" of escape.

The real triumph, insofar as an author may be able to state it, lies in the two men overcoming a set of moribund mores learned from an abnormal social superstructure, which had originally made them think they were enemies.

The song, far from being a senseless one, is sung by Poitier, the Negro, in the opening scenes is an individual expression of defiance and a source of annoyance to Curtis, the white man. At the end, the song is a gesture of strength and comfort with which the white man identifies.

To the two men, the sheriff represents law and oppression, pursuit and persecution. The sheriff represents an exploration of a character familiar to us all, the man whose humanist principles are crossed by what appears to be the acts he must approve for his own self-interest. The sheriff disapproves the use of the "killer" dogs to capture the escaping men. He is posed with the dilemma of "dogs" and guarantee of capture, or no "dogs" and the possibility of escape and the corresponding loss of his job. Again, we felt the triumph of principle more important than the mechanical act of capture or escape.

You said the picture tends to "send audiences away with questions in their minds" and asked "are we to gather that the new found brotherhood of the two is without hope of liberation?" We maintain, thematically, the men are liberated— liberated from hate.

If, having resolved this theme, we find a larger question arising from it, then we have succeeded most fully in expressing our intention. The question of freedom in its broadest sense can only be resolved by the people everywhere in the land, not by the authors. It is, indeed, today being resolved in Virginia, perhaps, tomorrow, in Little Rock.

Crowther printed the Young/Jacobs letter in the *Times* on February 8, but in an altered form. This in turn inspired Young to write Crowther a second time, on February 12:

On February 1st, in your column, you raised certain questions concerning the "symbol" aspects of *The Defiant Ones.*

Your questions were valid and provacative, and, in respect of them, Harold Jacob Smith and I, as co-authors of the script, attempted a clarification. We did this by means of a letter to you.

You were kind enough to print this letter, with its main contents intact, on February 8th.

I note however, with some surprise, that not only was my name eliminated as signatory to the letter, but that the first paragraph of the letter itself had been rewritten in order to make this omission plausible.

I grant there are no major issues involved, but, as a fellow writer, surely you can understand my wish to be identified not only with my work, but with any public discussion concerning the intent thereof.

I am aware that the circumstances would seem to preclude any public correction, but I would appreciate relief for my own puzzlement as to why such a mishap should occur.

If your time permits, I would be most grateful for a clarifying reply.

Crowther didn't acknowledge this second letter. But Ned Young's name, and pseudonym, came up in the *Times* several years later, on October 13, 1963, in an article by A. H. Weiler. The following is an excerpt:

Slated to go before the cameras on January 15 in Houston and Hollywood is *The Confessor,* which will be the first effort of director John Frankenheimer (*The Manchurian Candidate,* etc.) under the Mirisch banner. Henry Fonda and Tony Curtis will star in this psychological melodrama adapted by Nathan E. Douglas from the novel by Jackson Donahue published by World last June.

Mr. Douglas (real name: Nedrick Young) who, with Harold J. Smith, won the Academy Award for *The Defiant Ones,* treats of an educated man in *The Confessor,* who admits a murder he did not commit and is convicted, according to a spokesman for the company. "The point of the drama," our man added, "is a study of the compulsive personality as well as the crime and its unusual climax."

The defiant Ned Young received his final acknowledgment in the *Times* on September 18, 1968, on the occasion of his death. The heading of the obituary reads: "Nedrick Young,

54, Defied Blacklist—Writer Who Won Oscar for *Defiant Ones* Dies."

Nedrick Young (1914–1968) testified as an unfriendly witness before the House Un-American Activities Subcommittee in Los Angeles April 8, 1953. In one of his last public appearances he spoke at Carnegie Hall, September 22, 1961, on the effect of the Hollywood blacklist on American writers. His call for whatever sacrifices are necessary to reclaim our cultural heritage was loudly applauded: "From the time man first took chisel to stone tablet, the writer's credo has been simply this: the duly constituted authority must equate with my conscience, or one of us is doomed. It's an old story, but now something new has been added: monopoly—monopoly and terror. The historical brain-rack gets tighter. The powerful ones swallow up our press, invade our magazines, obscure our poetries, reduce our novels, destroy our theater, humiliate our traditions and our culture and warn us if we dare to retrieve them, we will be hit with the full recrimination of the blacklist—or whatever of their deadly punitive measures they can devise. . . . The time has come to un-silence ourselves. The time has come to fight back. The world is our home, my friends. If we wish to put it in order, let it be known." (DP)

62 UNION FILMS: AN INTERVIEW WITH CARL MARZANI

Cinéaste Editors Gary Crowdus *and* Lenny Rubenstein

D URING THE ECONOMIC STRUGGLES of the post World War
II years in the U.S., a film production collective known as
Union Films was engaged in the defense of working class
interests against the then rapidly-expanding power of big
business. Union Films produced a series of films for the
United Electrical, Radio and Machine Workers of America
and Carl Marzani served as writer/director on several of
them, including *Deadline for Action* (1946) and *The Great
Swindle* (1947).

Deadline for Action analyzes the post World War II
economic situation as experienced by one UE worker,
focusing on the nationwide strikes of 1946 when over two
million workers went out in protest over wage cutbacks. The
40-minute film features an animation and graphics sequence
explaining imperialism, including the role of multi-national
corporations and business inter-relationships overseas during the war.

The Great Swindle is a 30-minute film presenting the UE's
position versus the National Association of Manufacturers in
the latter's eventually successful propaganda campaign to
force termination of government price controls. An animation
sequence on inflation explains the relationship between

*From *Cinéaste* (Vol. 7, No. 2, Spring 1976). Reprinted by permission of
the publisher and Carl Marzani.

wages, prices, profits and monopoly control of key sectors of the American economy.

Carl Marzani was born in Italy and came to the U.S. as a youngster when his father, a socialist, had to leave the country when Mussolini came to power. In 1936, Marzani fought in the Spanish Civil War, joining the anarchist brigades in Barcelona. He later became a Marxist while studying at Oxford University and on his return to the U.S. joined the Communist Party, serving as a section organizer until he left the Party in the Fall of '42. During the war, he served with the Office of Strategic Services and gained his first film experience. After the war, while active with Union Films, Marzani became the first political victim of the Cold War, being indicted in January 1947 on a charge of defrauding the government (by collecting his salary!). He was convicted on eleven counts of which nine were thrown out by the Court of Appeals. The Vinson Supreme Court twice considered the remaining two counts and each time split 4–4 with Justice Douglas abstaining and Justices Black, Rutledge, Murphy and Frankfurter voting in favor of Marzani. A split vote allows the lower court's decision to stand and Marzani served 32 months of his three year sentence. While in jail he wrote his first book, *We Can be Friends: The Origins of the Cold War*. After he came out in 1951 he worked for the UE for four years and then, throughout the '50's and '60's, he remained active as a writer (including one novel, *The Survivor*) and as a publisher.

Today (1976) at 64, although "retired from the film field," he continues writing. His most recent work, *The Threat of American Neo-Fascism,* was published just before, and vindicated by, the Watergate scandal. He is now working on a book entitled *Orwell, Spain and 1992.* Mr. Marzani was interviewed in his New York home by *Cinéaste* editors Gary Crowdus and Lenny Rubenstein.

Q: How did you first get involved in filmmaking?

A: I got interested in making films purely for documentary and educational purposes during the war, when I made films on various economic and scientific subjects for the Joint Chiefs of Staff. We did a series of ten minute films—on target systems, one on synthetic rubber, how you make it, what the economics are, another film on ball bearings, and so on. Some of the other films I made for the government were fairly big, such as a 40-minute documentary called *War Department Report* in 1944. After the war, in 1946, I was asked by the UE to do a little film on the big CIO strikes of late '45 and '46. That was *Deadline for Action.* By the Fall of '46 it had grown into a much bigger film than was originally intended and that was the first big film I made outside the government.

Q: How many other people were involved with you in Union Films?

A: There were four of us—myself, an editor, a soundman and a cameraman. We had a contract with the UE—$50,000 per year to produce ten reels of film—and that gave us the financial backing. When I made *Deadline for Action,* you see, I had to rent the equipment—the film cost $20,000 and $5,000 went for rental of equipment. Well, we figured, that's no way to run a railroad, so we got ourselves a complete set-up. We got a brownstone at 111 West 88th Street and made it into a little 16mm studio, turning two floors into a cutting room and small sound stage. Then we slowly built it up by cutting down on the rental costs and operating like a small kibbutz—and in fact that's what we really were because we lived upstairs in the same building where we worked—and so by cutting costs we were able to produce a series of films and make a small but steady living.

We had some other contacts as well. We made a film for the West Coast fisherman's union, for instance, which was being attacked under the anti-trust law and this film was really their legal brief. There was a big struggle about whether or not it would be allowed to be shown in the courtroom and they finally allowed it to be shown without the soundtrack, which didn't help very much. We made some films for the Wallace movement such as *Dollar Patriots.* I made a film for Vito Marcantonio's campaign which was shown on the streets with a truck and rear-projection. We did a little bit of everything and our place became a center for other people to make films, using our cutting rooms, recording equipment, and so on.

Now, apart from *Deadline* and a few others, I didn't make too many of the films myself. I worked in a sort of producer/writer/director capacity, but you know how these things work—the editor is also a director, the cameraman is also a director, I mean, everybody did everything. My wife ran the distribution set-up for Union Films, because we also distributed the films to the union locals. We kept the prices very low for the locals—*Deadline,* for instance, rented for $15 and sold for $100, and we sold over 300 prints. We also helped the locals get projectors because we got a dealership in Bell and Howell and were able to pass on projectors at cost.

Q: Were there any other unions producing films at that time?

A: No, the nearest thing you had was the UAW which had a distribution set-up and they also commissioned a few films. There was also a small group of progressive people on the West Coast—Hubley was one—who were doing cartoons. But we were certainly the closest anybody ever came to really having a coherent, functioning and financed—at a low level but nevertheless regular—production and distribution set-up. But it was all peanuts in comparison to what could have been done, to what was envisaged. Because the CIO split took place as the Cold War got going and the split just stopped us. So none of this really got off the ground because films are always peripheral. It's expensive and unless you have continuous dedication and continuing work over time, you can't sustain it.

At that time the UE had some 600,000 members and was one of the three largest unions in the CIO. The UAW was also progressive at that time—this was before Walter Reuther came in. Our distribution started with the UE locals but we had planned, of course, to broaden into the CIO. I showed *Deadline* to Philip Murray of the CIO and Alex Kroll, the CIO Political Director, and they both approved of it. We also got a tremendous send-off in the *CIO News.* This was about four months before things got really tight.

Our goal was to put a couple of projectors in every town, so the UE would have a projector or if the UE local was not large, the UAW or some other local would have a projector which all unions could borrow. Not only Brandon but also the International Workers Order had a film distribution set-up of course, that was a Red outfit and they really got smashed but there were sources to get films for $5 or $10, so there were interesting possibilities. And looking down the road, we figured we'd get some films from socialist countries, nothing tremendous but, you know, if you start with a couple, over the years you can very readily build up a library.

My original intention, in fact, was to have a whole library of films, a book club, a magazine like *Life* magazine, and so on, for the CIO. Since you're working for other unions, you're all over the United States, so you would do films for agricultural workers, for the food and tobacco workers, for the auto workers, and so on. You would have a tremendous set of stills as well, so you could run a very good pictorial magazine. We also had ideas of going into film strips, you know, the totality of educational work. And it would have worked, unquestionably, because the money would have been available, we had the professional skills, we had the contacts with people who were willing to work. . . .

Q: And the time was ripe, too, for real political education.

A: Sure. It was the Cold War that smashed it. It was done consciously and deliberately, there was no nonsense about it. When *Deadline* came out, for instance, it came under violent attack within a matter of weeks. Frederick Woltman of the *World Telegram* had an 8-column heading on a story about the film, saying "*Deadline* Wins an Oscar in Moscow," implying it had been done with Moscow gold. At that time they still didn't know who the hell the people were because we didn't use any names. Unions Films was a collective and we deliberately didn't take individual credits.

Q: It was a tremendous opportunity down the drain.

A: The truth of the matter is that the Cold War set the labor movement back thirty years. It was designed for that purpose and they did it. The only thing they didn't get was a war. They got a lot of other stuff out of it—they smashed the left wing. I mean, the modern generation just doesn't know what the hell went on thirty years ago. *Labor's Untold Story** is just beginning to be read. I showed *Deadline* up at Columbia once and the kids just couldn't believe that in 1945 the cops were beating people just as badly as they do today. Or that someone was able to say 'imperialism.' Don't forget, *Deadline* is the first thing on record, before any other historian, the first

---

Labor's Untold Story by Richard O. Boyer and Herbert Morais is a history of the labor movement up to the Cold War.

film that says the United States has the major responsibility for the Cold War. Today that view is accepted in many universities, it's at least a respectable view, but it's taken thirty years.

Q: It was about this time, wasn't it, that you had some personal problems with the government?

A: Yes, partly as a result of *Deadline,* I was indicted. General Electric got together with the government and so I went out of circulation in March of '49. I was in jail during part of the appeal and during that time some films were made but then the outfit began to fall apart. By the time I got out of jail, I think it was in July of '51, the outfit was dispersed—the city had harassed us and literally zoned us out of existence—the equipment was gone and not only that but the UE itself was under attack, split and divided, and didn't have the money. In fact, I went to work for the UE as editor of *The UE Steward,* which was the UE's major leadership magazine for union stewards, and did a lot of educational publications work in the UE for years.

Q: Was this when *Labor's Untold Story* was published?

A: Yes, after I left the UE, about 1954–55, I became a publisher and *Labor's Untold Story* was one of the books we published for the UE. I was co-director with Angus Cameron of the Liberty Book Club which became Cameron Associates and when Cameron left it became Marzani and Munsell. We had a subscription book club where for $10 a year you got eight books. We also had a very distinguished list—we had the first book on the Rosenbergs, the first book on FBI informers, the first book on black armed self-defense, and so on. We also had an outlet for the blacklisted writers—we published novels and other writings by Ring Lardner, Alvah Bessie, Abe Polonsky, Albert Maltz. We also did an enormous amount of pamphlets, four or five every year on the Bay of Pigs, on Vietnam, the Warren Report—there wasn't a major issue we didn't put out something on. We were a major influence among two or three others—the *National Guardian, Monthly Review* during the years I call the American resistance to McCarthyism. Our office burned down in 1969, that's how we got out of business. It destroyed our stock, our lists, everything, and we had no insurance.

Q: You're working on a new book called *Orwell, Spain and 1992.*

A: Yes, the book is about Orwell's Spanish episode. I happen to be the only guy left around who was in the same front with him, 15 miles away. We never met because we had a big mountain between us but we were both close to the Ebro. Anyway, he wrote *Homage to Catalonia,* which many young people read today, and which is a great book about war but a lousy book about Spain. One of the things I want to do is to show that he was wrong and also that out of his mistakes he developed theories which have played into the hands of the ruling class, particularly in America—namely, the idea that fascism and communism are the same thing, that they're both totalitarian. The only other solution, he says, is anarchism but that doesn't work very well either, so the truth of the matter is that there's no way to change things, so stay away from politics because everybody always double-crosses you. That's all in there, you see, Orwell is the original do-your-own-thing guy. This I think is *disastrous,* it leads to terrorism, it leads to the Weatherpeople, to young provocateurs like the Symbionese Liberation Army—Christ, I hate to think what the FBI had to do with that!—it is a complete diversion and plays into the hands of the ruling class.

Another element in Orwell is that the oppressor and the oppressed are the same thing—in order to beat the oppressor, the oppressed has to become like the oppressor. So, again, what's the use of me fighting against you—you're the murderer but if I fight you, I'm going to end up a murderer too—as if self-defense is the same as aggression. Arthur Miller, in *After the Fall,* comes out and says, 'we're all victims, the informer and the person informed against are both victims'—well, what kind of crap is this, where are our values?

Another thing you get from Orwell is that the workers movements are betrayed from the top again and again. Well, you *don't* get it again and again—you get it sometimes, yes, and sometimes, no. John L. Lewis didn't betray the workers movement, Fitzgerald didn't betray the UE, Bridges didn't betray his union, so what kind of nonsense is this? Sure, some people betray; capitalists can buy people and some people sell out. With *1984,* Orwell went even beyond fascism and communism. He says there's no way out. If you want to see the future, he says, it's a boot stamped on the human face forever. He didn't quite mean it, but people read that and it's very disheartening, very despairing.

By the way, the tail end of all this is a book—thank God it came out because it shows how much nonsense all this is!—a professor at Berkeley wrote a book this year called *The Fascist Persuasion in Radical Politics* and he ends up by saying that Mussolini was a better socialist than the communists, I mean, literally, with all the footnotes and stuff. But Orwell started all this. And it was all unwittingly on Orwell's part—he didn't quite mean it that way, he meant to clarify, he meant to strengthen, to help the left. But he's been used—*1984* became, as Deutscher says, the super-weapon of the Cold War. The whole idea that communism and fascism are the same thing is such a crock of shit and so desperately wrong. . . . Well, this is something I feel very strongly about and the book will show the differences and sort of re-establish what I think is a proper intellectual position for the left.

Q: Getting back to your film work, some of the most impressive stuff in the UE films is the ingenious use of graphics to demystify and explain economic concepts like inflation.

A: Well, I'm a peculiar documentarist. I'm not anywhere in the same category as filmmakers like Joris Ivens who are much more emotionally directed, much more—I don't know how to put it—much more directed to a human element humanly expressed. I run much more to the presentation of ideas. The best thing about *Deadline,* to my mind, is that piece of animation which explains what the hell imperialism is. I don't think anybody, anywhere, has ever done as good a job as that. Nor do I think anybody has ever done the job on inflation that's in *The Great Swindle.* The point is that this is top economic stuff, it's not vulgarization at all, it's college level economics made available to working people and I'm ready to defend it against anybody, Galbraith or anybody else. This is serious stuff, and nobody had ever done that in film and nobody, I think, can do it as well as I can, even now, that is, how to present ideas on film, how to present a coherent view of an abstract subject.

Q: Of course, another one who was doing this in the 1930's, although in literary form, was Leo Huberman in *Man's Worldly Goods.*

A: Yes, that's right, it's a great book. I think I could put *Man's Worldly Goods* onto film. It takes the conceptual ability to see from the little to the big—so one can go from a strike, as *Deadline* does, to imperialism in one solid whole, because that's the way life is.

Q: What do you think are the chances for these sorts of trade union films being financed and produced today?

A: The tragedy today is that there is no political movement with the sufficient coherence. The Communist Party is small and much too rigid, too ossified. The other groupings are much too tiny, they don't amount to a hill of beans. And the left wing unions, of course, have more or less been smashed. The UE is still fairly decent but it hasn't got the strength and it just cannot do what it used to, it's got to defend itself. But it's coming, it's coming. I don't think the unions are going to stand by idly and let this kind of crap go on for the next ten years, no way, no way. I mean, it's all right for the ruling class to say, 'we can live with 8.5% unemployment,' but the unions can't.

Don't forget that today only 14% of American workers are organized—that's a terribly low figure. Of course, part of the reason is that the nature of work has shifted—there's much more service work, the factory workers per se are fewer in the totality. On the other hand, if the unions don't get off their tails and organize, the people will organize themselves. By the way, I think the ruling class is conscious of this and that's why I think we have a real potential for fascism in this country in the next ten to fifteen years. Whether they will or not is a different question but the potential is there, I don't think there's any question. The ruling class is in trouble—they're in trouble internationally, the market is shrinking, they can only do it by squeezing our allies and our allies resent it. We screwed Japan with this 'energy crisis,' for instance, and the Japanese know it.

Q: I guess the question is, is the left organized enough this time around, have they learned anything from the last time?

A: You know, I think progress is made. I grew up in the '20's and from 1924 to 1929 this country was a *desert.* It was worse than the McCarthy period—*nothing* moved, *nothing* existed. When you see the films of 1928 and '29 and see the shit that was in people's heads—they *believed* in the American Dream, they *believed* that hard work would pay off! But there's no worker today who believes that he can make it—very few, really, I mean, they're completely disillusioned. They think the government is a lot of crap. In the last two to three years the changes have been enormous. Figures published yesterday show that 80% of the American people don't think much of the FBI. Well, in the 1920's, 100% thought very highly of the FBI. I think there's a lot of change. For example, there are more Marxist teachers, economists and political scientists in the universities today than there were at the height of the New Deal. You used to count them in the hundreds, now you count them in the thousands. I think Marxism today is infinitely more influential in America than it has ever been. There's better work on Marxism being done all over the world, both in the socialist and non-socialist countries. In fact, some of the best work in America has been done by Marxists.

To get back to your original question, however, if I were doing this for the unions today, I'd print little booklets which would be given to every person in the audience so they could take home with them the basic charts, the basic facts and statistics, something they can get interested in and pass on to others.

But the most important thing is the whole distribution problem. I wouldn't have made *Salt of the Earth,* for instance, because you break your heart, you break your ass, and the showings are absolutely minimal. Now maybe someday things will change and it'll get its due, but the guys who made it will all be dead and they sure as hell can't eat off it. I was lucky, *Deadline* had 400 prints but that was the only one. *The Great Swindle* had only fifty prints and the others that were made had only thirty prints because the whole thing was disintegrating.

Another thing, you know, is that to my mind it's infinitely more important to get something 10% left into the public schools than to get something 90% left into the Higher Ground Cinema. Filmmakers today should remember that there are a lot of subjects which are not ostensibly left wing, like inflation, but which are enormously important. Or take the 'energy crisis'—you could do a job on what these fucking oil companies have done and there's not a union in this country which will not be offended by the oil companies and which will not accept a demand for nationalization of the energy industry. I mean, ten or twenty years ago this was a Red thing, right, but today people can see what they've done—it's the biggest, most incredible rip-off, it's so documented and so easy to see, and you can expose that. You don't have to say it's a Left approach, call it a consumer approach and you could take it to the high schools. If you avoid the rhetoric, even the economics teacher and the principal—you know, they drive cars, too—would agree with you.

Now a healthy 76, Carl Marzani is writing his memoirs, The Education of a Reluctant Radical. *He had to lay aside his book on Orwell to do a major book,* The Promise of Eurocommunism *(1981), "which should have been entitled the promise of Gorbachev." He is now finishing the Orwell book while working on his autobiography. (DP)*

63 HOLLYWOOD AND THE MYTH OF THE WORKING CLASS

Lynn Garafola

A FTER A LONG HIATUS, Hollywood has rediscovered the "working class." In quick succession have come *Rocky* and *Blue Collar, F.I.S.T.* and *Norma Rae,* films which have received full press coverage and, in some instances, enjoyed critical and financial success. They have also sparked considerable debate, particularly on the left—praised by some as marking new attitudes toward working-class life and damned by others as striking all time lows in sexism. Above all, they have been decried for their prevailing tone of cynicism toward working class life and institutions. While all these criticisms are to an extent justified, key questions about the way these films view the relationship of ethnicity, class, and race remain unasked. Beneath the veneer of the media's post-Vietnam "radicalism" lurks a profound yet unremarked irony. For what these films ultimately purvey is a nostalgia for old-time values and touchstones, closely attuned to the rightward drift of the country's political mood in the seventies.

The most striking thing about these films is that for Hollywood "working class" America is "ethnic." Since the release of *The Godfather* in 1972 audiences have been deluged with films portraying "ethnic" characters and situations. *Mean Streets, Taxi Driver, Saturday Night Fever,* and

From *Radical America* (Vol. 14, No. 1, Jan.–Feb. 1980). Reprinted by permission of the publisher and author. Radical America, 1 Summer St., Sommerville, MA 02143.

The Deer Hunter are but a sampling of a long list of titles which have reached the silver screen. The full extent of the blitz is underscored by the range of television shows centered around identifiably "ethnic" characters—*Kojak* and *Baretta, Petrocelli* and *Angie, Happy Days* and *Laverne and Shirley.*

Clearly, ethnicity is a major media theme of the seventies. Sylvester Stallone's "Rocky" and Tony (John Travolta in *Saturday Night Fever)* are Italian in descent, Johnny Kovacs (Stallone in *F.I.S.T.),* Slovak, Harvel Keitel, in *Blue Collar,* Polish. Their world is bounded by the ethnic ghetto of the decaying inner cities or the bedroom suburbs just beyond, their religion a Catholicism of a statuary rather than devotional nature, their language an English that suggests the presence of another tongue.

But is this pot pourri of Italians, Slovaks, and Poles a fair picture of the working class today?

Certainly, there was a time when working-class America was a mirror of the unmelted races of southern and eastern Europe. From 1880 onwards, millions poured through Castle Garden and Ellis Island from the most underdeveloped of Europe's empires and kingdoms to sweat in the factories and mills of America's cities. But the day when organizers, like those in Lawrence and Paterson, had to labor in more than a dozen languages has passed. In industry after industry, blacks and Latins have joined older generations of ethnic Americans on the assembly lines, while the children of the latter have slowly but perceptibly moved into middle-class and white-collar occupations. The blanket identification of "ethnic" and "working class" in the American media of the seventies is patently misleading.

What is true is that virtually every one of these films recreates that configuration, harking back to the heroic days of labor in the thirties or to a climate of unambiguous moral and social values. The emotional core of *F.I.S.T.* lies in the organizing struggles of the Teamsters during the Depression. This turbulent period, to which Stallone devotes fully sixty minutes of the film, is portrayed as the working class' "finest hour"—a time when people knew right from wrong and individuals rose to heroic deeds. Although set in the present, *Blue Collar,* too, draws on mythologized images of the thirties. As in the iconography of the period, the heroes are blue collar workers of heavy industry, men whose strength matches the raw power of the old-time assembly line. And the film's mood of disillusionment is sharpened by a sense of militant traditions betrayed.

If the depiction of labor betrays a retrospective yearning for heroes and unequivocal triumphs, that of the neighborhood reveals a similar nostalgia for the sense of community and "rootedness" that is increasingly absent from American life. (Whether it ever existed in the U.S. as it once did in Europe is a moot point. Terrence Malick's *Days of Heaven,* which follows workers on the move in the Southwest, uses the boxcar—as John Dos Passos did in *U.S.A.*—as a symbol for a country uprooted and transient even before World War I.) In *Rocky,* as in *Saturday Night Fever* and *F.I.S.T.,* the neighborhood is less a frame for events than a living protagonist. Indeed, these films draw their vitality from the concreteness of their locations—the rubbish that litters city curbsides, the distinctive character of frame or row houses.

Even more important, the neighborhood is a symbol of continuity: it rests on a web of mores and relationships that bind people to one another as well as to the past. Even if one leaves the "old neighborhood," as Travolta chooses to do when he heeds the call of Manhattan, it remains a psychic and physical touchstone. Nowhere is this symbolic dimension more clearly drawn than in *The Deer Hunter* where the rituals and neighborliness of the film's Slavic community symbolize American innocence in the face of the "alien savagery" of the Vietnamese. Even those who have condemned on political grounds director Michael Cimino's portrait of the war, have praised as authentic his vision of working-class life. In fact, Cimino's locale, a Ukrainian Catholic factory town, is more a film convention than a sociological reality, simply echoing the wedding scene in *The Godfather* and the male comraderie of *Mean Streets.* Although pockets remain, such communities are on the decline in the country today, and Cimino himself filmed not on location in the U.S. but in Canada.

It is not without significance that the emergence of Hollywood's "ethnic" theme coincides with an explosion of "ethnic," and especially Italian-American talent in the film industry, and the appearance of "ethnic power" on the country's political horizon. As both a reflection of and reaction to Black Power in the sixties, the recent growth of ethnic consciousness dates from the closing days of the Vietnam War and coincides with the publication of Richard Gambino's *Blood of My Blood* and Michael Novack's *Rise of the Unmeltable Ethnics,* some of the best known of the writings on this politically ambiguous phenomenon. As an affirmation of cultural values and challenge to remaining discrimination, "ethnic power" is a long overdue slap in the face of WASP economic and cultural hegemony. But to the extent that it finds political expression in backlash movements such as Mario Cuomo's short-lived Neighborhood Preservation Party, a force in New York's 1977 mayoral campaign, it represents a thinly-veiled attack on the hard-won advances of the minorities since the sixties.

As portrayed in these films, the working class is not only ethnic, but male, and not only male, but *macho.* With the exception of *Norma Rae,* whose protagonist is both a woman and an organizer, the women in *F.I.S.T., Blue Collar, The Deer Hunter,* and *Rocky,* when they appear at all, play second fiddle to the men.

The problem is not merely that their place is in the home, that they move from family to husband or that they are sweethearts, wives, and mothers. Certainly, the lives of many blue collar women have been marked out along conventional paths, and all too many have embraced the gender roles assigned by society. But, naturalistic veracity aside, the fact remains that the characters have been drawn to fit not only Hollywood's traditional images of women, but the stereotypes pandered by the most outspoken antagonists of contemporary feminism.

If damning by neglect is the pattern that emerges in most of these films, in others like *The Godfather, Saturday Night Fever,* and *New York, New York,* ethnic women are the objects of physical violence. Connie, Annette, and Francine in these films grate under the constraints of society's traditional roles. Whether demanding affection, a more equitable division of labor in the home or the freedom to pursue a career, all three voice dissatisfaction and independent needs. Yet in every instance, confrontation leads to violence. Annette is gang-banged by Tony's Bay Ridge pals in *Saturday Night Fever,* Connie in *The Godfather* is beaten black and blue by her husband, and Francine, eight months pregnant, is pummelled by Robert DeNiro in Scorsese's *New York, New York.* However, in setting the ethnic male against his powerless female counterpart, the filmmakers enact not only the drama of sexual warfare, but cultural warfare as well. The ethnic woman is transformed into a symbol of the ghetto itself, a link in the physical and cultural chain of ethnic continuity. The violence she provokes is a measure of group self-hatred and stems from the profound ambivalence underlying ethnic America's accommodation with its dual heritage and identity.

It is on the question of women's work that politics and nostalgia converge. At a time when over half the married women in America work—many, in fact, on assembly lines—Hollywood purveys traditional images of women and family life. Since *The Godfather,* Sunday dinners and weddings have become *de rigeur* symbols of old-time togetherness, destroyed in the passage to prosperity and Americanization. But, contrary to myths of America's long ago, the grandmothers and mothers of today's women did not merely tend their pots, particularly if they were working-class. Many labored in factories, others did home work—even after they were married.

Talia Shire in *Rocky* does in fact work. However, her cashiering job in a pet shop takes a back seat to the romantic plot. Making work a peripheral rather than central concern is hardly a sexist oversight as men's work in these films also serves as little more than a backdrop to the intrigue. For Hollywood, however, fitting windshields or driving trucks is more "real" than changing diapers or selling canaries. It is glamorous and action-packed. It also defines blue collar work in terms of the past, without reference to "post-industrial" patterns of employment in which the presence of women and the spectre of obsolescence figure prominently. For women's work, as indeed, a majority of jobs today performed by men, stands increasingly outside heavy industry in the white-collar and service sectors. Moreover, with the introduction of computers and automated equipment, it has become mechanized and humdrum as never before. As auto workers and miners, steelworkers and teamsters move into the ranks of labor's "aristocrats," a new proletariat of key punch operators and bank clerks has emerged. If the assembly line at General Motors epitomizes labor in the thirties, a word-processing unit is its symbol in the seventies.

Tendered under the guise of nostalgia, then, is a conservative ideology that seeks to turn back the clock to a family-centered past. It is no coincidence that this comes at a time when the White House is proclaiming the virtues of family life, the Catholic Bishops are throwing all their resources into anti-abortion campaigns, and insurance conglomerates are sparing no efforts to defeat the Equal Rights Amendment. Home though the U.S. may be to the women's movement, the ideology of "woman's place" has proved remarkably resilient. What has changed is the class focus of its family appeal. Where the fifties and early sixties gave us the suburban bliss of *Father Knows Best,* Hollywood in the late seventies dishes up the working-class ethnic family as the meat and potatoes of social stability—the offical answer to feminism, gay rights, open marriage, and the alternative lifestyles that have dotted the national horizon since the early seventies.

The past decade did not merely brush, it fundamentally altered the patterns of American life. Sons went off to war or into exile, daughters left home to take lovers and jobs, divorce rates soared, "gay" entered the popular vocabulary. Families looked at themselves and saw obsolescence on the wall and found their thoughts straying to the past—to tightly-knit immigrant communities where kin had banded together, to generations of ancestors whose survival stood in triumph over those who sought to destroy them.

Thus, at a time when the family was facing its greatest test, it was reborn as a symbol of permanence. Significantly, *The Deer Hunter* ends with a secular act of communion in which a surrogate family breaks bread together. This, like key scenes in *Roots* and other "working-class" films, calls upon an ideology that has not only been outstripped by the pace of change but runs counter to the ways people are actually conducting their lives. Beneath an occasionally radical facade, the appeal of these films rests on nostalgia and a ritualistic affirmation of a now departed *status quo.*

Another startling pattern that emerges in virtually every one of these films (as well as television programs like *Kojak* and *Petrocelli*) is the graphic contrast between the male protagonists and their female counterparts. Time and again, the "ethnic" hero—"swarthy," tough, and streetwise—is paired with women who are the very antithesis of identifiable ethnicity. Almost always (Talia Shire is a rare exception), the latter are blond, tall, and "ultrafeminine"; their accents like their backgrounds are "de-regionalized," their class origins obscured. Even Melinda Dillon, who plays Stallone's Slovak wife in *F.I.S.T.*, conforms to the pattern in physical appearance as much as in her speech.

Surely, it is no accident that most of the male characters are "Italian." (Harvey Keitel is an honorary "paisan" as Martin Scorsese's alter-ego in his early films; in *F.I.S.T.*, the hero is a Slav, but he is played by the "Italian Stallion" of *Rocky*.) For what the media understands by "Italianness" is a throwback to simpler, more primitive states of being: physical strength and violence, loyalty to outworn codes of honor, emotional spontaneity untempered by "middle-class" reflection, an uncomplicated sexuality that combines "instinct" with a protective chivalry and "respect."

But if to male middle-class America "Italianness" suggests a kind of barbaric atavism in which intellectual backwardness and undiluted *machismo* converge, it also has other connotations. Italians, particularly those from the South, are the black men of Europe; in their veins flows the blood of North Africa, and in contrast to the physical ideal of WASP America, they are not altogether "white." Among other things, therefore, these "working-class" films subliminally extol a *machismo* which weds sexuality to color. "Ethnicity" should thus be read as a codeword for "race"— race sufficiently "lightened" so as to remain acceptable to the moviegoing public, yet still "dark" enough to retain an exotic appeal.

In his pre-"born again" incarnation, Eldridge Cleaver had some perceptive things to say about the complex relationship of race and sex in American culture. White society, he wrote in *Soul on Ice,* created an image of the black male as a "Supermasculine Menial," whom it envies, fears, and despises. What we thus see in these films is a ritualized expression of very traditional American fears and desires. Transforming the heroes into "ethnics," however, kills two racial-sexual birds with one stone. It allows the white male audience to shed its middle-class codes of repression and identify vicariously with direct expressions of violence and sexual power (nowhere more completely than in the films of Martin Scorsese). On the other hand, to the extent that the celluloid heroes are "white," the fear of sexual emasculation by the black male is neatly sidestepped. Indeed, in films like *Rocky, Blue Collar,* and *Saturday Night Fever,* that fear is doubly neutralized by the introduction of black (or Latin) characters who enact in exaggerated form the same (white) roles. That they lose out in terms of audience sympathy has less to do with the intrinsic nature of their roles than an interpretation of those roles untempered by magnanimity or compassion. Travolta comes out a hero precisely because he hands over his prize to the Puerto Rican contenders, Rocky because of the grace and humility he shows under pressure.

If these films rely on stereotyping and code images to create their blue collar universe, the ethos they purvey is solidly middle-class. The guiding myth underlying *Saturday Night Fever* and *Rocky* is Horatio Alger: achievement and self-improvement, affluence and material accumulation. "Marrying up" into the ranks of homogenized blondness is one example of this. But the pattern appears with striking clarity in *Saturday Night Fever* where the solution to Tony's aimlessness is a subway ride to Manhattan. The Manhattan, however, to which Stephanie tries to lure him, is a far cry from the bright lights and Broadway glitter of myth. It is a specific phenomenon of the seventies: a landscape of renovated town houses and chic consumerism, hallmarks of the "gentrified" urbanites who make up the city's "New Class." To make it, Stephanie insists to Tony, you've got to get your head together, work hard, and mix with the right people. What she's really saying is that the American dream comes at the price of abandoning one's ethnic and working-class roots. To assimilated America, Brooklyn is no more than a colorful backdrop to be exploited for its accents and humor. "Real life" begins when the fantasies of America's image-makers have been taken to heart, and their myths have become articles of faith. With *The Godfather,* the cultural reality of ethnic America—invisible in the sixties—was resurrected. At the same time, a peculiar phenomenon emerged. Unlike European films such as Alain Tanner's *La Salamandre* or Lina Wertmuller's *All Screwed Up,* working-class identity was defined not in terms of work but as a lifestyle. Tailfin cars and juke-boxes, half-sentences and four-letter words—all of which were associated with black and working-class culture and recycled in the sixties into the counterculture—became the cinematic code for working-class life while the workplace retreated to the background. Like landscape in a genre painting, a Detroit assembly line added color. But the dramatic conflicts and action had their source elsewhere. If "real life" for Tony begins once he leaves Brooklyn, for Hollywood's other working-class heroes, it begins outside the factory gates.

Because class is a matter of lifestyle rather than economics, with the exception of *Norma Rae,* class conflict in these films is muted. The workplace appears as an isolated environment where bosses play a negligible role save for an occasional foreman and where there is no apparent connection between what happens on the shop floor and what happens on Wall Street. The real culprits of *F.I.S.T.* and *Blue Collar* are the unions—less because of their collusion with management than a generalized post-Watergate mistrust of bureaucratic institutions. Under a mask of critical liberalism, Hollywood projects onto the union and its membership the moral paralysis and cynicism associated with government. Cynicism, too, is the prevailing attitude toward collective action and the very notion of solidarity. Indeed, a typically American brand of individualism runs through these films, in which the "little man" takes on the Goliath of institutional corruption in the manner of an investigative reporter. His efforts, doomed to failure, are an object lesson in the pointlessness of political action, an appealing theme, no doubt, to the corporate conglomerates that now control Hollywood's major studios and distribution channels.

Hollywood's myth of the working class has been significantly shaped by Paul Schrader and Martin Scorsese, John Avildson and Sylvester Stallone, people who were touched by the catchwords of the sixties but unmarked by their radicalism. To a remarkable degree their films register the mood of the times. They have caught the pulse of the country, its uneasy accommodation with the changes of the past decade, its yearning for symbols of continuity. For Hollywood's new breed of filmmakers, the working class is ultimately a pretext in whose name corporate media voices the vague discontents of the seventies while discrediting the politics of change.

64 INDEPENDENT FILM AND WORKING-CLASS HISTORY: A REVIEW OF *NORTHERN LIGHTS* AND *THE WOBBLIES*

John Demeter

HOLLYWOOD'S CINEMATIC REDISCOVERY (and rewriting) of working class history parallels another recent development in American film—the appearance of a growing collection of independent, left, labor history films. *Northern Lights* (1978) and *The Wobblies* (1979) are two recent additions to a group that has included, among its more widely-known works, *Union Maids* (1976), *Harlan County* (1977) and *Babies and Banners* (1978).

Aesthetically and commercially, the two new arrivals are bringing a moderate degree of success and a growing "legitimization" of the genre: *Northern Lights* won the award for Best First Feature at the 1979 Cannes Film Festival, among other notices, and *The Wobblies* was selected for screening at the New York Film Festival last Fall. Following on *Harlan County's* Academy Award in 1977, one can only hope that the critical praise and exposure of both new films is pointing to a wider acceptance of this challenge to the media conglomerates' stranglehold on American film production and distribution.

Viewing the films politically, and in light of that long-term struggle, *Northern Lights* and *The Wobblies* present some lessons and questions for the "American Left" and the

From *Radical America* (Vol. 14, No. 1, Jan.–Feb. 1980). Reprinted by permission.

"independent cinema." Understanding that both these groups significantly overlap in these productions, we can see the films as a chance to reflect on the problems and potentials of that interrelationship. The five days of discussion, debate and struggle among the 400 participants at last June's "First U.S. Conference for an Alternative Cinema" was perhaps the clearest affirmation of the ties between left political activity and many independent media workers. While moving towards uniting these elements, the conference also reflected the problem of disorganization that both groups presently confront, and the funding/distribution dilemma faced by left film.

I was struck by one particular pairing mirrored both at the conference and in both *Northern Lights* and *The Wobblies*— that of elderly working class activists and 30-year-old filmmakers. It was a relationship that speaks quite clearly to the present and future alliance of film and political work.

The twelve interviewees of *The Wobblies* are aged 75 to 97, while the narrator of *Northern Lights* is 94. The overwhelming majority of media activists, meanwhile, at the Alternative Cinema Conference (including the producers of both films) came formed of the anti-war, black and women's movements of the '60's. The most visible presence of these activists' historical "roots" came in the person of three 70 year old producers whose work formed the base of the Communist Party's Film and Photo League in the '30's. In fact, the session chaired by these veteran activists (Tom Brandon, Leo Hurwitz and Leo Seltzer), at which they screened a number of their works, was one of the largest attended sessions at the conference.

The coming together of these two eras of politics and progressive media comes as no surprise. On one hand, it reflects a growing interest in some parts of the left to resurrect, study and analyze the historical roots of American working class and political radicalism. But at the same time, it also unveils a generational gap represented by the absence of left political leadership and progressive media representation from the '40's and '50's.

This disrupted history of both the people's movement and its media chroniclers presents, then, a major developmental problem for independent left cinema. The promising development of the new body of labor history films may help to overcome that disruption.

In serving as a link between present struggles and popular insurgencies of the past, *Northern Lights* and *The Wobblies* could not have come at a more opportune time. While *Union Maids* and *Babies and Banners* centered on the climactic trade union struggles of the '30's, particularly chronicling women's strategic roles in that period, the two newer films delve back even further, to the period before World War I that many historians consider the heydey of American socialism. In an era of widespread militant working class agitation, it was a time when populists and socialists alike were able to succeed electorally and by mass action in many areas of the country. It was also a period that witnessed a vicious and large scale response of state repression that suppressed and aided the demise of those movements.

As the near obliteration of much of this era from popular consciousness indicates, the repression was quite extensive. The historical and political importance of both films is thus magnified by their presentation of the first person witnesses of that period.

Northern Lights, a 90-minute dramatic "feature," is framed by the on-screen introduction and epilog of 94-year-old Henry Martinson. Martinson is a former organizer for the Nonpartisan League, the grass roots organization of populists and socialists, that swept to victory in North Dakota's state elections (1916) in an anticapitalist campaign directed against Eastern grain and banking interests. Shown reminiscing with an old diary at the outset, Martinson returns at the film's dramatic conclusion to speak of the need for continued struggle and presents us with the picture of an activist whose life-long dedication to socialism remained unaltered by the eventual demise of the NPL.

Providing most of the narration and anecdotal history in *The Wobblies* are the twelve octogenarian rank and file activists, whose insight and humor inject the film with a rare vitality and perspective. Addressing the audience at the screening of the film at the New York Film Festival, one of the film's subjects, 83-year-old Irma Lombardi, challenged viewers "to take it [the film] more seriously than just a good film." She added, "Of course, it's a nice picture, but it should bring home [to you] the sacrifice men and women paid."

Had either film been delayed, we would have stood to lose this first-hand testimony and witness. In fact, since the completion of *The Wobblies,* two of the interviewees have died. But each film's importance extends beyond its "timing." Both speak clearly, whether in matters of organizing and unionism or repression and fragmentation of the left, to areas of present-day urgency.

NORTHERN LIGHTS

Northern Lights is actually two stories. One is presented on film, the other is to be found in the three year odyssey of its directors, John Hanson and Rob Nilson, and their co-workers to fund, produce and distribute the work. The process of their work could produce a story almost as interesting as the film.

The film was produced by the San Francisco-based CineManifest for approximately $330,000. It grew out of the director's primary connection to the history of struggle of small farmers in the northern mid-west. Hanson was raised there and his grandfather was a NPL member and organizer; Nilson's grandfather was North Dakota's first filmmaker and had produced early footage of the NPL period. Their film seeks to retrace a lost heritage neither of the filmmakers remember learning anything about either from relatives or in public school.

With financial backing from the North Dakota Committee for the Humanities and Public Issues (an affiliate of the National Endowment for the Humanities), they began the research. Originally intended to form the middle film of a short documentary trilogy on the League and its history, *Northern Lights* evolved into a feature length dramatic work. With the personnel and experience of CineManifest behind them, the directors decided to ambitiously expand the project once further funding became available.

The filmmakers, actors and crew began travelling the state, researching the League and interviewing farmers and

historians. Their efforts won over the Divide County Historical Society in Crosby, North Dakota, which mobilized the
people of the county to provide clothing, props, farm machinery, old cars and the know-how to authenticate the period
piece. In addition to providing scene ideas, the farmers
played all but the three leading roles in the film, in some parts
speaking in their old Scandinavian dialect (sub-titled in the
film). In short, they participated in almost every phase of
production. Many parts of the film were played back at
different points for their reaction and criticism.

Given that history, it is no surprise that the world premiere
of the film was held on July 12, 1978 in Crosby, a town of
1,800 people. The film broke box office records at the town's
only theater, the Dakota, and audiences rose to give the film
a standing ovation. From Crosby, the crew travelled with the
film all across North Dakota running what they characterized
as a "grassroots political campaign." In addition to the
critical success the film enjoyed during its rural, small town
run, it proved able to financially support the outreach and
distribution campaign. The producers did find themselves
taxed by the many hours consumed in this type of work. It
was the personal commitment of the staff and crew that
supplanted the large media blitz most large studios can
bankroll.

Hanson described their apprehension in setting out for
Minneapolis and urban theaters: "The picture was in black
and white, no stars, no sex, had foreign languages with
subtitles and to top it off had a political theme." Runs in
Minneapolis, Madison and Seattle proved the work could
more than hold its own. After the trip to Cannes, the
unexpected award, and the ensuing enthusiastic reception
among European T.V. and film distributors, *Northern Lights*
was assured of a modicum of success. The testing of the
domestic market began again with a sweep through the
Northeast in the Fall of 1979.

"All of this has been very good for our egos," Hanson
commented, "but the question remaining is whether our
distribution path and future attempts modelled on ours are
economically viable." It appears that, at this time, it is not.
Short of a national network to support and sustain indepen-

dent film, questions of funding and distribution remain as the major hurdles.

All of this does not address the core of conscious political cultural work—the content, use and direction of the form. This remains problematic with the absence of a broad-based cultural formation or movement. That the aforementioned works have evolved in such an atmosphere speaks perhaps to the likelihood that conditions are ripe for this coalescing. But, leaving the larger questions aside, I'd like to discuss *Northern Lights* and *The Wobblies*—the films.

Northern Lights presents an instructive and vital addition to the predominantly documentary nature of most independent left film. Filmed in a grainy black and white, the film captures, in its bleak silhouettes and harsh contrasts, a sense of the land and its work that *Days of Heaven,* for all its lush cinematography, neatly opaqued. Focusing on the organizing efforts of farmer Ray Sorenson (Robert Behling) in the weeks before the successful NPL electoral campaign in 1916, the film is set against a backdrop of small, family wheat farms beset by harvest-threatening late fall blizzards. The film details Ray's reluctant entry into populist organizing at the urging of local League representatives. ("I've never met an organizer yet with a sense of humor," Ray comments.)

The young farmer opts at first to cynically ignore the organizer's overtures—"Is it fair to raise people's hope with all this talk?"—and work the harvest on his parents' farm with his brother John (Joe Spano). Heroically, Ray, John and neighboring farmers set to save not only their wheat but that of his fiance's ailing parents, in the midst of a howling blizzard. Had I not known that the blizzard was real, I would have credited it to brilliant studio-set special effects.

As was the case for many small farms at that time, it was the grain and banking interests that defined the "benefits" of the harvests. The farmers were forced to store their wheat and hope the fixed wholesale prices would rise. At this point, Ray's father dies and he must stand by helplessly with his fiance, Inga Olseness (Susan Lynch), as the local banker (played by *the* local banker) forecloses on her parents' farm and evicts them.

The conditions now gradually move Ray to consider more

active work with the Nonpartisan League. Sitting in a bar at the local grain elevator, he comments sardonically, "He [the dealer] steals the grain from you in the front and sells it back to you as liquor in the rear."

As Ray takes to the backroads of North Dakota, the film enters into its strongest portrayal—detailing the thankless, arduous task of winning over the isolated immigrant farmers, many of whom shared Ray's initial mistrust of "politics." The patience, humor and persistence of his efforts to defuse this cynicism is pictured, in both language and setting, quite realistically—a realism that connotes accuracy and humanism while avoiding romanticism. In fact, when one young farmer challenges Ray to wrestle him for his signing on with the NPL, I cringed in anticipation. But, it's Ray who's pinned, leaving the barn with the admonition that his opponent was the real loser.

But *Northern Lights,* beyond the historical narrative, is also a story of the tension between the political and personal aspects of Ray's life—his work on the farm and organizing with the NPL contrasted with his relationship to his brother, family and Inga. It is here that the film loses some of its probing, questioning edge.

The film does anchor its story, at its opening and conclusion, in the relationship of Inga and Ray. Following her partents' eviction and Ray's enlistment into the NPL, however, she is relegated to a sit-and-wait role. Inga serves to occasionally remind Ray of the "personal"—their postponed marriage, her loneliness. But she serves only to remind us of "questions" ("Sometimes the little things come first," "I don't know what the woman's role is now") the film evades tackling or confronting. Asked if it would have been inconceivable (historically) for Inga to have joined Ray in organizing, John Hanson referred to the few noted woman organizers of the time—Kate O'Hare, Emma Goldman and Mother Jones—and stated "she [Inga] would have had a hard time making it." "And there were local women who were very intelligent and persuasive in their own arenas but it would have been unrealistic," he added. "Realism" here, however, only subtly served to reinforce the stereotypical splitting of the personal and political. Ray's character remains very much the unemoting male organizer and the possible freedom in this dramatic form to delve briefly yet noticeably into that contradiction went untapped.

Northern Lights is at times stylistically selfconscious, producing some narrative dryness that was in no small way due to the economic pressures that forced an anti-improvisational manner in the filming. It still remains a very good film and one that will serve to bridge the long gap from *Grapes of Wrath, Salt of the Earth* and *Native Land* to new dramatic features chronicling an "unsanitized" people's history on film.

THE WOBBLIES

Made at a cost of approximately $180,000, *The Wobblies* culminates nearly five years of research by co-producers Stew Bird and Deborah Shaffer. While *Northern Lights* aids the rediscovery of North Dakota's Nonpartisan League, *The Wobblies* took on the task of resurrecting a national revolutionary labor organization whose erasure from popular consciousness was nearly as complete and vindictive as the persecution it buckled under at the outset of World War I. Made in the mold of *Union Maids* and *Babies and Banners, The Wobblies* is the most ambitious and politically direct labor history documentary to date.

The documentary grew from the script of "The U.S. Vs. William Haywood et al.," a play authored by Bird that was performed at the Labor Theater in New York in 1977. It was the personal contacts developed during the play's run, with ex-Wobblies who travelled to see it, that spurred on the work of the feature-length film.

With the research for the play as a base, Bird and Shaffer then began to construct a network of connections, with the Wobblies themselves, oral history projects, unions and leftists, that spanned the country. Eventually they were to anchor the film on interviews with twelve rank and file I.W.W. activists: Irma Lombardi, 83; Jack Miller, 89; Angelo Rocco, 95; James Fair, 80; Sophie Cohen, 77; Roger Baldwin, 95; Art Shields, 90; Nicholas Steelink, 89; Tom Scribner, 80; Dominic Mingone, 86; Nels Peterson and Katie Pintek, both 89. The group fairly represented the main arenas of struggle for the Wobblies in the period from 1905 to 1918: Paterson, New Jersey, Lawrence, Mass., and Philadelphia in the East; Bisbee, Arizona, Chicago, Illinois, and Seattle, Washington, in the Midwest and West.

Composed of nine men and three women, the group of interviewees included only one black. While this racial makeup accurately spoke to the outreach efforts of both mainstream and radical groups of the time, the directors were still frustrated in not being able to convey the I.W.W.'s progressive record among blacks and immigrants. As Shaffer explained, a large part of the I.W.W.'s work among black dock-workers took place in the organization's first years and nearly all the contacts they could track had died. Additionally, they were handicapped by the class and race bias of many historians, whose oral history and research work often deals only with white, male workers from that and following periods. She and Bird took up, in desperation, a six-month advertising and leafletting campaign around the docks of Philadelphia ("Was your grandfather a Wobblie?" read one leaflet) which resulted in their one black subject.

They encountered similar problems in the South, where the I.W.W. had brought many black and white workers together for the first time. The lack of written historical records in many rural parts of that area left the filmmakers unable to track many contacts. "If the film does anything," Stew Bird commented, "it will cause people to want to learn more [about the I.W.W.] . . . and their organizing down South."

With their twelve interviewees, the producers assembled a cinematic collage of rare film footage, stills, newspaper headlines and graphics to frame and elaborate the anecdotal history and reminiscences provided by the elderly activists. Complementing that portrait was the cultural work and its artifacts that provided people with perhaps one of the main contributions of the Wobblies—the cultural work embodied in their posters, leaflets and art work and their songs of struggle, satire and celebration. The music, particularly, is presented in the film quite movingly by Alice Gerard, Joe Glazer and Mike Seeger.

Underscored by the focus on rank and file Wobblie activists and their stories, the film also reflects the producers' attempt to present this history to a broader audience. And it is for this audience they attempted to debunk the many myths and false ideas that get resurrected along with the political history. "Nobody wants to deal with this period [1890–1920]," claimed Bird. "It's a period when the I.W.W. and the Socialist Party were very strong, a significant time for all labor, and people still continue to think that they didn't exist and that GM and Standard Oil, on the other hand, have been around as long as the U.S.," he added.

Both Bird and Shaffer point to the little-known realization that only twenty percent of the country's workers are now unionized as typical of the mythology that hinders trying to understand the conditions faced by the Wobblies. While unionism is a key element in the documentary (in fact the film shows the roots of many reforms—the eight-hour day and end of child labor—in radical not mainstream labor agitation), it is also an area where the film's weakness in presenting organizational history appears. While the producers acknowledge the I.W.W.'s preeminent position as the radical link in the period spanning the Knights of Labor and the C.I.O., that connection is unclear and not strongly supported in the film. The similarities in the I.W.W. and C.I.O.'s "industrial unionism" and the emergence of many of the latter's leaders from the ranks of the Wobblies is glossed over.

To be honest, the filmmakers flatly state that they were not attempting anything resembling a complete organizational history in the film. They are seeking to reach the rank and filers with the message that it was people like them who formed the base of groups like the I.W.W. "It's important for workers to understand that there's a history of radicalism in this country that's as American as apple pie," Bird related. That the film comes close to conveying just that message is in large part due to the humor, naturalness and conviction of the interviewees themselves.

There are many sharp and striking anecdotes and comments in the interviewee's recounting of the "bottom-up" history of their activism. My favorite was Jack Miller's definition of sabotage as "the conscious withdrawal of efficiency." Unfortunately, these glimpses are the only small sense we get in the film of the activists' lives outside of the workplace or their organizing, and the film suffers some from this lack of connection to day to day social concerns.

Beyond the strikers, confrontations on picket lines and stories of militant trade unionism, The Wobblies is also a story of the American radical movement and the widely feared organization that attempted to merge both the vanguard party and industrial union under one banner. In not attempting a complete organizational history, the film renders a sympathetic and at times, uncritical, view of the Wobblies. "The Wobblies' socialism was impossible to whitewash," explained Deborah Shaffer. And one result is a left labor history film that raises the vocabulary and parameters of socialist organizing in a direct, upfront style.

It becomes clear in the film why the I.W.W. represented such a direct challenge to American capitalism. What is not totally clear is why that vision disappeared. Much of the responsibility for their demise, although slightly overstated in the film, was of course due to one of the most widespread campaigns of repression this country has ever seen. And the film documents that with the newspaper headlines, accounts of the mass trials, deportations, lynchings and collusion between the A.F.L., the newly-formed F.B.I. (this was J. Edgar Hoover's first "case") and agents-provocateur. The directors even resurrected a Walt Disney propaganda cartoon from that era showing "Little Alice's Egg Farm" being infiltrated by the "Red Henski" (strikingly resembling Lenin) who agitates the chickens on to cries of "Smaller eggs" and "Shorter hours."

For all their charm and convincing accounts of the era, the Wobblies interviewed present little insight into what happened to the organization. As Irma Lombardi laments, "That's what hurt me. . . . I was looking forward and felt certain they would take over and then I never heard anything anymore." It is in this story of left fragmentation and division in the ranks of labor, spurred by repression, that the film speaks to the U.S. left and working class movement today. While incomplete, it can still serve as an adequate introduction to those contradictions.

Describing their attempts to recruit old antagonists to discuss the Wobblies in Bisbee, Arizona the directors realized the intensity with which the Wobblies were still viewed—

pro and con. "People still knew who was on either side, it [the forced deportations of I.W.W. members] was still a hot issue and people refused to talk to us," Bird recalled. That intensity will certainly follow the film today—particularly in its sharp portrait of the A.F.L.-I.W.W. rivalry.

In terms of audiences, *Northern Lights* and *The Wobblies* should prove particularly accessible to senior citizens, left and labor organizations, unions and ethnic groups. Beyond their educational and historical value, they can speak to a wider, if not mass, audience than previous works.

Reflecting on these two recent films, some critical points come to mind. As clearly as they and other films mentioned aid us in eradicating the national blind spot of radical and working class history, they also present a challenge to consider more closely the cultural presentation of that hidden history. Mass culture abounds with daily oversights and periodic attacks of amnesia that serve to blur our collective memory of the '60's—let alone periods two or three decades before.

While both works represent a clear growth of political cinema, both *Northern Lights* and *The Wobblies* demonstrate some lack of incorporation of the lessons of the Feminist Movement in this country. For all their manner of direct political orientation and historical insight, they still fall short of connecting work and political activity to people's everyday lives. There is still a separation of the personal and political, and lack of a fully dimensional portrayal of social and political life. The earlier films, *Union Maids* and *Babies and Banners* particularly, provided us with that orientation but without the full political context. So, perhaps, we're approaching that merger: demystifying the past and incorporating the lessons of our lifetime.

The session on independent films of the 1930s that John Demeter says attracted wide attention at the 1979 U.S. Alternative Film Conference at Bard College in New York was chaired by four (not three) 70-year-old veteran film activists. They were Tom Brandon, Leo Hurwitz, Leo Seltzer and David Platt (then 76). Demeter omitted my name in error, as he explained in a letter to me dated February 24, 1988. I was there as the former National Secretary of the Film and Photo League and former film critic of the Daily Worker. In fact I delivered the main address at the 1930s session. (DP)

65 WHO KILLED MARILYN MONROE?

Alvah Bessie

IN HER LAST PUBLISHED "INTERVIEW" (*Life,* Aug. 31, 1961), which was actually a very revealing piece of free association, Marilyn Monroe quoted Goethe as saying, "Talent is developed in privacy."

Then she added, "And it's really true. . . . But everybody is always tugging at you. They'd all like sort of a chunk of you. They'd kind of like to take pieces out of you. . . ."

"This industry," she said, "should behave [to its workers] like a mother whose child has just run out in front of a car. But instead of clasping the child to them, they start punishing the child."

On August 5, "the child," Marilyn Monroe, was dead of an overdose of nembutal. She was 36 years old.

No notes were left by the "sex symbol" of our time but in the *Life* article she put her finger on her murderers. For "they" is the motion picture industry and it is the motion picture industry that killed her.

If this sounds exaggerated, you need only cast a cursory glance at what had happened to this young woman, who was far from being merely a sex symbol. "That's the trouble," she told *Life's* associate editor, "a sex symbol becomes a thing. I just hate to be a thing."

And when she refused to be a thing she was cashiered. Her bankruptcy was announced triumphantly by Hedda Hopper in a front-page article in the *San Francisco Chronicle*

From the *San Francisco People's World* (August 18, 1962). Reprinted by permission of the author.

on June 19: "MARILYN MONROE is at the end of the road
. . . she has had it. . . . Fired by 20th Century-Fox, she
scarcely rates as an asset to any other producer who would
risk millions of dollars on her temperament and whims."

Naturally, Hopper said she felt "desperately sorry for her,"
but we scarcely need to be shocked by the sanctimonious
hypocrisy of a woman whose sole claim to notoriety lies in
the fact that she was one of the seven wives of the late
DeWolfe Hopper, for she had been gunning for Monroe ever
since her fame as a star was secure.

In a feature article in *Frontier* magazine (March, 1961) one
of the Hollywood 10 wrote:

> The bitch-goddesses hate her cordially and spare no pains to
> run her down, rip her up, castigate her for being late or
> "uncooperative" or not properly "grateful" to the industry. Of
> course her universal appeal is a sharp bone in the dry throats
> of the more dessicated (or obese) harpies of the gossip
> columns, but more important are other facts: she has not
> played the Hollywood game since her earliest days; she has
> not in ten years lent herself to the whole-cloth publicity which
> provides these parasites with their filet mignon and cham-
> pagne; she does not call up Dear Hedda or Louella Dear to let
> them "be the first to know. . . ."
>
> And still more important: she broke the Hollywood code,
> married a man held in contempt of Congress, stood by him
> while he was smeared all over the land and was finally
> vindicated by the higher courts. For there is no doubt that
> Miller's contempt is no small part of the contempt in which
> both she and America's leading dramatist are held by the
> movie columnists and gossips who are political reactionaries
> to a man or woman.

In the *Life* interview, Marilyn revealed a bit more about
what happened when Miller was on the rack: ". . . a certain
corporation executive said either he named names and I got
him to name names, or I was finished. I said, 'I'm proud of my
husband's position and I stand behind him all the way.'"

Miller did not name names and Monroe stood by him and
she revealed in her *Life* interview some of her own contempt
for the corporation executives who control the industry when
she said:

"After all, I'm not in a military school. This is supposed to be an art form, not just a manufacturing establishment."

Also—"I don't look at myself as a commodity, but I'm sure a lot of people have. Including, well, one corporation in particular, which shall be nameless. . . ."

Also—"And I want to say that the people—if I am a star—the people made me a star—no studio, no person, but the people did."

And—"If you've noticed in Hollywood where millions and billions of dollars have been made, there aren't really any kind of monuments or museums. . . . Gee, nobody left anything behind, they took it, they grabbed it and they ran—the ones who made the billions of dollars, never the workers."

For if Monroe was anything politically, she was a progressive. In *Redbook* magazine (August), she was asked if she had nightmares. "The H-bomb is my nightmare," she told the interviewer, and asked, "What's yours?"

Nor could she ever forget where she came from: the illegitimate child of a woman who has spent most of her life in a mental institution; farmed out to an orphanage and 12 foster homes; half-starved at times and kicked from pillar to post; "adopted" by religious fanatics and raped at the age of nine by a "friend of the family," she climbed from less than nothing to world-wide fame and financial affluence.

On top of this, she had suffered three marriage failures, one (or more) attempts at suicide and two miscarriages, and was tormented her entire life by the emotional instability almost inevitable to such a history. And the fact that this instability was one of the determinants of her death goes no distance at all to negate the fact that she was a victim of the industry's greed for profits and its determination to make its "hot property" toe the line of total conformity.

How else explain the vendetta that pursued her ever since she quit Hollywood cold in the '50s and went to New York to study at the Actors' Studio? At that time she was at the crest of her career and her films had made millions for her studio. But she wanted more: she wanted to become a fine actress instead of cheese-cake; she wanted better stories, better directors—and more money. And her studio capitulated.

But the vendetta persisted and there was nothing this

young woman did, whether it was to express a desire to play Grushenka in *The Brothers Karamazov,* to read books that were something more than superficial, to indicate that she took herself seriously, that was not utilized to make her the butt of ridicule and calumny.

The film that Arthur Miller wrote for her (*The Misfits*) was under attack before director John Huston rolled his first camera—and when it was released the avalanche of critical disdain for what was a progressive and a superior story was overwhelming.

The sniping at Monroe, as a person, continued daily and it came not only from Hopper but from Floribel Muir and Dorothy Kilgallen. From the sports writer Charles McCabe, the gents' room journalists, Walter Winchell, M. Miller, Herb Caen and Simon Lee Garth of *Confidential,* from the "fan" and "movie" magazines, from *San Francisco Chronicle* writers Lucius Beebe, Donovan McClure and Ron Fimrite, and even from such highbrow critics as Stanley Kauffmann of *The New Republic.*

The death of Clark Gable, immediately after *The Misfits* was finished shooting, was openly rumored to be Monroe's "fault." The break-up of her marriage with Miller, simultaneously, was attributed to a romance with Yves Montand, who starred with her in *Let's Make Love.*

Even her retreat to a psychiatric hospital in New York late in 1960 was made the occasion for snide comments by the harpies of the press whose sole allegiance is to what Hedda Hopper worships and wants to protect: the "risk [of] millions of dollars" on films that have to make more millions or they are worthless to their manufacturers.

Monroe is said to have cost 20th Century-Fox $6 million because she did not show up regularly on the set of *Something's Got to Give.* Elizabeth Taylor has cost the same studio many millions more because of her many illnesses and the time she took out to romance around Rome with her co-star in *Cleopatra.* But Fox will recoup those millions and make more, just as it would have made more with *Something's Got to Give* if it had shown concern for Monroe when she said she was ill.

Whether her illness was physical or psychological, only her physicians can tell. But Frank Sinatra was the only show-business personality to defend her at the time. He was quoted (United Press, July 20) as saying: "I was surprised by . . . Fox's action in shelving the film. It came time for the leaders of Fox to make a stand, and Miss Monroe was the whipping boy."

The "leaders" of Fox who had lost millions in the last five years—not because of Elizabeth Taylor or Marilyn Monroe, but because they made rotten films—have since ousted Spyros Skouras and reinstated Darryl Zanuck, as head. He will crack his riding crop, slam his desk with it, eliminate jobs and cut salaries.

But The Industry will be poorer for the loss of an adorable and magnetic personality who had the potential to become an artist instead of a sex symbol, or a "thing."

In 1956 Monroe told Pete Martin ("Will Acting Spoil Marilyn Monroe?"): ". . . I'm beginning to understand myself now. I can face myself more, you might say. I've spent most of my life running away from myself."

Even earlier, in 1952, *Life* (which, to its credit, has generally come to her defense, admired and understood her) said, "She is relaxed, warm, looks back on the hard knocks of her youth with no particular self-pity and only hopes they may have taught her a few things about people which will help her in her career. For, with all Hollywood at her feet, she is obsessed by an irrational childhood ambition; she wants very much to become an actress."

"The motivation [for her tardiness, her zeal for perfection]," said Jack Cole, her dance director, "is a terrible fear of failure. She is a great star without the background or experience. She is afraid and she is insecure." (*Life,* Aug. 15, 1960.)

And in the same article, the late Jerry Wald, who produced *Let's Make Love* for Fox, said, ". . . She is not malicious. She is not temperamental. She is a star—a self-illuminating body, an original, a legend. . . ."

The child christened Norma Jean Baker in Los Angeles' old General Hospital in 1926, had a childhood dream:

"I dreamed that I was standing up in church without my clothes on, and all the people there were lying at my feet on the floor of the church, and I walked naked, with a sense of freedom, over their prostrate forms, being careful not to step on anyone."

Some time during the night hours of August 4–5, Norma Jean Baker finally came to understand herself and the self-illuminating body burned out. Part of her childhood dream had come true: the people who made her a star had lain prostrate at her feet and she had walked naked and with a sense of freedom, being careful not to step on anyone.

But she had never been permitted or helped to become the artist she wanted to become and she finally understood herself and her situation in The Industry so well indeed that she ran away from herself forever.

66 LOOKING BACK FROM 1983: SOVIET FILMS AFTER WORLD WAR II

Jay Leyda

WHEN THE WAR ENDED in rejoicing and sorrow, the first effect on the Soviet film industry was a half-hearted effort to bypass the war as a subject, replacing it in the industry's themes by two purely political movements, "anti-cosmopolitanism" and the cold war.

In August 1948 the death of Andrei Zhdanov, responsible for much of the tight lacing of Soviet arts, offered no guarantee of less hindered filmmaking, for at the beginning of 1949 there was a strident and disgraceful campaign—against the "cosmopolitans." It is alongside Konstantin Simonov's definition of cosmopolitanism—as "the desire to undermine the roots of national pride because people without roots are easier to defeat and sell into the slavery of American imperialism"—that we must place, with astonishment, the filmmakers (nearly all of Jewish ancestry) who were the victims of this sweeping, poisonous attack. The first postwar issue in 1949 of *Iskusstvo Kino* labelled a "group of aesthetician-cosmopolitans in cinema" as including Leonid Trauberg (who had failed with his scenario on the scientist Popov), Mikhail Bleiman (his collaboration on *A Great Citizen* was not mentioned), and the critic-theoreticians Sutyrin, Otten, Kovarsky and Volkenstein. The evidence presented of their anti-patriotic behaviour was ridiculous:

From Jay Leyda, *KINO: A History of the Russian and Soviet Film,* 3rd. ed. Copyright © 1983 by Princeton University Press. Excerpt, pp. 398–404, reprinted by permission of Princeton University Press.

Trauberg had not praised *The Russian Question,* Bleiman had had an "intolerant attitude" to Pyriev's *Tales of the Siberian Land,* and Sutyrin had been impatient with Dovzhenko's published script of *Michurin.* A "cleansing of Soviet film-theory" was promised, menacingly. The first World Cinema volumes published in 1944 and 1945 on Griffith and Chaplin were used as damaging exhibits against Bleiman, a contributor to both; three other contributors were implicated without being named: Eisenstein, Kozintsev, and Yutkevich; the two last careers were seriously threatened for a time; Eisenstein[1] was protected by his death a year before. Another important name, Alexei Kapler, was dropped from all his script credits, including *Lenin in October* and *Lenin in 1918.* A third volume in the World Cinema project,[2] on John Ford, was quickly abandoned.

The films produced in 1949 and 1950 included a disproportionate number of anti-American subjects. After the Simonov-Romm *Russian Question* of 1947 nearly every Soviet film director rushed to write or direct a film on that villain, the United States. With Bolshakov frowning on continuing the Patriotic War on the screen, and the elimination of "the German" as villain, the dramatic convenience in these years of the American threat must have been as appealing to the film scenarist as the propaganda significance of revealing the Marshall Plan and related conspiracies. Alexandrov's *Meeting on the Elbe,* Kalatozov's *Conspiracy of the Doomed,* Romm's *Secret Mission,* Room's *Court of Honour,* were only the most notable contributions to a stream that by now (1983) is happily merely a trickle of sub-plots and stock characters. A counter-stream rushed as logically but imprudently from the other direction, with Hollywood turning out *The Iron Curtain, The Red Menace, I Married a Communist, Red Danube, Conspirator* at the depth of the cold war; scenarists there were no doubt just as relieved to have an artificial villain to replace the Japanese and German villains taken from them. Of course, neither stream ever reached the other's source—American screens were just as protected (by the Customs House) from anti-American films as were Soviet screens from anti-Soviet films.

Gerasimov, too, fired his verbal shot in the cold war when

he attended the Cultural and Scientific Conference for World Peace in New York in 1949. His characterization of the enemy's films was so clearly his description of Hollywood's films that no one could mistake him for diplomat or friend:

Some films state that to live better, to attain happiness, one must deceive, oppress and enslave, obtain profits by hook or by crook—shoving one's fellow-creatures around, pushing others out of the way and crushing everything in the path to make one's way to happiness at any cost. . . . Irrespective of whether they deal with wages, honour, love or matrimony the decisive argument in these films is violence, firearms, shooting, murder and death. The victor triumphs, he gains the right to happiness, though this is only for the time being since he is followed by another, a stronger one, who no longer depends on a revolver or a gun, but is equipped with a bomb.

And one of Eisenstein's last published articles was an attack on American films that one wishes had not been written, "Purveyors of Spiritual Poison."

Looking back at this embarrassment one sighs with relief that some of the most bitter anti-American films did not get beyond the script stage: Dovzhenko's *Farewell, America; Guarding the Peace,* written (before cosmopolitanism) by Bleiman, Kovarsky and Ermler; *Great Heart,* by Ehrenburg and Kozintsev; Arnstam's *Warmongers; The Man from Wall Street,* by Katayev and Kalatozov. It was no crime, artistically, to have composed such fierce invectives, even as weapons to protect the peace, but to have initiated so many of them, concentrating on this theme to the near-exclusion of others, was a mistake as absurd as the quantity of films at this time supporting Stalin's "personality cult."

The death of Stalin in 1953 and Khrushchev's temporarily secret report on him to the Twentieth Congress of the Communist Party in February 1956 are two dates within the postwar decade that cannot be ignored by any historian of a Soviet art. One striking aspect of Khrushchev's unexpected attack on the "personality cult" is that the only art repeatedly cited as misused to enhance the Stalin idolization is the art of the cinema:

. . . let us take, for instance, our historical and military films and some literary creations; they make us feel sick. Their true objective is the propagation of the theme of praising Stalin as a military genius. Let us recall the film *Fall of Berlin*. In it only Stalin acts, issuing orders from a hall in which there are many empty chairs . . . And where is the Military Command? Where is the Political Bureau? Where is the Government? What are they doing, what keeps them busy? There is nothing about them in the film. Stalin acts for everybody . . . Everything is shown to the nation in this false light. Why? In order to surround Stalin with glory, contrary to the facts and contrary to historical truth . . .

Stalin loved to see the film *The Unforgettable Year 1919* [1951], in which he was shown on the steps of an armoured train and where he practically vanquished the foe with his own sabre. Let Kliment Yefremovich [Voroshilov], our dear friend . . . write the truth about Stalin; after all, he knows how Stalin fought . . .

[Stalin] knew the country and agriculture only from films. And these films had dressed up and beautified the existing situation in agriculture. Many films so pictured collective farm life that the tables groaned beneath the weight of turkeys and geese. Evidently Stalin thought that it was actually so . . . The last time he visited the countryside was in January 1928, when he visited Siberia in connection with grain deliveries.

Nor was Stalin the only "personality" to exploit the film's possibilities. When Marshal Konyev later recited the vanities and exaggerations of Marshal Zhukov, he pointed out that when a film about Stalingrad was made (evidently the Virta-Petrov *Battle of Stalingrad*), Marshal Zhukov doctored the script to give himself an "undeserved role." By now the personality cult has lost some if by no means all of its film powers. Even showing the heroic Leader is no longer taboo.

A new type of film, two-edged in effect, was introduced on a broad scale in the early 1950s—partly the result of a scarcity of approved scenarios. Following the success of filmed collections of scenes from the repertoires of the Moscow Art and Maly Theatres, it was decided to make and distribute publicly film-recordings of complete theatre pro-ductions. During 1952 and 1953 twenty-five plays were filmed in the most important theatres of Moscow, Leningrad, and Kiev. The selection from the Maly Theatre concentrated on its Ostrovsky plays, while the Moscow Art Theatre offered Gorky's *Lower Depths,* Sheridan's *School for Scandal,* and their dramatization of *Anna Karenina*. Most of the other theatres showed Russian plays (favouring Ostrovsky), but plays by Lope de Vega and Goldoni were also recorded. Each of these uncondensed records was released in two full-length parts, and their popularity was marked. They competed on an equal footing with "normal" new films, for the recordings were always guided by experienced film directors (including Zarkhi, Solntseva, and Lukov) and film technicians, and of course they showed some of the best actors who were already familiar on the screen; young actors, too, for the productions of the post-war Theatre-Studio of Film-Actors were included in the recording programme. For those in Britain and America who see a more aggressive competitor in television it can be said that Soviet television, though widely used, has never rivalled the popularity of cinema as the Soviet theatre has. Many film energies, indeed, are devoted to preparing other purely theatre forms and works for film presentation. The most successful efforts to film opera have been Vera Stroyeva's disciplined adaptations of Mussorgsky's *Boris Godunov* (1955) and *Khovanshchina* (1959), both watched over by Dmitri Shostakovich; the most effective ballet-films have been Prokofiev's *Romeo and Juliet* (1955) and Plisetskaya's *Anna Karenina* (1975). Another original film drawn from the musical theatre is Shostakovich's *Katerina Izmailova* (1967), centred on the extraordinary dramatic soprano, Galina Vishnevskaya; all other roles are split between actor and singer.

When the major Soviet studios were evacuated in wartime to safer but cramped quarters in Alma-Ata and Stalinabad, the leading film school went with them. So, for a time, the most mature and immature filmmakers lived and worked in very close company, and their chief subject was the same—the war. One strikingly original approach to the subject emerged: groups of short fictional films were produced and circulated as "Fighting Film Albums". Literally everyone, before and after the evacuation to Central Asia, contributed to these, the best writers, directors, actors.[3] After the war such "almanac films" continued to be made. A continuing magazine series called *Fitil* (Fuse) of short comedies, anything from satire to slapstick—sometimes as short as a

single joke, varied the cinemas' programs. By 1982 the *Fitil*
series has reached No. 220! In addition to these, each studio
has occasionally brought together short films made by the
younger members of their staffs (fresh graduates from the
film school) under the titles of *Smiles, Street Adventures* and
the like.[4] It is unfortunate that foreign audiences never get a
chance to tap this stream of comedies and test films, to enjoy
making their own discoveries. At least three mature directors—Riazanov, Gaidai, Daneliya—have polished their comedy techniques to a point worth displaying abroad;[5] and
there are the gentle and wholly personal comedies made in
Gruzia (Georgia) that are also kept at home.

In the compilation film, the people at Mosfilm and the
Documentary Studios have learned how to gather and
manipulate archive footage for political and historical
themes. We lost Esther Shub (1894–1959) but gained a
recruit experienced in the fictional pavilions of Mosfilm:
Mikhail Romm. Romm did not intend *Ordinary Fascism*
(1966) to be his last blow against the cult of personality, but
his death left his next blow unfinished. So much buried and
"lost" newsreel footage has been unearthed (sometimes
literally!) that Soviet film and television viewers are seeing
their own history anew.

Few are left from the first generation of Soviet filmmakers,
and these few wisely divide their time between filming and
teaching. Those who died usually left plans or scripts
behind—the films they wanted to make. There has been no
attempt to explain the silence of Dziga Vertov's last years,
though his archive is sadly full of rejected ideas. No feature
film since *Lullaby* (1937) had been released over his name.[6]
Another loss: we'll never know what Parts II and III of *Ivan
Grozny* would have been if left in Eisenstein's hands. A
younger master also died too soon to realize a grand project;
the films of Vasili Shukshin (1929–1974) were so popular
that they alone would have financed *I've Come to Bring You
Freedom,* on the seventeenth-century uprising of Stenka
Razin.

Dovzhenko put aside many scripts before his death in
December 1956. Two of the films he tried to start (one a use
of Gogol's *Taras Bulba,* a project he had worked on since
1940)[7] were stopped with heart attacks that took him from

studio to hospital. His last plan came very close to realization; he told Georges Sadoul about it:

> In my new film there will be no mountain-peaks, no crimes, nothing to excite the spectator. All will be simple, without big effects . . .
>
> I have written a film trilogy that has for its frame and subject a Ukrainian village, my village. The first part—I have written it as a play—is set in 1930, during collectivization. The second part is an account of the fiery years of the Patriotic War, of the battles between the collective's farmers and the nazis. The third part comes up to our time. A great dam is built that places the village at the bottom of a new sea; the village dies under forty-five feet of waters that vitalize and impregnate the earth.
>
> I begin the production of this trilogy with its last part, *Poem About a Sea*. The title is perhaps too ambitious; I'd prefer *Prose About a Sea*. I have enjoyed planning my future work for the panoramic screen . . . In 1930, I saw such a giant screen [Fox Grandeur] in Paris and it made a profound impression on me. The long horizontal shape suits the elements in my next film: broad and monochrome steppes, stretching waters of a sea, airplanes, the idea of great spaces. . . .[8]

Poem About a Sea was prepared with great care. For two years before dramatic shooting was to begin Dovzhenko and two cameramen recorded the progress of the construction of the dam at Kakhovka. Compositions and details of the entire production were sketched by Dovzhenko, and the film's designer arranged these in a graphic continuity. Yulia Solntseva had worked on all stages of the preparation; the casting was completed, and on the night before studio shooting was to start Dovzhenko's heart stopped. His widow went ahead with the prepared production.[9] A more appropriate memorial to him was the renaming of the Kiev Studio as the Dovzhenko Studio.

Since the war years the young film industries of Soviet Asia have achieved a stability that did not seem probable before the war. It is one of the positive results of the temporary Asian wartime shelters for the studios of Moscow, Leningrad and Kiev—and the film school. Films from the republics of Uzbekistan and Turkmenia are proof and promise of more to come. The Kirghiz Studio is particularly fortunate in being headed by one of the most farseeing of Soviet writers, Chinghis Aitmatov. Not only does he nourish the studio with his stories,[10] but talented young Russian artists are welcomed by Kirghizfilm: Larissa Shepitko and Andron Konchalovsky made their first films under that roof, and the cameraman Sergei Urusevsky enjoyed directing his first film there. Inspired by the Kirghiz example, the Kazakh Republic has appointed a distinguished poet, Olzhas Suleimenov, to head their film enterprises.

Tbilisi has continued its tradition of encouraging young Georgian film talents.[11] The brothers Shengelaya, Eldar and Georgi, have pursued individual careers, courageous models for their contemporaries, Otar Ioseliani, Tengiz Abuladze, Lana Gogoberidze, Mikhail Kobakhidze. Other Georgians have shown their good work in Moscow studios— Kulidjanov, Daneliya, Khutsiev. Next door is Soviet Armenia and the troubled talent of Sergo Paradjanov—arrested on confused charges after making two of the most striking colour films in European film history, *Shadows of Forgotten Ancestors* and *Sayat Nova*. Question from the audience: What will he do now?

A great loss has been the early deaths of Vasili Shukshin and Larissa Shepitko. They had only enough time to show us their value to our future. The young originals, such as the remarkable critic Yuri Khanyutin, went through a certain amount of struggle with the administrators. This confrontation happens too often to be ignored, but this particular generation gap remains an unanalysed problem. Do the old men in charge of most of the world's movie businesses reject any film idea that goes beyond their formative film-going years?

It was sometimes after a long struggle, usually with the support of the Filmmakers' Union, that an "unusual" film would be allowed to find audiences abroad—that was the happy fate of *Andrei Rublyov* at Cannes, *Shadows of Forgotten Ancestors* at Mar del Plata, *The First Teacher* at Venice, *The Beginning* at New York. Of course, the world and domestic distribution of a *War and Peace* was attended by no anxieties, neither fiscal nor political. One man's solution was unique. After the crisis with *Rublyov*, Andrei Tarkovsky learned to bypass the mass audience, making beautiful puzzle films from which each flattered spectator could take away his interpretation as the only possible one. There were official obstacles, but never for long; foreign purchasers so discovered each of his handsome mazes.

Film festivals are good barometers of film health. After the war the international gathering at Moscow every other year began with lots of life and eagerness to be joining world films, but it is now more a market than a festival. But there are still two other Soviet film festivals where there is more hope. The Asian-African festival at Tashkent (on even-numbered years) is worth the long flight. When I consider that I first saw the work of Sembène (Senegal), Okeyev (Kirghiz Republic), Narliyev (Turkmenia), Sen (India) there, I am much in its debt. There is also an annual All-Union Film Festival that I have always wanted to attend, to see a cross section of the year's best, making for a more genuine competition—but there's no market reason to invite foreigners there.

One foreigner has reason to bless the Moscow Festival and film industry. When Akira Kurosawa thought that the Japanese film industry had deserted him and his career had ended, Mosfilm offered him a film of his own choice. After *Derzu Uzala* (1975), he was again employable, even in Japan.

Long ago, when I first saw Soviet films in New York, the quality that struck me first was that they looked quite unlike other films in the last months of the silent film. It was even less possible to compare the really extraordinary films (*October* and *Earth*, for example) with the biggest American films. But by the time World War II was over, the distinction was not so clear; apparently the war had produced an acceptable, international style—undisturbing, comforting, with a steadily diminishing ingredient of nationalism. As audiences grew younger—everywhere—many serious themes were pushed aside to leave room for "attractive" subjects, colourful or amusing, that could be trusted to represent their country as ambassadors of good will and good taste. At home (and this was certainly true of Soviet film production and distribution) the aim was to analyse every well-attended film to see how closely it could be imitated. In the film world national boundaries have never been very strictly defined. In the earliest years of film, almost a century ago now, this tendency to borrow successes can be regarded in a certain positive light: the swift international development of film ideas as well as techniques kept the audience constantly surprised and eager for more. Not all film-producing countries were strong enough to resist this increasing postwar pressure for entertaining product. Fortunately most of the Soviet studios employed artists who took their responsibilities and traditions seriously. But the war had decimated the first and second film-making generations (this was all too visible in the Ukrainian studios, even the one named after Dovzhenko) and the new film generation is convinced that their mission has been rewritten.

The bonus given to all studio workers was once measured by the quality of the films they had worked on, with all crews voting; now the main measure of the bonus is the number of tickets sold for each film. In spite of this new "incentive," whose damage is already apparent, positive surprises continue to emerge from all corners and capitals of the Soviet Union. Yet the greater a film's surprises the greater the obstacles erected between it and the Soviet—and world—audience.

Outside the Soviet Union as well as at Mosfilm and Lenfilm, the least discussable problem is the contradictions in the medium itself, an art and an industry. The sad, blank chapters in the careers of Stroheim and Flaherty have some motifs in common with the silences of Eisenstein and Dovzhenko. Though it is a discouraging notion to those workers and officials who give their lives to improving the physical circumstances of any film industry, it seems clear that the larger the "plant," the more convenient the equipment, the more organized the distribution apparatus—the greater the danger of the film growing less individual, more uniform, and less worth everyone's effort. Throughout Soviet film history, the films were finest when they had the individuality that any industrial administration, by its nature and purpose, was bound to distrust.

NOTES

1. E's Griffith essay is translated in *Film Form,* his Chaplin essay in *Film Essays.*
2. The ambitious plan was to publish individual volumes on foreign filmmakers of international importance.
3. See above, pp. 366–7, 446–8. The programme for this experiment was consolidated by Eisenstein, in a lecture given on 11 and 18 September 1941: No. 331 in "Published Writings," *Film Essays* (1982).
4. This good idea was introduced in Hungary, where the Balázs Béla Studio was organized especially to give the youngest film people a chance to show what they could do on their own, rather than as some senior's assistant.
5. Two outside sources that emphasize comedy production are Jeanne Vronskaya's *Young Soviet Film Makers* (London 1972) and Steven Hill's detailed report on "The Soviet Film Today," in *Film Quarterly,* Summer 1967.
6. To complete the record of Vertov's (wartime) film work: in 1941, *Soyuzkino-Journal* 77, 87; in 1943, *To You, the Front* (3 reels) and *News of the Day* 18; in 1945 *News of the Day* 4, 8, 12, 15, 20.
7. Other scripts from this period: *Opening the Antarctic* (1952), based on the 1819 notebooks of Thaddeus Bellinghausen, *Into the Depths of the Cosmos* (1954, on interplanetary travel), and the beautiful script on his childhood, *The Enchanted Desna,* realized by Solntseva in 1964.
8. *Les lettres françaises,* December 6–12, 1957.
9. Dovzhenko's script is translated in *Soviet Literature,* 6, 1957.
10. The three translated stories in Aitmatov's *Tales of the Mountains and Steppes* (Progress, Moscow 1969) have all been filmed.
11. The tradition began early. In preparing a recent Georgian retrospective for London, John Gillett discovered a forgotten work of stylized satire, *My Grandmother,* made in 1929 by K. Mikaberidze.

Significant changes have taken place in the realm of Soviet film art under Mikhail Gorbachev's glasnost, as witness the following report by Albert Prago on Alexander Askoldov's recently released 1967 film Commissar. *It appeared in the* Morning Freiheit, *a longtime chronicler and critic of Soviet anti-Semitism, on May 22, 1988:*

> *On a Thursday night in early May my wife and I drove from Queens into Manhattan in a driving, pelting rain to see a privately screened movie. To see a movie!*

But what a movie! We would drive through snow, sleet and hail to see Commissar *again . . . it's that good.*

Commissar *was produced in the Soviet Union in 1967, but hidden or suppressed or bureaucratized for twenty years. In 1987 it was sent to the international film festival in France and won a top prize. (The money, said the director-writer, went not to him but to the film ministry.)*

This extraordinarily moving film is an artistic triumph, melding all the arts and crafts of the movie-making industry beautifully and masterfully. The direction reminds one of the great Russian films of the 1920s—of Eisenstein and Pudovkin. The director has effectively merged realism with a spectacular impressionism, wonderful photography with exceptional camera technique, outstanding acting with excellent dialogue, lovely background music with studio and set sounds. Commissar *is quite a spell-binding tour de force.*

Why was this beautiful and powerful film held up for twenty years! Consider its content:

Year: Sometime during the Civil War.

Locale: a town (Berdichev) in the Ukraine.

Plot: A Red Army battalion commissar informs her superior officer that she's pregnant and is near term. After being mildly chastised, she is mustered out and is billeted in a tiny room of a hovel called home by a Jewish tinker, his wife, their six little children and a grandmother.

We see the Revolution through the eyes of a non-political Jewish worker and his passive but wonderfully compassionate wife. Their concern is survival—survival for the family and survival as Jews. When news comes that the Whites are advancing, the Jewish protagonist exclaims that he'll never realize his cherished dream of some day riding in a street car in Berdichev because "we'll all be dead." He complains that there have been many promises but none kept and things have simply gotten worse. It didn't make much difference, is his perception, whether the Reds or Whites were in town— Jews were blamed indiscriminately. They were a convenient scapegoat to be victimized in exceedingly troubled times. (Keep an especially vigilant eye out for a very poignant and tragically significant scene of five of the children acting out a pogrom)!

The woman Commissar, portrayed as supremely dogmatic and doctrinaire, undergoes a profound transformation. She is aided in a difficult birth by the Jewish couple and she sees at close quarters the special misery of her hosts. She cannot help but listen to the anguished cries of this Jewish father and the resigned hopelessness expressed by his beautiful wife. Living thus, midst the carnage of civil war, in the Jewish ghetto, the Commissar's world has been perceptibly widened.

In a fantasy sequence, the Commissar sees herself, carrying her newborn infant, following all the Jews in the town—men, women and children all wearing stars of David—into an awesome labor camp—a prophetic time projection. She stops short of entering the camp of death, and, no longer dreaming, returns to her revolutionary activity, but possessing a new, more humanist understanding. She has begun to see the special aspects of the oppression of Jews and, through the simple yet powerful descriptions by the young Jewish mother, she realises the terribly degraded status of women in Russia.

I must note that Commissar, *in which the Jewish theme—the principal thrust of the film—is so sympathetically presented, was done in 1967 when, paradoxically, anti-Semitism was a developing (although not new) phenomenon in the Soviet Union.*

At this special screening held at the Museum of Modern Art, during the question and answer period conducted by Alexander Askoldov, the Russian writer-director explained that near Kiev, the locale where the film was shot, there was a Babi Yar in every nearby town. (DP)

67 *JUDGMENT AT NUREMBERG:* AN INDICTMENT

David Platt

*J*UDGMENT AT *NUREMBERG* is a fine and courageous film, probably the best we have had on what the Nazis did and were and still are. It is an imaginative and absorbing reconstruction of the war crimes trial of high members of Hitler's Ministry of Justice and of the Judiciary. The trial of the judges was one of the 12 secondary war crimes trials (others in this group included the industrialists, generals and physicians) that were begun after the cases of the principal members of the Hitler gang were completed.

Though *Judgment at Nuremberg* is a fictionalized account of the judges' trial, it is nonetheless thoroughly and deeply rooted in fact. It was produced and directed by Stanley Kramer, who more than anyone now working in and out of Hollywood is carrying on the Roosevelt tradition in the movies. He has to his credit a long list of films in almost each of which there is imbedded a significant kernel of meaning. One of his recent works, *On the Beach,* was a trenchant commentary against nuclear insanity.

Judgment at Nuremberg is that rarity for Hollywood, a film of ideas. It is magnificently acted by Burt Lancaster, as a repentant Nazi judge; Richard Widmark, as an angry U.S. prosecutor, "a radical protégé of FDR," someone says of him, who is determined to win the maximum punishment of the Nazi judges; Judy Garland as the principal witness in the brutal frameup of an elderly Jew; Spencer Tracy as Judge

From *Jewish Currents* (January, 1962). © 1962. Reprinted by permission.

Haywood, a kindly, old-fashioned Republican liberal and admirer of Roosevelt; Maximilian Schell, as the forceful chief Counsel for the Defense; Montgomery Clift, as a victim of perverted Nazi science.

Prominent among the film's virtues is an illuminating discussion, particularly important for these times of fallout shelter hysteria and soft-pedalling of the annihilating character of nuclear war, of how, in the name of national security and patriotism, it is possible for a whole nation to run amuck and commit treason against itself and against the world.

In a powerful courtroom scene in which Lancaster holds the audience in a commanding grip, the former liberal judge who had deluded himself into justifying the gas chamber as the final solution for the Jewish question, tries to explain what happened to himself and to most of Germany under Hitler. "There were devils among us—Communists, liberals, Jews, Gypsies. They said that once the devils are destroyed our miseries will be destroyed." And he goes on to explain why those who, like himself, knew better, knew that the words were lies and worse than lies, went along with the fascists. It was, he said, "because we loved our country."

They loved their country, and so they kept silent when Hitler began shrieking his hate in the Reich; and when their neighbors were being dragged out in the middle of the night to Dachau they kept silent too.

"Where were we," the repentant criminal judge who had made a mockery of justice cried out in the Nuremberg courtroom, "when every village in Germany has a railroad terminal where cattle cars were filled with children who were being carried off to their extermination? Where were we when they cried out in the night to us? Were we deaf, dumb and blind?"

It is good to have a film like this that reminds us of the monstrous crimes that can be committed in the name of "love of country."

Abby Mann, who wrote the screenplay for Kramer's film adapted it from his own television play, which the now defunct CBS Playhouse 90 produced in the spring of 1959. This was the play that caused an uproar a few hours before the opening when its gas industry sponsor ordered the deletion of all references to Nazi gas extermination chambers.

It is one of the virtues of Mann's brilliant script that it never for one moment permits us to forget what happened in those gas chambers. A documentary film taken when British troops liberated Belsen and Buchenwald is used by the U.S. Prosecutor in *Judgment at Nuremberg* to show that it all began when a judge wearing a robe with a crooked swastika sewn into it framed and sentenced an innocent man.

There is a nightmarish shot of giant bulldozers pushing and burying huge mounds of flesh and bones which had become a menace to the living. "Break the body—break the spirit—break the heart"—that was the motto at Buchenwald, the prosecutor tells the court, and there follow shots of the huge piles of brushes, shoes and gold taken from the victims, shots of lampshades made out of human skin, of a human pelvis used as an ashtray, of the shrunken heads of murdered Polish workmen and other gruesome articles fashioned out of human hair and bone.

Among other things *Judgment at Nuremberg* gives us a powerful refutation of the contention of the Nazi judges' Defense Counsel that only a few Germans were aware of the full extent of the inhuman crimes committed by the Nazis. This theory was endorsed, by the way, by Gen. Lucius Clay in 1950 at a time when he was commuting some of the sentences meted out to the convicted war criminals at Nuremberg.

We see in this film about Germany in 1946–1948 that there are no more Nazis. Everybody hates Hitler. Nobody knew what was going on in the camps. There are only good Germans who, had they but known, would have done something about it. . . .

And so a German housekeeper who had lived a bare 30 miles from Dachau tells Judge Haywood that she knew nothing about Jews being murdered. "We were nonpolitical," she insists. "But Hitler did some good things," she tells him. A Mme. Berthold (Marlene Dietrich), aristocratic widow of an executed war criminal of the Junker class, cries over her cocktail, "we are not monsters. We didn't know. We hated Hitler and he hated us."

Nobody knew! Judge Haywood is soon straightened out
on the facts of life by Prosecutor Lawson, "Don't you know,"
he says, with eyes blazing, "that it was the Eskimos who
invaded Germany and took over. That's how all those terrible
things happened. It wasn't the fault of the Germans. It was
those darned Eskimos."

Three of the four Nazi judges completely reject the, to
them, fantastic notion that millions of Jews had died at the
hands of the Nazis. "It's impossible," one of them says
angrily, and at dinner time in the prison restaurant he asks a
fellow Nazi who had worked with Eichmann for clarification.

"It's possible," he replies, cool as a cucumber, and as
though the question asked had to do with slaughtering cows
for the market. He goes on to say it, "all depends upon your
facilities. Say you have two chambers which will accommodate two thousand people apiece. Figure it out. It's possible
to get rid of 10,000 in half an hour. You can tell them they are
going to take showers and then, instead of water, you turn on
the gas.

"It's not the killing that is the problem," he adds. "It's the
disposing of the bodies. That's the problem."

In other scenes, *Judgment at Nuremberg* takes a critical
look at U.S. postwar policy that shut its eyes to the rebirth of
Nazi ideas, encouraging and financing militaristic attitudes
and programs in West Germany. A Pentagon official on duty
in Nuremberg at the time of the Berlin blockade is seen
urging leniency for the Nazi judges. His grounds for this are
similar to the ones heard during the Hitler era. Russia is the
enemy to watch. Germany is the key to survival "and we are
going to need all the help we can get!"

One of the important aspects of Kramer's film is that it
does not go along with the official line. In the end, Judge
Haywood finds that he cannot honestly shut his eyes to the
murder of 6,000,000 Jews. The four judges, including the
repentent one, are given life imprisonment, over the dissenting vote of one of the three U.S. judges.

At this point the Counsel for the Nazis offers to bet the life
sentences won't last five years.

A final statement on the screen declares that of the 99 men
sentenced to prison by the time the judges' trials had ended
in 1949, not one is still serving his sentence as of 1961. By

1959, said the London *Jewish Chronicle* of November 29, 1959, no fewer than 1,000 former Nazi judges, almost all responsible for the deaths of thousands of liberals, Jews, anti-fascists and others, were again practicing at the same old stand in West Germany.

Kramer is to be saluted for a fearless and inspiring film.

68   CLAUDE LANZMANN'S *SHOAH:* ANNIHILATION

Amos Neufeld

S HOAH, A NINE-HOUR-LONG documentary film, is a compelling detailed inquiry into the annihilation of European Jewry during World War II. The film, made over a ten-year
period by Claude Lanzmann, is the most comprehensive
documentary yet made on this difficult and often incomprehensible subject. Acclaimed a masterpiece, *Shoah* is a work of
major importance and unparalleled impact, a film as rigorous
in its pursuit of detail as it is meditative in composition. Through
his use of detail, Lanzmann slowly draws us into the heart of
the abyss and leads us through its labyrinthine recesses.

Shoah—the Hebrew word for annihilation—is composed
around a series of interviews with the victims, perpetrators
and bystanders. The film does not contain a single frame of
archival footage; it is made entirely in the present. The
interviews are interwoven with contemporary scenes of the
death camps, Polish towns, rivers, fields and woods—the
landscapes of death as they appear today, their lush beauty
incongruously reclaimed by nature.

Trains, arriving at Treblinka and Auschwitz, like a refrain,
run through the film and punctuate it. They transport us to the
death camps and transport the past to the present.

Mr. Lanzmann has said that he wanted to refute the notion
that the Holocaust belongs to the past, that it is only a

From *Jewish Journal* (April 24, 1987). Reprinted by permission of the
author.

memory: "The film I have made is a counter-myth. It is an inquiry on the present of the Holocaust, or, at the very least, on a past whose scars are still so fresh and so inscribed in places and on minds that it appears with hallucinatory timelessness." Lanzmann has thoroughly succeeded in his mission. Anyone who sees Shoah will never again see Germany, Poland or this world of ours without seeing it through the lens of the Holocaust.

Lanzmann's camera probes and accuses. All the Poles interviewed admit that they knew about what was happening to the Jews. Polish peasants still living on the edge of former death camps, when asked how they feel about the extermination of the Jews, seem indifferent, even pleased. "If you cut your finger, it doesn't hurt me," says one Pole. They smirk; they claim they were affected by the horror they witnessed across the barbed wire, but, nevertheless, they continued to cultivate their fields beside death.

The Polish townsfolk of Chelmno tell the filmmaker that they are better off without the Jews: The Jews exploited and cheated them; before the war the Jews and Germans ran everything; Jews were rich, their women were beautiful because they didn't work. The Poles in the interview pile fantasy onto prejudice. Listening to them, one can't help but recall that Poles slaughtered Jewish survivors in pogroms after the war. A virulent strain of anti-Semitism exists today in Poland—even without Jews.

Lanzmann juxtaposes the past and the present to striking effect. He informs us that during the war, the Jews of Chelmno were imprisoned in the church before they were murdered. In the next scene, a crowd of Poles standing outside the church claims sympathy for their murdered Jewish countrymen, but in no time their anti-Semitism surfaces: they rationalize the murder of the Jewish Christ-killers; they deserved their fate, the crowd nods in agreement. The camera focuses and stays on a church procession. The head priest covers his face with a cross, but as the procession turns he is unmasked. Lanzmann then points the camera at the cross on the church steeple, silently accusing the church and the town of more than just indifference.

The Nazi officials who are interviewed, the men who made

it all possible, reject any responsibility. They claim to have known less than the Poles or the Jews. Franz Suchomel, former SS Unterscharfuhrer at Treblinka, dispassionately describes in exacting detail how the death camp worked. (He does not know that he is being filmed or the real purpose of the interview.) He explains his role in increasing the "efficiency" of the camp—how he reduced the time between the arrival of the Jews, gassing them and disposing of all the traces of extermination. He didn't want to panic the next arrivals, he explains: it would have reduced the efficiency of the death apparatus. "Auschwitz was an efficient death factory," he tells the filmmaker, "but Treblinka was merely a crude assembly line which functioned well anyhow!" There is a note of pride in his recollection. Throughout the interview the audience waits for a clue, a motive for this man's heinous crimes. We wait for a pang of conscience, a hint of remorse, but get none. This murderer, like most of the other Germans interviewed, seems to have amazingly escaped all sense of responsibility. Should not Treblinka have deeply scarred him? Or is there nothing in him to scar, no shred of humanity? Could this lack of humanity explain his ability to focus on the efficiency of death while in the clutches of the hellish world that he himself perpetuated, if not created.

Another macabre note is struck in interviewing Walter Stier, the German official in charge of dispatching the death trains to the gas chambers. He talks about "group rates," "vacation and tour packages" and "special trains." Listening to Stier, the viewer confronts the sheer absurdity of this man's denial. Stier acknowledges that his special trains, used to "resettle" Jews, went to concentration camps. But he claims he didn't know their ultimate destination. He was in charge of the Reich's railway, he says, not of extermination.

The perverse thinking of these men goes on. One German official who "administered" the Warsaw ghetto claims that he was really helping the Jews "maintain" themselves in the ghetto (even as they were starving to death and being deported to Treblinka for extermination). These men, for some strange reason, do not seem burdened by their crimes. Of all men, they seem to have found it easiest—and most convenient—to forget. And by forgetting them the world has allowed them to forget.

Remarkable as these interviews are, these murderers (all free men) remain a mystery; their hearts and minds, their callousness and savagery remain unfathomed.

Unlike them are the victims, men who have held onto their memory and humanity, even after having faced the nightmarish abyss which often overwhelmed them. We feel their agony. As they tell their stories, they sometimes cannot go on: in retracing their steps, they relive the painful events. Yet, they go on for the record, for the living and for the dead.

The victims that Lanzmann chose to interview worked as maintenance men in the bowels of death. These men poignantly relate to us how they faced the ultimate dilemma: they knew that their survival depended on their assistance in the destruction of their fellow Jews. Yet, in order for them to rebel and bear witness, they had to survive. In the face of this horrible decision many of the Jews in these special units committed suicide. As one of the survivors, Filip Muller says: we confronted life's infinite price.

Muller, a member of a special unit working in the gas chamber and crematorium, describes the terrible battle that took place every time the gas chamber doors were sealed: inside, the fierce struggle against death was horrible. One night, after having witnessed the savage beating of his fellow countrymen, Czech Jews who had refused to undress and enter the gas chamber and instead sang the Czech national anthem and "Hatikvah," Muller, terribly moved, and feeling the sheer despair and helplessness of that moment and that his life had lost all its meaning, walked into the gas chamber to join his countrymen. A few women approached him and told him that his death would not bring them back to life. He had to survive to bear witness to the cruelty and the injustice that they had suffered.

Shoah bears witness. It is a requiem of corroboration. Detail by detail *Shoah* recreates a world that some have called "another planet," but which nevertheless is ours to confront. Viewing the film, one is both profoundly moved and disturbed. *Shoah* may very well change the way we see things—as it should.

Lanzmann brings us face to face with the Holocaust, this awesome event which he merges with the present, integrating it as he thinks we must all do if we are to hold onto our humanity in the face of destruction.

The complete text—words and subtitles—of Claude Lanzmann's nine-hour documentary film, with a preface by Simone de Beauvoir, is available in a Pantheon (division of Random House) hardcover or paperback edition. (DP)

FINAL WORDS

David Platt

As I WRITE THIS in the summer of 1989, the first thing that crosses my mind is that the cold war has subsided, symbolized by the Washington-Moscow summit meetings and the standing ovation that a packed House Armed Services Committee meeting gave to Soviet Marshal Akhromeyev (Gorbachev's top military adviser) at the end of his four-and-a-half hour appearance there July 21. Who in one's wildest dreams of past years would have believed that this would happen in 1989, or that the Soviets that same year would grant permission to one of its major publications, Moscow's *Novy Mir,* to publish the long-banned Solzhenitsyn novel, *The Gulag Archipelago,* or permit a Soviet historian to reveal publicly for the first time that Stalin himself ordered the assassination of Leon Trotsky. As Nikolai A. Vasetsky wrote in *Literaturnaya Gazeta,* it was Col. Leonid Eitingon of the NKVD (Stalin's secret police) who gave $5,000 and a false passport to a Spanish communist, Ramon Mercader, who on August 20, 1940 smashed Trotsky's skull with an axe in Mexico. And a decade later (the McCarthy 1950s), the beating of war drums in our own country could be heard loud and clear from the moment the U.S. acquired a temporary monopoly of the H-bomb. American citizens were forthwith dubbed "red agents" and worse simply for expressing a desire for peaceful co-existence. Remember the *New York Times* dispatch from Hollywood (1950) that a motion picture dealing with the life and exploits of Hiawatha had been shelved because it was thought that the portrayal of his efforts as a peacemaker among the warring Indian tribes of his day (it brought about the Federation of Five Nations) might be considered helpful to communist propaganda for a similar co-existence. Cecil B. DeMille was then reported listening to taped speeches by General Van Fleet (U.S. commander in Korea) with a view to using him as the Voice of God in Paramount's *Ten Commandments* (*Newsweek,* 1950).

Regrettably, I was not able, for reasons of time and space, to deal with every significant controversial film of the century—silent and sound. If there is a second edition of this anthology, it should include material on Abel Gance's *Napoleon,* Charles Brabin's *Driven,* F. W. Murnau's *Sunrise,* Luis Buñuel's *Los Olvidados* and *Viridiana,* Robert Flaherty's *Nanook of the North,* Kurosawa's *Rashomon,* Roy Boulting's *Fame Is the Spur* and *Thunder Rock,* Herbert Kline's *Forgotten Village,* Joseph Losey's *Don Giovanni,* Roberto Rosselini's *Open City,* Nikolai Ekk's *Road to Life,* Manfred Kirchheimer's *We Were So Beloved,* and others.

Finally, a moment's silence in memory of the screenwriters, directors, producers, actors, historians and critics who died in recent years. Almost all contributed articles to the anthology: Honor to Bela Balasz, Alvah Bessie, Herbert Biberman, Thomas J. Brandon, Samuel Brody, Charles Chaplin, Lester Cole, Alexander Dovjenko, Sergie Eisenstein, Otis Ferguson, Lorraine Hansberry, Joris Ivens, Gordon Kahn, John Howard Lawson, Jay Leyda, Albert Maltz, Roger Manvell, Lewis Milestone, Samuel Ornitz, Harry Alan Potamkin, Jean Renoir, Harold Salemson, Adrian Scott, Gale Sondergaard, Robert Stebbins (Sidney Meyers), Philip Sterling, Dalton Trumbo, Dziga Vertov, Herman Weinberg, Michael Wilson.

CONTRIBUTORS

GRIGORI V. ALEXANDROFF assisted Eisenstein in the films *The Strike, Potemkin,* and *October,* of which he was coauthor and coeditor, and other works. He spent much time on *The General Line.* Experimenting with sound films, he produced *Romance Sentimentale* and *Internationale.* He accompanied Eisenstein to Hollywood. After 1935 he became involved in films of a kind of musical comedy which starred the singer Lyubov Orlova, whom he married. After the conclusion of the second 5-year plan, he produced the charming *Tanya.* In 1947 he produced the strange comedy *Spring.*

ALEXANDER BAKSHY was a prominent film theoretician and critic. His essay "The Kinematograph as Art," written in 1913 and first published in 1916 in *The Drama,* Chicago, was one of the earliest major statements on the cinema as an art medium. He was the film critic of *The Nation* from 1927 to 1933. See Harry Alan Potamkin's tribute to him in *The Compound Cinema,* by Potamkin and Lewis Jacobs (Teachers Press, Columbia University, 1977).

BELA BALASZ (1884–1949) authored four influential film volumes in his native Hungary, one of which, *Theory of the Film,* was translated into English by Edith Bone. No one, with the possible exception of Eisenstein, has written with greater eloquence and insight on the art of cinematography. Indispensable to film students is Joseph Zsuffa's recent biography of Balasz (University of California Press, 1986).

CEDRIC BELFRAGE (London-born) wrote on films for American and British publications before settling in New York.

There he cofounded and edited the radical newsweekly *National Guardian* until 1955, when he was deported from the United States at the behest of Joe McCarthy. Belfrage did translations from the Spanish in Mexico, where he lived for many years until his death in 1990 aged 85.

ALVAH BESSIE (1904–1985), one of the "Hollywood Ten," wrote novels, screenplays, and film criticism before, during, and after the McCarthy era. Bessie fought in Spain as a member of the Abraham Lincoln Brigade and wrote about it in *Men in Battle* and *Our Fight*, an anthology of writings by veterans of the Lincoln Brigade which he coedited with Albert Prago. Among his novels is *The Symbol*, a fictionalized account of Marilyn Monroe's life, which he adapted for a TV play in 1974. The story of the blacklisting of Bessie and others of the "Ten" is told elsewhere in this anthology, as well as in Bessie's *Inquisition in Eden* and Gordon Kahn's *Hollywood on Trial*.

HERBERT J. BIBERMAN (1900–1971) was a top Theatre Guild director of plays such as Sergei Tretyakov's *Roar China*, Maxwell Anderson's *Valley Forge*, and Lynn Riggs' *Green Grow the Lilacs*—the basis for the musical *Oklahoma!*, before going on to Hollywood to direct films. He was a founder of the Directors Guild and a force in the Hollywood Anti-Nazi League, the kind of social activism that contributed to his being blacklisted, as one of the "Ten," during the McCarthy era. The independently made 1954 film *Salt of the Earth*, which he directed from a screenplay by Michael Wilson, remains the most significant of his career.

THOMAS J. BRANDON (1910–1982), a pioneer labor film producer, distributor, and organizer of film societies, was a member of the National Board of the Film and Photo League in the early 1930s. Later he founded Brandon Films as a principal distributor of socially significant American and foreign feature films and documentaries. During World War II he was on the Committee of Seventeen which distributed films prepared by the Office of War Information and other government agencies. A large collection of his papers and documentary films is available for study at the Museum of Modern Art Film Study Center in New York.

SAMUEL BRODY (1907–1987) was a pioneer documentary filmmaker and a founder of the Film and Photo League, as well as one of the first in the USA to speak and to write about the Soviet silent film renaissance of the late 1920s. He was especially attracted to the ideas of Dziga Vertov, and did much to bring to public attention the originator of the "Kino-eye" and "Radio-ear"—a kind of socially-conscious "candid camera" technique for capturing on film "everyday life caught unaware." Brody's papers, including a taped interview with him by Brandon, as well as a few of the films he worked on at the Film and Photo League in the early 1930s and in the streets of Passaic, New Jersey, in the mid-1920s are accessible at the Museum of Modern Art. Brody's last film, unhappily a lost film, was the 28-minute 1965 award-winning documentary *The Roar of Many Waters,* which dealt with Black history, past and present.

KEVIN BROWNLOW, a British film historian, has done more than anyone involved with cinematic art to retrieve, restore, and revive the lost treasures of the silent screen. He is the author of numerous articles and two notable volumes on the silent era, *The Parade's Gone By* and *The War, The West and the Wilderness.* The third of the trilogy—it is devoted to the social problem film before the era of sound—is in the works.

RUSSELL CAMPBELL, a New Zealander who studied film at the London School of Film Technique, then at the University of Wisconsin and Northwestern University, went on to edit two texts on motion picture photography, and to found the *Velvet Light Trap,* a highly regarded journal of social film history and criticism, headquartered at the University of Wisconsin. He has also published a number of film essays and a book on radical U.S. films of the 1930s.

LESTER COLE (1904–1985) wrote a great many screenplays, including the excellent wartime anti-Nazi film *None Shall Escape* and several others of unusual value, before being cut down by the blacklist as one of the "Ten." In his autobiography, *Hollywood Red* (1981), he writes that his early influences were Maxim Gorky, Jack London, Hawthorne, Dreiser, all the Russian, French, Irish and English writers who "at that very moment, as for years before and many to come, were changing the minds and hearts of people all over the world." They changed his in the early 1920s. In 1925 he was "completely absorbed, living, laughing, crying in the world of literature and drama, feeling joy and fear and love and envisioning the nobility of fighting for a socialist life for all, along with the sense of agony that was the lot of most people struggling to survive in a world of hunger, cruel torture and pain. . . ." Read Cole's book to find out why federal authorities decided that he was a security risk. Incredibly, they had him put under surveillance for 32 years, "tracked, trailed and tailed" by paid informers and agents to see what he was writing and who his friends were.

GARY CROWDUS is the founding editor and publisher of the quarterly *Cineaste.*

HECTOR CURRIE is Associate Professor of Film at the University of Cincinnati, and the author of numerous articles on cinema and classic and modern drama. His 1972 book on film, *Encounter* (w. Donald Staples), has an introduction by John Howard Lawson.

JOHN DEMETER is an editor of the bimonthly *Radical America* (38 Union Square, Somerville, MA 02143), and a member of the Angry Arts Film Collective in that area.

SERGEI M. EISENSTEIN (1898–1948) first came to world attention with his cyclonic film *Battleship Potemkin* in 1925. Although he completed only seven films, such as *Potemkin, October, Alexander Nevsky, Ivan the Terrible, Part 1 and 2,* and one or two others, he remains one of the screen's most influential masters. His greatness lies not only in his finished films and contributions to the technique and art of the cinema, but, as with Leonardo da Vinci, also in the breadth of his visionary theoretical and philosophical principles. All students of film art should be grateful to Eisenstein's brilliant pupil Jay Leyda (1910–1988) for editing, translating, and publishing collections of Eisenstein's writings in English. (*The Film Sense, Film Form, Notes of a Film Director,* and *Film Essays,* all readily accessible to students at the Museum of Modern Art Film Study Center.)

OTIS FERGUSON (1907–1943) was the film critic of the *New Republic* in the 1930s.

LYNN GARAFOLA has written film criticism for *In These Times, Socialist Review, Commonweal, Radical America,* and other journals.

MAXIM GORKY (1868–1936) wrote several novels and a play that were made into films in the USSR, France, Japan and China. Pudovkin's 1926 silent film *Mother,* based on the Gorky novel of the same name, was voted one of the "12 Best Films of All Time," at Brussels in 1958, by a jury of historians from 26 countries. The same jury ranked Eisenstein's *Potemkin* as "The Best Film in the World" by 100 votes out of 117 cast. Soviet director Mark Donskoi also did a trilogy on the life of Gorky in the late 1930s, the best of which was *The Childhood of Maxim Gorky.* It had a cast of extraordinarily gifted actors headed by Varvara Massalitinova as the Grandmother and M. Troyanovski as the Grandfather. Gorky's play, *The Lower Depths,* was filmed by Jean Renoir in France in 1936 with a cast that included Jean Gabin, Louis Jouvet, Vladimir Sokolov and Robert Le Vigan. The play was also filmed by Chinese director Tse-Ling Wang in China in 1948 and in Japan by Akira Kurosawa in 1957.

ELSA GRESS-WRIGHT, a prominent Danish writer who lives in Marienborg, Denmark, was a close friend and neighbor of two world famous Danish screen artists: silent-film actress Asta Nielsen (1883–1972) and film director Carl Dreyer (1889–1968), maker of one of the all-time great films, *The Passion of Joan of Arc* (1928). *Celluloid Power* features essays on both these artists.

LORRAINE HANSBERRY (1930–1965) sat down to write a play in 1956 which, as she later wrote to her mother, "tells the truth about people, Negroes and life." The play, *A Raisin in the Sun,* opened in March 1939—and thus was marked a turning point in Black and American theatre because, as James Baldwin has written, "Never before in the entire history of the American theatre had so much of the truth of Black people's lives been seen on the stage." One might add that with this play Hansberry became, at 29, the only Black dramatist ever to win the Best Play of the Year Award of the New York Drama Critics. In 1961, Hansberry's film adaptation of the play was nominated for Best Screenplay and won a Cannes Film Festival Award. Published and produced in some 30 languages abroad and in thousands of productions across the U.S., *A Raisin in the Sun* was to become an American classic. It brought into the theatre a new black audience, and encouraged a new generation of black artists, playwrights, and performers. In its now legendary first cast and director, every one of whom was to make his/her own subsequent mark on theatre and film—Lloyd Richards, Sidney Poitier, Claudia McNeil, Ruby Dee, Diana Sands, Louis Gossett, Ivan Dixon, Glynn Turman, Douglas Turner Ward and Lonne Elder, III—it proclaimed unmistakably the resources and depths of black talent. Five years later, on January 12, 1965, during the run of her second play, *The Sign in Sidney Brustein's Window,* Lorraine Hansberry died of cancer. She was 34. In her short life she had participated, both as activist and artist, in some of the most momentous events of her time. In her plays she illuminated the lives and aspirations of ordinary people confronting, in their own ways, the fundamental challenges and choices of the age. "Her commitment of spirit . . . her creative literary ability and her profound grasp of the deep social issues confronting the world today," said Martin Luther King Jr. on her death, "will remain an inspiration to generations yet unborn."

GORDON HITCHENS is Associate Professor of Cinema (since 1972) at C. W. Post/Long Island University. He is also founder of *Film Comment* and its editor for 27 issues. He was guest editor for three special issues of *Film Culture* (edited by Jonas Mekas) on the Hollywood blacklist, the art of Chaplin, and the American films directed by Joris Ivens during World War II. Hitchens has been on/off consultant for years to Nippon Audio Visual Library (Film Archive) and to Hiroshima/Nagasaki Publishing Committee (producer of anti-war and anti-nuclear documentaries). For the past 15 years he has also served as U.S. representative to NYON (Switzerland) International Documentary Film Festival, as well as assisted at other international film festivals in East and West Germany and Italy. In January 1988 he won a Fellowship of $3,500 from the Writers Guild of America Foundation (New York) for his original feature-length screenplay *The Diamond Pilot*.

LEO HURWITZ was a founder of Frontier Films (with Paul Strand, Sidney Meyers, Irving Lerner, John Howard Lawson and others). For that pioneer 1936 organization he made *Heart of Spain* (w. Strand), on the Spanish Civil War (1937), and *Native Land* (1941), also with Strand. Paul Robeson was the narrator of this powerful plea for unions and workers' rights. Since then Hurwitz has produced 15 principal films, including the award-winning 1981 *Dialogue with a Woman Departed*. In 1947, after three years as a CBS producer and founding head of the news department, he made *Strange Victory*, a feature documentary about the Allied victory over German fascism and its implications for racism in the U.S. Blacklisted in the '50s for his political views, Hurwitz continued to work independently. In 1956 he wrote, directed and produced *The Museum and the Fury*, a study of World War II concentration camps. In 1961 he won an Emmy and a Peabody for his direction of the TV coverage of the Eichmann trial in Jerusalem. From 1969 to 1974 he headed New York University's Graduate Institute of Film and Television.

JORIS IVENS, a Netherlander who made his home in Paris, died there, at the age of 90. He was known all over the world as "a kind of Flying Dutchman" (French film critic Georges Sadoul's phrase) who made films of social struggle in many countries and always seemed to be present with his camera at crucial moments in history. But whether the film he undertook was *Rain, New Earth, Borinage, Spanish Earth, Indonesia Calling, Our Russian Front, Song of the Rivers* or *Easy Spring—600 Million People Are With You, China,* his purpose was always the same: to imbue deep poetic feeling into whatever political message he sought to communicate. As Ivens said in his 1984 interview with Deborah Shaffer in *Cinéaste* (reprinted in this anthology): "We are like poets. Poetry can outdo a novel by saying something precisely and concisely, by condensing things. . . . The power of poetry should play a large part in our work. Filming reality is copying it, but you have to go further than that, into art. I don't know if I've succeeded, but I still worry about it. Think about the genius of Dante, who in a poem could describe a battle scene as it looked from the air. When I was in a fighter plane during the war, it looked just as he had described it. How he did it, God knows, but he did it in his imagination. So you shouldn't be afraid to ask your imagination to do more than you think you can."

LEWIS JACOBS is a documentary filmmaker of distinction and a noted teacher of film courses on a university level, as well as a film historian whose books are essential reading for all students of the medium. Although his documentaries have won five medals at international competitions and 22 citations of merit for direction and cinematography, he is best known as the author of the classic, *The Rise of the American Film* (1939) and of such other film volumes as *The Emergence of Film Art* (1969), *The Movies as Medium* (1968), *The Documentary Tradition* (1971) and *The Compound Cinema: The Film Writings of Harry Alan Potamkin* (1977). Also, Jacobs was the founder (with David Platt) of the now legendary journal *Experimental Cinema* (1930). Forty years later, in the early 1970s, when it was rediscovered by another generation of film students for its advanced positions on the politics and aesthetics of film art, all the issues were reprinted in a handsomely bound volume by Arno Press, a subsidiary of The New York Times. Copies are available for study at the Museum of Modern Art Film Study Center.

PAUL JARRICO, Hollywood screen writer and producer, lived and worked abroad for many years following his blacklisting during the McCarthy era. He is best known today as the producer of the independently made 1954 film, *Salt of* *the Earth* (directed by Herbert Biberman from a screenplay by Michael Wilson).

DOROTHY B. JONES wrote film reviews and articles for *The Hollywood Quarterly* and other California journals during the war years. In addition to her MIT monograph on *The Portrayal of China and India in Hollywood Films: 1896–1955* (reprinted in large part in this anthology) she did a valuable study of Hollywood's contribution to the war effort in her capacity as head of the Film Reviewing and Analysis Section of the Hollywood branch of the U.S. Government's Office of War Information. See her article, "Hollywood War Films, 1942–1944," in *The Hollywood Quarterly* (October 1945), for her finding that of a total of 1,313 Hollywood films released between 1942 and 1944, about 45 or 50, or about 4 percent, significantly aided world understanding of the nature of the conflict.

ARTHUR KNIGHT was the film critic of the *Saturday Review* in the 1960s and author of the much-thumbed and oft-quoted *The Liveliest Art* (1957) as well as teacher of film courses at UCLA and other universities. One of his last works was to write the Foreword for Harcourt's 1985 anthology of reprints from *New Theatre and Film, 1934 to 1937,* the monthly New York magazine founded and edited by Herbert Kline.

LINDA KOWALL is a freelance writer and film historian whose articles have appeared in the *Philadelphia Inquirer, Pennsylvania Heritage, American Film,* and other publications. In 1984 she served as guest curator (w. Joseph P. Eckhardt) of the Siegmund Lubin exhibition sponsored by the National Museum of American Jewish history in Philadelphia and aimed at rescuing from oblivion the long-forgotten film pioneer.

RING LARDNER, Jr. (son of the famous American humorist) was a successful screen writer until blacklisted as one of the Hollywood Ten. His most important screenplays were the anti-Nazi *Cross of Lorraine* (1944) and *Tomorrow the World* (1945), and the 1942 Academy award-winning *Woman of the*

Year (w. Michael Kanin). More recently, Lardner turned to writing TV plays under pseudonyms, including one or two with other blacklisted film writers, and he also published a novel, *The Ecstasy of Owen Muir.* Today he is best known for his film and TV work on *MASH.*

JOHN HOWARD LAWSON (1895–1977) was a distinguished dramatist, screenwriter, historian and theatre and film theoretician. He wrote ten plays, including *Processional* (1925), *Success Story* (1932) and *Marching Song* (1937). He published two indispensable volumes for theatre and film students: *Theory and Technique of Playwriting* (later expanded to include Screenwriting) and *Film: The Creative Process.* His *Hidden Heritage* was a notable work of cultural history. Among his screenplays was *Blockade* (1937), Hollywood's first and only significant anti-Franco film on the Spanish Civil War (parts of the script were altered by front-office censors). His anti-Nazi wartime films *Action in the North Atlantic, Sahara* and *Counterattack,* were effective in their day. What was unique about Lawson was that the humanist writer and public-spirited citizen were tightly intertwined. In Hollywood he worked to organize the Screen Writers Guild in 1933, and was elected its first president. He helped establish the Screen Actors Guild as the powerful union it eventually became. In Boston, in the week before Sacco and Vanzetti were executed by the State of Massachusetts, he participated in last-minute efforts to save them. He once wrote that this was a turning point in his life and work. In the early 1930s he continued his political education by making two trips to the deep South, visiting Angelo Herndon and the "Scottsboro Boys" in their prison cells in Georgia and Alabama, and that was only the beginning of his work for social justice and social progress—work that in the McCarthy period would make him a central target of the witchhunters and blacklisters. Sufficient to add that he was one of the Hollywood Ten.

JAY LEYDA (1910–1988) wrote Charles Musser, his friend and collaborator, "was the leading film historian of his generation, and his *KINO: A History of the Russian and Soviet Film* (1960), remains perhaps the model one-volume history of a national cinema" (*Radical History Review,* 1988). In the mid-30s, after a short stay as a member of the New York Film and Photo League, Leyda went to Moscow to study with Sergei Eisenstein at the State Film Institute there. Within a year or two he was good enough to serve as apprentice director and still photographer on Eisenstein's unfinished and unreleased 1935 film, *Bezhin Meadow.* In addition Leyda was beginning to collect, translate, edit, and publish the Soviet director's theoretical writings, first in American periodicals, then in book form (*Film Sense,* 1942; *Film Form,* 1949; *Film Essays and a Lecture,* 1968, etc.). In 1941, when the United States and the Soviet Union were wartime allies, Leyda found work in Hollywood on such films as *The Bridge of San Luis Rey, Song of Russia* and *Mission to Moscow.* Later he held film posts at the Staatliches Filmarchiv in East Berlin, at the Cinemathèque Française in France and the British Film Institute in London. His years at the Chinese Film Archive in Beijing from 1959 to 1964 resulted in his book, *Dianying—Electric Shadows: An Account of Films and the Film Audience in China.* Leyda's scholarly interests extended to literature and music. He wrote and edited books about Melville, Emily Dickinson, Mussorgsky, and Rachmaninoff. At the time of his death Leyda was Filmwood Professor of Cinema Studies at the Tisch School of the Arts, New York University.

EDWIN LOCKE was in charge of photographic research for the U.S. Film Service during the Depression Decade and worked on such productions as *The Fight for Life* and *Ecce Homo.*

HERBERT G. LUFT, a Jewish journalist trapped in Nazi Germany, escaped to England in August 1939 after having been confined at Dachau during the previous winter. Since 1943 he has been working in Hollywood as an editor, production assistant, writer, and associate producer, and has contributed articles on the cinema in magazines the world over.

TIMOTHY J. LYONS is Professor of Mass Communication at Emerson College in Boston. He has previously served as faculty member and administrator of media arts programs at Temple University, University of Houston, Southern Illinois University at Carbondale, and Youngstown State University. His book *Charles Chaplin: A Guide to References and Resources* is considered the standard bibliographic work on Chaplin. He has also authored works on various topics in U.S. silent film history, media aesthetics and criticism, and legal aspects of mass communication research.

ALBERT MALTZ (1909–1985) wrote socially conscious dramas, novels, short stories, and screenplays during his 50-year career as a writer. Two of his documentary films, *Moscow Strikes Back* (1942) and *The House I Live In* (based on the Lewis Allan/Earl Robinson wartime song, 1945), won Academy Awards. The New York Film Critics Circle singled out the former as the Best War Documentary of 1942. His most memorable films were *This Gun for Hire* (1942), *Destination Tokyo* (1944) and *Pride of the Marines* (1945). The latter, which made effective statements against anti-Semitism, was premiered in 28 cities at Guadalcanal Day banquets under U.S. Marine Corps auspices (those were the days). Maltz's anti-Nazi novel, *The Cross and the Arrow* (1944), was issued in a special edition of 140,000 copies by a wartime government agency for American servicemen abroad. Other novels included *The Journey of Simon McKeever* (1949) and *A Long Day in a Short Life* (1957), reflecting his prison experiences as one of the "Hollywood 10" incarcerated for defying the McCarthy Committee. Maltz's long career, filled with controversy, included being raked over the coals in 1946 by the CP's cultural division for writing an article in *New Masses* suggesting that outstanding works of literature need not necessarily be connected with political propaganda, that the slogan "Art is a Weapon" should be revised to emphasize the word "art." He recanted his views but, as with Galileo, the "earth still moved." The Khrushchev revelations of Stalin's crimes lifted his blinders. In 1977 Maltz was among the 15 Americans who addressed an *Open Letter to Gustav Husak*, president of the Czecho-slovak Socialist Republic and general secretary of the CP of Czechoslovakia, appealing to him to honor the 1975 Helsinki

Accord—"a solemn commitment to respect the human rights of your citizens." The Letter condemned the jailing, blacklisting and harassment of those who signed Charter '77. "They perpetrated no crime in petitioning you to keep your word. It is you who commits a crime in abrogating your treaty obligations. And an even greater crime in making a mockery of socialist democracy. Do not tell us your internal affairs are none of our business. During the McCarthy period, when we ourselves were jailed, blacklisted and harassed, it was international outrage that helped us to regain our rights."

ROGER MANVELL (British-born, 1909–1987) was a dramatist, screenwriter, and professor of film at Boston University College of Communications in the last decade of his life, as well as the author of a number of books on film, among them a biography of Charles Chaplin. During World War II he worked at the British Ministry of Information, specializing in film. After the war he served as director of the British Film Academy for 12 years.

CARL MARZANI, at 76, is writing his memoirs, *The Education of a Reluctant Radical,* and putting the finishing touches to his long-delayed book on George Orwell. He is represented in this anthology with an interview in *Cinéaste* on his work as the founder of Union Films in the 1950s.

DAVID MATIS (1906–1988) was for many years the City Editor and UN Correspondent of the Yiddish *Morgen Freiheit.* In his later years he also served as an editor of the *Jewish Daily Forward.* His book, *The World of Charlie Chaplin,* published by YKUF in New York in 1959, remains the only study of this film genius in the Yiddish language. Eric A. Goldman, author of *Visions, Images, and Dreams—Yiddish Film Past and Present* (University of Michigan Press, 1979), acknowledges in his Dedication his debt to Matis as one of the three persons (the other two were his father, Ephraim L. Goldman, and film historian Jay Leyda) who influenced him to undertake his project. Matis was the first to recognize "the need for research on aspects of Jewish cinema and who brought together Yiddishkayt and cinema history."

LEWIS MILESTONE (1895–1980) was one of the 19 Hollywood screen artists called to Washington in October 1947 to testify before the House Un-American Activities Committee, but he was not one of the ten who were indicted. At the beginning of the Great Depression Milestone directed the powerful anti-war film *All Quiet on the Western Front* and the crackling newspaper story *Front Page. Of Mice and Men* followed a decade later. During World War II Milestone directed several outstanding anti-Nazi and anti-Axis films such as *Edge of Darkness, North Star, Purple Heart* and *A Walk in the Sun.* The decline of Hollywood under the impact of the McCarthy witchhunts inevitably affected the later work of this fine director.

PETER MORRIS, the founder and former Curator of the Canadian Film Archives, teaches film history and aesthetics at various universities in Canada. He was responsible for the English edition of Georges Sadoul's *Dictionary of Films* and *Dictionary of Film Makers* and is the author of several monographs on individual directors, *Shakespeare on Film,* and a forthcoming history of Canadian cinema.

AMOS NEUFELD, an Israeli-born poet living in New York, writes frequently on films for Jewish periodicals.

BERNARD L. PETERSON, Jr. is Professor Emeritus of English and Drama at Elizabeth City State University, Elizabeth City, North Carolina, a constituent institution of the University of North Carolina. He is the author of *Contemporary Black American Playwrights and Their Plays* (Greenwood Press, 1988), which was named an Outstanding Academic Book of 1988 by *Choice.* He is currently completing two additional books under contract to Greenwood: *Black American Writers for the Stage, Screen and Broadcasting* and *Encyclopedia of the Black American Musical Stage.*

DAVID PLATT was born on January 12, 1903, in Lugansk in the Ukraine, near Kiev, and was brought to this country the following year. Growing up in Pennsylvania he was a self-educated high-school dropout, who first studied the violin and then switched to films and journalism, supporting himself as a stenographer. He became a close friend of the socially conscious film scholar Harry Alan Potamkin, and in 1930 he founded the journal *Experimental Cinema.* He met Eisenstein in California. In 1934 he became National Secretary of the Film and Photo League, editing its journal *Film Front.* From 1933 to 1958 he was film critic for the *Daily Worker.* He began writing for *Jewish Currents* in 1958 and joined the Editorial Board in that year. In 1966 he began writing for *Morgen Freiheit,* becoming editor of the English pages a few years later. In 1980 he began a weekly classical music session for the senior citizens at the Brookdale Center in Long Beach, Long Island. He has a wife, Alice, and a son, David.

ABRAHAM L. POLONSKY directed his first feature, *Force of Evil,* and was the screen writer on others, when the McCarthy witchhunt was beginning to terrify Hollywood. Blacklisted for years and forced to work under pseudonyms on 15 feature films, Polonsky returned to directing, after 21 years, with *Tell Them Willie Boy Is Here* (1969). Long before that, however, he, together with writer Walter Bernstein (blacklisted because he was the instigator of an ad in *The New York Times* protesting against the blacklist) and the late Arnold Manoff, acquired control of the CBS television series *You Are There.* "This series," said Polonsky to interviewers later on, "was probably the only place where any guerrilla warfare was conducted against McCarthy in a public medium." The Polonsky-Bernstein-Manoff unit at CBS was able to produce plays about Socrates, Savonarola, Milton, Galileo, and others at a time when people were afraid to open their mouths to talk about the things that needed saying about freedom of thought, witchhunting, book-burning, freedom of speech and the press, etc. In Yugoslovia, during the blacklist years, Polonsky made *Romance of a Horsethief,* based on Joseph Opatoshu's Yiddish novel about Cossack-hating Jewish villagers. (See DP, *Jewish Currents,* October 1971.)

HARRY ALAN POTAMKIN (1900–1933) wrote some of the finest film criticism of his time in the six or seven years he was able to function as the critic of *Closeup* in England, *New Masses* and *Hound and Horn* in New York, and elsewhere. *The Nation* (weekly) said it all in its eulogy on his death in 1933: "Potamkin revealed in his reviews and articles a familiarity with the motion picture, past and present, as so complete as to inspire the same implicit confidence in his authority as a Bernard Berenson writing on Florentine paintings or a T. S. Eliot writing on Elizabethan poetry." *Hound and Horn's* tribute went further: "It is safe to say he knew more about the art of film than any one in this country, and except for the great Russian directors who were his friends and admirers, as much as anyone in the world." Read the Potamkin/Jacobs volume for the facts of his life and work. Born in Philadelphia in 1900, Potamkin—the fourth child of poor Russian immigrants—spent his early years doing odd jobs and dreaming of becoming a poet. The future film critic worked at the University of Pennsylvania for his tuition and contributed poems to school periodicals. When he turned to the new medium of films, what engaged his attention were the things that other critics overlooked as dull and unimportant. He wrote about women film directors; the child as part of the movie audience; film treatment of Jews, Blacks, and other minorities; capital-labor subjects; colonialism; and war.

JEAN RENOIR (1896–1979) belongs at the very top of the list of the French school of filmmakers: Abel Gance, Jacques Feyder, René Clair, Julien Duvivier, Marcel Carné, Germaine Dulac, Jean Repstein, Leon Poirier, Jean Benoit-Levy, among others. Two powerful influences shaped Renoir's film career: 19th-century impressionist painting—Auguste Renoir was his illustrious father—and the novels of Emile Zola, plus, of course, Zola's famous *J'Accuse* in defense of Alfred Dreyfus. Two of Renoir's film adaptations of Zola—*Nana* and *The Human Beast* (the latter with Jean Gabin as a symbol of alienated man, defiant, without hope or direction)—have rarely been surpassed as masterpieces of cinema with a social conscience. Two other Renoir films demand attention for their eloquent statements against war's affect on the human personality, the first, *Grand Illusion* (1937). Although it portrayed life in a World War One

German prison camp, one of its aims was to remind France and the world of the mortal danger to all free people arising from the agony of the Spanish Civil War that was unfolding in 1937, the year *Grand Illusion* was released. A perhaps even more powerful statement on French upper-class society on the eve of the occupation was Renoir's corrosive satire, *Rules of the Game,* issued in 1939. Only a mutilated version of this Renoir classic survives, however, thanks to Vichy regime censorship urged on by its Nazi watchdogs. This was an aesthetic crime exceeded only by the mutilation of von Stroheim's *Greed* and Eisenstein's *¡Que Viva Mexico!* During the occupation Renoir was forced into exile in Hollywood where he was able to make *This Land Is Mine,* about France at war, and several other exceptionally fine films.

LENNY RUBENSTEIN was, over the many years of *Cinéaste,* one of the editors (with Gary Crowdus, Editor-in-Chief), and he contributed many film reviews, interviews, and articles to the magazine.

MORRIS U. SCHAPPES was a founder and has been editor of *Jewish Currents* since 1958. A member of CCNY's English Department, from 1928 to 1941, he was dismissed as a result of the Rapp-Coudert Committee witchhunt and imprisoned for 13-½ months for refusing to be an informer. In 1981, CUNY's Board of Trustees apologized to him and some 40 others similarly fired for the injustice done them. He is the author of two volumes on American Jewish history: his third book, on Emma Lazarus, has just recently been published by the Jewish Historical Society of New York. From 1972 to 1976 he was Adjunct Professor of History at Queens College.

ADRIAN SCOTT (1912–1972), one of the "Hollywood Ten," has the distinction of being the producer of *Crossfire* (1947), the first full-length Hollywood film in which the theme of anti-Semitism was a significant part of the plot. The film was in the form of the familiar detective story. What was different was that one of the murder suspects, an ex-soldier, had a pathological aversion to "jewboys who live on easy street." But that was only one aspect of a film that connects blind, ugly hate with a loaded gun that can and does kill. Scott's connection with it contributed to his severe prison sentence. *Crossfire's* director, Edward Dmytryk, also one of the "Hollywood Ten," recanted his views while in stir in exchange for naming names.

LEO SELTZER, one of the most prolific of the filmmakers associated with the Film and Photo League in the early 1930s, went on to make films for NBC, CBS, Columbia Pictures, U.S. Information Agency, United Nations, National Film Board of Canada and many others. During the war years he directed training and public information films and was second unit director with John Huston on *Shades of Gray,* dealing with the treatment of war-related emotional problems, later released publicly as *Let There Be Light.* Seltzer's films won many awards, including an Academy Award for Best Documentary in 1948 and the Robert Flaherty Award in 1950. He has taught film technique at Brooklyn College, Columbia University, New York University, City College and elsewhere, and has appeared as guest lecturer at universities and film festivals the world over. His Film and Photo League films and photographs were featured on the 1987 Bill Moyers TV series, *A Walk Through the 20th Century,* in the section titled "The Reel World of News."

DEBORAH SHAFFER spent a year in New York at *Newsreal* after graduation in 1930. She then worked as Counsellor at the first legal abortion clinic and there made a documentary film called *How About You?* which started her filmmaking career, much of it dealing with Latin American subjects. She won an Oscar for Best Short Documentary Films for her *Witness to War: Dr. Charles Clements.* In 1977 she made her first 90-minute documentary, *The Wobblies.*

MAXIM SIMCOVITCH is the author of "The Impact of Griffith's *Birth of a Nation* on the Modern Ku Klux Klan" (chapter 6 in this volume).

ANTHONY SLIDE is Series Editor of The Scarecrow Filmmakers Series. He also wrote the following books, among others: *Early American Cinema, The Griffith Actresses,* and

The Idols of Silence. Scarecrow Press has published many of his works, including six volumes of selected film criticism, covering 1896–1960, one volume of selected film criticism of foreign films, covering 1930–1950, and *The Kindergarten of the Movies.*

GALE SONDERGAARD (1899–1985) was the actress wife of "Hollywood Ten" member Herbert Biberman (1900–1971) and a blacklist victim herself for many years because of her relationship with him. Of the scores of films Sondergaard made prior to and even after the end of the McCarthy era, none stands out more than her role as Mme. Dreyfus, wife of the central figure in the case, in the 1937 Warner Brothers film *The Life of Emile Zola,* directed by William Dieterle.

ROBERT STEBBINS (pseudonym of Sidney Meyers, 1906–1969) wrote astute film criticism for *New Theatre* magazine and other journals of the depression and anti-fascist decades, but he is remembered today for his filmmaking, as a founding member of Frontier Films. With Frontier he worked as writer-producer of *China Strikes Back,* as co-director of *People of the Cumberland,* and as sound editor on *Native Land.* During the war years he served as chief film editor for the Office of War Information. In 1948 he won the 1949 Venice Film Festival award for *The Quiet One,* a quietly moving documentary about a Harlem boy rescued from family neglect by the Wiltwyck School. Ten years later, he co-produced, with Ben Maddow and Joseph Strick, *The Savage Eye* which won the Edinburgh Prize for its sensitive portrayal of love and divorce in modern American society. Above all, Sidney Meyers is venerated today as an inspiring film teacher. He was, as an admirer once wrote, "an artist, a musician, a walking encyclopedia of the history of art." Before turning to films, Sidney was for several years a professional violinist and member of the Cincinnati Symphony Orchestra. But whether the subject under discussion was music, art, teaching or filmmaking, his great curiosity and enthusiasm had an impact on all who knew him or worked with him. This comes through with a special kind of beauty in the late Jay Leyda's 38-page tribute to him, titled *Vision Is My Dwelling Place,* published shortly after Meyers' death in 1969. Do not fail to read it at the Museum of Modern Art Film Study Center.

KYLE STEENLAND co-authored (with John Trimbur) "Film-makers Discover 'New' Native Americans" (chapter 60 in this volume).

PHILIP STERLING worked from 1936 to the end of 1939 on the New York City Writers Project as an associate editor of *The Film Index,* a 3-volume bibliography of the literature of the motion picture, Volume 1 of which (*The Film as Art*) was published by The Museum of Modern Art Film Library in 1941. Incredibly, the other two volumes were not published until 1985—44 years later. In his later years Sterling worked for 20 years (1945–1965) for the CBS Publicity Department, following which he wrote four books of biographies for young readers in collaboration with others, including a biography of Fiorello La Guardia. He also edited an anthology of Negro humor, *Laughing on the Outside;* a full-length biography of Rachel Carson, *Sea and Earth,* and a collection of interviews with teachers in black ghetto schools in Detroit, Cleveland, Boston, New York, Philadelphia and Washington: *The Real Teachers.* Before his death in September 1989 he made his home in New England with his wife Dorothy Dannen Sterling.

JOHN TRIMBUR co-authored (with Kyle Steenland) "Film-makers Discover 'New' Native Americans" (chapter 60 in this volume).

DALTON TRUMBO (1905–1976), the formerly blacklisted member of the "Hollywood Ten," was a former director of the Screen Writers Guild and founding editor of *The Screen Writer,* the Guild's official publication. In 1944, he was chairman of Writers for Roosevelt. Trumbo was a war correspondent in 1945 in Okinawa, Balikpapen (Dutch Borneo), and Luzon (Philippines). He wrote about the founding conference of the United Nations in San Francisco in 1945. During the blacklist period, Trumbo wrote films clandestinely, in the sense that producers sought him out, typically paid him very little, and used his work without screen credit.

As "Robert Rich," he won the Academy Award for writing *The Brave One.* In recent years, Trumbo has worked openly, and his credits under his own name include *Hawaii,* directed by George Roy Hill; *The Sandpiper,* directed by Vincente Minelli; *The Fixer,* directed by John Frankenheimer; *Lonely Are the Brave,* directed by David Miller; *Spartacus,* directed by Stanley Kubrick; and *Exodus,* directed by Otto Preminger. In March 1970, he was honored with the Laurel Award for Achievement by the Writers Guild of America/West. The presentation, made by Richard Murphy, the Guild's first Vice-President and its Screen Branch president, said it was ". . . the professional's recognition of a lifetime of professional work, the ultimate tribute of the Writers Guild." With the award was a citation stating that it is given "to that member of the Guild who, in the opinion of the current executive board of the Screen Branch, has advanced the literature of the motion picture through the years, and who has made outstanding contributions to the profession of the screen writer." See also Trumbo's 1949 38-page pamphlet, *The Time of the Toad,* written to inform the public and also to raise funds for the legal defense of the "Hollywood Ten."

JUDY VOCCOLA made, in the 1920s, a silent film on the Passaic textile strike, *Blood, Sweat and Tears,* with Sam Brody as the cameraman. It is distributed by the Museum of Modern Art and was among the films donated by Tom Brandon.

HERMAN G. WEINBERG (1908–1983) wrote and taught film criticism and film history on the college level for over 40 years. His 1970 volume, *Saint Cinema* (preface by Fritz Lang) contains a liberal assortment of his articles and reviews from 1929 on. One of Weinberg's main themes is that the glory and genius of film art is in its past. Thus the films that engage his deepest concern are the works of such masters as Griffith, Chaplin, Stroheim, Lubitsch, Murnau, Lang, Eisenstein, Rene Clair, Carl Dreyer, and a few other hallowed names. Weinberg's special attraction to students, once noted the film scholar Harry M. Geduld, is that he sees and writes about cinema with "a poet's sensibilities, discerning and winnowing out of the Himalayan heaps of celluloid dross the essence of all that is true, good and beautiful." Weinberg has also published *The Complete "Greed"* and *The Complete "Wedding March,"* detailed reconstructions with hundreds of still photos and ample text of those two mutilated masterpieces by Von Stroheim.

NAME INDEX

FILM INDEX

623